Renna Fielder

W9-BKI-099

SIXTH EDITION

Juvenile Delinquency
CAUSES AND CONTROL

ROBERT AGNEW
EMORY UNIVERSITY

TIMOTHY BREZINA
GEORGIA STATE UNIVERSITY

New York   Oxford
OXFORD UNIVERSITY PRESS

Oxford University Press is a department of the University of Oxford. It furthers the University's
objective of excellence in research, scholarship, and education by publishing worldwide.
Oxford is a registered trade mark of Oxford University Press in the UK and certain other countries.

Published in the United States of America by Oxford University Press
198 Madison Avenue, New York, NY 10016, United States of America.

© 2018, 2015, 2012, 2009 by Oxford University Press
© 2005, 2001 by Roxbury Publishing Company

For titles covered by Section 112 of the US Higher Education
Opportunity Act, please visit www.oup.com/us/he for the
latest information about pricing and alternate formats.

All rights reserved. No part of this publication may be reproduced, stored in a retrieval system,
or transmitted, in any form or by any means, without the prior permission in writing of Oxford University
Press, or as expressly permitted by law, by license, or under terms agreed with the appropriate
reproduction rights organization. Inquiries concerning reproduction outside the scope of the above
should be sent to the Rights Department, Oxford University Press, at the address above.

You must not circulate this work in any other form
and you must impose this same condition on any acquirer.

Library of Congress Cataloging-in-Publication Data

CIP data on file with Library of Congress
ISBN: 9780190641610

9 8 7 6 5 4 3
Printed by Webcom, Canada.

Contents

Handwritten note:
Reading Journals-4321
4. main concepts/ ideas learned
3. connections with course material or questions
2. ways reading shaped thoughts on delinquency
1. thought to share

PART 1

The Nature and Extent of Delinquency   1

3   How Much Delinquency Is There, and Is Delinquency Increasing?   45

4   Who Is Most Likely to Engage in Delinquency?   68

PART 2
The Causes of Delinquency: Theories   95

5   What Is a Theory and How Do We Test Theories?   97

PART 3

The Causes of Delinquency: Research   237

14 The Family   256

15 The School   275

20 The Police   370

21 Juvenile Court and Corrections   390

An Important Message for Instructors

Criminologists often complain about the limited impact of their discipline on public perceptions and crime control policy. We believe that a major reason for this limited impact lies with our introductory textbooks. Our texts are perhaps the chief way in which we communicate with the larger community. Yet, with a few notable exceptions, they do not provide students with a clear sense of what causes delinquency and what can be done to control it. Rather, our texts tend to overwhelm and confuse students. Students get lost in all the theories of delinquency that are presented; they have trouble drawing conclusions from the discussions of empirical research, since contradictory studies are often described, with little effort to sort them; and they are not provided with a good overview of the most promising approaches to delinquency control and prevention. If the readers of such texts were asked to explain why juveniles engage in delinquency or what should be done to control it, we venture to say that most would respond with blank stares or jumbled answers.

This book is very different from most delinquency texts now on the market, and those differences are described next.

MORE FOCUSED

The book is more focused than current texts. The dominant texts attempt to cover all the major research on delinquency. This text does not attempt to cover all major areas in the field. Rather, it devotes serious attention to what we consider to be the three major questions in the field: What is the nature and extent of delinquency? What are the causes of delinquency? What strategies should we employ to control delinquency? Students reading this text should be able to give reasonable answers to these questions. We are not sure that this is the case with many current texts.

At the same time, you may feel that this text does not devote adequate attention to certain topics. But the relatively low cost of this text should make it easy for you to cover whatever additional topics you like with supplemental readings. In fact, we encourage this approach. We believe it is important for students to read articles and other books that describe original research and discuss particular issues in detail. There are many wonderful articles and books on delinquency, like *Code of the Street* by Anderson (1999) and "The Saints and the Roughnecks" by Chambliss (1973). We think it would be unfortunate for students to take a delinquency course without being exposed to these materials. And we believe that this view is becoming more common, as reflected in the increased number of delinquency readers and "companion" texts being offered by publishers.

MORE SYNTHETIC APPROACH TO DELINQUENCY THEORY AND RESEARCH

This text differs from most current texts in that it employs a more "synthetic" approach to delinquency theory and research. Most texts spend a great deal of time describing delinquency theories and research but make little effort to synthesize such theory and research. For example, they describe (often superficially) the four or five different versions of strain theory that now dominate the literature. They also describe the research on each of these versions of strain theory, noting both supportive and nonsupportive studies. They do not, however, attempt to draw on this theory and research in the interest of developing an up-to-date, comprehensive version of strain theory. Students reading such texts get caught up in trying to memorize all the different versions of strain theory (and other theories) and the mixed evidence on each version. They come away confused and overwhelmed. Unlike virtually all other texts, our text does not describe the different versions of all the major delinquency theories. Rather, we attempt to synthesize the best of the current delinquency theories into a set of four "generic" theories: a strain-based theory, a social learning theory, a control-based theory, and a labeling-based theory. Since these generic theories represent a synthesis of the best of current theory and research, our empirical assessments of them are somewhat more optimistic than those found in other textbooks.

After presenting the four generic theories, we devote several chapters to the major research on the causes of delinquency, including the research on individual traits, family factors, school experiences, and delinquent peer groups and gangs. We make a special effort to state, in a clear, concise manner, the major conclusions that can be drawn from these different areas of research. At the same time, we make note of problems in the research, and we attempt to sort through contradictory studies where necessary. The final section of the book, Part 4, provides an overview of the police, the juvenile courts, and juvenile corrections. It then discusses four general strategies for controlling delinquency: deterrence, incapacitation, prevention, and rehabilitation. We describe the evidence on the effectiveness of these strategies and discuss ways to increase their effectiveness. While we provide examples of successful programs and policies in these areas, our major focus is on describing the general features of those programs and policies that appear to be the most successful.

Many instructors may object to this synthetic approach, especially as it applies to delinquency theories. We do not explicitly discuss certain popular theories. The four theories we present, however, dominate the delinquency literature, and we believe that they capture the essential ideas of most other theories. In particular, our discussion of these four theories presents the major arguments associated with rational choice, routine activities, self-control, life course, social disorganization, subcultural deviance, and certain aspects of conflict and feminist theories. To give a few examples, we describe how these theories explain patterns of offending over the life course, and in doing so we present the essential ideas from the leading theories of crime and the life course. We describe how these theories explain why crime is more likely in some situations than others, and in doing so we present the essential ideas of rational choice and routine activities theories. In addition, we describe how these theories explain why some communities have higher rates of delinquency than others, which allows us to present the essential ideas of social disorganization, subcultural deviance, and macro-strain theories. Like Bernard and Snipes (1996) and others, we believe that there are too many theories in criminology. We think that the essential ideas of most theories can be presented in terms of the four generic theories, making life much simpler for students and researchers and making criminology more useful for policy makers.

MORE STUDENT (AND INSTRUCTOR) FRIENDLY
We have done several things to make this text more student (and instructor) friendly. Unlike most other texts, this book is organized around questions rather than topics. For example, instead of a long section on "the sociodemographic correlates of delinquency,"

Part 1 of the text is entitled "Who Is Most Likely to Engage in Delinquency?" Students find questions more interesting than topics; questions invite students to become more actively involved in the learning process, and questions better convey what the research process is about—answering questions that researchers feel are interesting and important (see Goldsmid and Wilson, 1980). The subheadings under each question essentially form a sentence outline of the book. Students, then, can gain a quick overview of each chapter and part before reading it, and they can easily review the major points of each chapter/part after reading it.

The book also has a common theme: using the four delinquency theories to understand the basic facts about delinquency, to interpret the research on the causes of delinquency, and to evaluate and develop policies for the control of delinquency. For example, we stress that much of the research on delinquency was inspired by the four theories discussed and that all the research is interpretable in terms of these theories. To illustrate, the biopsychological research describes several traits that are conducive to crime, such as impulsivity and irritability. We stress that the effect of these traits on crime can be explained in terms of the four theories: Such traits increase strain, reduce concern for the costs of crime, make crime seem more rewarding, and increase the likelihood of negative labeling. The decision to use the four major delinquency theories as described helps students master the material, since the book comes across as an integrated whole rather than a series of discrete facts. Chapters build on one another, and certain points are re-emphasized throughout the text.

The book is written in a more informal, conversational style than is found in most texts. We believe this makes the material more interesting and accessible to students. Further, the book is divided into 25 relatively short chapters, each focusing on a particular topic, which makes it easier for instructors to assign readings. With other texts, instructors frequently end up assigning portions of a chapter (e.g., the four and a half pages that deal with strain theory). Students should also appreciate the fact that the chapters are shorter and generally more coherent than those in many other texts. **Although the chapters build on each other, they also can stand alone. This fact, along with the relatively short length and focused nature of the chapters, makes it possible for instructors to adopt the textbook flexibly.** Instructors may choose, for example, to assign some, but not necessarily all the chapters. And in most cases, it is reasonable to assign multiple chapters in a single week. (Note: See the sample syllabus included with the instructor resources for this textbook. Be sure to contact your local Oxford sales representative to gain access to the ancillary resource center).

Further, in the current edition of the text, "special topics" boxes are presented in most every chapter. The boxes, which cover events from the news, controversies, and case studies related to juvenile delinquency, are designed to stimulate student interest. We believe that students will find the material engaging and thought-provoking, and instructors can use the boxes as vehicles for launching classroom discussion. To this end, each box concludes with at least one discussion question.

Finally, each chapter contains a section titled Teaching Aids, including student exercises or controversial cases for students to consider, questions designed to test students' knowledge of the chapter, a list of key terms, and questions designed to encourage independent thinking and foster further discussion. Many of the teaching aids can form the basis for classroom activities and discussions. (Additional suggestions for class activities and lectures are contained in the *Instructor's Manual* that accompanies this text.)

Having said all this, we should note that this book does not contain a lot of illustrations or tables. These features are nice, but we avoid them for two reasons. First, we want to keep the cost of the book as low as possible. In our experience, students prefer a cheaper textbook to one with a lot of pictures. Second, many students ignore tables and figures, and many others are overwhelmed by them. Rather than presenting students with a lot of numbers, we prefer to stress the essential points that the numbers are designed to convey.

PROMOTES ACTIVE LEARNING

Our text attempts to promote active learning, especially the application of text materials. Most notably, students are provided with numerous examples of how one might use the major theories of delinquency to explain the basic facts about delinquency, to understand the research on the causes of delinquency, and to develop and evaluate programs and policies for controlling delinquency. Also, students are frequently asked to engage in such applications themselves. Students are asked, as well, to apply the text materials to their own lives. In particular, we pose questions for students throughout the text. And we do the same at the end of each chapter, in the sections titled Teaching Aids. This emphasis on the application of text materials is crucial in our view: it dramatically increases the students' understanding of the materials, which are of little use unless students develop the ability to apply them.

Further, the text not only describes what criminologists know about delinquency, it also gives students a sense of *how* criminologists know what they know, that is, how criminologists collect and analyze data. In particular, we spend much time discussing how criminologists measure delinquency, how they test theories—especially how they determine whether one variable causes another—and how they determine whether a program or policy is effective in controlling delinquency. Students, then, are not asked to accept the findings of criminology on faith. They are given a sense of what the research process is like. We frequently apply these materials, pointing to problems in research studies and noting the need for further research in certain areas. Further, we ask the students to apply these materials.

NEW TO THIS EDITION

- Greater emphasis throughout the textbook on the interplay of risk factors, with examples and illustrations showing how risk factors often work together in producing delinquency.
- New coverage of trauma, trauma-informed practice in juvenile justice, and cross-national differences in juvenile justice.
- Expanded coverage of police–community relations; "civil citation" diversion programs; Supreme Court decisions; children's exposure to violence; and concentrated poverty, including trends and causes as they relate to delinquency.
- Additional special topics boxes that discuss and analyze current events, controversies, and case studies related to juvenile delinquency. Each box concludes with questions designed to stimulate student interest and discussion.
- Each chapter has been updated to fully reflect the latest research on juvenile delinquency and juvenile justice, including up-to-date statistical information.

WE APPRECIATE YOUR FEEDBACK

We are most interested in receiving your impressions of the text, including things that you like and do not like (e.g., topics that we should devote more coverage to, sections that are unclear or too dry, statements that you disagree with, literature that we should have cited). We will consider your comments carefully when revising the text. Please e-mail the second author at tbrezina@gsu.edu or write to him at the Department of Criminal Justice and Criminology, Georgia State University, P.O. Box 3992, Atlanta, GA 30302-3992.

An Overview of This Book

The media are regularly filled with reports about juvenile crime. Not long ago, police in Minnesota foiled a teenager's plot to bring guns and explosives to school and to kill "as many students as he could." According to the criminal complaint, the 17-year-old had stockpiled handguns, automatic assault rifles, and bomb-making materials. He detailed plans for the school massacre in a 180-page notebook and had intended to carry out the attack on April 20, 2014—the fifteenth anniversary of the infamous shootings at Columbine High School. The date fell on Easter Sunday, however, when the school would be closed, so he decided to wait for another opportunity. Before he could attack, however, a neighbor reported suspicious activity to the police, leading to his arrest. The would-be attacker was reportedly a B student who was quiet and shy. According to a schoolmate, "He seemed like a good kid . . . . You'd never expect it from him" (Muskal, 2014).

This case and other incidents have led people throughout the country to ask a number of fundamental questions about juvenile delinquency: How common is juvenile delinquency? Is it increasing? Who is most likely to commit delinquent acts? What are the causes of juvenile delinquency? What can be done to control or prevent delinquency? These are the questions addressed in this book.

The book has four main divisions. The four chapters in Part 1 focus on the *nature and extent of delinquency*. These chapters deal with the "basic facts" about delinquency, such as: What is it? How widespread is it? Is it increasing? And who is most likely to commit delinquent acts?

The eight chapters in Part 2 focus on the major *theories* or explanations of the *causes of delinquency*. These chapters describe the four leading theories, or explanations, of delinquency, using them to explain why some juveniles are more likely than others to engage in delinquency; why some offenders engage in crime at high rates over much of their lives while others limit their offending to the adolescent years; why delinquency is more likely in some situations than others; and why some groups have higher rates of delinquency than other groups.

The six chapters in Part 3 focus on the *research* dealing with the *causes of delinquency*, much of which was designed to test the theories described in Part 2. The research examines the extent to which delinquency is caused by individual traits (e.g., low verbal intelligence, low self-control), family factors (e.g., broken homes, poor supervision), school factors, delinquent peers and gang membership, and a range of other factors, such as mass media violence, social media engagement, religion, drugs, and guns. The concluding chapter of Part 3 draws on this research and the leading delinquency theories to present an integrated or general theory of delinquency. This theory is used to explain many of the basic facts about delinquency presented in Part 1—for example, that some juveniles are more delinquent than others and that males are more delinquent than females.

The seven chapters in Part 4, the final section, focus on the *control and prevention of delinquency*. These chapters describe what the police, juvenile courts, and juvenile correctional agencies do to control delinquency. In particular, they describe how these agencies operate, how effective they are, what they might do to be more effective, and the extent to which they discriminate against certain groups in their efforts to control delinquency. These chapters then describe four general strategies for controlling delinquency that involve all these agencies as well as other groups: the "get-tough" strategies of deterrence and incapacitation, and the strategies of rehabilitation and prevention. These strategies address many of the causes of delinquency described in Parts 2 and 3.

We should note that this book does more than simply describe the major research on juvenile delinquency. It also describes how this research was carried out. That is, it tells how criminologists estimate the extent of delinquency, determine whether some factor causes delinquency, and determine whether some program or policy is effective at reducing delinquency. Not only will this information increase your understanding of the delinquency research, it will better enable you to evaluate the statements you hear about delinquency (and other topics) from friends, family, the media, politicians, and others. Furthermore, this book encourages you to apply the delinquency research. It encourages you, for example, to use the leading theories of delinquency to explain the basic facts about delinquency and to evaluate programs for reducing delinquency. It also encourages you to apply the delinquency research to your own life and to issues in the larger community.

We hope you find this book useful, and we are most interested in hearing any comments you might have about it—including suggestions for improving the next edition. You can email the second author at tbrezina@gsu.edu or write to him at the Department of Criminal Justice and Criminology, Georgia State University, P.O. Box 3992, Atlanta, GA 30302-3992.

Acknowledgments

We would like to thank several people for their help in preparing this book. They include Ron Akers and Gary Jensen, who encouraged the writing of the first edition and provided much useful feedback. Claude Teweles, who gave the time and freedom necessary to write this type of book. Frank Cullen, a valued friend and colleague, who has taught us much about crime and its control. Everett K. Wilson, whose ideas about teaching have had a tremendous influence on this book. The students in our juvenile delinquency classes. Dozens of individuals who provided valuable comments on all or portions of the book: Charles Amissah, Candice Batton, Thomas J. Bernard, Bonnie Black, Patricia Brennan, Kevin Bryant, Scott Decker, Michael Dindinger, Finn-Aage Esbensen, Joseph R. Franco, William Mark Franks, Stephanie Funk, Hua-Lun Huang, Michele Hussong, Seokjin Jeong, Marvin Krohn, David Mackey, Karen Miner-Romanoff, David L. Myers, Judge Robin Nash, Lois Presser, Dean Rojek, E. Scott Ryan, Joseph Sanborn, Frank Scarpitti, Randall Shelden, Sandra S. Stone, Sherod Thaxton, Charles M. Vivona, and Richard A. Wright. We would also like to thank the following reviewers who provided feedback on the fifth edition: Kevin Bryant, Benedictine College; Matthew Costello, Arkansas State University; George J. Day, Stephen F. Austin State University; Traci Etheridge, Richmond Community College; W. Mark Franks, University of Mississippi; Whitney M. Gass, Southern Arkansas University; Chenelle A. Jones, Ohio Dominican University; J. Scott Lewis, Penn State Harrisburg. Two additional individuals who assisted with the preparation of the current edition: Steve Helba and Beverly Crank. Robert Agnew thanks his wife, Mary, and children Willie and Jenny. Mary provided the support and encouragement necessary to write this book, while Willie and Jenny provided the inspiration. Timothy Brezina thanks his wife, Kellye, for her support and never-ending patience.

PART 1

The Nature and Extent of Delinquency

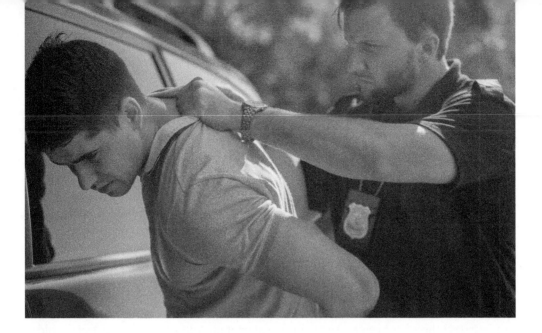

1 What Is Delinquency and How Does It Differ from Adult Crime?

"What is delinquency?" is a relatively easy question to answer. *Juvenile delinquency* **refers to violations of the criminal law by minors.** In most states, a minor is anyone under the age of 18. In some states, however, minors are defined as anyone under the age of 17 or even 16. So if a minor commits an act that would be a crime when committed by an adult, that minor has engaged in "juvenile delinquency" and may be considered a "juvenile delinquent." This definition, while correct, might lead you to believe that the only way delinquency differs from adult crime is in terms of age. Delinquent acts are committed by minors while crimes are committed by adults.

But juvenile delinquency differs from adult crime in a number of major ways besides the age of the offender. In particular, we tend to view juvenile delinquents differently than adult criminals, and we tend to treat juvenile delinquents differently than adult criminals—with an important exception, which we will note.

This chapter is in four sections. First, we describe how juvenile delinquents are viewed differently than adult criminals. Second, we describe how these different views of delinquents and adult criminals have led us as a society to treat them differently. We note, however, that there has been a trend to view and treat juvenile offenders— especially older, serious offenders—like adult criminals. Third, we discuss the "invention" of juvenile delinquency. People did not always view and treat juvenile delinquents differently than adult criminals. For most of history, in fact, juveniles who broke the law were viewed and treated very much like adults who broke the law. We briefly discuss some of the factors that led society to view and treat juvenile delinquents differently. Finally, we discuss how our view and treatment of juvenile offenders continues to evolve.

After reading this chapter, you should be able to:

- Define juvenile delinquency.
- Describe the major differences in the way that society views juvenile offenders and adult offenders.
- Describe the major differences in the way that society treats juvenile offenders and adult offenders.
- List the major ways in which juvenile court differs from adult court, and discuss the reasons for such differences.
- Explain what is meant by "the invention of juvenile delinquency."
- Describe how we came to view and treat juvenile offenders differently than adult offenders.

JUVENILE DELINQUENTS ARE VIEWED DIFFERENTLY THAN ADULT CRIMINALS

On the first day of our juvenile delinquency class, we play a trick on our students. We pass out a description of a crime that has occurred: Someone walks into a bank, points a gun at a teller, and demands money. It is a toy gun, but the teller believes it is real and gives the bank robber several hundred dollars. The robber later spends most of the money on luxury items before being caught. We ask the students what the court should do to this robber. Unbeknownst to the students, the robber is described as a "7-year-old boy" in half of the descriptions and a "32-year-old man" in the other half (the actual crime was committed by a 7-year-old boy).

After the students have considered the case for a few minutes, we ask for volunteers to tell us what they think should be done to the "bank robber." Some of the students describe what might be considered "mild" reactions on the part of the court: The robber should receive counseling, should be closely monitored for a period of time, should perform some community service, or the like. Other students describe what might be considered "tough" reactions on the part of the court; most commonly, they state that the robber should be locked up for several years. The students, of course, are confused by the responses of many of their classmates. Those with the 7-year-old robber wonder how some of their classmates could be so coldhearted as to recommend years of imprisonment, while those with the 32-year-old robber think some of their classmates are far too "soft" on crime.

We eventually tell the students that they are working with two different case studies and that this age discrepancy is the major reason for their different reactions. We then try to justify the trick we have played by telling the students that their different reactions to the 7- and 32-year-old robbers illustrate a very important point about juvenile delinquency: **Our society tends to view juvenile delinquents differently than adult criminals.**

If a juvenile breaks the law, the general public tends to view that person as imma-ture and in need of our guidance and help. There is no precise definition of *immaturity*, but notions of immaturity usually include one or more of the following: the individuals did not know that what they were doing was wrong; they did not appreciate the harm that their actions might cause; they could not control themselves; and they were easily led astray by others. (Data suggest that juveniles are more likely than adults to possess these traits, although there is no precise age at which individuals become "mature."[1] Rather, in-dividuals mature in a gradual manner and at different rates—although juveniles are less mature on average than adults.)

This immaturity partly stems from a lack of experience. Older juveniles are no longer closely supervised by parents, and they must increasingly learn to make decisions on their own. They lack experience at decision making, however, and so it is not surprising that they sometimes show poor judgment in the choices they make (see Zimring, 2005). This immaturity also has biological roots. A colleague of ours at Emory University coedited a book that focuses on the development of the adolescent brain (E. Walker and Romer, 2006). A central message of the book is that the "brain circuitry for pleasure and sensation develops rapidly during adolescence, while the brain circuitry responsible for behavioral control and inhibition lags behind" (C. Clark, 2007:6). As a consequence, adolescents have more trouble exercising self-control and resisting the influence of peers.

Given this view of juveniles as immature, most people tend to feel that juveniles do not deserve serious punishment. Rather, they need our help. So when a 7-year-old robs a bank, many students state that the major response of the court should be to provide that person with counseling. **But if an adult breaks the law, we generally view that person as someone who is responsible for his or her behavior and deserves to be punished.** So most students have no qualms about sending a 32-year-old who robbed a bank to prison for many years. *Maybe because they are still immature themselves.*

Many students take exception when juveniles are characterized in this way. They state that many juvenile offenders know exactly what they are doing and that these offenders should be punished just as severely as adults. They often describe some horrifying crime committed in the recent past by a juvenile, and they state that this juvenile surely deserves the most serious punishment the law can provide.

We realize that many people feel this way. Certain juvenile offenders—especially older juveniles who commit serious crimes—are not viewed as all that different from adult of-fenders. And in recent decades the justice system has been treating more of these offenders like adult criminals. So when we say that society views juvenile delinquents differently than adult criminals, an important exception should be noted. Older, serious juvenile offenders are often viewed like adult offenders. We will talk more about this exception toward the end of this chapter. Aside from this important exception, the general public still tends to view juvenile delinquents differently than adult criminals. We provide our students with a few additional examples to illustrate this point.

→ somewhat planned

There is the case of a 6-year-old girl in Florida who got into a fight with her 7-year-old friend. The 6-year-old girl repeatedly hit her 7-year-old friend with a piece of wood, while an older boy held the 7-year-old's arms behind her back. The 7-year-old's nose was damaged and her dress was soaked with blood by the time she arrived home to her mother. Her mother, of course, was outraged and immediately called the police. For legal reasons that we will not describe, there was some discussion of trying the 6-year-old girl as an adult. If tried as an adult, she would face a maximum penalty of fifteen years in prison and a $10,000 fine. This story made the national news, and people were outraged that such a young girl might be so severely penalized. They felt that the 6-year-old did not know what she was doing and that she needed guidance and help much more than punishment. Imagine the reaction, however, if a 30-year-old woman had committed this crime. People would be demanding the severest of penalties.

intent, knowledge of harm being done

To give another example, a 6-year-old boy in California was charged with savagely beating a month-old baby. He was accused of kicking, punching, and beating the sleeping baby with a stick, possibly causing permanent brain damage. The 6-year-old was said to have done this to seek revenge against the family of the baby for allegedly harassing him. We have asked our own students how the court should respond to this boy. This is a savage crime, but the young age of the boy led many of our students to talk of his immaturity and to argue that he is in desperate need of guidance and help. Again, imagine the difference in reaction if a 30-year-old man were charged with this crime.

With the exception of older juveniles who commit serious crimes, our society clearly views juvenile delinquents differently than adult criminals. In general, juvenile delinquents are viewed as immature and in need of guidance and help, while adult criminals are viewed as fully responsible for their behavior and deserving of punishment. To illustrate, one national poll found that only 21 percent of the public said that rehabilitation should be the most important sentencing goal for adults, but 50 percent said that it should be the most important sentencing goal for juveniles.[2]

JUVENILE DELINQUENTS ARE TREATED DIFFERENTLY THAN ADULT CRIMINALS

The difference in the way that juvenile and adult offenders are viewed has led us to treat juvenile delinquents differently than adult criminals (with an important exception, to be noted). In particular, our society has created a special set of laws that apply just to juveniles in order to more closely regulate their lives. We have created a special court for juvenile offenders, a court that places more emphasis on rehabilitation and less on punishment than does adult criminal court. And we have created special correctional programs for juveniles, programs that also focus more on rehabilitation and less on punishment—at least in theory.[3]

Special Laws for Juveniles: Status Offenses

Juveniles are delinquent if they commit any act whose violation by an adult would be a crime—acts like homicide, assault, rape, robbery, burglary, and larceny. However, in most states, juveniles can be arrested and referred to juvenile court for certain acts that are legal for adults. These acts are called *status offenses*, since they apply only to people with the status of juvenile.

The most common status offenses are running away from home, failure to attend school (truancy), refusing to obey parents (incorrigibility), liquor law violations (possession of alcohol, underage drinking), violating curfew, and engaging in certain consensual sexual activities. These activities are illegal for juveniles in all or many areas, but they are legal for adults; for example, it is illegal for juveniles to stop attending school. They can be arrested and taken to juvenile court in most states if they do so. It is perfectly legal for you, however, to stop coming to class.

The state felt that it was necessary to regulate the lives of juveniles more closely than the lives of adults. Rather than intervening only when juveniles committed a crime, the state felt it necessary to intervene when juveniles gave indications that they might be heading down the "wrong path"—a path that might lead to crime. Status offense laws, then, are directly tied to the view of juveniles as immature and in need of guidance or direction.

These status offense laws were **taken quite seriously until the late 1960s and early 1970s.** Juveniles who committed status offenses were frequently arrested and referred to juvenile court. They were often formally processed by the court, and they could be "adjudicated," or judged, "delinquent" by juvenile courts in nearly every state. And status offenders were sometimes subject to severe punishments. In particular, about half the juveniles in correctional institutions were there for status offenses like running away and being incorrigible. Status offense laws were especially likely to be enforced against females. Females were (and are) more closely supervised than males, and their sexual behavior, in particular, is more closely regulated. Females who committed status offenses like disobeying parents, running away from home, drinking, and having sex were more likely than boys to be arrested, referred to the court, and sent to institutions for such offenses. There is some evidence that this is still the case today (see Chapter 22 for a fuller discussion).

Status offense laws **came under heavy criticism during the 1960s and 1970s.** They were **often vague.** What, for example, does it mean to be incorrigible? Virtually all juveniles disobey their parents at some point. Also, these laws **often subjected juveniles who had not committed any criminal acts to severe penalties,** such as confinement in an institution (where they were exposed to serious offenders and sometimes subject to physical and sexual assault). Further, there was evidence that **poor, minority, and female juveniles were more likely to be punished for such offenses.** *yet male adults more common.*

In response to such criticisms, most states developed "diversion" programs designed to divert status offenders from the juvenile court. Rather than being formally processed by the court, most status offenders were dealt with informally by the court or were referred to special programs outside the court. Status offenders who were processed by the juvenile court were **no longer classified as "delinquents" in most states.** Rather, they were classified as Children in Need of Supervision (CHINS), Persons in Need of Supervision (PINS), or similar labels. This new designation was partly designed to reduce the stigma of a delinquent label. The federal government passed a law in 1974 that **strongly encouraged states to stop placing status offenders in institutions.** And evidence suggests that this law was largely effective: There has been a dramatic decline in the number of status offenders confined in institutions. Finally, a few states went so far as to **decriminalize status offenses.** Status offenses could no longer result in arrest and referral to the juvenile court; rather, status offenses were dealt with by social service agencies.

Nevertheless, status offenses are **still illegal in almost all states.** Several hundred thousand status offenders are arrested each year. In 2013, about 109,000 status offenders were formally processed by juvenile courts, over 7,300 were detained during court processing, and 3,800 were placed out-of-home as part of their "disposition" or sentence—most often for the offense of truancy (Hockenberry and Puzzanchera, 2015). So while status offenses are not treated as severely today as in the past, they are still taken seriously in many cases.

A Special Court for Juveniles: Juvenile Court

Every state has created special courts for juvenile offenders. *Juvenile court* differs from adult court in several fundamental ways, with the differences between the two courts reflecting our different views of juvenile delinquents and adult criminals. The differences between juvenile court and adult court have diminished in recent years, but they are still substantial.

First, the **goals of juvenile court are different from those of adult court.** Adult court determines whether individuals are guilty of committing specific crimes and then punishes them if they are convicted. Juvenile court was set up **not to punish juveniles but rather to guide and help them.** The court was supposed to act in "the best interests" of juveniles, providing them with the guidance and help that their parents should have provided. The court, in fact, was supposed to play the role of "superparent," assisting children whose parents had failed them. Judge Julian Mack, who helped develop the first juvenile court in the United States, said that the juvenile court should treat delinquents like "a wise and merciful father handles his own child" and that the goal of the court is "not so much to punish as to reform, not to degrade but to uplift, not to crush but to develop, [and] not to make [the delinquent] a criminal but a worthy citizen" (quoted in S. Singer, 2001:350). The goals of many juvenile courts have changed in recent years, with more courts coming to place an increased emphasis on punishing juveniles—especially older, serious offenders. Nevertheless, the juvenile court still places more emphasis on the goal of rehabilitation than does adult court. (This is not to say that the court always accomplishes or even tries to accomplish the goal of rehabilitation. As discussed later, there is often a large gap between goals and accomplishments.)

Second, the juvenile court **focuses more on the offender than on the offense.** Adult court focuses primarily on the offense(s) that the individual has committed. The punishment that individuals receive is based largely on their current and past offenses. Juvenile court is less concerned about punishing individuals for the specific offenses they have committed. Rather, it seeks to help juveniles. The court therefore focuses on the entire juvenile—not just the offense(s) that brought the juvenile to court. The court seeks to learn all it can about the juvenile, especially any personal, family, school, peer, or other problems the juvenile may have. And the actions that the court takes are supposed to address these problems—not simply respond to the juvenile's specific offense(s). Again, some changes are taking place in this area, with many juvenile courts putting more emphasis on the specific offenses that juveniles have committed and basing their response to juveniles largely on these offenses. Even so, there is still a substantial difference between juvenile and adult courts in this area.

Third, the juvenile court is **more informal and less adversarial than adult court.** Adult court provides accused individuals with numerous *due process rights* designed to protect them from being unfairly punished. These rights include the right to be represented by an attorney, the right to confront and cross-examine the witnesses against them, the right to proof beyond a reasonable doubt, and the right to a trial by jury. As a consequence of such rights, adult court is very formal, and it is adversarial in nature—at least in theory. The prosecution and defense attorneys are pitted against one another, arguing their cases before a judge or jury. The juvenile court, however, initially provided juveniles with few due process rights. It was felt that such rights were unnecessary, since the court sought to help rather than punish juveniles. Juveniles, then, did not need protection from unfair punishment. As a consequence, the juvenile court was more informal and less adversarial than adult court. Juveniles, for example, were not represented by attorneys. Often, the judge would simply talk with the juvenile—much like parents having a firm talk with their child. The judge might also question the police, witnesses, and others.

This informality has changed since the 1960s. In particular, a series of **Supreme Court decisions has granted juveniles most—although not all—of the due process rights available to adults.** The Supreme Court essentially argued that the juvenile court often fails to help the juveniles it processes and it often does punish them. They are sometimes confined in institutions, for example. They therefore deserve at least some of the due process protections available to adults. So juveniles now have such rights as the right to be represented by an attorney and to confront and cross-examine witnesses (see Chapter 22 for a fuller discussion). Juvenile court is now more formal and adversarial than it once was. But juveniles do not have all the rights available to adults; most notably, they lack the right to a trial by jury. Further, juveniles frequently waive their rights—sometimes with the encouragement of the juvenile court. In many courts, for example, less than half the juveniles are represented by an attorney. So while juvenile court has changed a great deal in recent decades, it is still less formal and adversarial than adult court—a difference that reflects the difference in goals between juvenile and adult court.

There are **still other differences between juvenile and adult court.** There are **differences in the terminology employed.** In juvenile court, the juvenile is not found "guilty" of a particular offense like robbery or burglary. The word "guilt" implies responsibility. Rather, the juvenile is *adjudicated* a "delinquent," regardless of the particular criminal offense(s) he or she committed. (In the case of status offenses, the juvenile is adjudicated a Person in Need of Supervision or whatever the label is for status offenders in that court.) Once a juvenile's status has been adjudicated, the judge does not announce a "sentence," which would imply punishment. Rather, the judge renders his or her *disposition* of the case.

Juvenile court hearings **are usually closed to the public and the media to protect the juvenile from adverse publicity and stigma.** Likewise, juvenile court records are usually unavailable to the public and media. Further, juveniles are often able to "seal," or erase, their juvenile court records if they stay out of trouble for a certain period of time. These policies are beginning to change; the public and media are being given greater access to juvenile court hearings and records. Nevertheless, the privacy of juvenile offenders receives much more protection than that of adult offenders. Adult court hearings are open to the public, adult court records are available to the public, and adult court records remain permanently available except under certain very special circumstances. The juvenile court tends to view delinquent acts as the mistakes of immature children, and it wants to minimize the damage that might result from such mistakes. One way to do this is to protect the privacy of juvenile offenders and to allow them to "erase" their records in certain cases.

There are also **differences in the sentences given out by juvenile and adult courts.** In particular, juvenile courts cannot impose the death penalty, and there are limits on the length of time for which juvenile courts can confine juveniles. Most juvenile courts cannot confine juveniles beyond their twenty-first birthday. This age limit often angers people because it means that juveniles who commit serious crimes cannot be confined for more than a few years (unless they are transferred to adult court). This age limit, however, has changed somewhat as many states have made it possible for juvenile court judges to confine juveniles for longer periods (and made it easier to try certain juvenile offenders as adults). Nevertheless, the sentences given out by juvenile courts are generally milder than those imposed by adult courts. There are still other differences between juvenile and adult court, and excellent summaries can be found in Bernard and Kurlychek (2010) and H. Snyder and Sickmund (2006).

Special Correctional Programs for Juveniles

Finally, the **view of juveniles as immature beings in need of guidance and help has led us to develop special correctional programs for them.** Juvenile correctional institutions protect juveniles from contact with adult criminals, who might exploit and corrupt them. And these institutions are more concerned with rehabilitation than with punishment.

Unfortunately, juvenile institutions often do not live up to their stated aim of rehabilitation. Again, there is often a large gap between goals and accomplishments. Nevertheless, juvenile institutions place more stress on the goal of rehabilitation than do adult institutions. Juvenile institutions are not called "prisons"; rather, they are called *youth development centers* or *training schools* or similar names that reflect their supposed emphasis on rehabilitation. A range of community-based programs designed to rehabilitate juveniles has also been developed. This is not to say that there is no concern with the rehabilitation of adult offenders, but rather that rehabilitation is a greater concern in the juvenile justice system.

In summary, the general public and the justice system tend to view most juvenile delinquents differently than adult criminals and tend to treat them differently as a result. As noted, however, our view of delinquents—especially older, serious offenders—has changed in recent years. And, related to this, our treatment of delinquents—especially older, serious offenders—has started to resemble our treatment of adult criminals.

HOW CAN WE EXPLAIN THE INVENTION OF JUVENILE DELINQUENCY?

It may sound strange to speak of the *invention of juvenile delinquency*. We do not mean to imply that juveniles did not commit delinquent acts in the past. Juveniles have always committed those acts we now label as "delinquent" and "status" offenses. In fact, there is reason to believe that some of these acts, such as fighting, drinking alcohol, and engaging in sex, were much more common at certain points in the past than they are today (see Empey et al., 1999).

When we speak of the invention of juvenile delinquency, we are referring to the special way that society views and treats juvenile offenders. As discussed in the preceding pages, the general public tends to view juvenile offenders as immature and in need of guidance and help. And juvenile offenders tend to be treated differently as a result: they are subject to a special set of laws that apply only to juveniles, they are sent to a special court, and they are placed in special correctional programs. Compared to adult criminals, much more emphasis is placed on their rehabilitation and much less on their punishment. **Juvenile offenders have not always been viewed and treated differently than adult criminals, however.**

Juvenile offenders were viewed and treated very much like adult offenders until the 1800s. There were no separate correctional facilities for juveniles in this country until the early to mid-1800s. The first juvenile court did not appear until 1899, and it was not until 1945 that all states had juvenile courts. Many status offense laws are also of recent origin. Laws requiring school attendance, for example, did not emerge until the late 1800s and early 1900s in most places. Even the word "delinquent" was not used until the 1800s. So the special way that we view and treat juvenile offenders is relatively new, having emerged in the last 100 to 200 years. As one of the first juvenile court judges stated, prior to the 1900s:

> No matter how young, . . . children [who committed crimes] were indicted, prosecuted, and confined as criminals, in prison, just the same as were adults. . . . The State kept these little ones in police cells and jails among the worst men and women to be found in the vilest parts of the city and town. (quoted in Zimring, 2005:35)

Criminologists have recently tried to explain the invention of juvenile delinquency— that is, why society and the law started to view and treat juvenile offenders differently than adult criminals over the last 100 to 200 years. Space prevents us from providing a full answer to this question, but we will describe the key features of the answer that has emerged from the research.[4]

Changing Conception of Children

Part of the answer has to do with our changing conception of children. Children past the age of 6 or 7 were not viewed much differently than adults until a few hundred years ago. The fact that children were viewed as adults is reflected in paintings from the 1600s and earlier, where the children have adult features and are dressed and posed like adults. The children, in fact, look like miniature adults. Children were also treated like adults: They lived and slept in large rooms with adults, drank alcohol, engaged in sexual behavior (willingly and unwillingly), began work at an early age, and were subject to severe punishments if they misbehaved. In fact, children were routinely subjected to treatment that would be classified as abusive today. Children who broke the law were treated very much like adults who broke the law. They were tried in the same courts and given the same punishments, including the death penalty and confinement in the same institutions as adults. Very young children, however, were usually exempted from state punishments, and older children sometimes received lighter punishments than adults.

However, **people's view of children began to change in the 1500s and 1600s.** Children began to be seen as different from adults—as immature and dependent on adults for guidance and protection. There are a variety of reasons for this change. The decline in the death rate of children is viewed as a major factor. Prior to this time, perhaps as many as two-thirds of all children died before the age of 20. Partly as a consequence, parents did not form strong attachments to their young children—it was emotionally risky to do so, since the children were not likely to live very long. Very young children were viewed with indifference, while older children were viewed as adults. The decline in the death rate, however, made it easier for parents to form close attachments to their children. As they formed such attachments, they were more inclined to view children as different from adults—as less developed and more in need of their special care and protection. Another factor contributing to this new view of children was the extension of education to broader segments of the population. Several factors increased the need for a formal education, including the increase in industry and trade and the invention of the printing press and subsequent spread of printed materials. Formal education also highlighted the immaturity and dependence of children because it widened the gap between what children knew and what adults knew. Still other factors can be listed, but the central point is that the new view of children paved the way for the invention of juvenile delinquency. **As people came to view children differently than adults, they were more inclined to view and treat juvenile offenders differently than adult offenders.**

Major Social Changes, Especially the Growth of Urban Slums

The new view of children, however, was not the only factor that led to the invention of juvenile delinquency. Also important were the major social changes that occurred in the United States during the 1800s and early 1900s (and in many other countries at the same or somewhat different times). The United States underwent a radical transformation during this time, moving from a largely rural to a largely urban society. Further, the urban areas that developed were populated by a large number of poor people, including many recent immigrants to the United States, and these areas were plagued by a range of problems, including crime. Before describing how these changes contributed to the invention of juvenile delinquency, let us first provide some more information on the nature of these changes.

At the end of the 1700s the United States was largely a rural society. In 1790, only 5.1 percent of the population lived in urban areas. There were only a few cities with populations over 2,500. By 1920, over 50 percent of the population lived in urban areas. Many cities experienced a tremendous increase in population over a very short period of time.

Chicago, for example, had a population of 5,000 in 1840. By 1890, it had a population of 1 million. This rapid growth in urban populations was largely due to the industrial revolution. Technological advances were improving farming techniques, so fewer people were needed to work the land. Many rural residents then moved to the city, hoping to find work in the newly emerging industries. Likewise, many people came to the United States from abroad, hoping to find work in those industries. In fact, it is estimated that in 1920 about half the residents of major urban areas were immigrants or the children of immigrants.

Many of the new urban residents were poor and they were not always able to find work, or at least work that paid a decent wage. As a result, **large slums began to appear. These slums suffered from a variety of problems:** poor housing, overcrowding, sanitation problems, health problems, and much crime and vice. **Many individuals became especially concerned about the children living in slums.** These children often spent much time on the streets, frequently stealing things and committing other crimes to survive. Their families and neighborhood residents seemed unable to control them, and there was concern that they were being corrupted by the "unwholesome" environment in which they lived. Some, however, felt that there was hope; they believed that with proper guidance from adults, the children in the slums might be diverted from a life of crime.

There are **two interpretations,** however, **about how this concern over poor children contributed to the invention of juvenile delinquency.** The first interpretation argues that **reformers were genuinely concerned about the plight of poor children growing up in the city.** These reformers were primarily middle-class women, many of them involved with charity or social welfare organizations. They felt that slum children needed protection from the evils of city life and should have more guidance and direction than they were receiving. So they lobbied to get special laws passed, laws that would more closely regulate the behavior of these children (e.g., status offense laws like those requiring school attendance). They also lobbied for the creation of a special court and special correctional facilities that would provide these children with the protection and guidance they needed. According to this view, then, the invention of juvenile delinquency sprang from the **desire of middle-class reformers to help children, especially poor urban children.**

A second interpretation argues that **many upper-class people were disturbed by the large concentration of poor people—especially immigrants—in the city.** They were concerned that people they frequently referred to as the "dangerous classes" might become a disruptive force in society. The upper class wanted to ensure that the poor did not threaten their privileged position, and one way they did this was by exercising greater control over their children. They lobbied for laws requiring slum-dwelling children to attend school so that they would be properly socialized. They lobbied for other laws designed to more closely regulate the children's behavior. The juvenile court was the institution designed to enforce these laws, even if it meant removing the children from their parents. And juvenile institutions were designed to teach proper discipline and respect for authority. According to this view, the invention of juvenile delinquency resulted from the **desire of upper-class people to protect their privileged position in society.**

Which interpretation is correct? A number of historians and criminologists have examined what is called the "child-saving movement." That is, they have examined individuals and groups who worked to pass status offense laws and create a separate juvenile court and juvenile correctional institutions. Each state and major city in the United States had its own group of *child savers*. Researchers have looked at whether the leaders of the child-saving movement were members of the middle or upper class. They have tried to examine the motives of the child savers on the basis of what they said and what they did. For example, do their statements indicate a genuine concern about the plight of children, or do they simply express a desire to control poor children and thereby protect "society"?

Were these children helped and protected or simply subject to greater control? Studies have examined the child-saving movements in such cities as Chicago, Los Angeles, New York, and Memphis (see the sources cited in note 7). Different studies reach different conclusions about which interpretation is correct, and there is no clear resolution of the issue yet. But it seems likely that both interpretations have some merit, with the invention of delinquency being partly motivated by a genuine concern for poor children and partly by a desire to control such children because of their perceived threat. (As an analogy, you might think of the response to the homeless in many urban areas today. Many individuals and groups truly care about the homeless and genuinely want to help them. Others, who view the homeless as dangerous and a threat to business activity, are more interested in controlling the homeless. A given city's response to the homeless is often motivated by both sets of concerns.)

Gender, Race, and the Invention of Delinquency

While the child-saving movement focused on both genders, there were certain important differences in how males and females were viewed and treated. Most notably, the child savers were more concerned about protecting females and their sexuality from the "evils" of city life. Consequently, females were more likely to be arrested and punished severely for sexual activity and acts that might put them at risk for sexual activity, such as running away from home (see Chavez-Garcia, 2007; Chesney-Lind and Shelden, 2004; Feld, 2008). The sexual activity of male juveniles, however, was often ignored or excused. As discussed in Chapter 22, there is still some evidence for a sexual double standard in the juvenile justice system, with females in many jurisdictions being more likely than males to be arrested and sanctioned for acts such as sexual behavior, running away, and being incorrigible.

The efforts of the child savers described in the preceding section focused on white youth. The child savers had little interest in black youth; and the justice system, during the 1800s and first part of the 1900s, was dominated by the racist belief that black offenders were brutish and could not be rehabilitated (Ward, 2012). So during this time, black youth who broke the law were sent to adult prisons, placed in convict-lease programs—where they engaged in forced labor, were subject to corporal punishment and execution, and, in certain cases, were sent to juvenile facilities that held only blacks. The latter facilities were inferior to those that held white youth and placed little emphasis on rehabilitation. Also, black juvenile offenders were excluded from many of the community treatment programs that were being developed, such as probation and apprenticeships. A black child-saving movement developed in response to this racist treatment, with the members of black women's clubs playing the major role. The black child savers tried to convince state officials to send black youth to the recently created juvenile facilities, but they were often unsuccessful given their limited political power. So the black child savers also worked with churches to create programs to help black juvenile offenders. Eventually, the efforts of the black child savers, along with those in the larger civil rights movement, put an end to the segregated juvenile justice system. But, as discussed in Chapter 22, there is still much work to be done. While there is no longer a "separate and unequal" juvenile justice system for black juvenile offenders, black juveniles are disproportionately involved in the juvenile justice system— even after controlling for race differences in offending (see Chavez-Garcia, 2007; and Ward's, 2012, excellent book, *The Black Child Saver: Racial Democracy and Juvenile Justice*).

In sum, it is important to remember that we did not always view and treat juvenile delinquents differently than adult criminals. Juvenile delinquency is a social invention—although there are important differences in how juvenile offenders from different gender and racial groups were (and are) viewed and treated.

OUR VIEW AND TREATMENT OF JUVENILE OFFENDERS CONTINUES TO EVOLVE

How we view and treat juvenile offenders continues to evolve (Bernard and Kurlychek, 2010). In the late 1980s, there was a dramatic shift in our view and treatment of juvenile offenders, especially older juveniles who commit serious crimes. Many argued that such offenders were a major threat, were little different from adult offenders, and should be punished as adults. But in the early 2000s, there was another shift, with many emphasizing the differences between juveniles and adults and the need to retreat from the harsh penalties that were imposed during the 1980s and 1990s. These trends are described next.

"Getting Tough" with Juvenile Offenders (Late 1980s Through the Early 2000s)

There was a dramatic increase in serious juvenile violence from the late 1980s to the mid-1990s. Further, many of the violent crimes committed by juveniles received massive publicity, such as the shootings committed by gang members in certain cities. Many people came to feel that this violence was not the work of "immature" juveniles who needed guidance and direction, but rather the work of "younger criminals" and "stone cold predators."[5] Also, many people came to feel that the juvenile court was not equipped to deal with such violence. In particular, they came to feel that such juveniles should be treated and punished like adults.[6] In a 2003 national survey, for example, 59 percent of respondents agreed that "juveniles between the ages of 14 and 17 who commit violent crimes should be treated the same as adults in the criminal justice system" (Pastore and Maguire, 2003).

As a consequence, there was a major movement to more severely punish juveniles, especially older juveniles who committed serious crimes. The goals of the juvenile court shifted, with more emphasis placed on holding juveniles accountable for their behavior and imposing punishment. The juvenile court became more likely to confine offenders in residential facilities. The number of confined juveniles increased during the 1980s and 1990s, peaking at 108,802 in 2000, even though juvenile crime started to decline in the mid-1990s (Sickmund, 2010). New methods of punishing juveniles came into wide use. One example is boot camps, which are military-style facilities that place much emphasis on discipline and physical labor. Another example is zero-tolerance policies in school systems, which mandate severe punishments—usually suspension and expulsion—for certain offenses. But perhaps the major thrust of the new get-tough initiatives involved making it easier to try older juveniles who committed serious crimes as adults. By 2000 the large majority of states had passed laws stating that older juveniles who committed certain serious offenses should be automatically sent to adult court (Griffin et al., 2011). Many of these juveniles were subsequently punished with confinement in adult prisons, some receiving sentences of life with no possibility of parole. The get-tough initiatives, it should be noted, disproportionately affected black and Latino youth (see Chapter 22).[7] The two cases described in Box 1.1, as well as the two cases that follow the boxed text, illustrate this shift in our view and treatment of juvenile offenders, especially older, serious offenders.

Case #1. One evening in 1997, a husband and wife were driving home with their two young children. They stopped at a convenience store in a crime-ridden neighborhood to buy soda. The wife got out of the car to make the purchase, while the husband and children remained in the car with the engine running and lights on. The parking lot adjacent to the store was a popular location for drug sellers. A 13-year-old known in the neighborhood as "Little B" approached the husband and told him to turn off his car lights (which were illuminating the drug market). The husband refused. Little B felt that he had been "disrespected" in front of the older drug dealers. He got a rifle that he had hidden nearby and

**Box 1.1   Child or Monster? Changing Views
of Serious Young Offenders Over Time**

The get-tough initiatives of the late 1980s and 1990s focused on older juveniles, yet there were also some efforts to get tough with *younger offenders*, although such efforts met with less success. Attempts to "throw the book" at very young offenders tend to provoke public outrage and face important legal obstacles, making it very difficult to treat members of that population like adult criminals. Nevertheless, the cases that follow help illustrate the change in attitudes toward serious juvenile offenders that occurred in the 1980s and 1990s. These two cases involve similar offenses that occurred about 25 years apart.

In 1971, in the Bay Area of San Francisco, a horrific scene was discovered. The body of a 20-month-old baby boy was found in a neighborhood play area. The baby had suffered a brutal beating—he had been pounced on and hit on the head with a brick—resulting in a ruptured liver, internal bleeding, and death. The police later determined that juveniles in the neighborhood were responsible for the killing, including two brothers, ages 7 and 10.

The oldest juvenile claimed that their intent was not to kill or injure the baby. Rather, while they were all playing together, the baby started to cry. The crying would not stop, so the brothers got mad and eventually hit the baby to make it be quiet. From there, he said, things just "got worse" (see transcripts from the *FRONTLINE* documentary "Little Criminals" at http://www.pbs.org/wgbh/pages/frontline/shows/little).

The public was shocked and saddened by news of the tragic death, but, for the most part, it was thought to be an anomaly, and few people could imagine charging the brothers with murder. This view was shared by one of the detectives involved in the case:

> [Kids] need supervision, period, and apparently these guys ran amok, and it's not their fault, really. . . . I think it would be criminal to [incarcerate] a 7-year-old and a 10-year-old. . . . We don't even do that to animals, for crying out loud. (quoted in Ferdinand, 1997)

Even the mother of the deceased infant shared this view. She emphasized that the two juveniles involved were just kids, and she expressed the hope that they would receive proper treatment. A juvenile court judge ruled in favor of therapy, ordering that the two brothers be placed "in a special home, where for two years they received extensive counseling and psychotherapy before being returned to their mother's custody. Their names were never made public" (Ferdinand, 1997).

About 25 years later, in the 1990s, a similar tragedy came to light in the Bay Area. This time, the juvenile believed to be responsible was only 6 years old. He had entered a neighbor's home with some other boys in search of a toy and came across an infant sleeping in a crib. He was accused of "mercilessly beating" the infant with a stick. Although the beating in this case did not result in death, the infant victim was left bloody, unconscious, and likely suffered permanent brain damage.

By the 1990s, the general public had become less patient with juvenile offenders. Reflecting a new get-tough stance toward youth crime, the 6-year-old suspect was informed of his legal rights and interrogated by seasoned detectives. Based on the facts of the case, the prosecutor decided to charge the boy with attempted murder. The prosecutor explained his decision in the following way: "It doesn't matter whether you're 6, or you're 106. If you do something that hurts somebody else, with knowledge of the wrongfulness of it, you're responsible for it, period."

(Continued)

(Continued)

Although members of the public protested the prosecutor's decision, the attention of court officials turned to a key legal issue: Was a 6-year-old boy competent to stand trial on an attempted murder charge? Could a 6-year-old understand, for example, the nature of a trial proceeding, such as the role of the judge and the possible outcomes? And what about the 6-year-old in this particular case? After all, he had been described as "mildly retarded" and had repeated kindergarten.

To resolve this legal issue, the juvenile court judge appointed several mental health experts. After interviewing the boy, one expert determined that he was indeed competent to stand trial, as he understood the "essentials" of a trial proceeding. The boy understood, for example, why he was being tried and that, "if things didn't go his way, he might not go home to see his mommy for a very long time." Furthermore, the expert expressed his opinion that the boy had all the characteristics of a "psychopath in the making." This novel diagnosis cast doubt on the ability of the boy to change and suggested that he would likely remain a threat to public safety. (Note: In the 1971 case, the outcomes of the juvenile offenders were mixed; the older boy avoided further trouble with the law, while the younger boy did not.)

A second expert for the court strongly disagreed. This expert did *not* believe the boy was competent to stand trial and explained that even a *gifted* 6-year-old would have difficulty appreciating the magnitude of a trial proceeding. He also criticized the first expert's diagnosis, especially the implication that the boy could not be helped: "There's no doubt in my mind but that we can effectively influence the life of any 6-year-old, the most violent 6-year-old included. And to desist from this, to reject that challenge, to turn away from that child is, I believe, very, very abusive."

In the end, the juvenile court judge ruled that the boy was *not* competent to stand trial. The boy was admitted to a facility for disturbed children where he received intensive therapy (reports suggest that he had been exposed to much violence in his short life, that he may have been abused by his mother's boyfriends, and that his mother lacked effective parenting skills). The prosecutor in the case, however, said he would "still press charges if the boy were later judged competent." (For a discussion of a more recent case, see the Teaching Aids section at the end of this chapter.)

Questions for Discussion

1. Based on the facts presented here, do you agree with the prosecutor's decision to charge the 6-year-old with attempted murder, so that the boy could be held responsible for his actions? Or do you agree with the view that, instead, efforts should be focused on the boy's treatment and rehabilitation? Justify the position you take.
2. In 1971, juvenile arrests in California were on the decline. Throughout the early to mid-1990s, juvenile arrests—especially arrests for serious violent crimes—had been increasing and received much coverage in the media. How might larger trends in juvenile crime (whether it was increasing or decreasing at the time) have affected the public's mood toward the juveniles in the two cases described earlier?

fired two shots into the car. The husband was killed in front of his two children. According to witnesses, Little B exclaimed that "This is still New Jack City!" referring to a movie about violent drug gangs.

Case #2. Our second case occurred in 1999, one month after two juveniles shot 13 other people to death at Columbine High School. A 15-year-old juvenile entered the commons area at Heritage High School in Conyers, Georgia. The juvenile was carrying a .22-caliber sawed-off rifle, and he started shooting into a crowd of between 150 and 200 students. He hit six of the students, although none died. He ran out of the school. Two of his classmates chased him. He pulled out a .357 Magnum handgun and fired at them but missed both. A letter was later found under the juvenile's bed. Part of it read:

> The one big question everybody is probably wondering is, Why? Well, for the sake of my brothers and sisters related to the Trenchcoat Mafia, that will have to remain a mystery to the public eye. I have been planning this for years, but I finally got pissed off enough to really do it. (quoted in Stafford, 1999:C1) [Note: The juveniles who killed 13 people at Columbine High School were said to be part of a group known as the "Trenchcoat Mafia."]

The response to these cases. These two juveniles elicited a different reaction from the community and juvenile justice system than the juvenile offenders described earlier in this chapter. With isolated exceptions, there was little talk of their immaturity and the need to guide and help them. Little B, in fact, was described in the media and by politicians as a "thug" and an "evil" in the city, among other things. Most people were outraged at the horrible crime he had committed and demanded that he be severely punished. Little B was tried as an adult and sentenced to life in prison. He will be eligible for parole after serving 14 years. The second juvenile was also tried as an adult and is now serving a 20-year term in prison; he will be eligible for parole when he is 33 years old.

These case studies illustrate an important point about the changing nature of juvenile delinquency: **Beginning in the late 1980s, older juveniles who committed serious crimes were viewed and treated less like "traditional" juvenile delinquents and more like adult offenders.**

Retreating from the Get-Tough Approach (Since the Early 2000s)

There is evidence that the way in which we view and treat juvenile offenders is again changing. In particular, the media, policy makers, and others are **once again starting to emphasize the differences between juveniles and adults, particularly the immaturity of juveniles. And this difference in view is leading to a retreat from the get-tough approach of the 1980s and 1990s.** There are several possible reasons for this change. There has been a dramatic decline in levels of delinquency, including serious delinquency, since the mid 1990s (see Chapter 3). People may feel less threatened by juvenile crime and so are perhaps less likely to embrace punitive or get-tough policies. New evidence on brain development over the life course has reinforced the view that juveniles are less mature than adults. As noted earlier, this evidence indicates that the brain continues to develop through the mid-20s, particularly that part of the brain responsible for the control of one's behavior. Also, evidence indicates that many of the get-tough approaches adopted in the 1980s and 1990s are not effective in reducing delinquency; in fact, they sometimes increase the likelihood of subsequent offending (see Chapter 23). This includes approaches such as trying juveniles as adults, confining them in institutions for long periods, placing them in boot camps, and zero-tolerance policies in the schools. For example, juveniles who are tried and punished as adults are somewhat more likely to offend than comparable juveniles tried in juvenile court (Feld and Bishop, 2012). Further, certain of the get-tough approaches are quite expensive and sometimes lead to the inhumane treatment of juveniles. Juveniles confined in adult prisons, for example, are more likely to be physically and sexually assaulted than those in juvenile facilities (see Mulvey and Schubert, 2012; Parsell, 2012).

As a result, **our treatment of juvenile offenders has changed somewhat since the early 2000s, with many of the get-tough approaches being scaled back or abandoned.** Fewer juveniles are being sent to institutions. The number of confined juveniles declined from 108,802 in 2000 to 54,148 in 2013, (Hockenberry and Puzzanchera, 2015). Many states have abandoned or are phasing out the use of boot camps. The federal government has recommended that certain other punitive measures, such as zero-tolerance policies in the schools, be ended (Hefling, 2014). At the same time, rehabilitative measures are being more widely used in many states (Lee, 2013). Such measures include drug treatment, after-school programs, and restorative justice approaches, which allow offenders to repair the harm they have caused through activities such as community service. We do not have good data on trends in the number of juveniles tried in adult courts (see Griffin et al., 2011). But since 2005 almost half the states have passed laws designed to reduce the likelihood that juveniles will be tried as adults or, if tried and sentenced, confined in adult prisons (Schwartz, 2013). Also, a few states have *raised* the age at which offenders are treated as adults. For example, Connecticut raised the age from 16 to 18, and New York is considering doing the same. Finally, the Supreme Court issued a series of major decisions stating that it is unconstitutional to impose certain severe sanctions on juveniles on the grounds that they are less mature than adults. These decisions are described next.

The juvenile death penalty. In early 2005, twenty states permitted the execution of individuals who committed their crimes when they were 16 or 17 years old. More than 70 such individuals were on death row at this time (see Sharp et al., 2007). Since 1973, 22 individuals who committed their crimes while they were juveniles have been executed. On March 1, 2005, the Supreme Court forbade the execution of individuals who committed their crimes before turning 18. The following comments about the case (Roper v. Simmons, 543 U.S. 551 [2005]) appeared in an article by Linda Greenhouse in the New York Times.

> Three general differences between juveniles under 18 and adults demonstrate that juvenile offenders cannot with reliability be classified among the worst offenders. First, as any parent knows and as the scientific and sociological studies . . . tend to confirm, "a lack of maturity and an undeveloped sense of responsibility are found in youth more often than in adults and are more understandable among the young. These qualities often result in impetuous and ill-considered actions and decisions."
>
> The second area of difference is that juveniles are more vulnerable or susceptible to negative influences and outside pressures, including peer pressure. The third broad difference is that the character of a juvenile is not as well formed as that of an adult. The personality traits of juveniles are more transitory, less fixed. . . .
>
> These differences render suspect any conclusion that a juvenile falls among the worst offenders. Once the diminished culpability of juveniles is recognized, it is evident that the penological justifications for the death penalty apply to them with lesser force than to adults. . . . The age of 18 is the point where society draws the line for many purposes between childhood and adulthood. It is, we conclude, the age at which the line for death eligibility ought to rest. (Greenhouse, 2005:A14)[8]

Life without parole for juveniles. In 2010, the Supreme Court ruled that juveniles who commit crimes in which no one dies cannot be sentenced to life with no possibility of parole (Graham v. Florida, 560 U.S. 48 [2010]). Thirty-seven states and the District of Columbia allowed such sentences (Liptak, 2010). And in 2012, the Supreme Court struck down laws that *mandated* a sentence of life without parole for murderers who committed their crimes under age 18 (Liptak and Bronner, 2012). More than 2,000 people had been sentenced under such laws. According to the Court, judges cannot impose a sentence of life without possibility of parole on juvenile murderers unless they have considered the defendant's age, level of maturity, life circumstances, and the nature of the crime (Miller v. Alabama, 567 U.S. 460 [2012]). In both the 2010 and 2012 decisions, the Supreme Court stated that children are less mature than adults and so should be treated differently by the justice system, particularly with respect to the most severe sanctions.

So our view and treatment of juvenile offenders continues to evolve. Juveniles are generally seen as less mature than adults and therefore less deserving of punishment, but more in need of guidance and help. But sometimes juvenile offenders, particularly older, more serious offenders, are viewed and treated more like adults. And at other times the differences between juveniles and adults are emphasized, and more effort is devoted to rehabilitating, rather than punishing, juvenile offenders. To learn how juvenile offenders are viewed and treated in other nations, see Box 1.2.

Box 1.2   Juvenile Delinquency & Juvenile Justice across the Globe

Juvenile delinquency is a global problem (Krohn and Lane, 2015). To get a better sense of this, we briefly summarize juvenile crime trends and juvenile justice practices in two very different countries: Brazil and China.

Brazil. In recent decades, Brazilian society has undergone major changes and tranformations. Emerging from a military dictatorship in the 1980s, Brazil experienced extreme inequality, economic instability, and increasing urbanization, with large numbers of people "living in city slums" (Diniz Filho and Lopes, 2015:27-28). These problems were associated with high rates of youth violence as well as violence against street youth committed by "self-appointed vigilante groups made up of off-duty policemen." (Note: The homicide rate in Brazil is about five times higher than in the United States—see Currie, 2016.) These developments prompted significant legal reforms, including laws granting protections to juveniles who commit "infractions" (acts that would be crimes if committed by adults). These protections give priority to rehabilitation and reintegration with family and community, with detention as a last resort.

In practice, however, many juveniles are confined in "educational detention facilities" where they remain idle; conditions are poor, and the detainees have been subject to violent abuse by guards. Further, "zero tolerance practices have permeated Brazil's culture in such a profound way that most citizens tacitly approve of police abuse as a legitimate resource to maintain public safety" (Diniz Filho and Lopes, 2015:35). Youth violence, however, continues to rise.

Nevertheless, there are encouraging signs. Certain Brazilian states have launched innovative violence prevention programs that provide incentives for youth to stay in school. These programs also prepare at-risk youth for employment. Evaluations of these programs are ongoing, but there is some evidence they may be helping to reduce crime (Diniz Filho and Lopes, 2015).

China. Although we have limited data on crime and delinquency in China, it is believed that China has traditionally been a low-crime country, where Confucian values encouraged people to "uphold the honor of their family, to think of the consequences of their behaviors to the groups to which they belong, and to be loyal to friends and rulers" (Dong, 2015:76). During the Cultural Revolution of the 1960s, however, traditional customs and values were challenged by social and political reformers and youth were encouraged to struggle against the existing social order.

By the 1980s, China experienced a "crime boom." The government responded with a "hard strike" campaign focused on punishment and deterrence, which included the

(Continued)

(Continued)

death penalty. This campaign targeted juvenile gang leaders and serious adult criminals. Although "hard strike" had a short-term deterrent effect, rates of juvenile delinquency continued to rise over the long run (Dong, 2015).

In the 1990s major legal reforms were enacted that require the entire society to play a role in the prevention of crime and rehabilitation of juvenile offenders:

> In practice, "education and rescue teams" are formed around juvenile delinquents, which comprise their parents, relatives, teachers, members of local neighborhood committees, and the police. . . . For different cases, [remedies] include victim-offender reconciliation, heart-to-heart talks between juvenile delinquents and representatives of the "education and rescue team," group discussion of juvenile delinquents' problems and offering criticisms and suggestions, and group study of laws and regulations. (Dong, 2015:81)

Serious and violent juvenile offenders can be sentenced to reformatories, where they wear uniforms and spend half their waking hours in educational activities and the other half performing labor. Although good crime statistics from China are difficult to obtain, available data indicate that China has a homicide rate that is about five times *lower* than that of the United States. (For more on international comparisons, see Krohn and Lane, 2015.)

Questions for Discussion
1. What lessons, if any, could be learned from these international comparisons, and from the experiences of Brazil and China?
2. It is said that China's "hard strike" campaign deterred crime for a time, but did not have lasting effects. Why might this be the case? (Note: see Chapter 23 for a discussion of police "crackdowns" in the United States.)

SUMMARY

You now know what juvenile delinquency is. The term refers to violations of the criminal law (and sometimes status offense laws) by minors. You also know that our society tends to view and treat juvenile delinquents differently than adult criminals—although older juveniles who commit serious crimes are something of an exception. Now that you know what delinquency is, we next want to examine the extent of delinquency and the characteristics of delinquents. Before doing that, however, we must present information on how delinquency is measured—which is the topic of Chapter 2.

TEACHING AIDS

Web-Based Exercises

The invention of delinquency. Watch the YouTube video, "Juvenile Court Documentary" by Shelby County, much of which focuses on the origins of the Memphis Juvenile Court. Relate the video to this chapter's discussion of the invention of juvenile delinquency. In particular, what forces lead to the creation of the court (e.g., the growth of slums in Memphis, street youth getting into trouble)? Who lobbied for the creation of the court? Was the court created to guide and help juveniles or to exercise greater control over them? Compare the arguments made in the video to those in the article by Randall G. Shelden and Lynn T. Osborne, "'For Their Own Good?': Class Interests and the Child Saving

Movement in Memphis, Tennessee, 1900–1917" (*Criminology*, vol. 27 [1989], pp. 747–767). Why do you think the video and the article by Shelden and Osborne present such different views on the origin of the court? Do you favor one view over the other? If so, why?

The evolving view and treatment of juvenile offenders. Drawing on YouTube or other websites, find a video that criticizes some method of responding to juvenile offenders, argues that we should respond to juvenile offenders differently, or both. This may be a contemporary video (e.g., one that criticizes placing juvenile offenders in adult prisons or argues for the use of some get-tough approaches) or a video from the past (e.g., one that criticizes the death penalty for juveniles). Many such videos can be found by using search terms like "juvenile delinquency," "juvenile court," "juvenile prison," "juvenile death penalty," and "get-tough juvenile delinquents." List the reasons why the video is critical of the response described or recommends an alternative response. Does the video support its argument by presenting a particular view of juveniles (e.g., as immature, as "street smart" and dangerous)? If possible, determine who produced or sponsored the video, describe the purpose of this group, and discuss what they may have hoped to accomplish with this video.

Controversial Case

As indicated in this chapter, there was a movement from the late 1980s to the early 2000s to treat older juveniles accused of having committed serious crimes as adults, trying these suspects in adult courts, and subjecting them to the same punishments as adults. While there has been a retreat from this approach in recent years, it is still the case that large numbers of older, serious juvenile offenders are tried and punished as adults. Even very young offenders still face the possibility of being tried as adults, as discussed shortly. Some individuals argue that we should abandon this practice, while others argue in favor of treating at least some juvenile offenders as adults.[9] The case study that follows is designed to get you to think about the extent to which juvenile offenders should be treated like adult offenders.

The "Slender Man" case. In the spring of 2014, a 12-year-old girl in Waukesha, Wisconsin, was stabbed 19 times and left for dead. Although the girl survived the attack and went back to school, the community was shocked to learn that the crime had allegedly been hatched by two other girls, friends of the victim. The two friends, who were also 12 years old at the time, told police they had developed an obsession with "Slender Man"—a fictional bogeyman character that appears in various stories and videos on the internet.

According to the girls, they came to believe that Slender Man "would harm them or their families if they didn't kill in his name" (Aradillas, 2017:105). Since 2014, both girls have been confined in separate facilities, having been charged with first-degree attempted murder. A newspaper report summarized the situation as follows:

> Anyone 10 or older charged with first-degree attempted homicide is automatically considered an adult under Wisconsin law. But defense attorneys have argued that the case belongs in juvenile court, saying the adolescents suffer from mental illness and won't get the treatment they need in the adult prison system. Experts testified that one of the girls has schizophrenia and an oppositional defiant disorder that requires long-term mental health treatment. The other girl has been diagnosed with a delusional disorder and a condition known as schizotypy, which a psychologist testified made her vulnerable to believing in Slender Man. (Associated Press, 2016)

In 2016, however, a Wisconsin judge ruled that the two girls should be tried as adults. He pointed to the extreme nature of the violence, the fact that it was planned in advance, and the fact that, if convicted, the juvenile court would have to release the girls at age 18. In contrast, if they are convicted in adult court they could be sentenced to prison for up to 65 years. The girls are now awaiting trial in adult court.

Do you think the two girls should be tried as adults or juveniles? If you believe they should be tried as adults, for how long should they be sentenced to prison if convicted? Justify the positions you take. (Note: For more on mental illness and juvenile justice, see Box 13.2 in Chapter 13; you may also have an interest in an HBO documentary on the case titled, *Beware of Slenderman.*)

TEST YOUR KNOWLEDGE OF THIS CHAPTER

1. What is juvenile delinquency?
2. Describe the major differences in the way that society views juvenile offenders and adult offenders.
3. What does it mean to say that juveniles are "immature"?
4. Describe the major differences in the way that society treats juvenile offenders and adult offenders. Discuss how these differences reflect our differing views of juvenile and adult offenders.
5. What is a status offense? Name at least five status offenses. What is the rationale, or reason, for having status offenses?
6. What are the major criticisms against status offense laws?
7. How have states responded to these criticisms?
8. List the major ways in which juvenile court differs from adult court. Discuss the reasons for such differences.
9. Describe the ways in which juvenile courts are becoming more like adult courts.
10. Describe how juvenile correctional institutions differ from those for adults.
11. Why are older juveniles who commit serious crimes being viewed and treated more like adult offenders?
12. What do we mean by "the invention of juvenile delinquency"?
13. How can we explain the invention of juvenile delinquency?
14. How has our view or conception of children changed over time? What are some of the reasons for the changes?

15. Describe the major social changes that occurred in the United States during the 1800s and early 1900s and how they contributed to the invention of juvenile delinquency.

16. There are two interpretations of how concern over the poor children in slums contributed to the invention of juvenile delinquency. Describe these interpretations. Describe how we might determine which is correct.

17. Describe how our view and treatment of juvenile offenders changed from the late 1980s to the early 2000s. What were the reasons for this change?

18. Describe how our view and treatment of juvenile offenders has changed since the early 2000s. What are the reasons for this change?

19. Why did the Supreme Court strike down laws that imposed the death penalty for juveniles? According to the Supreme Court, is it now permissible to impose a sentence of life with no possibility of parole on individuals who committed their crime(s) while juveniles? If so, under what conditions?

THOUGHT AND DISCUSSION QUESTIONS

1. Do you think status offenses should be illegal? Defend your answer. If status offenses should not be illegal, how should we respond to them, if at all? (It may help to consider each status offense in turn. For example, should running away from home be illegal? If not, how should we respond to juveniles who run away?)

2. Do you think older juveniles who commit serious crimes should be treated like adult offenders? Defend your answer.

KEY TERMS

- Juvenile delinquency
- Immaturity
- Status offenses
- Juvenile court
- Due process rights
- Adjudicated
- Disposition
- Youth development centers and training schools
- Invention of juvenile delinquency
- Child savers

ENDNOTES

1. See Feld, 1999; Rutter et al., 1998; E. Scott, 2002; Steinberg and Cauffman, 2000; Zimring, 1998, 2005.

2. See Applegate et al., 2009; Bishop, 2006; Cullen, 2006; Gerber and Engelhardt-Greer, 1996; Mears et al., 2007; A. R. Roberts, 2004; J. Roberts, 2004; also see Bernard and Kurlychek, 2010; Empey et al., 1999; Feld, 1999; Howell, 1997a; M. Moon et al., 2000; Roberts and Stalans, 1997; Tanenhaus, 2012; Triplett, 1996; Zimring, 1998.

3. See Bernard, 1992; Butts and Mitchell, 2000; Empey et al., 1999; Feld, 1998, 1999; Howell, 1997a, 2003a; Krisberg, 2005; Kupchik, 2006; Puzzanchera and Hockenberry, 2013; A. R. Roberts, 2004; J. Roberts, 2004; Rosenheim et al., 2002; H. Snyder and Sickmund, 2006; Tanenhaus, 2012; Zimring, 1998.

4. Also see Butts and Mitchell, 2000; Cullen, 2006; Feld, 1999; Howell, 2003a; Krisberg, 2005; Kupchik, 2006; H. Snyder and Sickmund, 2006; Tanenhaus, 2012; Zimring, 2005.

5. For excellent overviews of this topic, see Bernard and Kurlychek, 2010; Chavez-Garcia, 2007; Empey et al., 1999; Feld, 1999; Howell, 1997a; also see Aries, 1962; DeMause, 1974; Finestone,

1976; Platt, 1969; Salerno, 1991; Schlossman, 1977; Shelden and Osborne, 1989; Sutton, 1988; Tanenhaus, 2012; Ward, 2012.

6. See Cullen, 2006; Howell, 2003a; Tanenhaus, 2012; Zimring, 1998.

7. See Applegate et al., 2009; Cullen, 2006; Mears et al., 2007; Moon et al., 2000; Pastore and Maguire, 2003; Robert and Stalans, 1997; J. Roberts, 2004; Tanenhaus, 2012; Triplett, 1996; Zimring, 2005.

8. See Butts and Mitchell, 2000; Feld, 1999; Howell, 2003a; M. Jackson and Knepper, 2003; Ward, 2012.

9. For further information on juveniles and the death penalty, see Chapter 23 of this text; Bohm, 2003; Cothern, 2000; Feld, 1999:236–238; Howell, 2003a:37–39; Zimring, 2005.

2 How Is Delinquency Measured?

Now that you know what delinquency is, we want to answer two basic questions about it: How much delinquency is there in the United States, and is delinquency increasing? But before we can answer these questions (Chapter 3), we first have to discuss the different ways of measuring delinquency. As you will see, the way in which delinquency is measured often has a major impact on the conclusions that are drawn about the extent of delinquency and trends in delinquency. You might be groaning a bit right now, thinking, "Oh no, I don't want to read some technical discussion about how to measure delinquency!" But bear with us; this information is important. A lot of what you hear about the extent of delinquency and trends in delinquency is wrong or misleading. This section will help you understand why.

There are **three major ways of measuring the extent of and trends in delinquency:** (1) **"official" statistics** from the police, juvenile court, and juvenile correctional agencies; (2) **"self-report" data** from juveniles, with juveniles being asked about the offenses they have committed; and (3) **"victimization" data,** with people being asked whether they have been the victims of various crimes. This chapter describes each of these methods and their advantages and disadvantages.[1]

After reading this chapter, you should be able to:

- Describe the three major ways to estimate the extent of delinquency and trends in delinquency.
- Identify the strengths and weaknesses of each method.
- Indicate how these strengths and weaknesses impact estimates of the extent of and trends in delinquency.
- Explain why reports of the extent of delinquency or trends in delinquency are often misleading.

OFFICIAL STATISTICS—ESPECIALLY ARREST DATA FROM THE POLICE

Official statistics **include data from the police, the courts, and juvenile correctional agencies,** that is, data from the "official agencies" responsible for dealing with juvenile offenders. **The most commonly used official statistics are arrest data from the police.** Because only some of the juveniles arrested by the police are referred to juvenile court, and only some of the people referred to juvenile court are sent to juvenile correctional agencies, arrest data provide a more accurate indication of the extent of delinquency. We, therefore, focus on arrest data in this discussion (data from juvenile courts and correctional agencies are described in Chapter 21).

Each year the FBI collects data from the police and publishes these data in a report called *Crime in the United States: The Uniform Crime Reports*. The reports are available on the FBI's website at http://www.fbi.gov. Each report is divided into several sections. The first section contains information on the number of *crimes known to the police*. As the name implies, these are crimes that the police know about, both crimes that have been reported to the police and crimes that the police have discovered on their own. The second section contains information on the number of *crimes that have been "cleared" or solved by arrest*. Contrary to the impression you might get from the media, most crimes are not cleared by arrest. In 2015, less than half (46 percent) of the violent crimes known to the police were cleared by arrest, and only 19 percent of the property crimes known to police were cleared by arrest (see Box 2.1). The third section contains information on the **number of arrests** and the characteristics of the people who were arrested, including the most serious offense they were arrested for and the individuals' age, sex, and race. Note that the number of *crimes cleared by arrest* is not equal to the number of arrests. Sometimes

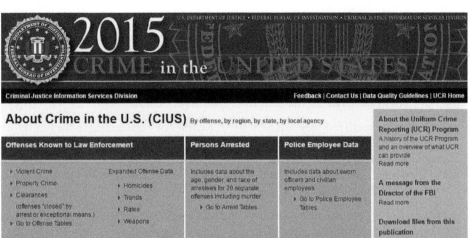

2015

CRIME in the UNITED STATES

U.S. DEPARTMENT OF JUSTICE • FEDERAL BUREAU OF INVESTIGATION • CRIMINAL JUSTICE INFORMATION SERVICES DIVISION

Criminal Justice Information Services Division   Feedback | Contact Us | Data Quality Guidelines | UCR Home

About Crime in the U.S. (CIUS) By offense, by region, by state, by local agency

Offenses Known to Law Enforcement		Persons Arrested	Police Employee Data
▸ Violent Crime	Expanded Offense Data	Includes data about the age, gender, and race of arrestees for 28 separate offenses including murder	Includes data about sworn officers and civilian employees
▸ Property Crime	▸ Homicides		
▸ Clearances	▸ Trends	▸ Go to Arrest Tables	▸ Go to Police Employee Tables
(offenses "closed" by arrest or exceptional means.)	▸ Rates		
▸ Go to Offense Tables	▸ Weapons		

▸ **Caution Against Ranking**

Additional Reports

▸ **Federal Crime Data**
The second report from the UCR Program looking at Federal Crime reporting. This year's report includes 2015 data from FBI and ATF cases as well as traditional offense information from other federal agencies.

▸ **Human Trafficking**
Report from the UCR Program's Human Trafficking data collection. The content includes general information about human trafficking as well as data provided by agencies that reported human trafficking offenses in 2015.

▸ **Cargo Theft**
Report from the UCR Program's Cargo Theft data collection. The content includes general information about cargo theft as well as data provided by agencies that reported cargo theft incidents in 2015.

About the Uniform Crime Reporting (UCR) Program
A history of the UCR Program and an overview of what UCR can provide
Read more

A message from the Director of the FBI
Read more

Download files from this publication
Access a compressed file with all of the spreadsheets and PDFs in this publication

Go to previous editions of CIUS
Visit the UCR publications page

A summary of crime in the Nation in 2015
Go to an overview of this publication

An addendum about changes to the rape data
The offense definition of rape, as well as the collection and presentation of rape data, have changed.
Read more

Box 2.1   Do the Crime, Avoid the Time? The Apprehension of Offenders as the Weak Link in the Juvenile Justice Process

Viewers of television crime shows, such as *CSI: Crime Scene Investigation,* may be surprised to learn that, in the real world, most crimes that come to the attention of the police go unsolved. Despite recent advances in forensic and other crime-fighting technologies, the arrest and punishment of offenders remains far from certain. Few may appreciate this fact more than the offenders themselves.

In one study, researchers examined young people who self-reported a very high rate of serious offending over a two-year period (specifically, these youths reported 20 or more serious "index" offenses, such as aggravated assaults, burglaries, and auto thefts). It turned out that only 4 percent of these youth had been arrested for an index offense during the period under study (an additional 18 percent had been arrested for something other than an index offense). Apparently, police were unable to solve these index crimes, or perhaps the crimes were never reported to the police to begin with. The more crime an individual commits, the greater the odds of arrest; however, researchers estimate that the "likelihood of arrest is close to zero" until one reports in excess of 20 index offenses (Dunford and Elliott, 1984:81). (In the next chapter, we examine these data more closely.)

It appears that many young offenders come to appreciate the uncertainty of arrest or apprehension, and this is true even among those offenders who have been arrested

(Continued)

(Continued)

and punished in the past. In a large survey of incarcerated juveniles, respondents were asked to estimate the likelihood that they would be arrested again should they reoffend. A sizable percentage (39 percent) believed they would **not** be arrested. (However, most believed that, if they were caught, they would be punished, and punished more severely than in the past). As the authors of the survey observe:

> Perhaps these youth feel they will be better at eluding law enforcement in the future, or perhaps they recognize the considerable challenge that officers face in solving crime and apprehending those responsible. Whatever their reasoning, youth's answers [in the survey referred to] suggest that arrest or apprehension is the weakest link in the sanctioning process. (Sedlak and Bruce, 2010:9)

If offenders believe that the overall odds of apprehension are low, then this fact may help explain their attraction to delinquency. Moreover, getting away with delinquency and outwitting the authorities may be rewarding and may increase the likelihood of repeat offending. In the words of one offender:

> The worst thing that can happen to a kid, or a guy—is to go out and do something [a crime] and be successful the first time out. I got a proposition to drive a car in a bank job, so I went. Everything went off good. . . . I was just going to drive a [getaway] car once; I'd give it a try. And it worked out so good, so, like I say, if you're a success, it feels good. So we kept going. (quoted in Laub and Sampson, 2003:181–182)

Furthermore, some offenders may work to develop their apprehension-avoidance skills, as illustrated by the following young man, who was not incarcerated but remained active on the streets at the time of the interview):

> A lot of people look at me, or look at criminals, and we're depicted as dumb folks. . . . But I ain't no dummy, by far, OK? Criminals these days are smarter, man, a lot smarter. Because the more cops come up with the different things, like these cameras on the street corner, there's a lot more challenges you got to get up to. [The offender then described how he reads *Popular Mechanics* and other magazines to stay ahead of new car alarm systems and other crime control technologies.] (quoted in Brezina and Topalli, 2009)

Questions for Discussion

1. What impressions have you or your classmates received from watching television crime shows, such as *CSI*? Have you been under the impression that most crimes in the real world are "solved," with the persons responsible being arrested? Do you think the average viewer is able to separate fact from fiction?
2. Much crime-control legislation has focused on increasing the severity of punishment, with heavier fines, jail time, or longer prison sentences for various offenses. Do you think these punishments can deter crime if offenders perceive a low likelihood of arrest or apprehension?

multiple crimes might be cleared by a single arrest. For example, an individual may be arrested for several burglaries. And sometimes a single crime is cleared by the arrest of many people. For example, several people may be arrested for a single burglary. Juveniles usually commit their crimes in groups, and it is often the case that several juveniles are arrested for a single crime (see Chapter 16 for further discussion).

Information on the extent of delinquency and trends in delinquency comes from
the clearance and arrest data. These data (unlike the "crimes known to the police" data)
contain information on the age of the offender. So they allow us to estimate such things as
the number of crimes committed by juveniles, the number of arrests that involve juveniles,
the most serious offense these juveniles were arrested for, and whether juvenile arrests are
increasing or decreasing. Most media reports regarding the extent of and trends in delinquency are based on these clearance and arrest data.

The FBI Crime Reports focus on what are known as "Part I," or "index," offenses
and "Part II" offenses. The *Part I, or index, offenses* are eight relatively serious violent
and property crimes: *criminal homicide, forcible rape, robbery, aggravated assault, burglary, larceny-theft, motor vehicle theft, and arson.* (Note: Recently, the FBI added human
trafficking crimes to the Part I offenses. Because data on these crimes remain limited, we
do not focus on them in this chapter.) The FBI reports both "crimes known to the police"
and clearance/arrest data on these offenses. The top half of Table 2.1 provides a definition of each of these offenses. Read these definitions and then try to answer the following
multiple-choice question:

> Your roommate steals your TV from the living room of your apartment while you are
> attending class. Is this a:
>
> a. burglary
> b. larceny-theft
> c. robbery
> d. all of the above

The *Part II offenses* consist of 20 additional offenses as well as a category for "all
other offenses." These offenses are listed in the bottom part of Table 2.1. Note that
this list includes one status offense: curfew violation. Also, liquor law violations often
involve the status offense of drinking under age. Arrests for all other status offenses are
included in the "all other offenses" category. The FBI reports arrest data for the Part II
offenses only.

The data from the FBI have several advantages. They are collected from police
departments representing approximately 95 percent of the U.S. population. They have
been collected since 1930, so they provide long-term information on trends in crime. And
certain evidence suggests that the "crimes known to the police" data provide a moderately
accurate measure of the extent of and trends in certain types of serious crime, particularly
homicide and serious instances of certain other crimes like robbery, burglary, and motor
vehicle theft (see Gove et al., 1985). But at the same time, a number of problems are associated with the FBI data, particularly the arrest data.

Problems with Arrest Data

Arrest data greatly underestimate the extent of most forms of delinquency and may
sometimes provide misleading information about trends in delinquency. There are several reasons for this underestimation, including the following.

Most delinquent acts do not become known to the police. There are three reasons
for this. **First,** the police usually find out about a crime when someone else—usually the
crime victim—reports it to them. But surveys of crime victims indicate that only about
40 percent of all crime victimizations are reported to the police. Not surprisingly, serious crimes are more likely to be reported to the police than minor crimes. Serious crimes
include those where a weapon is used, the victim is injured, and/or there is a significant
financial loss. Crimes involving strangers are also more likely to be reported to the police.
And crimes against adults are more likely to be reported to the police than crimes against

TABLE 2.1 Part I and Part II Offenses

Part I or Index Offenses

1. **Criminal Homicide:** (a) Murder and nonnegligent manslaughter: the willful (nonnegligent) killing of one human being by another. Deaths caused by negligence, attempts to kill, assaults to kill, suicides, and accidental deaths are excluded. Justifiable homicides are also excluded. (b) Manslaughter by negligence: the killing of another person through gross negligence. Deaths of persons due to their own negligence, accidental deaths not resulting from gross negligence, and traffic fatalities are not included in the category manslaughter by negligence.
2. **Rape:** The penetration, no matter how slight, of the vagina or anus with any body part or object, or oral penetration by a sex organ of another person, without the consent of the victim.
3. **Robbery:** The taking or attempting to take anything of value from the care, custody, or control of a person or persons by force or threat of force or violence and/or by putting the victim in fear.
4. **Aggravated assault:** An unlawful attack by one person upon another for the purpose of inflicting severe or aggravated bodily injury. This type of assault is usually accompanied by the use of a weapon or by means likely to produce death or great bodily harm. Simple assaults are excluded.
5. **Burglary:** The unlawful entry of a structure to commit a felony or a theft. Attempted forcible entry is included.
6. **Larceny-theft:** The unlawful taking, carrying, leading, or riding away of property from the possession or constructive possession of another. Examples are thefts of bicycles, motor vehicle parts and accessories, shoplifting, pocket-picking, or the stealing of any property or article that is not taken by force and violence or by fraud. Attempted larcenies are included. Embezzlement, confidence games, forgery, check fraud, etc., are excluded.
7. **Motor vehicle theft:** The theft or attempted theft of a motor vehicle. A motor vehicle is self-propelled and runs on land surface and not on rails.
8. **Arson:** The willful or malicious burning or attempt to burn, with or without intent to defraud, a dwelling house, public building, motor vehicle or aircraft, personal property of another, etc.

Part II Offenses

Other assaults

Forgery and counterfeiting

Fraud

Embezzlement

Stolen property: buying, receiving, possessing

Vandalism

Weapons: carrying, possessing, etc.

Prostitution and commercialized vice

Sex offenses (except forcible rape and prostitution)

Drug abuse violations

Gambling

Offenses against family and children

Driving under the influence

Liquor laws

Drunkenness

Disorderly conduct

Vagrancy

All other offenses

Suspicion

Curfew and loitering law violations

SOURCE: Federal Bureau of Investigation, 2016.

juveniles (see Finkelhor and Ormond, 1999; Watkins, 2005). **Second,** crimes like drug use and gambling do not have a "victim" in the usual sense of the word—that is, someone who feels that he or she has been injured. It is unlikely that the participants in these crimes will notify the police. And **third,** it is physically difficult for the police to detect most crimes on their own. Obviously they cannot detect crimes that occur in private, but they also have trouble detecting crimes that occur in public. The police in a patrol car may pass a given spot on their beat once or twice a day, if that often, so they are unlikely to come upon crimes in progress. The police therefore do not even know about the large majority of crimes that occur, especially the less serious crimes. As a result, even the "crimes known to the police" data greatly underestimate the extent of crime, with the exception of homicide and serious instances of a few other crimes.

Even when crimes become known to the police, the police do not catch the offender in most cases. As we discuss further in Chapter 20, the police are unlikely to catch the offender unless they discover the offender at the scene of the crime, or unless someone can identify the offender to them; this is one reason why police are more likely to catch offenders who commit violent crimes than those who commit property crimes. Most violent crimes involve people who know one another, so the victim can often identify the offender (or the police have a good idea of who the offender might be). But for nonviolent crimes, which constitute the vast majority of crimes, the police usually do not catch the offender.

The police do not arrest most of the suspected offenders they catch. As you will learn in Chapter 20, the police have a lot of discretion over whether to arrest suspected offenders. They exercise that discretion by releasing most of the suspected offenders they encounter. **Several factors influence whether the police make an arrest;** the seriousness of the offense is most important. But other factors also have an impact. The attitude of the victim or complainant is quite important. Does the victim press for arrest? If so, the police will usually make an arrest. If the victim argues against arrest, the police will usually let the offender go. As discussed in Chapter 22, the characteristics of the offender—including race, class, and sex—often influence the likelihood of arrest. The characteristics of the police department may also be important. Some police departments encourage officers to informally resolve criminal matters, while others encourage officers to make arrests.[2] Also, police departments occasionally crack down on certain offenses, like drug crimes, prostitution, curfew violation, and truancy. The police are more likely to search for and arrest individuals committing such crimes during a crackdown. For example, the transit police in the city of Atlanta instituted a crackdown against truancy, and as a result the number of juveniles apprehended for truancy increased by almost 200 percent over a two-year period.

Research has shown that only about 20 percent of the crimes known to the police are cleared by arrest. (As indicated earlier, this percentage varies by type of crime. In 2015, 62 percent of all murders and 54 percent of all aggravated or serious assaults were cleared by arrest, versus 13 percent of all burglaries and 13 percent of all motor vehicle thefts.)

Police data reported to the FBI are sometimes inaccurate. On top of all this, the police sometimes report inaccurate data to the FBI. Sometimes these inaccurate reports are the result of unintentional errors on the part of the police, and sometimes the police deliberately distort crime data in an effort to make themselves look good—for example, by *"unfounding" crime reports*. The police usually investigate crime reports by citizens to determine whether a crime has occurred and what type of crime has occurred, if any. If they feel that a crime has not occurred, they "unfound" the crime report. And that "crime" does not become part of the "crimes known to the police" data reported to the FBI. Some police departments have lowered their crime rates by unfounding a large percentage of the crimes reported to them. The police in our hometown of Atlanta were accused of wrongly unfounding a large number of crimes in 1996. An external audit found some support for this accusation. For example, Atlanta reported 392 rapes to the FBI in 1996. This represented an 11 percent decrease in rapes compared to 1995. The external audit, however, concluded that the Atlanta police wrongly unfounded 56 rapes in 1996. If these 56 rapes had been reported to the FBI along with the other rapes, the number of rapes in Atlanta would have increased 2 percent from 1995 (Martz, 1999).

Another common way in which the police distort crime data involves **reclassifying crimes** from more to less serious categories. For example, police officials may reclassify aggravated assaults as simple assaults or burglaries as larcenies. A report in the *New York Times* stated that about one-quarter of the felonies or serious crimes recorded in a New York City precinct in 2002 were improperly downgraded to misdemeanors or minor crimes. As a result of this downgrading, the precinct reported a 7.4 percent drop in serious crime compared to 2001. But when the improperly downgraded crimes were reclassified as felonies, the precinct had a 15 percent increase in serious crime. According to the news report, precinct commanders in New York City were under much pressure to keep crime rates down, and some claim that this occasionally led certain officials to "shave numbers" (Rashbaum, 2003).

The FBI arrest data report only the most serious offense for which the person is arrested. For example, suppose a juvenile robs someone while under the influence of an illicit drug. The juvenile may be arrested for both robbery and drug abuse, but only the robbery arrest will be shown in the FBI data. The FBI data on drug abuse arrests indicate only the number of arrests for which drug abuse is the most serious charge. Many additional drug abuse arrests may have been made, but these arrests are not reported by the FBI because drug abuse is not the most serious charge. (Note: The National Incident-Based Reporting System [NIBRS] was designed to provide more complete data on juvenile arrests, but not enough states participate in the program at this time to permit generalizations to the United States as a whole [see Bierie, 2015].)

Summary
Arrest data, then, vastly underestimate the extent of delinquency. This underestimation is **especially true for minor delinquency,** which is less likely to become known to the police and is less likely to result in arrest. Further, **arrest data may provide misleading information on trends in delinquency.** Suppose, for example, that arrest data show an increase in juvenile delinquency over time. This increase could be due to a number of factors. Perhaps victims have become more likely to report crimes to the police (e.g., the percentage of violent crimes reported to the police increased from 43 percent in 1993 to 49 percent in 2009—see Truman and Rand, 2010). Perhaps complainants have become more likely to press for arrest (e.g., stores have become more likely to press for arrest in shoplifting cases). Perhaps police departments have become more likely to encourage officers to make arrests (e.g., some police departments have adopted zero-tolerance policing, where even minor violations of the law may result in arrest). Perhaps the police have cracked down on certain types of crime, like drug use or gun-related crimes. Perhaps the police are turning in more accurate crime reports (data suggest that crime reports have become more accurate in recent decades). Or perhaps juvenile delinquency really is increasing. It is sometimes the case that we cannot tell which factor or factors are responsible for a change in arrest rates.

SELF-REPORT DATA

Given the problems with arrest data, criminologists have tried to develop alternative ways to measure the extent of delinquency. The major alternative they have developed is *self-report data*. Self-report data are obtained by asking juveniles about the extent of their delinquency. Sometimes the juveniles are interviewed, and sometimes they fill out questionnaires. Most self-report surveys focus on delinquency committed during the previous year, to minimize problems with memory. In almost all cases, self-report surveys are anonymous, or respondents are assured that their answers are confidential. A popular self-report measure of delinquency is shown in Table 2.2. Take a few minutes to answer the questions in this measure (although you should not record the answers in this book in case it is lost or borrowed).

Self-report surveys of delinquency did not come into wide use until the 1960s, but they are now the major method criminologists use to measure delinquency. The major advantage of self-report data is that they provide an estimate of all delinquency committed by juveniles, regardless of whether that delinquency is known to the police or has resulted in arrest. As a consequence, self-report data indicate that delinquency is far more extensive than arrest data suggest. But before we continue our discussion of self-report data, let us address a question that we know is on your mind.

HOW DO WE KNOW THAT JUVENILES ARE TELLING THE TRUTH?

Most people have the same reaction to self-report surveys: How do researchers know that juveniles are telling the truth? They are asking juveniles whether they have engaged in a range of illegal behaviors, some of which are strongly condemned and subject to severe punishment. It is reasonable to think that many juveniles will underreport their delinquency. Researchers have tried to estimate the accuracy of self-report data in several ways. None of these ways are perfect, but taken together they provide a rough estimate of the accuracy of self-report data (see Thornberry and Krohn, 2000, for an excellent overview of this issue).

1. **Official record comparisons.** Most commonly, researchers compare the self-reported delinquent acts of respondents with their police or court records. They determine whether respondents report the offenses for which they have been arrested or convicted.[3] The failure of respondents to report such offenses suggests that self-report data are inaccurate. Reporting such offenses suggests that self-report data may be accurate. It does not, of course, prove that self-report data are accurate. People may admit to offenses for which they have been arrested or convicted but fail to report other offenses.

2. **Comparisons with peer, family, or school reports.** Certain researchers have estimated the accuracy of self-reports by determining whether respondents report the delinquent acts that their friends, parents, and/or teachers attribute to them (e.g., Gold, 1966). Failure to do this suggests that self-report data are inaccurate. If respondents do report acts mentioned by others, that suggests that self-report data may be accurate.

3. **Lie-detector tests.** Certain researchers have used lie-detector tests or the threat of lie-detector tests to estimate the accuracy of self-report data (e.g., Clark and Tift, 1966; Hindelang et al., 1981). For example, juveniles in one study were interviewed about the extent of their delinquency. They were then interviewed again, but this time they were

TABLE 2.2	A Popular Self-Report Measure of Delinquency

How many times in the last year have you

1. Purposely damaged or destroyed property belonging to your parents or other family members?
2. Purposely damaged or destroyed property belonging to a school?
3. Purposely damaged or destroyed other property that did not belong to you (not counting family or school property)?
4. Stolen (or tried to steal) a motor vehicle, such as a car or motorcycle?
5. Stolen (or tried to steal) something worth more than $50?
6. Knowingly bought, sold, or held stolen goods (or tried to do any of these things)?
7. Thrown objects (such as rocks, snowballs, or bottles) at cars or people?
8. Run away from home?
9. Lied about your age to gain entrance or to purchase something (lied about your age to buy liquor or get into a movie)?
10. Carried a hidden weapon other than a plain pocketknife?
11. Stolen (or tried to steal) things worth $5 or less?
12. Attacked someone with the idea of seriously hurting or killing him/her?
13. Been paid for having sexual relations with someone?
14. Had sexual intercourse with a person of the opposite sex other than your wife/husband?
15. Been involved in gang fights?
16. Sold marijuana or hashish ("pot," "grass," "hash")?
17. Cheated on school tests?
18. Hitchhiked where it was illegal to do so?
19. Stolen money or other things from your parents or other members of your family?
20. Hit (or threatened to hit) a teacher or other adult at school?
21. Hit (or threatened to hit) one of your parents?
22. Hit (or threatened to hit) other students?
23. Been loud, rowdy, or unruly in a public place (disorderly conduct)?
24. Sold hard drugs, such as heroin, cocaine, and LSD?
25. Taken a vehicle for a ride (drive) without the owner's permission?
26. Bought or provided liquor for a minor?
27. Had (or tried to have) sexual relations with someone against their will?
28. Used force (strong-arm methods) to get money or things from other students?
29. Used force (strong-arm methods) to get money or things from a teacher or other adult at school?
30. Used force (strong-arm methods) to get money or things from other people (not students or teachers)?
31. Avoided paying for such things as movies, bus or subway rides, and food?
32. Been drunk in a public place?
33. Stolen (or tried to steal) things worth between $5 and $50?
34. Stolen (or tried to steal) something at school, such as someone's coat from a classroom, locker, or cafeteria, or a book from a library?
35. Broken into a building or vehicle (or tried to break in) to steal something or just to look around?
36. Begged for money or things from strangers?
37. Skipped classes without an excuse?
38. Failed to return extra change that a cashier gave you by mistake?
39. Been suspended from school?
40. Made obscene telephone calls (calling someone and saying dirty things)?

How often in the last year have you used:

41. Alcoholic beverages (beer, wine, and hard liquor)?
42. Marijuana or hashish ("grass," "pot," "hash")?
43. Hallucinogens ("LSD," "mescaline," "peyote," "acid")?
44. Amphetamines ("uppers," "speed," "whites")?
45. Barbiturates ("downers," "reds")?
46. Heroin ("horse," "smack")?
47. Cocaine ("coke")?

SOURCE: Elliott and Ageton, 1980.

told that their answers would be evaluated using a "psychological stress evaluator" that detects dishonest responses. They were then asked a variety of questions, including the same questions they had previously been asked about the extent of their delinquency. The researchers then determined whether the juveniles changed their answers in the second interview.

4. **Comparisons with drug tests.** Researchers have estimated the accuracy of self-reports of drug use by comparing such reports to estimates of drug use obtained from analyses of urine, saliva, or blood (e.g., Akers et al., 1983).

5. **Comparisons between groups known to differ in their level of delinquency.** Researchers have also estimated the accuracy of self-reports by comparing the self-reported delinquency of groups known to differ in their level of delinquency. For example, they have compared the self-reported delinquency of institutionalized delinquents to that of high school students (e.g., James Short and Nye, 1958). If there is little difference in self-reported delinquency between these groups, that suggests that self-report data are inaccurate. If the institutionalized delinquents have a higher level of self-reported delinquency, that suggests that self-report data may be accurate.

Again, none of these methods is perfect, but taken together they allow researchers to form a rough estimate of the accuracy of self-report data. **Overall, they suggest that self-report data provide a moderately accurate estimate of the extent of delinquency.** Most juveniles are reasonably honest in their responses, although there is some underreporting (and even a little overreporting) of delinquency. Data suggest that this underreporting is greatest for serious offenses. That is, juveniles are more likely to conceal serious offenses than minor ones. Underreporting may be especially likely to occur among individuals who possess low self-control or various cognitive limitations (e.g., forgetfulness or inability to concentrate). For example, one recent study finds that underreporting is more common among young people who suffer from attention deficit hyperactivity disorder, or ADHD (Sibley et al., 2010). Other individuals may be uneasy about revealing personal information, or they may worry about the possibility of contributing to racial or ethnic stereotypes. Certain data suggest that black males are more likely to underreport the extent of their delinquency, although findings here are somewhat mixed.[4]

Problems with Many Self-Report Surveys

While self-report surveys appear to provide a moderately accurate estimate of the extent of delinquency, they do have some problems (see Thornberry and Krohn, 2000, for a full discussion). One problem is that there are **very few long-term, nationwide self-report surveys of delinquency.** While the federal government collects data from police departments on an annual basis, the government has no comparable program for the collection of self-report data. Most self-report surveys are administered by university professors (who may receive government funding for their research). Their surveys usually focus on the extent of self-reported delinquency in a single city or region at one point in time. Only a few national self-report surveys have been done. As a result, estimates of the extent of self-reported delinquency in the United States and trends in such delinquency are somewhat limited.

A second problem is that **many self-report surveys underestimate the extent of serious delinquency.** One reason for this has already been indicated: data suggest that respondents sometimes underreport serious delinquent acts. Three additional reasons for the underestimation of serious delinquency are described next. (Some of the more recent self-report surveys, however, have taken significant steps to obtain better estimates of serious delinquency. These steps are described in the following section.)

Many self-report surveys employ measures of delinquency that focus on minor offenses and employ vague response categories. The early self-report surveys and some recent self-report surveys employ questions identical or similar to the ones in Table 2.3. Take a moment to examine these questions. You will immediately notice that the questions focus on minor forms of delinquency. There is a reason for this. Most self-report surveys, especially the early surveys, examine samples of only a few hundred juveniles. Serious delinquent acts, like serious assaults and rapes, are not common, so only a small number of juveniles will report such acts in a sample of a few hundred. As a consequence, there are too few instances of these acts to allow for any meaningful analyses. Many self-report researchers therefore focus on the more frequently occurring minor offenses.

Further, notice the response categories for each delinquency question ("no," "once or twice," "several times," "very often"). Respondents who commit an act 10 times will probably select "very often," but so will respondents who commit an act 100 times. The response categories do not distinguish offenders who commit an act a few times from those who commit an act scores or even hundreds of times. This lack of precision is a serious problem. Recent data indicate that there is a small group of high-rate offenders, each of whom commits hundreds of delinquent acts per year. These offenders account for a majority of all delinquent acts in some studies. But the response categories used in the survey shown in Table 2.3 do not provide an accurate count of the number of delinquent acts committed by these offenders. So not only do some self-report surveys focus on minor delinquency, but they often also provide an imprecise estimate of the extent of delinquency.

Juveniles often report trivial acts on self-report surveys—acts that would probably not be considered delinquent by law enforcement officials. Examples of trivial acts would be sipping a little wine at the dinner table with your parents' permission or playfully shoving one of your siblings. While juveniles might report these as underage drinking and minor assault, it is quite unlikely that law enforcement officials would see them as such. Trivial events are most likely to be reported in response to questions about minor delinquent acts. In one study, over 75 percent of the minor assault reports were classified by the researcher as trivial (Elliott et al., 1989:15). Trivial events, however, are sometimes reported when respondents are questioned about serious delinquent acts like aggravated assault.

TABLE 2.3	An Early Self-Report Measure of Delinquency

Have you ever:
1. Driven a car without a driver's license or permit?
   No _____
   Once or twice _____
   Several times _____
   Very often _____
2. Skipped school without a legitimate excuse?
   (Same response categories as above.)
3. Defied your parents' authority (to their face)?
4. Taken little things (worth less than $2) that did not belong to you?
5. Bought or drunk beer, wine, or liquor (include drinking at home)?
6. Purposely damaged or destroyed public or private property that did not belong to you?
7. Had sexual relations with a person of the opposite sex?

SOURCE: Nye, 1958.

Most self-report surveys tend to undersample the most serious delinquents. Self-report surveys are usually based on school or household samples. For example, a researcher might try to survey a sample of students from several schools in a city. Or a researcher might try to survey juveniles from a sample of households in a city. The researcher first selects the juveniles to survey and then tries to obtain their permission to conduct the interview or to elicit their agreement to complete the questionnaire. It is usually necessary to obtain the permission of their parents or guardians as well.

These strategies have the advantage of reaching broad samples of juveniles—both those who have been arrested and those who have not. These strategies, however, tend to undersample the most serious delinquents, including those who commit the most offenses and those who commit very serious offenses. If you sample school students, you miss students who have dropped out of school, are suspended, or are truant. These students tend to be the more serious offenders. This undersampling is a less serious problem if the researchers sample households; but even here they are likely to miss juveniles who live on the street or spend a lot of time on the street. Such juveniles tend to be more serious offenders (see Hagan and McCarthy, 1997a, 1997b). Furthermore, there is reason to believe that the more serious offenders (and their parents) are less likely to agree to participate in the survey (Brame and Piquero, 2003). In fact, it is often the case that 30 percent or more of the juveniles who are selected in the initial sample refuse to participate in the survey or cannot be reached. As a consequence, data suggest that most self-report surveys undersample serious delinquents (see Cernkovich et al., 1985).

In sum, there is reason to believe that **many self-report surveys underestimate the extent of serious delinquency.** This underestimation occurs because (1) serious offenses are more likely to be underreported, (2) measures of delinquency often focus on minor offenses and employ vague response categories, (3) respondents often report trivial acts, and (4) most self-report surveys tend to undersample serious offenders.

Recent Self-Report Surveys Have Made Much Progress in Overcoming the Preceding Problems

Criminologists have made much progress in overcoming the preceding problems. As a consequence, contemporary self-report surveys often provide much more accurate information about the extent of delinquency, including serious delinquency (see Thornberry and Krohn, 2000, 2003). Criminologists have overcome the preceding problems in several ways.

New methods of administering self-report surveys have been developed, methods **that appear to substantially reduce the amount of underreporting.** One of the most promising of these methods is the *audio computer-assisted self-administered interview.* This rather long name basically refers to a technique whereby juveniles are interviewed by a personal computer. The computer screen presents the juveniles with questions, including questions about the extent of their delinquency. They also hear these questions over a headset at the same time they are presented on the screen. The juveniles then respond to each question by striking the appropriate key on the computer. As Thornberry and Krohn (2000:62–63) point out, this approach has several advantages. Among other things, it overcomes the reading problems that sometimes arise when a respondent is asked to fill out a questionnaire. Also, "the respondent does not have to reveal potentially embarrassing behavior directly to another person," as happens in interviews (also see C. Turner et al., 1998).

Another promising method involves the use of a *life event calendar.* Before reporting any delinquent offenses, survey respondents are first asked to plot important life events and circumstances on a calendar that covers, for example, the previous year. For instance, the respondent may indicate where they were living during various time periods or where they went to school. They then fill in the calendar by recalling specific life events, such as a birthday celebration, a concert or sporting event, meeting a new friend, or working at a new job. In the end, the calendar provides a framework for the respondent's memories and experiences, thereby enhancing the recall of delinquent behavior, such as involvement in a fight or illicit drug use at a party (see N. Morris and Slocum, 2010).

Many recent self-report surveys also **employ better measures of delinquency.** In particular, they **obtain accurate counts of the number of delinquent acts committed.** Further, they **focus on both minor and serious offenses** (such surveys collect larger samples of juveniles, which allows them to examine the less frequently occurring serious offenses). The self-report delinquency measure in Table 2.2 is an example of a measure that focuses on both minor and serious delinquency and that tries to accurately measure the number of times delinquent acts have been committed. This measure was developed by Elliott and associates and has served as a model for measures in many recent self-report studies (see Elliott and Ageton, 1980).

Further, certain of these recent surveys **make an effort to eliminate trivial acts from their delinquency counts.** Researchers ask respondents a series of follow-up questions about the delinquent acts they report, which allows them to classify such acts as trivial or nontrivial. The trivial acts are then excluded from the estimates of delinquency.

Finally, certain of these surveys **make a special effort to include serious offenders in their samples.** For example, they oversample juveniles in neighborhoods that have high delinquency rates. Also, they screen juveniles before including them in the survey, making a special effort to detect and recruit serious offenders in their survey (see Thornberry et al., 1995; Thornberry and Krohn, 2003).

These recent self-report studies are not free of problems. For example, researchers still encounter some difficulty in recruiting the most serious offenders, and there may still be some underreporting of delinquency. Nevertheless, these surveys represent a major improvement over earlier self-report surveys, and there is good reason to believe that they provide reasonably accurate estimates of the extent of delinquency—serious and minor—in most groups.

VICTIMIZATION DATA

The problems with police data have also motivated criminologists to develop another way of estimating the extent of crime and delinquency: *victimization data.* **Victimization data are obtained by asking people to report on their experiences as crime victims.** Several victimization surveys were conducted in the 1960s, and the federal government started compiling victimization data on an annual basis in the early 1970s through the administration of the *National Crime Victimization Survey.* Each year people ages 12 and older in approximately 90,000 households throughout the United States are asked about their experiences as crime victims. These households are selected so as to be representative of all households in the United States. Data from the National Crime Victimization Survey allow researchers to estimate the total amount of crime and delinquency in the United States. These victimization data are published annually in a report titled *Criminal Victimization* (see Truman and Morgan, 2016; also look for victimization data on the website of the Bureau of Justice Statistics: http://www.bjs.gov).

The respondents in the victimization survey are asked if they have been the victims of crime, including aggravated assault, simple assault, rape/sexual assault, robbery, burglary, motor vehicle theft, and larceny. (They are not, of course, asked if they have been the victims of homicide.) If they reply that they have been the victim of one of these crimes, they are asked a number of questions about this victimization. For example, they are asked whether they reported the victimization to the police, and if not, why not. In 2015, less than half of all victimizations were reported to the police (47 percent of violent crime victimizations and 35 percent of property crime victimizations). Prior research indicates that the most common reason for not reporting is that the victimization is a private or personal matter. Respondents are also asked if they saw the person(s) who victimized them. If so, they are asked about the age, sex, and race of this person(s), among other things. On the basis of their responses, researchers can estimate the number of people who have been victimized by young people and trends in such victimization over time.

Like self-report data, victimization data provide information on both crimes that have come to the attention of the police and crimes that have not. They also provide much information on the experiences and characteristics of crime victims.

Problems with Victimization Data

There are, however, problems with using victimization data to estimate the extent of delinquency (see Cantor and Lynch, 2000, for an excellent overview).

1. **Victimization data focus on only a few violent and property crimes committed against individuals ages 12 and older.** They do not provide any information on crimes such as drug use and on status offenses. They do not provide any information on crimes committed against businesses—like shoplifting at department stores. And they do not provide any information on crimes committed against people younger than 12 years of age.

2. **Certain groups with high rates of criminal victimization are undersampled, such as homeless people, transients, and institutionalized persons.**

3. **There is evidence that many crime victims do not report their victimizations to the interviewers.** There are a variety of reasons for this nonreporting, including memory loss and embarrassment. Data suggest that victimizations by family members, friends, and acquaintances are often not reported to the interviewer. There have been some attempts to increase reporting; for example, the wording of the survey has been changed to better prompt respondents to report certain kinds of victimization. To illustrate, respondents are now encouraged to report crimes by friends and family members with the following prompt:

> People don't often think of incidents committed by someone they know. Did you have something stolen from you OR were you attacked or threatened by (a) someone at work or school, (b) a neighbor or friend, (c) a relative or family member, or (d) any other person you've met or known?

Such prompts and other changes have substantially reduced the extent of underreporting, but there is reason to believe that much underreporting still occurs for certain crimes (see Cantor and Lynch, 2000; Mosher et al., 2002).

4. **The victim often does not see the offender and so cannot estimate the offender's age.** This is especially likely for property crimes. One study found that the victim saw the offender in only 6 percent of all burglaries and motor vehicle thefts and in 4 percent of all household larcenies (Hindelang, 1981). The victim, of course, does see the offender in most violent crimes. The victim, however, can only make a rough estimate of the offender's age. In particular, it is often hard to distinguish older juveniles from young adults.

For these reasons, victimization data are somewhat limited in the information they provide about the extent of and trends in delinquency. The discussion in Chapter 3 therefore draws primarily on arrest and self-report data. However, we will note certain relevant findings from victimization data. And we will also briefly discuss the extent to which juveniles are crime victims, as well as offenders.

SUMMARY

There are three major ways to measure the extent of delinquency and trends in delinquency: arrest, self-report, and victimization data. Each has its advantages and disadvantages. With the exception of homicide, arrest data vastly underestimate the extent of delinquency and may provide misleading information on trends in delinquency. Arrest data are especially likely to provide misleading information on minor crimes, since these crimes are the least likely to be reported to the police and the least likely to result in arrest. Self-report data provide a better estimate of the extent of delinquency since they focus on all offenses, both those that have come to the attention of the police and those that have not. Many self-report surveys, however, tend to focus on minor offenses committed in the general population. Such surveys provide less accurate estimates of the extent of serious delinquency. Several recent self-report surveys, however, likely provide reasonably accurate estimates of both minor and serious delinquency. Victimization data also attempt to measure both crimes that have come to the attention of the police and those that have not. But victimization data suffer from several problems; most notably, they focus on a small number of crimes, and victims usually have not seen the offenders who committed the crime—with the exception of violent crimes.

As you can see, measuring delinquency is not a simple matter. It is easy to produce estimates of the extent of delinquency and trends in delinquency, and we are exposed to such estimates on a regular basis in the media. Most estimates, however, are problematic for the reasons indicated here. The situation is not as bad as it might appear, however. We can often use our knowledge of these data sources to judge which provides the best estimate of the extent of delinquency or trends in delinquency in a particular situation. And it is sometimes the case that the three data sources agree with one another. We can, of course, be more confident in the conclusions we draw when this is the case.

TEACHING AIDS

A Challenge

A criminologist is asked to estimate the extent of delinquency in City X. The criminologist decides to interview all the high school students in the city, asking them the questions shown in Table 2.4. Eighty percent of the high school students and their parents agree to participate in the interviews (returning consent forms to the criminologist). The interviews are conducted during school hours on a certain day. Ninety percent of those who agreed to participate in the survey are in school that day and complete the interviews. Based on their responses to the questions in Table 2.4, the criminologist produces

---

TABLE 2.4	A Self-Report Measure of Delinquency

Respondents are asked whether they engaged in the following offenses in the prior year, with the response categories for each offense ranging from "never" to "five or more" times.

1. Taken something not belonging to you worth under $50?
2. Taken something not belonging to you worth over $50?
3. Got something by telling a person something bad would happen to them if you did not get what you wanted?
4. Got into a fight?
5. Used marijuana?
6. Consumed alcohol?
7. Skipped a day of school without a real excuse?

SOURCE: Adapted from Gold, 1966.

an estimate of the extent of delinquency in City X. Is this estimate accurate? If not, list all of the reasons why accuracy has not been achieved. (These reasons are listed after the Key Terms for this chapter.)

Practical Advice: Three Things to Beware of When Others Discuss the Extent of and Trends in Delinquency (and a Challenge)

We often hear a lot about delinquency from family members, friends, the news media, and politicians. Unfortunately, a lot of the information that is presented is misleading or wrong. The following is a list of three things you should be wary of when others are discussing delinquency. These are not the only things you should be wary of, but they are among the more common ways that misleading information is conveyed about the extent of and trends in delinquency. **Your challenge:** Draw on this chapter and the next three chapters to expand this list (also see Mosher et al., 2002).

1. **The sensational case.** The news media, politicians, and others will often focus on a sensational crime, such as a crime committed by a famous person, a gruesome crime, and/or a crime with many victims. There will be much discussion of this crime, and the impression will be given that this type of crime (or crime in general) is more extensive or is increasing faster than is actually the case. School shootings represent a well-known example. The media devoted major attention to school shootings from the 1990s to the present, often implicitly or explicitly suggesting that school violence was common and that it was increasing. But as we discuss in Chapter 15, school violence, especially of a serious nature, is quite uncommon. Further, such violence has been decreasing. This is not, of course, to claim that all media reports focusing on sensational crimes are misleading. Rather, it is to suggest that you should be cautious in generalizing from one or a few crimes to crime. If possible, examine what official, self-report, and victimization data say about the type of crime being discussed.

2. **The reliance on one data source.** Reports on crime are usually based on a single data source, often official statistics from the FBI's *Uniform Crime Reports*. But, as indicated in this chapter, each data source has some major disadvantages (and advantages). We should therefore be cautious when we hear a report based on a single source. In particular, we should keep the advantages and disadvantages of that source in mind. We should also ask what other data sources say about the same issue. If the different data sources are in agreement, we can be more confident about the information presented. If the data sources disagree, we need to delve into the possible sources of this disagreement. Mosher et al. (2002:1–2) present a good example of this point. The FBI *Uniform Crime Reports* that were released in 2001 indicated that crime rates had increased for the first time in many years. The news media reported headlines such as "Decade-Long Crime Drop Ends," and commentators were trying to make sense of the increase. Two weeks later, data from the National Crime Victimization Survey were released, and they indicated that the crime rate had decreased by 15 percent. A subsequent headline read "Crime Is: Up? Down? Who Knows?"

3. **Percentage changes based on a small number of cases.** Others will sometimes report that there has been a large percentage increase or decrease in crime. So, for example, drawing on the *Emory Campus Annual Security Report*, someone might report that there was a 63 percent increase in drug law arrests from 2013 to 2014. This might lead you to think that drug abuse had become much more common on the Emory University campus in the space of a year. In fact, the number of drug law arrests increased from eight in 2013 to thirteen in 2014. When you are dealing with a small number of cases, a small change in raw numbers can produce a large change in percentages. This, in turn, can convey a misleading impression about trends in crime. It's quite unlikely that there was actually a

63 percent increase in drug abuse on the Emory campus from 2013 to 2014. So be sure to look at the raw numbers involved when you hear others talk about what percentage crime increased or decreased. (Note: This illustration also shows the dangers of relying on one data source. Arrest data are clearly a poor way to estimate the extent of or changes in drug use in this case. Most drug abuse incidents do not result in arrest, and the number of drug arrests may be influenced by many factors in addition to the actual extent of drug abuse. Can you list several such factors?)

Web-Based Exercise: Measuring the Extent of Rape

As noted in this chapter, the National Crime Victimization Survey generally reports more crime than the police data presented by the FBI, since the Victimization Survey picks up many crimes not reported to the police. But this should not be taken to mean that the Victimization Survey provides an accurate measure of all crime. Most notably, it has been charged that the Victimization Survey greatly underestimates the extent of rape. For a discussion of why this may be the case, see the article by Emily Bazelon (2013) titled "We've Been Measuring Rape All Wrong" at http://www.slate.com. The Bureau of Justice Statistics (BJS), which oversees the Victimization Survey, is now examining ways to more accurately measure the extent of rape and sexual assault. For a brief description of what they are doing, along with their publications on rape and sexual assault, visit their information webpage at http://www.bjs.gov/index.cfm?ty=tp&tid=317. Alternately, visit the BJS website, at http://www.bjs.gov. Click on "Crime Type," hold the cursor over "Violent Crime," and click on "Rape and Sexual Assault."

TEST YOUR KNOWLEDGE OF THIS CHAPTER

1. What are the three major ways of estimating the extent of and trends in delinquency?
2. Why is it important to know something about these methods, including their advantages and disadvantages?
3. What are "official statistics"? Why are arrest data the main source of official data on the extent of and trends in delinquency?
4. What are the major types of information you would find in the FBI's report in *Crime in the United States: The Uniform Crime Reports*?
5. List the eight Part I, or index, offenses. List any four Part II offenses.
6. Why is it that the number of crimes "cleared" by the arrest of juveniles usually does not equal the number of arrests that involve juveniles?
7. What are the major advantages and disadvantages of arrest data? Why do arrest data vastly underestimate the extent of delinquency?
8. How have researchers tried to estimate the accuracy of self-reports of delinquency (i.e., how do they estimate whether juveniles are telling the truth on self-report surveys)? What conclusions do researchers draw about the accuracy of self-report surveys?
9. Many self-report surveys suffer from a number of problems that cause them to underestimate the extent of serious delinquency. What are these problems?
10. How have researchers tried to overcome these problems?
11. What are the major advantages and problems with victimization data?

THOUGHT AND DISCUSSION QUESTIONS

1. City X experienced a 30 percent increase in the juvenile *arrest* rate. List all the possible reasons for this increase *other than a real increase in the rate of delinquency* (e.g., the arrest rate may have increased because crime victims have become more likely to report crimes to the police).

2. We state that none of the methods for estimating the accuracy of self-reports is perfect. Is it possible to develop a method that would precisely estimate the accuracy of self-reports of delinquency? If not, why not?

3. Describe how you might best estimate the extent of delinquency or crime on your campus (indicate the method or methods of data collection you would use and the steps you would take in employing these methods).

KEY TERMS

- Official statistics
- *Crime in the United States: The Uniform Crime Reports*
- Crimes known to the police
- Crimes cleared by arrest
- Part I, or index, offenses
- Criminal homicide, forcible rape, robbery, aggravated assault, burglary, larceny-theft, motor vehicle theft, and arson
- Part II offenses
- Unfounding crime reports
- Self-report data
- Audio Computer-Assisted Self-Administered Interview
- Life event calendar
- Victimization data
- National Crime Victimization Survey

ANSWERS TO THE CHALLENGE

The criminologist would not produce an accurate estimate of the extent of delinquency in City X because:

1. Only high school students were interviewed, so the delinquency of juveniles not in high school (e.g., high school dropouts, middle school students) is not estimated.

2. Twenty percent of the high school students did not agree to participate in the survey, so their delinquency is not estimated. The more serious delinquents may be more likely to be in this missing group.

3. Ten percent of the students who agreed to participate in the survey were not present on the day of the interviews, perhaps because they were truant or cutting class, so their delinquency is not estimated. Again, the more serious delinquents may be more likely to be in this missing group.

4. Many juveniles may underreport their level of offending, especially serious offending, since a face-to-face interview is used (versus a technique like the Audio Computer-Assisted Self-Administered Interview).

5. The measure of delinquency in Table 2.4 tends to focus on minor offenses and employs vague response categories.

6. No effort was made to distinguish trivial from nontrivial acts and to eliminate the trivial acts from the delinquency count.

ENDNOTES

1. For fuller discussions, see Bernard, 1999; Cantor and Lynch, 2000; Cernkovich et al., 1985; Elliott, 1982; Elliott and Ageton, 1980; Elliott et al., 1989; Farrington et al., 1996; Gove et al., 1985; Hindelang et al., 1979, 1981; Huizinga and Elliott, 1986; Patrick Jackson, 1990; Maxfield, 1999; Mosher et al., 2002; O'Brien, 2000; Reiss and Roth, 1993; Rutter et al., 1998; Sullivan and McGloin, 2014; Thornberry and Krohn, 2000, 2003; Weis, 1986; E. Wells and Rankin, 1995.

2. See David Smith, 1984; J. Wilson, 1976; also see Chappel et al., 2006.

3. See Farrington et al., 1996; Hindelang et al., 1981; Huizinga and Elliott, 1986; Paschall et al., 2001; Piquero et al., 2014; Thornberry and Krohn, 2000.

4. See Farrington et al., 1996; Hindelang et al., 1981; Huizinga and Elliott, 1986; Mosher et al., 2002; Piquero et al., 2014; Thornberry and Krohn, 2000; Weis, 1986.

3 How Much Delinquency Is There, and Is Delinquency Increasing?

This chapter focuses on the two simple questions asked in the title: How much delinquency is there in the United States? Is delinquency increasing? Simple questions, however, often have complex answers. This complexity can be frustrating at times, but you will have a much fuller understanding of the extent of and trends in delinquency after reading this chapter. We first focus on the extent of delinquency in the United States, presenting estimates from arrest, self-report, and victimization data. We then focus on trends in delinquency, again presenting estimates from arrest, self-report, and victimization data. These data sources do not always agree with one another, but we think there are some conclusions that can be safely drawn about the extent of and trends in delinquency. One such conclusion is that there has been a dramatic decrease in serious delinquency in recent years, and we end this chapter by discussing some possible reasons for this decrease.

We should warn you that any discussion in this area is going to contain a lot of numbers. We try to keep the numbers to a minimum, and we encourage you to focus on the central points that are being made and to avoid getting caught up in the specific numbers. Much of the information that follows comes from the Office of Juvenile Justice and Delinquency Prevention's *Statistical Briefing Book* (http://www.ojjdp.gov/ojstatbb). It is a good place to look if you ever want to know anything about the extent of delinquency, trends in delinquency, the characteristics of delinquents, or a range of other topics.

After reading this chapter, you should be able to:

- Describe the extent of delinquency using arrest data and self-report data.
- Identify the characteristics of those most likely to be victims of crime.
- Describe trends in delinquency using arrest data, self-report data, and victimization data.
- Explain why there are no simple answers to questions of how much delinquency there is or how much it is changing over time.
- Offer explanations for the dramatic decline in serious crime since the mid-1990s.

HOW MUCH DELINQUENCY IS THERE?
How Many Juveniles Are Arrested, and What Are They Arrested For?

As you know, arrest data vastly underestimate the extent of delinquency. Most delinquent acts do not come to the attention of the police, and acts that do come to the attention of the police usually do not result in arrest. This is especially true for minor crimes. Nevertheless, many juveniles are arrested each year.

Table 3.1 shows the estimated number of juvenile arrests in 2014 broken down by type of crime. The top part of the table focuses on Part I, or index, crimes, while the bottom part focuses on Part II crimes. Overall, there were about 1 million juvenile arrests. That number does not mean that 1 million different juveniles were arrested. Many juveniles were arrested more than once.

About 288,000 of these arrests were for Part I crimes. Note that arrests for property crimes are much more common than arrests for violent crimes. In fact, well over half of all Part I arrests are for larceny-theft. Larceny-theft, in fact, is the crime with the highest number of arrests. About 736,000 arrests were for Part II offenses, with the most arrests being for "other assaults," disorderly conduct, drug abuse violations, liquor law violations, curfew violations, and vandalism.

Overall, note that the number of arrests tends to be higher for minor crimes than for serious crimes. For example, 800 juvenile arrests were for homicide and 3,300 were for rape. About 178,000 juvenile arrests were for larceny-theft, however.

TABLE 3.1	Estimated Number of Juvenile Arrests, 2014
Total	**1,024,000**
Part I (Index) Offenses	
Criminal homicide (murder and nonnegligent manslaughter)	800
Rape	3,300
Robbery	19,400
Aggravated assault	30,100
Burglary	40,300
Larceny-theft	178,000
Motor vehicle theft	12,700
Arson	3,200
Part II Offenses	
Other assaults	139,100
Forgery and counterfeiting	1,200
Fraud	4,300
Embezzlement	500
Stolen property (buying, receiving, possessing)	10,400
Vandalism	45,200
Weapons (carrying, possessing, etc.)	20,700
Prostitution and commercialized vice	700
Sex offenses (except rape and prostitution)	9,400
Drug abuse violations	112,600
Gambling	600
Offenses against the family and children	3,400
Driving under the influence	7,000
Liquor law violations	53,300
Drunkenness	6,500
Disorderly conduct	80,800
Vagrancy	900
All other offenses (except traffic)	186,000
Curfew and loitering	53,700

SOURCE: Office of Juvenile Justice and Delinquency Prevention, *Statistical Briefing Book* (http://www.ojjdp.gov/ojstatbb).

These data, while useful, may be a little difficult to interpret. One way to help interpret them is to look at *arrest rates*. Arrest rates show the number of juvenile arrests per 100,000 juveniles ages 10 to 17 in the population (very few juveniles under age 10 are arrested). Arrest rates are useful because they give us an idea of the probability that a juvenile will be arrested. The overall juvenile arrest rate was about 3,000 per 100,000 juveniles. In other words, there were about 3,000 juvenile arrests for every 100,000 juveniles ages 10 to 17 in the population (or about 3 arrests per 100 juveniles). The arrest rate for Part I violent crimes was about 158 per 100,000 juveniles (or about 0.2 arrest per 100 juveniles). The arrest rate for Part I property crimes was about 693 per 100,000 juveniles (or about 0.7 arrest per 100 juveniles).

We want to add a note of caution: The fact that there were nearly 1 million juvenile arrests does not mean that juveniles committed 1 million crimes. We earlier stated that juveniles usually commit their crimes in groups. As a consequence, several juveniles are often arrested for a single crime. For example, several juveniles might be arrested for a single act of vandalism. To estimate the number of crimes committed by juveniles, it is best to look at the number of crimes cleared by the arrest of juveniles. *Clearance data* allow us to estimate the number of Part I crimes committed by juveniles (clearance data are not reported for Part II crimes). While about 288,000 juveniles were arrested in 2014 for Part I crimes, only about 183,000 Part I crimes were cleared by the arrest of juveniles.

You know that arrest data vastly underestimate the extent of delinquency. Self-report data, discussed in the following section, provide a more accurate estimate of the extent of delinquency.

How Much Self-Reported Delinquency Is There?

We have the students in our juvenile delinquency courses fill out a short survey on the first day of class. Among other things, the survey asks whether they ever committed any of 14 different delinquent acts as juveniles. Some of these acts are status offenses, like running away and truancy. Some are minor crimes, like petty larceny and trespassing. And some are more serious crimes, like burglary and robbery. The students are always shocked by the results. We typically find that anywhere from 90 to 100 percent of the students have committed at least one of the delinquent acts. And it is often the case that about half the class has committed at least 7 of the 14 delinquent acts. Keep in mind that most of our students have done quite well in school and are pursuing a college degree. A certain percentage of them will go on to become doctors, lawyers, business managers, and leaders in their communities. (Look at the self-report survey in Table 2.2 again. How many of the delinquent acts have you committed?) Self-report surveys typically find that 90 percent or more of all juveniles have engaged in at least some forms of delinquency—usually minor delinquency but often a few instances of more serious delinquency as well.

We do not, however, want you to think that we are picking on juveniles. Two criminologists conducted a self-report survey of crime among criminologists (M. Robinson and Zaitzow, 1999). They describe their motivation for doing such a survey by stating, "We were in an airplane on our way back from a recent American Society of Criminology meeting [and] we overheard from the seats directly in front of us two criminologists discussing what they had taken (i.e., stolen) from the conference hotel." They began to wonder just how common crime was among criminologists. So they surveyed 522 criminologists from throughout the United States, most of whom had doctoral degrees and half of whom were faculty members at colleges and universities. The large majority of these criminologists had engaged in one or more crimes at some point in their lives. For example, 55 percent had committed theft, 22 percent had committed burglary, 60 percent had used illicit drugs, and 25 percent had physically attacked another person. Self-report data, then, indicate that delinquency (and crime) is common, even among students like yourselves and the faculty who teach you. Keep this in mind when we are examining topics like the causes of delinquency. To some extent, we are examining your (and our) behavior.

As indicated earlier, not many self-report surveys have been administered to juveniles throughout the United States. But a few such surveys exist. The most recent is the 2014 Monitoring the Future survey. **The Monitoring the Future survey is administered to a sample of about 2,500 high school seniors throughout the United States each year.** While the survey provides national data on the extent of self-reported delinquency, it does have certain problems. It focuses on high school seniors, thereby missing dropouts and students who were suspended or truant when the survey was administered. As indicated earlier, such juveniles are more likely to be serious offenders. It does not examine many delinquent offenses, especially serious offenses like homicide and rape. And it employs vague response categories. In particular, it uses the response category "five or more times," so that researchers cannot distinguish someone who committed an act 5 times from someone who committed the same act 100 times. Nevertheless, the data in Table 3.2 provide an idea of the extent of delinquency in this group.

Note that certain forms of delinquency are quite common, particularly status offenses and minor forms of delinquency. For example, the large majority of high school seniors have drunk alcohol and have argued or fought with their parents in the past year (the status offense of "incorrigibility"). And a substantial percentage of students have engaged in petty theft and fighting. More serious forms of delinquency are less frequent but not uncommon. For example, about 8 percent of high school seniors reported that they "hurt someone badly enough to need bandages or a doctor" in 2014.

The best self-report survey conducted on a national level is the National Youth Survey (see Elliott et al., 1985). This survey was administered to a sample of 1,725 adolescents ages 11 through 17 throughout the United States in 1977. These adolescents were asked about the extent of their delinquency in 1976. The same group of adolescents was surveyed several additional times through the 1990s, but they, of course, turned from adolescents into adults as the surveys progressed. Elliott and his associates looked at a total of 47 delinquent acts, including status offenses, minor crimes, and serious crimes (see Table 2.2 for a list of these acts). They took care to precisely measure the number of times each act was committed, avoiding the use of vague response categories. They found that the average number of delinquent acts committed by a juvenile in 1976 was 52 (there is reason to believe this number is similar today, as indicated by the trend data presented in the next section). So while FBI data indicate that there are 3 arrests per 100 juveniles, self-report data indicate that there are at least 5,200 self-reports of delinquency per 100 juveniles (52 × 100). And while arrest data indicate that there were about 1 million juvenile arrests in 2014, self-report data suggest that the 33 million juveniles between ages 10 and 17 in the United States engaged in hundreds of millions of delinquent acts in 2014.

Again, self-report data indicate that most of these delinquent acts are status offenses and minor crimes. More serious crimes are less frequent, although they are not uncommon, particularly in certain subgroups. For example, Elliott (1994) found that 36 percent of 17-year-old African American males and 25 percent of 17-year-old white males committed at least one serious act of violence over the course of a year. Serious acts of violence include aggravated assaults, robberies, and rapes; all involve some injury or the use of a weapon.

The large discrepancy between arrest data and self-report data highlights the fact that **most delinquent acts do not come to the attention of the police or result in arrest.** Dunford and Elliott (1984) used the National Youth Survey to explore the relationship between self-reported delinquency and arrest data. They classified youth according to the number of delinquent acts they self-reported in a two-year period and then examined the percentage of youth in each group who had been arrested at least once during the same two-year period. They found that the probability of arrest was quite low, even among youths who had committed a large number of offenses. For example, only 7 percent of the youths who self-reported between 101 and 200 delinquent acts were arrested. Only 19 percent of the youths who self-reported over 200 delinquent acts were arrested. Overall, the probability that a youth will be arrested for a given delinquent act is well under 1 percent. The probability of arrest is low even for those who commit serious offenses. For example, Elliott (1995) estimated that the probability of arrest for a serious violent offense (aggravated assault, rape, robbery) is about 2 in 100 (also see Farrington et al., 2007).

TABLE 3.2   The Extent of Self-Reported Delinquency Among High School Seniors, 2014.

During the Last 12 Months How Often Have You	Not at All (%)	Once (%)	Twice (%)	3 or 4 Times (%)	5 or More Times (%)	Rate (# Acts per 100 Juveniles)
1. Argued or had a fight with either of your parents?	15.1	12.0	15.3	24.0	33.6	282.6
2. Hit an instructor or supervisor?	97.3	1.5	.7	.3	.3	5.3
3. Gotten into a serious fight in school or at work?	90.4	5.6	2.1	1.1	.8	17.1
4. Taken part in a fight where a group of your friends were against another group?	86.7	7.6	2.9	2.0	.8	23.4
5. Hurt someone badly enough to need bandages or a doctor?	91.8	4.3	2.1	1.0	.8	15.5
6. Used a knife or gun or some other thing (like a club) to get something from a person?	97.6	1.1	.8	.2	.4	5.3
7. Taken something not belonging to you worth under $50?	79.3	9.3	5.2	3.3	3.0	44.6
8. Taken something not belonging to you worth over $50?	93.0	3.4	1.5	1.2	.9	14.5
9. Taken something from a store without paying for it?	78.9	9.0	4.5	3.7	3.9	48.6
10. Taken a car that didn't belong to someone in your family without permission of the owner?	96.1	1.9	1.0	.3	.7	8.3
11. Taken part of a car without permission of the owner?	97.4	1.3	.6	.1	.6	5.8
12. Gone into some house or building when you weren't supposed to be there?	77.8	9.3	6.3	3.5	3.1	47.9
13. Set fire to someone's property on purpose?	98.2	1.0	.3	.1	.4	3.9
14. Damaged school property on purpose?	93.8	2.9	1.7	.5	1.1	13.3
15. Damaged property at work on purpose?	98.0	1.0	.4	.2	.3	3.9
16. Used alcohol at least once in 2014?		60.2				
17. Used marijuana at least once in 2014?		35.1				

SOURCE: Monitoring the Future survey (http://www.monitoringthefuture.org).

What can we **conclude** about the extent of delinquency according to self-report data? Delinquency is far more common than arrest data suggest. Most juveniles engage in delinquency. They generally commit status offenses and minor crimes, but serious crimes are not uncommon.

We have focused on self-reported delinquency in the United States, but a large international survey allows us to place these self-report data in cross-national context. Between 2005 and 2007, self-report data were collected from young people (ages 12–15) in the United States and 30 other nations, mostly in Europe. The findings indicate that the percentage of youth involved in serious violent delinquency is highest in the United States, Ireland, Germany, and the Netherlands, Young people in the United States and other prosperous nations also have some of highest levels of participation in serious property offenses (for a discussion of factors that may help to explain the high rate of serious delinquency in the United States, see Chapters 17 and 24). Further, the findings suggest that cross-national differences in relatively minor delinquencies, such as shoplifting, partly reflect differences in opportunity. Participation in shoplifting tends to be most common in prosperous nations such as the United States. The lowest rate of shoplifting "can be found in Armenia where consumer goods are rare" (Enzmann et al., 2010:165).

How Many Juveniles Are Victimized, and How Many Victimizations Are Committed by Juveniles?

Victimization data provide another alternative to arrest data. As indicated earlier, victimization data tell us a lot about crime victims. Such data have somewhat less to say about the number of victimizations committed by juveniles, largely because crime victims usually do not see the person who victimized them. Nevertheless, victimization data do provide some information about the number of violent crimes committed by juveniles.

Table 3.3 shows the number of victimizations experienced by U.S. residents age 12 or older in 2014, as estimated by the National Crime Victimization Survey. About 21 million victimizations were reported in 2014, including 5.4 million violent victimizations and 15.3 million property victimizations. That amounts to about 2 violent victimizations for every 100 people age 12 or older and 12 property victimizations for every 100 households. As you can see, people are most often the victims of larceny-theft. Victimization data, like arrest and self-report data, indicate that property crimes are more common than violent crimes, and minor crimes are more common than serious crimes.

TABLE 3.3	Number and Rate of Victimizations, 2014	
	Number	Rate
All crimes	20,648,040	
Rape/sexual assault	284,350	1.1
Robbery	664,210	2.5
Aggravated assault	1,092,090	4.1
Simple assault	3,318,920	12.4
Household burglary	2,993,480	23.1
Motor vehicle theft	534,370	4.1
Theft	11,760,620	90.8

SOURCE: Truman and Langton, 2015.

Note: Rate of victimization is per 1,000 persons age 12 or older, or per 1,000 households.

Who is most likely to be victimized? Who do you think is most likely to be victimized by crime: young or old, male or female, white or African American, Hispanic or non-Hispanic, poor or rich?

Young people have higher rates of victimization than older people for violent crimes (data for property crimes are reported for households rather than for individuals). Rates of violent victimization are highest for those between 12 and 17 years old. Rates of victimization generally decline with age and are lowest among those 65 or older. To illustrate, about 3 out of every 100 people ages 12 to 17 were the victims of violence in 2014, a rate about 10 times higher than those ages 65 and over. As dramatic as this difference is, there are data suggesting that the National Crime Victimization Survey substantially underestimates the extent of victimization against young people. Data from other surveys suggest that at least 50 of every 100 adolescents are the victims of violence each year and that more than 25 of every 100 are the victims of theft (Finkelhor et al., 2005, 2009).

Males have higher rates of victimization than females for violent crimes, with the exception of serious intimate partner violence (which includes rape/sexual assault, robbery, or aggravated assault committed by the victim's spouse, boyfriend, or girlfriend). About 2.1 of every 100 males were the victims of violence in 2014, versus about 1.9 of every 100 females. Data from previous years, however, indicates that females are about 4 times more likely than males to be the victims of serious intimate partner violence. About 1.6 acts of serious intimate partner violence per 1,000 females were reported in 2011 (S. Catalano, 2013). These estimates, however, should be viewed with much caution. Data suggest that the National Crime Victimization Survey substantially underestimates the amount of rape and other violence against women. In particular, other data suggest that 15 to 20 percent of all females will be the victims of a completed or attempted rape at some point in their lives, with at least half of these rapes occurring before the age of 18 (Black et al., 2011; Tjaden and Thoennes, 1999, 2006; also see Fisher and Cullen, 2000). Based on data from the 2010 National Intimate Partner and Sexual Violence Survey, an estimated 1.3 million women were raped in the 12 months prior to the survey (too few males in the survey reported rape to provide a reliable 12-month estimate). Nearly 1 in 5 women (18.5%) have been raped at some point in their lives, compared to 1 in 71 men (1.4%). For females, more than half (51.1%) of these rapes were committed by intimate partners (current and former spouses, cohabiting partners, and dates or boyfriends). As indicated by Gove et al. (1985), intimate partner violence is much less likely to be reported in the National Crime Victimization Survey than is violence committed by strangers (for more on intimate partner violence, see Box 7.2 in Chapter 7).

African Americans are somewhat more likely than whites to be victims of violence. About 2.3 of every 100 African Americans were victims of violence in 2014, versus about 2 of every 100 whites. The rate of violent victimization among Hispanics (1.6 per 100) was lower than that of white non-Hispanics (2.0) and African American non-Hispanics (2.3). ("Hispanics" are defined as persons of Spanish-speaking origin; they may identify themselves as white, African American, or members of other racial groups.)

Data from previous years indicate that **people with lower incomes** are generally more likely to be victims of violence. In 2005, for example, about 4.1 of every 100 people in households with incomes of less than $7,500 were victims of violence, versus about 1.7 of every 100 people in households with incomes of $75,000 or more. **The relationship between household income and property crime is somewhat mixed.** In 2008, about 5.7 of every 100 households with incomes lower than $7,500 were burglarized, versus 1.6 of every 100 households with incomes of at least $75,000. The differences in property crime between lower- and higher-income households are much smaller for theft, however.

In sum, the victims of violence tend to be young, male (except for rape/sexual assault), African American, and poor. The relationship between household income and property crime is somewhat mixed, but lower-income households are more likely to be burglarized.

How many victimizations are committed by juveniles? What do victimization data tell us about the number of crimes committed by juveniles? As indicated, crime victims are asked whether they saw the person(s) who victimized them. They rarely see the offender(s) in property crimes like larceny and burglary, but they almost always see the offender in violent crimes like assault, rape, and robbery. Victims who saw the offender(s) are asked to estimate the offender's age. The information that victimization data provide about the extent of juvenile delinquency, therefore, is largely limited to violent crimes (although see Hindelang, 1981, regarding property crime). Data from 2014 indicate that juveniles ages 12 to 17 committed about 174,000 serious violent crimes (rape/sexual assault, robbery, and aggravated assault), or about 6.9 serious violent crimes per 1,000 juveniles ages 12 to 17 (Federal Interagency Forum on Child and Family Statistics, 2016). These estimates exceed by several times those provided by FBI arrest and clearance data (e.g., about 53,000 juveniles under age 18 were **arrested** for these crimes in 2014). So victimization data show that violent crime among juveniles is far more extensive than arrest data indicate, although not as extensive as indicated by self-report data.

Summary

You have been presented with a lot of numbers and may be feeling a little overwhelmed right now. Again, try not to get too caught up in all the numbers. Focus on the basic points being made by these numbers. These points include the following:

1. Arrest, self-report, and victimization data provide different estimates of the extent of delinquency in the United States. Arrest data provide the lowest estimates, and self-report data provide the highest. You should be able to explain why this is the case, drawing on the discussion of the advantages and disadvantages of each type of data (see Chapter 2).
2. Self-report data probably provide the most accurate estimate of the extent of delinquency. At least 90 percent of all adolescents engage in delinquency at some point, and, on average, each juvenile commits about 52 delinquent acts per year.
3. All three data sources indicate that minor offenses are more common than serious offenses and that property crime is more common than violent crime, although minor or simple assault is common.

IS JUVENILE DELINQUENCY INCREASING?

As Bernard (1992) points out, most people think that juvenile delinquency is worse now than in the past. In fact, they often think of the past as the "good old days," a time when it was safe to walk the streets and juveniles almost never committed serious crimes like murder and rape. It is easy to understand why people feel this way. The media regularly report on the horrible crimes committed by juveniles (see Box 3.1). But what do the data show? Is delinquency increasing, decreasing, or staying the same? Once more, we must examine arrest, self-report, and victimization data. As you will see, they sometimes disagree with one another regarding trends in delinquency. Nevertheless, an examination of these data sources will allow us to draw some tentative conclusions about trends in delinquency. Our focus is on **trends in delinquency since the early 1980s.**

Box 3.1   Are Today's Youth More Violent than Previous Generations? Sorting Fact from Fiction

[In earlier times] it was a rare day when you saw a man under 25 up for a felony. Today it's the rule. And today when one of these kids robs a bank he doesn't rush for a businesslike getaway. He stays around and shoots up a couple of clerks. Not long ago I asked such a boy why, and he said: "I get a kick out of it when I see blood running."

[In earlier times] juvenile delinquency, in general, meant such things as truancy, minor vandalism and petty theft. Today, the term includes armed robbery, assault and even murder.

Do these quotations reflect your own sentiments about young offenders today, and perhaps that of your friends and family members? Would you be surprised to learn that these quotations are over 50 years old? The first quotation is from a New York City judge in 1954—a time period that many people associate with social order and stability. The second quotation is from the head of the FBI in 1964 (quoted in Bernard, 1992:33). Similar concerns about a rising tide of out-of-control, violent youth can be traced back to the 1940s, 1930s, and 1920s. Further, historians have uncovered complaints about "rotten" and inconsiderate youth dating back hundreds and even thousands of years. As summarized by author Frank Donovan, it seems that "every generation since the dawn of time has denounced the rising generation as being inferior in terms of manners and morals, ethics and honesty" (quoted in Bernard, 1992:31).

It is not difficult to see how adults would form a negative impression of the younger generation. As mentioned earlier, the media regularly report on the horrible crimes committed by young people. In such reports, we often hear claims that a certain type of delinquency is increasing. "Expert" commentators may even offer explanations for the alleged increase, and viewers are left with the impression that serious juvenile offending was less common in earlier times. If you pay close attention to such reports, however—and we encourage you to do so in the future—you may find that claims about juvenile crime are frequently exaggerated and lack supporting data (or are inconsistent with the major data sources described in this book).

A dramatic example involves the "superpredator" myth. During the mid-1990s, following a real increase in the rate of serious juvenile crime, some expert commentators jumped to conclusions. Not only did they predict that the problem would grow worse, but they attributed the rise in youth crime to a new and remorseless breed of young offenders: that is, to a new group of "superpredators." As the authors of a 1996 book titled *Body Count* described:

America is now home to thickening ranks of superpredators—radically impulsive, brutally remorseless youngsters, including ever more preteenage boys, who murder, assault, rape, rob, burglarize, deal deadly drugs, join gun toting gangs, and create serious communal disorders. . . . [H]ere come the superpredators. (quoted in Brownstein, 2000:120)

Although other experts dismissed the superpredator story as "hogwash," it was picked up by the national press with such headlines as "Teenage Time Bombs: Violent Juvenile Crime Is Soaring and It's Going to Get Worse" (Brownstein, 2000:121). There was one major problem with the superpredator story, however. The predicted juvenile crime wave failed to materialize. In fact, as we describe later in this chapter, the rate

(Continued)

(Continued)

of serious juvenile offending has *declined dramatically* since the publication of *Body Count*. Although the juvenile crime rate has fluctuated in recent years, it remains far below the level of the early to mid-1990s (when some of your professors may have come of age). Today's youth, then, are **not** more violent than the previous generation.

Nevertheless, alarmist reports of a rising juvenile crime wave tend to be repeated every decade (Bernard, 1992). In fact, the same experts who promoted the superpredator story in the 1990s did not hesitate to warn of another possible juvenile crime wave in the following decade. In a book published in 2001 titled *The Will to Kill,* the authors write: "Over the next 6 years, the number of teens, ages 14 to 17, will swell by about 15 percent, which may indeed bring increased problems of . . . drug abuse, joblessness, and, of course, violence" (J. Fox and Levin, 2001:87).

Questions for Discussion
1. Why do you think media reports of a juvenile crime wave are repeated every decade, regardless of the facts?
2. After reading this chapter, try to answer the following question: Did the 2001 prediction of a possible juvenile crime wave come to pass?

Are Juvenile Arrests Increasing?

When examining trends in juvenile arrests, it is best to look at **arrest rates** rather than the number of arrests. Arrest rates are usually presented as the number of arrests per 100,000 juveniles ages 10 to 17 in the population. Arrest rates have the advantage of controlling for changes in the size of the juvenile population. If there is an increase in the number of juveniles, then the number of juvenile arrests will likely increase because there are more juveniles to be arrested. This will occur even if the typical juvenile is no more or less delinquent than before. For example, there was a dramatic increase in the number of juvenile arrests during the 1960s and early 1970s. But part of this increase was because there were more juveniles to be arrested. As a result of the post–World War II baby boom, the number of juveniles between 10 and 17 years of age increased from about 25 million in 1960 to over 33 million in 1975. The arrest rate is not influenced by changes in the size of the juvenile population, since it shows the number of arrests per 100,000 juveniles. Changes in the arrest rate, then, provide a better indication of whether juveniles are becoming more or less delinquent.

The two graphs in Figure 3.1 show changes in the juvenile arrest rate for Part I violent crimes (homicide, aggravated assault, robbery, rape) and Part I property crimes (burglary, larceny, motor vehicle theft, arson). Take a moment to look at these graphs; some of their ramifications are suggested in the paragraphs that follow.

Property crime. The rate of property crime was reasonably stable from the early 1980s to 1994, with perhaps a modest increase in rates during the late 1980s and early 1990s. The rate has been declining since the mid-1990s, dropping from over 2,500 arrests per 100,000 juveniles in 1994 to less than 1,300 arrests per 100,000 juveniles in 2006. By 2006, the rate of juvenile property crime dropped to its lowest level since the 1960s. This downward trend was interrupted between 2006 and 2008, when the overall rate of juvenile property crime began to increase again by a modest amount (though it remained far below the rates recorded in the early to mid-1990s). Beginning in 2010, the downward trend continued, reaching a historic low by 2014 (about 693 arrests per 100,000 juveniles). **In fact, the 2014 juvenile arrest rate for property crime was lower than at any point in the past 30 years.**

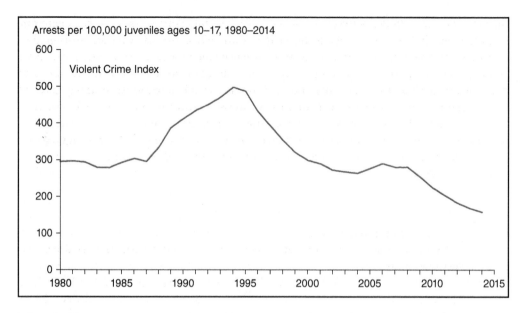

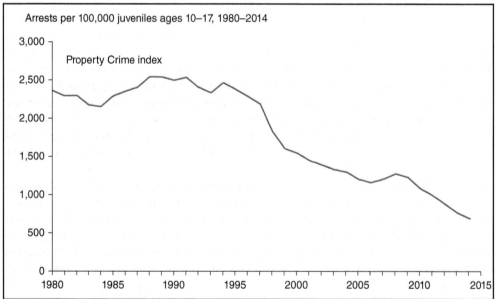

FIGURE 3.1 Trends in the Juvenile Arrest Rate for Part 1 Violent and Property Crimes

SOURCE: Office of Juvenile Justice and Delinquency Prevention Statistical Briefing Book, 2017.

It should be noted that trends for particular types of property crime sometimes differ from the overall trend shown in Figure 3.1. For example, the modest increase in the property crime rate in recent years (2006–2008) was due mainly to an increase in juvenile arrests for larceny-theft. In contrast, the rate of juvenile arrests for arson and motor vehicle theft continued a steady downward trend.

Violent crime. The rate of violent crime arrests was reasonably stable from 1980 to 1988. It then increased by more than 60 percent between 1988 and 1994. This increase did much to draw attention to the juvenile crime problem, with the media running numerous stories about juvenile violence during this time. Violent crime arrests then declined from 1994 through the early 2000s. Between 2004 and 2006, violent crime rates increased again but remained well below their levels in the early to mid-1990s. This increase led to some discussion over whether the dramatic drop in violence since the mid-1990s had come to an end (see Butts and Snyder, 2006; Zimring, 2007). But then the juvenile violent crime rate decreased once again between 2006 and 2014. **In fact, by 2014, the juvenile arrest rate for violent crime was at its lowest level in more than three decades.** As with property crime, trends for particular types of violent crime sometimes differ from the overall trend. Much of the latest decrease in violent crime is due to a lower rate of juvenile arrest for aggravated assault. The juvenile arrest rate for robbery, however, increased slightly between 2006 and 2008.

Trends in murder rates. We want to draw special attention to the crime of murder, since trends in the arrest rate for murder have been the subject of much discussion in the media and in the criminology literature.[1] The juvenile arrest rate for murder more than doubled between 1987 and 1993. This increase was especially dramatic because the arrest rate for murder among those over 25 declined during this period. Further, the increase in the juvenile arrest rate for murder was entirely due to an increase in gun-related murders. The juvenile arrest rate for nongun murders was stable (see Blumstein and Wallman, 2006; Blumstein and Rosenfeld, 1998; Snyder, 2003).

There has been much discussion about **why the juvenile arrest rate for gun-related murders increased so dramatically during the late 1980s and early 1990s.** Among other things, some evidence suggests that the increase was due to the spread of crack cocaine during the mid- to late 1980s. Juveniles became heavily involved in the crack trade, and they often armed themselves for protection (you are unlikely to call the police for protection if you are a crack dealer). So guns became more common among certain juveniles. This led other juveniles to feel that they had to carry guns for protection. The end result was that guns spread throughout the juvenile population, and disputes that used to be settled with fists or knives came to be settled with bullets (Blumstein and Rosenfeld, 1998; Blumstein and Wallman, 2006; Cork, 1999).

The increase in juvenile homicides (and serious violence more generally) has also been linked to certain social changes that led to an increase in gangs (see Braga, 2003; Greenwood, 2002). These changes include a decline in manufacturing jobs, especially in inner-city neighborhoods; an increase in single-parent families; and tensions involving recent immigrants to the United States (see Chapter 16 for further discussion). Such changes likely contributed to the dramatic growth in gangs during the 1980s and early to mid-1990s (W. Miller, 2001). As discussed in Chapter 16, gang members are more likely than nonmembers to possess and use guns.

The juvenile arrest rate for murder declined sharply from 1994 to 2004, with the decline more than erasing the previous increase in arrest rates for murder. There has also been much discussion about the reasons for this decline and the more general decline in violent and property crimes—a topic that we address shortly. Beginning in 2005, the arrest rate for juvenile murder increased again by a modest amount, but this increase was interrupted by another drop from 2008 to 2014. Despite some fluctuation in recent years, the arrest rate for juvenile murder remains well below its levels in the early to mid-1990s. To illustrate, the rate peaked in 1993, with 12.8 juveniles per 100,000 being arrested for murder. The arrest rate for juvenile murder in 2014 was 2.2 per 100,000, about one-sixth of the 1993 rate.

Overall, arrest data suggest the following about trends in delinquency since the early 1980s: (1) rates of property crime were fairly stable from the early 1980s to 1994, with perhaps a modest increase in the late 1980s and early 1990s, then rates declined sharply after 1994, and have since continued a general downward trend, despite some year-to-year fluctuations; (2) rates of violent crime were stable through the late 1980s, increased sharply from 1988 to 1994, then declined sharply until 2004, and have since continued a general downward trend despite some year-to-year fluctuations in the mid-2000s. We have focused on Part I crimes. We should note that trends in Part II crimes are somewhat varied, although arrests for most such crimes have declined in recent years. Perhaps the most striking trends in arrests for Part II crimes involve drug abuse and curfew/loitering violations. There was a dramatic increase in the arrest rates for drug abuse and curfew/loitering violations in the mid-1990s—followed by decreases in the arrest rates for these crimes in the later 1990s and 2000s. (There is good reason to believe that much of the increase in curfew/loitering arrests reflects changes in the law and police practices. Many cities, for example, responded to the increase in juvenile violence by instituting curfews for juveniles or more strictly enforcing existing curfew laws.)

Is Self-Reported Delinquency Increasing?

The Monitoring the Future survey described earlier provides information on trends in self-reported delinquency. Again, these data focus on high school seniors. They do not contain information on certain serious crimes, like murder and rape. Rather, they tend to focus on minor offenses or minor instances of more serious offenses (for reasons indicated in Chapter 2). Also, their use of the response category "5 or more times" means that they underestimate the extent of delinquency. Nevertheless, these data provide some indication of trends in delinquency—especially minor delinquency—among high school seniors throughout the United States.[2]

The graph in **Figure 3.2 shows trends in the rate of self-reported property crime and violent crime from 1980 to 2014.** In particular, it shows the number of property and violent crimes reported each year per 100 high school seniors. We focus on four property crimes: larceny under $50, larceny over $50, shoplifting, and auto theft (there is no good

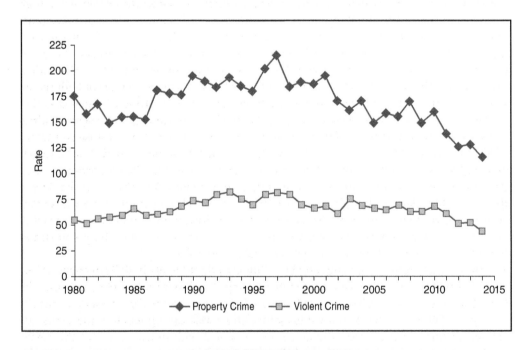

FIGURE 3.2 Trends in the Rate of Self-Reported Delinquency of High School Seniors (Rate = Number of Acts per 100 Seniors)

SOURCE: Monitoring the Future survey (http://www.monitoringthefuture.org)

measure of burglary in the survey). And we focus on three violent crimes: serious assault, group fights, and robbery. Take a moment to examine the graph in Figure 3.2. Focus on long-term trends, rather than short-term or year-to-year fluctuations in the delinquency rate. These short-term fluctuations may be due to chance, but substantial changes in the crime rate that last for several years likely reflect real changes.[3]

Property crime. The rate of property crime was generally stable during the early to mid-1980s, increased by a modest amount during the late 1980s and 1990s, then declined by a modest amount during the 2000s. To illustrate, the average rate of property crime each year from 1980 to 1986 was 159.6 property crimes per 100 high school seniors. The average rate of property crime per year from 1987 to 2002 was 188.2 property crimes per 100 seniors. The average rate from 2003 to 2014 was 148.9 per 100 seniors. These data are somewhat at odds with arrest data. While arrest data also show a modest increase in rates of property crime during the late 1980s, arrest data show a more dramatic decline in rates of property crime since the mid-1990s.

Violent crime. It is more difficult to discern clear patterns in the rate of self-reported violence. Rates of violence were fairly stable during much of the 1980s but then increased somewhat during the late 1980s and 1990s. To illustrate, the average rate of violence each year from 1980 to 1988 was 59.6 violent acts per 100 high school seniors. The average rate of violence each year from 1989 to 1998 was 76.3 violent acts per 100 seniors. There has been a slight decrease in the rate of violence since 1998, with the average rate of violence from 1999 to 2014 being 63.7 acts per 100 seniors. These data are also somewhat at odds with arrest data. Arrest data show a larger increase in violence in the late 1980s. Also, arrest data show a larger decline in violence beginning in the mid-1990s.

Drug use. Figure 3.3 shows trends in drug use, using data from the Monitoring the Future study of high school seniors. In particular, Figure 3.3 shows the percentage of high school seniors who used an illicit drug in the last 30 days. Illicit drugs include marijuana, LSD and other hallucinogens, crack and other forms of cocaine, heroin and other narcotics, amphetamines, barbiturates, and tranquilizers (not under a doctor's orders). As can be seen, there was a dramatic decrease in illicit drug use from the early 1980s to 1992. Illicit drug use then increased a good deal during the 1990s, with the percentage of high school seniors reporting illicit drug use almost doubling. This increase attracted much attention in the media and was a major issue in the 1996 presidential campaign. A major antidrug initiative was launched by the federal government in response to this increase (see Office of National Drug Control Policy, 1999, 2007). And illicit drug use did in fact decrease beginning in the early 2000s. Since 2006, however, data indicate that the proportion of illicit drug users began to creep up again, although it remains far below that observed during the early 1980s. (Note: Other data on illicit drug use, including data on younger juveniles, largely confirm these trends; see Federal Interagency Forum on Child and Family Statistics, 2016. We should note, however, that trends in the use of particular drugs sometimes differ from the general trends in illicit drug use just described.)

In sum, self-report data suggest the following about trends in delinquency: (1) The rate of property crime was generally stable during the early to mid-1980s, increased by a modest amount during the late 1980s and 1990s, then declined by a modest amount during the 2000s; (2) the rate of violent crime was stable during much of the 1980s, increased during the late 1980s and generally remained high during much of the 1990s, then decreased slightly since 1998; and (3) the rate of illicit drug use decreased during the 1980s and early 1990s, increased during the 1990s, decreased during the early 2000s, and increased again by a modest amount in recent years.

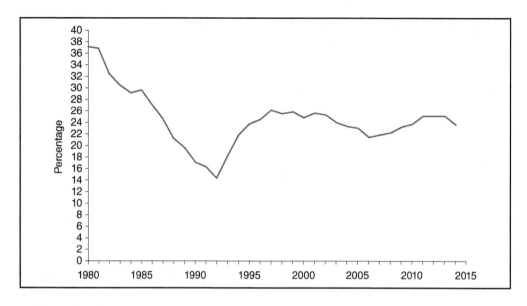

FIGURE 3.3 Percentage of High School Seniors Using Illicit Drugs in the Last 30 Days

SOURCE: Monitoring the Future survey, as reported by the Federal Interagency Forum on Child and Family Statistics, 2016.

Are Victimizations Committed by Juveniles Increasing?

We can use the National Crime Victimization Survey to estimate the rate of violent crime victimizations committed by juveniles ages 12 through 17. Data indicate that this rate was moderately stable during much of the 1980s, increased during the late 1980s and early 1990s, declined dramatically from 1993 to 2002, and has continued a general downward trend since 2002 despite some year-to-year fluctuations. These trends are illustrated in Figure 3.4, which focuses on aggravated assaults, robberies, rapes, and homicides committed by juveniles ages 12 to 17 (the homicide data are from police reports).

So victimization data, like arrest data, indicate that the violent crime rate for juveniles was reasonably stable during the early to mid-1980s, increased in the late 1980s and early 1990s, declined sharply through the early 2000s, and has continued a general downward trend. Unfortunately, victimization data on trends in property crime by juveniles are largely lacking.

Summary

We began with a simple question: Is juvenile delinquency increasing? But, as you can see, the answer is anything but simple. The answer varies somewhat by type of crime and by data source. Nevertheless, we can draw some general conclusions.

Property crime. Arrest and self-report data disagree somewhat regarding trends in property crime. Both arrest and self-report data suggest that rates of property crime were fairly stable during much of the 1980s, with a modest increase during the late 1980s. But arrest data show that rates of property crime have declined sharply since the mid-1990s, while self-report data show a relatively modest decline. One possible explanation for this difference is that arrest data are biased toward serious crimes and the more serious instances of less serious crimes, while self-report data are biased toward minor crimes. In particular, the Monitoring the Future survey does not measure the crime of burglary; in addition, it likely picks up large numbers of trivial property crimes, and it undersamples those juveniles most likely to engage in serious property crime. So we might **tentatively**

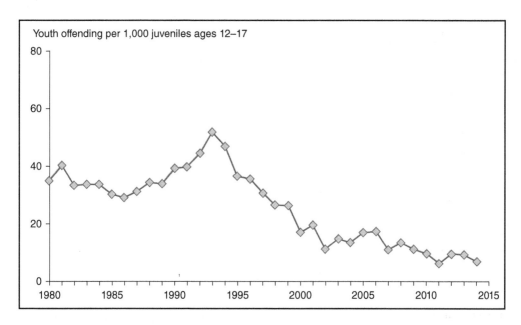

FIGURE 3.4 Trends in the Rate of Violent Victimizations Committed by Juveniles Ages 12–17

SOURCE: Federal Interagency Forum on Child and Family Statistics, 2016.

conclude that there was **an overall sharp decline in serious property crime from the mid- to late 1990s to 2014, and a relatively modest decline in minor property crime.**

Violent crime. Arrest and victimization data indicate that rates of juvenile violence were generally stable in the early to mid-1980s, increased substantially in the late 1980s and early 1990s, decreased substantially from the mid-1990s to early 2000s, and continued on a modest downward trend, despite some year-to-year fluctuations. Self-report data, however, show a more modest increase in violence during the late 1980s and a more modest decrease since 1998. We lean toward the arrest and victimization data when it comes to trends in serious violence. For reasons indicated earlier, arrest and victimization data probably do a better job of measuring serious violence. So we would conclude that **rates of serious violence increased dramatically in the late 1980s and early 1990s, declined sharply through the early 2000s, and continued on a general downward trend.** We lean toward the self-report data for trends in less serious violence. So **rates of less serious violence increased by a modest amount during the late 1980s and early 1990s and decreased by a modest amount since the late 1990s.**

Drug crime. It seems safe to conclude that **overall rates of illicit drug use declined substantially during the 1980s and early 1990s.** All major self-report data indicate such a decline. Arrest rates for drug abuse during this period are relatively stable, but arrest rates for drug abuse are heavily influenced by police practices as well as by true levels of drug abuse. It also seems safe to conclude that **rates of drug use increased substantially from about 1992 to the early 2000s.** Both self-report and arrest data are in agreement here. **Rates of illicit drug use declined once again throughout the early to mid-2000s,** with this decline evident in both self-report and arrest data. According to multiple self-report surveys, however, **the rate of illicit drug use began creeping up again after 2006.** (Arrest data show a decline, but for reasons stated previously, we tend to rely on self-reports when interpreting drugs use trends.)

HOW CAN WE EXPLAIN THE DRAMATIC DECLINE IN SERIOUS CRIME SINCE THE MID-1990S?

As indicated, there is good reason to believe that there has been a dramatic decline in the rates of serious violent and property crimes since the mid-1990s. In fact, these rates are now at historic lows. Crime and delinquency remain serious problems, of course, but the general downward trend we observe is encouraging. And it is important to determine why this decline has occurred. Doing so may help us better predict future trends in crime and may even help us influence those trends. For example, if we determine that certain police practices contributed to the decline, we might make an effort to continue or increase the use of such practices.

Unfortunately, it is often difficult to determine whether particular factors contributed to the decline. Researchers need to demonstrate that a particular factor changed around the time that crime rates declined and that there is good reason to believe that this change affected crime rates. But this is not always possible. Nevertheless, there is some reason to believe that **several factors may have contributed to the decline in juvenile crime rates.**[4]

Two such factors are the **decline in crack use** and in the **turf disputes among crack dealers.** As indicated earlier, the increase in crack use in the 1980s likely contributed to the increase in serious juvenile violence during this time. Juveniles became heavily involved in the crack trade; they armed themselves for protection, given the dangers involved; other juveniles responded by arming themselves; and, as a consequence, disputes that used to be settled with fists came to be settled with guns. Crack use, however, began to decline in the 1990s, partly because attitudes toward crack became more negative as people became aware of the devastating effects of this drug. Also, competition among crack dealers decreased as dealers established their territories. As a consequence, juvenile involvement in the crack trade declined, and the trade itself became less violent. This, in turn, contributed to a decrease in the carrying and use of guns by juveniles.

The decline in crime rates was also probably influenced by **improvements in the economy** during the 1990s. Among other things, the percentage of children living in poverty fell sharply from 1993 through the early 2000s, especially for African American children (Federal Interagency Forum on Child and Family Statistics, 2007). Reductions in poverty contribute to **better parenting practices and improved school performance,** which in turn contribute to lower delinquency (see Bellair and Roscigno, 2000; Chapters 14 and 15 in this text). Also, unemployment declined to the point that **teenagers with few skills and a limited education were able to get jobs.** Data suggest that employment reduces crime, especially when illegal opportunities to make money—like selling crack—are on the decline (see Allan and Steffensmeier, 1989; Grogger, 2006; Zimring, 2007). Further, improvements in the economy likely contributed to the **decline in gangs** that began in the mid-1990s, with this decline also contributing to the reduction in crime rates (see Chapter 16). Economic factors alone, however, cannot explain why serious juvenile crime remained relatively low into the late 2000s, despite a major economic recession (2007–2009) and an increase, once again, in poverty (see Chapter 12).

Improvements in police practices may have also contributed to the decline in crime rates, although the data here are less clear-cut. Many cities adopted new methods of policing. Evidence suggests that certain of these methods are effective at reducing crime. These include efforts to crack down on particular types of crime, such as drug selling and gun carrying, to crack down on gangs, and to crack down on locations with high rates of crime. These methods also include certain types of "community policing," such as problem-oriented policing ,where the police attempt to address the underlying problems that contribute to crime. (These methods and the evidence on their effectiveness are described in Chapter 20.) However, we lack good data on the extent to which these methods were adopted by police departments across the country. Also, many cities experienced substantial reductions in crime even though they did not adopt such methods to any significant degree (see Conklin, 2003; Eck and Maguire, 2006; Zimring, 2007, 2011). Even so, some criminologists feel that new methods of policing helped contribute to the reduction in crime rates.

Further, **the increased use of prevention and rehabilitation programs** during the 1990s may have contributed to the decline in crime rates. These programs include efforts to help troubled families, to help children do better in school, to provide mentors for at-risk and delinquent children, to mediate gang disputes, and to provide teenagers with organized recreational activities (see Chapter 24 for a discussion of rehabilitation and prevention programs). However, we lack good data on the extent to which effective rehabilitation and prevention programs were employed during the 1990s.

Another factor that may have contributed to the decline is **the higher rate at which juvenile offenders were incarcerated** in the 1990s. Confining more juvenile offenders may prevent crime in two ways: the confined juveniles are unable to commit crimes on the street, and their confinement may deter others from crime. It is estimated that increased rates of confinement accounted for about one-fourth of the reduction in **adult** crime during the 1990s (see Blumstein and Wallman, 2006; Conklin, 2003; Zimring, 2007). But the rate at which juveniles were confined increased at a much slower pace than the rate at which adults were confined, so **increased rates of confinement probably account for only a small portion of the decrease in juvenile crime rates** (see Chapter 23).

Scholars are now exploring **the role of immigration** in the crime decline. Although past studies have linked immigration-related tensions to gang problems (see Chapter 16), research indicates that, on average, immigrants are less violent than third-generation Americans (see Chapter 4 for further discussion). Moreover, since 1990, America has experienced a large wave of immigration, with the foreign-born population increasing by 56 percent—representing an additional 11 million individuals. This wave of immigration was followed by a dramatic *decrease* in violent crime, as we have seen. This fact may seem counterintuitive, as many people assume that immigration leads to more crime (and people often assume that crime is rising, regardless of the facts). But at least two studies now show that the increase in the immigrant population contributed to the *decline* in violent crime (Stowell et al., 2009; Tim Wadsworth, 2010). (Reading this chapter, you may have noticed a theme emerging: namely, that common sense and conventional wisdom are often poor guides to understanding social problems like crime and delinquency. You will encounter other examples in the chapters ahead.) The role of additional factors, including technological developments (e.g., new security devices, availability of smartphones) and improvements in health and safety (e.g., reduced exposure to lead and lower levels of alcohol consumption), are being explored as well.

In sum, many factors likely contributed to the decline in rates of serious offending that began in the mid-1990s. There is now some concern that the downward trend in serious violent crime may be coming to an end. At the time of this writing, the latest official crime data indicate that, while the property crime rate continued to drop, the rate of violent crime in 2015 was 3 percent higher than that recorded in 2014 (FBI, 2016). This uptick in serious violent crime was not the result of a nationwide crime surge; rather, it was largely the result of a dramatic spike in homicide in a small number of cities, such as Chicago, Baltimore, and Washington, DC. The reasons for this spike are not yet clear, but criminologists and law enforcement officials point to the possible influence of gangs, drug markets, and policing issues in these cities. There is now a lively debate over the actions of the police, and whether the spike in violence was the result of police adopting a less aggressive stance toward crime. Some claim that, given recent protests over police shooting deaths, the police are now more reluctant to confront potential offenders—the so-called

"Ferguson effect" (for an overview of this debate and a discussion of relevant evidence, see Beckett, 2016; for more on policing, see Chapter 20).

Yet, despite this tragic spike in violence, it is important to emphasize that the national crime rate remains at historic lows—far below that of the early 1990s. Whether it will be possible to keep the crime rate down in the future will likely depend on such things as trends in the economy and the extent to which the United States makes use of effective crime control strategies, including new methods of policing (see Chapter 20), better methods of sanctioning juvenile offenders (see Chapter 23), and effective methods of rehabilitating offenders and preventing delinquency (see Chapter 24). All these things are important because they impact the causes of delinquency, described in Chapters 6 through 18.

TEACHING AIDS

Exercise: The Extent of and Trends in Campus Crime

Colleges and universities are required to collect data on the extent of crime on campus and to make that data available to the public. We would like you to obtain data on the extent of crime on your campus during the previous two years (you can probably obtain such data by visiting the office or website of your campus police or security force). Then do the following.

1. Figure out what data are being reported. In particular, what crimes are listed and what types of data are available on each crime (e.g., number of crimes known to the police, number of arrests).

2. Look at the number of crimes listed for each type of crime. Do you think these numbers provide an accurate indication of the extent of crime on your campus (e.g., the extent of liquor law violations, drug offenses, sexual assaults)? If not, list all your reasons for believing that such data may underestimate the extent of campus crime.

3. Determine whether the number of crimes increased, decreased, or stayed the same over the previous two years. In particular, calculate the percentage change in the number of crimes. Do this for each type of crime. (For example, you might find that the number of liquor law violations increased 50 percent from 2015 to 2016.) Do you think these data provide a good indication of the true amount of change in the extent of crime? If not, list all the reasons why not.

4. How might you go about better determining the extent of crime on campus and trends in crime? (Note: See Fisher et al., 1998, for an example of a victimization survey conducted on 12 college campuses. The researchers found that more than 33 percent of the students they surveyed had been the victims of crime during the academic year. Furthermore, "the main predictor of violent victimization was a lifestyle that included high levels of partying on campus and the recreational use of drugs" [Fisher et al., 1998:671; also see Hart, 2003].)

Web-Based Exercise: Finding the Latest Information on the Extent of and Trends in Crime and Delinquency

FBI data collected from the police. Each year the FBI releases data on the extent of and trends in crime in the prior year, including data on "offenses known to law enforcement" and "persons arrested." You should:

1. Visit the **FBI's homepage** (www.fbi.gov).
2. Click on the "Resources" tab at the top of the page.
3. Click on **"Crime Statistics."**
4. Under "Publications," click on "Crime in the United States," and then click on the year of the latest complete *Uniform Crime Reports/Crime in the United States* volume.
5. Click on **"Offenses Known to Law Enforcement."** Examine the number and rate of index, or Part I, crimes committed in the most recent year. What are the most

common and least common crimes? Describe trends in the rate of crime over the last several years. (Note: These data are usually provided in Table 1 of each volume of *Uniform Crime Reports*).

6. The "Offenses Known to Law Enforcement" data focus on crimes committed by both adults and juveniles. We have to examine arrest data to estimate the extent of delinquency. But only some of the offenses known to law enforcement are "cleared" by arrest. Click on "**Clearances**" and indicate the percentage of crimes cleared by arrest or "exceptional means."

7. Click on "**Persons Arrested**." Examine the number of juveniles arrested for Part I and Part II offenses (these data are usually provided in Table 41). What crimes are juveniles most often arrested for?

8. Explore the FBI data on your own. For example, examine trends in juvenile arrests over time (usually in Table 32). Examine sex and race differences in delinquency.

Victimization data. You might also examine the latest victimization data reported by the Bureau of Justice Statistics.

1. Visit the **Bureau of Justice Statistics homepage** (www.bjs.gov).
2. Click on "**Victims**."
3. Click on "**Crime characteristics and trends**."
4. Scroll down to "**Publications and Products**."
5. Find the publication titled "**Criminal Victimization**" (look for the latest year available). Open the PDF. What do these data say about the extent of and trends in crime? How do they compare to the FBI "Offenses Known to Law Enforcement" data? Why might there be differences between these two sources of data (see the discussion near the end of Chapter 2)?

Self-report data. We report self-report data from the annual Monitoring the Future survey and certain other sources. Another major source of self-report data on delinquency, particularly violence and drug use, is the **Youth Risk Behavior Surveillance System (YRBSS)** of the CDC (Centers for Disease Control and Prevention). The YRBSS in based on a national, school-based survey of 9th–12th grade students conducted every two years by the CDC and on state, local, and tribal surveys conducted by health agencies and governments (see the YRBSS website for further information). You should note that these data provide information on the **prevalence** of violence and drug use (that is, the percentage of youth who committed the act in question at least once during the prior 12 months). They do **not** indicate how many times each youth committed the act.

1. Visit the website for the **Youth Risk Behavior Surveillance System** at http://www.cdc.gov/healthyyouth/yrbs/index.htm.
2. Click on the box "**Youth Online Data Analysis Tool**."
3. Following the instructions provided, explore the data. You can examine the extent of selected types of violence and drug use in the United States as a whole, in particular states, in particular cities and counties, by males and females, by race/ethnic groups, and by grade. You can also examine trends in self-reported violence and drug use since 1991 (click "**View all years**" to examine trends).
4. Drawing on these data, how would you respond if asked the following questions: How much juvenile violence and drug use are there in the United States? Is juvenile violence and drug use increasing?
5. How do these self-report data differ from the victimization and FBI data above? For example, do they examine the same or somewhat different types of crime? Do they examine the same or somewhat different populations or samples?

TEST YOUR KNOWLEDGE OF THIS CHAPTER

1. What general conclusions can we draw about the extent and nature of delinquency from arrest data (e.g., how widespread is delinquency, what types of crime are most common)?
2. What is the "arrest rate"?
3. What do clearance data show?
4. Why is the number of juveniles arrested greater than the number of crimes cleared by the arrest of juveniles?
5. What general conclusions can we draw about the extent and nature of delinquency from self-report data?
6. Why are estimates of the extent of delinquency based on self-report data so much larger than those based on arrest data?
7. Who is most likely to be victimized?
8. Why is it that victimization data provide so little information about the characteristics of people who commit property crimes?
9. Why do we argue that arrest rates should be examined when investigating trends in delinquency?
10. Drawing on arrest data, describe the major trends in property and violent crimes since the early 1980s.
11. Describe the major trends in arrest rates for murder. How have criminologists explained the sharp increase in arrest rates for murder in the late 1980s and early 1990s?
12. Drawing on self-report data, describe trends in violent crime, property crime, and illicit drug use since the early 1980s.
13. Drawing on victimization data, describe trends in violent crime since the early 1980s.
14. Drawing on all data sources, we reach general conclusions about trends in property crime, violent crime, and illicit drug use since the early 1980s. What are they?
15. Describe those factors that may have contributed to the large decline in serious crime rates in the 1990s. Briefly note any problems in the evidence linking these factors to the decline in crime rates (e.g., indicate that we lack good data on the extent to which effective rehabilitation and prevention programs were employed in the 1990s).

THOUGHT AND DISCUSSION QUESTIONS

1. Self-report data suggest that 90 percent or more of all adolescents engage in delinquency at some point. Why do you think delinquency is so common among adolescents? How might we explain the fact that a small portion of adolescents—10 percent or less—manage to refrain from delinquency? (See Chapter 10; Agnew, 2003a; and Moffitt, 1993, for discussions of these issues.)
2. Despite the decline in serious crime since the late 1990s, many people believe that delinquency has increased. How might we explain this?
3. Give an example of a situation where the juvenile arrest rate remains the same but the number of crimes committed by juveniles increases. (Hint: The number of persons under age 18 will increase by 4 million in the next 20 years.)
4. Data suggest that while rates of serious delinquency declined sharply during the 1990s, rates of minor delinquency declined at a more modest pace. How might we explain this difference in trends?

5. Do you think rates of serious delinquency will remain at historic lows? Justify your response.

6. Why do you think rates of illicit drug use have started to creep up again since 2006?

KEY TERMS

- Arrest rates
- Clearance data

ENDNOTES

1. For examples, see Blumstein, 1995; Blumstein and Rosenfeld, 1998; Blumstein and Wallman, 2006; Braga, 2003; Cook and Laub, 1998; Cork, 1999; J. Fox and Zawitz, 1999; National Institute of Justice, 1998a; Messner et al., 2005; Ousey and Lee, 2004; Zimring, 1998, 2007.

2. See Browning and Huizinga, 1999; Huizinga et al., 2003; McCord et al., 2001; Steffensmeier et al., 2005; and Snyder, 2012 for additional self-report data on trends in delinquency.

3. Jensen and Rojek (1998), McCord et al. (2001), and Osgood et al. (1989) have conducted similar analyses using earlier data from the Monitoring the Future survey.

4. See the discussions in Blumstein, 2002; Blumstein and Rosenfeld, 1998; Blumstein and Wallman, 2006; Conklin, 2003; LaFree, 1999; Ousey and Augustine, 2001; Ousey and Lee, 2004, 2007; Messner et al., 2005; Steffensmeier and Harer, 1999; Stowell et al., 2009; Wadsworth, 2010; Zimring, 2007, 2011.

4 Who Is Most Likely to Engage in Delinquency?

Suppose that you encountered a group of people, some young and some old, some male and some female, some white and some African American, and some lower class and some middle class. Further, suppose that you wanted to divide this group in two: criminals on the one side and noncriminals (or less serious criminals) on the other. What characteristic would best allow you to do this: age, gender, race, or social class?

If you are like many people, you probably think that race and class do the best job of distinguishing criminals from noncriminals. This view is often fostered by the media, which tend to portray crime as a problem that is concentrated in poor African American communities. But in fact, age and gender do a far better job of distinguishing criminals from noncriminals. In particular, adolescent males have crime rates that far exceed those of other groups. Of course, not all adolescent males engage in crime. While age and sex are strongly related to crime, the relationship is far from perfect. Nevertheless, age and gender are more strongly related to crime than class and race.

This chapter examines the *sociodemographic characteristics* **of delinquents.** We focus on the relationship between delinquency and social class, race/ethnicity, gender, and age. (Social class is usually measured in terms of the occupational prestige, education, and/or income of the juvenile's parents.) Once more, you will find that simple questions often have complex answers. This is especially the case when we ask whether lower-class juveniles are more delinquent than middle-class juveniles and whether African Americans are more delinquent than whites. Also, you will find that arrest, self-report, and victimization data sometimes disagree about the characteristics of delinquents. Nevertheless, we think that there are a number of conclusions that can safely be drawn about the characteristics of delinquents. We think that you will find some of these conclusions rather surprising, because we suspect that they will challenge your view of the typical juvenile delinquent.

After reading this chapter, you should be able to:

- Explain why studies have produced contradictory findings regarding the relationship between social class and delinquency.
- Draw tentative conclusions about the relationship between social class and delinquency.
- Describe and explain the complex relationship between race and delinquency.
- Describe the relationship between age and delinquency.
- Describe the relationship between gender and delinquency.
- Describe the different types of delinquents.

IS SOCIAL CLASS RELATED TO DELINQUENCY?

Before we talk about social class in our juvenile delinquency courses, we tell the students about a trait known as "tolerance of ambiguity." Some individuals have a low tolerance of ambiguity. That is, they have a strong need for definite, clear-cut answers. When they take a course, they want to be told what is right and what is wrong—no "ifs, ands, or buts." They get very uneasy, even upset, if they are told that the studies in an area contradict one another or that the relationship between certain factors depends on other factors. We mention this trait to you for a good reason: we want to warn you in advance. If you have a low tolerance of ambiguity, you might get a little uneasy with the following discussion on the relationship between social class and delinquency.

Most people assume that lower-class juveniles are more delinquent than middle-class juveniles. A large number of studies have tried to determine whether this is true, but these studies often contradict one another. In fact, you can find studies that support just about any position you like. Many studies find that lower-class juveniles are more delinquent than middle-class juveniles. Many studies find that lower-class and middle-class juveniles engage in about the same amount of delinquency. And a few studies even find that middle-class juveniles are more delinquent than lower-class juveniles. The conclusions that criminologists draw about the relationship between social class and delinquency reflect these studies. Some prominent criminologists argue that there is little or no relationship between class and delinquency, while others argue that lower-class juveniles are more likely to engage in at least some types of delinquency. So we ask a simple question: Are lower-class juveniles more delinquent than middle-class juveniles? But the answer is anything but simple.[1]

We want to help you make sense of the contradictory research on this topic. The best way to do that is by providing you with a historic overview of the research on the relationship between class and delinquency. At the end of this overview, we'll draw two general conclusions about the relationship between class and delinquency, one well supported by the data and the other more tentative.

Early Studies Based on Arrest Data

Until the 1960s, the main way of measuring delinquency was through the use of arrest data or police reports. Criminologists asked whether lower-class juveniles were more likely to be arrested or to come in contact with the police than higher-class juveniles. The FBI does not provide any information on the social class of arrested individuals. But researchers compared the juvenile arrest rates of lower- and higher-class communities. And, less commonly, they compared the arrest records of lower- and higher-class juveniles.

Virtually every study found that lower-class communities had much higher arrest rates than higher-class communities (see the discussion on communities in Chapter 12). Also, most studies found that lower-class juveniles were more likely to be arrested or have police reports than middle-class juveniles (see especially Braithwaite, 1981). One of the best studies in this area looked at all juveniles who were born in Philadelphia in 1958 and lived there from the ages of 10 through 17—a total of 27,160 juveniles. It was found that 42 percent of the lower-class males had a police record, compared to 24 percent of the higher-class males (Tracy, 1990).

On the basis of these studies, criminologists came to the conclusion that social class was strongly associated with delinquency. In fact, criminology textbooks from the 1960s and before often state that one of the most important and best-supported facts about delinquency is that it is concentrated in the lower classes. This belief led criminologists to construct a number of theories to explain why delinquency was concentrated in the lower classes. And billions of dollars were spent on the War on Poverty in the 1960s and early 1970s, partly on the assumption that poverty was a major cause of crime and delinquency. Criminologists, however, experienced a major shock in the 1960s.

Early Self-Report Studies

Self-report surveys of delinquency came into wide use during the 1960s, and most of these surveys found **little or no relationship between social class and delinquency.** This result challenged a fundamental belief of most criminologists, as well as of policy makers and the general public. (Victimization data cannot be used to examine the relationship between social class and delinquency, since crime victims are not asked to estimate the class of the people who victimized them.)

The finding that lower- and middle-class adolescents are equally delinquent seems to challenge our personal experiences. Lower-class neighborhoods, for example, seem unsafe to us, while middle-class neighborhoods seem quite safe. This finding also seems to challenge common sense. It is easy to think of reasons why lower-class adolescents should be more delinquent than middle-class adolescents, but it is difficult to think of reasons why lower- and middle-class adolescents should be equally delinquent. Nevertheless, numerous self-report studies during the 1960s and 1970s found little or no relationship between class and delinquency. Further, some evidence suggested that the relationship between social class and arrest rates was becoming weaker over time (Tittle et al., 1978). As a consequence, many criminologists came to feel that class was unrelated to delinquency. A major review article published in 1978, in fact, was titled "The Myth of Social Class and Criminality" (Tittle et al., 1978).

If class is unrelated to delinquency, **how can one account for the findings from arrest data?** It was said that arrest data were biased. Only a small number of delinquent offenses were reported to the police and, of those, only a small number resulted in arrest. It was claimed that offenses committed by lower-class juveniles were more likely to come to the attention of the police and were more likely to result in arrest. (Chapter 22 discusses the evidence on police discrimination against lower-class juveniles.)

Likewise, if class is unrelated to delinquency, **how can one account for the perception that lower-class juveniles are more delinquent?** A fascinating study by Chambliss (1973) suggests why perceptions regarding the relationship between social class and delinquency may be wrong. Chambliss examined two groups of adolescent males in a high school: the "Saints" and the "Roughnecks." The middle-class Saints were well liked and respected by their teachers and members of the community. In fact, the Saints included some of the top students in the school. The lower-class Roughnecks were disliked and seen as delinquents by their teachers and community residents. Chambliss, however, discovered that the two groups were about equally delinquent. Why, then, were they perceived so differently? Chambliss lists three reasons. **First,** the delinquency of the Saints was less visible. The Saints went to great lengths to hide their delinquency; for example, their greater access to cars allowed them to commit many of their delinquent acts in remote locations. **Second,** the Saints had a better demeanor: they were respectful and apologetic when caught doing something wrong. The Roughnecks, however, were often hostile. As a consequence, people tended to assume that the Saints were basically "good kids" who would occasionally "sow their wild oats," while the Roughnecks were "troublemakers." **Finally,** people were simply biased in favor of the Saints and against the Roughnecks; this bias reflected their beliefs about what lower-class and middle-class people were like. This bias, in turn, influenced their perceptions of the two groups—what they noticed and how they interpreted what they noticed (see Box 4.1).

Finally, if class is unrelated to delinquency, **how can we account for all the good reasons linking class to delinquency?** The findings of one intriguing study indicate that while higher-class juveniles are less likely to engage in delinquency for some reasons, they are more likely to engage in delinquency for other reasons (B. Wright, Caspi, Moffitt, Meich, and Silva, 1999). For example, higher-class juveniles are less likely to engage in delinquency because they have less need for money. But higher-class juveniles are more likely to engage in delinquency because they have greater "social power"; that is, they are better able to avoid detection and are better able to resist the efforts of others—teachers and police, for example—to punish them. These effects tend to cancel one another out, so one finds that social class has little relationship to delinquency.

By the late 1970s many criminologists were stating that there was little or no relationship between social class and delinquency. Several criminologists, however, challenged this conclusion.

Criticisms of the Early Self-Report Studies

Some criminologists said that the early self-report studies suffered from several problems and that these problems account for their failure to find any relationship between social class and delinquency.[2]

Box 4.1 Devils in Disguise? The Dynamics of Middle-Class Delinquency

In his classic study of the "Saints and Roughnecks," Chambliss observed that the middle-class Saints, while highly delinquent, were viewed by adults in their community as essentially "good boys" with bright futures. This was the case even though the Saints were engaged in delinquency nearly every day and even though some of their behavior was potentially dangerous. For example, the Saints would remove the barricades around road construction sites and, under the cover of darkness, wait for unsuspecting motorists to crash. It was surprising to Chambliss (1973:26) that "no one was seriously injured as a result of the Saints' activities."

As described earlier, there are several possible reasons for the positive reputation enjoyed by the Saints. Because of their middle-class backgrounds, parents and teachers rarely suspected them of delinquent activity (they did not fit the stereotype of the lower class delinquent). As a result, the Saints were trusted by adults, enjoyed access to automobiles, were able to escape adult supervision, and thus managed to conceal their delinquency. During the rare occasions when their delinquency was discovered, authority figures tended to dismiss their activities as simple pranks or momentary lapses of judgment—not as indicators of their essential character. The polite, respectful, and apologetic demeanor of the Saints encouraged such reactions.

In the paragraphs that follow, we illustrate these dynamics with quotations from other middle-class delinquents. We also highlight two processes that facilitate the concealment of delinquent involvement, including parental ignorance and the exercise of manipulative power.

In the example of the Saints, we see that authority figures were largely ignorant of the young men's delinquent activities and that most of these activities went undetected. We learn from Chambliss that it was easy for the Saints to hide their delinquency. For example, because teachers viewed them as good students, it was easy for them to fabricate excuses for skipping class and receive the benefit of the doubt. This tendency toward ignorance may apply to adults more broadly, however, especially among parents. As criminologist Marcus Felson observes:

> Because our society so often associates bad behavior with bad parenting, parents have a strong incentive to hear and see no evil done by their own children. This encourages them not to dig too deeply to find bad facts, not to believe those that come to their attention, and to find excuses for those they cannot deny. (Felson, 1998:11)

Yet even determined parents may remain ignorant of their child's delinquency, as illustrated by the following quotation. In this case, a father (a middle-class professional) assumed that he could judge the character of his daughter's friends and thereby steer his child away from delinquent peers. As the daughter explained, this parenting strategy backfired:

> One of my best friends [T.] looked real sweet, didn't wear make-up, and dressed conservatively. . . . I did too. My dad was always encouraging me to go out with [T.] instead of my other friends because he thought the rest were trouble. But [T.] was the wildest one! The first time she smoked pot was in the 5th grade. And she would steal stuff. When she got drunk she thought it was funny to steal things because she knew no one would suspect her. (quoted in Brezina and Aragones, 2004:521)

(Continued)

(Continued)

This same daughter commented on the ease with which she had concealed delinquent involvement not only from her parents but from school officials:

> In high school I did all that stuff . . . got drunk and high. But I was also a pep club officer, on the student council, and an office assistant to the principal's office. I was asked to [be an office assistant] because [they thought] I was such a "goody goody." But I roamed the halls, and pulled my friends out of class . . . and we would go to the bathroom and do Whippets [inhale nitrous oxide]. And in the 80s they had the big "Just Say No" [to drugs] campaign and I was selected as the representative to the "Just Say No" state conference! (quoted in Brezina and Aragones, 2004:520–521)

The ignorance of adults may stem partly from false assumptions or stereotypes, such as the belief that delinquents can be detected by their appearance or that middle-class youth are unlikely to be delinquent. But young people may play an active role in fostering such ignorance by helping create the illusion of conformity. By charming others and by appearing responsible, some delinquent youth are able to gain the trust of adults and escape supervision. As Tittle (1995:152) describes, they know how to "appear sincere, to be complimentary, to be lovable, and most important, how to use knowledge they [have] about adult authorities to their own advantage." In short, by wielding manipulative power over adults, some adolescents are able to get away with more mischief than other youths, as described by the following middle-class delinquent:

> Me and a buddy borrowed my dad's car for a night out. We drove to our hangout and had exactly two beers each—just as we had planned it. We called home . . . called my parents and told them to come pick us up because we couldn't drive. They were expecting us to be *really* smashed. [When my parents arrived] they couldn't believe we had called home after only a couple of beers. They thought we were *so "responsible."* Ha, ha, ha. . . . Compared to my brothers and sisters—after that—I got away with murder. (quoted in Brezina and Aragones, 2004:524, emphases in original)

Questions for Discussion

1. Like the adults in the "Saints and Roughnecks" study, many people falsely assume that there is a strong association between social class and delinquency, with the typical lower-class youth being much more delinquent than the typical middle-class youth. What do you think accounts for this assumption?
2. The quotations presented earlier come from middle-class youth. Do you think lower-class youth would have the same ability to exercise manipulative power over adult authorities? Why or why not?

First, the early self-report studies **focused on minor delinquent acts.** That is, they used measures that focus on status offenses and minor delinquent acts like petty theft and simple assault. Many of these studies, for example, employed the measure of delinquency shown in Table 2.3 (from Chapter 2). Or, if the studies did consider serious acts, these acts were not examined separately. Rather, the researchers created general scales that measured the extent to which adolescents engage in both minor and serious delinquency. The more frequently occurring minor offenses have a much greater influence on counts of delinquency than the less frequently occurring serious offenses (see Elliott and Huizinga, 1983:153–154). The early self-report studies, then, do not tell us anything about the relationship between class and serious delinquency. They simply suggest that class is unrelated to minor delinquency. It may be that class is related to serious delinquency. In this area, some criminologists note that arrest data contain a higher portion of serious offenses than self-report data. This may be why arrests are typically related to social class, while self-reports of delinquency are not.

Second, the early self-report studies **often used delinquency measures with truncated response categories, like "5 or more times."** So someone who commits an act 5 times is included in the same category as someone who commits the act 100 times. Again, this is a serious problem because there is a small group of high-rate offenders who commit an enormous number of delinquent acts. The early self-report surveys, however, did not accurately measure the delinquency of these high-rate offenders. These high-rate offenders, committing scores or even hundreds of delinquent acts, are not distinguished from juveniles committing only a few delinquent acts. It may be that the lower class has more high-rate offenders than the middle class. And if the delinquency of these high-rate offenders was accurately measured, one might well find that the lower class engages in more delinquency than the middle class.

Third, the early self-report studies **often employed problematic measures of social class.** Most notably, they **failed to examine very poor juveniles.** Many of the early self-report studies examined only a few hundred juveniles from one or a few schools; there are not enough very poor juveniles in these studies to examine separately. In other cases, researchers failed to distinguish the very poor juveniles from other groups. For example, the very poor are combined with the working class. It may be that delinquency is higher among the very poor, but that there is no difference in delinquency between the working and middle classes. So it is important to examine the very poor separately, and criminologists have now experimented with different methods for better identifying the very poor. For example, they focus on juveniles whose parents receive welfare benefits (see Brownfield, 1986; Farnworth et al., 1994). Also, the early self-report studies **failed to measure the duration of poverty** or the length of time that juveniles have been poor. Many juveniles experience short periods of poverty, while others live in poverty for long periods. We would expect long-term or persistent poverty to have a stronger effect on delinquency (see Farnworth et al., 1994; Jarjoura et al., 2002).

The Later Self-Report Studies

Several criminologists have conducted self-report studies that attempt to correct for some or all of the problems discussed in the preceding section. Perhaps the most prominent of these studies are the analyses of the National Youth Survey (NYS) conducted by Elliott and associates (Elliott and Ageton, 1980; Elliott and Huizinga, 1983). The NYS was described earlier. It examines both minor and serious delinquency. It accurately measures the number of delinquent acts that juveniles commit. And Elliott and associates distinguish lower-class juveniles from both working- and middle-class juveniles (although they do not measure the duration of poverty). What do their analyses of the NYS data reveal about the relationship between social class and delinquency? Their major findings are as follows.

1. **There are few or no class differences in most types of minor delinquency.** Table 4.1 reports the average number of delinquent acts committed by lower-, working-, and middle-class juveniles for several types of delinquency. Note that the averages are quite similar for the minor types of delinquency.

2. **The lower class is more likely to engage in serious delinquency.** As indicated in Table 4.1, the average number of violent crimes committed by a lower-class juvenile is about four times as high as the average number committed by a middle-class juvenile.

TABLE 4.1	Average Number of Self-Reported Delinquent Acts Committed by Lower-, Working-, and Middle-Class Juveniles in 1976			
	Violent Crimes	Property Crimes	Public Disorder Crimes	Status Offenses
Lower class	12	14	14	14
Working class	8	9	16	14
Middle class	3	7	14	16

SOURCE: Elliott and Ageton, 1980.

Note: Violent crimes include sexual assault, aggravated assault, simple assault, and robbery. Property crimes include vandalism, burglary, auto theft, larceny, stolen goods, fraud, and joyriding. Public disorder crimes include carrying a concealed weapon, hitchhiking, disorderly conduct, drunkenness, panhandling, making obscene phone calls, and marijuana use. Status offenses include runaway, sexual intercourse, alcohol use, and truancy.

The average number of property crimes committed by a lower-class juvenile is about twice as high as the average number committed by a middle-class juvenile.

3. **The reason that lower-class juveniles have a higher average rate of serious delinquency is that there are more high-rate offenders in the lower class.** For example, 2.8 percent of the lower-class juveniles commit more than 55 serious violent acts per year, whereas only 0.8 percent of the middle-class juveniles commit more than 55 violent acts per year. This point is very important. The lower class has a higher average rate of serious crime not because the typical lower-class juvenile is more involved in serious crime than the typical working- or middle-class juvenile. Most lower-class juveniles commit very few serious crimes. Rather, most of the serious crimes are committed by a small group of high-rate offenders. These high-rate offenders make up only a very small proportion of the lower class, but these high-rate offenders are two to three times more common in the lower class than in the middle class. And that is why the average rate of serious crime is higher in the lower class.

There have been several attempts to replicate the findings of Elliott and associates. That is, other researchers have examined serious delinquency separately from minor delinquency, have accurately measured the extent of delinquency, and/or have focused on the very poor. Not all of these attempts at replication have resulted in the same conclusions as Elliott and associates. Certain studies, in particular, have found that social class is unrelated to both serious and minor delinquency (e.g., Weis, 1987). Other studies, however, tend to support the work of Elliott and associates, although some of these studies find that social class has only a moderate association with serious delinquency.[3] In addition, two studies have examined the effect of persistent poverty on delinquency (Farnworth et al., 1994; Jarjoura et al., 2002). These studies have found that the length of time a juvenile lives in poverty does make a difference, with **those juveniles experiencing persistent poverty being more likely to engage in delinquency.**

Taken as a whole, we believe that the previous studies provide some support for the critiques of the early self-report surveys. They demonstrate that it is important to examine serious delinquency separately from minor delinquency; to accurately count the number of delinquent acts that are committed; to pay special attention to the very poor; and to examine the duration of poverty. When these steps are taken, researchers tend to find a relationship between class and *serious* delinquency. At the same time, most find little or no relationship between class and *minor* delinquency.

Summary

You can see why there is still some confusion in the field about the relationship between social class and delinquency. Again, we began with a simple question, but the answer turns out to be quite complex. Nevertheless, we believe that some general conclusions can be drawn about the relationship between social class and delinquency.

1. **There is good reason to believe that social class is largely unrelated to minor delinquency.** The large majority of self-report studies come to this conclusion. Arrest data tend to focus on more serious delinquency, so they are of limited relevance here.

2. **It is likely that social class is moderately related to serious delinquency, with lower-class juveniles having higher average rates of such delinquency.** The average rates of serious delinquency may be higher in the lower class because there are more high-rate offenders in the lower class—not because the typical lower-class juvenile is more delinquent than the typical working- or middle-class juvenile. Most of the better self-report studies suggest a relationship between class and serious delinquency, as do most studies based on arrest data. Further, there is little doubt that lower-class communities have higher rates of serious crime. As Braithwaite (1981:37) points out, "It is hardly plausible that one can totally explain away the higher risks of being mugged and raped in lower-class areas as a consequence of the activities of middle-class people who come into the area to perpetrate such acts."

ARE RACE AND ETHNICITY RELATED TO DELINQUENCY?

As with social class, the data on race and ethnicity and delinquency are somewhat contradictory, but there are some conclusions that criminologists can more or less safely draw.[4] Our focus is on African Americans and whites because most data deal with these groups. Unfortunately, we lack extensive data on other race and ethnic groups, including Latinos, Asians and Pacific Islanders, and American Indians. And there are often problems with the data we do have. For example, studies often fail to distinguish between the major Latino groups in the United States, such as Mexican Americans, Puerto Ricans, and Cuban Americans. While these groups have much in common, they also differ in important ways. To illustrate, Puerto Ricans are United States citizens, while many Mexican immigrants struggle with citizenship-related problems (see Cintron, 2006). Whenever possible, however, we note what the data say regarding the delinquency of racial and ethnic groups other than whites and African Americans.

We first describe what arrest, self-report, and victimization data have to say about the relationship between race/ethnicity and delinquency. We then draw two general conclusions about the relationship. And we finish by discussing whether the relationship between race and serious delinquency is explained by race-related differences in social class.

Arrest Data

The racial composition of the juvenile population (ages 10 to 17) in 2014 was 75.9 percent white, 16.4 percent African American, 5.9 percent Asian or Pacific Islander, and 1.8 percent American Indian. Latinos are an ethnic group, and most Latinos classify themselves as white. Mexican Americans constitute the largest share of Latinos, followed by Puerto Ricans and Cuban Americans. About 23 percent of the juvenile population was Latino in 2014, but the FBI does not report arrest data on Latinos and non-Latinos. Several individual studies, however, suggest that Latinos have higher arrest rates than non-Latinos for at least certain crimes—with Latino rates often falling between African American and white rates (D. Hawkins, Laub, and Lauritsen, 1998; Riedel, 2003).

Arrest data indicate that African Americans are disproportionately involved in delinquency. African Americans accounted for 34 percent of all juvenile arrests in 2014, whites accounted for 63 percent, Asians and Pacific Islanders accounted for 1 percent, and American Indians accounted for another 1 percent (the percentage for American Indians should be interpreted cautiously, since arrests by tribal police and federal agencies are not recorded in the FBI arrest data). African Americans were especially likely to be arrested for more serious violent offenses, accounting for 57 percent of murder arrests, 33 percent of rape arrests, 71 percent of robbery arrests, and 42 percent of aggravated assault arrests. African Americans were less likely to be arrested for property crimes, although they were still disproportionately arrested for such crimes. For example, they accounted for 36 percent of all larceny-theft arrests.

It is important to note that race differences in arrest rates have declined in recent years. In 1980, the juvenile arrest rate for Part I violent crimes was six times higher for African Americans than for whites. In 2014, it was five times higher.

Criticisms of Arrest Data

Arrest data suggest that African Americans are more likely to engage in most forms of delinquency, especially serious violence, but arrest data, as you know, have a number of problems. Only a small percentage of the crimes that are committed come to the attention of the police, and only a small percentage of these crimes result in arrest. Perhaps crimes committed by African Americans are more likely to come to the attention of the police and result in arrest. The data in this area are somewhat complex, but they suggest that African Americans who commit a given offense are often more likely to be arrested than whites who commit the same offense (see Chapter 22 for a full discussion). As a consequence, it is important to examine the relationship between race and delinquency using self-report and victimization data. These data sources have the advantage of measuring delinquent acts that do and do not result in arrest.

Self-Report Data

There are certain dangers in using self-report data to study the relationship between race and delinquency. As indicated in Chapter 2, **some** evidence suggests that African American males may be more likely than other groups to underreport their delinquency in self-report surveys. Nevertheless, it is instructive to examine what self-report data say about the relationship between race and delinquency.

Most early self-report surveys find that there is little or no relationship between race and delinquency. African Americans and whites are about equally delinquent. As you know, however, the early self-report surveys suffer from a number of problems: a focus on minor offenses, the use of truncated response categories, and the undersampling of serious offenders.

Later self-report surveys that correct for these problems find a more complex relationship between race and delinquency, a relationship similar to that found for social class and delinquency. These studies include the National Youth Survey, described earlier, the National Longitudinal Study of Adolescent Health (Add-Health), and studies conducted in Seattle, Denver, Rochester, and Pittsburgh.[5] The results of these studies may be summarized as follows.

1. **African Americans and whites report similar levels of minor delinquency.**

2. **African Americans are more likely to engage in serious delinquency, although not to the extent implied by arrest data.** For example, in their analysis of the 1976 National Youth Survey, Elliott et al. (1989) found that African Americans had a rate of serious assault about 2.5 times higher than the white rate. Arrest data, however, suggested

that the African American rate for serious assault was about 5 times higher than the white rate.

3. The average rate of serious crime among African Americans is higher because there are more high-rate offenders among African Americans (see Elliott and Ageton, 1980). This point requires emphasis: African Americans have a higher rate of serious crime **not** because the typical African American is more criminal than the typical white. Most African Americans commit no or very few serious crimes. Rather, most serious crimes are committed by a small group of high-rate offenders. These high-rate offenders make up only a small proportion of African American juveniles, but they are about twice as common among African Americans as among whites.

Asian Americans, Latinos, and Native Americans. While most self-report data focus on whites and African Americans, limited self-report data suggest the following: Asian Americans have the lowest rates of offending, followed by whites, Latinos, and African Americans, with Native Americans having the highest offending rates. Some self-report studies suggest that Latino and African American juveniles have similar rates of offending, while others suggest that Latinos have lower rates of offending than African Americans.[6]

Does immigration increase delinquency? Self-report and arrest data might lead you to conclude that immigration increases crime, since most immigrants to the United States are now Latinos. You would not be alone in this belief: most U.S. residents believe that immigration increases crime (Martinez and Lee, 2000; Press, 2006). Research, however, suggests that recent immigrants to the United States have lower rates of crime than U.S. natives.[7] This is especially the case when the immigrants live in communities with a high proportion of other immigrants. (Findings, however, vary somewhat by immigrant group and the city being examined.) Researchers have explained the lower crime rate of immigrants in several ways. Among other things, recent immigrants tend to have strong family ties, strong social ties to their neighbors, and high rates of employment, although often in blue-collar jobs.

Related to this, there is evidence that first-generation immigrants (those who are foreign born) have lower crime rates than second-generation immigrants (those whose parents are foreign born). Second-generation immigrants, in turn, have lower crime rates than third-generation immigrants. Sampson et al. (2005), for example, found that first-generation immigrants in Chicago had self-reported rates of violence about half as high as those of third-generation immigrants. Given these data, it may be more accurate to say that residence in the United States increases the crime rate of immigrants than it is to say that immigration increases the crime rate of the United States.

Victimization Data

There are no victimization data on the relationship between social class and delinquency, but such data have been collected for race. Crime victims are asked to identify the race of the person or persons who victimized them. Such data are limited, however; as a general rule, only victims of violent crimes see the offender. Nevertheless, victimization data from previous years suggest that African Americans are disproportionately involved in violent crime. In particular, data from 1998 indicate that African American juveniles had rates of serious violent offending 2.4 times higher than whites (Lynch, 2002).[8] This race difference, however, was not as large as that revealed by arrest data. In 1998, African American juveniles had an arrest rate for serious violent crime that was 3.9 times as high as white juveniles. Like arrest data, victimization data indicate that race differences in offending have declined over time. African American juveniles had rates of serious violent offending that were 6.1 times as high as white rates in 1992 but only 2.4 times as high in 1998.

Data also indicate that African American juveniles are more likely than white juveniles to be the **victims** of serious violence (Rennison, 2001). African American juveniles, for example, are about four times as likely as white juveniles to be the victims of homicide (Snyder and Sickmund, 2006). Criminologists know that most crimes are **intraracial:** African Americans tend to victimize other African Americans, and whites tend to victimize other whites. The fact that African Americans have higher victimization rates for serious violence suggests that they have higher offending rates as well.

Is Race Related to Delinquency?

We believe it is safe to draw the following conclusions about race and delinquency.

1. **There is little or no relationship between race and minor delinquency.** Self-report surveys consistently find little relationship between race and minor delinquency. Arrest and victimization data are less relevant here, since they tend to focus on more serious delinquency.

2. **African Americans are more likely than whites to engage in serious delinquency, especially serious violence.** The relationship between race and serious delinquency, however, is probably not as strong as suggested by arrest data. Arrest data, victimization data, and most of the better self-report surveys indicate that African Americans are more involved in serious delinquency, although self-report and victimization data suggest that arrest data exaggerate the involvement of African Americans in such delinquency. **The greater involvement of African Americans in serious delinquency may reflect the fact that there are more high-rate offenders among African Americans.**

3. **Race differences in serious delinquency have declined in recent years.**

Are Race Differences in Serious Delinquency Explained by Social Class?

Given the history of discrimination in this country, it should come as no surprise that race and social class are related. African Americans are more likely to be members of the lower class than whites (although most African Americans are **not** members of the lower class). As discussed, lower-class individuals are more likely to engage in serious delinquency than higher-class individuals. So it is reasonable to ask whether African Americans are more likely to engage in serious delinquency because they are more likely to be in the lower class.

Researchers have examined this issue by comparing the delinquency of lower-class African Americans to that of lower-class whites and by comparing the delinquency of middle-class African Americans to that of middle-class whites. Class is usually measured in terms of family income, parents' occupational prestige, and/or parents' education. If social class explained the higher rate of serious delinquency among African Americans, we would expect that lower-class African Americans and whites would have similar levels of serious delinquency. Likewise, we would expect that middle-class African Americans and whites would have similar levels of delinquency.

The data suggest that social class explains some but not all of the association between race and serious delinquency. For example, comparisons find that lower-class African Americans are still more likely to engage in serious delinquency than lower-class whites, but race differences in delinquency are reduced somewhat when the researchers take account of class.

Researchers, however, have recently pointed out that the life circumstances of poor African Americans are often quite different from those of poor whites. Most notably, poor African Americans are much more likely than poor whites to live in disadvantaged communities—that is, communities in which a high percentage of the other people are poor and a low percentage have the advantages of holding well-paid, high-status jobs and having good educations. As Sampson and Bean (2006:12) state, "Whereas less than 10 percent of poor whites typically live in extreme poverty areas, almost half of poor blacks live in such areas." High-poverty neighborhoods suffer from a range of problems, such as an absence of jobs, a high percentage of single-parent families, inferior schools, and few conventional role models. As Sampson and Lauritsen (1997:338) state, "Even given the same objective socioeconomic status, African Americans and whites face vastly different environments in which to live, work, and raise their children." African Americans are more likely to live in high-poverty areas for several reasons, including the effects of past and present discrimination in housing and jobs. So it is misleading to simply compare poor African Americans to poor whites. One must also take account of the type of community in which the individuals live.[9]

A few studies have attempted to take account of community context. That is, they have attempted to compare African Americans and whites who live in high-poverty communities, as well as African Americans and whites who live in higher-class communities. Such comparisons are difficult to make, since it is hard to find more than a few whites who live in high-poverty communities. But limited data suggest that race differences in delinquency are substantially reduced when researchers take account of the types of communities in which African Americans and whites live.[10] More research is needed in this area, but we may tentatively conclude that **much—perhaps all—of the race difference in serious delinquency is explained by the fact that African Americans are more likely to be poor and to live in high-poverty communities**, which suffer from a host of problems that are conducive to delinquency (see Chapter 12 for a discussion of such communities).

IS AGE RELATED TO DELINQUENCY?

The data on social class, race, and delinquency are complex and frustrating. The data on the relationship between age and delinquency, however, are fairly straightforward. Arrest, self-report, and victimization data generally agree with one another in this area.[11]

Crime rates are highest for people in mid- to late adolescence. The graphs in Figure 4.1 show the relationship between age and the 2015 arrest rates for Part I property crimes and Part I violent crimes. Arrest rates for property crime peak in mid- to late adolescence and then decline rapidly. A 16-year-old, for example, is about two times more likely to be arrested for a property crime than a 35-year-old. Arrest rates for violent crime peak in late adolescence and early adulthood and then decline somewhat more slowly. An 18-year-old, for example, is about twice as likely to be arrested for a violent crime as a 40-year-old. These data should be interpreted somewhat cautiously. Some evidence suggests that juvenile offenders may be more likely to be arrested than adult offenders, perhaps because juvenile offenders do not plan their crimes as carefully or are more conspicuous because they tend to commit their crimes in groups (see H. Snyder, 1999). As a result, these data may exaggerate the juvenile contribution to crime. Also, it should be noted that the relative involvement of juveniles in crime has declined somewhat from a high point reached in the mid-1990s. Juveniles accounted for 19 percent of all Part I violent crime arrests in 1995 versus 11 percent in 2014, and juveniles accounted for 35 percent of all property crime arrests in 1995 versus 15 percent in 2014.

Nevertheless, self-report and victimization data tend to show similar patterns. **Rates for property crime tend to peak in mid-adolescence and decline rapidly thereafter. Rates for violent crime peak somewhat later, in late adolescence/early adulthood, and decline more slowly.** Although not illustrated in a graph, rates of illicit drug use tend to peak in the late teens and early 20s, but the peak varies somewhat by type of drug (e.g., inhalant use peaks in the early to mid-teens). There is little doubt, then, that most crimes reach a peak during mid- to late adolescence.

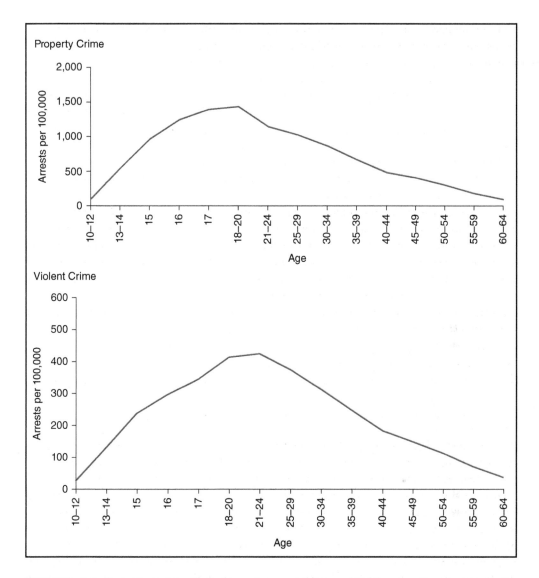

FIGURE 4.1 Relationship Between Age and Arrest Rates for Property and Violent Crime, 2015

SOURCE: Federal Bureau of Investigation, *Crime in the United States, 2015;* U.S. Census Bureau, *Population Estimates* (http://www.census.gov).

Crime rates may peak during adolescence because there are a fixed number of criminals who increase their rate of offending during adolescence. Or they may peak because there is an increase in the number of criminals during adolescence; that is, new criminals appear. What do the data show? Do criminals start committing more crimes during adolescence, or is there an increase in the number of criminals during adolescence? The data tend to support both explanations. The peak in crime rates during adolescence occurs partly because many juveniles start committing crimes when they become adolescents. Most of these juveniles then stop committing crimes when they become adults, or at least they substantially reduce their level of offending. Also, there is some evidence that offenders commit more crimes during their adolescent years—although not all studies show this.

Criminologists have recently devoted much attention to explaining these patterns, and you should ask yourself the following questions.

1. Why do so many juveniles start committing criminal acts when they become adolescents?
2. Why do most of these adolescent offenders stop committing criminal acts when they become adults?
3. Why do offenders commit more crimes during adolescence?

(We address these questions in Chapter 10.)

We should note that the relationship between age and crime is somewhat different for females and for African Americans. Female offending, especially violence, tends to peak at a slightly earlier age than male offending. And African Americans are less likely than whites to stop offending when they become adults. Elliott (1994), for example, used data from the National Youth Survey to study African Americans and whites who had committed serious violent crimes as juveniles. He found that the African Americans were almost twice as likely as the whites to continue committing such offenses in their 20s. Elliott and others explain this finding by arguing that African Americans have more difficulty obtaining decent work when they enter adulthood. In the words of Steffensmeier and Allan (1995:103):

> In the inner cities of this nation, where the labor market for young adults is dominated by marginal jobs with low hours, low pay, high turnover, and limited benefits and opportunities for advancement, the other goals of conventional life—marriage, family, community involvement—are more difficult to attain, and the proportion of the population still attracted to illegitimate alternatives will be greater.

A note on out-of-control toddlers. When we state that crime peaks in mid- to late adolescence, you should not take this to mean that toddlers and children are relatively well behaved. The peak in adolescent crime refers to property crimes such as larceny and burglary, status offenses such as running away and truancy, and more serious violent crimes such as aggravated assault and robbery. Lahey and Waldman (2005) refer to these as "developmentally-late conduct problems." Several recent studies show that toddlers and children regularly engage in other types of misbehavior, especially minor forms of aggression (e.g., hitting, kicking, biting).[12] In describing one study in this area, Lahey and Waldman (2005:18) state that "nearly half of all toddlers hit, kick, intentionally break things, take other children's toys, state untruths, and resist the authority of adults from the time they can walk and talk." These "developmentally-early conduct problems" appear to peak at ages 2 to 4 for most individuals and then decline sharply by preadolescence. Individuals with the highest levels of developmentally early conduct problems, however, are more likely to have the highest levels of developmentally late conduct problems. That is, the out-of-control toddlers are more likely to become adolescent offenders. This relationship, however, is far from perfect and is truer of boys than girls.

IS GENDER RELATED TO DELINQUENCY?

The data on the relationship between gender and delinquency are also fairly straightforward.

Arrest, self-report, and victimization data (where applicable) agree on the following facts about gender and delinquency: Males have a higher rate of delinquency than females. Gender differences in delinquency are greatest for serious violent and property crimes. They are lowest for minor crimes and status offenses, with males and females having similar rates of involvement in certain minor crimes and status offenses. Males have higher rates of delinquency because there are more male than female delinquents and because male delinquents commit more offenses than female delinquents. In particular, there are more male than female high-rate offenders. We elaborate on some of these points later. We also point to a key area of disagreement between arrest and self-report data.[13]

Arrest Data

Arrest ratios. Overall, there were about 2.4 male juveniles arrested for every female juvenile arrested in 2014. The ratio of male to female arrests is highest for serious violent and property crimes. For example, males are about 12 times more likely to be arrested for murder, 9 times more likely to be arrested for robbery, and 7 times more likely to be arrested for burglary. Sex ratios are lowest for minor crimes and status offenses. For example, males are about 1.4 times as likely to be arrested for larceny-theft and nearly twice as likely for simple assault. Females are more likely than males to be arrested for only two offenses: prostitution and running away (the FBI has stopped collecting data on runaways, but data from 2008 indicate that females accounted for 56 percent of runaway arrests). (We discuss the higher female arrest rate for running away in Chapter 22, when examining gender discrimination in the juvenile justice system.)

What crimes are males and females arrested for? Males generally commit more crimes than females, but do males commit different types of crime than females? The preceding discussion might lead you to believe that males commit serious crimes, whereas females commit less serious crimes. This belief is not correct. Consider the four crimes for which male and female juveniles are most frequently arrested. For male juveniles, 19 percent of all arrests are for "all other offenses" (including status offenses like incorrigibility and truancy); 15 percent are for larceny-theft; 12 percent are for simple assaults; and 12 percent are for drug abuse violations. For female juveniles, 25 percent of all arrests are for larceny-theft; 17 percent are for "all other offenses"; 17 percent are for simple assaults; and 9 percent are for disorderly conduct. **Thus, both males and females are most often arrested for minor crimes.** Further, males and females are arrested for many of the same minor crimes—larceny-theft, "all other offenses," and simple assault.

At the same time, there are some differences in the types of crimes for which males and females are arrested. **A greater portion of all male arrests are for serious crimes** (although such crimes constitute only a small portion of all male arrests). About 6 percent of all male arrests are for serious violent crimes, versus 3 percent of all female arrests. And about 6 percent of all male arrests are for the serious property crimes of burglary and motor vehicle theft, versus 2.3 percent of all female arrests. **By contrast, a greater portion of all female arrests are for larceny-theft (most often shoplifting) and status offenses.** Historically, the status offense of running away has accounted for a greater portion of all female arrests, though the FBI no longer tracks data on this offense. Further, some

data suggest that a large portion of the female arrests for "all other offenses" involve the status offense of incorrigibility (Chesney-Lind and Shelden, 2004:11).

Trends in male and female delinquency. Even though males are generally more likely to be arrested than females, the proportion of all arrests accounted for by females has been increasing over time. In 1980, females accounted for 18 percent of all juvenile arrests for Part I offenses. Today, females account for 31 percent of all Part I arrests. This increase has occurred for both violent and property crimes. Arrest rates generally **increased faster for females** than males from the mid-1980s to the mid-1990s. Then arrest rates **declined more slowly for females** than males from the mid-1990s. As a result of these trends, the gender gap in arrest rates is much lower than it once was. In 1980, male juveniles were 8.3 times more likely to be arrested for violent crimes than female juveniles. By 2014, males were only 4.3 times more likely to be arrested for violent crimes. In 1980, male juveniles were 4 times more likely to be arrested for property crimes than females. By 2014, males were only 1.8 times more likely to be arrested for property crimes.

Self-Report Data

Like arrest data, self-report data reveal that males have higher rates of delinquency than females, with gender differences in delinquency being greatest for serious crimes and lowest for minor crimes and status offenses. Self-report data also indicate that while males generally commit more delinquent acts than females, females commit a broad range of delinquent acts. Females, for example, steal, fight, and use drugs—they just do so less frequently than males. There is, however, one key area in which self-report data are at odds with arrest data.

Self-report surveys do not indicate that the proportion of all offenses committed by females is increasing.[14] The limited self-report data we have on trends in delinquency suggest that the gender ratio in delinquency has been fairly stable since the late 1960s. This has led some researchers to question the accuracy of arrest data; they claim that the increase in female arrests may reflect changes in police practices or the behavior of those who report crimes to the police. In particular, Steffensmeier et al. (2005) make a rather convincing argument that this is the case, at least with respect to violent crime.

Trends in female violence. Steffensmeier et al. (2005) point out that the proportion of violent crime arrests accounted for by female juveniles has increased a good deal since 1980. This is especially true for the crime of assault. For example, girls accounted for 21 percent of simple assault arrests in 1980 versus 36 percent in 2014. Steffensmeier et al. note that such arrest data have led some researchers and people in the news media to conclude that girls really are becoming more violent. This alleged increase in female violence is frequently explained by arguing that in the past, girls were taught to be submissive and weak, whereas now they are taught to be assertive and strong. It is said that this change in socialization practices is reflected in many movies and video games, such as *Hunger Games* and *Tomb Raiders,* where the lead character is a female who engages in much violence.

Steffensmeier et al., however, also use two self-report surveys and victimization data to examine gender trends in violence. These alternative data sources do not indicate that the percentage of violent crimes committed by females has increased since 1980. Rather, the percentage has stayed about the same. Steffensmeier et al. believe that the self-report and victimization data are more accurate, and that the share of violence committed by females has not really increased. How, then, do we explain the increase shown in arrest data? Steffensmeier et al. offer several explanations, all involving changes in police practices since 1980.

The researchers assert that the police have become more likely to make arrests for types of violence in which females most often engage. In particular, the police have become more likely to make arrests for minor violence. While males are much more likely to engage in serious violence than females, rates of minor violence are more similar for males and females. The increased likelihood of arrest for minor violence therefore raises the percentage of violent crime arrests accounted for by females. Also, Steffensmeier et al. say that the police have become more likely to make arrests in cases involving domestic or family violence. While males are much more likely than females to commit violent acts against strangers and acquaintances, rates of family violence are more similar for males and females. So, again, this change in policy increases the percentages of violent crime arrests accounted for by females.

Further, Steffensmeier et al. argue that the police have become more likely to "charge up" minor forms of violence. So a violent act that might have resulted in a charge of simple or minor assault in the past now results in a charge of aggravated or serious assault. Finally, Steffensmeier et al. argue that the police have become less tolerant of female offenders. In the past, the police were more likely to deal with female violent offenders in an informal manner or to charge them with status offenses, such as incorrigibility. Today, they are more likely to charge such offenders with violent crimes.

Steffensmeier et al. discuss the factors that have led to these changes in police practices. These factors include the rise of "zero-tolerance" policies, which encourage the police to make arrests even in the case of minor crimes (see Chapter 20). They include the increased social concern with domestic violence, with many police departments implementing mandatory arrest policies in this area. And they include the feminist movement, which has contributed to the more similar treatment of male and female offenders. Their central point, however, is that the increase in the percentage of violent crime arrests involving females reflects a change in police practices rather than a real increase in female violence (also see Steffensmeier and Schwartz, 2009; Zahn et al., 2008).

Summary
Overall, the following conclusions can be drawn about the relationship between gender and delinquency.

1. **There is little doubt that males generally have higher rates of delinquency than females, with gender differences in delinquency being greatest for serious violent and property crimes.** Males have higher rates of delinquency because there are more male than female offenders and because male offenders commit more offenses on average than female offenders.

2. **While males commit more offenses than females, females commit a broad range of offenses.** Contrary to certain stereotypical views, female offending is not limited to a few sex-related offenses such as prostitution. Females, like males, fight, steal, use drugs, and engage in other delinquent acts. They just do so less than males. At the same time, a relatively greater proportion of all male offenses involve serious crimes, and a relatively greater proportion of all female offenses involve larceny-theft and status offenses.

3. **Arrest data suggest that gender differences in delinquency have become smaller since 1980, but self-report and victimization data point to more stability than change.** Some evidence suggests that the increase in the percentage of arrests involving females reflects a change in law enforcement practices more than a real increase in female delinquency (Feld, 2009).

ARE THERE DIFFERENT TYPES OF DELINQUENTS?
We have been talking about delinquents and nondelinquents, with an occasional reference to high-rate and serious offenders. As you might imagine, though, dividing juveniles into delinquents and nondelinquents is a bit simplistic. There are many types of delinquents.

As mentioned earlier, for example, delinquents differ greatly in their frequency of delinquency. Some delinquents commit only a few offenses each year, while others commit hundreds—thus, we have low-rate and high-rate delinquent offenders.

Criminologists are now devoting much attention to the identification of different types of delinquents. As you will see, this is an important task. The factors that cause juveniles to become one type of delinquent may differ from those that cause them to become another type. For example, the factors that cause juveniles to become low-rate offenders may differ from those that cause them to become high-rate offenders. Also, the existence of different types of delinquents has important implications for society's efforts to control delinquency. For example, we may want to focus our control efforts on high-rate offenders, since they commit so many delinquent acts. Further, high-rate offenders may require different types of intervention programs than low-rate offenders.

This section briefly reviews the research on the different types of delinquents. While criminologists still have much to learn in this area, some generally accepted conclusions can be drawn about the types of delinquent offenders.[15]

An Overview of the Research on the Different Types of Delinquents

Researchers try to classify delinquents into different types on the basis of such things as their frequency of offending, the types of offenses they commit, and when they start and stop offending. The major research in these areas is reviewed next.

How many offenses do juveniles commit?   Both arrest and self-report data indicate that juveniles vary a great deal in the frequency of their delinquency. Self-report surveys typically find the following. A small percentage of juveniles—10 percent or less in most studies—refrain from delinquency. A much larger percentage of juveniles—a majority in all studies—commit a small to moderate number of delinquent offenses each year. And a small percentage of juveniles commit an enormous number of offenses each year. The relative size of this high-rate group depends on the cutoff point that is used, but it is usually about 5 to 15 percent of all juveniles.

For example, Dunford and Elliott (1984) examined the frequency of offending using self-report data from the National Youth Survey. They found that about 11 percent of the juveniles did not report any delinquent acts over a two-year period. About 34 percent reported 1 to 10 delinquent acts during this period. About 41 percent reported 11 to 100 acts. About 8 percent reported 101 to 200 delinquent acts (one to two delinquent acts per week). And about 6.5 percent reported 201 or more delinquent acts (at least two delinquent acts per week).

In some studies, the high-rate offenders account for a majority of all delinquent offenses and for the large majority of serious delinquent offenses. For example, a major study in Philadelphia found that 7.5 percent of the juvenile males accounted for 61 percent of all juvenile arrests, including 61 percent of the homicide arrests, 65 percent of the aggravated assault arrests, 76 percent of the forcible rape arrests, and 73 percent of the robbery arrests (Tracy et al., 1990). Clearly, then, at a minimum, one can distinguish high-rate offenders from lower-rate offenders.

What types of offenses do juveniles commit?   Criminologists once assumed that juveniles specialized in particular types of crimes. For example, it was argued that some juveniles specialized in property crimes like larceny and burglary, others specialized in violent crimes, and still others specialized in drug use and sales (e.g., Cloward and Ohlin, 1960). Recent data suggest that there is some specialization in juvenile offending—but not nearly as much as previously believed. Most juveniles who commit more than a few offenses tend to commit a variety of offenses. There is, however, some specialization against this backdrop of diversity. One of the best studies in this area found that some juvenile offenders are more likely than others to engage in violence—although these "violent offenders" also commit other types of crime (Osgood and Schreck, 2007). It is possible that further research will find that some offenders are also more likely than others to engage in such crimes as drug use and theft. Juvenile offenders, then, tend to commit a range of offenses—although they may favor some offenses more than others. (Note: Adult offenders are more likely to specialize in particular types of crime than juvenile offenders.)

If we move beyond particular types of crime, data suggest that some offenders commit primarily minor offenses, while others commit a mixture of minor and serious offenses. (It is rare for an offender to commit only serious offenses; individuals who commit serious offenses usually commit minor offenses as well.) In particular, the large majority of juvenile offenders commit a range of minor offenses, plus the occasional serious offense.

A much smaller percentage of juvenile offenders commit a range of both minor and serious offenses. Even though most offenders commit a variety of offenses, it is possible to distinguish between offenders who commit primarily minor crimes and those who commit both minor and serious crimes. And several researchers have distinguished minor from serious offenders. An analysis of data from the 1976 National Youth Survey found that about 8.6 percent of the juveniles could be classified as "serious" offenders, meaning that they had committed at least three Part I or serious offenses during 1976. These serious offenders accounted for more than three-fourths of all the Part I offenses, and they also committed a large number of minor crimes and status offenses. Most of the remaining juveniles committed a small to moderate number of minor crimes and status offenses (Dunford and Elliott, 1984; Elliott et al., 1989).

When do juveniles start to commit delinquent acts and when do they stop? Studies in this area find much variation among offenders. Some offenders start committing delinquent acts in childhood, while others wait until late adolescence. And some offenders stop committing crimes in adolescence, while others continue to offend well into the adult years. The most common pattern is for offenders to start committing crimes in late childhood to mid-adolescence and to stop committing crimes in late adolescence. Individuals who follow this pattern have been described as *adolescence-limited offenders*, since their offending is largely limited to their adolescent years (see Moffitt, 1993, 1997). These adolescence-limited offenders are partly responsible for the fact that rates of offending peak during mid- to late adolescence (see the discussion on age and crime).

There is a much smaller group of offenders who begin to engage in delinquent or "antisocial" behavior as young children. They lie, steal, cheat, and engage in aggressive behavior at an early age; their parents and others commonly describe them as "troublesome" or "difficult." Studies suggest that these individuals are more likely to offend at high rates, to commit serious offenses, and to continue offending as adults than juveniles who start committing delinquent acts at a later age. In fact, the "early onset" of delinquency is one of the best predictors of the frequency, seriousness, and duration of offending. We should note, however, that the early onset of delinquency does not guarantee that a person will have problems later in life. For example, only about half of the juveniles with an early onset of delinquency become adult offenders. Nevertheless, there is a small group of individuals who offend from early childhood well into adulthood. These individuals have been referred to as *chronic offenders*, and they may be distinguished from the adolescence-limited offenders.

Are there any patterns to juvenile offending over the life course? Juveniles vary a good deal in the frequency of their offending, the seriousness of their offending, and the ages at which they start and stop offending. Despite this variation, there are certain common patterns in juvenile offending over the life course.

First, studies suggest that there is a general tendency to move from less serious to more serious offending. For example, minor delinquency like petty theft and status offending tends to precede more serious delinquency like burglary and aggravated assault. And alcohol use tends to precede marijuana use, which tends to precede hard drug use. Most juveniles, of course, do not advance all the way from minor to serious offending. Most remain at the level of minor offending. But those who engage in serious offending usually begin their careers with minor offending.

Second, studies suggest that there is a general tendency for the frequency of offending to increase during early to mid-adolescence and to decrease during late adolescence and adulthood. This behavior pattern is especially true for adolescence-limited offenders. It is less true for chronic offenders, but some data suggest that even chronic offenders increase their level of offending somewhat during adolescence (see D'Unger et al., 1998).

What Are the Different Types of Delinquents?

As indicated, juvenile offenders differ in terms of the frequency of their offending, the seriousness of their offending, and the ages at which they start and stop offending. Researchers have drawn on these differences to describe the major types of delinquent offenders. Some descriptions focus on the frequency of offending, distinguishing low-rate from high-rate offenders. Some focus on the seriousness of offending, distinguishing minor from serious offenders (or serious violent offenders). Some focus on the duration of offending, distinguishing adolescence-limited from chronic offenders. And some descriptions focus on two of the previous dimensions—the frequency and duration of offending, for example (D'Unger et al., 1998; also see Loeber et al., 1991). It is probably best, however, to classify offenders using all three dimensions. Although these dimensions are related to one another (e.g., high-rate offenders are more likely to be serious offenders), the relationship is not perfect (e.g., certain high-rate offenders commit only minor crimes).

Some researchers are beginning to classify offenders using all three dimensions. At one extreme, we have **high-rate, serious, chronic offenders.** Data suggest that only a small percentage of juveniles fall into this group: perhaps 5 percent or so of the juvenile population. Nevertheless, this small group is an important one, given the enormous amount of crime, especially serious crime, they commit. Data suggest that members of this group are more likely to be male, poor, and African American (although race may be important because of its correlation with individual- and community-level social class). At the other extreme, we have **low-rate, minor, adolescence-limited offenders.** Between these two extremes there are several groups. It is unclear what percentage of juveniles fall into each of these groups. The answer depends, in part, on the type of data used (arrest versus self-report) and the definitions employed for high-rate, chronic, and serious offending. For example, how many delinquent acts must juveniles commit each year before they can be classified as high-rate offenders?

In any event, it is important to keep in mind that there are different types of delinquent offenders. These types will come up again when we discuss the causes of crime. Some evidence suggests that the causes of high-rate, serious, chronic offending differ somewhat from the causes of less extreme types of offending. These types will also come up when we discuss strategies to control delinquency. In particular, there has been a major movement to crack down on the more extreme types of delinquents, especially those who commit serious crimes.

SUMMARY

We can draw the following major conclusions about the characteristics of delinquents:

1. Males have higher rates of delinquency, especially serious delinquency, than females. There are more male offenders, and male offenders offend at higher rates than female offenders.

2. Rates of delinquency peak in mid- to late adolescence and decline rapidly thereafter. This peak and decline occurs largely because there is an increase in the number of offenders during adolescence, but data also suggest that rates of offending increase during adolescence as well.

3. Lower-class juveniles are more likely to engage in serious delinquency than higher-class juveniles. This difference exists because there are more high-rate offenders in the lower class. There is little or no relationship between class and minor delinquency.

4. African Americans are more likely to engage in serious delinquency, especially violent delinquency, than whites. Again, data suggest that this difference occurs because there are more high-rate offenders among African Americans. There is little or no relationship between race and minor delinquency.

5. Juveniles differ a great deal in the frequency, seriousness, and duration of their offending.

Part 2 of the book focuses on the causes of delinquency. We will try to explain the basic facts about delinquency presented in this chapter and Chapter 3. Most notably, we will try to explain why some juveniles commit more delinquent acts, commit more serious delinquent acts, and offend for longer periods than other juveniles. We will also try to explain why certain groups have higher rates of delinquency than other groups. Why, for example, are males more delinquent than females?

TEACHING AIDS

Exercise 1: Perceptions of Race and Crime

One of the central points made in this chapter is that the perceptions many people have of juvenile delinquents are mistaken. In particular, many people think that class and race are the factors that best distinguish delinquents from nondelinquents, when in fact age and gender do a much better job of differentiating delinquents from nondelinquents. As indicated in this chapter, class and race are largely unrelated to minor delinquency. They are related to serious delinquency but not as strongly as gender and age. For example, studies that examine the predictors of violent delinquency typically find that gender is a much stronger predictor than race (e.g., Felson, Deane, and Armstrong, 2008; J. Kaufman, 2005). Further, lower-class juveniles and African Americans have higher rates of serious crime not because the typical lower-class or African American juvenile is involved in serious crime but because high-rate offenders are more common among the lower-class and African Americans. Such offenders, however, constitute a very small percentage of all lower-class and African American juveniles.

Nevertheless, many people still view African Americans and poor people as strongly involved in delinquency. One study provides an excellent illustration of this point; it focuses on the factors that influence perceptions of neighborhood crime rates (Quillian and Pager, 2001). This study examined people living in a variety of neighborhoods in three cities: Chicago, Seattle, and Baltimore. These people were asked to estimate the level of crime in their neighborhoods (e.g., "How much crime would you say there is in your own immediate neighborhood?"). The researchers then examined the factors that influenced perceptions of neighborhood crime levels. They found that one of the strongest factors was the percentage of young African American men in the neighborhood (the percentage of poor people in the neighborhood also had an effect). People living in neighborhoods with a higher percentage of young African American men were much more likely to say that crime was a problem, *even after* the researchers took account of the neighborhood's actual level of crime (measured by crimes known to the police and victimization data); the economic characteristics of the neighborhood; the physical appearance of the neighborhood (as rated by trained staff); neighborhood problems (e.g., teenagers hanging out on the street, noise); the age, sex, education, income, and personal victimization experiences of the respondents; and other factors. These findings held for both white and African American residents, although whites were more likely than African Americans to associate young African American men with crime.

The researchers summarized their study by stating that their "results suggest that the strong mental association between race and crime has a powerful influence on perceptions of neighborhood crime levels, *beyond any actual association between race and crime*" (Quillian and Pager, 2001:746; emphasis added).

1. What accounts for the perception among many people that race is strongly associated with crime?
2. What can be done to counter this perception?

Exercise 2: Why Do Asian Americans Have Lower Crime Rates?

Both arrest and self-report data indicate that Asian Americans have much lower crime rates than other race and ethnic groups. Why might this be the case? In responding to this question, be sure to consider such things as community characteristics, socioeconomic status, family factors, school factors, peer factors, and values and beliefs. (For excellent examples of research on this question, see Jang, 2002, and McNulty and Bellair, 2003; for an overview of research in this area, see Unnithan, 2006. Also, it is important to note that Asian Americans comprise many different groups, and these groups sometimes differ from one another in their backgrounds and current circumstances. Jang [2002] divides Asian Americans into four regional groups: Far Eastern [e.g., Chinese, Japanese, and Korean], East Asian [e.g., Filipinos], Southeast Asian [e.g., Vietnamese, Laotian, Cambodian, Thai], and South Asian [e.g., Indian, Pakistani].)

Exercise 3: Explaining the Association Between Gender and Crime

We present several basic facts about the characteristics of delinquents in this chapter. One of the key facts is that males are more likely to engage in delinquency than females, especially serious violent and property crime. We suspect that this is true of the males and females in your class (you might verify this with a self-report survey of the students in your class). We discuss the relationship between gender and delinquency at several points in this text, with an extended discussion in Chapter 18. For now, we would like you to try to answer the following questions.

1. Why do you think males have higher rates of delinquency than females?
2. Do you think that the causes of delinquency among males are the same as those among females?
3. Do you think the gender difference in levels of delinquency will ever diminish?

Exercise 4: Girls' Delinquency

Visit "Girls' Delinquency," the website of the Office of Juvenile Justice and Delinquency Prevention, or OJJDP, the federal agency responsible for dealing with juvenile delinquency. The site (http://www.ojjdp.gov/programs/girlsdelinquency.html) describes the work of the Girls' Study Group, a group of researchers and practitioners with expertise in girls' delinquency. The OJJDP created the Girls' Study Group partly because of reports that girls' violence was increasing faster than that of boys. Also, the bulk of criminological research has focused on boys, so our knowledge of girls' delinquency was deficient in many areas— something the OJJDP wanted to help remedy. The group was charged with examining the trends in girls' delinquency, the nature and causes of girls' delinquency, and how girls' delinquency might be reduced. Explore the website, browsing through some of the publications produced by the Girls' Study Group. Then examine the publication titled "Violence by Teenage Girls: Trends and Context." What types of data are examined in this report? What does each type of data say about the trends in girls' violence? Why is there some disagreement between data sources? What are the major "contexts" (targets, settings, contributing factors) of girls' violence? What do the authors conclude about trends in girls' violence?

TEST YOUR KNOWLEDGE OF THIS CHAPTER

1. What do we mean by the "sociodemographic characteristics" of juveniles?
2. How is social class usually measured?
3. Describe the relationship between social class and delinquency according to arrest data.
4. Describe the relationship between social class and delinquency according to the early self-report studies. How did researchers explain the difference in findings between the early self-report studies and studies using arrest data? How did researchers account for the perception that lower-class juveniles are more delinquent? How did researchers account for all of the good reasons linking class to delinquency?
5. Describe the major criticisms of early self-report studies.
6. Describe the major findings of later self-report studies.
7. Describe the relationship between social class and delinquency according to victimization data. (Hint: this might be a trick question.)
8. Provide a summary of the relationship between social class and delinquency.
9. Describe the relationship between race, ethnicity, and delinquency according to arrest data. Why might arrest data provide a biased view of this relationship?
10. Describe the relationship between race, ethnicity, and delinquency according to self-report data. Be sure to distinguish between the early and later self-report studies. Also, note any similarities and differences between the findings from self-report and arrest data.

11. Describe the relationship between race and delinquency according to victimization data, noting any similarities and differences between the findings from victimization and arrest data.

12. What do we mean when we ask whether the relationship between race and delinquency can be explained by social class? What do the data in this area indicate? Why is it important to consider both an individual's social class and the class composition of the community in which the individual lives?

13. Provide a summary of the relationship between race, ethnicity, and delinquency.

14. Describe the relationship between immigration and delinquency.

15. Describe the relationship between age and delinquency (be sure to distinguish between property and violent crimes). Describe how the relationship between age and delinquency differs somewhat for females and African Americans.

16. Describe the relationship between gender and crime (be sure to distinguish between serious and less serious crimes).

17. Describe trends in female violence according to arrest, self-report, and victimization data. How can we account for differences between these data sources?

18. Describe what the research says regarding differences between juveniles in (a) the number of delinquent acts committed, (b) the types of delinquent acts committed, and (c) when the juveniles start and stop committing criminal acts.

19. Describe the two major patterns of juvenile offending over the life course.

20. What are the major types of juvenile offenders?

THOUGHT AND DISCUSSION QUESTIONS

1. Arrest data, early self-report studies, later self-report studies, and victimization data occasionally disagree regarding the characteristics of delinquents (e.g., whether African Americans have higher rates of delinquency, whether rates of male and female delinquency are becoming more similar). Point to an area of disagreement and discuss how one might decide which data sources are more accurate or how one might reach a compromise position between the data sources. (Note: You will need to consider the advantages and disadvantages of each data source, as discussed in this chapter and in Chapters 2 and 3.)

2. Reread the discussion about the Saints and the Roughnecks (in the section entitled Is Social Class Related to Delinquency?). Were there similar groups in your high school? Do you think that our perceptions of upper- and lower-class delinquency are biased for the three reasons indicated by Chambliss (1973)?

3. Can you think of any reasons why middle- and upper-class juveniles might be more likely to engage in delinquency than lower-class juveniles (see B. Wright, Caspi, Moffitt, Meich, and Silva, 1999)?

4. Why do you think rates of serious delinquency among whites and African Americans have become more similar in recent years?

5. Pick a race or ethnic group other than African Americans and whites. Find whatever information you can about levels of delinquency in this group and about the ways in which the life circumstances of this group (e.g., level of poverty, family relations, discrimination experienced) may have influenced levels of delinquency. (You might begin by looking at certain of the sources in note 4 and at indexes to journal articles and reports, like *Sociological Abstracts, Criminal Justice Abstracts,* and the

National Criminal Justice Reference Service Abstracts Database (https://www.ncjrs
.gov/App/ AbstractDB/AbstractDBSearch.aspx).

6. Why do you think so many juveniles start committing criminal acts when they become adolescents? And why do most of these adolescent offenders stop committing criminal acts when they become adults? (Note: Chapter 10 addresses these questions.)

7. A distinction was made between "high-rate, chronic, serious offenders" and "low-rate, adolescence-limited, minor offenders." Do you think the causes of delinquency differ between these two groups of offenders? (Note: Chapter 10 addresses this issue.)

KEY TERMS

- Sociodemographic characteristics
- Adolescence-limited offenders
- Chronic offenders

ENDNOTES

1. For selected studies and overviews of the research in this area, see Agnew et al., 2008; Bjerk, 2007; Braithwaite, 1981; Elliott and Ageton, 1980; Elliott and Huizinga, 1983; Farnworth et al., 1994; Hagan, 1992; Harris and Shaw, 2000; Hay et al., 2007; Heimer, 1997; Hindelang et al., 1979, 1981; Jarjoura et al., 2002; Tittle and Meier, 1990; Tittle et al., 1978; B. Wright, Caspi, Moffitt, Meich, and Silva, 1999.

2. See Bjerk, 2007; Brownfield, 1986; Elliott and Ageton, 1980; Farnworth et al., 1994; Hagan, 1992; Hindelang et al., 1979, 1981; Jarjoura et al., 2002; Thornberry and Farnworth, 1982.

3. See Bjerk, 2007; Brownfield, 1986; Farnworth et al., 1994; Jarjoura et al., 2002; Loeber, Farrington, Stouthamer-Loeber, Moffitt, and Caspi, 1998.

4. For selected studies and overviews of the research on race/ethnicity and delinquency, see Cintron, 2006; Elliott and Ageton, 1980; Elliott et al., 1989; Felson, Deane, and Armstrong, 2008; French, 2006; Hagan and Peterson, 1995; Harris and Shaw, 2000; D. Hawkins, Laub, and Lauritsen, 1998; Hindelang, 1978; Hindelang et al., 1981; Huizinga and Elliott, 1987; J. Kaufman, 2005; Lauritsen, 2005; Lauritsen and Sampson, 1998; McCluskey, 2002; McNulty and Bellair, 2003; Mears and Bhati, 2006; Morenoff, 2005; Sampson and Lauritsen, 1997; Sampson et al., 2005; Traver et al., 2002; Velez et al., 2003; S. Walker et al., 2004.

5. See Elliott and Ageton, 1980; Elliott et al., 1989; Farrington et al., 1996, 2003; Felson, Deane, and Armstrong, 2008; Hindelang et al., 1981; Huizinga and Elliott, 1987; J. Kaufman, 2005; Kelley et al., 1997; Lauritsen, 2005; Liberman, 2007; Morenoff, 2005; Office of Juvenile Justice and Delinquency Prevention, 1999a; Peeples and Loeber, 1994.

6. See Felson, Deane, and Armstrong, 2008; French, 2006; D. Hawkins, Laub, and Lauritsen, 1998; Jang, 2002; J. Kaufman, 2005; Lauritsen, 2005; McNulty and Bellair, 2003; Morris et al., 2006; Sampson et al., 2005; C. Smith and Krohn, 1995.

7. For an excellent overview, see Sampson, 2008; also see Bui, 2009; Martinez and Lee, 2000; Martinez and Nielsen, 2006: Morenoff, 2005; Nielsen et al., 2005; Press, 2006; Sampson and Bean, 2006; Sampson et al., 2005; Velez, 2006.

8. See H. Snyder and Sickmund, 1999:192; also see Bishop and Leiber, 2012; Hindelang, 1981; Lauritsen, 2005; Liberman, 2007; Tonry, 1995.

9. For a fuller discussion of these issues, see Chapter 12 in this text and Bishop and Leiber, 2012; Crutchfield et al., 2006; Hawkins, Laub, and Lauritsen, 1998; Lauritsen and Sampson, 1998; Mears and Bhati, 2006; Sampson and Bean, 2006; Sampson and Lauritsen, 1997; Sampson et al., 2005; Sampson and Wilson, 1995; Velez et al., 2003.

10. See Peeples and Loeber, 1994; also see Bellair and McNulty, 2005; Bishop and Leiber, 2012; Crutchfield et al., 2006; C. Johnson and Chanhatasilpa, 2003; J. Kaufman, 2005; Krivo and Peterson, 1996; Liberman, 2007; McNulty and Bellair, 2003; Sampson, 1985, 1987; Sampson and Bean, 2006; Sampson et al., 2005; Velez et al., 2003.

11. For overviews and selected studies, see Bushway et al., 2003; Cook and Laub, 1998; Elliott, 1994; Elliott et al., 1989; Farrington, 1986, 1994, 2005; Farrington et al., 2003; Greenberg, 1977, 1985; Hirschi and Gottfredson, 1983; Huizinga, 1995; Kelley et al., 1997; Le Blanc and Loeber, 1998; Moffitt, 2006; Osgood et al., 1989; A. Piquero et al., 2003; A. Rowe and Tittle, 1977; Sampson and Laub, 1993b; H. Snyder, 2003; H. Snyder and Sickmund, 1999; Steffensmeier and Allan, 1995, 2000; Steffensmeier et al., 1989; Warr, 1993; Zimring, 2005.

12. See Broidy et al., 2003; Lahey and Waldman, 2005; Nagin and Tremblay, 2005a, 2005b; for information on "child delinquents," see Loeber et al., 2003.

13. For overviews and selected studies on gender and delinquency, see Canter, 1982; Chesney-Lind, 2001; Chesney-Lind and Shelden, 2004; Daly, 1998; Elliott et al., 1989; Federal Bureau of Investigation, 2003; Goodkind et al., 2009; Hindelang et al., 1981; Jensen and Rojek, 1998; Kelley et al., 1997; Poe-Yamagata and Butts, 1996; Steffensmeier, 1993; Steffensmeier and Allan, 1996, 2000; Steffensmeier and Schwartz, 2009; Zahn et al., 2008.

14. See Canter, 1982; Chesney-Lind and Shelden, 2004; Goodkind et al., 2009; Huizinga et al., 2003; Steffensmeier, 1993; Steffensmeier and Schwartz, 2009; Zahn et al., 2008; and trend data from the Monitoring the Future survey as reported in the Sourcebook of Criminal Justice Statistics; also see Jensen and Rojek, 1998.

15. For overviews and selected studies in this area, see Caspi and Moffitt, 1995; Chung et al., 2002; L. Cohen and Vila, 1996; Deane et al., 2005; DeLisi et al., 2013; Dunford and Elliott, 1984; D'Unger et al., 2002; D'Unger et al., 1998; Elliott et al., 1989; Farrington, 1986, 1994, 2005; D. Hawkins, 2003; Howell, 1997a, 2003a; Howell, Krisberg, and Jones, 1995; Huizinga, 1995; Huizinga et al., 2003; Kelley et al., 1997; Le Blanc and Loeber, 1998; Loeber et al., 2003; Loeber, Farrington, and Waschbusch, 1998; Moffitt, 1997, 2006; Osgood and Schreck, 2007; A. Piquero, 2000; A. Piquero et al., 2003; A. Piquero and Mazerolle, 2001; A. Piquero et al., 1999; Sampson and Laub, 1993a; C. Sullivan et al., 2006; Thornberry et al., 1995; Tolan and Gorman-Smith, 1998; Visher, 2000.

PART 2

The Causes of Delinquency

THEORIES

The next eight chapters focus on what is probably the most frequently asked question about delinquency: What causes it? In particular, these chapters present the leading theories or explanations of delinquency. There are numerous theories of delinquency, especially if we count the different versions of more general theories.[1] For example, there are several major versions of strain theory (Agnew, 1992; Berkowitz, 1993; Cloward and Ohlin, 1960; A. Cohen, 1955; Colvin, 2000; Elliott et al., 1979; Greenberg, 1977; Merton, 1938). As a consequence, most introductory texts in delinquency end up describing 20 or more different delinquency theories. And, not surprisingly, many of these theories are superficially described; there is simply not enough space to adequately describe them all. Based on our experience, this approach typically overwhelms and confuses students. Students struggle to keep track of all the different theories, the evidence on these theories, and the relationship between these theories. We take a different approach in this text.

We attempt to "synthesize" the best of the current delinquency theories into a smaller set of "generic" theories, theories that we believe represent our best answers to the question, What causes delinquency? Four major generic theories are presented in Chapters 6 through 9: **strain theory, social learning theory, control theory,** and **labeling theory.** These theories are used to explain **why some individuals are more likely than others to engage in delinquency.** They do so by arguing that some individuals develop traits and are in social environments that create a predisposition for delinquency.

Theories of delinquency, however, attempt to explain more than individual differences in offending (see Tittle, 2000). Theories also try to explain **patterns of offending over the course of the individual's life.** For example, they try to explain why some individuals offend at high rates for much of their lives, while others limit their offending largely to the adolescent years. Chapter 10 addresses this issue, drawing heavily on the four theories presented in Chapters 6 through 9. Further, theories try to explain **why individuals are more likely to engage in delinquency in some types of situations than others.** For example, they try to explain why individuals are more likely to engage in delinquency when they are involved in unstructured, unsupervised activities with peers. Chapter 11 addresses this issue, again drawing heavily on the theories presented in earlier chapters. Finally, theories try to explain **why some groups have higher rates of delinquency than other groups.** Chapter 12 addresses this issue, with a focus on explaining why some communities have higher rates of delinquency than other communities. Once again, we draw heavily on the theories presented in earlier chapters. We address other group differences in delinquency, including age and gender differences, later in the book—especially in Chapter 18.

But before we describe the theories of the causes of delinquency, we describe what a theory is and how we test theories in Chapter 5.

ENDNOTE

1. For overviews, see Akers et al., 2016; Bernard et al., 2015; Cullen et al., 2014; Cullen et al., 2006; Shoemaker, 2009.

5 What Is a Theory and How Do We Test Theories?

The leading theories or explanations of delinquency are presented in Chapters 6 through 12. But before presenting these theories, we need to address three basic questions in this chapter: (1) What is a theory? (2) Why is it important to study theories of delinquency? (3) How do we go about testing theories or testing ideas derived from them? In particular, how do we determine whether some factor causes delinquency?

After reading this chapter, you should be able to:

- Provide a definition for a theory.
- Describe and differentiate the basic parts of a theory.
- Describe why theories are important in the explanation and response to delinquency.
- Describe the major steps involved in testing a theory.
- Identify the four conditions for making causal statements.

WHAT IS A THEORY?

A *theory* is an attempt to explain something or describe the causes of something. Most of you probably already have theories of delinquency in mind. You may believe, for example, that poverty causes delinquency or that poor parental supervision causes delinquency (or that several factors cause delinquency). The delinquency theories that we examine herein simply represent the efforts of criminologists to explain delinquency.

When criminologists develop theories of delinquency, however, they draw not only on their own experiences and creative abilities (as you do, when you develop your theories). They also draw on previous theories and research regarding delinquency. Their theories, then, are based on a large body of information. Further, the theories they develop are tested, and the results of such tests are used to develop still better theories or explanations of delinquency.

What Are the Basic Parts of a Theory?

Theories usually have several parts. Let us take the following simple theory as an illustration: Child abuse causes delinquency. Abuse makes children angry, and they often take this anger out on others through delinquency.

First, this theory lists what it is that we want to explain. In our case, we want to explain **juvenile delinquency**. In particular, we want to explain why some juveniles are more delinquent than others. As indicated in the introduction to Part 2 of this book, the delinquency theories we examine attempt to explain (1) why some individuals are more likely than others to engage in delinquency, (2) patterns of offending over the course of the individual's life, (3) why delinquency is more likely in some types of situations than in others, and (4) why some groups have higher rates of delinquency than other groups. These theories typically focus on a wide range of delinquent acts, including violent acts, property crimes, drug offenses, and status offenses.

Second, the theory lists what we believe to be the cause of juvenile delinquency: child abuse. In the language of social research, child abuse is our *independent variable* and juvenile delinquency is our *dependent variable*. That is, delinquency is said to depend on child abuse. Most theories of delinquency are more complicated than our simple theory and list several independent variables or causes of delinquency. (**A variable is anything that can differ from person to person.** Sex is a variable, since one can be male or female. Income, education, and beliefs regarding violence are also variables.) Theories of delinquency also sometimes discuss the relationship between these independent variables. For example, they argue that income influences beliefs regarding violence.

Third, the theory explains why the independent variable causes delinquency. In particular, we claim that child abuse causes delinquency because it angers the child, who then strikes out at others. You can probably think of other reasons why child abuse might cause delinquency. Child abuse, for example, may teach children that violence is an appropriate way to deal with one's problems. Or child abuse may reduce the child's respect and affection for parents, thereby making it difficult for parents to properly raise their children. **The leading theories of delinquency often share many of the same independent variables;** these theories are most **sharply distinguished from one another in terms of their description of why these independent variables cause crime** (see Agnew, 1995a).

Many delinquency theories also have a fourth part. In the preceding example, we claim that child abuse causes delinquency. Studies provide some support for this theory: namely, that abused children are somewhat more likely than nonabused children to engage in delinquency (see Chapter 14). But not all abused children have high rates of delinquency. Child abuse increases the likelihood of delinquency, but it does not result in delinquency in all cases. Many theories try to specify the conditions under which a variable like child abuse is most likely to cause delinquency.

The simple theory we stated did not do this. We might, however, argue that child abuse is most likely to cause delinquency when the child is also having problems at school (Zingraff et al., 1994). **Certain theories list factors that influence the likelihood that the associated independent variables will cause delinquency.** Such factors are sometimes called *conditioning variables*, since they specify the conditions or circumstances under which the independent variables are most likely to cause delinquency (see Cullen, 1984, for an extended discussion of conditioning variables in crime theory).

You now know the basic parts of a theory, and we will make reference to them in the descriptions of the delinquency theories presented in subsequent chapters.

Why Is It Important to Study Theories of Delinquency?

It is important to study theories for several reasons. First, **these theories help explain the "basic facts" about delinquency, which we discussed in previous chapters.** In particular, they help explain why certain individuals are more likely to engage in delinquency than others; why individuals are more likely to engage in crime at certain points in their life, like adolescence; and why some groups have higher rates of delinquency than others. For example, they help explain why males are more delinquent than females.

Second, **most of the research on the causes of delinquency is guided by these theories or can be interpreted in terms of them.** These theories are basically "educated guesses" about why juveniles engage in delinquency. Most of the research conducted by criminologists—like surveys and field studies—represents an attempt to test and extend these theories. Chapters 13 through 19 describe this research.

Third, **these theories can help society prevent and control delinquency.** The theories point to the major causes of delinquency, and prevention and control programs are more likely to be successful to the extent that they target those causes. Chapters 20 through 25 describe a number of successful programs that are based on or compatible with these theories.

Finally, **these theories can help us better understand our own behavior and the behavior of those around us.** As brought out in Chapter 3, most of us have committed at least minor delinquent acts. Most of us know individuals who have committed delinquent acts. And most of us live in communities where delinquency is a problem.

HOW DO WE TEST THEORIES OF DELINQUENCY (OR DETERMINE WHETHER SOME FACTOR CAUSES DELINQUENCY)?

As indicated, theories are basically educated guesses about what causes delinquency. That is, they describe factors that may cause delinquency. It is therefore important that we test theories to determine if they are true. But how do we go about determining if some factor really does cause delinquency? For example, how do we determine whether child abuse causes delinquency? This question is relevant not only to the causes of delinquency but also to all areas where causal statements are made. It is relevant to many of the other courses you are taking and to your daily lives. You are constantly exposed to causal statements like the following: mass media violence causes crime, secondhand smoke causes cancer, and certain human activities cause climate change. The discussion that follows will not only help you better understand the research on the causes of delinquency, but it will also help you better judge the accuracy of these sorts of claims.

The Scientific Method

Suppose you believe that child abuse causes delinquency. That is your theory of delinquency. You may have good reason to believe that this theory is correct. It may be supported by your personal experiences; perhaps you know someone who was abused and turned out to be delinquent. The theory may make much sense to you; you can think of many good reasons why abuse might lead to delinquency. The theory may be held by other people whom you respect. It is, nevertheless, still important to test the theory. Personal experiences do not provide a sufficient basis for judging the accuracy of a theory. Even though you may know an abused individual who turned out to be delinquent, that does not prove that abuse causes delinquency. It may be that abused and nonabused individuals are equally likely to engage in delinquency; you just happen to know one of the abused individuals who engages in delinquency. It is dangerous to generalize from this one individual to all abused individuals. Also, the fact that this theory makes sense to you or is supported by others does not mean that it is correct. Many people, for example, believe that low self-esteem is a major cause of delinquency, and this belief makes much sense to them. The data, however, suggest that self-esteem has little or no effect on delinquency (Blackburn, 1993; Jang and Thornberry, 1998).

How, then, do we determine whether our theory that abuse causes delinquency is correct? We test our theory against data gathered from juveniles. Social and behavioral scientists have developed a number of guidelines for us to follow in this process: guidelines for collecting and analyzing data. These guidelines form the core of the *scientific method*, and they describe the steps that we should follow to provide an accurate test of our theories. A brief overview of these guidelines is provided next (see Babbie, 2016; Champion, 2005, for fuller discussions).

Carefully Define Your Independent and Dependent Variables

The first step in testing our theory involves carefully defining our independent and dependent variables (remember, the independent variable is what causes the dependent variable). For our theory, we must carefully define what we mean by abuse and delinquency. For example, does abuse constitute only physical aggression, or does it also include such things as inappropriate sexual contact, verbal harassment, and physical neglect (e.g., the failure to provide adequate food, clothing, medical care, and shelter)? Suppose we decide to limit our definition of abuse to physical aggression. What constitutes such aggression? If a parent softly spanks her or his child for a misdeed, is that aggression? If not, what is the dividing line between physical contact that is abusive and contact that is not abusive? As you can see, it is sometimes difficult to carefully define variables. Nevertheless, it is important: We cannot test our theory that abuse causes delinquency unless we can precisely define abuse and delinquency. For the purposes of our example, let us define abuse as any deliberate act of physical violence against the child (see English, 1998, for a discussion of efforts to define child abuse).

In evaluating any piece of research, you should **carefully examine the definitions of all variables: Are these variables precisely defined, and do the definitions seem reasonable?** For example, you might criticize the definition of abuse just presented. This definition excludes acts that many people would define as abusive, such as verbal abuse, physical neglect, and certain forms of sexual behavior. Further, it includes certain acts that many people would not define as abusive, such as spanking.

Decide How to Gather Data to Test Your Belief or Theory

Second, you must decide how you will gather data to test your belief or theory. Criminologists gather data from juveniles in three major ways. As you will see, each method has certain advantages and disadvantages.

Surveys. The most common way to gather data is by surveying juveniles. Surveys **involve asking people questions, either by interviewing them or having them fill out questionnaires.** For our theory, we might ask a sample of juveniles how many times their parents deliberately hit them in the last year and how many times they have engaged in certain delinquent acts in the last year. We would then have data on the extent of their abuse and delinquency. We could use the data to begin to explore whether abuse causes delinquency. In particular, we could determine whether abused juveniles are more likely to engage in delinquency than nonabused juveniles.

Surveys have the advantage of allowing us to study a large number of juveniles. Further, if we select these juveniles carefully, we can ensure that they are similar to or representative of all juveniles. As a consequence, we can generalize from our survey to all juveniles. For example, suppose we find that child abuse causes delinquency in the sample of juveniles we survey. Since these juveniles are representative of all juveniles, we have some basis for concluding that child abuse causes delinquency among all juveniles. At the same time, surveys do have certain disadvantages. Most notably, there is the danger that some juveniles will not provide accurate answers to our questions. They may, for example, forget some of the things that they have done or that others have done to them. Also, they may lie to us in an effort to make themselves look good.

Experiments. Criminologists also collect data by doing experiments on juveniles. In an experiment, **you do something to a group of people and then observe the consequences.** For example, you show them a violent video and then observe whether they act in a more aggressive manner.

As we will discuss in Chapter 19, properly conducted experiments are a good way to determine if something causes something else. Many laboratory experiments, however, have been criticized as artificial. Conditions in the lab may not adequately reflect conditions in the real world, so when someone behaves a certain way in the lab, it does not necessarily mean that he or she will behave the same way in the outside, or "real," world. For example, a laboratory experiment may reveal that juveniles often respond to violent cartoons by hitting an inflated doll in a playroom. This behavior, however, does not necessarily mean that they respond to violent cartoons in the real world by hitting other people. Further, ethical considerations often prevent social scientists from doing experiments on the causes of delinquency. For example, we would not want to abuse a group of juveniles and then determine whether they become more delinquent. Likewise, we would not want to create conditions of poverty, broken homes, or poor grades to study such alleged causes of delinquency. Such ethical considerations are why experiments are used less often than surveys when studying the causes of delinquency. Experiments are more often used to determine whether programs are successful at reducing or preventing delinquency, and we discuss them further in Chapter 19. Nevertheless, experiments are sometimes used to study the causes of delinquency. For example, numerous experiments have investigated the impact of media violence on juveniles. Juveniles are exposed to media violence (e.g., a clip from a violent TV show), and researchers then observe the consequences of this exposure on their behavior (e.g., are they more aggressive to a toy clown in the playroom?).

Field studies. Finally, criminologists collect data by studying juveniles, including delinquents, "in the field." That is, **criminologists sometimes go out into the community and study juveniles firsthand** in an effort to determine the causes of delinquency. Such studies usually **involve a combination of observation and intensive interviewing** (see Lofland and Lofland, 1995, for an excellent overview). Criminologists, for example, may spend time observing the behavior of gang members in a particular community. What do they do each day? How do they get along with one another, with family members, with school officials and others? What do they talk about? Criminologists may also conduct intensive interviews with the gang members. Intensive interviews differ from the interviews associated with surveys. Survey interviews are usually highly structured: respondents are asked to answer a set of predetermined questions, and each question usually has a list of predetermined answers from which they must choose. For example, the survey interviewer may ask: "How many of your friends have been arrested?" and respondents must select their answer from a list that includes "all," "most," "some," or "none." *Intensive interviews* are much less structured. The interviewer usually has a list of topics to explore, but there are few predetermined questions, and respondents can answer each question in their own words. Intensive interviews have been described as "guided conversations." Field studies, then, involve a combination of "looking, listening, and asking" (Lofland and Lofland, 1995:70).

Field studies provide a much more detailed picture of social life than is provided by surveys and experiments. Researchers directly observe juveniles over an extended period of time and have long conversations with them. As a consequence, they get a fuller picture of the circumstances in which juveniles live and the factors that influence their behavior. Also, since the researcher directly observes juveniles, field studies are less affected by the fact that juveniles are sometimes unable or unwilling to provide accurate answers to survey questions.

At the same time, field studies have certain limitations. It is difficult for a criminologist to observe and intensely interview more than a small number of juveniles. As a consequence, we need to be much more cautious about generalizing from a particular field study to all juveniles. A field study, for example, may find that the members of a particular gang are heavily involved in selling drugs. But since only one of the many thousands of gangs in the United States was studied, there is some danger in concluding that all or most gangs are heavily involved in selling drugs. The results of a field study, however, can be verified with additional field studies of different gangs and sometimes with surveys. There are also limits to what can be observed. Most families, for example, would probably be reluctant to have a researcher in their home observing them. Further, the presence of the researcher might change the behavior being observed. Parents might be reluctant to abuse their kids, and juveniles might be reluctant to commit delinquent acts if there is an observer present. Finally, the researchers' biases may influence what researchers observe and how they interpret what they observe.

Despite these limitations, field studies have provided criminologists with important information about the causes of delinquency—information that would have been difficult or impossible to obtain with surveys and experiments. Field studies, in particular, have played a key role in helping us understand the role of gangs and community characteristics in causing delinquency.[1] We describe the findings from a number of field studies throughout this book.

Each method of collecting data, then, has its own special set of advantages and disadvantages. Ideally, researchers studying the causes of delinquency will use all three methods when feasible and ethical.

Develop Measures of Your Independent and Dependent Variables

Since most research on the causes of delinquency employs surveys, we will **focus on survey research** for the remainder of this discussion. Once you have decided to conduct a survey, you need to decide how you will measure your variables. That is, you need to **decide what questions you will ask the juveniles in your sample** to measure variables like child abuse and delinquency. You want to make sure that your questions reflect the definitions you have developed. At the same time, you want to make sure that your questions will be properly understood by your respondents, many of whom may be young and of limited intellectual ability. In some cases, it is an easy matter to develop questions. For example, if you want to measure a variable like age, you can simply ask juveniles, "How old are you?" In other cases, it is much more difficult to develop good questions. For example, how do you measure a variable like "low self-control" (defined in Chapter 13)? This variable has several components, including impulsivity and a preference for risky activities. Researchers have measured low self-control by asking respondents whether they agree with a series of questions, such as "I often act on the spur of the moment without stopping to think," and "Sometimes I will take a risk just for the fun of it" (see Grasmick et al., 1993). Responses to these questions are then used to develop an overall measure of low self-control.

Textbooks on social research, like Babbie (2016) and Champion (2005), provide guidelines for researchers to follow in developing good measures. In evaluating a piece of research, you should **ask yourself whether there are any potential problems with the measures employed.** As you may recall from earlier chapters, one major issue in delinquency research involves the way delinquency is measured. Many researchers measure delinquency by using arrest data. Arrest data, however, suffer from several problems, including the fact that they overlook the vast majority of delinquent acts, which do not come to the attention of the police. As a consequence, most criminologists studying the causes of delinquency now rely on self-report measures of delinquency. Such measures are not free of problems; but if properly constructed, they are generally thought to provide a more reliable indicator of delinquency. Researchers, however, place greatest confidence in findings that hold for both self-report and arrest measures. We can be more confident, for example, that child abuse really does cause delinquency if it affects both self-reported delinquency and arrests. Fortunately, the research based on arrest data and the research based on comparable self-report measures have generally produced similar results about the causes of delinquency, although there are some exceptions.

Select a Sample of Juveniles to Survey

There are about 33 million juveniles between the ages of 10 and 17 in the United States. But it is not necessary to survey all of them. **If researchers carefully select a *sample* of one or two thousand juveniles, they can accurately generalize from this sample to all juveniles in the United States.** If the researchers find, for example, that abused juveniles are more delinquent than nonabused juveniles in this sample, they can be reasonably confident that they would find the same thing if they surveyed all 33 million juveniles ages 10 to 17 in the United States. Researchers must, however, carefully select their sample so that it is *representative* of all juveniles in the United States. What do we mean by "representative"? We mean that the characteristics of the juveniles in our sample should be similar to those of all juveniles in the United States. The two groups should be proportionately similar in terms of delinquency and all the potential causes of delinquency—including variables like class, race, sex, and age. How do we ensure that our sample is similar to or representative of all juveniles? The best way to do this is to collect a *random sample*.

    A random sample is collected such that each juvenile in the population has an equal chance of being selected. For example, imagine that we had put the names of all juveniles in the United States in an enormous hat. We then thoroughly mixed the names up and had a blindfolded person pull out 2,000 names. We would have a random sample, and we could be reasonably sure that the juveniles in this sample were similar to or representative of all juveniles in the United States. Researchers do not collect random samples in quite this manner; rather, they have developed more sophisticated techniques for randomly sampling juveniles from a population (see Babbie, 2016; Champion, 2005). Unfortunately, it is often difficult for researchers to collect random samples of juveniles—even random samples of juveniles from a single city. There is no list containing the names of every juvenile in the United States (or in cities or states within the United States). Even if there were such a list, it is often hard to locate certain juveniles, and if you do locate them, they may refuse to participate in your survey.

    As a consequence, most studies of delinquency are based on samples that are not quite representative of all juveniles or that are of questionable representativeness. For example, researchers commonly collect random samples of students from high schools (e.g., they select every 20th student on the rolls from all the high schools in a city or from a random sample of high schools in the United States). As indicated earlier, however, many juveniles have dropped out of school, are suspended, or are absent from school the day the survey is administered. This is especially likely to be true of lower-class juveniles and serious delinquents. Also, many students will refuse to participate in the survey, or their parents will refuse to allow them to participate. So the final sample of students is not representative of all juveniles. As a consequence, criminologists have to be cautious when generalizing from their sample to all juveniles. In fact, some researchers have claimed that the use of unrepresentative samples—including school samples—has led scientists to draw some inaccurate conclusions about the causes of delinquency (e.g., Bernard, 1984; Cullen, 2011; Hagan and McCarthy, 1997a, 1997b). The extent to which the sample is unrepresentative obviously depends on the particular survey, and some of the more recent surveys on juvenile delinquency have gone to great lengths to select more representative samples of juveniles. In particular, researchers have made a special effort to make sure that serious delinquents are included in the sample (see Thornberry et al., 1995; Thornberry and Krohn, 2003). In any event, when you are evaluating a piece of survey research, you should **ask whether the sample is representative of the population from which it is drawn. And if it is not representative, how might that affect the results?** (Good researchers will usually address these issues in their research reports.)

Analyze the Data You Have Collected

Once researchers have developed their measures and selected their sample, they administer the survey. Most delinquency surveys today contain hundreds of questions (remember, it may take several questions to measure a single variable) and are administered to as many as 1,000 or more juveniles. Researchers enter all the data they have collected into a computer and then analyze this data using certain statistical techniques. Before researchers can conclude that some independent variable like child abuse causes delinquency, **they must demonstrate four things: that the independent variable is associated with delinquency; that the association is not due to chance; that the association is not due to third variables; and that the independent variable precedes delinquency in time.** These are the four conditions for making causal statements. Let us describe each of them in turn (see Hirschi and Selvin, 1967, for a fuller discussion).

Association. Before we can say that our independent variable causes delinquency, we must demonstrate that our independent variable is associated, or correlated, with delinquency. For example, before we can say that child abuse causes delinquency, we must demonstrate that abused juveniles are higher in delinquency. This requirement makes sense. If child abuse causes delinquency, then we would expect abused juveniles to be more delinquent than nonabused juveniles. (This is an example of a *positive association*: A high score on our independent variable is associated with a higher level of delinquency. Positive association is illustrated in Figure 5.1A: as the level of abuse increases, the level of delinquency also increases.) To give another example, suppose we argue that poor school grades cause delinquency: students with higher grades have more to lose by engaging in delinquency and should therefore be lower in delinquency. If this argument is correct, school grades should be associated with delinquency: Those with high grades should be less delinquent than those with low grades. (This is an example of a *negative association*: A high score on our independent variable is associated with a lower level of delinquency. This negative association is illustrated in Figure 5.1B: as grades increase, the level of delinquency decreases.)

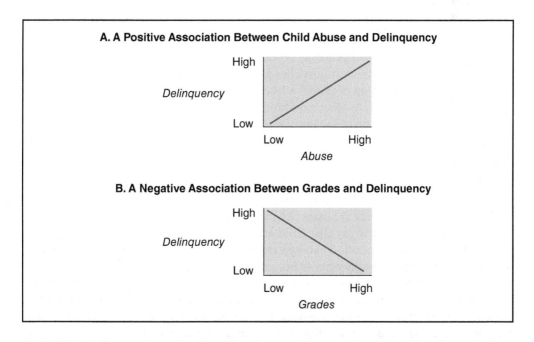

FIGURE 5.1 Examples of a Positive Association and a Negative Association

It is important to emphasize that **most associations are far from perfect.** Do not expect to find that all abused juveniles are delinquent and that all nonabused juveniles are not delinquent. Instead, you might find that 30 percent of all abused juveniles are high in delinquency compared to 17 percent of all nonabused juveniles. **Delinquency is caused by a large number of variables, most of which have small to moderate associations with delinquency** (see Box 5.1). So when you read that low grades or broken homes are associated with delinquency, you should not assume that all or even most juveniles with low grades or from broken homes are delinquent (or that all juveniles with high grades or from intact homes are nondelinquent). What you can safely assume is that juveniles with low grades and juveniles from broken homes are somewhat more likely to engage in delinquency than juveniles with high grades and juveniles from intact homes.

Most of the statistics employed by researchers summarize the association between the independent and dependent variables. These statistics usually tell the researcher how much delinquency increases or decreases when the independent variable increases by a certain amount. For example, they might tell the researcher that juveniles commit an average of five fewer delinquent acts every time school grades increase by one unit (from D to C, C to B, etc.). See Babbie (2016) and Champion (2005) for an overview of such statistics.

Association not due to chance. Suppose we find that child abuse and delinquency are associated, with abused juveniles being more delinquent than nonabused juveniles. Does that mean that child abuse causes delinquency? It does not.

The association may be due to chance. For example, suppose you randomly sample 10 students from your school. You find that 40 percent of the blue-eyed students in your sample are delinquent, whereas only 20 percent of the brown-eyed students are. So there is an association between eye color and delinquency. But this association may be due to chance. If you surveyed **all** the students at your school, you might find that eye color is unrelated to delinquency (e.g., 30 percent of the blue-eyed students are delinquent and 30 percent of the brown-eyed students are delinquent). But, by chance, your sample of 10 happened to include more blue-eyed delinquents than brown-eyed delinquents. The fact that two variables are associated does not prove that one causes the other; the association may be due to chance.

The likelihood that a given association is due to chance becomes smaller as the sample size increases. Larger samples generally produce more accurate results, although increases in sample size beyond 2,000 or so juveniles produce only small increases in accuracy (see Babbie, 2016, for a discussion of factors affecting the accuracy of sample results, including sample size). Also, if you have collected a random sample, you can estimate the probability that any association you find is due to chance. For example, you can say that the probability that the association between child abuse and delinquency is due to chance is less than 1 in 20 (5%) or less than 1 in 100 (1%). Researchers state that such associations are **"statistically significant."**

Association not due to third variables. Now suppose we have demonstrated that child abuse and delinquency are associated and that it is unlikely that this association is due to chance. Can we now say that child abuse causes delinquency? Unfortunately the answer is still no. The association between child abuse and delinquency may be caused by a third variable that is causally prior to both original variables.

Let us provide an example from actual research. Criminologists have found that there is an association between IQ and delinquency: People with low IQs are higher in delinquency. Further, it is quite unlikely that this association is due to chance. Does that mean that low IQ causes delinquency? Many criminologists argue that it does not. They claim that the association between IQ and delinquency does not mean that low IQ

Box 5.1   What about Free Will and Personal Responsibility?

We once observed an interview in which an influential politician was asked, "Do you believe that smoking causes lung cancer?" The politician stated that, no, he could not see how smoking could be a *cause* of lung cancer. After all, he explained, he was aware of several life-long heavy smokers who did not develop the disease.

Apparently, this politician was under the impression that the term "cause" implies an inevitable one-to-one relationship between smoking and lung cancer (i.e., "all heavy smokers develop lung cancer"). This is not how medical experts use the term, however. When they use the term "cause," they are simply pointing to a causal *association* between the two, in which smoking increases the *risk* or *probability* of cancer. Likewise, this is how the term is used in criminology. When you hear a criminologist state that child abuse or some other factor is believed to be a "cause" of delinquency, it may help to remind yourself that he or she is referring only to an increased risk or probability of delinquency (and usually only a modest increased risk). It may also be helpful to replace the term "cause" with "risk factor."

Keep in mind that any complex behavior such as delinquency is shaped by *multiple* risk factors. Typically, a single factor like child abuse, by itself, will contribute to only a modest increase in the risk of delinquency. However, when abused individuals are exposed to additional risk factors, such as delinquent peers or failure in school, their risk for delinquent behavior becomes more substantial.

The fact that criminological research is based on observed probabilities means that the possibility of free choice or "free will" is *not* eliminated. As the influential criminologist David Matza (1964) emphasized, we have the unique capacity as humans to reflect on our past experience and, ultimately, to transcend this experience. In other words, it is possible for us to reflect on our past behavior, on the causes of such behavior, and work to overcome these causes or risk factors. It may be difficult to do so, but it remains a possibility (also see Agnew, 2011).

Research on the children of alcoholics provides a good example. Much research indicates that a family history of alcoholism is a risk factor for the development of substance abuse (a risk that appears to be rooted in both social and biological factors). This relationship is especially evident among the sons of alcoholic fathers. Yet there is nothing inevitable about this relationship. Rather, the research merely points to a pattern or trend. While the sons of alcoholic fathers are four to eight times more likely than the sons of nonalcoholic fathers to develop alcoholism themselves, only about one-third do so (Vitaro et al., 1996). In fact, many children of alcoholics refrain from alcohol use all together. Some abstain from alcohol because "they have seen the negative consequences of their parents' drinking" and "fear they will become alcoholics themselves"; others abstain because they have found support in self-help groups (J. Walker and Lee, 1998:524). In other words, the abstainers have overcome or transcended the risk posed by their family history.

Overcoming background risk factors may be relatively easy for some individuals but very difficult for others. For example, it may be easier for individuals who possess high levels of self-awareness and think a lot about their own behavior, as suggested by research on the children of alcoholics (Rogosch et al., 1990). It may also be easier for individuals who feel in control of their behavior and, instead of simply reacting emotionally to the bad events in their past, view this past history as a challenge to overcome (see Laub and Sampson, 2003). It may be relatively difficult to overcome

(Continued)

(Continued)

background risk factors for individuals who have many risk factors stacked against them, who feel helpless, and who do not perceive many options (Agnew 1995c, 2011; also see the discussion of punishment and free will at the end of Chapter 13, in the "Teaching Aids" section).

The fact that individuals can, under the right conditions, overcome their past has important implications for personality responsibility and offender rehabilitation. Some people are troubled by criminological research because they worry that the identification of risk factors will provide excuses for offenders. Our experience, however, suggests that an understanding and appreciation of risk factors need not diminish personal responsibility. To provide an example, the second author of this textbook worked as a resident counselor in a treatment center for troubled youth. Not surprisingly, the files on these youth indicated the presence of many important risk factors in their backgrounds, including severe child abuse and neglect, exposure to alcohol in the womb (fetal alcohol syndrome), and exposure to parental crime and drug use. Yet, instead of letting those past experiences serve as an excuse, the treatment staff was relentless in their efforts to hold these youth accountable for their behavior. They demanded that the young residents take ownership of their current behavior problems and make better choices in the future, and they administered appropriate punishment for failure to comply (they also rewarded compliance). In fact, the staff regularly exclaimed, "It's your responsibility to get your behavior under control!"

The staff felt justified in holding these youth accountable for their behavior because they were also providing tools designed to help these youth overcome background risk factors. For instance, in therapy sessions the youth gained insight into the factors that triggered their anger and acting out. In addition, they learned how to better deal with their past experiences, including specific techniques for managing their emotions and behavior. These therapeutic efforts were informed by knowledge of the risk factors to which the youth had been exposed.

Questions for Discussion

1. Before reading this chapter, what was your impression of criminological research? When you heard experts refer to the "causes" of crime and delinquency were you confused, like the politician described earlier? If such misunderstandings are common, how might this influence public acceptance (or rejection) of social science research and the crime control recommendations that follow from such research?

2. How do you feel about the search for the causes of crime and delinquency? Like others, do you worry that this search will provide excuses for offenders? Or do you believe that this search is necessary to help society prevent and control crime? Explain your position.

3. To help individuals overcome background risk factors, such as a family history of alcoholism, perhaps interventions could be designed to increase self-awareness (see Chassin et al., 1988). Can you think of other possibilities?

causes delinquency. Rather, it is due to the fact that both IQ and delinquency are caused by the same third variable. In particular, they claim that the third variable, social class, affects both IQ and delinquency (see Figure 5.2). Lower-class people have lower IQs and are higher in delinquency. That is why low IQ is associated with high delinquency—not because low IQ causes delinquency but because both IQ and delinquency are caused by the same third variable, social class. (Try to think of another association between two variables that may be caused by a third variable. Hint: A popular example involves the

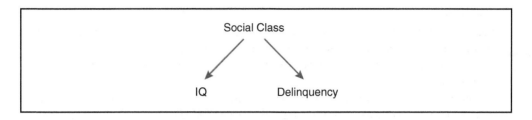

FIGURE 5.2 **Some Claim that Social Class Affects both IQ and Delinquency**

following three variables: number of storks in an area, area birthrate, and urban/rural location—see Babbie, 2016.)

Before we can argue that the independent variable in our theory causes delinquency, we must also demonstrate that the association between our independent variable and delinquency is not caused by a third variable. How do we do this? Let us continue with the example. Again, many criminologists argue that people with low IQs are more likely to be delinquent because they are more likely to be lower class, not because they have low IQs. Likewise, they argue that people with high IQs are less likely to be delinquent because they are more likely to be higher class, not because they have high IQs. If these arguments are correct, the association between IQ and delinquency should disappear if we examine just lower-class people. That is, IQ should be unrelated to delinquency in a sample of lower-class people: Lower-class people with low IQs should be about as delinquent as lower-class people with high IQs. Likewise, the association should disappear if we examine just higher-class people: higher-class people with low IQs should be about as delinquent as higher-class people with high IQs. If IQ is no longer associated with delinquency when we examine lower-class people separately from higher-class people, that finding suggests that the original association between IQ and delinquency is due to social class, and we can no longer claim that IQ causes delinquency.

What if the association does not disappear? What if we find that lower-class people with low IQs are more delinquent than lower-class people with high IQs, and that higher-class people with low IQs are more delinquent than higher-class people with high IQs? This finding means that the association between IQ and delinquency is not caused by the third variable of social class. And, in fact, that is what researchers have found: IQ is still associated with delinquency even when the analysis is limited to lower-class people only or higher-class people only (e.g., Hirschi and Hindelang, 1977).

Researchers, then, determine whether the association between an independent variable and delinquency is caused by a third variable by *"controlling" for the third variable, or "holding it constant."* We examined the association between IQ and delinquency separately for each category of social class—lower and higher. If the association disappears, that suggests that it was caused by our third variable. (We realize that these arguments may be difficult for some of you to follow. We encourage you to consult with your classmates and to try to come up with examples of your own; also see the discussion in Hirschi and Selvin, 1967:73–87.)

When you are evaluating a piece of research, you should **ask yourself whether any of the reported associations might be caused by a third variable.** Is there some causally prior third variable that might account for the association between the independent variable and delinquency? Are there any third variables, for example, that might account for the association between child abuse and delinquency? Most researchers will try to anticipate third variables that might account for the associations they report and then control for them. This is not always done, however.

Correct causal order. Suppose you find that child abuse is associated with delinquency and that, moreover, the association is not due to chance and appears not to be caused by a third variable. Can you now state that child abuse causes delinquency? If not, why not?

It may be that the association between child abuse and delinquency exists because delinquency causes child abuse. Juveniles who commit delinquent acts may upset their parents, and the upset parents may react by striking their children. Much recent data, in fact, suggest that the behavior of juveniles often has a large effect on how others, including their parents, treat them. Children who are difficult to raise, for example, are more likely to be rejected and to elicit negative reactions from their parents (see Rutter et al., 1998:171–174).

Before we can say that child abuse causes delinquency, we must demonstrate that the abuse preceded the delinquency in time. That is, the abuse came first and the delinquency followed. This is usually accomplished by conducting a *longitudinal survey*. We survey the same group of juveniles over time. For example, during our initial survey we ask a sample of juveniles about the extent of their delinquency and whether their parents hit them. Then we survey the same group of juveniles one year later, once again asking them about the extent of their delinquency. These two surveys allow us to determine whether abused juveniles engage in more **subsequent** delinquency than nonabused juveniles.

It is difficult to do longitudinal surveys of this type, since it is often hard to keep track of a large group of juveniles over time. Much research on the causes of delinquency suffers from the fact that it is not longitudinal (such research is said to be *cross-sectional*, since it looks at juveniles at one cross section in time). Nevertheless, several excellent longitudinal surveys of delinquency have been conducted (e.g., Elliott et al., 1985; Thornberry et al., 1995; Thornberry and Krohn, 2003). One interesting finding to emerge from these studies is that variables sometimes have a *reciprocal effect* on one another. For example, research suggests that associating with delinquent peers and delinquency are reciprocally related. Associating with delinquent peers causes delinquency, and delinquency causes a juvenile to associate with delinquent peers (see Chapter 16).

SUMMARY

Determining whether your beliefs or theories about the causes of delinquency are correct is not an easy matter. There are a number of guidelines that should be followed when collecting and analyzing data, but it is often difficult to follow them all, and some research on the causes of delinquency is suspect as a result. Perhaps a variable is not well defined or measured. Perhaps an unrepresentative sample is employed. Perhaps the researchers failed to control for relevant third variables. Perhaps the research is not longitudinal. Given these problems, criminologists sometimes need to be cautious when making causal statements. We will try to indicate when that is the case in the discussions that follow. At the same time, there are some areas that permit the making of causal statements with some confidence. Certain areas have been well researched, and a range of studies have come to similar conclusions. Criminologists do not like to place too much faith in a single study. But if a number of different studies agree—especially well-conducted studies that use different measures and samples—we are more confident in our conclusions.

TEACHING AIDS
Some Challenges

The data that follow are not real; answers to the challenges are given after the Key Terms.

1. Researchers decide to sample 100 students at your college or university. They set up a table in front of the main dining hall during dinner. They then ask passing students to fill out their survey until 100 students have responded. Do these 100 responders constitute

a random sample of the students at your school? If not, why not? How would you collect a random sample of students at your school?

2. A researcher finds that 90 percent of all delinquent boys played violent video games before they became delinquents. Does this prove that playing video games causes delinquency among boys? If not, why not?

3. A researcher finds that 50 percent of all spanked juveniles are delinquent compared to 30 percent of all nonspanked juveniles. Does this prove that spanking causes delinquency? If not, why not?

4. After analyzing data from many years, a researcher finds that delinquency is much more common during a full moon. Does this prove that a full moon causes delinquency? If not, why not? (Note: This is a rather tough challenge.)

Web-Based Resources for Your Criminological Research Project

This chapter describes how criminologists conduct research on the causes of delinquency. It is unlikely that you will collect and analyze data on the causes of delinquency at this point in your career. However, you might do a research project that involves examining the reports of criminologists and others. For example, suppose you were to do a report on the causes of acquaintance rape among college students. Where would you begin? Your library should have useful resources to draw on, including databases such as Sociological Abstracts and PsycINFO. In addition, there are many useful resources available on the web. One such resource is Google Scholar, which can be accessed at https://scholar.google.com. By typing keywords into the search box (e.g., **IQ** and **delinquency**) you can identify studies that have been published on your topic of interest. Two additional resources on the web are

A. The Abstracts Database of the **National Criminal Justice Reference Service (NCJRS)**. Visit the NCJRS website at https://www.ncjrs.gov. Click **Library**, then click **NCJRS Abstracts Database Search.** If you type **Acquaintance Rape College Students** into the **General Search** box, you will get a good number of hits, including articles in academic journals, books and book chapters, and government reports. Also, try using a few related search terms, such as "sexual assault" and "sexual violence." You will get many additional hits. By reading through the titles and abstracts (click on **Abstract**), you can determine which are most relevant to you. For example, some will focus on the prevention of rape rather than its causes. Some will focus on stranger rape rather than acquaintance rape. You should begin your research by focusing on reports that provide summaries or overviews of the topic, such as book chapters, reviews, and the "review of the literature" sections that appear near the start of research reports. In some cases, the documents listed in your search will be available through the NCJRS website (click on PDF), in other cases you will have to find them in a library (check your library, or click on **Find in a Library**).

B. The NCJRS Abstracts Database focuses on academic research. Depending on your research project, you may want to supplement such research with media reports. For example, suppose you are doing a report on the effectiveness of zero-tolerance policies in the school system or whether zero-tolerance policies are disproportionately applied to blacks and Latinos. In addition to looking at the academic research, you might want to examine media reports. Such reports provide information on things such as the current status of zero-tolerance policies in many school systems, the position of the U.S. Department of Justice or attorney general on zero-tolerance policies, and recent statements on zero-tolerance policies by groups such as the National Education Association. An excellent source of information on media reports is **The Crime Report** website at http://www.thecrimereport.org. By using their search feature, you can get scores of hits when you enter **zero tolerance.** Also, spend some time exploring the site, including the list of topics under **Resources.** If you are not sure what topic you would like to examine in a research paper, this is an excellent source for ideas.

TEST YOUR KNOWLEDGE OF THIS CHAPTER

1. What is a theory? What are the basic parts of a theory?

2. Why is it important to study theories of delinquency?

3. What is meant by the "scientific method"?

4. List and briefly describe the major steps in testing a theory (or determining whether some factor causes delinquency).

5. List and briefly describe the three major methods of gathering data to test theories. Describe the advantages and disadvantages of each method.

6. How do the "intensive interviews" that are part of field studies differ from the interviews that are part of surveys?

7. What is a random sample? Why is it important to collect random samples? Related to this, what is a "representative" sample?

8. Many researchers who study delinquency try to collect random samples of students in high schools. Do such surveys result in a "representative" sample of juveniles? If not, why not?

9. When analyzing their data, researchers must satisfy four conditions before they can conclude that some factor or variable causes delinquency. What are these four conditions?

10. What do researchers mean when they state that two variables are "associated"? Give an example of a positive association and a negative association. What is meant by the statement that most associations are far from perfect?

11. What do researchers mean when they state that an association is probably due to chance?

12. When researchers say than an association is "statistically significant," what do they mean?

13. What do researchers mean when they state that they have "controlled for" a third variable or "held it constant"?

14. What is a "longitudinal survey"? Why is it important to conduct longitudinal surveys?

15. What is a "reciprocal effect"? Give a plausible example of a reciprocal effect.

THOUGHT AND DISCUSSION QUESTIONS

1. Develop a simple theory of delinquency other than those discussed in this chapter. Identify the independent variable(s), dependent variable, and explanation of why the independent variable(s) causes the dependent variable in your theory. Describe a plausible "conditioning variable" for your theory.

2. Describe how you would ideally test the simple theory of delinquency you developed in question 1.

3. Give an example of how you would determine whether some factor causes delinquency by doing an experiment. Give an example of how you might examine some possible cause(s) of delinquency by doing a field study.

4. Draw a "two-variable table." At the left side of this table will be your dependent variable, "delinquency," and it will have two categories: "low" and "high." At the top of your table will be your independent variable, and it will also have two categories: "low" and "high" (or two other categories of your choice, like "yes" and "no" or "male" and "female"). Fill in the table with percentages that indicate a strong association

between your independent variable and dependent variable. Then fill in the table with percentages that indicate no association between your independent variable and dependent variable. Remember that percentages must always add up to 100; also, when filling in the percentages, remember that you are comparing one category of your independent variable to the other (e.g., you are comparing the percentage of males who are high in delinquency to the percentage of females who are high in delinquency).

5. Give a plausible example of an association that is due to a third variable. Create a diagram like that shown in Figure 5.2 to illustrate your example.

6. How would you go about determining whether the association you just described is, in fact, due to the third variable you list?

7. Can we ever "truly" determine (with 100 percent confidence) that some factor causes delinquency? Justify your response.

KEY TERMS

- Theory
- Independent variable
- Dependent variable
- Conditioning variable
- Scientific method
- Surveys
- Experiments
- Field studies

- Intensive interviews
- Sample
- Representative sample
- Random sample
- Positive association
- Negative association
- Association not due to chance

- Association not due to third variables
- "Controlling" for the third variable, or "holding it constant"
- Longitudinal survey
- Cross-sectional survey
- Reciprocal effect

ANSWERS TO THE CHALLENGES

1. The sample of 100 responders is probably not a random sample of students. It is probably the case that some students are less likely to pass by the dining hall during dinner than other students; for example, those who live off campus or in fraternity or sorority houses are probably less likely to pass by the dining hall during dinner. Also, some of the students who do pass by the dining hall are probably less likely to fill out the survey than others; for example, those who are busy or have little interest in the topic of the survey may be less likely to fill out the survey. So it is *not* the case that each student on campus has an equal chance of being in the sample. Rather than being representative of all students, the sample of 100 responders is likely biased toward students who live on campus, are not in fraternities or sororities, have more free time, care about the topic of the survey, and so on. You might collect a random sample of the students in your school by obtaining an up-to-date list of students, then selecting every tenth student on that list (if there are 1,000 students in your school and you want a sample of 100) or using a table of random numbers to select 100 students from the list (see Babbie, 2010).

2. The researcher cannot safely conclude that playing video games causes delinquency among boys. The main reason for this is that the data do *not* demonstrate an *association* between playing violent video games and delinquency. Most adolescent boys play violent video games at some time. As a consequence, it is likely the case that most delinquent boys *and most nondelinquent boys* have played violent video games (e.g., 90 percent of all nondelinquent boys may have played violent video games). To demonstrate that playing violent video games causes delinquency among boys, we must *determine whether*

boys who play violent video games are more likely to engage in delinquency than boys who do not play violent video games (and, of course, we must do so by using a random or representative sample of boys and good measures). If we find an association between playing violent video games and delinquency, we must then try to demonstrate that the association is not due to chance and that the association is not caused by a third variable (e.g., maybe poor parental supervision leads to violent video game playing on the one hand and delinquency on the other). Since the example states that the delinquents played violent video games *before* they became delinquent, causal order is not a problem.

3. These data demonstrate that there is an association between spanking and delinquency, with spanked juveniles being more likely to engage in delinquency (we are assuming that the researcher has a representative sample of juveniles and good measures of spanking and delinquency). But these data do *not* prove that spanking *causes* delinquency. The association may be due to chance. The association may be caused by a third variable (e.g., parental criminality may be such a variable; criminal parents may be more likely to spank and more likely to cause their children to engage in delinquency, perhaps because they are poor role models). And the association may be due to the fact that the delinquency of the child causes the parent to engage in spanking rather than spanking causing delinquency.

4. These data demonstrate an association between a phase of the moon and delinquency (delinquency is more common during a full moon). It is unlikely this association is due to chance if the researcher analyzed data from many years. It is hard to think of a third variable that causes a full moon on the one hand and delinquency on the other (email us if you come up with a good candidate). And it is quite unlikely that delinquency causes a full moon. So these data do strongly suggest that a full moon causes delinquency. These data, of course, are not real; but an astute student in one of our classes nevertheless came up with the following explanation about how a full moon might cause delinquency. Since it is lighter outside when the moon is full, people are more likely to go outside at night. And this creates more opportunities for delinquency (among other things, delinquency is more likely when juveniles are associating with one another in the absence of authority figures).

ENDNOTE

1. For examples, see E. Anderson, 1990, 1999; Campbell, 1984; Decker and Van Winkle, 1996; Hagedorn, 1988; Jody Miller, 2001; Joan Moore, 1991; Padilla, 1992; M. Sullivan, 1989.

6 Strain Theory

Does Strain or Stress Cause Delinquency?

According to *strain theory*, **when juveniles experience strain or stress, they become upset,** and they sometimes engage in delinquency as a result. They may engage in delinquency to reduce or escape from the strain they are experiencing. For example, they may engage in violence to end harassment from peers; they may steal to reduce their money problems; or they may run away from home to escape abusive parents. They may also perform delinquent acts to seek revenge against those who have "wronged" them. And they may engage in illicit drug use in an effort to feel better. Strain is not the *only* reason that juveniles offend—some delinquencies may be committed for reasons that have little to do with strain or stress. But strain theorists argue that strain plays a key role in many delinquent acts and is therefore a leading cause of delinquency.

After reading this chapter, you should be able to:

- Explain why, according to strain theory, juveniles engage in delinquency.
- Describe the major types of strain associated with delinquency.
- Describe the effects of strain on juveniles, especially their emotional states.
- Identify and provide examples of the coping strategies employed by young people to deal with both strain and the negative emotions produced by strain.
- Explain why only *some* strained youth resort to delinquency.

Many of the delinquent acts that you may have committed or come close to committing can probably be explained by using strain theory. You experienced some type of *strain* or stress; most probably, someone did something to you that you did not like. Perhaps someone insulted you or did not give you something you wanted. You became angry and frustrated as a result, and you thought about or actually committed some delinquent act. In this area, studies indicate that a large number of violent acts start off with one person insulting another or otherwise doing something that the other person does not like.[1]

Some young people are exposed to severe and persistent strains, making a delinquent response even more likely. Consider the following case of Jane, a young woman who experienced severe strain on a daily basis:

> Jane, a sixteen year old girl, ran away from home because of daily physical abuse at the hands of her father and seventeen year old brother. . . . She often tried to stay over at a friend's house to escape her brutal home life. . . . A run away report was made by Jane's father, but Jane stated, "Before I go back there, I'll kill myself." (McFarlane and Miller, 2005:5)

There are several versions of strain theory. The first modern version of strain theory was presented by Robert K. Merton in 1938. To explain crime, Merton's strain theory highlighted one type of strain, involving the inability of individuals to achieve culturally prescribed success goals (or "goal blockage"). According to Merton, American culture encourages everyone to strive for monetary success and upward social mobility even though many lower-class individuals lack the legitimate means necessary to attain such goals. When the success goals of individuals are blocked, they may become frustrated and resort to illegitimate or criminal paths to monetary success, such as drug dealing, theft, or prostitution.

Merton classified such individuals as "innovators"—they pursue unconventional (illegal) paths to success when the socially approved paths are blocked or unavailable. Merton recognized, however, that such innovation is only one possible response to strain. Other responses or adaptations to strain include *conformity* (the continued pursuit of success through legal means, despite the odds), *ritualism* (acceptance of failure, while still obeying society's rules), *retreatism* (in which individuals give up on the culturally prescribed goals and means, perhaps retreating into drug use), and *rebellion* (individuals reject the cultural system that defines certain goals and means as desirable). Nevertheless, while these alternative responses are possible, Merton argued that strain increases the likelihood that at least some people will innovate and resort to crime.

It is important to note that Merton developed his strain theory partly in reaction to pathological theories that were popular in his day, which traced the causes of crime to abnormal psychological or biological characteristics. Merton advanced the opposite view, arguing that crime and delinquency more often represent *normal* reactions, by otherwise *normal* people, to abnormal or stressful conditions (see Merton, 1938:672, note 2). Merton was not trying to say that offending behavior is acceptable or excusable, only that psychological or biological disorder is not a prerequisite, or necessary ingredient, for crime or delinquency to occur. In other words, **strain theory advances the view that otherwise ordinary people can be pressured into crime or delinquency by difficult or frustrating circumstances. In this view, delinquent responses to strain are psychologically understandable and therefore predictable.** (At the same time, certain biological or psychological traits may make a delinquent response especially likely. We discuss this possibility later in the chapter.)

Merton's account was enormously influential and spawned many revised versions of strain theory, the most prominent being those of A. Cohen (1955), Cloward and Ohlin (1960), Greenberg (1977), Elliott et al. (1979), Agnew (1992), Berkowitz (1993), and Colvin (2000). These revised versions identify other important types of strain beyond the inability to achieve monetary success. Although each version of strain theory is unique in some way, all basically try to do two things: **Describe the major types of strain that lead to delinquency, and describe the conditions under which strain is most likely to lead to delinquency.** All strain theorists recognize that strain usually does not lead to delinquency—it does so only under certain conditions. As a consequence, such theorists describe the "conditioning variables" that influence the likelihood that strain will result in delinquency.

Rather than describe each version of strain theory, we present a generic version that incorporates the central arguments of the major strain theories, although this generic theory draws most heavily on Agnew's (1992, 2006a, 2006b) general strain theory.

WHAT ARE THE MAJOR TYPES OF STRAIN?

Researchers often measure strain by presenting juveniles with lists of strainful events and conditions and asking them which events/conditions they have experienced.[2] Certain of these lists contain more than 200 items, including things like parents divorcing, parents arguing or fighting, a close friend dying or becoming seriously ill, not being selected for a much-wanted extracurricular activity, disagreements with teachers, disagreements with friends, breaking up with a romantic partner, and money problems. Theorists have tried to categorize these types of strain in various ways and to list the types of strain that are most strongly related to delinquency. Two general categories of strain have been linked to delinquency: the failure to achieve your goals, and the loss of positive stimuli/presentation of negative stimuli.

The Failure to Achieve Your Goals

All strain theorists argue that a major type of strain is the failure to achieve your goals. And several theorists argue that the inability of adolescents to achieve certain goals contributes to much delinquency. These goals include money, status/respect, thrills/excitement, and autonomy from adults.

Money. Certain strain theorists argue that money is the central goal in the United States (see especially Merton, 1968; Cloward and Ohlin, 1960). All people, poor as well as rich, are encouraged to work hard so that they might make a lot of money. Further, money is necessary to buy many of the things people want, including the necessities of life and all those luxury items to which most people are regularly exposed. Money is said to be important for adolescents as well as for adults, since adolescents need money for such things as clothing, social activities, automobiles, and drugs (see Greenberg, 1977). Many adolescents, however, are not able to obtain the money they need through legal channels, such as parents and work. This inability is especially true of poor adolescents, but it may also be true of many middle-class adolescents. As a consequence, such adolescents experience strain and may attempt to get money through illegal channels, such as theft, selling drugs, and prostitution. Studies provide some support for this argument.

Several field studies have found that criminals and delinquents often report that they engage in income-generating crime because they want money but cannot easily get it any other way.[3] In particular, researchers have asked individuals like burglars, robbers, shoplifters, drug addicts, and prostitutes why they engage in crime. Perhaps the most common response is that they have a **desperate need for money,** and crime is the only way or the easiest way for them to get it. It is important to note, however, that they usually do not need money for necessities like food and shelter; rather, they need it for things like partying, gambling, and drugs. Nevertheless, in their view they desperately need cash.

The fact that some delinquents report monetary strain, however, does not prove that such strain is a cause of delinquency. Many individuals who experience monetary strain do not engage in delinquency. Many of you, for example, have probably been in situations where you wanted more money than you had, yet you did not engage in crime. To establish that monetary strain is a cause of delinquency, criminologists must demonstrate that people who are high in monetary strain are more likely to engage in delinquency than people low in such strain (see the discussion of "association" in Chapter 5). Surprisingly, only a few studies have tried to do this, and most suffer from serious problems.[4] Some data, however, suggest that crime is more common among people who are dissatisfied with their monetary situation; such dissatisfaction is higher among lower-class people and people who state that they want "a lot of money."[5] So there is limited support for the idea that monetary strain is related to delinquency. More research is needed in this area, however.

Status/respect. Closely related to the desire for money is the desire for status and respect (see A. Cohen, 1955). People want to be positively regarded by others and want to be treated respectfully, which at a minimum involves being treated in a just or fair manner (see Agnew, 1992). Data suggest that anger is often the result of disrespectful or unjust treatment (Agnew, 1992, 2006a). Although people have a general desire for status and respect, the desire for "masculine status" is said to be especially relevant to delinquency.[6]

There are class and race differences in views about what it means to be a "man," although most such views emphasize traits like independence, dominance, toughness, competitiveness, and heterosexuality (see Messerschmidt, 1993; Oliver, 1994). Most male juveniles experience difficulties in their desire to be viewed and treated as men, particularly given the emphasis of the school system on docility and submission (see Greenberg, 1977; Messerschmidt, 1993). Certain juveniles, however, experience special difficulties in this area, especially lower-class and minority group members.[7] **Such juveniles may attempt to "accomplish masculinity" through delinquency.** They may engage in delinquent acts to demonstrate that they possess traits like toughness, dominance, and independence. And they may attempt to coerce others into giving them the respect they believe they deserve as "real men." In this connection, they may adopt a tough demeanor, respond to even minor shows of disrespect with violence, and occasionally assault and rob others in an effort to establish a tough reputation. There have been no large-scale tests of this idea, although several field studies provide support for it.[8]

For example, Oliver (1994) conducted intensive interviews with 41 lower-class African American males about their participation in violent events. He discovered, like other researchers, that many of these events were precipitated by what were seen as challenges to masculinity. He asked one of his respondents, "Why do you think so many fights among black males are centered around manhood?" and received the following reply:

> I believe with us, the black man, that our manhood is very important to us. That's about the only thing we have to hold on to—besides our families—is our manhood. And when that's threatened, it's time to fight. "I'm going to show you I'm not a punk," "I'm going to show you I'm not a faggot"—you know, that sort of thing. I've seen fights where words were exchanged for at least ten, fifteen minutes and they just stood there and exchanged words with one another, and one guy told the other guy, "Look, just leave me alone," and the other guy just kept on you know, "Fuck you punk," and the other guy was getting tired of the exchange of words, being called punk, faggot, sissy, so forth, that he just went ahead and punched the guy, and a fight occurred. (Oliver, 1994:90)

There is reason to believe that concern with one's manhood or masculine status is not limited to African American males, although African American males and lower-class males may have more trouble "accomplishing masculinity" through legal channels—as a result of the discrimination and limited opportunities they encounter (see Messerschmidt, 1993). In any event, the previous quote makes clear how threats to one's masculine status sometimes lead to crime.

Thrills/excitement. Individuals who have a strong desire to engage in thrilling or exciting activities are sometimes referred to as "sensation seekers" (see H. White et al., 1985). They gain much pleasure from engaging in risky, even life-threatening activities. As argued in Chapter 13, there is some reason to believe that this desire for thrills/excitement is in part biologically based. In any event, many individuals discover that they have trouble satisfying this desire through legal channels. This may be especially true of juveniles, who are confined in school for much of the day and prevented by adults from engaging in a range of risky behaviors. Such juveniles, then, may attempt to satisfy their desire for thrills/excitement through delinquent acts, like aggression, theft, and drug use. Several studies provide support for this argument. Criminals and delinquents often state that they engage in illegal acts "for the thrill of it" or because of the "rush" they get from it. Further, juveniles with a strong need for thrills and excitement are more likely to engage in delinquency.[9]

To illustrate, J. Katz (1988) asked the students in his criminology classes to report on their shoplifting experiences. He discovered that many of the shoplifting incidents committed by these largely upper-middle-class students were motivated not by material need, but rather seemed to be motivated by a desire for thrills or excitement—as suggested by the following quotes:

> Once outside the door I thought Wow! I pulled it off, I faced danger and I pulled it off. I was smiling and I felt at that moment like there was nothing I couldn't do. (Katz, 1988:64)

> The experience was almost orgasmic for me. There was a build up of tension as I contemplated the danger of the forbidden act, then a rush of excitement at the moment of committing the crime, and finally a delicious sense of release. (Katz, 1988:71)

Autonomy from adults. Several researchers have argued that a major goal of most adolescents is to achieve autonomy from adults.[10] Autonomy may be defined as freedom from the control of others. Adolescents come to desire autonomy as they physically and socially mature. Adults, however, often deny adolescents the autonomy they desire. Although adolescents have more autonomy than children, their behavior is still subject to much control; a broad range of behaviors are prohibited or restricted. Most notably, adolescents find their desire for autonomy frustrated in the school system with its extensive regulations and emphasis on authoritarian styles of teaching (see Greenberg, 1977). Parents may also continue to restrict the freedom of adolescents. The denial of autonomy may lead to delinquency for several reasons: delinquency may be a means of asserting autonomy (e.g., sexual intercourse or disorderly behavior), achieving autonomy (e.g., stealing money to gain financial independence from parents), or venting frustration against those who deny autonomy.

Some data support these arguments. Adolescents often demand greater autonomy from parents and teachers, and they frequently clash with these individuals over issues involving autonomy. Such issues include doing chores, clothing, appearance, schoolwork, interpersonal relations, and rules for such things as bedtime and curfew (see Agnew, 1997). Agnew (1984) examined the relationship between the need for autonomy and delinquency and found that adolescents with a strong need for autonomy were angrier and more frustrated and, partly as a consequence, more likely to engage in delinquency than other adolescents (also see Brezina, 2008; Chen, 2010; A. Piquero and Brezina, 2001).

Strain, then, may result from the failure to achieve one's goals. We have listed four goals that are said to be important to most adolescents: money, status/respect, thrills/excitement, and autonomy from adults. Strain may also result from the failure to achieve other goals, and thus any test of strain theory should attempt to determine what goals the people being examined consider important. For example, one goal that many college students consider important is good grades. And many college students experience strain when they find that they are unable to achieve this goal through legitimate channels—like studying. We have the students in our juvenile delinquency courses fill out a survey on the first day of class; among other things, we ask them what grade they would ideally like to get in the class and what grade they realistically expect to get. Not surprisingly, almost all the students state that they would ideally like to get an A (sometimes one or two students with more modest ambitions state that they would like a B). Such ideal goals have something of the utopian in them and probably are not taken seriously by many students. We find, however, that roughly 70 percent of the students state that they realistically expect to get an A. The percentage of students who actually end up getting an A, however, is usually between 25 and 30 percent. Many students thus experience strain. Based on existing research (Ford and Schroeder, 2009), we suspect that some of these students respond to such strain with deviance, such as cheating on exams or excessive alcohol use.

In one such course, we administered an anonymous survey to learn more about the reasons that students give for academic cheating. Here is how some of our own students explained their cheating behavior:

> It is very important to get high marks in college. [I cheated because] I felt the pressure to do well, but didn't have enough time to study. (Brezina, 2000b:74)

> A bad professor gave an unreasonable assignment. I felt like I had no choice but to cheat to get a decent grade. (Brezina, 2000b:74)

Note how both quotes refer to goal blockage; in this case, the perceived inability to achieve good grades through legitimate means.

Many of the same students said they knew cheating was wrong, but they cheated nonetheless. Some students said they felt guilty or ashamed as a result of their cheating. These observations suggest that, for some individuals, the experience of strain may be sufficient to overpower their better judgment, at least temporarily. Perhaps we can all relate to this phenomenon. When we become angry or frustrated in response to goal blockage or other type of strain, we may say or do things we later regret. When looking back on our regrettable behavior, we may explain to others or to ourselves that "I was not myself" or "I lost my head." As stated earlier, strain theorists argue that strain increases the likelihood of delinquency or "acting out" even among otherwise normal individuals.

Loss of Positive Stimuli/Presentation of Negative Stimuli

The types of strain described thus far all involve what might be called "nonevents." The individual wants or expects something—like money or autonomy or a good grade—but does not get it. The second major category of strain involves negative events or conditions. Juveniles lose something they value (*loss of positive stimuli*) or are *presented with noxious or negative stimuli*. For example, the juvenile may break up with a boyfriend or girlfriend, someone may take something from the juvenile, or someone may insult or physically assault the juvenile. In short, people treat the juvenile in a negative manner—in a way that she or he does not like. Such negative treatment may upset or anger the juvenile and, as indicated earlier, delinquency may be the result.

Several studies have asked juveniles about the types of events that anger or upset them (see Agnew, 1997, for an overview). The answers inevitably focus on interpersonal problems, typically interpersonal problems with parents, siblings, teachers, friends, and romantic partners. Juveniles report that they became angry or upset because these others insulted them, physically assaulted them, disciplined or sanctioned them when they did not deserve it, pressured them, overburdened them, got into conflicts with them, or rejected them. Studies have found that many of these negative events and conditions increase the likelihood of delinquency. This is especially true of those events and conditions that are likely to be viewed as unjust and serious in nature.

In particular, **delinquency has been linked to the following types of negative treatment** (see especially Agnew, 2001a, 2001b, 2006a):

1. **Parental rejection.** Parents who reject their children show little interest in them, provide little support and affection to them, and often display hostility toward them (see Chapter 14).

2. **Parental supervision and discipline that is very strict, erratic, excessive given the infraction, and/or harsh (use of humiliation, insults, threats, screaming, and/or physical punishments)** (see Chapter 14).

3. **Child abuse and neglect.** See Chapter 14.

4. **Negative school experiences.** These include low grades, poor relations with teachers (e.g., teachers treat the juvenile unfairly, belittle or humiliate the juvenile), and the experience of school as boring and a waste of time (see Chapter 15).

5. **Abusive peer relations.** These include insults and ridicule, gossip, threats, attempts to coerce, and physical assaults.[11]

6. **Criminal victimization.** Many studies suggest that being the victim of a crime, especially a violent crime, substantially increases the likelihood of offending.[12]

7. **Homelessness.** Youths living on the street encounter a broad range of strains or stresses, like the inability to obtain food and shelter, frequent conflicts with others, and criminal victimization (Hagan and McCarthy, 1997a; Hoyt et al., 1999).

8. **Experiences with prejudice and discrimination based on ascribed characteristics like gender and race/ethnicity.**[13]

A study by Wilkinson (2002) illustrates some of these strains, especially abusive peer relations and criminal victimization. The study involved intensive interviews with 125 adolescent males who had recently committed violent acts. The interviews suggested that these acts were usually prompted by strains like the following:

- a range of abusive behaviors that made the respondent feel "dissed, challenged, or played," with such behaviors including insults, bumps, "grilling" (staring at the respondent in a way seen as inappropriate), and threats;
- competition over girls, including advances on "one's girl" by another man;
- physical attacks;
- material attacks, including the theft or attempted theft of one's possessions; and
- disputes centered on the drug trade, including attempted robberies, turf disputes, and disputes over the price, quantity, or quality of the drugs being sold.

Jody Miller's (2001) field study of female gang members in St. Louis and Columbus indicates that these sorts of strains are not limited to males. For example, Miller (2001:116) states:

> Young women acknowledged that male–female relationships were often a source of strife between and among gang members. Most often, they described the source of conflict as two girls fighting over a particular boy. . . . Tonya recalled when "this girl named Patricia threatened a girl named Dana 'cause she tried to take her dude." . . . Alecia said members of her gang, the 2–1s, often fought with female members of the 2–2s because young women in both groups competed for the attention of male members of 2–2.

For more on gender, strain, and delinquency, see Box 6.1.

Box 6.1   Gender, Strain, and Delinquency

As described in Chapter 4, males have a higher rate of delinquency than females and this is especially true for serious offenses. Strain theory can be used to explain the gender difference we observe in delinquent behavior (Broidy and Agnew, 1997).

In studies that examine a wide range of stressful life events, females typically report that they experience as many stressors as males. So the high rate of male offending cannot be explained in terms of gender differences in the overall level of stress or strain. In fact, some studies find that females experience a greater number of stressful life events. Strain theorists, however, highlight gender differences in the *types* of stressors that individuals experience.

It is said that males are more likely than females to experience those stressors that are especially conducive to offending, including stressors that are likely to be seen as unjust, severe, and that create some incentive or pressure to engage in delinquency. For example, data indicate that males are more likely than females to be punished harshly, to have negative experiences at school, to experience violent victimization, and to be homeless (Agnew, 2006a). Females, of course, experience many of these same strains, but not at the same rate as males (see Chapter 18 for a special note on the role of sexual abuse in the development of female delinquency). So one reason that strain theorists give for the high rate of male offending is that, generally speaking, males are more likely than females to experience the types of strain that are most likely to lead to delinquency.

(Continued)

(Continued)

A second reason for the high rate of male delinquency involves gender differences in the response to strain. According to strain theorists, the high rate of male offending is due, in part, to the fact that males are more likely than females to deal with strain by resorting to delinquent coping strategies. This fact is related to the different ways that males and females tend to react to strain. Females, for example, may tend to blame themselves for the experience of strain and may be more likely to react with some combination of anger, depression, fear, anxiety, and shame. In contrast, it is said that males are relatively quick to blame others, to view negative experiences as a challenge or insult, and to react with moral outrage. The experience of moral outrage, in turn, is especially conducive to serious violence and property offenses (for more on gender differences in the reaction to strain, see Agnew, 2006a).

Thus, according to strain theorists, the experience of strain is "gendered," as is the relationship between strain and offending: males are more likely to experience those strains conducive to delinquency and to cope with them in a delinquent manner. Initial studies provide some support for these arguments, although the research findings are mixed. For instance, in comparison to females, some studies find that males experience a higher level of physical punishment and violent victimization (Hay, 2003; Kaufman, 2009). Although females tend to experience about the same level of anger in response to strain, some studies find that, in comparison to males, females are more likely to experience nonangry emotions along with anger, such as fear, anxiety, and depression. Nonangry emotions, in turn, tend to reduce the likelihood of delinquent coping (Ganem, 2010; but see De Coster and Zito, 2010). Overall, in response to strain, it appears that females are more likely than males to adopt legitimate, nondelinquent coping responses (for reviews, see De Coster and Zito, 2010; Ngo and Paternoster, 2013; for more on the explanation of gender differences in offending, see Chapter 18).

Questions for Discussion

1. Relative to males, what types of strain might females experience at a higher rate? When you think of strains that may be especially relevant to female offending, what types of strain come to mind?
2. When answering the questions above, did you consider gender discrimination, partner abuse, or sexual abuse? Would you classify any of these strains as being conducive to crime or delinquency? Explain.
3. Some gender theorists argue that, relative to males, females tend to be more concerned about protecting and maintaining their relationships with others. Males, in contrast, are said to be less concerned with others, as males often believe that they are (or should be) tough, independent, and competitive. Assuming these generalizations are valid, how would these different gender orientations affect the reaction to strain, and the likelihood of a delinquent response?

WHAT IMPACT DOES STRAIN HAVE ON THE JUVENILE?

Strainful events and conditions make juveniles feel bad—angry, frustrated, depressed, anxious, and the like. These negative feelings, in turn, create pressure for corrective action. That is, juveniles want to do something to alleviate their bad feelings. And delinquency is one possible response. The emotions of anger and frustration are said to be especially conducive to a delinquent response, since they energize the individual for action, create a desire for revenge, and lower inhibitions. And certain studies indicate that strain increases the likelihood of delinquency partly because it increases the adolescent's level of anger/ frustration.[14]

It is important to emphasize, however, that there are **several possible ways to cope with strain and the negative emotions associated with strain. Only some of these coping strategies involve delinquency.**

Adolescents may cope by **cognitively reinterpreting the strain they experience so as to minimize its impact.** Agnew (1992) lists three major *cognitive coping* strategies, summarized in these phrases: "It's not that important." "It's not that bad." "I deserve it." Imagine, for example, an individual who is unable to achieve his monetary goals. This individual may minimize the failure to obtain enough money by claiming that money is not that important, perhaps claiming that other goals, such as having good friends, are more important. Or this individual may come to exaggerate the amount of money he has, claiming that he really has enough money to satisfy his needs. Or this individual may state that he is to blame for his lack of money. This may not reduce feelings of depression, but it is likely to reduce anger at others. All these cognitive coping strategies reduce the likelihood that individuals who use them will react to strain with delinquency.

Adolescents may also employ *behavioral coping* **strategies, attempting to act in ways that reduce the strain they are experiencing. Certain of these strategies may involve nondelinquent behavior.** Adolescents, for example, may get a job to earn money; they may avoid the peers who harass them; or they may negotiate with the teachers who frustrate them. **Other behavioral strategies for reducing strain, as indicated earlier, involve delinquency** (e.g., stealing money or attacking the peers who harass you).

Some studies find that such delinquent strategies may "work" for the offender, providing short-term relief from strain or negative emotions (for a review, see Brezina, 2000a). For example, when participants in a laboratory experiment were angered, the participants who retaliated with aggression experienced a subsequent reduction in angry arousal (see Patterson, 1982:146–147). In other words, strained and angry individuals may experience a certain amount of emotional relief or satisfaction when they attack the perceived source of strain, at least in the short run. This fact may help explain the appeal of delinquent coping for many strained adolescents.

Finally, adolescents may engage in *emotional coping*. Rather than trying to reduce their strain or cognitively reinterpret it, they act directly on the negative emotions that result from strain. They may attempt to reduce their negative emotions through **nondelinquent strategies** like exercise, deep breathing, listening to music, or other relaxation techniques. Or they may employ **delinquent strategies**, such as the use of illegal drugs (see Box 6.2).

The existence of these different coping strategies, some involving delinquency and some not, raises a major question for strain theorists.

Box 6.2   Coping with Strain: The Role of Drugs and Alcohol

Adolescents experiment with drugs and alcohol for a variety of reasons. Consistent with strain theory, it appears that *some* of these reasons involve attempts to cope with strain or stress. In a study titled, "Why Do Adolescents Use Drugs?," Jill Novacek (1991:483–488) and her associates surveyed several thousand adolescents to learn more about their motives for substance use and abuse. They find the "day-to-day struggle to cope" to be a common theme in the reports of regular users. The young people in their survey frequently stated that they used drugs or alcohol to "escape from my problems," "to get along in the world," "to relieve nervousness," and "because

(Continued)

(Continued)

I was depressed." Moreover, some studies observe a statistical relationship between strain and adolescent drug use: young people who report high levels of strain tend to be frequent users of drugs and alcohol, even after controlling for other relevant factors (Agnew and White, 1992; Carson et al., 2009; Ford and Schroeder, 2009).

It is not too difficult to understand the seductive appeal of drugs and alcohol among strained, nervous, and depressed adolescents. Other research indicates that the use of drugs and alcohol can provide short-term relief from depression and despair, allowing individuals to "self-medicate" (for a review, see Brezina, 2000a). Of course, a strategy of self-medication may only create more problems in the long run and lead to drug or alcohol dependency.

Questions for Discussion

1. Substance abusers may find it very difficult to avoid drugs or alcohol, even when loved ones plead with them to stop using. How might strain theorists explain this fact?
2. To reduce the problem of adolescent substance abuse, what strategies do you think strain theorists would recommend?

WHY ARE SOME JUVENILES MORE LIKELY TO COPE WITH STRAIN THROUGH DELINQUENCY?

Strain theorists have argued that several factors influence whether or not people will respond to strain with delinquency (see Agnew, 1992, 2001b, 2006a, 2006b; Agnew et al., 2001).

Strain is more likely to lead to delinquency when it involves areas of life that the individual considers important. For example, challenges to masculinity are more likely to result in delinquency among individuals who attach great importance to their masculine identity. Likewise, threats to autonomy are more likely to lead to delinquency among individuals who strongly desire autonomy. If strain affects a central area of a person's life, it will be more difficult to ignore it or define it away by using the cognitive strategies described in the preceding section.

Strain is more likely to lead to delinquency among individuals with poor *coping skills* **and resources.** Some individuals are better able to legally cope with strain than others. For example, they have the verbal skills to negotiate with peers and adults, or they have a high level of "self-efficacy," believing that they have the ability to solve their problems. A variety of factors influence an individual's ability to legally cope, including financial resources, intelligence, problem-solving skills, interpersonal skills, and self-efficacy. Individuals who lack these skills and resources, however, may find that delinquency is the only way they can cope with their strain.

Strain is more likely to lead to delinquency among individuals with few *conventional social supports*. Family, friends, and others often help us cope with our strain, providing advice, direct assistance, and emotional support. Individuals who lack such supports are more likely to find themselves in a situation where delinquency is their only means of coping (see Cullen, 1994).

Strain is more likely to lead to delinquency when the costs of delinquent coping are low and the benefits are high. In particular, delinquent coping is more likely when the juvenile has little to lose from delinquency, does not believe that delinquency is wrong in her particular case, and is in a situation where the likelihood of getting caught and sanctioned in a meaningful manner is low. Delinquent coping is also more likely when the juvenile believes that delinquency will result in certain benefits, like the reduction of her strain (see Brezina, 2000a). As a simple illustration, strain theory would predict that people are more likely to respond to monetary strain with theft if they encounter an open cash register and no one is around.

Finally, strain is more likely to lead to delinquency among individuals who are disposed to delinquency: that is, among individuals who have a preexisting tendency to engage in delinquent behavior. The individual's disposition to engage in delinquency is influenced by a number of factors (see Agnew, 1992, 2001a). Among other things, individuals are more disposed to respond to their strain with delinquency if they were reinforced for delinquent responses in the past, if they have been exposed to models who have responded to similar strains with delinquency, and if they believe that delinquency is a desirable or justifiable response in their situation. Individuals are also more disposed to respond to strain with delinquency if they possess certain personality traits, like irritability and low self-control (see Chapter 13). Individuals with these traits are easily upset and have trouble controlling themselves.

A variety of factors, then, may influence whether individuals respond to strain with delinquency. Research on whether these factors do in fact condition the effect of strain on delinquency has produced mixed results. **Some studies find that the sorts of factors just listed increase the likelihood that individuals will respond to strain with delinquency.** For example, Mazerolle and Maahs (2000) found that strain was more likely to lead to delinquency when juveniles associated with delinquent peers and had weak moral beliefs (did not strongly condemn delinquency). And Agnew et al. (2001) found that strain was more likely to lead to delinquency among individuals who were irritable and low in self-control. But other studies have failed to find the expected patterns.[15]

It is possible that a delinquent response to strain is most likely when *multiple* factors are present: that is, when strained individuals possess *many* of the factors just listed—not just one or two (Agnew, 2013). Gang members, for example, are likely to have strong ties to delinquent peers and to be exposed to others who model delinquent responses to strain. In addition, they may have poor coping skills and resources and may be in situations where delinquency is rewarded. For a number of reasons, then, gang members can be expected to have a strong tendency to cope with strain in a delinquent manner. Researchers are now exploring this possibility, although a good test of the idea has yet to be conducted (see Brezina, 2017).

SUMMARY

At its core, strain theory is rather simple: strain makes people upset, and they **may** respond with delinquency (see Figure 6.1). As you can see, however, this rather simple idea has been the subject of much elaboration. In particular, there has been much discussion of the major types of strain that contribute to delinquency and the factors that condition the effect of strain on delinquency. The data provide some support for strain theory, suggesting that the inability to achieve certain goals and the experience of certain negative events increase the likelihood of delinquency. The research on factors predicted to condition the effect of strain on delinquency has been more mixed, but recent data suggest that at least some of these factors increase the likelihood that juveniles will respond to strain with delinquency.

TEACHING AIDS
Case Studies

Cases involving juvenile violence are regularly in the news. News reports frequently indicate that the perpetrators of such violence have often been the victims of peer abuse, an assertion supported by surveys and field studies of violent juveniles (e.g., Lockwood, 1997;

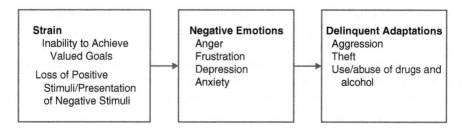

FIGURE 6.1 A Simple Diagram Illustrating the Core Arguments of Strain Theory

Wilkinson, 2002, 2003). Not long ago, we read a news account about two teenagers who were arrested for planning a "Columbine-style" attack on their high school. Officials allege that the two teens plotted to kill students and staff using shotguns and explosives, before killing themselves. The article focused on one of the teenagers who had been arrested, reporting that he wanted to kill classmates who had teased him about living in a trailer park. According to the boy's lawyer, he was constantly taunted by his classmates for being "trailer trash" (Associated Press, 2007). Such teasing, of course, does not justify the mass slaughter that the teenagers were allegedly planning. Other cases, however, cause one to wonder about the extent to which the strain or abuse suffered by certain juvenile offenders should be taken into account when sanctioning them. A few such cases follow. What is your reaction to them? To what extent do you think we should take account of the strain suffered by juvenile offenders when deciding how to respond to them?

Case 1. The sexual exploitation of children has received much attention in our home state of Georgia. Traditionally, many child prostitutes were arrested, placed in youth detention centers while they awaited court processing, and sometimes sanctioned by being sent to juvenile institutions. (Note: See the discussion of gender and delinquency in Chapter 18.) This approach has changed dramatically in recent years. The state passed tougher laws against those who exploit children. The state also enacted laws that encourage law enforcement agencies to view child prostitutes as "victims of human trafficking" rather than "juvenile delinquents in need of punishment." In addition, funds have been set aside for safe homes, where victims can obtain food, shelter, and counseling. These changes were prompted, in part, by media coverage of the problem, especially graphic newspaper accounts of children such as "Natalie":

> Natalie's story puts a human face on the issue of prostituted children... Natalie is no longer prostituting. She and her parents and older sister are in counseling, and Natalie says she's coping with anger and depression. "It was traumatizing what I went through and what other girls went through," she said. . . . She says she ran away [at age 15] because of pressures at home and at school. She lost her virginity to [a pimp] who raped her soon after she left home the first time. She never knew his name. She escaped from him, but ended up with another pimp, an 18-year-old who cut Natalie's hair and put her into skimpy clothes. . . . She admits she fell hard for her pimp. "He said I wouldn't have to do this forever and that he hits me because he loves me," Natalie recalled. "I believed it. I bought into all of it. My brain shut off. I didn't care about having to do prostitution for him. I felt devoted to him and wanted to do everything to be with him."
>
> The men who paid Natalie for sex "were mostly white and Mexican guys, with some Asians. They were college students, to guys in their 70s," she said. Most had girlfriends or wives.

Natalie remembers getting her last phone call from a man looking for a "date." "He sounded perfectly fine. He didn't sound sketched out at all," Natalie said of the man who turned out to be an undercover police detective. Natalie was taken into custody, and her pimp was arrested when they showed up at a local hotel for Natalie's prearranged date. The family is slowly putting the pieces of their lives back together, but it's been a struggle, Natalie's mom said. Natalie hopes to return to high school in the fall. (Green, 2011)

Case 2. A guest editorial in our local newspaper discussed the reasons for some of the incidents of school violence that periodically make the headlines. Selections from this editorial follow.

The media keep asking "Why?" They have been told, but they refuse to hear. They bring out experts. "It's the guns. The video games, movies, and CDs!" they say. But those people who have the privilege of being asked to give their opinions to a national audience are probably the same ones who had the privilege of growing up popular. Those of us who didn't can understand. . . . I remember once as a freshman, the varsity jocks hung me up on a coat hook in the locker room. The coach thought it was funny. There were no repercussions for their actions. As a 5 foot 2 sophomore, a football player didn't like something I said to him, and the result was my trip to the hospital for a fractured clavicle. The police weren't even called. . . . To this day, when I hear of these horrible shootings, I know right away the answer to the question, "Why?" When a person has so much power over you that they feel that they can do anything to you and get away with it, no matter whom you turn to . . . what are you supposed to do? You can't leave. You can't walk away. You have only one option: Remove the menace yourself. As rational adults, we can argue that there are always options. The confused teenager does not see that. . . . When I was a teenager, I got a gun. I had it in my pants at a movie theater when I saw one of my regular tormentors. By the grace of God, this guy wasn't in the mood to confront me that night. . . . Later that night. . . . I realized what could have happened. . . . That kid is lucky to be alive. If he had died, he would have had himself to blame as much as me. (Honohan, 2001) (Note: See the discussion of antibullying programs in Chapter 24.)

Web-Based Exercise: Applying Strain Theory

The theories or explanations of delinquency described in this text are all illustrated in popular songs, both past and present. Drawing on YouTube, iTunes, or another web source, find a song that illustrates strain theory. A good example is "Runaway Love" by Ludacris, although there are many other songs relevant to strain theory. (If your instructor allows it, a few students might play the songs they selected in class; it helps if they also show the lyrics to the songs.) Then ask: What strains are illustrated in the song? What impact do these strains have on the person(s) experiencing them? What are some of the reasons why this person(s) may have coped with the strains through delinquency? This exercise can also be used with the other theories you will examine.

TEST YOUR KNOWLEDGE OF THIS CHAPTER

1. Describe the essential arguments of strain theory in a few sentences, explaining why strain increases the likelihood of delinquency.
2. Each version of strain theory tries to do two things. What are they?
3. What are the two major types of strain?

4. The failure to achieve four goals is said to contribute to much delinquency. What are these goals?

5. List four of the negative events or conditions that contribute to delinquency.

6. Describe the major ways in which individuals cope with strain and the negative emotions associated with strain.

7. What factors increase the likelihood that juveniles will cope with strain through delinquency?

THOUGHT AND DISCUSSION QUESTIONS

1. How might strain theory explain forms of deviance like cheating and excessive drinking on college campuses?

2. Develop a set of survey questions that measure the key independent and conditioning variables in the explanations for cheating and excessive drinking that you developed in question 1.

3. How might strain theory explain school violence? (Note: See Brezina et al., 2001.)

4. What recommendations based on strain theory would you make for reducing crime? (Note: See Agnew, 2001a.)

5. Some students may worry that strain theory provides excuses for offenders. For example, defense lawyers have been known to use the "abuse excuse" in courts, arguing that their clients should be held less responsible because of past child abuse. Do you believe it is the intent of strain theorists to provide excuses for offenders? Is it possible to view strain or abuse as a cause of delinquency, and at the same time hold young people accountable for their actions? (Note: See Box 5.1 in Chapter 5.)

KEY TERMS

- Strain theory
- Strain
- Loss of positive stimuli and presentation of negative stimuli
- Cognitive coping
- Behavioral coping
- Emotional coping
- Coping skills
- Conventional social supports

ENDNOTES

1. See R. Felson, 1993; R. Felson and Steadman, 1983; Lockwood, 1997; Luckenbill, 1977; Oliver, 1994; Wilkinson, 2002, 2003.

2. See Agnew, 2006a; Compas, 1987; Kohn and Milrose, 1993; Williams and Uchiyama, 1989.

3. See Agnew, 2006c; E. Anderson, 1990; Jankowsi, 1995; MacLeod, 1995; Padilla, 1992; Sullivan, 1989; R. Wright and Decker, 1997.

4. See Agnew, 1994a, 1995b; Agnew et al., 1996; Burton and Cullen, 1992; Rebellon et al., 2009.

5. See Agnew, 1994a:423–426, 2006a; Agnew et al., 1996; S. Baron, 2004, 2007; Burton and Dunaway, 1994; B. Wright et al., 1999a.

6. See Agnew, 1997, 2006a; E. Anderson, 1994, 1999; Greenberg, 1977; Majors and Billson, 1992; Messerschmidt, 1993; Oliver, 1994.

7. See Agnew, 2006a; E. Anderson, 1994, 1999; Greenberg, 1977; Majors and Billson, 1992; Messerschmidt, 1993.

8. See Anderson, 1994, 1997, 1999; Bucher, 2011; Fagan, 1998; Majors and Billson, 1992; Messerschmidt, 1993; Oliver, 1994; for relevant quantitative studies, see Kreager, 2007; Krienert, 2003.

9. See Agnew, 2006a; Le Corff and Toupin, 2009; H. White et al., 1985; P. Wood et al., 1997; P. Wood et al., 1993.

10. See Agnew, 1997; Greenberg, 1977; Moffitt, 1993, 1997.

11. See Agnew, 2006a; Colvin, 2000; De Coster and Kort-Bulter, 2006; Hay et al., 2010; Lockwood, 1997; Rusby et al., 2005; L. Wallace et al., 2005; Wilkinson, 2002; but see Moon et al., 2009.

12. See Agnew, 2002, 2006a, 2006b; Begle et al., 2011; Carson et al., 2009; Eitle and Turner, 2002; Hay and Evans, 2006; Kaufman, 2005, 2009; Manasse and Ganem, 2009; Shaffer and Ruback, 2002; Spano et al., 2006.

13. See Agnew, 2006a, 2006b; Burt et al., 2012; Eitle, 2002; R. Katz, 2000; Martin et al., 2010; McCord and Ensminger, 2003; Simons et al., 2003; Unnever et al., 2009.

14. See Agnew, 1985a, 1992, 1997, 2001a, 2006a, 2006b; Agnew and Brezina, 1997; Agnew and White, 1992; Aseltine et al., 2000; S. Baron and Hartnagel, 1997; Brezina, 1998; Broidy, 2001; Capowich et al., 2001; Ellwanger, 2007; Hagan and McCarthy, 1997a; Hay, 2003; Hay and Evans, 2006; Hoffmann and Cerbone, 1999; Hoffmann and Miller, 1998; Jang and Johnson, 2003; Landau, 1998; Mazerolle and Piquero, 1997, 1998; Mazerolle et al., 2003; Moon et al., 2009; Paternoster and Mazerolle, 1994; N. Piquero and Sealock, 2000, 2004.

15. See Agnew, 2001a, 2006a, 2006b; Agnew and White, 1992; Aseltine et al., 2000; Bao et al., 2007; S. Baron, 2004, 2007; S. Baron and Hartnagel, 2002; Capowich et al., 2001; Hay and Evans, 2006; Hoffmann and Cerbone, 1999; Hoffmann and Miller, 1998; Hoffmann and Su, 1997; Jang and Johnson, 2003; M. Johnson and Kercher, 2007; Mazerolle and Piquero, 1997; Moon et al., 2009; Paternoster and Mazerolle, 1994.

7 Social Learning Theory

Do Individuals Learn to Be Delinquent from Others?

*S*ocial learning theory **says that juveniles learn to engage in delinquency from others.** These others reinforce juveniles for delinquency, teach them beliefs that are favorable to delinquency, and expose them to delinquent models. As a consequence, the juveniles come to view delinquency as something that is desirable or at least justifiable in certain situations.

After reading this chapter, you should be able to:

- Use social learning theory to explain why juveniles engage in delinquency.
- Describe the mechanisms by which individuals learn to engage in delinquency.
- Discuss how reinforcements and punishments encourage and/or discourage delinquent behavior.
- Explain the difference between negative and positive reinforcement and negative and positive punishment.
- Describe the types of beliefs conducive to delinquency.
- Identify the conditions under which individuals are most likely to imitate a model.

Consider the words of the following gang member, describing how he first became attracted to gang life:

> [In elementary school] I was really into my studies, and I didn't get involved in any stuff that the gang was doing. But then I began to see that they had the girls, that people listened to them, and stuff like that. I never expected to become one of them . . . [but] I kind of admired what they stood for and the way people used to like them. (Padilla, 1992:60–90)

Consistent with social learning theory, this quote suggests that exposure to delinquent peers eventually led the boy to view gang life as something desirable or rewarding. Presumably, this view contributed to the boy's future gang involvement. He went on to describe how he was later recruited into a gang:

> [O]ne day I met this [older] guy . . . he had been in the gang all his life. . . . After a while he started teaching me the tricks, how to burn people, how to deal, how to do this, and I made him lots of money. He started turning me on to the gangs, the colors, the hand signals, and everything—how it was done, how you shook someone's hand when you were on the street, and who to eye for. (Padilla, 1992:60–90)

The primary version of social learning theory in criminology is that of Akers, and the description that follows draws heavily on his work (Akers, 1985, 1998; Akers and Jensen, 2003; Akers et al., 2016; also see Bandura, 1973, 1986; Patterson et al., 1992). Akers's theory, in turn, represents a reformulation and elaboration of Sutherland's differential association theory (see Matsueda, 1988; Sutherland et al., 1992).

Edwin H. Sutherland was a pioneer in the field of criminology. The influence of his "differential association" theory of crime, presented in its final form in 1947, is still felt today. In his theory, Sutherland emphasized the role of socialization in the development of criminal behavior as opposed to mental defects or genetic influences. Specifically, he argued that criminal behavior is learned through communication and interaction with others. Further, Sutherland asserted that offenders learn the techniques of committing crime as well as the attitudes and rationalizations that promote criminality. He did not specify exactly how such things are learned, however.

Drawing on subsequent developments in behavioral psychology, Burgess and Akers (1966) elaborated on differential association theory by identifying the specific mechanisms by which individuals learn criminal and delinquent behavior. For example, they argued that much learning takes place via "operant conditioning": individuals tend to repeat behaviors that are rewarded and avoid behaviors that are punished. This elaborated version of differential association theory is known as the Akers social learning theory and is currently a leading theory of crime and delinquency. In this chapter, we describe the theory in some detail, along with the various learning mechanisms that Akers and his colleagues helped identify.

JUVENILES LEARN TO ENGAGE IN DELINQUENCY FROM OTHERS

According to social learning theory, juveniles learn to engage in delinquent behavior in the same way they learn to engage in conforming behavior: through association with or exposure to others. Primary or intimate groups like the family and peer group have an especially large impact on what juveniles learn. This is not surprising, since juveniles usually spend a lot of time with family members and friends and are quite close to them. Juveniles also learn how to behave from people in their school, religious community, neighborhood, and other settings. Further, juveniles do not have to be in direct contact with others to learn from them; for example, they may learn from observing people in the media or interacting with others via the internet.

Whether juveniles learn to conform or engage in delinquency depends primarily on the nature of the people they associate with. If they associate with others who engage in delinquency/crime and hold beliefs favorable to delinquency, they are likely to learn to engage in delinquency. In this area, data indicate that juveniles are much more likely to engage in delinquency if intimate others like their friends, parents, and siblings engage in delinquency/crime. In fact, having delinquent friends is perhaps the strongest predictor of subsequent delinquency, other than prior delinquency (see Chapter 16 for a fuller discussion).[1]

The fact that associating with delinquent others increases the likelihood of delinquency provides strong support for social learning theory, but it does not prove that the theory is correct. Associating with delinquent others may increase delinquency for reasons related to strain or other theories (see Agnew, 1995a; Warr, 2002). For example, juveniles who associate with delinquent peers may be more likely to engage in delinquency because they are higher in strain; delinquent peers are more likely to abuse one another and get into conflicts with outsiders (see Colvin, 2000:72–81; Chapter 16). To prove that social learning theory is correct, we would have to demonstrate that juveniles **learn** to engage in delinquency from delinquent others.

Much of social learning theory involves a description of the mechanisms by which juveniles learn to engage in delinquency from others. According to the theory, juveniles learn to engage in delinquency when others (1) differentially reinforce their delinquent behavior, (2) teach them beliefs favorable to delinquency, and (3) provide delinquent models for them to imitate. We describe each of these learning mechanisms next and examine what the research says about their role in fostering delinquency.

The Differential Reinforcement of Delinquency

Other individuals may teach us to engage in delinquency through the reinforcements and punishments they provide for our behavior. **We are more likely to engage in delinquency when others have reinforced our delinquency in the past and we anticipate that they will continue to reinforce our delinquency.** Let us illustrate this point with a simple example. When Jody Miller (2001) asked certain female gang members in her study why they sometimes sell drugs, they told her that they do it for the money (a major reinforcer). In the words of one gang member:

> They just sell it [drugs] to get them some money 'cause they need some. Whatever they need they'll make the money and then probably won't sell drugs no more until they

need something else. And then they'll just go buy them some drugs and sell it and that's it. (Miller, 2001:145)

So these gang members sell drugs because doing so has been reinforced in the past with money and they anticipate that drug selling will continue to be reinforced with money. Social learning theory, however, has taken this simple idea—that we are more likely to engage in delinquency when it is rewarded or reinforced—and elaborated on it in several important ways.

The Frequency, Amount, and Relative Probability of Reinforcement

Social learning theory argues that reinforcement is not an all-or-nothing matter. In particular, if we want to best predict delinquency, we need to examine the *frequency* with which it is reinforced, the *amount* of reinforcement received or expected, and the *relative probability of reinforcement*. Delinquent behavior is more likely to occur when it (1) is frequently reinforced and infrequently punished; (2) results or is expected to result in large amounts of reinforcement (e.g., a lot of money, social approval, or pleasure) and little punishment; and (3) is more likely to be reinforced than alternative behaviors.

These three factors—the frequency, amount, and relative probability of reinforcement/ punishment—are easy to understand if you think of a concrete example. Let's begin with the frequency of reinforcement and punishment. This simply means that juveniles are more likely to commit a delinquent act like fighting if they are frequently reinforced and seldom punished for fighting. Juveniles who win most of their fights and receive praise from their friends are more likely to fight than juveniles who lose most of their fights and are ridiculed. We tend to repeat behaviors that are reinforced and avoid those that are punished. As for the amount of reinforcement and punishment, juveniles who receive or expect to receive a lot of reinforcement and little punishment for fighting are more likely to fight than juveniles who receive little reinforcement and much punishment. The relative probability of reinforcement refers to the likelihood that delinquent acts will be reinforced relative to other behaviors. For example, juveniles who get into conflicts with others might resolve these conflicts through fighting or through negotiation. They are more likely to choose fighting if fighting is more likely to result in reinforcement than negotiation. The term *differential reinforcement* means simply that different behaviors have different probabilities of being reinforced. We are more likely to engage in behaviors with the highest probabilities of reinforcement. We encourage you to think of additional examples involving the frequency, amount, and relative probability of reinforcement/punishment.

Positive and Negative Reinforcement

Reinforcement may be positive or negative. In *positive reinforcement*, **the behavior results in something good—some positive consequence.** This consequence may be in the form of money, the pleasurable feelings associated with drug use, attention from parents, approval from friends, or an increase in social status. For example, suppose you shoplift a video game with your friends. Your friends congratulate you for the theft and you spend the afternoon playing the game with them. The approval of your friends and the pleasure you get from playing the game function as positive reinforcers for your shoplifting. **In** *negative reinforcement*, **a behavior results in the removal of something bad—a punisher is removed or avoided.** For example, suppose your friends have been calling you a coward because you refuse to use drugs with them. You eventually take drugs with them, after which time they stop calling you a coward. Your drug use has been negatively reinforced.

Punishment

Reinforcement increases the likelihood that a behavior will be repeated, and **punishment reduces the likelihood that a behavior will be repeated.** Like reinforcement, punishment may be either positive or negative. *Positive punishment* **involves the presentation of something bad.** For example, you engage in a delinquent act, and your parents spank you or verbally reprimand you. *Negative punishment* **involves the removal of something good.** For example, your parents punish your delinquency by reducing your allowance or prohibiting you from watching your favorite TV show.

The Sources of Reinforcement and Punishment

Our behavior is reinforced and punished primarily by family members, friends, teachers, neighborhood residents, and others, although family members and friends are the major sources of reinforcement and punishment for juveniles. The key role that **other people** play in reinforcing and punishing our behavior is the major reason that social learning theory is called "social learning" theory.

Social learning theory, however, also recognizes that individuals may engage in *self-reinforcement* **and punishment.** Individuals usually adopt or internalize standards for their behavior from others—parents, for example. They may then evaluate their own behavior using these standards, praising themselves when they meet these standards and criticizing themselves when they do not (see Akers, 1998:72–75; Bandura, 1973:207–221, 1986:335–389).

Finally, social learning theory recognizes that some delinquent acts may be *intrinsically reinforcing* **or punishing.** Perhaps the best example is drug use; individuals sometimes experience a "high" or pleasurable feeling from drug use that is intrinsically reinforcing (or reinforcing in and of itself, independent of the reactions of others). There is also evidence that some individuals experience a range of delinquent acts as intrinsically reinforcing. This is said to be especially true of "sensation seekers," who often receive a "rush" or "thrill" from the delinquent acts they commit. For example, P. Wood et al. (1997) asked a sample of prison inmates about "the types of feelings a person may get when committing different crimes." Many of the inmates said that such feelings included positive emotions like being "on a high or rush," "pumped up," "on top of the world," and "happy/excited" (college undergraduates were much less likely than the inmates to list such positive emotions). These intrinsic reinforcers are sometimes referred to as **nonsocial** reinforcers, since it is assumed that they are not derived from others. It is still possible, however, that social factors—including the beliefs and attitudes that one learns from others—may influence the extent to which individuals experience delinquent acts as "intrinsically reinforcing" (see Box 7.1).

In any event, social learning theory argues that the major sources of reinforcement and punishment for us are other people, especially intimate others like family members and friends.

Some Individuals Are More Likely to Be Reinforced for Delinquency than Others

According to social learning theory, some individuals are more likely to be reinforced for delinquency than others. **Sometimes this reinforcement is deliberate.** For example, the parents of aggressive children often deliberately encourage and reinforce aggressive behavior outside the home (E. Anderson, 1994; Bandura, 1973). E. Anderson (1994:86) states that some families in inner-city communities tell their children that they should respond to provocations with aggression. Furthermore:

> Many parents actually impose sanctions if a child is not sufficiently aggressive. For example, if a child loses a fight and comes home upset, the parent might respond, "Don't you come in here crying that somebody beat you up; you better get back out there and whup his ass. I didn't raise no punks! Get back out there and whup his ass.

Box 7.1　Hooked on Delinquency

Drawing on social learning theory, criminologist John D. Baldwin (1990) argues that some young people can "get hooked" on crime and delinquency, similar to the way that some individuals get hooked on drugs or alcohol. According to Baldwin, the activities of childhood typically lose the ability to arouse or excite individuals as they grow older. As children move into adolescence they usually seek out new experiences and new sources of sensory stimulation. Some adolescents may find delinquency to be a significant source of stimulation. For example, they may experience "sneaky thrills," excitement, or an adrenalin rush during the commission of a delinquent act. As the following quotes suggest, some young people get hooked on these emotional rewards:

> "It's like an addiction [shoplifting]. I like the feeling I get when I might get caught. . . . It's a buzz. An adrenaline buzz. I love that feeling. . . . [In the store] I'm really scared, but once I get away, I'm exhilarated." (Cromwell et al., 1999:65)

> "[Stealing a car is] a thrilling thing to me. To be able to get away with it. I mean, it would just give me goose pimples." (Copes, 2003:324)

Other criminologists observe that such behaviors can activate a dopamine-dependent reward process in the brain, leading to an intrinsically pleasurable "neurophysiologic high" (Gove and Wilmoth, 1990). Of course, not all individuals find crime or delinquency to be rewarding or addictive. Some studies indicate that individuals with strong moral beliefs are less likely to experience delinquency as rewarding, perhaps because they end up feeling more shame or guilt than pleasure (in other words, these individuals exercise self-punishment: Brezina, 2009; Brezina and Piquero, 2003; also see Wood et al., 1997). But for some individuals, delinquency appears to be reinforced by the emotional (nonsocial) rewards they reap from such behavior.

Questions for Discussion
1. Criminologists often describe delinquent behavior as "highly resistant to change." Most anyone who has worked with troubled youth would probably agree with this description. How would social learning theorists explain this fact? Why is it so difficult to change the behavior of delinquent offenders?
2. If it is true that delinquency represents an important source of sensory stimulation for some individuals, what delinquency control or prevention strategies might follow from this observation? Can you think of any alternative, legal sources of stimulation that delinquent offenders could be encouraged to pursue?

If you don't whup his ass, I'll whup your ass when you come home." Thus the child obtains reinforcement for being tough and showing nerve.

At other times, the reinforcement for delinquency is less deliberate (see Patterson et al., 1989; Patterson et al., 1992). Two common scenarios will illustrate what we mean. First, a mother repeatedly asks her son to clean up his room. The son ignores her. The mother eventually starts to yell at and threaten her son. The son yells back at his mother and then slams the door to his room and locks it. The mother, exasperated with her son's behavior, leaves. Without intending to do so, the mother has just negatively reinforced her son's belligerent behavior (the son has learned that, if he remains defiant, his "nagging" mother will eventually go away). Second, a father takes his daughter to the supermarket.

The daughter says she wants a candy bar at the checkout line, but the father refuses. The daughter repeatedly asks for the candy bar, but the father continues to refuse. Eventually, the daughter is screaming for the candy bar and attempting to hit her father. Everyone is now watching and the embarrassed father gives his daughter the candy bar. The daughter stops screaming and eats the bar. In this instance, the father has positively reinforced his daughter's screaming and hitting by giving her a candy bar. Also, the daughter has negatively reinforced the father for giving in to her demand (she stopped screaming after she got the candy bar).

Not only are some individuals **more likely** to be reinforced for delinquency, but some are also **less likely to be reinforced for conventional behavior.** Many parents, for example, often ignore or otherwise fail to reinforce the conventional behavior of their children (Patterson et al., 1989; Patterson et al., 1992). For example, they ignore a child who brings home good grades or displays good manners at a social function, rather than praising him or her. **In some cases, conventional behaviors may even be punished.** For example, behaviors like studying or cooperating with teachers are punished in certain peer groups. And youth detained in juvenile institutions often reinforce behaviors like fighting and punish behaviors like cooperating with the staff.

According to social learning theory, individuals in these types of environments—where delinquency is more likely to reinforced and conventional behavior is more likely to be ignored or punished—should be higher in delinquency. Again, we tend to repeat behaviors that are reinforced and avoid those that are punished.

Intermittent Reinforcement

Delinquents, of course, are rarely reinforced for every delinquent act they commit. Only some of their delinquent acts are reinforced. For example, it may be the case that only every third or fourth delinquent act, on average, results in significant reinforcement. This type of schedule is referred to as an *intermittent schedule of reinforcement* (as opposed to a *continuous schedule of reinforcement*, in which every act is reinforced). Such intermittent schedules, however, are usually sufficient to maintain a behavior. (For example, witness the behavior of slot machine players: they continue to pour money into the machine even though they are only occasionally reinforced.) In fact, behaviors that are reinforced on an intermittent schedule are more difficult to eliminate than those reinforced on a continuous schedule. As Bandura states, "Behavior that has been reinforced on a thin unpredictable schedule is exceedingly difficult to extinguish because one's efforts are sustained by the belief that the actions will eventually prove successful" (1973:186).

Discriminative Stimuli

Juveniles usually find that their delinquency is more likely to be reinforced in some situations than in others. For example, smoking marijuana with your friends may result in much reinforcement, including the approval and companionship of your friends. Smoking marijuana in front of your parents, however, may result in far more punishment than reinforcement. Individuals soon learn to distinguish between situations in which delinquency is likely to be reinforced and those in which it is likely to be punished. They do so based on *discriminative stimuli*, such as the presence of friends or parents. Juveniles, of course, are most likely to commit delinquent acts in situations where the probability of reinforcement is highest. A recent study in the Netherlands confirms that the probability of delinquency is greatest when young people are "hanging out" with their friends in public in the absence of adult supervision, as opposed to spending time indoors in the presence of adults (Weerman et al., 2015).

Research on the Reinforcement and Punishment of Delinquency

Numerous studies have examined the effect of reinforcement and punishment on delinquency and aggression.[2] **Experimental studies** have focused on the effects of reinforcing or punishing aggressive behavior. For example, children might be rewarded with praise or with marbles for hitting a toy clown. These experiments usually indicate that such reinforcement or punishment has a strong effect on subsequent aggression (which might be measured by how often the child continues to hit the toy clown). Other experimental studies have examined the punishments applied by the police and juvenile justice agencies. As discussed in Chapters 20 and 23, such punishments reduce delinquency *when they are properly applied.* That is, such punishments are effective when individuals are properly monitored and consistently sanctioned for rule violations in an appropriate manner.

Surveys and field studies have examined the impact of reinforcement and punishment on various types of delinquency. As indicated in Chapters 14 and 15, these studies indicate that delinquency is less likely when parents and teachers closely monitor the behavior of juveniles and consistently punish them for rule violations. And as discussed in Chapter 23, surveys indicate that individuals are less likely to engage in delinquency when they believe that the likelihood of arrest is high and the likelihood of reinforcement is low (also see Matsueda et al., 2006). Akers and his colleagues conducted one of the best surveys examining the effects of reinforcements and punishments.[3] They asked a sample of adolescents about the punishments and reinforcements they received (or expected to receive) from their parents and friends for using drugs. They obtained a range of responses. Some adolescents, for example, reported that their friends encouraged their drug use, while others said that their friends threatened to turn them in to the authorities. They also asked adolescents about the effects that drugs had on them (or, in the case of nonusers, the effects that they expected drugs to have). The responses ranged from mostly good effects to mostly bad effects. Akers and his colleagues found that drug use was higher among those respondents who said they were usually reinforced and seldom punished for such use.

Studies, then, suggest that reinforcements and punishments have an important effect on behavior. Further, studies suggest that reinforcements and punishments help explain why associating with delinquent others—such as delinquent friends—increases the likelihood of delinquency. Delinquent others lead us into delinquency partly because they are more likely to reinforce our delinquency and less likely to punish it. It is important to note, however, that reinforcements and punishments do not fully explain the effect of delinquent friends on delinquency (see Akers, 1999; Krohn, 1999; McGloin, 2009). Delinquent friends increase the likelihood of delinquency for other reasons as well (more on this later).

BELIEFS FAVORABLE TO DELINQUENCY

Other individuals may not only reinforce our delinquency, they may also teach us beliefs favorable to delinquency. Most individuals, of course, are taught that delinquency is bad or wrong. They eventually accept or "internalize" this belief, and they are less likely to engage in delinquency as a result. For example, suppose we were to ask you why you do not burglarize houses or rob people. You would probably reply that burglary and robbery are wrong. This value is what you have been taught all your life—by parents, friends, and others—and you have come to believe it. Some individuals, however, learn beliefs that are favorable to delinquency, and they are more likely to engage in delinquency as a result.

When we speak of "beliefs favorable to delinquency," **we do not mean that some people believe that serious delinquent acts like burglary and robbery are generally good or acceptable.** Few people, including delinquents, generally approve of serious delinquent acts.[4] Surveys and interviews with juveniles suggest that **beliefs favoring delinquency fall into three categories,** and data suggest that **each type of belief increases the likelihood of delinquency.**[5]

Generally Approve of Minor Delinquency

Some juveniles generally approve of certain minor forms of delinquency, such as sexual intercourse between consenting adolescents; certain forms of gambling, truancy, and curfew violations; and certain forms of alcohol and "soft" drug use. For example, a nationwide survey of high school seniors in 2015 found that 42.4 percent believed that using marijuana should be "entirely legal" (see the Monitoring the Future survey at http://www.monitoringthefuture.org). Presumably, these seniors generally approve of marijuana use. Organizations such as the Partnership for Drug-Free Kids are trying to counter this belief in the hopes of reducing drug use. The stated purpose of their "Above the Influence" antidrug media campaign is to "help teens stand up to negative pressures or influences," including the pressure to use drugs and alcohol. A website for the campaign provides information on various drugs and emphasizes the harmful consequences of their use. The effects of marijuana are summarized in the following manner:

> THE BOTTOM LINE: Marijuana has the potential to cause problems in your daily life, or make existing problems worse. It limits your brain's effectiveness, slows down thinking, and impairs coordination and judgment. And while you're young and still maturing, marijuana can have a long-lasting, negative impact on your developing brain. (Visit the website at http://www.abovetheinfluence.com)

> The campaign also attempts to reach teens through a variety of social media outlets and by speaking in the language of teens. For example, a short YouTube video produced by the campaign shows a teenager at a party drinking several beers in a row and then passing out. The video concludes by asking the viewer: "If you're not in control, then who is? Live above the influence."

For a review of research on the effectiveness of antidrug media campaigns, see Ferri et al., 2013. For a review of research on the effects of marijuana use, see Volkow et al., 2014.

Conditionally Approve of Delinquency, Including Some Serious Delinquency

Some juveniles conditionally approve of, justify, or excuse certain forms of delinquency, including some serious delinquent acts. These juveniles believe that delinquency is generally wrong but that some delinquent acts are excusable, justifiable, or even desirable in certain conditions. Many juveniles, for example, will state that violence is generally wrong but that it is justified if you have been insulted or provoked in some way. This idea is at the heart of E. Anderson's (1999) work on the **"code of the street."** Anderson argues that many individuals in disadvantaged communities are unable to achieve respect or status through conventional channels, such as getting a good education and then a prestigious job. Some of these individuals cope by trying to achieve respect by adopting a tough demeanor and responding to disrespectful treatment with violence. Many such individuals come to believe that violence is justified or even desirable when others treat them in a disrespectful manner. One study (Stewart and Simons, 2006) measured the extent to which individuals have adopted the code of the street by asking them to indicate how much they agreed with statements such as the following:

> When someone disrespects you, it is important that you use physical force or aggression to teach him or her not to disrespect you.

> If someone uses violence against you, it is important that you use violence against him or her to get even.

> People do not respect a person who is afraid to fight physically for his or her rights.

Researchers have found that many juveniles agree with such statements and that such juveniles are more likely to engage in violence.[6]

Sykes and Matza (1957) argue that **the excuses and justifications employed by juveniles assume five basic forms,** each of which specifies the conditions in which crime is justified/excused.

1. *Denial of responsibility:* Delinquents claim that delinquency is excusable when a person is not responsible for his or her behavior (e.g., "I was drunk and didn't know what I was doing," or "My parents abused me and I can't help myself.").

2. *Denial of injury:* Delinquents claim that delinquency is excusable when no one is harmed by it (e.g., "Insurance will cover the loss," or "I was just borrowing the car.").

3. *Denial of the victim:* Delinquents claim that delinquency is justifiable when the victim deserves it (e.g., "The store owner is dishonest," or "She started it by insulting me."). This justification is closely related to the code of the street, which claims that violence is justified when others treat you in a disrespectful manner.

4. *Condemnation of the condemners:* Delinquents claim that delinquency is justifiable or excusable when those who condemn them also engage in questionable behavior (e.g., "All the cops and politicians are crooked," or "My parents drink and that's just as bad as using marijuana.").

5. *Appeal to higher loyalties:* Delinquents claim that delinquency is justifiable when it serves some higher purpose ("I did it to help my friends" or "to protect my turf").

Other researchers have listed additional justifications and excuses.[7] Not all juveniles accept such justifications/excuses, but those who do are more likely to engage in delinquency.[8]

Many of us employ such justifications/excuses when we engage in deviant acts, minor or otherwise. Suppose, for example, you wake up one morning and do not feel like going to class. You may believe that cutting class is generally bad, but you tell yourself that in your case it is justified because you are not feeling well (a form of "denial of responsibility"). What other sorts of justifications/excuses do students employ for cutting class and for other forms of deviance like cheating on exams (see Agnew and Peters, 1985; McCabe, 1992)? Do these justifications/excuses fall into the categories described by Sykes and Matza, or are additional categories necessary?

General Values Conducive to Delinquency

Some juveniles hold certain general values that are conducive to delinquency. These values do not explicitly approve of or justify delinquency, but they make delinquency appear a more attractive alternative than might otherwise be the case. Theorists have listed three general sets of values in this area. The first is **an attraction to "excitement," "thrills," or "kicks."** The desire for excitement can be satisfied through legitimate as well as illegitimate means, but criminal activities hold a special appeal, since they have the added element of danger—of "experimenting with the forbidden." Individuals who value excitement, then, are more likely to find crime an attractive alternative in a given situation. The second value involves **a disdain for hard work and a desire for quick, easy success.** Many delinquents, for example, are said to have "grandiose dreams of quick success." Crime, of course, would have an obvious appeal to those who place a low value on hard work and a high value on money and pleasure. Finally, delinquents are said to place **a high value on toughness—on being "macho."** Macho includes being physically strong, being able to defend yourself, not letting others "push you around," and showing bravery in the face of physical threat. Such individuals will clearly view delinquent activities like fighting in a more favorable light than people without those values.

Where Do the Beliefs Favorable to Delinquency Come From?

Juveniles learn the beliefs favorable to delinquency from others, including family members, friends, community residents, and the media. Data suggest that delinquent friends are an especially important source of such beliefs.[9] **Also, juveniles often come to adopt such beliefs after engaging in delinquency.**[10] In particular, juveniles who engage in delinquency—for whatever reason—often find it advantageous to adopt such beliefs. Such beliefs allow them to neutralize whatever guilt they might feel and to reduce the likelihood of punishment by others (which is why young children often try to convince their parents that the victims of their delinquency deserved it). Once such beliefs have been adopted, however, they make further delinquency more likely, since they define delinquency in a favorable light or at least allow a juvenile to justify or excuse delinquent behavior.

These beliefs also help explain why associating with delinquent others, like delinquent friends, increases the likelihood of delinquency. Delinquent friends teach the juvenile beliefs favorable to delinquency, and these beliefs in turn increase the likelihood of delinquency. Beliefs, however, do not fully explain the effect of delinquent friends on delinquency (see Akers, 1999; Krohn, 1999; Megens and Weerman, 2012). Also, it is important to note that factors other than association with delinquent peers influence the adoption of beliefs favorable to delinquency. Most notably, the experience of certain strains appears to increase the likelihood that individuals will adopt such beliefs. As indicated, individuals who cannot achieve respect through legal channels may come to believe that violence is sometimes an acceptable method for achieving respect. Also, individuals in high-crime communities with poor police protection may come to believe that violence is justified if one is threatened or provoked (Brezina et al., 2004; Stewart and Simons, 2006). Further, researchers have argued that individuals who cannot achieve monetary success through legal channels may come to believe that theft, drug selling, and prostitution are sometimes justified (Agnew, 2006a; Cloward and Ohlin, 1960).

THE IMITATION OF DELINQUENT MODELS

People's behavior is not only a function of their beliefs and the reinforcements and punishments they receive, but also of the behavior of those around them. In particular, people often imitate or model the behavior of others, especially when they have reason to believe that such imitation will result in reinforcement. It is perhaps for this reason that we are most likely to imitate a model when we "like or respect the model, see the model receive reinforcement, see the model give off signs of pleasure, or are in an environment where imitating the model's performance is reinforced" (Baldwin and Baldwin, 1981:187).

We should note that some people may inadvertently model delinquent or aggressive behavior for juveniles, just as they inadvertently reinforce delinquency/aggression. Parents, for example, may punish aggression in their children by spanking or beating them, or parents who smoke or drink may warn their children about the dangers of drug use. In each case, the parents are modeling the type of behavior they wish to stop in their child.[11]

We should also note that we do not have to be in direct contact with the models we imitate (D. Payne and Cornwell, 2007). In fact, a good deal of research has focused on the extent to which juveniles model the aggressive behavior of those in the media, especially television. The media often show glamorous characters engaging in frequent and extreme forms of violence. Such characters often receive much reinforcement and little punishment for their aggression. As Bandura (1973:101) states, "The modern child has witnessed innumerable stabbings, shootings, stompings, stranglings, muggings and less blatant but equally destructive forms of cruelty before [he or she] has reached kindergarten age." The negative impact of media violence is discussed in Chapter 17.

Data from a wide range of studies demonstrate the importance of imitation (see Akers, 1998; Akers et al., 2016; Bandura, 1973, 1986). A large number of **experimental studies** have exposed individuals to aggressive models and then observed the impact of such exposure on the subjects' behavior. Such studies typically demonstrate an increase in aggression. Likewise, several **survey studies** have examined the effect of imitation on delinquency. One study, for example, examined the effect of imitation on "courtship violence" (the use of physical violence against dating partners; Sellers et al., 2003). Imitation was measured by asking respondents whether they had "actually seen any of the following role models use physical actions (hitting, slapping, etc.) against a spouse or partner: (1) father or stepfather, (2) mother or stepmother, (3) siblings, (4) other relatives, (5) friends, (6) actors on TV/movies, and (7) others" (Sellers et al., 2003:116). The researchers found that those who had witnessed more physical violence were more likely to engage in courtship violence themselves (for more on the social learning of intimate partner violence, see Box 7.2).

Box 7.2   Social Learning and the Cycle of Family Violence

Millions of Americans are affected by intimate partner violence (IPV) each year. Intimate partners include a current or former lover, partner, or spouse. Over their lifetimes, one in four women (24.3 percent) and one in seven men (13.8 percent) aged 18 and older have been the victim of severe physical violence by an intimate partner. IPV has been described as a major public health problem that costs society billions of dollars each year in the form of medical and mental health care, lost productivity (e.g., missing days of work), and criminal justice system expenditures (for further information visithttp://www.cdc.gov/violenceprevention/intimatepartnerviolence).

Evidence suggests that the roots of IPV perpetration can often traced, in part, to the abuser's family of origin. Many studies find that childhood exposure to violence is a risk factor for violence in adult relationships and may include witnessing IPV as a child or being the victim of child abuse or maltreatment. This phenomenon is referred to as the "intergenerational transmission of violence" or the "cycle of family violence." Social learning theory is often invoked to explain this cycle. According to social learning theorists, children who are exposed to early acts of family violence are, in essence, being exposed to violent models, which they later imitate as adults. They may also grow up to believe that physical aggression is a normal, acceptable, or justifiable method for dealing with interpersonal conflict.

To see how researchers have applied social learning concepts to the study of IPV, it is helpful to review an example of such research. In a study titled, "A Test of Social Learning and Intergenerational Transmission among Batterers," Jennifer Wareham and her colleagues (2009) administered a survey to over 200 men who were enrolled in domestic violence programs for batterers. Ordinarily, to determine whether childhood experiences predict violence in adult relationships, researchers would also want to survey men with no history of battering. In this case, however, the researchers wished to determine whether childhood experiences and social learning shape the *types* and *severity* of violence exhibited by men in domestic violence programs. (Note: These men were enrolled in the programs for a variety of reasons, from admitting to verbally and emotionally abusing a partner to arrest for physically assaulting a partner.)

(Continued)

(Continued)

To measure early violence exposure, the men were asked to report how frequently they received childhood punishments of the following types: "kicked or hit with a closed fist," "spanked with a belt or other instrument," or "had something thrown at you" (childhood maltreatment). They were also asked to indicate how often in childhood they witnessed "one parent hit another parent." A series of questions were designed to measure social learning mechanisms. For example, the men were asked to anticipate how their family or close friends would react to their use of violence against a partner—whether these others would "call the police" or "encourage it" (differential reinforcement). Other questions in the survey asked the respondent if he believed it was necessary or justifiable to use violence against a partner in various situations (beliefs favorable to aggression); if he had observed friends, coworkers, or people in the media hit a partner; and if he was influenced by these models (imitation).

Like many other investigations, the findings of this study indicate an association between childhood maltreatment and the use of violence against intimate partners. Compared to the men who reported little or no childhood maltreatment, the men in this study who reported high levels of childhood maltreatment (e.g., frequently being kicked or hit with a closed fist) reported more frequent use of violence against their intimate partners, even after controlling for other factors in their background, such as socioeconomic status. The acts of violence ranged from slapping a partner to kicking them, hitting them with a fist, and choking them. Having witnessed one's parents hit each other was not associated with the frequency of IPV, however (though other studies find a link here; for a review, see Wareham et al., 2009).

In addition, the findings indicate that many of the social learning mechanisms added to the explanation of IPV. For instance, differential reinforcement and imitation also contribute to frequent use of IPV in this sample of men. This was mainly true for the acts of violence that were classified as relatively minor in the study (e.g., slapping a partner and threatening to hit a partner). Finally, in the case of minor IPV (but not serious IPV), social learning mechanisms appear to be responsible for the effect of childhood maltreatment. In other words, childhood maltreatment contributes to minor IPV because men who have been maltreated tend to score high on measures of social learning (e.g., they anticipate favorable responses to their use of violence and have been influenced by violent models).

The authors of this study conclude that both early violence exposure and social learning mechanisms play a role in the development of IPV, and that social learning theory can help explain the cycle of family violence. Overall, it appears that "early relationships between children and their parents set a foundation of 'normative' and acceptable behaviors" that may lead some individuals to repeat the dysfunctional patterns of behavior found in their family of origin (Wareham et al., 2009:171).

Questions for Discussion

1. In the study just described, social learning factors partially explained the development of IPV. Can you think of other factors that may contribute to IPV but were not examined in this study?
2. Although many studies of IPV focus on adults, adolescent dating violence has also been described as a serious problem. In fact, women between the ages of 16 and 24 are at greatest risk of nonfatal IPV (when they are most likely to be dating), and 32 percent of in-school adolescents report being psychologically or physically abused by a romantic partner (see Gomez, 2011). Would you expect childhood exposure to violence to increase the risk of dating violence perpetration? Would you expect it to increase the risk of dating violence *victimization*? Why?

Likewise, **field studies** reveal the importance of imitation. Consider, for example, this quote from a juvenile delinquent in a public housing project in Boston:

> We were all brought up, all we seen is our older brothers and that gettin' into trouble and goin' to jail and all that shit. . . . We seen many fucking drugs, all the drinking. They fucking go; that group's gone. The next group came. It's our brothers that are a little older, y'know, twenty something years old. They started doing crime. And when you're young, you look up to people. You have a person, everybody has a person they look up to. And he's doing this, he's drinking, he's doing that, he's doing drugs, he's ripping off people. Y'know, he's making good fucking money, and it looks like he's doing good, y'know? So bang. Now it's our turn. We're here. What we gonna do when all we seen is fuckin' drugs, alcohol, fighting, this and that, no one going to school? (MacLeod, 1995:117)

Individuals who are exposed to delinquent models, then, are more likely to engage in delinquency themselves. Furthermore, imitation helps explain the effect of associating with delinquent others on delinquency, although it only explains part of the effect (see Akers, 1999; Krohn, 1999).

SUMMARY

Social learning theory has much support. Data indicate that people in our environment have a strong impact on whether we become delinquent and that this impact is partly explained by the effect these people have on our beliefs regarding delinquency, the reinforcements and punishments we receive, and the models we are exposed to (see Figure 7.1). Social learning theory and control theory, described in Chapter 8, are the leading explanations of delinquency (Ellis and Walsh, 1999).

TEACHING AIDS
Controversial Cases

The basic ideas behind social learning theory are straightforward: Individuals are more likely to engage in delinquency when others reinforce their delinquency, teach them beliefs favorable to delinquency, and model delinquency for them. And, based on this, you might think that most people would agree that we should not reinforce delinquency, teach beliefs favorable to delinquency, and model delinquency. But, as the four case studies that follow illustrate, things are sometimes not quite so simple.

Case 1. To spank or not to spank. Most people in the United States believe that "it is sometimes necessary to discipline a child with a good hard spanking" (for further information, visit www.childtrends.org). And most parents spank their children at some point. Many who do so claim that the practice is justified by the well-known biblical injunction: Spare the rod and spoil the child. There has been a fair amount of research on the relationship between

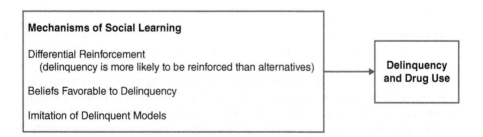

FIGURE 7.1 Simple Diagram Highlighting the Major Mechanisms Involved in the Learning of Delinquent Behavior

spanking and delinquency (e.g., Farrington et al., 2003; Gershoff and Grogan-Kaylor, 2016; Simons et al., 2007; Straus, 1994). Most such research suggests that frequent spanking may increase the likelihood of delinquency somewhat (at least among whites; it does not appear to have this effect among African Americans). Part of the reason for the effect of spanking on delinquency is explained in terms of social learning theory: Parents who spank provide their child with a violent model and teach them that violence is sometimes an appropriate way to deal with one's problems. What do you think? Should parents spank their children?

Case 2. To lock up or not to lock up   We often respond to juvenile offenders, especially serious offenders, by confining them in institutions. In theory, such institutions are supposed to rehabilitate the youth who are sent there. In practice, things are sometimes rather different. One newspaper article on juvenile detention centers in our home state of Georgia began as follows:

> One thing the two childhood friends knew: They had to have a good plan to survive inside the gray concrete walls of the Metropolitan Regional Youth Detention Center. Kelsey Richardson, a sixth grader at Brown Middle School, tried to be macho, squinting his eyes and feigning a bravado much larger than his wispy physique. Dratez Wilcox, 5-foot-5 and 125 pounds but the larger of the two, took the "keep quiet, blend in" approach. The 13-year-old boys didn't want to be "ratpacked"—jumped and beaten by groups of boys—for pointless reasons: not handing over their snacks or accidentally sitting in someone's chair in the TV lounge. Both boys are among dozens of former teenage inmates who painted life inside the state's largest juvenile detention facility as a state-sanctioned "Lord of the Flies," where children survive by using their fists or the filed-down shanks of pens, wire or paper clips, or, as a last resort, by feigning attempts of suicide so they'll be moved to a more secure cell and constantly monitored. . . . By all accounts, many of the youths . . . are unruly and violent, and trying to keep them under control is a stressful, taxing job. They threaten guards, teachers and nurses and often make good on their promises with physical violence (Dyer, 2000:A10).

Social learning theorists sometimes argue that correctional institutions are little more than "schools for crime." They segregate juvenile delinquents from conventional others and confine them with other juvenile delinquents, who often reinforce their delinquency, model delinquency, and foster beliefs favorable to delinquency. What are your thoughts? In particular, do you feel we should try to reduce the number of juvenile offenders who are sent to institutions? Do you feel we should modify juvenile institutions? If so, how? (See Chapter 21 for a discussion of juvenile institutions.)

Case 3. Growing up in an urban war zone.   Earlier we said that some parents deliberately encourage their children to engage in violent acts, sometimes reinforcing them for violence and punishing them when they fail to resort to violence. There are several reasons for this, one of which is described by Geoffrey Canada (1995:6), who has worked with poor families in New York and Boston:

> I have counseled so many children who've said they acted violently because their parents told them to. Parents often give instructions similar to those my mother gave my brother: fight back or I will beat you when you get home. Many times children as young as six and seven would bring weapons to school, or pick up bottles, bricks, or whatever was at hand. When asked about their violent behavior they'd often say their parents told them to "get something and bash his head in." The children were telling the truth. In the more than twenty years I have spent counseling, teaching, and running programs for poor, inner-city children, I have seen a steady stream of parents who have given their children these instructions. The parents, inevitably single women raising children in the midst of an urban war zone, come with similar stories of children being

victimized again and again. Institutions do nothing to protect the child. The child coming home scared, scarred, looking to them for protection that they could not provide. The parents feeling as if they had no alternative. Accept it, this is a violent world, so teach them to cope by acting more violently than the others.

What would you do if you were a single parent raising a child in an "urban war zone," the child was being regularly victimized, and school officials and the police seemed unable to stop it? (See the discussion of antibullying programs in Chapter 24, as well as the answers that Geoffrey Canada provides in his book.)

Case 4. Social learning theory and binge drinking on college campuses. Binge drinking has been called the foremost public health problem on college campuses. Binge drinking is usually defined as the consumption of five or more drinks in one sitting. (A drink equals a 12-ounce beer or wine cooler, a 6- to 8-ounce glass of wine, or a shot of hard liquor.) Recent surveys suggest that nearly 40 percent of college students have engaged in binge drinking during the past month (for further information, visit https://www.niaaa.nih.gov). As Durkin et al. (2005:256) state, binge drinkers are more likely to experience negative consequences such as "blackouts, hangovers, missing class, falling behind in their studies, doing something they later regretted, arguing with friends, getting involved in physical fights, and getting into trouble with the police." Further, binge drinking has negative consequences for others on campus, including "being verbally insulted or abused, being physically assaulted, having one's property damaged, experiencing unwelcome sexual advances, and having sleep or study disturbed because of the conduct of intoxicated students" (Durkin et al., 2005:257).

How would social learning theory explain binge drinking? In particular, why are some students more likely than others to engage in binge drinking according to social learning theory? Test your explanation by (1) developing a set of questions to measure binge drinking and your key independent variables, (2) having the students in your class answer these questions (by filling out an anonymous questionnaire), and (3) determining if your independent variables are associated with binge drinking. For example, you might ask students what proportion of their best friends on campus binge drink (or drink five or more drinks in a sitting). Then you can determine whether the students with a high proportion of binge drinking friends are more likely to binge drink themselves. If you like, you can compare your study to that of Durkin et al. (2005), who used social learning theory to explain binge drinking among students at four colleges.

Discuss the results with your classmates. Address questions such as the following: Does it matter who you associate with? How do individuals select their friends? How do individuals form their beliefs regarding alcohol and binge drinking? (And, related to this, why do individuals have different beliefs in this area?) Are students regularly exposed to others who binge drink? What factors influence whether students imitate the behavior of these other binge drinkers?

Web-Based Exercise: Learning to Hate

You can obtain information on hate groups in the United States, including those in your state or local area, on the website of the Southern Poverty Law Center at http://www.splcenter.org. Click on **Hate Map**. Many hate groups are skinhead and neo-Nazi groups that include juveniles. You may wonder why the people in such groups think and act as they do; their actions sometimes include violence against the members of particular racial, ethnic, religious, and other groups. Social learning theory can shed much light here. Visit YouTube and view several of the "Skinhead USA" clips that focus on a skinhead/neo-Nazi group in Alabama. (WARNING: The videos contain rough language and dialogue, including the use of derogatory terms to describe the members of certain racial, religious, and other groups.) Then draw on social learning theory to explain how the members of this group have learned to hate. Be sure to consider the different mechanisms of social learning, including differential reinforcement, beliefs favorable to delinquency (hate), and exposure to delinquent (hateful) models. Do you think strain theory can also be used to understand the beliefs and behavior of those in this group?

TEST YOUR KNOWLEDGE OF THIS CHAPTER

1. Describe the essential arguments of social learning theory in a few sentences.
2. Next to prior delinquency, what is probably the best predictor of subsequent delinquency?
3. Individuals who associate with delinquent others, like delinquent friends, are much more likely to engage in delinquency. We stated that this fact strongly supports social learning theory but does not prove that the theory is correct. Why do we make this statement?
4. What are the three major mechanisms by which individuals learn to be delinquent from others?
5. Define and then give examples involving the frequency, amount, and relative probability of reinforcement and punishment.
6. Define and then give examples of positive and negative reinforcement. Do the same for positive and negative punishment.
7. List the three major sources of reinforcement and punishment. Which source of reinforcement is most important according to social learning theory?
8. Define and give an example of intermittent reinforcement. Do the same for discriminative stimuli.
9. What are the three major types of "beliefs favorable to delinquency"? Give two examples of each type (e.g., list two "general values conducive to delinquency").
10. List and give an example of each of the five justifications or excuses for delinquency developed by Sykes and Matza.
11. Where do "beliefs favorable to delinquency" come from?
12. What factors influence whether we imitate the delinquent behavior of others?
13. Give an example of how a parent might unintentionally or inadvertently reinforce delinquent or aggressive behavior. Give an example of how a parent might inadvertently model delinquent or aggressive behavior.
14. Describe the evidence in favor of social learning theory (evidence dealing with the effects of associating with delinquent others, reinforcements, beliefs, and imitation on delinquency).

THOUGHT AND DISCUSSION QUESTIONS

1. How might social learning theory explain a form of deviance like cheating on exams?
2. Develop a set of survey questions that measure the independent variables in the explanation for cheating you developed in question 1.
3. Describe how you might test social learning theory, or a portion of it, by doing an experiment and by doing a field study.
4. Many studies indicate that there is a strong association between having delinquent friends and engaging in delinquency. Does this association demonstrate that having delinquent friends causes delinquency? If not, why not? (See Chapter 16 for a fuller discussion of this question.)

5. Strain theory draws on social learning theory to some extent in explaining delinquency. Describe how.

6. What recommendations would a social learning theorist make for reducing delinquency? (In your response, describe things that should and should not be done to reduce delinquency.)

7. Some criminologists are concerned that social learning theory overlooks the role of individual differences.[12] For example, certain psychological or biological traits may render some individuals especially susceptible to the influence of delinquent peers or the effects of drugs and alcohol. Can you think of any specific traits that may impact the learning of delinquency? (See Chapter 13 for a full discussion of individual traits.)

KEY TERMS

- Social learning theory
- Frequency, amount, and relative probability of reinforcement
- Differential reinforcement of delinquency
- Positive and negative reinforcement

- Positive and negative punishment
- Self-reinforcement
- Intrinsically reinforcing
- Intermittent and continuous reinforcement
- Discriminative stimuli

- Denial of responsibility
- Denial of injury
- Denial of the victim
- Condemnation of the condemners
- Appeal to higher loyalties

ENDNOTES

1. See Akers, 1998; Akers and Jensen, 2003; Aseltine, 1995; Chapple, 2005; Elliott et al., 1985; Elliott and Menard, 1996; Ferguson et al., 2009; Gordon et al., 2004; Gorman and White, 1995; Haynie, 2001, 2002; Haynie and McHugh, 2003; Haynie and Osgood, 2005; Haynie and Payne, 2006; Huizinga et al., 2003; McGloin, 2009; Pratt et al., 2010; Thornberry Freeman-Gallant et al., 2003; Thornberry, Krohn et al. (with Porter), 2003; Thornberry, Krohn et al. (with Tobin), 2003; Warr, 2002; Weerman and Smeenk, 2005.

2. For overviews, see Akers, 1985, 1998; Akers et al., 2016; Bandura, 1973; Brauer, 2009; Matsueda et al., 2006; Patterson et al., 1992; Rebellon, 2006; Rebellon and Manasse, 2004; Warr, 2002.

3. See Akers et al., 1979; also see Akers, 1998; Krohn et al., 1985; Patterson et al., 1992; Thornberry et al., 1994.

4. See Agnew, 1994a; Matza, 1964; Short and Strodtbeck, 1965.

5. See Agnew, 1994b, 1995b; Akers, 1998; Akers et al., 1979; Heimer, 1997; Markowitz and Felson, 1998; Maruna and Copes, 2005; Stewart and Simons, 2006; Thornberry et al., 1994; Q. Zhang, Loeber, and Stouthamer-Loeber, 1997.

6. Agnew, 1994b; Brezina et al., 2004; Decker et al., 1997; Sheley and Wright, 1995; Stewart and Simons, 2006, 2010.

7. See Bandura, 1990; Conklin, 1992; Maruna and Copes, 2005; Minor, 1981.

8. See especially Matza and Sykes, 1961; also see Agnew, 1995b; Curtis, 1974; England, 1960; Maruna and Copes, 2005; Morris and Copes, 2012; W. Miller, 1958; Stewart and Simons, 2006, 2010; Topalli et al., 2014; Vaz, 1967.

9. See Agnew, 1995b; Akers, 1998; Brezina et al., 2004; Heimer, 1997; Matsueda and Heimer, 1987; Megens and Weerman, 2012; Stewart and Simons, 2006; Thornberry, 1998; Thornberry et al., 1994; Warr and Stafford, 1991.

10. See Agnew, 1995b; Brezina et al., 2004; Heimer, 1997; Thornberry et al., 1994; Topalli et al., 2014; Q. Zhang et al., 1997.

11. See Bandura, 1986; Heimer, 1997; Patterson et al., 1992.

12. See Beaver et al., 2011; Button et al., 2007; H. Miller, 2010.

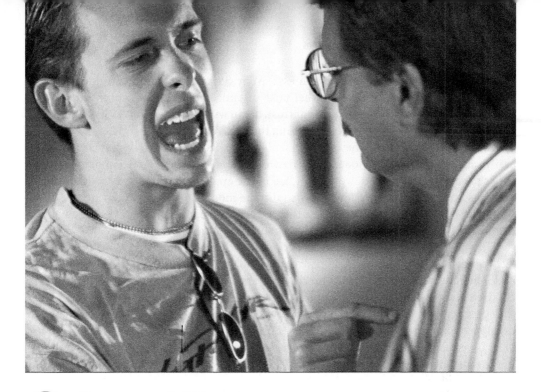

8 Control Theory

Do Weak Controls Result in Delinquency?

Strain and social learning theorists ask: "Why do juveniles engage in delinquency?" They then focus on the factors that push or entice juveniles into committing delinquent acts. **Control theorists,** in contrast, **begin with the question "Why do juveniles conform?"** Unlike strain and social learning theorists, control theorists take the existence of delinquency for granted. They argue that all people have needs and desires that are more easily satisfied through delinquency than through legal channels. For example, it is much easier to steal money than to work for it. So, in the eyes of control theorists, **delinquency requires no special explanation; it is usually the most expedient way for people to get what they want.** These theorists argue that, rather than explaining why people engage in delinquency, we need to explain why they do not.

This argument may strike you as odd. Most of us take conformity for granted and feel that delinquency is in need of explanation. If you observe the behavior of very young children, however, you begin to appreciate the argument of control theorists. When little children want something, they simply take it, whether it belongs to them or not. When they get angry, they often hit and shove others. And when their verbal skills are sufficiently developed, they often lie and deceive others. Their behavior, however, usually does not impress us as odd; we say that the children are simply trying to satisfy their needs and desires in the most direct, expedient way possible. Control theorists ask why most older juveniles and adults do not do the same.

After reading this chapter, you should be able to:

- Explain how control theory differs from strain and social learning theories of delinquency.
- Recognize the areas of overlap between control and social learning theories.
- Identify the major types of control.
- Explain how each type of control serves to inhibit delinquency.

WHY DO JUVENILES CONFORM (AND SOMETIMES DEVIATE)?

According to control theorists, **people do not engage in delinquency because of the controls or restraints to which they are subject.** While strain and social learning theory focus on the factors that push or entice the individual into delinquency, control theory focuses on the factors that restrain the individual from engaging in delinquency. These restraints might be portrayed as a wall holding the individual back from delinquency, as shown in Figure 8.1.

Let us provide some examples of these controls or restraints. Each year we ask the students in our juvenile delinquency courses the following question: **"Why are you not a delinquent?"** (or, in some cases, "Why are you a delinquent?"). Students then write their responses on a sheet of paper. Here are some examples of the most common types of responses: "I know the difference between what's right and wrong." "My parents raised me to respect the laws and follow them." "I was disciplined by my parents." "It's at odds with my belief in right and wrong, which comes from my religion." "I feel too guilty when I do something wrong." "Because I am afraid of getting caught." "My family would be greatly disappointed." "My parents would disown me." "My parents would kill me." "I'm worried about what my friends would think or say." "The consequences could somehow affect my college career and my other career goals." "I have many plans for the future and delinquency may hinder or destroy my future." "It would look bad on my résumé" "I have more to lose than to gain from being delinquent." "I can control my anger instead of resorting to violence when I am in a conflict."

These responses nicely illustrate many of the controls or restraints that prevent people from engaging in delinquency (at least frequent or serious delinquency). We refrain from

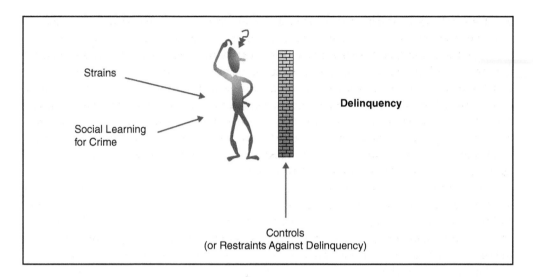

FIGURE 8.1 Control Theory Focuses on the Factors That Hold Individuals Back from Delinquency

engaging in delinquency because we believe it is wrong and because we fear that we will be caught and sanctioned in some way. We might get arrested, hurt people we care about, jeopardize our education and future career, and so on. Our beliefs and fear of sanctions, then, act as controls or restraints on our behavior: they help explain our conformity.

Control theory argues that **people differ in their levels of control, or in the restraints they face to engage in delinquency. Some individuals are high in control;** for example, they believe that delinquency is very wrong and that they would be heavily sanctioned if they committed a delinquent act. They would upset their beloved parents, their friends would leave them, they would lose their scholarship to college, they would ruin their chances of getting into law school, and so on. According to control theory, such individuals should be less likely than others to engage in delinquency.

Other individuals, however, are low in control; for example, they believe that delinquency is only a little bit wrong and that they would not be heavily sanctioned if they committed a delinquent act. They do not care what their parents think about them, their friends would not leave them, they have no scholarship to lose, and they have no plans for going to law school. According to control theory, such individuals should be more likely to engage in delinquency. Nothing is holding them back from delinquency, and so they are free to pursue their wants and desires in the most expedient way possible, which often involves delinquency. So if they see something they want, they may steal it. If someone upsets them, that person may be hit.

How Is Control Theory Similar to and Different from Social Learning Theory?

If you have been following this discussion closely, you may have noticed that there is some overlap between control theory and social learning theory. Social learning theory has a lot to say not only about the factors that cause delinquency but about the factors that prevent delinquency. In this area, both control theory and social learning theory argue that delinquency is less likely when it is sanctioned or punished and when conformity is reinforced. Individuals may be sanctioned by others, like parents and school officials, and they may sanction themselves if they believe that delinquency is wrong. Both theories, then, focus on the extent to which delinquency is prevented through sanctions. There is, however, a crucial difference between the theories.

Social learning theory also focuses on the extent to which delinquency is motivated through modeling, beliefs, and reinforcement. Some individuals are said to have a relatively strong motivation for delinquency because they have been exposed to delinquent models, have learned beliefs favorable to delinquency, and have been reinforced for delinquency. Social learning theory, then, is broader than control theory since it focuses on both the factors that prevent delinquency and the factors that motivate it. Theorists like Akers (1985) and Conger (1976) have argued that social learning theory is a more powerful theory as a result and that it is capable of incorporating control theory.

Control theorists, however, argue that it is not important to examine the motivation for delinquency. They claim that the motivation for delinquency is more or less equally strong for everyone: we all have unfulfilled wants and desires that could more easily be satisfied through delinquency. **Delinquency is said to be largely a function of differences in the level of control.** As Travis Hirschi, the leading control theorist has stated:

> Control theories assume that the potential for asocial conduct is present in everyone, that we would all commit delinquent acts were we not somehow prevented from doing so. The important differences between delinquents and non-delinquents are not differences in motivation; they are, rather, differences in the extent to which natural motives are controlled.[1]

WHAT ARE THE MAJOR TYPES OF CONTROL (OR RESTRAINTS TO DELINQUENCY)?

Control theories basically describe the major types of control or the major restraints to delinquency. Control theories enjoyed a rise in popularity following the publication, in 1969, of Hirschi's groundbreaking book, *Causes of Delinquency.* Drawing on the works of earlier control theorists, Hirschi formulated a clear statement of the control theory perspective and offered his own version of control theory, which emphasized the strength of the individual's bond to society. According to Hirschi (1969), emotional attachments to others, moral beliefs, and other "elements of the social bond" help restrain delinquent impulses. Hirschi also provided an initial test of his "social bonding" theory using data from a survey of adolescents. Due in part to his systematic approach to theory construction and testing, Hirschi's version of control theory became one of the most respected and frequently tested theories in the field of criminology (Akers et al., 2016). In more recent years, Hirschi has come to place more importance on the role of self-restraint, as outlined in M. Gottfredson and Hirschi's (1990) influential "self-control" theory of crime and delinquency.

The theories of Hirschi (1969) and M. Gottfredson and Hirschi (1990) remain the leading control theories, but major versions of control theory have also been developed by Reiss (1951), Toby (1957), Nye (1958), Reckless (1961), Matza (1964), Briar and Piliavin (1965), Kornhauser (1978), Sampson and Laub (1993a), and Laub and Sampson (2003). These versions differ in terms of the particular types of control that are said to inhibit delinquency, but most seek to answer the same basic question: Why don't more of us commit crime/delinquency more often? What is stopping or inhibiting us? Rather than describing the different types of control in all these theories, we present a generic version of control theory that draws from them.

This generic theory lists four major types of control, with certain types having two or more components. The first type is *direct control*, which refers to the efforts of others to directly limit the juvenile's behavior by (1) setting rules for the juvenile, (2) monitoring the juvenile's behavior, (3) sanctioning the juvenile for rule violations and delinquency, and (4) reinforcing the juvenile for conventional behavior. The second type of control or restraint is the juvenile's **stake in conformity,** which refers to things that the juvenile might lose by engaging in delinquency. Juveniles with a lot to lose should be less likely to engage in delinquency. A juvenile's stake in conformity is a function of his or her (1) emotional attachment to conventional others and (2) actual or anticipated investment in conventional activities (like getting an education). The third type of control is **belief,** which refers to the juvenile's beliefs regarding delinquency. Juveniles who believe that delinquency is wrong should be less likely to engage in delinquency. The fourth type is **self-control,** which refers to the juvenile's ability to exercise self-restraint. Self-control is usually indexed by several personality traits, such as impulsivity or the tendency to act without thinking about the consequences of one's behavior. Control is highest, then, when others try to control the juvenile's behavior, when the juvenile has a lot to lose by engaging in delinquency, when the juvenile believes that delinquency is wrong, and when the juvenile has the ability to exercise self-restraint.

Direct Control

When most people think of control, they think of **direct control: someone watching over the juvenile and sanctioning him or her for deviance.** Much direct control is exercised by the justice system—the police, courts, and correctional agencies. The police try to watch juveniles and arrest suspected offenders, while the courts and correctional agencies sanction offenders. A fair bit of research has examined the extent to which these "official" efforts to exercise direct control are effective. That is, do the sanctions administered by the justice system control or "deter" delinquency? This research is discussed in some detail in Chapters 21 and 23, as part of a larger discussion of the juvenile justice system. Direct control, however, is not exercised by the justice system alone. It is also exercised by parents, school officials, neighborhood residents, and others. In fact, these "unofficial" efforts to exercise direct control are far more common and influential than the efforts of official agencies like the police and courts. Parents are the major source of direct control. Given their longstanding and intimate relationship with the juvenile, parents are in a much better position to detect and sanction delinquency in their children than are representatives of the justice system.

Direct control has four components: setting rules, monitoring behavior, sanctioning deviance/delinquency, and reinforcing conventional behavior.

Setting rules. Direct control is enhanced to the extent that parents and others provide the juvenile with clearly defined rules that prohibit delinquent behavior and that limit the opportunities and temptations for delinquency. These rules may specify whom the juvenile associates with; for example, parents may forbid or strongly discourage their children from associating with juveniles who seem prone to delinquency. The rules may specify where the juvenile can and cannot go; for example, some parents may forbid their children from spending time in unsupervised locations, such as the street. The rules may specify the activities in which juveniles can and cannot engage; for example, some parents may forbid their children from attending unsupervised parties. The rules may specify what the juvenile can and cannot have; for example, parents may limit the spending money of their children or refuse to allow them to dress in a certain way. These rules may also specify time restrictions for the juvenile; for example, parents frequently impose curfews on their children.

Monitoring. Direct control involves more than just setting rules. It also involves monitoring juveniles' behavior to ensure that they comply with the rules and do not engage in delinquency. Monitoring may be direct or indirect. In *direct monitoring*, the juvenile is under the direct surveillance of a parent or other conventional "authority figure." In *indirect monitoring*, the parent or authority figure does not directly observe the juvenile but makes an effort to keep tabs on what the juvenile is doing. The parent, for example, may ask the juvenile where he or she is going, may periodically phone or text him or her, may ask others about the juvenile's behavior, or the like. Juveniles obviously differ in the extent to which their behavior is monitored. In some cases, a parent meets the juvenile when he or she arrives home from school and the juvenile is seldom out of the sight of adults. In other cases, the juvenile's parents are seldom at home, or the juvenile spends much time on the street or in other locations where monitoring by conventional adults is minimal.

Elijah Anderson (1999) conducted a field study of residents in a poor, inner-city community in Philadelphia. He found that most parents in this community tried to monitor their children's behavior, but parents who were part of what Anderson called "street-oriented families" were a prominent exception. In the words of Anderson (1999:69):

> At an early age, often even before they start school and without much adult supervision, children from street-oriented families gravitate to the streets, where they must be ready to "hang," to socialize competitively with peers. These children have a great deal of latitude and are allowed to rip and run up and down the streets. They often come home from school, put their books down, and go right back out the door. On school nights many eight- and nine-year olds remain out until nine or ten o'clock (teenagers may come home whenever they want to).

Setting rules and monitoring behavior should restrain delinquency: the rules prohibit delinquency and limit the temptations and opportunities for delinquency, while monitoring increases the likelihood that rule violations/delinquency will be detected. Several studies have examined the relationship between setting rules, monitoring, and delinquency, with most such work focusing on parents.[2] The studies tend to find that higher levels of rule setting/monitoring are associated with moderately lower levels of delinquency, although certain data suggest that overly strict parents may be ineffective or that they may even increase delinquency (perhaps for reasons related to strain theory).

Sanctioning delinquency. Parents and others may closely supervise the child—setting rules and monitoring behavior—but they may fail to effectively sanction delinquency/deviance when it occurs. Direct control, then, is enhanced to the extent that delinquency/deviance is effectively sanctioned. What do we mean by "effectively sanctioned"? Effective sanctions are consistently applied. Studies indicate that the failure to punish and the inconsistent use of punishment contribute to delinquency. Effective punishments are also fairly applied; that is, the child is punished only when he or she deserves it and the punishment fits the offense (e.g., the child is not severely punished for trivial infractions). Further, effective punishments are not overly harsh. Data suggest that punishments using physical violence and verbal abuse are not effective; in fact, they tend to increase delinquency.[3] Such punishments may create "fear and resentment" in the child and "break the bonds of respect" between parent and child (Sampson and Laub, 1993a:68, 73). Many researchers recommend punishments like verbally condemning an act and explaining why it is wrong, imposing a time out, withdrawing privileges, and requiring the juvenile to perform certain tasks (e.g., Patterson and Gullion, 1977; Straus, 1994).[4]

Reinforcing conventional behavior. Parents and others should not only sanction delinquency but also reinforce conventional behaviors that compete with or provide alternatives to the delinquency. For example, suppose your child frequently resorts to violence when he or she gets into disputes with others. You should not only punish your child for such violence, you should also teach the child how to resolve disputes through verbal means, and you should reinforce the child when he or she does so.

To further illustrate the components of direct control, the Partnership for Drug-Free Kids, a nonprofit organization, encourages parents to keep their children safe and healthy by setting rules, monitoring activities, sanctioning misbehavior, and reinforcing prosocial behavior. The organization produces informational guides, videos, and parental "tool kits" that communicate messages like the following:

> Lots of parents are afraid to set limits. They think it will build a wall between them and their teen. In truth, limits actually show your teen that you care. . . . Depending on your teen's personality and routine, you might consider setting boundaries that spell out [for example] what she can and can't do after school. (Note: This is prime time for experimenting with drugs and alcohol. Having an adult around during these hours is one of the most effective ways to keep kids clean.)

In addition to setting rules and monitoring behavior, these materials also stress the importance of sanctioning: "There's got to be a price for stepping over the line. (Otherwise, why would a teen pay attention to limits?) Let your teen help you define the consequences." Finally, these materials encourage parents to comment regularly on their child's positive qualities and to compliment them when they are doing well (reinforcement). For further information, visit http://www.drugfree.org.

Stake in Conformity

The efforts of others to directly control juveniles' behavior are a major restraint to delinquency. These efforts, however, are more effective with some juveniles than with others. For example, all juveniles are subject to more or less the same direct controls at school: the same rules, the same monitoring, and the same sanctions if they deviate. Yet some juveniles are very responsive to these controls, while others commit deviant acts on a regular basis. There are several reasons for this difference, but one fundamental reason is that some juveniles have more to lose by engaging in deviance. These juveniles have what has been called a strong *stake in conformity*, and they do not want to jeopardize that stake by engaging in deviance/delinquency (see Toby, 1957). For example, imagine two students: One has an A average and dreams of going to Harvard, and the other has a D average and dreams of dropping out of school. Who do you think is going to be more responsive to the threat of school sanctions?

An individual's stake in conformity—what a person stands to lose by engaging in delinquency—functions as another major restraint to delinquency. Those with a lot to lose will be more fearful of being caught and sanctioned and so will be less likely to engage in delinquency. A stake in conformity has two components: (1) emotional attachment to conventional others and (2) the actual or anticipated investment in conventional society.

Emotional attachment to conventional others. If we have a strong emotional attachment to conventional others, like parents and teachers, we have more to lose by engaging in delinquency. Our delinquency may upset people we care about, cause them to think badly of us, and possibly disrupt our relationship with them. For example, many of the students in my juvenile delinquency class report that they do not engage in delinquency because they do not want to hurt their parents or cause their parents to think badly of them. People's emotional bond to conventional others, then, is one major component of their "stake in conformity."

Studies generally confirm the importance of this bond.[5] Individuals who report that they love and respect their parents and other conventional figures are usually lower in delinquency. Individuals who do not care about their parents or others have less to lose by engaging in delinquency and so are more "free" to act on their desires. The association between emotional attachment and delinquency, however, is usually small to moderate. And we should note that an attachment to delinquent others does not reduce delinquency, since delinquency is not likely to jeopardize the relationship with these others. Attachment to delinquent others often increases delinquency, as one would expect from social learning theory.[6]

Actual or anticipated investment in conventional activities. A second major component of a person's stake in conformity is his or her investment in conventional society. Most people have put a lot of time and energy into conventional activities, like "getting an education, building up a business, [and] acquiring a reputation for virtue" (Hirschi, 1969:20). And they have been rewarded for their efforts in the form of good grades, material possessions, a good reputation, and the like. Juveniles may also expect their efforts to reap certain rewards in the future; for example, they may anticipate getting into college or professional school, obtaining a good job, and living in a nice house. In short, they have a large investment—both actual and anticipated—in conventional society. They do not want to jeopardize that investment by engaging in delinquency. Once again, they have too much to lose. Studies usually indicate that delinquency is moderately lower among juveniles who like school, are doing well in school, and have high educational and occupational expectations.[7]

As an illustration of someone with a low investment in conventional activities, consider this quote from a juvenile offender in a study of youth in a Boston public housing project by MacLeod (1995:124):

> I didn't really care to try in school. . . . You ain't got a chance of getting a good job, even with a high school diploma. You gotta go on to college, get your Masters and shit like that to get a good paying job that you can live comfortably on. So if you're not planning on going to college, I think [working to get good grades in high school is] a waste of time.

The youth who made this quote ended up dropping out of school and getting a job, only to be laid off a short time later. As MacLeod pointed out, he was "out of school, out of work, and out of money"; furthermore, he did "not have much to which he could look forward." We present additional examples in Box 8.1.

Box 8.1   "Dead by 25, So Who Cares?" Future Uncertainty and Delinquency

According to control theorists, anticipated investments in conventional society serve to inhibit delinquency. For example, young people who look forward to a college education, a rewarding conventional career, or a family of their own have much to lose by engaging in illegal behavior. Not wanting to jeopardize their future plans, such individuals will have an incentive to "think twice" before engaging in unlawful conduct.

But what about young people who *see no future at all?* In particular, children who grow up in "urban war zones" (described at the end of Chapter 7) may lose faith in the future when exposed to high levels of serious violence. A survey of school children in Chicago revealed that in certain inner-city neighborhoods, nearly 25 percent had witnessed someone being killed (C. Bell and Jenkins, 1993). In a similar survey of students in inner-city Cleveland, 33 percent of male students reported that they had been shot or shot at (M. Singer et al., 1995). And research indicates that such youth may come to doubt their future, as suggested by the following young men:

> Where I'm from you never know if you gonna live one minute to the next. It's like a war out there. People die every day. You can go to sleep and hear gunshots all night man, all night. Bullets be lying in the street in the morning. (quoted in Brezina et al., 2009:1113)

(Continued)

(Continued)

> Life is short. I don't know what the chance is [of me getting killed in the near future]. Might be dead by 25, so who cares? (quoted in Brezina et al., 2009:1115)

Consistent with the expectations of control theorists, studies in this area find that a sense of "futurelessness" is associated with elevated levels of delinquency (e.g., Agnew, 2002; Brezina et al., 2009; Piquero, 2016). Compared to their more optimistic peers, young people who believe they have a good chance of dying an early death are more likely to engage in theft, robbery, and assault. Presumably, young people who feel uncertain about their future have "less to lose" by engaging in illegal conduct. As a result, they tend to focus on satisfying their immediate desires and have less reason to worry about the long-term consequences of their actions:

> Life is short, so it's smart to get yours now. . . . Ain't no point in being scared because you cannot know [what] you gonna die from. . . . If I see something I want I take it right then because that might be your only chance in this world to get some. Somebody might be shootin' dice on the curb or something, I walk up and take all the money. So like that. (quoted in Brezina et al., 2009:1117–1118)

Exposure to community violence has been linked to poor school performance, "difficulty forming healthy [emotional] attachments to others," and impulsivity (Harris, 2009:136; Monahan et al., 2015). Therefore, it has been suggested that such exposure may be another factor preventing young people from developing other stakes in conformity. Recognizing these and other negative outcomes, lawmakers in California made it easier for affected children to obtain the help they need to cope, providing up to $5,000 for mental health counseling (Harris, 2009). More generally, mental health experts are now recommending that individuals who exhibit behavior problems be assessed for their exposure to violence and other potentially traumatic experiences. (For more on "trauma-informed" care, see Box 21.1 in Chapter 21.)

Questions for Discussion
1. Some people believe that young offenders will be deterred by the threat of more severe sanctions, such as longer prison sentences. Do you think the young offenders quoted here would be responsive to such threats? Why or why not?
2. What interventions beyond mental health counseling are needed to address the problem of exposure to community violence? Can you think of additional possibilities?

Belief

Imagine that you had the opportunity to steal something that you wanted but could not afford. Imagine further that you were certain that you would not be caught and sanctioned. Would you do it? Some of you will say yes; the absence of direct controls and the feeling that you have nothing to lose are enough to result in your delinquency. Others, however, will say no. A major reason for rejecting the opportunity is that you have come to believe that delinquency is wrong. This belief functions as a major restraint against delinquency. It is an important restraint, since we all are sometimes tempted to engage in crime and the probability of external sanction is low. (The belief that delinquency is wrong may help explain the gender gap in delinquency, since females are more likely than males to hold this belief—see Box 8.2).

The extent to which people believe that delinquency is wrong is at least partly a function of an individual's level of direct control and stake in conformity. Did the person's parents provide a clear set of rules that condemned delinquency? Did the parents monitor

Box 8.2   Gender, Moral Beliefs, and Delinquency

As we have seen, males generally engage in more delinquent acts than girls. In Chapter 6, we presented the explanation that strain theorists provide for this gender gap in delinquency (see Box 6.1). And in Chapter 7, we highlighted the mechanisms of social learning, which could also be used to explain the gender gap. Social learning theorists, for example, might explain the higher rate of male delinquency in terms of delinquent peer influence: males are more delinquent because they are more likely to associate with delinquent peers. These peers, in turn, model, provide reinforcement for, and teach beliefs that promote delinquent behavior (evidence indicates that males are in fact more likely than females to have delinquent friends).

Control theorists take a different approach. Instead of asking why males have a higher rate of delinquency, they are more apt to ask, "Why aren't girls just as delinquent as boys? What is *stopping* girls from engaging in delinquency at the same rate?" One possible answer to these questions has to do with gender differences in restraint. In particular, females are more likely than males to believe that delinquency is wrong. As described earlier, this belief serves as an important control or restraint against delinquency. Thus, instead of focusing on motivations or enticements, control theorists tend to focus on the factors that serve to *inhibit* delinquency among young people.

This issue was explored in a research study by Daniel Mears and his colleagues (1998). After examining data from a national survey of adolescents, the researchers found that, relative to males, females are more likely to view delinquency as "very wrong." For example, 51 percent of females in the survey regard "hitting someone" as very wrong, compared to 34 percent of males. These beliefs, in turn, reduce the probability of delinquency, though they do not eliminate delinquent behavior. But moral beliefs serve another important function: they help counteract the influence of delinquent peers. Further inspection of the data revealed that, even when females have delinquent friends, they are less likely than males to be influenced by such friends (females, e.g., may be less likely to "go along" with their peers who express the intention to engage in delinquency). In fact, among females with very strong moral beliefs, the influence of delinquent peers was eliminated.

In sum, the study by Mears et al. highlights the role of belief as an important restraint. Males have higher rates of delinquency partly as a result of having more delinquent friends—a fact that is consistent with a social learning explanation of the gender gap. But this is not the whole story. Consistent with control theory, another reason for the gender gap is that females have stronger moral beliefs than males (on average). As a result, females are more restrained than males, and they are less likely to be led astray by delinquent friends. Finally, other research indicates that young people with strong moral beliefs are less likely to associate with delinquent peers in the first place (Brezina and Piquero, 2007).

Questions for Discussion

1. Why do girls have stronger moral beliefs about delinquency than boys, on average? What may explain this gender difference in belief? (Note: Later in this chapter we address some of the sources of belief).

2. Consider the other types of control discussed in this chapter (direct control, stake in conformity, and self-control). How might boys and girls differ with respect to these other types of control? What gender differences, if any, would you expect to find?

behavior and punish delinquency? Such actions serve to teach children that delinquency is wrong. Were the children strongly attached to their parents? Such attachment increases the likelihood that the children will adopt parental beliefs. Finally, do they have a large investment in conventional society? People are more likely to accept conventional beliefs when it is to their advantage to do so.

So individuals who are low in direct control and have a low stake in conformity are less likely to believe that delinquency is wrong. Such individuals often have an *amoral orientation to delinquency*: they believe that delinquency is neither good nor bad. As a consequence, their beliefs do not restrain them from engaging in delinquency. Their beliefs do not propel or push them into delinquency; they do not believe that delinquency is good. Their amoral beliefs simply free them to pursue their needs and desires in the most expedient way. Unlike social learning theorists, most control theorists argue that few people define delinquency as good or acceptable. Rather than being taught that delinquency is good, control theorists argue that some juveniles are simply not taught that delinquency is bad.

Studies suggest that juveniles do differ in the extent to which they condemn delinquency. Most juveniles define delinquent acts, especially serious acts, as generally wrong. A significant minority of juveniles, however, have a somewhat amoral view of delinquent acts. For example, a national sample of adolescents was asked, "How wrong is it for someone your age to hit or threaten to hit someone without any reason?" Seven percent of the respondents replied "a little bit wrong," while 93 percent said "wrong" or "very wrong." Individuals with amoral beliefs are somewhat more likely to engage in delinquency.[8] (Studies, however, also suggest that many juveniles do have beliefs favorable to delinquency, as described in Chapter 7 on social learning theory.)

Self-Control

Several types of control have been listed, including direct control, stake in conformity, and beliefs regarding delinquency. Some individuals are less responsive to these controls than others, however. These individuals **have trouble restraining themselves from acting on their immediate desires.** For example, if someone provokes them, they are more likely to get into a fight. Or if someone offers them drugs at a party, they are more likely to accept. They do not stop to consider the negative consequences of their behavior. Rather, they simply focus on the immediate, short-term benefits or pleasures of the delinquent act. In the words of M. Gottfredson and Hirschi (1990:87), they are more "vulnerable to the temptations of the moment." Such individuals are said to be low in *self-control.*

Self-control is usually indexed by several personality traits, including impulsivity, a strong preference for immediate over delayed rewards, a preference for risky activities, high activity levels, and little ambition or motivation (see Grasmick et al., 1993; A. Piquero, 2008b).[9] Many of these traits are discussed in Chapter 10. And such traits have been measured with survey items like the following (from Grasmick et al., 1993; respondents are asked to agree or disagree with each item):

1. I act on the spur of the moment without stopping to think.
2. I do things that bring me pleasure here and now.
3. I find it exciting to do things for which I might get in trouble.
4. I take risks just for the fun of it.
5. I feel better when I am on the move than when I am sitting and thinking.
6. I try to avoid projects that I know will be difficult.

There has been a great deal of research on self-control since the early to mid-1990s. This research has established that low self-control is an important cause of delinquency— likely one of the most important causes.[10] (The other types of control that we have listed, however, also affect delinquency—even after we have accounted for levels of self-control.[11]) The fact that self-control has a large effect on delinquency has recently stimulated much research on the factors that affect one's level of self-control.

Why is it that some individuals are low in self-control? Gottfredson and Hirschi (1990) argue that low self-control is our natural state; that is, individuals initially lack the ability to restrain themselves from acting on their immediate desires. People must be taught to exercise self-control. Gottfredson and Hirschi go on to argue that parents play the central role in this process. In particular, self-control is most likely to result when parents have a strong emotional bond to their children, establish clear rules for behavior, closely monitor their children, and consistently sanction them for rule violations (i.e., exercise direct control over them). As a result of such factors, most children eventually learn to exercise some self-restraint over their behavior. Some parents, however, fail to teach their children to exercise self-control. Data provide some support for these arguments, suggesting that factors like parental attachment, monitoring, and discipline have an important effect on the development of self-control.[12]

Recent research, however, suggests that other factors also influence the development of self-control. For example, studies suggest that teachers, peers, and neighbors may also help juveniles develop self-control.[13] There is some evidence that certain stressful life events, such as physical abuse at an early age, impede the development of self-control (Kort-Butler et al., 2011). Likewise, criminal victimization tends to weaken the self-control of adolescents in the near term, perhaps because victimized young people become angry and lose sight of the possible consequences of their actions (Agnew et al., 2011; Monahan et al., 2015). Further, research suggests that at least some of the traits that make up self-control have a biological basis (Chapter 13; Cauffman et al., 2005; John Paul Wright and Beaver, 2005; John Paul Wright, Beaver, Delisi, and Vaughn, 2008). Many of these traits, for example, have a strong genetic basis—with individuals inheriting a predisposition for these traits from their parents.

Is it possible to alter one's level of self-control? Certain criminologists argue that one's level of self-control is established early in life, before age 10, and is relatively stable thereafter (Gottfredson and Hirschi, 1990). Studies do find that the trait of self-control is somewhat stable, such that people who are low in self-control at one point in time tend to be low at a later point in time. Self-control, however, is far from perfectly stable. Some people experience increases or decreases in self-control during the adolescent years and beyond. These increases and decreases are caused by changes in such factors found to affect self-control, such as parenting practices, school factors, and the nature of one's peers.[14] This is an important finding, with implications for controlling delinquency (see Chapter 24).

SUMMARY

Control theory asks why people conform, not why they deviate. And it says we conform because of the controls or restraints placed on our behavior. In particular, conformity is most likely when others attempt to directly control our behavior, when we have a large stake in conformity, when we believe that delinquency is wrong, and when we are able to control our own behavior. Conversely, delinquency is most likely when these forms of control are low or absent (see Figure 8.2). In such cases, individuals are free to satisfy their needs and desires in the most expedient way—which is often through delinquent acts. The data are generally supportive of control theory, and, as indicated earlier, control and social learning theories are the leading explanations of delinquency.

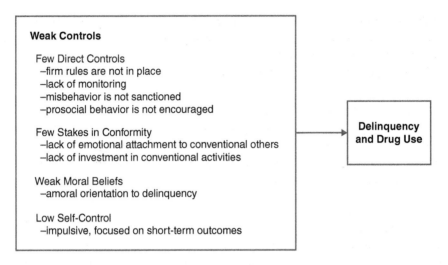

FIGURE 8.2 According to Control Theory, Weak Controls Increase the Likelihood of Delinquency

TEACHING AIDS
Controversial Issue: The Nature of Human Nature

Control theorists hold a particular view of human nature. They believe that people "naturally" pursue their self-interest, seeking to maximize their pleasure and minimize their pain. This pursuit of self-interest is what explains crime, since criminal acts like theft and violence are often the easiest or most expedient way for people to get what they want. It is easier to steal money, for example, than it is to work for it. Crime, then, requires no special explanation. In particular, people do not need to be taught to engage in crime, nor are strains necessary to push them into crime. Rather, all people sometimes experience situations where crime is the most expedient way to satisfy their needs and desires. The only thing that prevents them from engaging in crime is the controls or restraints they face. This view is well expressed by one of the leading control theorists:

> Control theories all assume that all people are alike in that they tend to pursue self-interest—they seek pleasure and try to avoid harm. Because most criminal and deviant acts satisfy human needs and desires, control theories assume constant motivation for deviance. They further assume that individuals will engage in deviance if some form of restraint is not present. (M. Gottfredson, 2006:79)

Data presented in Chapter 4 suggest that there may be some basis for this view. Describing recent research on young children, Lahey and Waldman (2005:18) state that "nearly half of all toddlers hit, kick, intentionally break things, take other children's toys, state untruths, and resist the authority of adults from the time they can walk and talk."

Some scholars, however, have challenged this view of human nature. Frans De Waal, in particular, attacks the view that "morality is a thin crust underneath which boil human passions that are invariably antisocial, amoral, and egoistic" (De Waal, 2003:8). He claims that people are "naturally" social, inclined to cooperate with one another. This inclination is said to be evolutionarily based. Cooperation makes it easier to secure food and protect oneself against predators. Those individuals who are inclined to cooperate with others, then, are more likely to survive and pass their genes on to others. Further, De Waal argues that with time, this inclination leads people to assist others even when there is no direct benefit in doing so:

> All species that rely on cooperation—from elephants to wolves and people—show group loyalty and helping tendencies. These tendencies evolved in the context of a close-knit social life in which they benefited relatives and companions able to repay the favor. The impulse to help was therefore never totally without survival value to the ones showing the impulse. But . . . the impulse became divorced from the consequences that shaped its evolution. This permitted its expression even when payoffs were unlikely, such as when strangers were beneficiaries. (2003:12)

De Waal draws on animal research to support his arguments about our "natural" tendency to cooperate with and help others, even when it is not in our self-interest to do so. For example, he notes that "rhesus monkeys refuse to pull a chain that delivers food to themselves if doing so shocks a companion. One monkey stopped pulling for 5 days, and another for 12 days after witnessing shock-delivery to a companion. These monkeys were literally starving themselves to avoid inflicting pain upon another" (2003:17–18).

Which view of human nature do you think is more accurate: (1) humans as self-interested creatures who seek to maximize their pleasure and minimize their pain or (2) humans as social creatures who show some concern for one another? How might we test or evaluate the accuracy of these views? Might both views have some merit? If the second view is more accurate, does that mean that control theories have little to say about the explanation of crime? If the first view is more accurate, does that invalidate strain and social learning theories?

Controversial Methods for Increasing Direct Control

Parents are the major source of control over their children, but unfortunately, many parents fail to exercise adequate control. For example, they fail to exercise sufficient direct control over their children. A number of programs have been developed to deal with this fact; some try to get parents to exercise more control, and some try to increase the control exercised by other groups, such as schools and communities. Most of these programs, like parent training programs and after-school recreational programs, arouse little controversy (descriptions of these programs are provided in Chapter 24). Certain of these programs, however, have aroused a good deal of controversy. One example is drug testing in schools, designed to improve the monitoring of student behavior. (The U.S. Supreme Court has ruled that such testing is constitutional for those in athletic programs and other extracurricular activities.) Another example is curfews, also designed to increase direct control over juveniles. (The effectiveness of drug testing and curfews in controlling delinquency is discussed in Howell, 2003a.)

The importance of direct control has received new attention given certain high-profile cases involving cyberbullying. In one case, 12-year-old Rebecca Sedwick jumped to her death after reportedly being bullied by her peers for months, both physically and online. A message posted on her social media site said she should "drink bleach and die" (for more on this case, see Chapter 17). A social media expert offered the following comments on the case:

> In most cases of cyber-bullying, parents reject the accusations that their children could perpetrate such heinous acts. The father of one of the girls accused of bullying Rebecca Ann Sedwick claimed that "none of it is true . . . my daughter's a good girl and I'm 100 percent sure that whatever they're saying about my daughter is not true," despite the proof the Sheriff claims to possess. . . . What role have the parents of bullies played in these cases? Why are parents giving young children smart phones with 24/7 access to social networks? More importantly, why are they not diligently monitoring their kids' online activity? Pre-teens typically don't have the funds or ability to purchase internet-enabled devices or authorize internet and mobile contracts for access to social

networks. If parents are going to provide such access to their children, they must be held accountable for their online activities, including cyber-bullying. (Fiorella, 2014)

Some jurisdictions have passed parental liability laws, making parents liable for the criminal behavior of their children in certain circumstances—for example, when parents fail to provide adequate supervision. Efforts to enforce such laws have not fared well in the court system. Even so, do you think parents should be held responsible for the delinquent acts of their children in certain circumstances? If so, under what sorts of circumstances? What should be done to the "offending" parents?

Web-Based Exercise: Where Do Theories Come From?

The theories you are reading about in this text were developed by many criminologists, each of whom drew on the work of many other criminologists. Certain of the leading criminology theorists were interviewed as part of the Oral History Project of the American Society of Criminology (ASC). The ASC is the leading organization for academic and research criminologists. You should:

1. Visit the website of the ASC at http://www.asc41.com.
2. Click on **Resources**" then click on **Oral History Project**.
3. Interviews with a good many criminologists are listed. Robert Merton and Albert Cohen were instrumental in developing strain theory, Ronald Akers in developing social learning theory, Travis Hirschi in developing control theory (listed under panels), and Medna Chesney-Lind in explaining female offending (read about her work at the end of Chapter 18). Skim through these and other of the interviews to get a sense of how criminologists developed their theories. This text does not discuss the work of particular theorists in detail, rather we focus on generic versions of each theory. But these generic versions draw heavily on these theorists and others. If you take additional courses in criminology, you will likely study the work of these theorists in more detail.

TEST YOUR KNOWLEDGE OF THIS CHAPTER

1. Describe the essential arguments of control theory in a few sentences.
2. Rather than focusing on the causes of delinquency, control theorists focus on the causes of conformity. Why?
3. Describe the similarities and differences between control theory and social learning theory.
4. What are the major types of control or restraints to delinquency?
5. Describe the major components of direct control.
6. What are the characteristics of effective sanctions?
7. Describe the two components of "stake in conformity," and indicate why they reduce delinquency.
8. Give two examples of each of the components of stake in conformity.
9. What is meant by "anticipated investment in conventional society"?
10. What is meant by belief?
11. Unlike social learning theorists, control theorists do not argue that juveniles are taught beliefs favorable to delinquency. What do control theorists argue regarding beliefs?
12. List or briefly describe three of the personality traits that make up low self-control.
13. Why are some individuals low in self-control, and is it possible to alter one's level of self-control?

THOUGHT AND DISCUSSION QUESTIONS

1. Do you think that the justice system (police, courts, correctional agencies) does a good job of exercising direct control (setting rules, effectively monitoring behavior, effectively sanctioning deviance)? Explain your answer. (See Chapter 23 for a full discussion.)

2. How might control theory explain forms of deviance like cheating on exams and excessive drinking?

3. Develop survey questions to measure the independent variables in your explanation of cheating and drinking.

4. Describe, in detail, a high school student who is low in self-control (e.g., describe the person's relationship with parents, grades, and beliefs regarding delinquency).

5. To reduce delinquency, what recommendations might a control theorist offer?

KEY TERMS

- Control theory
- Direct control
- Direct and indirect monitoring
- Stake in conformity
- Amoral orientation to delinquency
- Self-control

ENDNOTES

1. See Hirschi, 1977:329; also see Agnew, 1993; Britt and Gottfredson, 2003; Goode, 2008a; M. Gottfredson, 2006; Kornhauser, 1978:46–50; Paternoster and Bachman, 2001.

2. See Browning and Huizinga, 1999; Burton et al., 1995; Costello and Vowell, 1999; Farrington, 1996a; Fulkerson et al., 2008; Hagan, 1989; Hawkins, Herrenkohl et al., 1998; Hoeve et al., 2009; Huizinga et al., 2003; Ingram et al., 2007; Lahey et al., 2008; Loeber, Farrington, Stouthamer-Loeber, and Van Kammen, 1998; Loeber and Stouthamer-Loeber, 1986; Nye, 1958; Patterson et al., 1992; Sampson and Laub, 1993a; Simons, Simons, Chen, Brody, and Lin, 2007; J. Snyder and Patterson, 1987; Thornberry, Krohn et al. (with Porter), 2003; Tilton-Weaver et al., 2013; Vazsonyi and Belliston, 2007; Vermeersch et al., 2008; Wells and Rankin, 1988; J. Wright, Beaver, Delisi, and Vaughn, 2008; K. Wright and Wright, 1995.

3. See Agnew, 1983; Alyahri and Goodman, 2008; Evans et al., 2012; Hipwell et al., 2008; Loeber and Stouthamer-Loeber, 1986; McKee et al., 2007; Nye, 1958; Patterson et al., 1992; Ratchford and Beaver, 2009; Sampson and Laub, 1993a; J. Snyder and Patterson, 1987; Straus, 1994; Wells and Rankin, 1988; K. Wright and Wright, 1995.

4. For additional information on the factors influencing the effectiveness of punishment, see Bandura, 1973:222–227; Quay, 1983; and Snyder and Patterson, 1987; also see Patterson and Gullion, 1977, for a child-training manual.

5. See Costello and Vowell, 1999; Hirschi, 1969; Hoeve et al., 2012; Jang, 1999; Loeber and Stouthamer-Loeber, 1986; Longshore et al., 2005; Mack et al., 2007; Özbay and Özcan, 2008; Rankin and Kern, 1994; Sampson and Laub, 1993a; Stewart, 2003; B. Wright, Caspi, Moffitt, and Silva, 1999; K. Wright and Wright, 1995; also see Kempf-Leonard, 1993, for an overview.

6. See Agnew, 1991b; Akers, 1998; Conger, 1976; Felson and Staff, 2006; Jensen and Brownfield, 1983; Özbay and Özcan, 2008.

7. See Agnew, 1991a, 2003b; Chapple, McQuillan, and Berdahl, 2005; Costello and Vowell, 1999; Hawkins and Lishner, 1987; Hirschi, 1969; Jang, 1999; Kempf, 1993; Maguin and Loeber, 1996; Matsueda et al., 2006; Sampson and Laub, 1993a; Stewart, 2003; Thornberry, Krohn et al. (with Porter), 2003; B. Wright, Caspi, Moffitt, and Silva, 1999.

8. See Chapple, McQuillan, and Berdahl, 2005; Hirschi, 1969; Kornhauser, 1978; Longshore et al., 2005; Stewart, 2003.

9. This conception of low self-control differs somewhat from that of M. Gottfredson and Hirschi (1990); most notably, M. Gottfredson and Hirschi view the trait of irritability as a component of low self-control, while we view irritability as part of a separate personality dimension. See Chapter 13 for further discussion.

10. See Burt et al., 2006; Burton et al., 1998; Cauffman et al., 2005; Evans et al., 1997; Goode, 2008b; Grasmick et al., 1993; Hay and Forrest, 2008; Hirshi, 2004; LaGrange and Silverman, 1999; Le Blanc, 1993; Longshore, 1998; Moffitt et al., 2011; Piquero and Boufford, 2007; Piquero and Tibbetts, 1996; Polakowski, 1994; Pratt and Cullen, 2000; Rebellon et al., 2008; Simons et al., 2007; Vazsonyi and Belliston, 2007; P. Wood et al., 1993; B. Wright, Caspi, Moffitt, and Silva, 1999.

11. See Cheung and Cheung, 2008; De Li, 2004; Longshore et al., 2005; Piquero and Bouffard, 2007; Tittle et al., 2004; B. Wright, Caspi, Moffitt, and Silva, 1999.

12. See Botchkovar et al., 2015; Burt et al., 2006; Cullen et al., 2008; M. Gottfredson, 2006; Hay, 2001a; Meldrum, 2008; Nofziger, 2008; Pratt et al., 2004; Rebellon et al., 2008; Simons et al., 2007; Vazsonyi and Belliston, 2007; Unnever et al., 2003; J. Wright and Beaver, 2005.

13. See Burt et al., 2006; Cullen et al., 2008; Meldrum, 2008; Pratt et al., 2004; Teasdale and Silver, 2009; B. Wright, Caspi, Moffitt, and Silva, 1999.

14. See Burt et al., 2006; Hay and Forrest, 2006; Longshore et al., 2005; Piquero et al., 2010; Winfree et al., 2006; B. Wright, Caspi, Moffitt, and Silva, 1999.

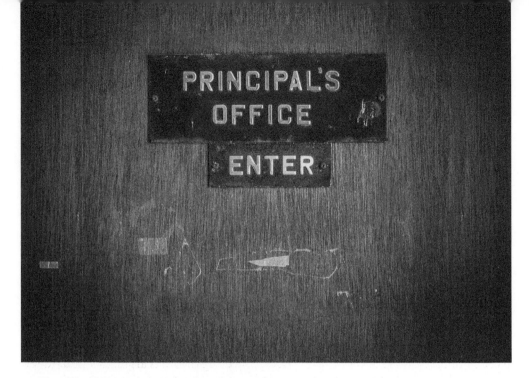

9 Labeling Theory

Does the Reaction to Delinquency
Lead to Further Delinquency?

S train, social learning, and control theories focus on the characteristics of juveniles and their environment. These theories describe how such characteristics lead juveniles to engage in delinquency. *Labeling theory* **focuses on the reaction to delinquency: both the** *official reaction* **by the justice system and the** *informal reaction* **by parents, peers, teachers, and others.** Labeling theory describes how the reaction to delinquency sometimes leads offenders to engage in further delinquency.

After reading this chapter, you should be able to:

- Describe the central ideas of labeling theory.
- Identify and describe the major types of reaction to delinquency examined by labeling theorists.
- Explain why the harsh/rejecting reaction may lead to further delinquency.
- Identify factors that increase the likelihood of a harsh/rejecting reaction.
- Explain why some juveniles are more likely than others to respond to a harsh/rejecting response with further delinquency.
- Describe the types of research that have been conducted to test labeling theory.

As stated above, labeling theorists focus on the reaction to delinquency and how this reaction impacts future behavior. In particular, **labeling theorists argue that individuals who are labeled "delinquent" are often viewed as "bad" or "evil" people.** And this view **leads others to reject them and treat them in a harsh manner.** This "harsh/rejecting" response **increases the likelihood of further delinquency** because of how the juveniles subjected to this response tend to react:

1. They experience a reduction in control, partly because conventional others do not want to associate with them, and they have trouble obtaining a stake in society.
2. They experience an increase in strain, since they have more trouble achieving their goals and others treat them in a harsh manner.
3. They experience an increase in the social learning for crime because they are forced to associate with delinquent others (since conventional others reject them).
4. They come to view themselves as the type of people who commit delinquent acts, because that is how others view and treat them.

As is apparent, labeling theory draws heavily on strain, social learning, and control theories. And, to a large extent, labeling theory may be viewed as an elaboration or extension of these theories. But, again, labeling theory is distinguished by the fact that it focuses on how others react to the juvenile's delinquency and the impact of this reaction on the juvenile. Labeling theory, then, does not try to explain the juvenile's initial acts of delinquency, the acts that result in labeling. Rather, the theory tries to explain why some juvenile offenders are more likely than others to continue engaging in delinquency and perhaps move on to more serious delinquency (see Chapter 10 for additional explanations of why some individuals continue to engage in delinquency). This difference between labeling and other theories is illustrated in Figure 9.1.

We begin by providing a brief overview of labeling theory, noting that the theory addresses several questions about the reaction to delinquency. We then present a generic version of labeling theory that draws from the leading versions of labeling theory, including those of Tannenbaum (1938), Lemert (1951, 1972), Becker (1963), Matza (1969), Paternoster and Iovanni (1989), Matsueda (1992), Heimer and Matsueda (1994), Sampson and Laub (1997), and especially Braithwaite (1989, 2002) and Sherman (1993, 2000). This generic theory describes the different ways in which others react to delinquency, with a focus on the harsh/rejecting reaction. It describes why the harsh/rejecting reaction increases the likelihood of further delinquency. It discusses why some juvenile offenders are more likely

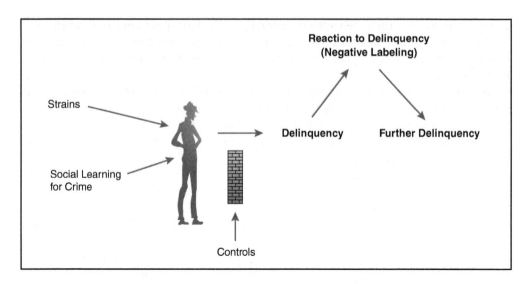

FIGURE 9.1 Labeling Theory Focuses on the Reaction to the Juvenile's Delinquency and Argues That This Reaction Sometimes Leads to Further Delinquency

than others to experience this reaction. And it argues that the effect of the harsh/rejecting reaction on delinquency is conditioned by the characteristics of juvenile offenders. That is, it argues that some juvenile offenders are more likely than others to respond to the harsh/rejecting reaction with further delinquency. The chapter concludes with a discussion of the evidence on labeling theory.

It is important to examine labeling theory not only because it helps us explain why some juvenile offenders continue to offend but also because it has had and continues to have a major impact on the juvenile justice system. In particular, labeling theory explicitly addresses the issue of how we should (and should not) react to delinquency. Labeling theory is the primary inspiration behind the "restorative justice" approach to delinquency, which is having a major impact on the juvenile justice system in certain areas. This approach, described briefly in this chapter and more fully in Chapter 23, involves an alternative way of reacting to delinquency—one that is designed to reduce the likelihood of further delinquency.

BACKGROUND ON LABELING THEORY

Labeling theorists ask five major questions about the reaction to delinquency.

First, labeling theorists ask **why certain acts are defined as delinquent or status offenses.** For example, why is using marijuana generally defined as a delinquent offense (see Becker, 1963)? Why are behaviors like skipping school and drinking alcohol defined as status offenses? We do not address this question in this chapter, although this question was addressed to some extent in Chapter 1, where we discussed the invention of juvenile delinquency. As part of that discussion, we examined the development of status offense laws. We presented a common argument made by labeling theorists: Powerful groups in our society have a large impact over what behaviors are and are not defined as illegal. These groups generally act in their own self-interest, so they work to get those behaviors that they find threatening or morally objectionable defined as illegal (see Jensen and Rojek, 1998; Paternoster and Bachman, 2001). As indicated in Chapter 1, for example, there is some evidence that upper-class individuals in the late 1800s and early 1900s felt threatened by the many poor children hanging out on the street, sometimes engaging in crime. As a result, they lobbied for the passage of status offense laws, like those requiring that juveniles attend school or be home by a certain hour.

Second, labeling theorists ask **how others react to delinquency.** They describe several major ways of reacting, including the harsh or rejecting reaction described earlier. This reaction is said to be especially common in the United States (Braithwaite, 1989).

Third, labeling theorists ask **what impact the reaction to delinquency has on further delinquency.** Most attention has focused on the harsh/rejecting reaction, since this reaction is said to increase the likelihood of further delinquency. Labeling theorists, then, make a rather provocative argument: The way in which we often react to delinquency in the United States has the effect of increasing delinquency.

Fourth, labeling theorists ask **why some juvenile offenders are more likely than others to experience the harsh/rejecting reaction.** Part of the answer has to do with the nature of a juvenile's delinquency. Juveniles engaging in more frequent and serious delinquency are more likely to experience the harsh or rejecting reaction. But the likelihood of experiencing this reaction is also influenced by factors beyond the juvenile's delinquency, such as the juvenile's race or ethnicity, social class, and gender.

Fifth, labeling theorists ask **whether some juvenile offenders are more likely than others to respond to the harsh/rejecting reaction with further delinquency.**

The answers that labeling theorists have provided to questions two through five are presented next.

HOW DO OTHERS REACT TO THE JUVENILE'S DELINQUENCY?

The police, courts, parents, school officials, and others may react to a juvenile's delinquency in several ways. Labeling theorists focus on three major types of reaction: Some may react in a harsh or rejecting manner, others may fail to respond to the juvenile's delinquency, and still others may condemn the juvenile's delinquency but accept the juvenile.

Harsh/Rejecting Reaction

The *harsh/rejecting reaction* is said to increase the likelihood of further delinquency. This reaction has two essential features. First, juveniles are labeled "delinquents," and this label **leads others to view them as "bad" or "evil" or "dangerous" people.** That is, others do not just view the juvenile's **behavior** as bad, they also view the **juvenile** as bad.

Second, this view of juveniles as bad **leads others to reject the juveniles and treat them in a harsh manner.** Others do not want to associate with or help the juveniles because they dislike and/or are fearful of them. Others treat the juveniles harshly; that is, they treat the juveniles in ways that are disrespectful, unfair, excessively punitive, and/or abusive (see especially Sherman, 1993).

Many labeling theorists focus on **the ways in which official agencies, like the police and courts, react to delinquency (or suspected delinquency).** It is said that these agencies often view juvenile offenders as bad or dangerous people and treat them in a harsh manner. To illustrate, a juvenile in a community with a gang problem described his relations with the police as follows:

> I wasn't a gangbanger. I used to hang out with them; they are my friends. The police started messing with me. They would pull me into their car and harass me. I kept telling them I was not a banger. But they don't believe anything we tell them. They asked me questions about this and other friends, guys from the hood who are gangbangers, and since I wouldn't tell them what they wanted to hear, they would say things like,

"Yes, you are one of those hoodlums from this street. We've been watching you for a long time, and now we got you, and you're going to pay."

One day I was with my girlfriend and my friend and his girl—it was like the four of us. So we were walking by the neighborhood. . . . The police saw us and pulled us over to a corner. They went through their shit—you know, "Who you be?" "Where are the other boys?" So, we didn't say nothing. They got really pissed and, in front of our girls, told us to kneel down and sing "Jingle Bells." So, there we are singing "jingle bells, jingle bells, jingle bells" for these pricks. . . . I wanted to kill them fuckers. How are you supposed to feel when they do that to you for no reason and then in front of your girl? And there's a lot of shit like that that goes on all the time. (Quoted in Padilla, 1992:83)

This juvenile did end up becoming a gang member, and he said he did so partly because of the way the police viewed and treated him. According to labeling theorists, being treated in a harsh or rejecting manner by the official agencies like the police often has this type of negative effect. Official agencies have much power over suspected offenders, and their actions can have a major effect on them. Further, the actions of official agencies may lead others to view juveniles as bad and treat them in a harsh or rejecting manner. Being arrested by the police, for example, may lead parents, teachers, and community residents to view and treat the juvenile as a "bad" person.

Contemporary labeling theorists also focus on **the "informal" reactions to delinquency by parents, teachers, and others.** Many labeling theorists argue that these informal reactions are just as important, if not more important, than official reactions. These informal reactions are more common than official reactions; for example, most offenders have encounters with the police infrequently, but they may have encounters with their parents every day. And these informal reactions often involve intimate others that the juvenile cares about (see Paternoster and Bachman, 2001; Triplett and Jarjoura, 1994).

Data from surveys and field studies suggest that parents, peers, teachers, and others may also view juvenile offenders as bad and treat them in a harsh or rejecting manner. Parents may become overly strict with their delinquent children or reject them, perhaps "throwing" them out of the house. Other parents in the community may tell their children to avoid the juvenile offenders. Teachers and other school officials may harshly sanction offenders and segregate them in special classes or schools for "troublemakers," and employers may refuse to hire offenders.

To illustrate, a juvenile offender described his experience and that of his friends in elementary school by stating that "the teachers would put it in our heads, you know. . . 'You guys are the troublemakers,' and 'You guys are too loud,' and 'You're too this, and you just don't want to listen, and you just want to sit in your chairs and lay there'" (Padilla, 1992:71). This offender was put in a special class for the "learning disabled," a class that he said was for "the bad ones." And he was treated in a harsh manner by his teachers; for example, he was regularly blamed for delinquent acts that came to the attention of school authorities.

Failure to Respond to the Juvenile's Delinquency

A second way of reacting to the juvenile's delinquency involves the failure to respond to the delinquency. That is, others may do little or nothing in response to the juvenile's delinquency. In most cases, this is because **others never find out about the delinquency.** As we discuss in Chapter 20, the police fail to detect the large share of delinquency that occurs. The same is probably true of parents and others. One study, for example, reported that about one in five teenagers has sex before age 15 (a status offense in most states). The study went on to report that only about one-third of the parents of sexually active 14-year-olds knew that their children were having sex (Lewin, 2003). Another study found that 39 percent of mothers and 62 percent of fathers of active gang members did not know their children were gang members. (Most of the gang members did not live with their fathers [Decker and Van Winkle, 1996:236].) So the failure to respond to delinquency is due largely to the fact that others are unaware of the juvenile's delinquency.

But even if the juvenile's delinquency is detected, **it may be ignored or subject to only a mild sanction.** For example, the police do not arrest most of the suspected juvenile offenders they encounter but instead release them, often with a warning (see Chapter 20). And juvenile courts do not formally process almost half of the suspected juvenile offenders that are referred to them (see Chapter 21). There are a number of reasons for this. Police and/or court officials may feel that the juvenile offender is basically a "good kid" who doesn't deserve to be sanctioned, they may lack good evidence to arrest or formally sanction, or they may be overwhelmed with more serious cases. Likewise, we know that some parents fail to sanction the delinquent behavior of their children, even when detected. The parents may also believe that their children are basically good kids who do not deserve serious sanctions. Or, if they have been overwhelmed by their children's behavior, they may have given up trying to discipline them. For example, one gang member who described his parents' reaction to his gang membership said, "My parents just say fuck it. He ain't going to listen. He going to do what he wants to do" (Decker and Van Winkle, 1996:244).

Some labeling theorists **argue that failure to respond to the juvenile's delinquency is a good strategy.** In particular, they claim that most juveniles engage in delinquency at one point or another, but this delinquency tends to be occasional and minor, and most juveniles "grow out of it" if left alone. According to these theorists, efforts to control the juvenile's delinquency run the risk of labeling the juvenile a "bad kid" and making matters worse. Ignoring the juvenile's delinquency avoids all the negative effects associated with the harsh/rejecting reaction. Certain labeling theorists, then, advocate a policy of *radical nonintervention*, claiming that the best way to reduce delinquency is to do as little as possible about it.[1]

Labeling theorists, in particular, have argued that the police should handle cases informally whenever possible rather than arresting juveniles. Juvenile court officials should divert juveniles from the court whenever possible, either outright releasing them or placing them in programs outside the court system. If court officials do formally process and sanction offenders, the offenders should be placed, whenever possible, in community-based programs rather than institutions. Finally, status offenses and many minor delinquent acts, like marijuana use, should be legalized or at least decriminalized (e.g., treated as violations of civil rather than criminal law, say, like "speeding" violations). Many of these recommendations were partly implemented by the juvenile justice system during the 1960s and 1970s, when labeling theory was at the height of its popularity (see Akers et al., 2016; Matsueda, 2001; Chapter 21).

Increasingly, however, labeling theorists are **moving away from the position that ignoring delinquency is a good strategy.** While ignoring delinquency may avoid the negative effects associated with the harsh/rejecting reaction, it may nevertheless increase delinquency by reducing direct control. It may also reduce the likelihood that juveniles will condemn delinquency and develop self-control, since these traits often result from direct control. Rather than ignoring delinquency, many labeling theorists now advocate a third type of reaction to delinquency.

"Condemn the Delinquency but Accept the Juvenile" Reaction

Many contemporary labeling theorists now argue that **the juvenile's delinquency should be condemned but in a way that is accepting of the juvenile** (recall the saying: "Condemn the sin, but love the sinner."). In particular, others should sanction the juvenile for his or her delinquency, emphasizing that the delinquency is morally wrong. The sanctions, however, should not be overly harsh. Further, the juvenile should not be rejected; rather, conventional others, like parents and teachers, should maintain close ties to the juvenile, even as the sanctions are being administered (see especially Braithwaite, 1989, 2002). The best way to appreciate this reaction is with an example.

Imagine that parents find out that their child has vandalized a local store. The parents explain to the child why they disapprove of this act. Among other things, they describe the harm that the act caused to the store owner and others in the community. If they are successful, the child will feel some shame and guilt for the act. The parents, however, do not condemn the child. For example, they do not tell the child, "You're no good," or "You're a rotten kid." The parents also sanction the child but in a way that is not overly harsh. Perhaps they require the child to apologize to the store owner, repair the damage or pay for the repairs, and do some community service (as opposed to beating the child, forcing the child out of the house, or trying to have the child "locked up"). And the parents continue to express their love and support for the child, forgiving the child once the sanctions have been administered (as opposed to rejecting the child).

Hay (2001b) measured this type of reaction by asking juveniles questions like the following:

1. When your parents are reacting to a rule violation they consider important, how much importance do they place on:
   a) Convincing you that what you did was immoral or unfair.
   b) Making you feel guilty or ashamed for what you did.
   c) Having you make up for your actions by apologizing or helping erase any harm that was done.
2. Do your parents see you as a good person even when they are upset with you?
3. Do your parents treat you with respect when they are disciplining you?
4. How likely is it that your parents would tell you that you are a "bad kid" when disciplining you?
5. How likely is it that your parents would tell you that they forgive you after disciplining you?

Labeling theorists argue that this *"condemn the delinquency but accept the juvenile" reaction* does not have the negative effects associated with the harsh/rejecting reaction.

In particular, it does not reduce control, since the juvenile maintains close ties to conventional others. It does not increase strain, since the juvenile is not treated in a harsh or rejecting manner. It does not foster the social learning of delinquency, since the juvenile is not driven to associate with delinquent others. And it does not lead the juvenile to view him- or herself as a bad person, since the parents and others condemn the juvenile's behavior rather than the juvenile. Further, this type of reaction does not have the negative consequences that result from ignoring delinquency, since the juvenile is sanctioned. This sanction imposes direct control on the juvenile and helps the juvenile learn to condemn delinquency, since parents and others try to convince the juvenile that his or her delinquency is morally wrong.

It is easy to understand how people like parents might go about condemning the juvenile's delinquency but accepting the juvenile. But how might official agencies like the police and courts react in this manner? According to labeling theorists like Braithwaite (1989, 2002) and Sherman (2000), the police and/or the courts should respond to most juvenile offenders by using the *restorative justice approach*. This approach focuses on making offenders aware of the harm they have caused and having them repair that harm. But it does so in a way that does not condemn the offender, is not overly harsh, and maintains or restores the offender's ties to conventional society.

The core part of the *restorative justice* **approach involves a** *conference* **between the offender, the victim, family members of the offender and victim, and selected community representatives.** This **restorative justice conference** takes the place of a court hearing. The first part of the conference examines the harm caused by the offender's delinquency. Among other things, the victim tells the offender about the harm she or he has suffered and asks questions of the offender (e.g., "Why did you do it?" "Why did you pick me?"). The focus is on making the offender appreciate the harm caused by his or her behavior, not on condemning the offender. In fact, the victim and others often come to realize that the offender is a troubled juvenile, not a "monster" or "evil" person. In the second part of the conference, everyone—including the offender—develops a plan to repair the harm. The plan often involves an apology to the victim, restitution to the victim, and community service. Harsh sanctions like incarceration are avoided. The offender is forgiven once the harm is repaired, and efforts are made to maintain or restore the offender's ties to conventional society. For example, efforts may be made to help the offender with school or employment problems. This approach is discussed further in Chapter 23 (also see Bazemore, 2000; Braithwaite, 2002). Data on its effectiveness are encouraging, suggesting that it is often more effective at reducing offending than approaches that are more harsh or rejecting in orientation.

Summary
The essential point of labeling theorists is that others often respond to delinquency in ways that increase the likelihood of further delinquency, with labeling theorists focusing on the harsh/rejecting reaction to delinquency.

WHY DOES THE HARSH/REJECTING REACTION LEAD TO FURTHER DELINQUENCY?
The harsh/rejecting reaction tends to reduce control, increase strain, and foster the social learning of crime; further, it leads juveniles to view themselves as the type of people who engage in delinquent acts. We elaborate on each of these points in the following sections.

Reduces Control
Conventional others view the juvenile offender as a bad or evil person, and, as a consequence, they avoid the offender or treat him or her in a harsh manner. This **reduces direct**

control, since others, like parents and teachers, avoid the juvenile or employ overly harsh methods of discipline. It **reduces the juvenile's stake in conformity,** since emotional ties between the juvenile and others, like parents and teachers, are weakened.[2] Also, the juvenile's investment in conventional society is weakened. Being labeled a delinquent, for example, disrupts relations with school authorities and jeopardizes the individual's future educational and occupational plans.[3] To illustrate, a study by Sweeten (2006) examined the effect of arrest and court appearance on the likelihood of dropping out of high school. Sweeten examined a national sample of adolescents and took account of a range of "third variables," including school grades, achievement test scores, educational expectations, poverty status, and self-reported delinquency. Sweeten found that "first-time arrest during high school nearly doubles the odds of dropout, while a court appearance nearly quadruples the odds of dropout" (2006:473). Similar studies find that formal contact with the police during adolescence can have lasting effects on the individual's stake in conformity, increasing the risk of unemployment in adulthood. Unemployment, in turn, is related to adult crime (Lopes et al., 2012; Farrington and Murray, 2014). Further, **the juvenile's beliefs may be weakened as well.** Juveniles are less likely to condemn delinquency if they are subject to weak direct controls and have a small stake in conformity. Finally, the experience of being viewed and treated as a bad person may weaken their resolve to exercise self-control.

Increases Strain

Others treat the juvenile in a harsh manner, thereby increasing levels of strain (Sampson and Laub, 1997; Stewart, Simons, Conger, and Scaramella, 2002). In particular, others may make it **more difficult for the juvenile to achieve his or her goals.** Employers, for example, may refuse to hire the juvenile (the blockage of monetary goals). The juvenile may be more closely monitored by parents, teachers, and police (the blockage of autonomy goals), and the juvenile may be treated in a disrespectful manner by these others (the blockage of status goals). Also, **the juvenile may experience the loss of positive stimuli and presentation of negative stimuli.** Conventional peers may avoid the juvenile. The juvenile may then associate with delinquent peers, where the likelihood of abuse is higher. Parents, teachers, and justice officials may employ harsh methods of control. Further, the experience of such harsh treatment may **increase the juvenile's level of irritability,** which in turn increases the juvenile's sensitivity to strains and likelihood of responding to strains in an aggressive manner (see Chapter 13).

Increases the Social Learning of Delinquency

Conventional others often try to avoid the juvenile, so the juvenile is **more likely to associate with delinquent others** as a result (M. Adams and Evans, 1996; Heimer and Matsueda, 1994; L. Johnson et al., 2004; Restivo and Lanier, 2015; Wiley et al., 2013). To illustrate, Bernburg et al. (2006) examined whether contact with the juvenile justice system (e.g., arrest, court involvement) influenced the likelihood that juveniles would subsequently associate with delinquent peers or join gangs. They took account of a range of "third variables" in their analysis, including self-reported delinquency, prior levels of delinquent peer association, and prior gang membership. Bernberg et al. (2006:77) found that "youths who experience juvenile justice intervention are significantly more likely to be members of gangs during the successive period relative to [comparable youths] who have no intervention experience. . . . Juvenile justice intervention increases the odds of gang membership by a factor of 5.2." Likewise, they found that juvenile justice intervention increases the likelihood of associating with delinquent peers. This, of course, increases the likelihood that juveniles will be differentially reinforced for delinquency, exposed to delinquent models, and taught beliefs favorable to delinquency. Further, labeled juveniles are more likely to develop beliefs favorable to delinquency as they seek to rationalize or justify their behavior to themselves and others.

Creates a Delinquent Self-Concept

Labeling theory is derived from a perspective in sociology known as **symbolic interactionism.** A central tenet of this perspective is that our *self-concept*—the way in which we view ourselves—is a function of how others view and treat us (see Matsueda, 2001). Suppose, for example, that others view and treat you as an intelligent person (e.g., teachers give you good grades, your parents tell you how smart you are, and your peers eagerly solicit your opinion on important issues). Eventually, you will come to view yourself as intelligent. Further, you will act on the basis of this self-concept; that is, you will act like an intelligent person. For example, you may participate frequently in class, regularly voice your opinions to others, and plan on obtaining an advanced education.

The same logic applies if others view and treat you as a bad person. **You may come to view yourself as a bad person and act accordingly** (M. Adams et al., 2003; Heimer and Matsueda, 1994; Matsueda, 1992). This does not happen immediately. It is not the case that someone calls you a delinquent or a bad kid, and you suddenly alter your self-concept. It happens gradually, if at all. Some juveniles are able to maintain a positive self-concept even in the face of harsh or rejecting treatment by others (see Rogers and Buffalo, 1974). Others alter their self-concept and behavior. As one juvenile offender stated, "If the teachers and everyone else thought we were bad, we started to show that we were. So, we started doing a lot of bad things" (Padilla, 1992:74).

WHAT DETERMINES WHETHER JUVENILES EXPERIENCE THE HARSH/REJECTING REACTION?

Only some of the juveniles who engage in delinquency are subject to the harsh/rejecting reaction described earlier. What determines whether juveniles experience this reaction from others?

The most important factor is **whether juveniles engage in delinquency, especially frequent and/or serious delinquency that becomes known to others.** We should note that delinquency is not an absolute requirement for a harsh or rejecting response from others. Occasionally, juveniles are falsely accused of delinquent behavior and subject to a harsh or rejecting response. Cases involving falsely accused criminals are frequently in the news, and a number of falsely accused individuals are sentenced to death. In fact, over 150 people on death row have been exonerated since 1973. In most cases, however, the harsh/rejecting reaction is stimulated by actual delinquency.

As indicated in Chapter 1, this harsh/rejecting reaction is especially common with serious offenders. The harsh/rejecting reaction to young serious offenders grew in popularity in the late 1980s and 1990s. The justice system and many people in the general public viewed serious offenders as bad people who posed a major threat to our society and deserved harsh sanctions. For example, a book on crime by several prominent authors stated:

> America is now home to thickening ranks of juvenile "superpredators"—radically impulsive, brutally remorseless youngsters, including ever more preteenage boys, who murder, assault, rob, burglarize, deal deadly drugs, join gun-toting gangs, and create serious communal disorders. (W. Bennett et al., 1996:27)

The justice system, in turn, punished many of these offenders, especially the older ones, more harshly in an effort to isolate them from conventional society (by confining them in institutions) and to make them suffer for their misdeeds. As we discussed in Chapter 1, many states have begun to retreat from this "get tough" approach and are now placing greater emphasis on treatment and rehabilitation, even for serious and violent offenders. Nevertheless, the harshest penalties are generally reserved for juveniles who commit the most egregious offenses. And it is still the case that large numbers of older, serious juvenile offenders are tried and punished as adults. Other factors influencing whether juveniles experience the harsh/rejecting reaction include **the sociodemographic characteristics of the juvenile (and the juvenile's parents).** In particular, lower-class juveniles, the members of certain minority groups, and older juveniles are said to be more likely to experience the harsh/rejecting reaction. Such juveniles are less able to resist the efforts of others to treat them in a harsh or rejecting manner, and/or they fit the stereotype of a delinquent. In particular, lower-class juveniles (and their parents) are more likely to lack the financial resources, connections, reputation, and negotiating skills to convince others to ignore the delinquency or treat it in a mild manner. Furthermore, lower-class juveniles, the members of certain minority groups, and older juveniles fit the stereotype of serious delinquents (see the discussion of race in Chapter 4). We discuss these issues in Chapter 22 when we examine discrimination by the juvenile justice system. For now, we note that the evidence suggests that poor individuals and members of certain minority groups are sometimes treated more harshly than others by juvenile justice officials, even after we take account of their level of delinquency (for an example involving race, misbehavior, and the reaction of school officials, see Box 9.1).

Box 9.1   Race, Punishment, and the School-to-Prison Pipeline

Kyle Thompson is described as a "soft-spoken, 115-pound" high school freshman and football player. Last year he got into a tug-of-war with a teacher over a "hit list" he created, which identified students he wanted to tackle on the football field. As a result of this incident, he was handcuffed and ultimately expelled from school (Abdullah, 2014). When Kyle became depressed over the following summer, his worried mother brought him to a therapist. She described the fallout from the incident in the following manner:

> It's changed him. It makes me so sad . . . He still avoids people. He doesn't want to be around people from his own school. He's very embarrassed. He doesn't want to talk about it. I just tell him what you did was not criminal and you're not a criminal. (Abdullah, 2014)

Kyle is also a young black male. In 2013, an investigation by the U.S. Department of Justice found that students like him have been suspended, expelled, and subject to school-based arrest at a much higher rate than other students, even for minor rule violations. In one Mississippi school district, the department found that "black students frequently received harsher disciplinary consequences, including longer suspensions, than white students for comparable misbehavior, even where the students were at the same school, were of similar ages, and had similar disciplinary histories." Not only is this practice unlawful and discriminatory, but child advocates worry that such overly harsh reactions set up young black men for failure. They note that students who are repeatedly suspended and expelled from school are at risk of future incarceration. In short, overly harsh penalties may help create a "school-to-prison pipeline" (Fowler, 2011).

Although evidence of racial bias in school punishment has not surfaced in all reports (see Wright et al., 2014), several recent studies confirm that suspension or expulsion from school increases the risk of future involvement in the criminal justice

(Continued)

(Continued)

system—for both minority and nonminority youth—even after taking into account the child's level of problem behavior (Mowen and Brent, 2016; Ramey, 2016; Wolf and Kupchik, 2017). This outcome has been interpreted in terms of labeling theory:

> By creating the impression that a boy is a "troublemaker" and cutting him off from important educational resources, including classroom time and extracurricular opportunities, school punishment can contribute to a process of criminalization that significantly increases the odds of involvement in the criminal justice system. (Ramey, 2016:135)

Facing legal consequences, the school district mentioned above agreed to work with the Department of Justice to end discriminatory practices and create a more supportive learning environment. The corrective steps the school district agreed to take include (1) training staff to ensure that disciplinary consequences are fair and consistent, (2) providing supports and interventions for students before excluding them from school, (3) limiting the use of suspension and expulsion for minor misbehavior, and (4) "prohibiting school officials from involving law enforcement officers to respond to behavior that can be safely and appropriately handled under school disciplinary procedures." The school district superintendent embraced the reforms: "If a student's shirt is out or they're rolling their eyes at a teacher, is that misbehavior? Yes and it needs to be addressed. Does that student need to be kicked out of school for that? No" (Cherry, 2013).

A Justice Department official stated in 2014 that racial discrimination in student discipline is not limited to one or two school districts; rather, it occurs throughout the nation. Further, child advocates worry that the increasing presence of police officers in the nation's schools may be contributing to overly harsh punishments for some students, helping fuel the school-to-prison pipeline. Rigid zero-tolerance policies have also been cited as a contributing factor (for more on zero-tolerance policies, see the Teaching Aids section at the end of this chapter). In 2014, the U.S. Departments of Education and Justice issued legal guidance to school administrators, informing them that they must avoid discrimination in student disciplinary practices, and that harsh and exclusionary punishments may be used only as a last resort. In the words of the attorney general, "A routine school disciplinary infraction should land a student in the principal's office, not in a police precinct" (Abdullah, 2014).

Questions for Discussion
1. Why would young black males be treated more harshly than white youth who engage in similar behavior? What are some possible explanations for this differential treatment? (Note: You can draw on the material presented in this chapter to help answer these questions).
2. Critics have described the use of out-of-school suspension as an outdated and counterproductive response to student misbehavior. Can you think of alternative sanctions that could be used to punish students but, at the same, keep them involved in the learning process?

The situation with respect to **gender** is more complex. Males fit the stereotype of a serious delinquent, and some data suggest that males are more likely than females to be arrested and severely sanctioned for serious offenses. However, things are different when it comes to status offenses, especially status offenses that involve sexual behavior or the possibility of sexual behavior, like running away. Females are more likely than males to be arrested and severely sanctioned for such offenses. This reflects a double standard regarding sexual behavior. Female juveniles who engage in sexual behavior are more likely to be viewed as "bad," subject to efforts to control their behavior, and treated in a harsh manner (see Chapter 22; Bartusch and Matsueda, 1996:150; Chesney-Lind and Shelden, 2004).

Finally, **juveniles who are low in control and who associate with delinquent others** are more likely to experience the harsh/rejecting reaction. Such juveniles fit the stereotype of a delinquent or "bad person"; in particular, they do not get along with their parents and teachers, they do poorly at school, they have amoral beliefs or beliefs favoring delinquency, and they belong to delinquent peer groups or gangs. Also, such juveniles are less able to resist the efforts of others to treat them in a harsh or rejecting manner. They lack close ties to conventional others who might assist them, they have poor reputations, and they have poor problem-solving skills. Finally, such juveniles tend to associate with others who are more likely to treat them in a harsh or rejecting manner. Among other things, such juveniles are more likely to have parents and teachers who dislike them or are weakly attached to them—which increases the likelihood of harsh treatment.[4]

So juveniles are most likely to experience the harsh/rejecting reaction when they engage in delinquency that becomes known to conventional others, especially frequent and serious delinquency; when they are poor, members of certain minority groups, and older; and when they are low in control and associate with delinquent peers. Such juveniles fit the stereotype of a delinquent or bad person, they (or their parents) are less able to resist the efforts of others to treat them in a harsh or rejecting manner; and/or they are more likely to associate with others who respond in a harsh or rejecting manner.

Certain of these points are illustrated in Chambliss' (1973) classic study of the Saints and the Roughnecks, described in Chapter 4. As you may recall, the middle-class Saints were liked and respected by members of the community and were viewed as "good boys who just went in for an occasional prank." The lower-class Roughnecks were viewed as "tough, young criminals who were headed for trouble," and they were "constantly in trouble with the police and community." The two groups, however, were about equally delinquent. Chambliss argued that the Saints and the Roughnecks were viewed and treated so differently for three reasons. The Saints were better able to hide their delinquency from others, partly because their access to cars allowed them to commit their delinquent acts in out-of-the-way places. The Roughnecks' delinquency, by contrast, was often committed in the center of town, where it was highly visible. The Saints were better able to resist the efforts of others to treat them in a harsh or rejecting manner. For example, the Saints were polite and apologetic when confronted by suspicious police officers and teachers, and this deflected harsh treatment. The Roughnecks, however, reacted with hostility and disdain when confronted by others, and this encouraged harsh treatment. Finally, the middle-class, high-achieving Saints did not fit the stereotype of serious delinquents, whereas the lower-class Roughnecks did.

ARE SOME JUVENILES MORE LIKELY THAN OTHERS TO RESPOND TO THE HARSH/REJECTING REACTION WITH FURTHER DELINQUENCY?

Imagine a group of juvenile offenders who are being treated in a harsh or rejecting manner. According to some labeling theorists, certain of these offenders are more likely than others to respond to this treatment with further delinquency.[5] In particular, a delinquent response is most likely among offenders who are **low in control, believe that delinquency is a desirable or justifiable response, and are high in strain.**

You can appreciate why such offenders are more likely to respond with delinquency if you think back to our discussion of strain theory in Chapter 6. The harsh or rejecting treatment received by these offenders is a type of strain; that is, people treat the offenders in a negative manner. As indicated in Chapter 6, juveniles are more likely to respond to strain with delinquency if they are low in control. Among other things, they lack the resources to respond in a nondelinquent manner, they have less to lose through delinquency, and they give less thought to the consequences of their behavior. Likewise, they are more likely to respond to strain with delinquency if they believe that delinquency is a desirable or justifiable response (because they have been reinforced for delinquency or anticipate reinforcement, have been taught beliefs favorable to delinquency, and have been exposed to delinquent models). Finally, they are more likely to respond to strain with delinquency if they are experiencing other strains. These other strains reduce their ability to cope in a legal manner, since individuals experiencing several strains are easily overwhelmed. And these other strains make them irritable, which increases their sensitivity to negative treatment.

Consider, for example, two students who are treated in a harsh or rejecting manner by a teacher. One student is closely monitored by parents, has good grades, believes that delinquency is wrong, associates with conventional peers, and is generally treated well by others. The other student is poorly monitored by parents, is flunking out of school, believes that one should respond to disrespectful treatment with violence, associates with delinquent peers who often reinforce violence, and is experiencing many other strains. It is clear that the second student is more likely to respond to the harsh or rejecting treatment with violence, for all the reasons indicated in the preceding paragraph.

Some juvenile offenders, then, are more likely than others to respond to harsh or rejecting treatment with delinquency. Unfortunately, juvenile offenders most likely to respond to harsh or rejecting treatment with delinquency are also the juveniles most likely to be treated in a harsh or rejecting manner.

THE EVIDENCE ON LABELING THEORY

The generic labeling theory that we have just presented has not yet been well tested. In particular, the **ideal test** of the theory would involve the examination of three groups of comparable offenders: the first received the harsh/rejecting reaction, the second received the "failure to respond to delinquency" reaction, and the third received the "condemn the delinquency but accept the juvenile" reaction. If labeling theory is correct, those who received the harsh/rejecting reaction should be much more likely to engage in further delinquency than those who received the "condemn the delinquency but accept the juvenile" reaction and perhaps somewhat more likely to engage in delinquency than those who received the "failure to respond to delinquency" reaction. Further, a full test of labeling theory should determine whether the factors that we described condition the effect of the harsh/rejecting reaction on delinquency.

Most tests of labeling theory fall far short of this ideal.[6] Let us illustrate this with an example. Perhaps the major way that researchers have tested labeling theory is by **comparing arrested delinquents to comparable delinquents who have not been arrested.** These tests assume that the arrested delinquents are more likely to have experienced the harsh/rejecting reaction. Therefore, the arrested delinquents should be more likely to engage in subsequent delinquency. Most such tests find that the arrested delinquents do have higher levels of subsequent delinquency, but not all tests find this.[7] Such tests, however, suffer from certain major problems.

First, **while arrested juveniles may be somewhat more likely to experience the harsh/ rejecting reaction, many arrested juveniles do not have this experience.** In particular, many arrested juveniles are treated in a respectful manner by the police and courts, experience only mild sanctions, and have few problems with others—like parents and teachers.[8] For an in-depth illustration, see Box 9.2. Further, some arrested juveniles are placed in programs that increase their level of control, reduce their strain, and/or foster the social learning of conventional behavior.

Box 9.2 When Arrest Becomes "Normal"

As we have suggested, one cannot assume that an arrest inevitably leads to a harsh or rejecting reaction. This point is illustrated in a powerful way by Paul Hirschfield's (2008) study of official sanctions in a low-income section of Chicago, in an area suffering from a high rate of juvenile arrest.

Hirschfield interviewed a number of young males who described arrest as being so common in their experience that it was regarded as "no big thing." Many of these young men attended schools "surrounded by male peers who have been or will be arrested" (Hirschfield, 2008:584). In response to arrest, their teachers and parents responded with mild sanctions or indifference:

> It's just I got a lot of lectures from all the teachers. [Arrest] didn't really change anything, because that wasn't a good neighborhood. I wasn't the only one sitting there getting arrested and stuff. It was a lot of other people getting arrested too; [we] had to just talk to the teachers. (Hirschfield, 2008:589)

> [My mom and grandmother] didn't really react to [arrest] no way. They just came and get me, you know what I'm saying? "You ain't getting the five dollars this week." Something like that and then didn't do nothing. (Hirschfield, 2008:587)

(Continued)

(Continued)

In fact, some of the young men said their arrest and detention elicited positive reactions, at least from their fellow peers:

> [After being locked up] then I was a role model. (Pause). I wasn't a role model, but `everybody looked up to me at school, like, all "Yeah, that's Jay right there; he cool right there." (Hirschfield, 2008:597)

In short, it appears that arrest has become something of a "rite of passage" within certain segments of Chicago's inner-city poor, being viewed as a normal part of adolescence or even a regular path to adulthood. Hirschfield attributes this troubling development, in part, to existing policies of mass arrest and mass incarceration. In particular, the heavy policing of inner-city communities has resulted in the arrest of some serious offenders but also a large number of minor offenders. The latter arrests are viewed by some members of the community as "petty" or "bogus" (e.g., arrests for marijuana possession or arrests that involve suspected improper action by the police). When the arrest of minor offenders is so prevalent in the larger community, the arrest of one particular individual is not necessarily viewed as a statement of that individual's true character or basic "goodness." And when the arrest of minor offenders is so prevalent, it becomes easier for the arrestees themselves to minimize the personal importance of arrest.

In addition, it is possible that some young people have adapted to their disadvantaged position in society by developing an oppositional identity (Hirschfield, 2008). Instead of adopting and internalizing the standards of mainstream society (which tends to look down on them), they have developed their own standards and definitions of status or success, which may include the definition of arrest or incarceration as a "badge of honor" and as an indictor of guts, toughness, or nerve.

Questions for Discussion
1. The young people quoted here did not experience the harsh/rejecting reaction as a result of their arrest. What type of reaction did they receive? (Recall the three major types of reactions.)
2. Following the arrest of the young people quoted here, what type of reaction would contemporary labeling theorists recommend? (Provide an example.) Do you think the recommended approach would be difficult for parents and teachers to implement in the communities described by Hirschfield? Could it still be effective in such communities?

Second, **we cannot assume that the nonarrested juveniles experience the "condemn the delinquency but accept the juvenile" reaction.** Most of the nonarrested juveniles probably had their delinquency ignored, a reaction that increases the likelihood of further delinquency. And some of the nonarrested juveniles probably experienced the harsh/rejecting reaction. While these juveniles have not been arrested, their parents and others may have labeled them as "bad" and treated them in a harsh or rejecting manner. So, determining whether arrested juveniles have higher rates of subsequent delinquency than nonarrested juveniles is not a good way to test labeling theory.

To properly test labeling theory, **we must develop better measures of the three major ways of reacting to delinquency.**[9] A few studies have tried to do this, although their measures are still far from perfect. For example, Paternoster et al. (1997) examined how the police treated adults arrested for domestic violence. Some were treated in a respectful manner; the police took the time to listen to them, did not handcuff them in front of their spouses or partners, and did not use force. Others were treated in a more disrespectful manner, one that had elements of the harsh/rejecting reaction. The researchers found that those treated in a disrespectful manner were more likely to reoffend, even when prior levels of violence were accounted for. Another set of studies examined the way in which parents viewed their children. Some parents viewed their children in a negative light, stating that their children often "get into trouble" or "break rules." And this negative view increased the likelihood that those children would engage in subsequent delinquency, even when a range of "third variables" like prior delinquency of the children had been accounted for. This negative view increased the likelihood of delinquency for many of the reasons listed earlier; most notably, it increased the likelihood that the children would form a delinquent self-concept and associate with other delinquents.[10] More research is needed on labeling theory, however, particularly research that better measures the different reactions to delinquency.

As stated earlier, most tests of labeling theory are less than ideal, as they simply compare arrested delinquents to similar delinquents who have not been arrested. Nevertheless, studies of this type are still useful as they help us to better understand how and why official interventions can lead to further delinquency. Consistent with the generic version of labeling theory presented in this chapter, several recent studies confirm that the experience of arrest can reduce control, increase strain, increase association with delinquent peers, and contribute to a delinquent self-concept—thereby increasing the risk of further delinquency.[11] In light of such findings, it may be possible to disrupt the relationship between arrest and repeat offending with programs that help delinquent youth maintain social bonds, cope with strain, and avoid delinquent peers (see Wiley et al., 2013).

Interestingly, one study finds that the experience of arrest increases the odds of being arrested again in the future, even after taking into account the juvenile's behavior. Another study finds that dropping out of school increases the likelihood of arrest, even when there is no actual increase in delinquent behavior. It is possible that an "arrestee" or "dropout" label may lead to increased scrutiny and monitoring by the police, resulting in an increased likelihood of future arrest and a deepening involvement in the justice system (Liberman et al., 2014; Na, 2017).

In addition, there is some evidence that "high risk" juveniles are especially likely to respond to arrest with further delinquency, especially if they have a history of delinquent behavior (Morris and Piquero, 2013). Ward et al. (2014) find that if juveniles with a history of violent offenses are stopped or questioned by the police, this intervention tended to increase the probability of repeat offending. Among nonviolent juveniles, however, no such effect was observed. The authors of this study conclude that the nonviolent youth may have been protected from labeling effects because, on average, they have greater stakes in conformity, have fewer delinquent peers, and for these reasons are less likely to respond in a delinquent manner.

Additional research on labeling effects will be important, because labeling theory has implications for how we respond to delinquency. As described earlier, labeling theory is already having an important impact on how we respond, as reflected in the restorative justice approach. Future research in this area may suggest additional ways to minimize the occurrence of harsh/rejecting reactions, or the likelihood that such responses will result in further delinquency (see Liberman et al., 2014; Wiley et al., 2013).

SUMMARY

Labeling theory focuses on the reaction to delinquency. It is said that the way in which official agencies and others react to delinquency may increase the likelihood of further delinquency. Labeling theorists examine three major types of reaction, devoting most of their attention to the harsh/rejecting reaction in which offenders are viewed as bad, rejected by conventional others, and treated in a harsh manner. This reaction is said to increase the likelihood of further delinquency by reducing control, increasing strain, fostering association with delinquent peers, and leading the offender to form a delinquent self-concept. Juvenile offenders of certain types are said to be more likely than others to experience this reaction and to respond to it with further delinquency. The "condemn the delinquency but accept the juvenile" reaction, by contrast, is said to reduce subsequent offending. This reaction avoids the negative effects of the harsh/rejecting reaction, imposes direct control, and fosters the development of internal control. Additional research is needed to fully test labeling theory, but recent studies provide tentative support.

TEACHING AIDS
Controversial Issue #1: Going Too Far?
Zero-Tolerance Policies in the Nation's Schools

Many school districts have adopted strict zero-tolerance policies that mandate suspension or expulsion for certain disciplinary infractions. Initially, these policies targeted weapons violations and matters of school safety, but often they were extended and applied to minor rule violations.

The assumption behind zero tolerance is that swift and certain punishment will serve as a deterrent, and that the removal of rule violators will create an environment more conducive to learning.

However, because the punishments are automatic and do not take into account the intent of the rule violator, zero-tolerance suspensions and expulsions have been applied in cases that some describe as absurd:

> A 10-year-old girl found a small knife in her lunchbox placed there by the mother for cutting an apple. Although she immediately handed over the knife to her teacher, [under the school district's strict zero-tolerance policy] she was expelled from school for possessing a weapon. (Skiba et al., 2008:852)

> In another case, an adolescent [boy] was expelled for violating school rules by talking to his mother on a cell phone while at school—his mother was on deployment as a soldier in Iraq and he had not spoken with her in 30 days. (Skiba et al., 2008:852)

In 2006, the American Psychological Association (APA) convened a task force to review the impact of zero-tolerance policies in the nation's schools. Although the task force recognized a possible need for zero-tolerance expulsions in cases that pose a clear threat to safety, they concluded that the broader use of such punishments is misguided: "Many infractions," they argue, "do not require the severe and unbending consequences of zero tolerance" (Skiba et al., 2008:857).

Further, the task force found little evidence that zero-tolerance policies increase safety or improve behavior. Instead, the removal of large numbers of students from school may exacerbate behavior problems in the long run, increasing their likelihood of school failure as well as contact with the juvenile justice system. In the end, the task force recommended alternative reactions to most cases of rule violation, including greater flexibility and discretion in the application of punishment, punishments appropriate to the offense, counseling and other in-school interventions for problem students, and a "restorative justice" approach.

More recently, during the Obama administration, schools were urged to abandon overzealous zero-tolerance policies. The U.S. attorney general described such policies as outdated and ineffectual, noting that they raised concerns that youth could become saddled with a serious record for minor school infractions (Hefling, 2014). Further, education experts worry that zero-tolerance policies may disproportionately affect minority youth and contribute to the "school-to-prison pipeline" (see Box 9.1).

Do you agree with the recommendations of the APA task force? Or do you believe that a strict zero-tolerance approach is necessary to maintain school discipline? How do you think labeling theorists would react to this approach? Would they agree with the task force? What additional predictions would they make about the impact of zero-tolerance policies on school delinquency? Finally, what do you think the task force had in mind when they recommended a "restorative justice" approach to school discipline? How would this work in practice? Describe a few examples.

Controversial Issue #2: Is It Sometimes Best to Ignore Delinquency?

Some labeling theorists argue that the best way to control delinquency is to do as little as possible about it—a policy of "radical nonintervention." Such theorists contend that efforts to control delinquency, including many efforts to treat or rehabilitate delinquents, often make matters worse by portraying delinquents as a problem and as different from nondelinquents. Therefore, such efforts carry a high risk of labeling delinquents as "bad" and prompting the harsh/rejecting reaction. The policy of radical nonintervention involves tolerating much behavior that we now define as delinquent, dramatically limiting the role of the juvenile justice system and carefully structuring interventions so that they do not label or stigmatize juveniles as "bad." Schur (1973:154–155) describes this policy as follows:

> Radical nonintervention implies policies that accommodate society to the widest possible diversity of behaviors and attitudes, rather than forcing as many individuals as possible to "adjust" to supposedly common societal standards. This does not mean that anything goes, that all behavior is socially acceptable. But traditional delinquency policy has proscribed youthful behavior well beyond what is required to maintain a smooth-running society or to protect others from youthful depredations.

> Thus, the basic injunction for public policy becomes: leave kids alone whenever possible. This effort partly involves mechanisms to divert children away from the courts but it goes further to opposing various kinds of intervention by diverse social control and socializing agencies.... [P]olicies [should] favor collective action programs instead of those that single out specific individuals, and voluntary programs instead of compulsory ones.

To what extent do you agree with the policy of radical nonintervention? In particular, do you feel that the justice system and others (e.g., parents, school officials) sometimes go "too far" in trying to control delinquency and thereby make matters worse? If so, do you think acts now defined as delinquent or status offenses should sometimes be ignored? Or do you think they should respond in other ways, like those embodied in the restorative justice approach? Justify your responses.

Web-Based Exercise: Applying Labeling Theory (Race and Labeling)

An earlier web exercise asked that you find a song that illustrates strain theory. In this exercise, use web resources, such as YouTube, to find a video that illustrates labeling theory, perhaps a video clip from a movie (e.g., *The Breakfast Club*), a TV show (e.g., *The Wire*), or a news broadcast. As an illustration, examine how a group called "The Cranky Sociologists" applied labeling theory to clips from *The Wire* at http://thecrankysociologists.com/2013/05/04/the-wire-and-labeling-theory. One of the key points made in this application (and in this chapter) is that the members of less powerful groups are likely to be negatively labeled or to experience the harsh/rejecting reaction. This includes the members of certain minority groups and lower-class juveniles. As an illustration, view the following YouTube video, which discusses delinquency and racial stereotypes: "What Would You Do? Racism in America, Part 1", available at https://www.youtube.com/watch?v=_cCQU0jt4cs.

TEST YOUR KNOWLEDGE OF THIS CHAPTER

1. Describe the essential arguments of labeling theory in a few sentences.
2. How is labeling theory different from and similar to the other major theories of delinquency?
3. Does labeling theory try to explain all delinquency?
4. What major questions do labeling theorists ask about the reaction of others to delinquency?
5. List and briefly describe the three major types of reaction to delinquency examined by labeling theorists. Indicate whether each type of reaction should increase or decrease the likelihood of subsequent offending. Explain why the reaction should have this effect.
6. What is meant by official and informal reactions to delinquency?
7. Why do some labeling theorists argue that the failure to respond to the individual's delinquency is a good strategy? What specific recommendations do such labeling theorists make for controlling delinquency (e.g., recommendations regarding the police, courts, and laws)?
8. How do juvenile justice agencies implement the restorative justice approach to delinquency? How does this approach reflect the "condemn the delinquency but accept the juvenile" reaction?
9. Why does the harsh/rejecting reaction increase the likelihood of subsequent delinquency?
10. What is an individual's self-concept? According to symbolic interactionism, how is the self-concept formed? How is self-concept relevant to labeling theory?
11. What factors influence whether juveniles experience the harsh/rejecting reaction? Why do these factors influence the likelihood of experiencing the harsh/rejecting reaction?
12. What factors influence whether juveniles will respond to the harsh/rejecting reaction with further delinquency? Why do these factors influence the likelihood of a delinquent response?
13. Ideally, how should researchers go about testing labeling theory?
14. The major way in which labeling theory has been tested is by comparing the subsequent offending of arrested delinquents to that of comparable nonarrested delinquents. What are the major problems with this type of test?
15. Describe the evidence on labeling theory.

THOUGHT AND DISCUSSION QUESTIONS

1. How might labeling theory explain deviant behaviors like cheating on exams and excessive drinking?
2. Develop survey questions to measure the independent variables in your explanation of cheating and drinking in question 1.
3. Suppose you are a labeling theorist. What advice would you give to parents and teachers about responding to delinquency? What advice would you give to police and court officials about how to best control delinquency?

KEY TERMS

- Labeling theory
- Official reaction to delinquency
- Informal reaction to delinquency
- Harsh/rejecting reaction
- Radical nonintervention
- "Condemn the delinquency but accept the juvenile" reaction
- Restorative justice approach
- Restorative justice conference
- Self-concept

ENDNOTES

1. See Akers et al., 2016; Matsueda, 2001; Schur, 1973.

2. See Ambert, 1997; Hay, 2001b; Sampson and Laub, 1997; Stewart et al., 2000; Stewart, Simons, Conger, and Scaramella, 2002.

3. See Bernburg and Krohn, 2003; De Li, 1999; Hagan, 1991; Sampson and Laub, 1997; Sweeten, 2006.

4. See Braithwaite, 1989; Hay, 2001b; Triplett and Jarjoura, 1994.

5. See Bernburg and Krohn, 2003; Bernburg et al., 2006; Hagan, 1991; Jackson and Hay, 2013; Sampson and Laub, 1997; Sherman, 1993, 2000; Sweeten, 2006.

6. For overviews of the research on labeling theory, see Akers et al., 2016; Farrington and Murray, 2014; Jensen and Rojek, 1998; Paternoster and Iovanni, 1989; Sampson and Laub, 1997; Shoemaker, 2004.

7. See Chapter 23; Bernburg and Krohn, 2003; Bernburg et al., 2006; Farrington, 1977; Farrington and Murray, 2014; Gold and Williams, 1969; Huizinga et al., 2003; L. Johnson et al., 2004; Lopes et al., 2012; Palamara et al., 1986; Restivo and Lanier, 2015; Sampson and Laub, 1997; Douglas Smith and Brame, 1994; Stewart, Simons, Conger, and Scaramella, 2002; Wiley et al., 2013.

8. See Hirschfield, 2008; Jensen and Rojek, 1998; Paternoster and Iovanni, 1989; Sherman, 1993, 2000; Shoemaker, 2000.

9. For additional problems with tests of labeling theory, see Jensen and Rojek, 1998; Paternoster and Iovanni, 1989; Farrington and Murray, 2014.

10. See Adams and Evans, 1996; Braithwaite et al., 2006; Hay, 2001b; Heimer and Matsueda, 1994; Matsueda, 1992; Sherman, 2000; Ward and Tittle, 1993; L. Zhang and S. Zhang, 2004; also see Losoncz and Tyson, 2007.

11. Bouffard and Piquero, 2010; Jackson and Hay, 2013; Kavish et al., 2016; Restivo and Lanier, 2015; Wiley et al., 2013; Wiley et al., 2016.

10 The Life Course

How Do We Explain Different Patterns of Offending over the Course of a Lifetime?

The theories of delinquency described in the last four chapters focus on explaining why some individuals engage in more delinquency than others. But there are also other facts about delinquency that are in need of explanation. Not only do some individuals engage more frequently in delinquency than others, but **individuals also exhibit different patterns of offending over the course of their lives.**[1] As we pointed out in Chapter 4, most individuals increase their level of offending when they enter adolescence and then reduce it when they enter adulthood. This is referred to as the *adolescence-limited* pattern of offending, since offenses are largely limited to the adolescent years. A smaller number of individuals, however, offend at high rates over much of their lives. Even though these *life-course persistent* offenders make up only 4 to 10 percent of the population, they are an important group—accounting for a large share of all delinquency, including perhaps a majority of all serious delinquency. This chapter seeks to explain patterns of offending over the life course, focusing on the adolescence-limited and life-course persistent patterns.

After reading this chapter, you should be able to:

- Describe the pattern of offending that characterizes adolescence-limited offenders.
- Discuss the major biological and social changes that take place during adolescence and that increase the likelihood of delinquency.
- Draw on the leading theories of delinquency to explain why these changes increase delinquent behavior.
- Describe the pattern of offending that characterizes life-course persistent offenders.
- Explain why life-course persistent offenders offend at high rates over the course of their lives.

The first part of this chapter presents an integrated theory that explains why most individuals increase their offending during adolescence and then decrease it during adulthood. This theory draws heavily on the work of Agnew (1997, 2003a), Farrington (1986, 2006), M. Felson (2002), Greenberg (1977), Moffitt (1993, 2006), Osgood et al. (1996), Patterson et al. (1989), Raine (2002a), Sampson and Laub (1993a), Steffensmeier and Allan (1995, 2000), Thornberry and Krohn (2001), Walsh (2002), and Warr (2002), among others. The theory basically argues that **the biological and social changes associated with adolescence lead to an increase in strain, a reduction in control, and an increase in the social learning for crime.** This integrated theory, then, may be viewed as an elaboration of strain, control, and social learning theories.

The second part of this chapter presents an integrated theory that explains why a small percentage of individuals offend at high rates over much of their lives. This theory draws heavily on the work of Lahey and Waldman (2005), Moffitt (1993, 1997, 2006), Patterson et al. (1989), Sampson and Laub (1993a), and Thornberry and Krohn (2001, 2005). The theory argues that **certain biological and social factors cause some individuals to experience, over the course of their lives, high levels of strain and low levels of control, as well as an increase in social learning.** This integrated theory also represents an extension of strain, control, and social learning theories—as well as labeling theory.

Recent research has begun to identify other patterns of offending besides the adolescence-limited and life-course persistent patterns. Some individuals, for example, offend at low rates over much of their lives (e.g., Benson, 2002; Moffitt, 2006). And there is now some debate over how many different patterns of offending there are and how to best describe these patterns (see Laub and Sampson, 2003; Nagin and Tremblay, 2005a, 2005b). The adolescence-limited and life-course persistent patterns, however, are major patterns, and most attention has focused on them.

WHY DO MOST INDIVIDUALS INCREASE THEIR LEVELS OF OFFENDING DURING ADOLESCENCE?

The best self-report surveys suggest that 90 percent or more of all adolescents engage in delinquency. Typically, such adolescents commit a small to moderate number of minor offenses, like petty theft, minor acts of vandalism, fighting, drinking under age, marijuana use, sexual intercourse, truancy, and curfew violation. For example, one college student describes an adolescent shoplifting incident as follows:

> There we were, in the most lucrative department Mervyn's had to offer, two curious (but very mature) adolescent girls: the cosmetic and jewelry department. . . . We didn't enter the store planning to steal anything. In fact, I believe we had "given it up" a few weeks earlier; but once my eyes caught sight of the beautiful white and blue necklaces alongside the counter, a spark inside me was once again ignited. . . . Those exquisite puka necklaces were calling out to me, "Take me! Wear me! I can be yours!" All I needed to do was take them to make it a reality. (Quoted in J. Katz, 1988:54)

What is it about adolescence that causes most juveniles to engage in delinquency? Certain of the biological and social changes associated with adolescence lead to a reduction in control, an increase in the social learning for crime, and an increase in strain. We first describe these biological and social changes and then discuss how they impact control, social learning, and strain.

The Biological and Social Changes Associated with Adolescence

Certain of the changes associated with adolescence are biological in nature.[2] Perhaps the most visible of these changes is the increased physical and sexual maturation of adolescents. Adolescents come to resemble adults, and among other things, this leads adolescents to desire many of the privileges of adults—especially increased autonomy and sexual relations. Other of the biological changes associated with adolescence are less visible. Adolescent males experience increased levels of certain hormones, like testosterone. Some claim that this leads to an increase in irritability, so adolescents are quicker to take offense at slights and become angry. Also, some evidence suggests that a portion of the adolescent's brain—the prefrontal cortex—is not yet fully developed. The prefrontal cortex is involved in the control of emotions, among other things, so adolescents may be less able to exercise self-control than adults.

Other of the changes associated with adolescence are social in nature. Adolescence is a period of transition from childhood to adulthood, a time when individuals prepare for adult family and work roles. Reflecting this fact, adolescents are given **some, but not all** of the privileges and responsibilities of adults. It is felt that these privileges and responsibilities will help adolescents prepare for adult roles but that adolescents are not able to handle all the privileges and responsibilities of adulthood. Five of the privileges and responsibilities extended to adolescents are listed next.

1. **More autonomy than children (but less than adults).** For example, parents relax the rules they impose on adolescents, allowing them more freedom to do such things as choose their friends, get involved in romantic relationships, and stay out late at night. State agencies allow adolescents above a certain age to drive automobiles.

2. **More material resources than children (but less than adults).** For example, parents give adolescents more spending money and access to cars. Adolescents are also allowed to earn money through after-school and summer jobs.

3. **Higher status than children (but less than adults).** Adolescents are no longer viewed and treated as "kids" or children, although they are not viewed and treated with as much respect as adults.

4. More responsibility for managing their behavior and relations with others. Parents and teachers hold adolescents more responsible for their behavior (although not as responsible as adults in most cases). Related to this, adolescents are more often expected to cope on their own when problems arise (but not to the same extent as adults).

5. More responsibility for their educational and career goals. Adolescents are expected to give serious thought to their educational and career goals and to devote more effort to the pursuit of these goals. **Related to this, school becomes more demanding.**

There is more homework, teachers grade in a more rigorous manner, and there is heightened competition with other students. The fact that adolescents have some but not all of the privileges and responsibilities of adults is reflected in the responses that a sample of college students gave when they were asked whether they thought they had reached adulthood. Almost two-thirds of the students chose the response category "in some respects yes, in some respects no" (Arnett, 1997). The feeling among teens that they are "caught in between" childhood and adulthood is also a persistent theme in popular music. This theme was evident, for example, in the title of a Britney Spears' song ("I'm Not a Girl, Not Yet a Woman") and in a line from the lyrics of a No Doubt song, "Sixteen": "'Cause you're caught between, you're only sixteen." Can you think of any contemporary songs that reflect this same theme?

The biological changes and the limited privileges and responsibilities associated with adolescence lead to a **reduction in control,** an **increase in the social learning for crime,** and an **increase in strain.**

A Reduction in Control

Individuals experience a reduction in control as they move from childhood to adolescence. This is especially true of **direct control.** Parents grant adolescents more autonomy than children. In particular, parents relax the rules they impose on adolescents. Among other things, adolescents are given more freedom to leave home without parental supervision. As a consequence, adolescents spend much less time with their parents, which reduces direct monitoring. In fact, time spent with parents declines by almost half as juveniles move from childhood to adolescence (Larson et al., 1996). Likewise, teachers exercise less direct control over adolescents than children. Adolescents attend larger schools, are in larger classes, and are more likely to change classes several times a day. These facts reduce the extent to which teachers can effectively monitor behavior.

Adolescents may also **experience a reduction in their stake in conformity.** Their ties to parents and teachers sometimes suffer as they get into disputes with elders over issues involving the privileges and responsibilities of adolescence. For example, adolescents and parents argue about things like curfews, appropriate dress, access to the family car, and the amount of time that should be spent on homework. Further, many adolescents experience a reduction in grades and satisfaction with school, reflecting the increased demands at school and the reduced support provided by school officials.

Finally, adolescents often **become less likely to condemn delinquency and to exercise self-control.** The influence of parents on adolescent beliefs regarding delinquency is often reduced, since adolescents have weaker ties to parents and stronger ties to peers, who sometimes challenge parental beliefs. Also, the biological changes mentioned earlier often result in a reduction in self-control, with adolescents showing less command over their emotions.

Individuals, however, **experience an increase in control when they leave adolescence and enter adulthood.** Adults usually develop strong ties to their families and jobs, which increase their direct control and stake in conformity. Several studies suggest that such ties result in reductions in offending (see the reviews in Cernkovich and Giordano, 2001; Laub and Sampson, 2001, 2003). Further, data suggest that adults experience an increase in self-control. This occurs partly for biological reasons; hormonal surges subside and the prefrontal cortex of the brain becomes fully developed. Also, the increased ties of adults to family and work (and the reduced ties to peers) foster beliefs that condemn crime.

An Increase in the Social Learning for Crime

Social learning theory focuses on the extent to which juveniles associate with others who teach beliefs favorable to delinquency, model delinquency, and reinforce delinquency, with the theory arguing that delinquent peers are especially likely to engage in these activities. Data suggest that adolescents are much more likely than children and adults to associate with such peers. For example, one study based on a national sample of adolescents found the following: at age 11, approximately 9 of 10 respondents reported that none of their friends had used alcohol during the past year; at age 18, this figure had fallen to approximately 1 in 10 (Warr, 1993; also see Elliott and Menard, 1996). Similar, although less dramatic, figures were reported for other forms of delinquency. Further, adolescents spend more time with their peers, place more importance on peer activities, and are more loyal to their peers than are children and adults. A good part of the association between age and crime is explained by the increased association of adolescents with delinquent peers (Warr, 2002; also see Lam et al., 2014).

But why are adolescents **more likely than children and adults to associate with delinquent peers?** Part of the answer lies in adolescents' greater freedom to associate with delinquent peers. Adolescents are subject to less direct control than children. And they do not have the family and work responsibilities of adults. Further, adolescents have more exposure to delinquent peers, since they spend more time on the street and attend large secondary schools populated by peers, including delinquent peers. Finally, adolescents are more attracted to delinquent peers. Adolescents are somewhat alienated from parents and teachers and are often drawn to delinquent peers because such peers possess many of the adult privileges they desire. Delinquent peers, in particular, usually drink, engage in sex, stay out late, have money, and demand to be treated with respect by others.

An Increase in Strain

Adolescents experience more strain than children and adults (see Agnew, 1997, 2003a; Greenberg, 1977). Adolescents are **more likely to have trouble achieving their goals.** In particular, adolescents come to desire many of the privileges of adults, like increased autonomy, money, and status. This desire partly stems from the fact that adolescents are physically mature and have certain adult responsibilities, which fosters the belief that they deserve adult privileges. Also, adolescents see that many of their peers, especially delinquent peers, have these privileges (see Agnew, 2003a; Moffitt, 1993).

At the same time, adolescents are often denied the money, autonomy, and status they desire. For example, parents limit their spending money and restrict their activities, and teachers and other adults sometimes treat them in a demeaning manner. As a consequence, adolescents become frustrated and may turn to delinquency. Delinquency may be a means of obtaining adult privileges (e.g., via curfew violation or income-generating crimes), seeking revenge against those who deny adult privileges, or coping with the emotional problems that result from the denial of adult privileges (e.g., drinking to make oneself feel better). Children, by contrast, are not as interested in adult privileges as adolescents are. And adults are better able to obtain such privileges through legal channels. Adults, for example, are legally entitled to drink, stay out late, and engage in certain sexual activities. And adults are better able to obtain the money they need through work.

Adolescents are also **more likely to experience the loss of positive stimuli or presentation of negative stimuli.** In particular, adolescents live in a larger and less protected social world than do children and adults, which increases the likelihood that they will be negatively treated by others. Adolescents leave elementary school and enter larger, more impersonal, and more diverse secondary schools. Partly as a consequence, they come to interact with a larger and more diverse group of peers, including delinquent peers. Much of their interaction with peers occurs away from adults, especially in the evenings and on weekends. This dramatic increase in the size of their social world is itself likely to be stressful, but it also increases the likelihood of negative treatment, since adolescents are interacting with many more people—often in unsupervised settings. As adolescents become adults, however, their social world begins to narrow again, and they have more control over the nature of this world (e.g., they have some choice over where they live and work). Some data support the argument that adolescents experience more strains or stressors than children and adults (see Agnew, 1997, 2003a).

Finally, adolescents are **less able to legally cope with the strains they experience** (Hoffmann, 2010). Adolescents have **fewer coping skills and resources than adults.** In particular, the biological conditions associated with adolescence make adolescents more sensitive to strains and more likely to react to them in a delinquent manner. Adolescents also have less experience at coping and fewer coping resources, like money and power, than adults. Owing to their limited power, for example, adolescents are "compelled to live with their family in a certain neighborhood; to go to a certain school; and, within limits, to interact with the same group of peers and neighbors" (Agnew, 1985a:156). If any of these contexts is aversive, there is often little that adolescents can do to legally cope. Adults, however, can divorce their partners, move to new neighborhoods, change jobs, and change their friends if they experience strain in any of these arenas. Adolescents have more coping skills and resources than children have, but children are usually under the protection of adults, who cope on their behalf. Further, adolescents are often **more disposed to delinquency.** They are more likely to associate with delinquent peers, for example, who provide delinquent models, teach beliefs favorable to delinquency, and reinforce delinquency. Adolescents, then, are more likely to cope with strain through delinquency than are children or adults.

Summary

The biological and social changes associated with adolescence lead to a reduction in control, especially direct control; an increase in the social learning for crime, as reflected in the marked increase in association with delinquent peers; an increase in strain; and an increase in the likelihood of coping with strain through delinquency. That is why most individuals increase their levels of offending during adolescence.

About 5 to 10 percent of adolescents are shielded from the effects described in this section and manage to refrain from delinquency. For example, they experience delayed puberty, they remain closely supervised by parents, and/or they avoid contact with delinquent peers. They may avoid contact with delinquent peers because they have strong ties to their parents and teachers, possess strong moral beliefs about delinquency, or are unusually timid and shy; or they may be in settings where delinquent peer groups are less common—such as all-female schools (see Brezina and Piquero, 2007; Moffitt, 1993, 2006; Owens and Slocum, 2015; A. Piquero et al., 2003, 2005).

WHY DO A SMALL PERCENTAGE OF INDIVIDUALS OFFEND AT HIGH RATES OVER MUCH OF THEIR LIVES?

While most individuals tend to limit their offending to the adolescent years (see Box 10.1), about 4 to 10 percent of the population become "life-course persistent" offenders. Such individuals start offending at high rates early in life, they engage in both minor and serious crimes, and their offending often continues well into middle age.

Box 10.1   Growing Out of Delinquency

Most individuals limit their offending to the adolescent years. As they enter adulthood, they develop attachments to work and family, move away from a "peer-oriented" lifestyle, and experience a decline in delinquent peer associations. They also gain more control over their lives, are better able to cope with strain, and increasingly adopt a prosocial identity (Rocque et al., 2016). These and other factors contribute to desistance from delinquency, or the termination of delinquent involvement.

To achieve a better understanding of the desistance process, Peggy Giordano and her colleagues (2003) followed a sample of delinquent offenders over time, interviewing them during adolescence—when they were confined to institutions—and then again in adulthood. In the interviews, the "desisters" describe how their attitudes toward delinquency changed over time as they began to appreciate the negative consequences of their behavior. They also described how, with age and life experience, they were better able to resist negative peer influences and had learned to become more selective in their friends:

> I don't want to do any of that [anymore]. Drinking, drugs, I just know where it got me and I don't want to get back into all that stuff. . . . [Now] I just stay away from trouble and people that I think is going to get me into trouble. I just don't need it. (Giordano et al., 2003:304)

> I'm my own person [now]. I don't . . . look, hell when I was younger. . . people would say let's go do this, let's go do that. I'd probably just go along with, you know, just go along with it when I was little. But not anymore. (Giordano et al., 2003:308)

The development of such maturity may be encouraged or facilitated by certain life changes, such as landing a good job, achieving success in school, entering a stable relationship with a conventional partner or spouse, or becoming a parent (Blomberg et al., 2012; Laub and Sampson, 2003; Schubert et al., 2016; Zoutewelle-Terovan et al., 2014). For example, Laub and Sampson (2003) observe that marriage often proves to be a crucial turning point in the lives of young male desisters like Leonard. As a young man, Leonard had been involved in serious delinquency and had served time for burglary and auto theft. But then Leonard met his future spouse. She refused to tolerate any misbehavior and did not hesitate to exert direct control. Before they married she delivered an ultimatum to Leonard, "Your friends or me." Later, when Leonard wanted to quit his job because he wasn't making enough money, she told him, "You quit, you leave." Leonard remained married, stayed with his employer for 43 years, and never returned to crime.

For other men, the relationship with a spouse provided a new sense of direction and belonging. For some former offenders, "a wife was one of the first people to care about them and for them" (Laub and Sampson, 2003:136–137).

Relatively few studies have examined the impact of marriage on female offenders. These studies have produced mixed results, but some find that marriage promotes desistance among females as well as males (e.g., Bersani et al., 2009). In addition, some studies find that the transition to motherhood appears to be an influential turning point for some women, prompting them to turn away from delinquency, drugs, and alcohol (Giordano et al., 2002; Kreager et al., 2010).

Cultural expectations also encourage the development of maturity and desistance. Although most adolescents flirt with delinquency, this behavior is generally seen as

(Continued)

(Continued)

age-inappropriate if it continues into adulthood. Adult status, in turn, is defined by such activities as marriage, parenthood, and the completion of school. People who do not "settle down" and desist from delinquency are likely to be viewed by others as immature or worse (Massoglia and Uggen, 2010). It is possible that many individuals respond to this cultural pressure and desist from delinquency, in part, to avoid such negative labels.

Questions for Discussion

1. Some people believe that serious offenders can't be changed. What does research on the different patterns of offending, and on desistance in particular, suggest about the possibilities of behavioral change?
2. Has your own perspective on delinquency changed with age? Do you view "hell-raising" or "criminal-mischief" types of behavior differently, now that you have begun the transition to adulthood? If so, how have your views changed? Is it possible to pinpoint a time, event, or series of events that led you to view delinquency in a different way? If you were to become (or already are) a parent, how would (did) that change your perspective?

One can get the flavor of these life-course persistent offenders by considering the case of a 10-year-old boy described in the *New York Times*. Even though this boy had not yet reached adolescence, it appears that he was already involved in much crime. According to the article:

> He caused trouble. But he was 10. How much trouble could he cause? He yanked out shrubs, or pounded them with his bat. He peeled the siding off neighbors' houses. He pelted dogs with rocks. He shoved classmates, and heckled them. . . . [Authorities] accused him of molesting and murdering 3-year-old Amir Beeks, after spiriting him from a library. Authorities said he beat Amir with a baseball bat . . . and left the 3-year-old to die inside a storm drain at the edge of his yard. . . . Because of his age, the suspect is not being publicly identified by the police. Those in Woodbridge [where the murder occurred] already know who he is. Many of his neighbors tell of having sampled his caustic nature. "Since I knew him, he's always been bad," said a 10-year-old who had been a classmate of the boy. . . . "No one wanted to play with him because he was so mean." He was the scourge of the neighborhood. Other children might annoy neighbors by trampling across their lawns. His neighbors said that he would yank out flowers or smack shrubs with his baseball bat. He would scrawl on fences. He would throw rocks at neighborhood pets. Any animal he saw would become a target. "Anything you could think of doing he was already into" [said a neighbor]. (Kleinfield, 2003)

It seems clear that this boy had gone far beyond the occasional, largely minor delinquency typical of adolescence-limited offenders. It is not clear whether he will continue to offend at a high rate throughout his life, but his early history of high-rate and serious offending is typical of most life-course persistent offenders.

What accounts for life-course persistent offending? Life-course persistent offenders differ from the adolescence-limited offenders in that they tend to suffer from a number of related problems early in life. Most notably, they have traits conducive to crime, like low self-control and irritability, and they experience poor parenting. These problems tend to persist over time; and they contribute to additional problems later in life, like poor school performance, association with delinquent peers, employment problems, and marital problems. All of these problems result in a reduction in control, an increase in social learning for crime, and an increase in strain. That is why these individuals offend at high rates over much of their lives.

Traits Conducive to Crime

Life-course persistent offenders tend to have a number of personality traits conducive to crime. Most notably, they tend to be **irritable and low in self-control.** That is, they are quick to anger, and they have trouble restraining themselves from acting on their immediate impulses. In popular terms, they might be described as "mean" and "out of control." Although data are limited, the 10-year-old offender described in the *New York Times* article seems to fit this characterization.

Life-course persistent offenders **develop these traits early in life.** Certain **biological factors** increase the likelihood of developing these traits (see Chapter 13). In particular, these traits are inherited from parents to some degree, and they may also result from experiencing certain "biological harms," like birth complications and exposure to lead and other toxic substances. **Poor parenting practices** also increase the likelihood of developing these traits. In particular, these traits are more likely to develop when parents fail to teach their children how to control their anger and exercise self-control. Parents, for example, may fail to effectively sanction children for angry outbursts and acting on immediate desires. Some of the neighbors of the 10-year-old boy described earlier said that the boy was poorly supervised by his blind father and that other family problems may have been present. The traits of irritability and low self-control are especially likely to develop when individuals with a biological predisposition for them experience poor parenting.

The traits of irritability and low self-control increase offending for reasons related to control, social learning, and strain theories. Individuals with these traits are, by definition, lower in self-control; that is, they have trouble restraining themselves from crime. These individuals are more likely to find crime rewarding, since they are often angry with others and they have a strong need for the immediate gratification of their desires. And these individuals are more easily upset by strains and disposed to respond to strain with crime. So, if provoked, they are more likely to become upset and respond in an aggressive manner.

Poor Parenting

Life-course persistent offenders tend to experience poor parenting early in life. Their parents often reject them, fail to effectively supervise and discipline them, and treat them in a harsh or abusive manner. **There are several causes of this poor parenting** (see Chapter 14; Patterson et al., 1992). The parents themselves may be irritable and low in self-control, which increases the likelihood that they will neglect their children or respond to them in a harsh manner. The parents may be poor; data suggest that the stressors associated with poverty are a major cause of poor parenting. And the children may be irritable and low in self-control, hence quite difficult to manage, with the result that parents may give up trying to enforce discipline or become so angry that they treat the children in a harsh or abusive manner. (So poor parenting and irritability and low self-control are reciprocally related. Having kids who are irritable and low in self-control is a major cause of poor parenting, and poor parenting is a major cause of irritability and low self-control.)

Poor parenting also increases offending for reasons related to control, social learning, and strain theories. Juveniles who experience poor parenting are, by definition, subject to poor direct control by parents, as well as being weakly bonded to parents. Such juveniles also experience social learning for crime, since their abusive parents function as deviant models for them, sometimes teach them beliefs conducive to crime, and sometimes reinforce aggressive behavior. And such juveniles are high in strain, since their parents treat them in a harsh or abusive manner.

High Rates of Offending over the Life Course

Life-course persistent offenders, then, tend to start out as troubled individuals in troubled families. Their traits and family environment lead them to engage in high rates of deviance at an early age. They are aggressive; they lie, cheat, and steal; they are difficult to control; and they devote little effort to conventional pursuits like schoolwork.

Such individuals offend at high rates over the life course partly because **their traits and poor family experiences persist over time.** That is, individuals who are irritable and low in self-control as children tend to be irritable and low in self-control as adults. And individuals who experience poor parenting as children tend to have family problems as adolescents. This persistence partly stems from the fact that the causes of irritability/low self-control and poor parenting tend to persist over time. For example, the biological factors that cause irritability, and the poverty that causes poor parenting, often persist over time. The negative traits and parenting practices also persist because their consequences contribute to their continued existence. For example, irritability and low self-control contribute to poor parenting, which then contributes to further irritability and low self-control.

These traits and poor parenting experiences contribute to high rates of offending over the life course because **they lead to problems in school, among peers, in marital relations, and at work.** Juveniles with these traits and experiences are more likely to dislike and perform poorly at school and work; they simply do not have the discipline and skills that are necessary to do well in these settings. Also, these juveniles are more likely to elicit negative reactions from others. Individuals with these traits and experiences are not pleasant people, and they often exasperate and irritate others. As a consequence, they are more likely to be avoided or treated in a negative manner by others. For example, school officials may place them in special tracks or schools for "problem" students. Conventional peers may reject them, causing them to associate with delinquent peers. Romantic partners may reject them or treat them harshly, and employers may fire them or refuse to hire them in the first place. These additional problems also contribute to high rates of offending over the life course by reducing control, fostering the social learning of crime, and increasing strain. (These arguments, of course, are similar to those made by labeling theory, which argues that the individual's delinquency often elicits reactions from others that contribute to further delinquency.)

Summary

Life-course persistent offenders tend to experience poor parenting and to develop traits conducive to delinquency early in life. These traits and poor parenting contribute to high rates of offending over the life course partly because they tend to persist over time and partly because they lead to additional problems with peers, school, romantic partners, and employers.

Unlike adolescence-limited offenders, life-course persistent offenders do not stop offending when they become adults, since their offending is **not** rooted in the biological and social changes associated with adolescence. Rather, it is rooted in ongoing problems that originate during childhood. Further, the family, school, and other problems experienced by life-course persistent offenders are more serious than those experienced by adolescence-limited offenders. This also makes it more difficult for life-course persistent offenders to escape from a life of crime.

The arguments described with respect to life-course persistent offenders have limited support. A few recent studies suggest that life-course persistent offenders are more likely than other individuals to have traits conducive to crime and to experience poor parenting early in life, and that these early problems create additional problems over the life course—problems usually more severe than those experienced by the adolescence-limited offenders.[3]

However, we note that not all juveniles who experience poor parenting and irritability/low self-control early in life become life-course persistent offenders. While such juveniles have a much greater risk of becoming life-course persistent offenders, some manage to substantially reduce their levels of offending when they become adults. This usually occurs because they obtain decent jobs; make good marriages; or have other life-changing experiences, like participation in the military or involvement in effective rehabilitation programs. It is not yet entirely clear why some of these individuals are able to turn their lives around while others are not, but this topic is receiving a good deal of attention from criminologists.[4]

SUMMARY

The integrated theories in this chapter try to explain patterns of offending over the course of the individual's life. The first theory focuses on the "adolescence-limited" pattern of offending and the second on the "life-course persistent" pattern. Both these theories represent extensions of strain, social learning, and control theories. The first theory argues that certain of the biological and social changes associated with adolescence lead to a reduction in control, an increase in the social learning for crime, and an increase in strain during adolescence. The second theory argues that certain biological and social factors lead some individuals to experience low levels of control, much social learning for crime, and high levels of strain over a good portion of their lives.

TEACHING AIDS

Web-Based Exercise: Comparing Adult and Juvenile Offenders

In this chapter we have argued that patterns of offending can be explained, in part, in terms of social changes occurring over the life course. Some of these changes involve time use, including how people spend their time and who they spend their time with. As we have seen, individuals tend to spend less time with their parents and more time with their peers as they move from childhood to adolescence. We now ask you to consider how adolescent time use may differ from adult time use, and how such differences may impact offending.

Visit the website for the Department of Justice, Office of Juvenile Justice and Delinquency Prevention at http://ojjdp.gov. Select the **Statistics** tab on the left-hand side of the page, and then select the **Offending by Juveniles** tab. Under **Related FAQ**, click on the **Comparing Offending by Adults and Juveniles** tab. In this section you will see a question that reads: "What time of day are adults and juveniles most likely to commit violent crime?" Click on the **Answer** tab. What do you think explains the difference you see between juveniles and adults?

Controversial Issue: An Evolutionary Theory of Adolescence-Limited Offending

One of the first modern theories of crime and delinquency, that of Lombroso (1911), explained life-course persistent offending in terms of evolutionary theory. A large portion of the habitual offenders who committed serious crimes were said to be "genetic throwbacks," individuals who were not as evolved as other people. These genetic throwbacks were savages in the midst of modern society, and it was their savage or primitive nature that led them to engage in crime. Lombroso described certain of the physical characteristics of these individuals, like enormous jaws, flattened noses, arm span greater than the individual's height, and prehensile feet (feet capable of grabbing or picking up things). Individuals with such characteristics resemble the stereotypical "caveman."

Lombroso's theory was discredited when research revealed that most of the characteristics he listed failed to distinguish criminals from carefully matched samples of noncriminals. And evolutionary theories of crime—as well as biological theories of crime more generally—fell into decline for much of the twentieth century. Also contributing to this decline was the fact that many people were disturbed by the racist elements of the early evolutionary theories (certain race and ethic groups were sometimes said to be biologically predisposed to crime). Many people were also disturbed by the policy implications of these theories. Certain of these theories, in particular, contributed to the eugenics movement, which sought to prevent certain categories of people from reproducing (for overviews, see Rafter, 1997; Bernard et al., 2015).

However, evolutionary (and biological) theories of crime have experienced a revival in recent decades. The new evolutionary and biological theories are much more sophisticated than the older theories. These new theories, however, still elicit some controversy. Evolutionary theories have been used to explain both life-course persistent and adolescence-limited offending.[5] As Ellis and Walsh (1997:232) point out, all such theories are based on a "simple but powerful idea: to the degree that a particular characteristic is prevalent in the population, it is likely to have contributed to the reproductive success of the individuals currently living."

One evolutionary theory of adolescence-limited offending argues that when males reach puberty they become involved in an effort to find a mate, protect that mate from rivals, and produce children. Males who are aggressive and attractive to females are more likely to be successful in this effort. As D. Rowe (2002:54) states, "The teenage boy needs to quickly establish his reputation [for aggression, among other things] and to acquire the material things that make him attractive to the opposite sex, which can be anything from a surfboard to a low-rider car." Aggressive and attractive males, then, are more likely to reproduce and thereby pass their genes on to their children. But once males find a mate and produce children, competition with other males becomes less critical. In fact, competition can be costly, threatening the physical well-being of males and reducing their ability to care for their children. Rather, males who provide material support and parenting help are more likely to have their children survive and do well, and these children then pass their genes on to still others. So, engaging in supportive behavior now provides a reproductive advantage.

According to this theory, then, the evolutionary process selects for males who are aggressive in adolescence (when seeking and protecting mates) and more supportive in adulthood (when raising children). Such males are most likely to have their genes passed on to others. This theory is said to explain such things as the increase in testosterone during adolescence and the decline during adulthood. And, more generally, it is said to explain why adolescents are generally more aggressive than children and adults (see Rowe, 1996, 2002).

This theory has not yet been fully tested, but certain data are said to be compatible with it. For example, Rowe (1996) states that the rapid increase in male testosterone levels during adolescence is correlated with an increase in both sexual activity and delinquency. And marriage is said to result in a decrease in testosterone levels. Can you think of additional ways in which we might test or explore the accuracy of this theory? If correct, does this theory mean that the social conditions associated with adolescence have little effect on adolescence-limited offending? How might evolutionary theory explain the fact that males are more likely to engage in most forms of crime than females (see Ellis and Walsh, 1997; Rowe, 1996)? What are the policy implications of evolutionary theories (see Ellis et al., 2012; Raine, 1993; Rowe, 1996, 2002)? What is your overall reaction to such theories?

TEST YOUR KNOWLEDGE OF THIS CHAPTER

1. Describe the adolescence-limited and life-course persistent patterns of offending.
2. Briefly describe the integrated theories of adolescence-limited and life-course persistent offending presented in this chapter.
3. Why are adolescents granted some, but not all, of the privileges and responsibilities of adulthood? Describe some of the privileges and responsibilities granted to adolescents.
4. Describe how these privileges and/or responsibilities may reduce control, foster the social learning of crime, and increase strain.
5. Why do most adolescents reduce their level of offending when they become adults?
6. How do life-course persistent offenders differ from adolescence-limited offenders (in terms of traits and early life experiences)?
7. Why do the traits and family experiences of life-course persistent offenders tend to persist over time?
8. Describe how these traits and family experiences reduce control, foster the social learning of crime, and increase strain.
9. Why do these traits and family experiences lead to school, peer, marital, and work problems? Describe how arguments in this area are similar to those made by labeling theorists.
10. Adolescence-limited offenders reduce their level of offending when they become adults. Why don't life-course persistent offenders do the same?
11. Describe why some of the individuals who experience poor parenting and irritability/low self-control early in life do not become life-course persistent offenders.

THOUGHT AND DISCUSSION QUESTIONS

1. Is it possible to alter the biological and social changes associated with adolescence in ways that reduce offending? If so, how?
2. Can you think of additional reasons, beyond those presented in this chapter, why adolescents are more likely to engage in crime than children and adults?
3. Even though they are a small percentage of the population, life-course persistent offenders account for a large share of all delinquency, especially serious delinquency. How should we respond to them? For example, some argue that juvenile justice agencies should focus their resources on such offenders, attempting to identify them as early as possible, offer them treatment, and punish them severely if treatment is not effective. Do you agree?

KEY TERMS

- Adolescence-limited offending
- Life-course persistent offending

ENDNOTES

1. For overviews of the theories and research in this area, see Agnew, 2003a; Benson, 2002; Cullen et al., 2014; Farrington, 2005, 2006; Gibson and Krohn, 2013; Laub and Sampson, 2003; Le Blanc and Loeber, 1998; Moffitt, 1993, 1997, 2006; Nagin and Tremblay, 2005a; Piquero and Mazerolle, 2001; Sampson and Laub, 1993a; David Smith, 2002; Thornberry, 1997; Tittle, 2000.
2. For overviews, see Benson, 2002:69–70; Raine, 2002a; Walsh, 2002; John Paul Wright, Tibbetts, and Daigle, 2008.

3. See Agnew, 2005; Aguilar et al., 2000; Barnes et al., 2011; Brame et al., 1999; Farrington, 2005; Farrington et al., 2009; Fergusson et al., 2000; Gibson and Krohn, 2013; Lahey and Waldman, 2005; Moffitt et al., 2001; Moffitt and Harrington, 1996; Patterson et al., 1989; Patterson et al., 1998; Simons et al., 1994, 2002; Thornberry and Krohn, 2005; Thornberry, Krohn et al. (with Porter), 2003; Turner et al., 2007; Wiesner and Capaldi, 2003; B. Wright, Caspi, Moffitt, and Silva, 1999.

4. See Farrington et al., 2009; Giordano et al., 2002, 2003, 2007; Laub and Sampson, 2001, 2003; Laub et al., 2006; Schubert et al., 2016; Shover, 1996; Simons et al., 2002, M. Turner et al., 2007.

5. For excellent overviews, see Barber, 2008; Cullen et al., 2014; Ellis and Walsh, 1997; Raine, 1993; Rowe, 2002; Walsh, 2002.

11 Is Delinquency More Likely in Certain Types of Situations?

The theories examined thus far focus on the factors that create a general *predisposition* or willingness to engage in delinquency. Such factors include high levels of strain, social learning for crime, low levels of control, and (in some cases) being labeled a delinquent. Individuals who are predisposed to delinquency tend to commit more delinquent acts than others, as indicated in Chapters 6 through 9. And certain individuals tend to commit more delinquent acts during adolescence, when their predisposition to delinquency is strongest, as indicated in Chapter 10. But **even the most predisposed individuals do not commit delinquent acts all the time. In fact, they spend most of their time engaged in nondelinquent activities.** Decker and Van Winkle (1996:118–119) make this point in their field study of gang members:

> Gang members spend much of their time together being "normal" teenagers or young adults: hanging out at each others' homes, in parks, on street corners, and at fast food joints, malls, skating rinks, bowling alleys, and youth clubs. When we asked subjects "What do you do the most with other gang members?" the dominant answer was "hang out" (or one of the many equivalents—"chill out," "playing," "hang," "fuck around"). . . . Nearly two-thirds of the responses involved fairly innocuous and non-criminal behaviors.

Whether predisposed individuals engage in delinquency depends heavily on the types of situation they encounter. The first part of this chapter draws on strain, control, and social learning theories to describe those situations most conducive to delinquency. The second part discusses the factors that influence the likelihood that predisposed individuals will encounter such situations. The arguments made draw heavily on the work of Akers (1990), Birkbeck and LaFree (1993), L. Cohen and Felson (1979), Colvin (2000), Cornish and Clarke (1986), Marcus Felson (2002, 2006), Richard Felson (1993), Finkelhor and Asdigian (1996), Leslie Kennedy and Forde (1999), Miethe and McCorkle (2001), Osgood et al. (1996), Sherman et al. (1989), Tedeschi and Felson (1994), and Wilcox et al. (2003).

After reading this chapter, you should be able to:

- Identify the types of situation that are most likely to result in delinquency.
- Draw on the leading theories to explain why these situations are conducive to delinquency.
- Explain why some juveniles are more likely than others to encounter situations that are conducive to delinquency.

Describing the situations most conducive to delinquency not only helps predict when predisposed juveniles will engage in delinquency but also has important policy implications. In particular, it is sometimes difficult to reduce the individual's predisposition for delinquency. But it may still be possible to reduce the amount of delinquency the individual commits by **altering the situations he or she encounters.** For example, we know that delinquent acts are more likely to be committed in the hours immediately after school (especially the more serious violent offenses), when juveniles are more likely to be involved in unstructured, unsupervised activities with peers (Soule et al., 2008). We might, therefore, reduce delinquency by creating structured after-school programs for juveniles (see Chapter 24).

WHAT TYPES OF SITUATIONS ARE MOST CONDUCIVE TO DELINQUENCY?

While the leading delinquency theories focus on the factors that predispose juveniles to delinquency, we can draw on these theories and certain other research to describe situations of the types most likely to result in delinquency. In particular, juveniles are most likely to engage in delinquency when (1) they are provoked or face other situational strains; (2) alcohol or drugs are being used, which will increase the likelihood of delinquent coping; (3) the costs of delinquency are seen as low (i.e., control is low); and (4) the benefits of delinquency are seen as high (i.e., the anticipated reinforcement for delinquency is high).[1]

Strain Theory: Situational Strains

Strain theory argues that delinquency is most likely to occur in situations where individuals are subject to strain. Several types of situational strain have been described in the literature. The most common type is **provocations by others,** especially verbal and physical attacks that are perceived as deliberate. Several researchers state that such attacks are especially likely to provoke a violent response, particularly when males are attacked by other males.[2] Such attacks involve the presentation of negative stimuli, and they may also be seen as threats to an individual's status, especially among certain males who view the attacks as threats to their masculine status, or "manhood."

Using data from a national sample of adolescents, Agnew (1990a) found that more than 60 percent of the juveniles engaging in assault said they did so because they were intentionally provoked in some way. Among other things, they said that they were insulted, annoyed, threatened, molested, or that their property had been damaged or taken. Being provoked or mistreated by others was also the main reason given for vandalism and running away. Provocations, however, were not a major cause of income-generating crimes, like theft.

A study by Lockwood (1997) also highlights the central role of provocations in producing violence. Lockwood interviewed 110 middle school and high school students from schools with high rates of violence. These students discussed 250 violent incidents in which they had been involved. About half these incidents occurred at school; others occurred in public areas (e.g., sidewalks, streets, and parks) and in homes. Most of the incidents involved acquaintances (58 percent); others involved friends (16 percent) and family members (15 percent). Only 11 percent involved strangers. The most common setting for a violent incident, then, was an encounter with an acquaintance at school. These violent incidents almost always began when one student did something the other student did not like—that is, when one student provoked the other. The most common provocation was "offensive touching," such as pushing, grabbing, hitting, or throwing something. Other provocations included interfering with someone's possessions, refusing to comply with someone's request, saying something bad about someone to someone else, verbally teasing someone, and deliberately insulting someone. Such provocations typically led to an argument, the argument escalated, insults were exchanged, and violence was the result. Violence was performed to end the disliked behavior, seek revenge, and/or save face (also see Garofalo et al., 1987; Wilkinson, 2002).

It is important to stress that **many offenders are not the innocent victims of provocations by others.** Data suggest that many offenders mistreat others and, in doing so, elicit negative reactions from the victims (see R. Felson, 1993; Jensen and Brownfield, 1986). The offenders then respond to these negative reactions with delinquency. A school bully, for example, may regularly "pick on" or harass another juvenile. When the harassed juvenile complains, the bully may respond with violence, claiming that he or she was "provoked." Many offenders behave in ways that call forth "provocations," or negative responses, from others.

When offenders are provoked, they may immediately attack the victim. As just suggested, however, offender and victim more commonly engage in a series of verbal exchanges. The offender, for example, may demand that the victim apologize. The victim may refuse. The offender may then insult the victim. The victim, in turn, may reply with an insult. Neither the victim nor the offender is willing to back down, and violence eventually results. Onlookers, if present, often contribute to the escalation of hostilities by encouraging violence.

Other types of situational strain have received less attention, although **data suggest that income-generating crimes are often produced by a desperate need for cash.** In particular, individuals are in situations where they believe they desperately need money, perhaps to purchase drugs, pay off gambling debts, finance their partying lifestyle or "high living," or survive on the street. Many engage in crimes like shoplifting, burglary, robbery, drug selling, and prostitution to get the money (see, e.g., T. Bennett and Wright, 1984; R. Wright and Decker, 1997). Still other situational strains involve **threats to autonomy** (e.g., parents or teachers prevent adolescents from engaging in a desired activity) and the **loss of positive stimuli** (e.g., romantic breakups, the murder of a friend).

There have been some **efforts to reduce crime by reducing situational strains.** For example, areas with lots of bars often have high rates of violence, especially when the bars close and the patrons pour out onto the streets. The inebriated patrons often get into confrontations with one another, and many of these confrontations are settled in a violent manner. Some jurisdictions have attempted to reduce the likelihood of such confrontations or provocations by staggering bar closing hours, so that not everyone pours out onto the street at the same time. To give another example, soccer violence in Britain has been reduced by separating rival fans in the stadium and taking steps to ensure that fans do not spend longs periods of time waiting around before or after the game.[3] (See Chapter 24 for additional information.)

Strain Theory: Situational Factors That Increase the Likelihood of Delinquent Coping

Predisposed individuals, then, are more likely to engage in delinquency when they are in strainful situations. But not all predisposed individuals respond to strainful situations with delinquency. Leslie Kennedy and Baron (1993), for example, found that this was the case with the punk rockers they examined in their field study. While the punk rockers were known for their violent behavior, Kennedy and Baron (1993:100) state:

> [We were] quite surprised at the amount of verbal abuse that [the punk rockers] absorbed without retaliatory measures. Passersby frequently made derogatory remarks about members' sexual preferences and "manliness." The members' appearance also made them the center of attention. Individuals passing by the group often stared and often made negative comments. This type of response was more noticeable when members were alone, away from the group, walking the downtown streets.

Kennedy and Baron go on to state that the punk rockers were more likely to retaliate in some situations than in others. For example, retaliation was more likely when the punk rockers were together and away from busy streets, where passersby might intervene.

More generally, a delinquent response to situational strain is most likely when **features of the situation increase the individual's sensitivity to strain, reduce the individual's ability to legally cope, reduce the perceived costs of delinquency, and increase the perceived benefits of delinquency.** In this area, **the use of alcohol and certain drugs like barbiturates** may increase the likelihood of a delinquent response by increasing the individual's sensitivity to provocations. Such drugs may also reduce the individual's ability to engage in legal coping, like negotiating with others. For example, one 17-year-old daily crack user stated:

> It doesn't seem to matter if you're on or off crack. . . . [Y]ou're crazy both times. If you're high, you think someone's goin' do something to you, or try an' take your stuff.

If you're comin' down or waiting to make a buy or just get off, you seem to get pissed off easy. . . . A lot of people been cut just because somebody looked at them funny or said somethin' stupid. (Quoted in Inciardi et al., 1993:104).

Further, such drugs may reduce the individual's awareness of and concern with the costs of delinquency.[4] For example, one shoplifter stated:

When I'm drunk or stoned, it's like I'm invisible. No, it's like I'm Superman. I ain't scared of nothing. Nobody can touch me. It seems like that's what always gets me in trouble. I'll just walk in and take something and walk out. (Quoted in Cromwell et al., 1999:65)

Other situational factors that increase the likelihood of delinquent coping are discussed in the following sections. They include the presence of attractive targets, the absence of capable guardians, and the presence of delinquent peers. These factors lead the juvenile to conclude that the costs of delinquent coping are low and the benefits are high. (Also see the discussion of guns in Chapter 17; some evidence suggests that the presence of guns in a situation increases the likelihood of delinquent coping.)

Social Learning and Control Theories: The Benefits and Costs of Delinquency

We treat social learning and control theories together here, since the arguments they make overlap to some extent. According to both theories, **crime is most likely in situations where the benefits of delinquency are seen as high and the costs as low.** The benefits of delinquency may be **tangible,** like money or property, and they may be **intangible**— for example, social approval and the thrills or excitement associated with the crime (see J. Katz, 1988). Agnew (1990a) found that most of the juveniles who had stolen things said they did so because they needed to obtain a certain item or because the act was fun or enjoyable. The costs of delinquency include the **likelihood of being caught** and punished, as well as the **"moral costs"** of committing the crime: that is, how bad or guilty would the juvenile feel if he or she committed a crime in that situation?

Few researchers argue that juveniles carefully consider all the benefits and costs of delinquency in a particular situation. Most juveniles (and adults) are not that rational or thoughtful. Researchers argue, however, that most juveniles give at least some thought to the rewards and costs of delinquency. For example, juveniles in a particular situation may not pause and carefully calculate the probability that they will be caught and punished if they commit a delinquent act. At the same time, they usually do not commit delinquent acts when their parents are present or the police are nearby. Thus, they give some rough consideration to the costs (and benefits) of delinquency. For example, offenders are generally more likely to attack smaller or weaker targets than larger or stronger ones. This fact partly explains why males are more likely to engage in aggression than females (R. Felson, 1996). The amount of consideration given to costs and benefits varies by the characteristics of the juvenile. For example, some juveniles are very impulsive; they often commit crimes with little thought of the consequences. Other juveniles, however, are more thoughtful (see Loughran et al., 2016; Tibbetts and Gibson, 2002).

Several researchers have discussed the features of a situation that influence the individual's calculation of benefits and costs. In the language of social learning theory, we might describe these features as "discriminative stimuli" (see Chapter 7); they indicate the probability that a delinquent act will be reinforced or punished in a given situation. For example, imagine a predisposed offender who encounters a luxury car parked on a deserted street with the key in the ignition. The features of this situation are such that the predisposed offender is likely to conclude that the benefits of auto theft are high and the costs are low. But if the same offender encounters an old, beat-up car in a well-lit parking lot with an attendant, he or she will likely conclude that the benefits of auto theft are low and the potential costs are high. More generally, individuals are more likely to believe that the benefits of crime are high and the costs are low when attractive targets for crime are available, capable guardians are absent, and delinquent peers are present.

Attractive Targets

The benefits of delinquency are more likely to be seen as high and the costs as low in situations where an *attractive target* is present.[5] With respect to property, **attractive targets are (1) visible and accessible, (2) valuable, (3) easy to move and/or concealable, (4) enjoyable,** and **(5) unlikely to provoke guilt if the targets are to be stolen.** In particular, predisposed offenders must be able to see the target and gain access to it. The target must be valuable, like cash or jewelry. It must be easy to move, like a cell phone or automobile (which can be driven). Related to this, many attractive targets are also easily concealed in one's pocket or a bag, which makes shoplifting much easier. Items like refrigerators and washing machines are valuable but are seldom stolen because they are difficult to move and conceal. The ideal targets have a high value in proportion to their weight. Marcus Felson (1998), for example, reports that washing machines cost about $5 per pound, while other electronic goods cost much more per pound and so are more likely to be stolen. Further, attractive targets are enjoyable to the adolescents who take them. This is one reason why adolescents are more likely to steal cell phones, liquor, cosmetics, and clothing (versus vitamins and milk). Finally, the target should be unlikely to provoke guilt in the offender if it is to be stolen, perhaps because the item belongs to someone who is disliked or because the offender believes that insurance will cover the owner's loss.

With respect to people, **attractive targets are (1) visible and accessible, (2) thought to possess valuable items like cash and jewelry, (3) unlikely to offer effective resistance,** and **(4) unlikely to provoke guilt if an attack is carried out.** Predisposed individuals may believe that others possess valuable items for a variety of reasons; for example, the others may display or "flash" lots of money, have just exited ATMs or check-cashing establishments, wear expensive clothes or jewelry, or handle large sums of money in their occupation (e.g., people involved in drug dealing or prostitution—see Box 11.1). The perceived likelihood that others will offer effective resistance depends on things such as their size, whether they are part of a group, and whether they are intoxicated. (See Tark and Kleck, 2004, for a study examining the ways victims offer resistance and the effectiveness of such resistance in preventing injury and property loss.) Also, some categories of people are seen as less likely to call the police (e.g., undocumented immigrants or those involved in illegal activities). Finally, certain targets are less likely to provoke guilt than others because offenders believe the targets deserve to be victimized (because, e.g., they provoked the offender or are rival gang members) or that they will not be seriously harmed by their victimization (because, e.g., their insurance will cover the loss). For example, the criminologists studying the punk rockers known for their violence reported the following attitude:

> When asked about their targets, members informed the researcher that their targets or victims were "geeks." The term geek suggested a subcultural neutralization of the victim's humanity. Geeks were unworthy of respect or fear. They were lower on the cultural totem pole than any of the other groups that gathered downtown. A geek was unfit even to be a member of a rival group. (L. Kennedy and Baron, 1993:102)

There have been efforts to reduce crime by **making targets less attractive.** Some of these efforts involve reducing the value of targets. The robbery of bus drivers, for example, was dramatically reduced when transit companies installed theft-proof change boxes on buses and required exact change (which reduced the amount of money that drivers carry). Other efforts

---

Box 11.1 Are Drug Dealers Attractive Targets?

Imagine for a moment that you are a young offender, willing to rob and steal from others. Would you consider robbing a drug dealer? What would be the pros and cons of targeting a drug dealer? Would a drug dealer qualify as an "attractive target"?

If you were able to think like a robber, certain benefits may have occurred to you: namely, drug dealers often carry large amounts of cash, drugs, or both and are unlikely to call the police if robbed. At the same time, you may have wondered about the risk or potential cost involved in robbing a drug dealer. Although dealers are unlikely to call the police, they may retaliate with lethal violence (with death being an extremely high cost!). Further, drug dealers may feel *compelled* to retaliate in a dramatic way. Otherwise, they may become known on the streets as "easy targets," inviting further victimization.

To understand why some robbers select drug dealers as their targets, Bruce Jacobs and his colleagues (2000) interviewed a number of so-called drug robbers in St. Louis. Drug robbers, they learned, are well aware of the risk of retaliation and make some attempt to weigh this potential cost against possible benefits. But because the robbers adopt strategies that are designed to reduce the likelihood of retaliation (thereby minimizing the potential cost), they still view drug dealers as attractive targets overall. For example, they may select drug dealers that are considered "soft" and unlikely to retaliate; they may instill fear so that their victims will think twice about retaliating' or they may wear disguises (making it difficult for the victim to retaliate at a later date). Here is how the drug robbers described such strategies:

> [The drug dealer I robbed] had all this dope and money but he was . . . real soft, you know what I'm saying? He was more like a little girl. . . . [He] had some tough [friends] but he stayed by his self. (Jacobs et al., 2000:178)

> "Get on the ground, don't move or you're dead, motherfucker!" . . . and a host of [other expletives] were reportedly voiced with a tone so fearsome as to leave no doubt that the [robber] was not to be messed with, ever. (Jacobs et al., 2000:178)

> I wear a [ski] mask so they can't see my face. . . . [Some] of them, I be right in they faces laughing, and they don't even know I'm the one that robbed them last night. . . . That's cold ain't it? (Jacobs et al., 2000:184)

Question for Discussion
1. Criminologists observe that offenders tend to have high rates of criminal victimization. That is, offenders often become crime *victims*. Can you think of other factors that may increase the vulnerability of offenders to victimization, beyond the factors described previously (possession of cash, drugs, and reluctance to call the police)?

---

employ certain "target-hardening" techniques that make targets less visible, less accessible, or more difficult to move. Antitheft devices on automobiles and burglar bars on windows are examples. Still other efforts increase the ability of targets to offer effective resistance. For example, individuals purchase guns (see Chapter 17), obtain large dogs, or take self-defense classes. Finally, there have been efforts to increase the moral costs of committing crimes against certain targets. For example, stores try to educate shoppers about the harm caused by shoplifting, and retailers in certain areas try to improve relations with community residents. (For more information, see the web exercise at the end of this chapter; also see Chapter 24.)

The Absence of Capable Guardians

The costs of delinquency are likely seen as low when there is no one around who might interfere with the crime. Individuals who might interfere are sometimes described as *capable guardians* (see M. Felson, 1994, 2002). The police often function as capable guardians, but it is more common for ordinary people to play this role. For example, the presence of people walking the street at night is often enough to prevent a robbery. The presence of neighbors during the day is often enough to prevent a burglary, and the presence of teachers in the school cafeteria is often enough to prevent fights. Offenders fear that if they are seen committing a crime, guardians may intervene, either directly, by confronting the juveniles, or indirectly, by calling the police. Parents, respected teachers, and other capable guardians with strong ties to juveniles are said to be especially effective at preventing crime, since juveniles are more responsive to them.

There have been efforts to reduce crime by **increasing the likelihood that others will intervene.** For example, convenience stores are frequently the target of robberies. Research suggests that the likelihood of robbery can be reduced by altering the staffing and layout of such stores. In particular, potential offenders are less likely to rob stores if two clerks rather than one are on duty, if the cashier is visibly stationed in the middle of the store rather than off to the side, and if the store is surrounded by businesses that are open in the evening. Potential offenders avoid such stores because one clerk may intervene on behalf of the other and because the offenders do not want to risk encountering or being noticed by people who might intervene. To give additional examples, parking lots with attendants have lower rates of auto theft than those without, and large households have lower rates of victimization than small households. (See Chapter 24 for more information.)

The Presence of Delinquent Peers

The presence of peers, especially delinquent peers, also influences the perceived costs and benefits of delinquency in a particular situation. **Peers often reduce the costs of delinquency** by preventing retaliation from others, by helping the juvenile commit delinquent acts, and by convincing the juvenile that such acts are justifiable or excusable (thereby reducing the moral costs of crime). The presence of delinquent peers **may also increase the anticipated benefits of delinquency,** since delinquent peers often reinforce delinquent acts. Leslie Kennedy and Baron (1993), for example, state that the punk rockers in their study were more likely to respond to provocations with violence when their friends were around partly because they anticipated their friends would reward such a response. Given these arguments, it should perhaps come as no surprise that most delinquent acts occur when peers are present (see Chapter 16).

Summary

Delinquency is most likely when predisposed offenders are provoked or experience other situational strains, when situational factors like alcohol and drug use increase the likelihood of delinquent coping, when the perceived benefits of crime are seen as high, and when the perceived costs are seen as low. Benefits are most likely to be perceived as high and costs as low when attractive targets are available, capable guardians are absent, and delinquent peers are present.

These statements may seem straightforward, but they have led to a number of important, not-so-obvious conclusions about delinquency. In particular, researchers have argued that the level of delinquency is dependent not only on the number of predisposed offenders but also on such things as the frequency of provocations, the supply of attractive targets, the presence of capable guardians, and the presence of delinquent others. In this area, we briefly described several crime control programs that reduced levels of offending not by reducing the predisposition for delinquency but by, for example, reducing the frequency of provocations, reducing the supply of attractive targets, and increasing the presence of capable guardians (for a detailed example of this approach, see Box 11.2).

> ### Box 11.2   Preventing Sexual Assault in Australia: A Focus on Situational Factors

Young people are responsible for a sizable proportion of known sex offenses. In the United States, juveniles account for about 20 percent of all those arrested for forcible rape and other sexual offenses. In Queensland, which is the second-largest state in Australia, juveniles account for about 25 percent of the perpetrators of sexual offenses known to the police (Smallbone and Rayment-McHugh, 2013). To help prevent sexual assault and to stop youth sex offenders from reoffending, a team of psychologists at Griffith University in Australia developed a comprehensive community-based intervention. One of the goals is to identify and address the **situational factors** that are conducive to youth sexual assault.

To illustrate, the team received a report of six youth who had committed sexual assault in a small, remote community in north Queensland. Over a period of several years, the team made weekend visits to the community to assess the problem and implement treatment strategies. Their assessment focused, in part, on **youth routine activities**. They interviewed family members, residents, and observed the settings where sexual assaults took place. They learned that many of the assaults had occurred in an abandoned house. They also became aware of areas in the community frequented by unsupervised groups of youth.

Although the intervention included individual treatment for the six youth who had committed sexual assault (e.g., techniques for developing self-control, education about appropriate sexual behavior), more time was spent working with the family members of these youth in an effort to strengthen parenting skills, increase adult supervision, and reduce the amount of time that youth spent in unsupervised, unstructured activities with their peers:

> Situational interventions were begun early to increase guardianship by family members and to reduce opportunities for [sexual violence and abuse]. . . . Increased supervision of children and youth was arranged before, during, and after community events, lighting was increased at night-time events, and . . . scheduling [of formal, supervised pro-social recreational activities] was focused on periods of increased risk. (Smallbone and Rayment-McHugh, 2013:10)

The intervention team reports that, to their knowledge, none of the six youth have committed another sexual offense, although some have been in trouble for other delinquent behaviors.

Question for Discussion

1. Imagine that you are a member of an intervention team and that your task is to identify the situational factors that contribute to general delinquency in your own community (e.g., vandalism, fights, drug activity). How would you go about identifying such factors? What would you look for? What questions would you ask family members, residents, business owners, school officials, or the police?

WHAT FACTORS INFLUENCE THE LIKELIHOOD THAT PREDISPOSED OFFENDERS WILL ENCOUNTER SITUATIONS CONDUCIVE TO DELINQUENCY?

Sometimes individuals who are predisposed to delinquency **deliberately seek out situations that are conducive to delinquency.** They are more likely to look for opportunities to commit property crimes than violent crimes. Predisposed offenders might actively search for good homes to burglarize or "soft" individuals to rob. Several studies, however, suggest that such searching behavior is not as wide-ranging as some people believe (see Bottoms and Wiles, 2002; Miethe and McCorkle, 2001). Individuals tend to search for targets in areas that are convenient and familiar to them, so they select targets near their homes, near the places they frequent (like school and recreational sites), and along the routes they frequently travel (like the routes to and from school and the mall). Selection of targets in these areas requires less effort on their part, and offenders feel less conspicuous and more secure in these areas, since they know them well. Offenders, however, usually do not commit property crimes too close to home because they might be recognized. Violent crimes, on the other hand, are frequently committed close to home or in the juvenile's home, since they often involve family members, friends, and acquaintances.

At other times, predisposed offenders **do not deliberately seek out situations that are conducive to crime.** Rather, they **encounter such situations during the course of their everyday, routine activities**—attending school, going to work, and hanging out with friends. For example, a juvenile might spot a tempting target for burglary while on the way to school or might encounter a good opportunity for shoplifting while hanging out with friends at the mall. Violent crimes are especially likely to emerge out of everyday activities. Such crimes are usually not planned but rather stem from the frictions of everyday life, such as disputes at school.

Certain factors influence the likelihood that individuals will find or encounter situations that are conducive to crime. Most prominent among these factors is the nature of the individual's routine, or everyday, activities (see especially M. Felson, 2002).

The Nature of the Individual's Routine Activities

The nature of individuals' *routine activities* refers to what people do each day, with whom they do it, when they do it, and where they do it. As argued next, routine activities of certain types increase the likelihood of being in situations conducive to crime.

What juveniles do and with whom they do it. Juveniles who spend a lot of time in **unstructured, unsupervised activities with peers,** especially delinquent peers, are more likely to encounter situations conducive to crime.[6] Unstructured activities include hanging out, riding around in a car, going to parties, and certain other recreational activities. Unsupervised activities are those from which capable guardians, like parents and teachers, are absent. Individuals who spend a lot of time in unstructured, unsupervised activities with delinquent peers are more likely to be in situations where capable guardians are absent and delinquent peers are present. This lowers the perceived costs of delinquency and increases the perceived benefits. Also, such individuals are more likely to be in provocative situations, since delinquent peers often provoke one another and get into conflicts with others.

When they do it. Crimes involving juveniles are more frequent on school days and tend to occur before, during, and in the few hours after school (D. Gottfredson and Soule, 2005; H. Snyder and Sickmund, 2006). This temporal pattern is easily explained, since it is at these times that peers are most likely to be involved in activities with one another, often in unstructured, unsupervised settings (e.g., hanging out before or after school, interacting in school hallways or the cafeteria). It should be noted, however, that drug use displays a somewhat different temporal pattern. Drug use is less likely during school hours. While it might be easy to obtain and take drugs during school hours, the lingering effects of drug use might be detected by teachers. Drugs are more likely to be used after school and especially on weekends.

Where they do it. Public settings are generally more conducive to delinquency than private settings. In fact, each hour spent in public space is about 10 times more risky than an hour spent at home (M. Felson, 1994:39). Also, data suggest that certain locations are especially conducive to delinquency. Delinquency is most likely in settings that bring young people together in the absence of capable guardians. Such settings include the area around schools and the routes to and from school. As indicated, much crime occurs as juveniles are leaving school. When crime does occur in school, it is more likely to occur in hallways and restrooms than in classrooms, where teachers are typically present. Other locations where juveniles congregate—such as youth centers, shopping malls, movie theater parking lots, and restaurants—are also characterized by high rates of juvenile offending. These areas have been described as juvenile crime "magnets" or "hot spots" (Bichler et al., 2014; Weisburd et al., 2009).

Factors Influencing Routine Activities

Age and gender have especially strong effects on routine activities. Adolescents are much more likely than other age groups to engage in unstructured, unsupervised activities with peers. This fact partly explains why crime rates peak in adolescence. Also, males are more likely than females to engage in unstructured, unsupervised activities with peers. This fact partly explains the gender difference in delinquency (see Osgood et al., 1996). Routine activities are also influenced by many of the factors that affect the juvenile's predisposition for delinquency, like the juvenile's **level of parental supervision, commitment to school, and level of self-control.** In particular, such factors increase the likelihood of engaging in routine activities that involve exposure to situations conducive to delinquency (see Simons et al., 2014). For example, juveniles who are poorly supervised by parents are more likely to engage in unstructured, unsupervised activities with peers.

We should also note that **larger social and technological changes may affect levels of delinquency insofar as such changes influence the nature of routine activities.** For example, increases in parental work, single-parent families, and multicar households have led to a sharp decline in parental supervision since the 1950s. Parents are less likely to be home after school, they are less likely to engage in shared activities with their children, and they grant their children more freedom than in the past. Children today, for example, have fewer chores or duties around the house, later curfews, and greater access to automobiles. This decline in parental supervision, in turn, has led to a change in the routine activities of juveniles: juveniles now spend more time with peers, away from parents. This may partly explain the large increase in juvenile crime rates during the 1960s and early 1970s.

To give another example, technological advances are shaping the way that adolescents socialize with their peers. The majority of teenagers in the United States now have their own cell phones and more than half text-message others daily. This new form of unstructured, virtual socializing with peers is often done discreetly, beyond parental awareness. In short, new technologies make it easier for adolescents to plan delinquent activities with their friends and more difficult for parents to exercise supervision and control. Although this development has not led to an increase in the overall rate of juvenile crime (recall that rates of serious juvenile crime have declined substantially since the mid-1990s), it may have consequences for individual youths and certain types of delinquent activity. For instance, one study found that, in comparison to juveniles who seldom phone, email, or text-message their friends, juveniles who spend large amounts of virtual time with their friends tend to report more frequent use of alcohol and marijuana. This finding holds even after taking into account a number of third variables, such as self-control, parenting style, and time spent in the actual presence of peers (Meldrum and Clark, 2015).

Certain other technologies, such as personal computers and game devices, may help **reduce** juvenile crime. Time spent indoors playing video games, for example, is less conducive to delinquency than time spent on the street or in the juvenile crime hot spots mentioned earlier. We examine the impact of computers, video games, and social media in Chapter 17. (For more on the impact of larger social and technological changes on routine activities and situations conducive to crime, see Marcus Felson [1998]. Felson argues that the large decrease in crime that began in the mid-to-late 1990s partly reflects the fact that people are using credit or debit cards more than cash.)

Summary

Individuals may deliberately seek out situations conducive to delinquency, or they may encounter such situations during the course of their everyday, routine activities. Individuals who frequently engage in unstructured activities with peers in the absence of authority figures are especially likely to find themselves in situations conducive to delinquency. Adolescents, males, and those who are poorly supervised by their parents, among others, are more likely to fall into this category.

SUMMARY

Delinquency is most likely to occur when predisposed juveniles encounter situations conducive to delinquency. In the situations most conducive to delinquency, (1) juveniles are provoked or experience other situational strains, (2) factors like alcohol or drug use increase the likelihood of delinquent coping, (3) the perceived benefits of delinquency are high, and (4) the perceived costs are low. These factors interact in their effect on delinquency; that is, each factor conditions the effect of the other factors on delinquency. For example, provocations are more likely to lead to delinquency when the costs of delinquency are low and the benefits are high.

Predisposed individuals may seek out situations conducive to delinquency. Also, predisposed individuals may encounter such situations during the course of their everyday or routine activities. Most notably, individuals who engage in unstructured, unsupervised activities with peers are especially likely to find themselves in situations having these four characteristics.

TEACHING AIDS
Applying the Research: Examining the Routine Activities of College Students

The routine activities in which people engage not only influence the likelihood that they will engage in crime but also influence the likelihood that they will be crime victims (e.g., by influencing their exposure to predisposed offenders, how well guarded they or their property are, how attractive they or their property are as crime targets). Thus individuals who spend a lot of time out alone at night drinking in bars are more likely to be victimized. Such individuals are more likely to encounter predisposed offenders, they are less likely to offer effective resistance (since they have been drinking), and it is less likely that capable guardians will come to their assistance.

Mustaine and Tewksbury (1998a) examined whether the routine activities of students in nine colleges and universities influenced the extent to which they were victims of minor theft (property worth less than $50) and major theft (property worth more than $50). The students were asked about a wide range of routine activities (what they do, when they do it, where they do it, with whom they do it). The following activities and individual and/or community characteristics were found to influence the likelihood of major theft:

- Threatened another with a gun (increases likelihood of major theft)
- Threatened another with no weapon (increases)
- Frequently eats out (increases)
- Neighborhood is too noisy (increases)
- Dog in residence (decreases)

- Installed extra locks (decreases)
- Belongs to many clubs and organizations (increases)
- Leaves home often for studying (increases)
- Lower social class (increases)
- Unemployed (increases)

The finding that people who engage in illegal activities are more likely to be the victims of crime has also been reported in other studies. It is usually argued that such persons are more likely to associate with other criminals. Also, it may be that such persons are less likely to call the police if victimized, making them more attractive targets for crime. How would you explain the association between the other routine activities and characteristics listed here and the likelihood of being a victim of major theft? (See the discussion in Mustaine and Tewksbury, 1998a, if you need assistance.)

Web-Based Exercise: Crime Prevention Through Environmental Design

In this chapter we described "target-hardening" techniques that have been used to reduce the attractiveness of potential crime targets. This strategy is related to a broader multidisciplinary approach known as Crime Prevention Through Environmental Design (CPTED). To better understand the principles behind this approach, visit the Seattle Police Department's CPTED webpage at http://www.seattle.gov/police/prevention/neighborhood/cpted.htm.

Drawing on the recommendations listed on the Seattle PD's web page, describe how you would implement CPTED on your college campus. What changes would you make to the built environment of your campus or dormitory to reduce the likelihood of crime? If you were to design a new college campus, what CPTED design features would it incorporate?

TEST YOUR KNOWLEDGE OF THIS CHAPTER

1. What do we mean when we state that some individuals are "predisposed" to delinquency? What major factors influence the individual's predisposition to delinquency?
2. Briefly describe the types of situation in which predisposed individuals are most likely to engage in delinquency.
3. We state that it is possible to reduce juveniles' level of offending without affecting their predisposition to delinquency. Give three examples of how this might be done.
4. What types of situational strain increase the likelihood of delinquency? Give an example of a provocation likely to prompt a delinquent response.
5. What types of situational factors increase the likelihood that juveniles will cope with these strains in a delinquent manner? Why do the use of alcohol and certain other drugs increase the likelihood of delinquent coping?
6. What major factors affect the individual's perceptions of the costs and benefits of crime in a situation?
7. Do juveniles give careful thought to the costs and benefits of crime? If your answer is no, does that mean that costs and benefits are irrelevant?
8. Describe the major features of attractive property and person targets.
9. What is a capable guardian?
10. Describe how the presence of delinquent peers may affect the perceived costs and benefits of crime.

11. Give an example of efforts to reduce delinquency by (a) reducing situational strains, (b) reducing the attractiveness of property targets, (c) reducing the attractiveness of person targets, and (d) increasing the presence of capable guardians.

12. What is meant by "routine activities"?

13. Describe the routine activities that increase exposure to situations conducive to crime. Why does engaging in unstructured, unsupervised activities with delinquent peers increase exposure to situations conducive to crime?

14. Describe those factors that increase the likelihood that one will engage in routine activities that increase exposure to situations conducive to crime.

THOUGHT AND DISCUSSION QUESTIONS

1. Describe the situational characteristics most conducive to cheating on exams and to minor theft on your college campus. How might such characteristics be altered to reduce cheating and theft?

2. Describe the routine activities that increase the likelihood that college students will be the victims of violence.

3. Are juveniles who are predisposed to delinquency more likely to encounter situations conducive to delinquency? Why (or why not)?

KEY TERMS

- Predisposition to delinquency
- Attractive targets
- Capable guardians
- Routine activities

ENDNOTES

1. For overviews and examples of the research in this area, see Agnew, 1990a, 2006; Akers, 1990; Birkbeck and LaFree, 1993; Bottoms and Wiles, 2002; Brantingham and Brantingham, 1984; Briar and Piliavin, 1965; Clarke and Cornish, 1985; Clarke and Eck, 2005; L. Cohen and Felson, 1979; L. Cohen et al., 1981; Colvin, 2000; Cornish and Clarke, 1986; M. Felson, 1987, 1994, 2002, 2006; R. Felson, 1993, 1997; Finkelor and Asdigian, 1996; Garofalo et al., 1987; Hindelang et al., 1978; Jensen and Brownfield, 1986; L. Kennedy and Baron, 1993; L. Kennedy and Forde, 1990, 1996, 1999; Madero-Hernandez and Fisher, 2013; Massey et al., 1989; Matsueda et al., 2006; McCarthy, 1995; Miethe and McCorkle, 2001; Miethe and Meier, 1990, 1994; Mustaine and Tewksbury, 1998a; Osgood et al., 1996; Sampson and Wooldredge, 1987; Sherman et al., 1989; Tedeschi and Felson, 1994; Wilcox et al., 2003; Wilkinson, 2002.

2. See especially Athens, 2005; Colvin, 2000; L. Hughes and Short, 2005; L. Kennedy and Forde, 1999; Tedeschi and Felson, 1994; Wilkinson, 2002; Wilkinson and Carr, 2008.

3. For further examples, see Clarke, 1992, 1995; Clarke and Eck, 2005; Eck, 2002; M. Felson, 2002, 2006; Geason and Wilson, 1989; Sherman et al., 1989.

4. See Assaad and Exum, 2002; Bernasco et al., 2013; R. Felson and Burchfield, 2004; R. Felson, Teasdale, and Burchfield, 2008; H. White and Gorman, 2000; H. White et al., 2002.

5. See Clarke and Eck, 2005; L. Cohen and Felson, 1979; M. Felson, 2002, 2006; Finkelhor and Asdigian, 1996; Wilcox et al., 2003.

6. See Agnew and Petersen, 1989; A. Anderson and Hughes, 2009; Bernasco et al., 2013; R. Felson, 1997; Haynie and Osgood, 2005; Hoban and Wierman, 2016; Hundleby, 1987; Jensen and Brownfield, 1986; Lotz and Lee, 1999; Maimon and Browning, 2010; Office of Juvenile Justice and Delinquency Prevention, 1999a; Osgood and Anderson, 2004; Osgood et al., 1996; Riley, 1987; Vazsonyi et al., 2002; Weerman et al., 2013; Wikström and Svensson, 2008.

12 Group Differences in Delinquency

How Can We Explain Group Differences,
Particularly Community Differences,
in Rates of Delinquency?

W e have so far examined how the leading theories of delinquency explain why some individuals engage in more delinquency than others, why individuals exhibit different patterns of offending over the life course, and why individuals are more likely to commit delinquent acts in some situations than in others. In this chapter we shift our focus from individuals to groups and examine how the leading theories explain **why some groups have higher delinquency rates than others.** There are many groups we might examine, but this chapter focuses on communities, including neighborhoods and cities. The central question addressed is: **Why do some communities have higher rates of delinquency than others?**

The discussion in this chapter provides **a model for explaining group differences in delinquency rates.** As you will see, the major way such differences are explained is by arguing that group characteristics affect levels of strain, control, the social learning for crime, and labeling. (Chapter 18 draws on the leading theories, as well as the research inspired by these theories, to explain still other group differences in delinquency—including gender, age, class, and race and ethnic differences. Our discussion of these group differences is delayed until Chapter 18, since it draws heavily on the research presented in Chapters 13 through 17.)

After reading this chapter, you should be able to:

- Describe the common characteristics of high-crime communities.
- Describe trends related to the growth, and decline, of neighborhoods suffering from economic deprivation.
- Draw on the leading theories to explain the high rates of crime and delinquency found in deprived communities.
- Describe the role of street culture (especially the "code of the street") in the development of youth violence.

We begin this chapter by describing the characteristics of communities that have high rates of crime. We then describe how these characteristics reduce levels of control, increase the social learning for crime, and increase levels of strain—thereby accounting for the high rates of crime in these communities. We also draw on labeling theory, noting that high rates of crime in a community often have consequences that increase the likelihood of further crime. The arguments draw heavily on the work of Agnew (1999), Akers (1998), E. Anderson (1999), Bernard (1990), Bursik and Grasmick (1993), Kornhauser (1978), Sampson and Groves (1989), Sampson and Raudenbush (1999), Sampson and Wilson (1995), Shaw and McKay (1942), and Sutherland et al. (1992).

This chapter, which completes our discussion of the leading theories of delinquency, ends with a brief overview of strain, control, social learning, and labeling theories.

WHY ARE CRIME RATES HIGHER IN SOME COMMUNITIES THAN IN OTHERS?

There is little doubt that some communities have much higher crime rates than others. We are sure that many of you can think of neighborhoods in your hometowns that have relatively high crime rates or at least are reputed to have high crime rates. One neighborhood with a high crime rate was described in our hometown newspaper in an article titled "A Bad Way to Die":

> Willie Arnold's first mistake that sweltering July night was to buy crack cocaine from a man he hardly knew on Beatie Avenue in Southwest Atlanta. His second mistake was to return to that street, known as one of the worst drug-infested neighborhoods in the city, to complain about the drugs he had bought. It was his last mistake. The gripe got

Arnold killed, beaten and kicked to death in the front yard of a Beatie Avenue house as dozens of people watched and cheered the aggressors on. . . . The attack took about 35 minutes, as the men and women involved took breaks so they could ultimately beat on the victim some more. Even a couple of children, younger than 10 years of age, participated in the assault, kicking and punching Arnold a few times as he wailed and writhed on the grass. No one tried to stop the beating. No one dared. "If something bad happens around here, you keep quiet, you don't tell on your neighbors for fear of your life" [said a Beatie Avenue resident]. When the attack was over, not much remained of Arnold's head and torso but a bloody mass crushed into the weeds and gravel of an unkempt front lawn. (Longa, 1998)

It is also the case that some cities have higher crime rates than others. Each year the FBI publishes data on the crime rates of cities throughout the United States, and newspapers and TV stations often carry stories about the city with the highest crime rate (the "crime capital" of the United States) or the highest murder rate (the "murder capital"). Among the 30 largest cities in the United States, Baltimore had the highest homicide rate for the year 2015, with 55 homicides per 100,000 residents. (By contrast, New York City had 4 homicides per 100,000 residents.) You might look up the crime rate in your city and compare it to that of other cities (see the latest edition of the FBI's *Uniform Crime Reports* at https://ucr.fbi.gov). (You should be aware, however, that the FBI data are not well suited for comparing crime rates in different cities—except for homicide rates and perhaps the rates of certain other serious crimes [see Gove et al., 1985]. Among other things, cities differ in the extent to which victims report crimes to the police and in police record-keeping practices.)

There has been much research on the characteristics of neighborhoods and cities with high crime rates. Although the results of this research are sometimes contradictory, researchers now have a reasonably good idea what those characteristics are. Most of the research has focused on crimes committed by both adults and juveniles, but some data suggest that the conclusions that follow apply to juvenile delinquency alone.[1]

WHAT ARE THE CHARACTERISTICS OF HIGH-CRIME NEIGHBORHOODS AND CITIES?

Generally speaking, urban communities have higher crime rates than suburban and rural communities, although the relationship between the degree of urbanization and crime is not as strong as many people think (Maguire and Pastore, 2003; Pratt and Cullen, 2005). Some urban communities have relatively low crime rates, while some rural communities have relatively high rates (Egan, 2002; Osgood and Chambers, 2000). Rather than the level of urbanization, the most important characteristics distinguishing high- from low-crime communities are the levels of economic deprivation, residential instability, family disruption in the community, and proximity to high-crime/poor communities.[2]

Economic deprivation. The most distinguishing characteristic of high-crime communities is that they are economically deprived. Deprivation has been measured in a variety of ways, including the average or median family income level in an area, the percentage of families below the poverty line ($24,600 for a family of four in 2016), the percentage of adult males who are unemployed, the percentage of families that receive welfare, and the average or median educational level. These measures are highly correlated, and they are often combined into more general measures of economic deprivation. Virtually all studies indicate that deprived cities and neighborhoods have more crime than other communities (see Land et al., 1990; Pratt and Cullen, 2005). For example, a study of neighborhoods in Columbus, Ohio, examined the relationship between the percentage of residents below the poverty line and neighborhood crime rates (based on crimes known to the police). Neighborhoods with extremely high levels of poverty (40 percent or more of the residents below the poverty line) had violent crime rates that were approximately five times as high as neighborhoods with low levels of poverty (5 percent or fewer below the poverty line). The difference in property crime rates was less extreme but still substantial (Krivo and Peterson, 1996).

Several criminologists have argued that researchers should consider not only the extent to which community residents are poor but also the extent to which they are **advantaged.** By advantaged, we mean having high incomes, advanced educations, prestigious jobs, or all three. Two communities may have identical levels of poverty (e.g., 25 percent of residents below the poverty line). One community, however, may be a "mixed-class" community in which a substantial number of residents earn high salaries, have college degrees, and work in managerial and professional jobs. The other community may have few such advantaged residents; rather, most other residents may be just above the poverty line. Researchers argue that the advantaged residents may reduce levels of crime in the community for several reasons. For example, they may use their resources to secure better police protection, improve the quality of local schools, and limit the number of bars in the community. They may also act as role models and mentors for youth in the community. Certain data support these arguments, suggesting that the presence of advantaged residents in a community is associated with lower levels of crime—even after we take account of poverty levels (e.g., Kubrin and Weitzer, 2003b; Sampson and Raudenbush, 1999).

Residential instability. High-crime communities also tend to have high rates of *residential instability*; that is, **people frequently move into and out of the community.** Residential instability is often measured by the percentage of residents who lived in different houses five years ago and the percentage of housing units that are renter occupied. Residential instability is more common in poor communities. New immigrants to the city often locate in poor communities because they cannot afford to live elsewhere, so people are frequently moving into the community. And the residents of poor communities often move elsewhere as soon as they are able, so people are frequently moving out of the community. Some data suggest that residential instability is related to crime only in poor communities: that is, poor communities with high rates of instability have higher crime rates than poor communities with low rates of instability. Instability may be unrelated to crime rates in wealthier communities.

Family disruption. High-crime communities tend to have higher rates of family disruption. Disruption is usually measured by the percentage of families headed by females and/or the percentage of residents who are divorced or separated. Economic deprivation is a major cause of family disruption, since, among other things, it leads to a decline in the proportion of males who are able to support a family.[3] Nevertheless, data indicate that family disruption has an independent effect on community crime rates. In fact, certain data suggest that family disruption partly explains the effect of economic deprivation on community crime rates. That is, economic deprivation affects community crime rates partly through its effect on family disruption (Sampson, 1985, 1987).

Close proximity to high-crime/economically deprived communities. High-crime communities tend to be adjacent to other high-crime or economically deprived communities. Criminals often commit crimes in nearby communities, so areas that are close to high-crime communities tend to have higher crime rates for this reason. Also, areas that are close to economically deprived communities tend to have higher crime rates because these communities have fewer jobs, good schools, and other resources on which to draw. So, if you live in a poor community, it is better to live in a poor community surrounded by wealthier communities than in one surrounded by other poor communities. If you are surrounded by wealthier communities, you might have easier access to such things as decent jobs, good schools, and various social services.

Is race or ethnicity related to community crime rates? High-crime communities tend to have a higher percentage of African American and Hispanic residents. Data, however, suggest that **much or all of the association between race/ethnicity and community crime rates is due to third variables like economic deprivation, residential instability, family disruption, and proximity to high-crime communities.** For example, African Americans are more likely than whites to live in communities characterized by high rates of poverty, residential instability, family disruption, and proximity to high-crime communities. According to data from the 2013 American Community Survey, 25.2 percent of poor African Americans versus 7.5 percent of poor whites lived in high-poverty neighborhoods (where 40 percent or more of the residents are below the poverty line; Jargowsky, 2015). When we control for, or take account of, third variables like economic deprivation, the association between race or ethnicity and community crime rates is substantially reduced or eliminated in most studies.[4] So, for example, studies tend to find that very poor communities have similar rates of crime, regardless of whether they are populated by African Americans or whites.

Summary
Economic deprivation, residential instability, family disruption, and proximity to high-crime/poor areas lead communities to develop high rates of crime. High-crime communities have a higher percentage of African Americans and Latinos because race/ethnicity is associated with factors like economic deprivation; the relationship between race/ethnicity and community crime rates is substantially reduced when we take account of these factors.

ARE COMMUNITIES WITH CHARACTERISTICS CONDUCIVE TO CRIME BECOMING MORE COMMON?
Most of the data we have on trends in community characteristics deal with economic deprivation. During the 1960s, 1970s, and 1980s, the urban decay and violence associated with high-poverty neighborhoods were of major concern in the United States. Further, the

number of people living in such neighborhoods was increasing dramatically. During the 1990s, however, this concern dissipated, as the number of people living in high-poverty neighborhoods dropped by 25 percent. This improvement was related to a booming economy and federal housing policies that encouraged cities to replace public housing projects with mixed-income housing (Atkin, 2003).

Unfortunately, this positive trend was short lived. In fact, since the year 2000, the trend has completely reversed. **From 2000 to 2013, the number of high-poverty neighborhoods rose again, reaching a record high.** The number of people living in such neighborhoods also increased. In the year 2000, 7.2 million Americans lived in high-poverty neighborhoods. By 2013, the number rose to 13.8 million—a 91 percent increase. This is the "highest number of high-poverty neighborhood residents ever recorded" (Jargowsky, 2015:4). As Jargowsky (2015:2) observes:

> After the dramatic decline in concentrated poverty between 1990 and 2000, there was a sense that cities were "back," and that the era of urban decay—marked by riots, violent crime, and abandonment—was drawing to a close. Unfortunately, despite the relative lack of public notice or awareness, poverty has reconcentrated.

So despite some improvement during the 1990's, **we have witnessed a long-term historical trend toward the increasing concentration of poverty, with more high-poverty neighborhoods, and more people living in these neighborhoods.** There are several reasons for this long-term trend.[5]

1. Working- and middle-class people moved out of mixed-income communities, leaving the poor behind. This is **especially true of African American communities.** As late as the 1960s, many inner-city African American communities contained a mix of poor, working-class, and middle-class residents. Working- and middle-class African Americans were prevented from living in the suburbs by discriminatory housing policies. As these discriminatory practices declined, working- and middle-class African Americans started to move to the suburbs—which increased the concentration of poor African Americans in the inner city (Quillian, 1999).

In recent decades, much population growth and development has occurred in new "outer suburban" communities, as affluent people of all races have been moving further away from central city neighborhoods, and even beyond the older "inner ring" suburban neighborhoods that were located just outside of city centers. This growth has often come at the expense of central city and inner-ring suburban neighborhoods: "taxpayers funded all the new infrastructure needed to facilitate suburban expansion—roads, schools, water and sewer, and so on—even as existing infrastructure was abandoned and underutilized in the urban core" (Jargowsky, 2015:13). Although some central-city neighborhoods have experienced economic renewal through a process of gentrification, in which more affluent residents relocate to "in town" areas and raise average incomes, this form of change has driven up property values, taxes, and rents—pushing lower-income residents out of the central city to older suburban locations (which then become new locations of concentrated poverty).

Ferguson, Missouri, provides an example of the concentration of poverty that has spread from inner-city areas to suburban outskirts. Ferguson is an older inner-ring suburb of St. Louis—one of the most rapidly gentrifying cities in the nation. In recent decades, the population of Ferguson shifted, becoming increasingly populated by African Americans. In addition, the poverty rate increased dramatically—about 30 percent of its neighborhoods are now high-poverty neighborhoods (Jargowsky, 2015). In 2014, Ferguson became a flashpoint for racial and economic tensions when the streets erupted in protest following the fatal police shooting of an 18-year-old African American man named Michael Brown.

2. The government placed public housing projects in poor inner-city communities, which further increased the concentration of low-income people there. Despite efforts in recent decades to promote the development of mixed-income housing, the availability of affordable housing remains limited outside central city and older suburban areas. According to Jargowsky (2015:14), the richer "suburbs have used exclusionary zoning to keep out affordable housing, so the poor and low income people can only live in the central city and dying suburbs that are being abandoned as wealthier people move further and further out to the fringes for larger houses, bigger bathrooms, and walk-in closets."

3. The economic situation of poor people, especially those in the inner city, declined as a result of several major changes in the economy. Most notably, **low-skill jobs paying a decent wage became scarcer.** There was a decline in the number of manufacturing jobs, partly due to technological changes and partly due to the movement of manufacturing jobs from the central city to suburban areas and overseas. For example, Philadelphia, Chicago, New York, and Detroit have lost more than half their manufacturing jobs since the 1960s (W. Wilson, 1996). The wages in manufacturing jobs also became less competitive, owing to such factors as foreign competition, the increase in the size of the workforce, and the decline of unions. There was an increase in low-skill jobs in the service sector (e.g., sales, food service), but most of these jobs had low salaries and were located at a distance from inner-city communities. There was also an increase in high-skill jobs in the technology and information-processing areas, but these jobs were beyond the reach of most inner-city residents. Changes in the job market, then, have made it much more difficult for unskilled workers—particularly those in inner-city communities—to earn an adequate living.

Addressing the problem of concentrated poverty represents an ongoing national challenge, although we are learning more about the impact of certain public policy approaches (see Box 12.1). For more on public policies that may help reduce concentrated poverty, see Jargowsky, 2015.

Box 12.1   Moving to Opportunity: An Experiment

Between 1994 and 1998, the Moving to Opportunity (MTO) experiment allowed a large number of extremely poor inner-city families to move to low-poverty areas. This ambitious experiment in public policy involved more than 4,000 families living in public housing in Baltimore, Boston, Chicago, Los Angeles, and New York. These families were randomly assigned to different groups. The families in the "experimental group" received a housing voucher that allowed them to move to low-poverty neighborhoods, while the families in the "control group" did not receive such a voucher. The housing vouchers were effective. Though few families in the experimental group moved to truly affluent areas, many were able to enter neighborhoods that were lower in poverty. Moreover, family members reported feeling safer in their new neighborhoods (Gennetian et al., 2012).

The MTO experiment also provides a unique opportunity to learn about the impact of such a move on youth outcomes. Can children who are born into the conditions of concentrated poverty overcome any accumulated deficits and disadvantages by moving into a neighborhood that's lower in poverty? When the experiment began, many of the children that were affected were under the age of 12. In a follow-up study, researchers examined the well-being of these children in the year 2007, when the young people

(Continued)

(*Continued*)

were between the ages of 10 and 20 (Gennetian et al., 2012). It was anticipated that the children in the experimental group would benefit from their family's move to an improved neighborhood and that they would display more positive outcomes than children in the control group.

The results of the experiment, however, were mixed. The results were disappointing in terms of academic achievement, as test scores of the youth in the experimental and controls group were about the same. This outcome may not be surprising, given that many of the children who moved into improved neighborhoods still ended up in low-performing schools. In fact, some of these children stayed in the same low-performing schools they had been attending before the move.

More surprising are the results that relate to other youth outcomes. Overall, the youth in the experimental and control groups had the same level of self-reported delinquency (e.g., assault, gang involvement, vandalism) and the same probability of being arrested for violent offenses. But youth in the experimental group were *more* likely to be arrested for property offenses.

When researchers turned their attention to the female youth, the findings were more encouraging. Compared to their counterparts in the control group, the females in the experimental group were less likely to have "serious behavioral and emotional problems." They were less likely, for example, to report feeling sad, hopeless, or worthless. They also had fewer problems with obedience or getting along with others.

In sum, it appears that girls were more successful than boys in adapting to life in a low-poverty neighborhood. The results of qualitative research may help us understand these gender differences as well as some of the disappointing results of the MTO experiment. According to one interview-based study, boys in the experimental group often had difficulty adjusting to their new neighborhoods, in part, because they did not feel welcomed. For example, these boys continued to engage in the same activities they had become accustomed to in their old neighborhoods, such as hanging out on the street corner, in basketball courts, or in vacant lots. But because these activities were not the norm in their new communities, their new neighbors viewed them with suspicion. In the words of one boy:

> You can't really [hang out in the neighborhood] because it's like mixed [in this area] with like white and black. . . . So if you see a group of black people and then like white people look out the window and call the police and they just say, "You gotta leave," and there's nowhere to go. Like they don't want us to be together, like if we're together they say, "You gotta go." (Clampet-Lundquist et al., 2011)

Because the girls in the experimental group were more likely to spend time indoors or going to the mall or to the movies, their activities were less likely to be viewed as a problem in their new neighborhood. Related to this, boys in the experimental group were more likely than those in the control group to report being questioned or hassled by the police. Among the girls, there was a little difference between the groups in terms of their experience with the police (Clampet-Lundquist et al., 2011).

Despite these mixed short-term results, recent evidence suggests that moving to a lower-poverty neighborhood while young (under the age of 13) was still beneficial to both males and females in the *long run*, with increased rates of college attendance and higher incomes. Older children did not reap these same benefits, however, suggesting that the amount of time spent in high-poverty neighborhoods may impact long-term outcomes (Chetty et al., 2016).

(Continued)

Overall, given the mixed results, the MTO experiment appears to reveal the limits of an individual-level approach to the problem of concentrated poverty (Sampson, 2008; Rosenfeld et al., 2013). While moving individual families (extremely poor families) into improved neighborhoods resulted in certain desirable outcomes—especially for younger children—other challenges remained. For example, apart from living in a more desirable neighborhood, the parents in the experimental group often faced many of the same challenges they faced before their move, including lack of job skills, lack of job contacts, lack of transportation, and the challenges of raising children in a low-income, single-parent household. Further, the new neighborhoods often remained racially segregated. These facts may suggest a need for direct support and services for struggling families (Duncan and Zuberi, 2006) or for neighborhood-level interventions. The results of a "natural experiment" that took place in Colombia are suggestive, as it involved an effort to transform entire neighborhoods. Following a large-scale redevelopment effort designed to connect residents with jobs and attract businesses to economically deprived areas, the violent crime rate dropped dramatically in neighborhoods that had been plagued by drug-related gangs (see Cerdá et al., 2012; for more on the MTO experiment, see the excellent MTO symposium in the July 2008 issue of the *American Sociological Review*).

Question for Discussion

1. As stated in the foregoing discussion of MTO, a surprising finding is that boys in the experimental group had a higher rate of arrest for property crimes, even though they reported the same level of delinquency as boys in the control group. Assuming that the actual levels of delinquency in the two groups are about the same, how might we explain the higher rate of arrest among boys in the experimental group? How would labeling theorists explain this higher rate? (Hint: See the discussion of the Saints and Roughnecks in Chapters 4 and 9.)

WHY ARE DEPRIVED COMMUNITIES HIGHER IN CRIME?

High-crime communities are high in crime for two fundamental reasons. First, crime-prone individuals may be attracted to these communities, or they may be more likely to live in them because they (or their families) cannot afford to live elsewhere. Second, the characteristics of high-crime communities may cause individuals to engage in crime. **High-crime communities, then, may both attract or select for crime-prone individuals and cause these individuals to engage in crime.** Data suggest that both explanations have some merit, although there is still some uncertainty about the size of the causal effect of communities on crime.[6] In this section, we examine the ways in which the characteristics of high-crime communities may cause crime.

Not surprisingly, researchers argue that the characteristics of high-crime neighborhoods cause crime for reasons related to strain, control, social learning, and labeling theories.

Deprived Communities Are Higher in Strain

Strain theorists argue that the residents of deprived communities are more likely to experience the types of strain described in Chapter 6: The failure to achieve positively valued goals, the loss of positive stimuli, and the presentation of negative stimuli. Also, the residents of such communities may be less able to cope with their strain through legitimate channels.[7]

Goal blockage. It is clear that the residents of such communities are less able to achieve the goal of economic success. In particular, the schools are generally inferior, and residents have less access to jobs in general and to stable, well-paying jobs in particular. Manufacturing and service-sector jobs (e.g., retail sales, restaurant work) are often located at a distance from deprived communities, so they are less accessible, relatively few individuals in the community have job contacts or job information, and there are fewer individuals in the community to teach and model the skills and attitudes necessary for successful job performance. As a consequence, residents may be more likely to engage in theft, drug selling, prostitution, or other illicit income-generating activities. The frustration that results from goal blockage may result in violent behavior as well.

Related to this, residents in these communities are also less able to achieve social status, including "masculine status," through conventional means. One field study of crack dealers in a poor New York City community, in fact, is titled "In Search of Respect" (Bourgois, 2003). As the author of this study states, "One message the crack dealers communicated clearly to me is that they are not driven solely by simple economic exigency. Like most humans on earth, in addition to material subsistence, they are also searching for dignity and fulfillment. In the Puerto Rican context this incorporates definitions of respeto [respect]" (2003:324). Unfortunately, the residents of deprived communities often have trouble achieving respect or status through legal channels, such as getting a good education and then a prestigious job. As a consequence, they may attempt to achieve this status through illegitimate means, or they may strike out at others in their frustration. These arguments have not received a good test, but much data are compatible with them (see Agnew, 1999; Kingston et al., 2009; Kubrin and Weitzer, 2003b; Messerschmidt, 1993).

Loss of positive stimuli/presentation of negative stimuli. The residents of high-crime communities are also subject to a range of other strains. In addition to economic hardships of various types, they are more likely to experience family disruption and the strains associated with such disruption, such as family conflict. They are more likely to experience problems at school owing to lack of good preparation for school and the inferiority of schools they're eligible to attend. They are more likely to get into interpersonal conflicts because they often compete with others for scarce resources like money. As Elijah Anderson (1999:37) states, "Life in public often features an intense competition for scarce social goods in which 'winners' totally dominate 'losers.'" And, not surprisingly, they have higher rates of criminal victimization and child abuse.

A few studies have attempted to test these ideas.[8] Warner and Fowler (2003), for example, measured strain by asking neighborhood residents whether they or anyone in their household had "(1) received verbal threats or insults, (2) felt cheated by someone, [and] (3) been harassed by the police" (2003:514). They found that the residents of deprived communities were more likely to experience strains of these types and that the strains increased neighborhood levels of violence. To give another example, Joanne Kaufman (2005) found that the residents of deprived communities were more likely to witness and be the victims of violence. Witnessing or being victimized by violence, in turn, increased the residents' likelihood of engaging in violence.

Coping with strain. Finally, it has been argued that the residents of high-crime communities may be less able to cope with strain through legitimate channels. Among other things, they have fewer coping resources, like money and power. They are also less likely to receive assistance or support from others in their community (see the discussion of control theory in the next section). Furthermore, it has been argued that residents' continued experience with strain increases their underlying level of anger and their sensitivity to slights. That is, they develop what has been called a "short fuse."[9] Finally, they are subject to less control and are more likely to be predisposed to crime for reasons related to social learning theory (discussed later). All these factors increase the likelihood that residents will respond to strain with crime (see Warner and Fowler, 2003, for a study in this area).

Deprived Communities Are Lower in Control

According to control theorists, **the characteristics of deprived communities reduce the ability and willingness of residents to exercise effective control** (see Chapter 8 for a description of control theory). This includes the ability and willingness of parents to control their children, of school officials to control students, and of community residents to control one another. In particular, the residents of high-crime communities **are less likely to exercise effective direct control.** For example, community residents are less likely to engage in activities like "taking note of and/or questioning strangers, watching over each other's property, assuming responsibility for supervision of general youth activities, and intervening in local disturbances" (Sampson, 1986a:27).

Wilkinson (2007) provides a nice illustration of this point. She interviewed several hundred "active violent offenders" in two very poor, high-crime communities in New York City. Among other things, she asked these offenders what adults in their neighborhood do when they see juveniles engaging in various types of crime. One hundred percent of the offenders said that the adults in their neighborhoods "walk away or do nothing" when they see older juveniles fighting on the street, while 74.3 percent said adults walk away or do nothing when they see juveniles selling drugs. In describing how adults respond to drug sellers on the street, one offender stated that "half of them walk across the street and the other half they just walk right through them and act like they ain't even there. They try to ignore it. They don't want nothing to do with it." Another offender was asked why most adults ignore drug selling. He replied: "Cause they don't want no beef. You stick your nose in my mother fucking business, you getting popped . . . you'll be dead" (Wilkinson, 2007:205).

Communities where residents are willing to work together to exercise direct control over others are said to be high in *collective efficacy*. The extent of collective efficacy in a community has been measured in part by asking residents how much they trust one another and get along together. Efficacy is also measured by asking residents how likely it is that their neighbors "could be counted on to take action if: (1) children were skipping school and hanging out on a street corner, (2) children were spray-painting graffiti on a local building, (3) children were showing disrespect toward an adult, (4) a fight broke out in front of their house, and (5) a fire station closest to home was threatened with a budget cut" (Sampson, 2006:153; also see Sampson et al., 1997; Simons et al., 2005).

The residents of deprived communities are also **less likely to provide juveniles with a stake in conformity,** which includes establishing close ties to juveniles and helping them succeed at school and work. And the residents are **less likely to socialize juveniles so that they condemn delinquency and develop self-control.** Elijah Anderson (1990) provides an excellent illustration of these points in his description of the community he called Village-Northton. The Northton community was once a mixed-income African American community with a relatively low crime rate. Juveniles in the community often received assistance from many adults, including adults outside their families. These adults, referred to as *old heads*, would often function as surrogate fathers, providing guidance, encouragement, financial aid, and help in finding jobs. More generally, they served as conventional role models. As Anderson states, they "served the black community well as visible, concrete symbols of success and moral value, living examples of the fruits of hard work, perseverance, decency, and propriety" (E. Anderson, 1990:58). In recent years, however, the working- and middle-class residents of the community have moved to more affluent areas, so there are fewer old heads to assist youths. The old heads that remain have less influence, partly because decent-paying jobs in the inner city have become scarcer, making it difficult for the old heads to assist youths and undermining their lessons about the rewards of hard work and a conventional lifestyle. Partly as a consequence, crime rates have increased (see Parker and Reckdenwald, 2008).

The residents of high-crime communities are less likely to engage in these types of control for at least four reasons.[10]

1. The residents of such communities have **trouble finding decent work.** As a result, they often struggle to deal with a range of economic and other problems; moreover, many are emotionally distressed and lack the skills and resources to legally cope with their own problems or assist others. These factors **undermine the ability of parents to exercise effective control over their children.** In particular, these factors often lead to the breakup of families and a host of family problems (see Chapter 14). Furthermore, these factors **undermine the efforts of community residents to exercise effective control over juveniles in the broader community.**

2. Community residents are **less likely to have ties to their neighbors and to care about their community.** They do not own their own homes, which lowers their investment in the community. They often hope to move to a more desirable community as soon as they are able, which also lowers their investment in the community. People are constantly moving into and out of their community, which makes it difficult for them to form ties with their neighbors. In fact, they may have trouble recognizing many of their neighbors. As you might imagine, these factors make residents reluctant to get involved in community affairs, including such risky activities as confronting delinquents in their neighborhood.

3. Residents are **less likely to support or form community organizations,** including educational, religious, and recreational organizations. This lack of participation is partly a consequence of the residents' limited resources and their lower attachment to the community. Their failure to get involved in community organizations further reduces control, since these organizations often help supervise, assist, and guide youth. Such organizations also help ensure that outside agencies—like the police and city government—are more responsive to community needs. For example, these organizations may lobby for better schools and more police protection.

4. Community residents are **less likely to have a good working relationship with the police.**[11] The residents of deprived communities are more likely to hold negative attitudes toward the police. In one study of three high-crime communities in Philadelphia, for example, more than 60 percent of the young people expressed negative views of the police (Carr et al., 2007). These views at least partly stemmed from negative experiences with the police. The police in deprived communities are more likely to use force against suspects and engage in misconduct. According to Carr et al. (2007:467), the young people in their study stated they had negative views of the police because they were "stopped for no good reason, . . . harassed or treated roughly, or . . . [they] encountered dishonest or lackadaisical police." Also, the residents of deprived communities are more likely to view the police as ineffective. As Anderson (1999:321) states, based on his field study of a deprived Philadelphia community, the residents "believe the police are unlikely to come [if called] or, if they do come, may even harass the very people who called them." As a consequence of these views, the residents of deprived communities may be less likely to call the police when problems arise. Carr et al. (2007) found that less than 10 percent of the respondents said they would call the police if they saw a group of young people misbehaving (also see Warner, 2007). These views may also reduce the willingness of residents to intervene on their own, since they believe they cannot count on the police to support them if necessary. The result, then, is a reduction in direct control.

Theories that explain community crime rates in terms of control theory are called *social disorganization theories*, since they essentially argue that there has been a breakdown of control in the community, leaving the community disorganized.

Data provide some support for the arguments just enumerated. Factors like economic deprivation, residential instability, and family disruption reduce the extent to which community residents engage in effective parenting, know and trust their neighbors, intervene in neighborhood problems, get involved in community organizations, and develop good relations with the police. The same factors, in turn, directly influence crime rates or indirectly influence crime by allowing for the development of delinquent peer groups (discussed later).[12]

Deprived Communities Foster the Social Learning of Crime

Social learning theorists argue that economic deprivation, residential instability, and family disruption increase community crime rates because they lead to the development of delinquent groups—that foster the social learning of crime (see Akers, 1998; Sutherland et al., 1992). Related to this, learning theorists argue that the residents of deprived communities are more likely to develop beliefs favorable to delinquency, forming what have been called *delinquent or criminal subcultures*.

Delinquent groups. Delinquent peer groups, gangs, drug-selling organizations, and prostitution rings are said to be more common in deprived communities partly because **control is low** in such communities, so residents are less able to stop the groups from forming or operating. Also, such groups are more likely to form in these communities for reasons related to **strain theory.** Among other things, the people are poor and often have little prospect for a better life. So illicit methods of making money, like drug selling, theft, and prostitution, have more appeal.

As a consequence of such groups, juveniles in the community are provided with more opportunities to make money through delinquent channels. For example, opportunities to sell drugs are readily available. Juveniles are also more likely to be exposed to criminal models, like drug sellers on the street corner. And juveniles are more likely to become involved in delinquent groups, including delinquent peer groups and gangs. The members of such groups, of course, are more likely to model crime, teach beliefs conducive to crime, and reinforce crime.

Field studies and surveys provide some support for these arguments.[13] In particular, the research suggests that delinquent groups are more common in deprived neighborhoods and that they foster crime in the ways indicated earlier. For example, as Elijah Anderson (1999:29–30) states:

> In the impoverished inner-city neighborhood, the drug trade is everywhere, and it becomes ever more difficult to separate the drug culture from the experience of poverty. The neighborhood is sprinkled with crack dens located in abandoned buildings or in someone's home. On corner after corner, young men peddle drugs the way a newsboy peddles papers. . . . At times they sell drugs to passing motorists, who stop in broad daylight and hold up traffic during the transaction. . . . [S]mall children will occasionally be sitting in the back seat.

Beliefs favorable to delinquency. There is also some evidence suggesting that community characteristics like economic deprivation may lead some community residents—especially juveniles—to **develop beliefs favorable to delinquency.**[14] Such beliefs include a strong emphasis on toughness and the view that delinquency is justifiable or excusable under certain conditions (see Chapter 7). Juveniles with such beliefs are, of course, more likely to respond to a range of temptations and provocation with delinquency.

The origin of such beliefs may be partly explained by using strain theory. Individuals who cannot obtain money through legitimate channels may attempt to use delinquent channels, such as theft and drug selling. In the process, they may come to justify or rationalize their delinquency. For example, they may claim that while theft in general is bad, it is justified or excusable if decent jobs are unavailable. Also, individuals who cannot obtain the more general goal of social status through legitimate channels may attempt to obtain it through violence. That is, they may attempt to coerce or intimidate others into treating them with respect. Among other things, these attempts may take the form of maintaining a tough demeanor, responding to even minor shows of disrespect with violence, and occasionally "campaigning for respect" by assaulting others (see especially E. Anderson, 1999). Such individuals may come to believe that violence is often justified and that it is important to be tough. Such "beliefs favorable to delinquency" may then spread through the community as these individuals interact with others. Finally, individuals who feel they cannot turn to the police for help may come to believe that they are justified in engaging in violence if provoked or insulted (see Kubrin and Weitzer, 2003b).

A number of field studies and certain surveys suggest that **such beliefs are more common in deprived communities,** although it is important to stress that only a small percentage of the residents fully subscribe to them.[15] Even so, such beliefs can still have a large effect on community crime rates. As Anderson (1999) points out, many juveniles who do not subscribe to these beliefs must nevertheless act as if they do. Many juveniles, for example, may **not** place a strong emphasis on toughness, but they must act tough if they want to avoid being regularly victimized by others (especially by juveniles who do value toughness). For more on this point, see Box 12.2.

Box 12.2   Neighborhood Street Culture and Youth Violence

As we first described in Chapter 7, Elijah Anderson (1999) argues that violence in disadvantaged communities is fueled in part by an informal code of conduct or "street code" that prescribes physical retaliation in response to various provocations. In essence, young people in these communities learn that to avoid repeat victimization, one must send an important message to others: "I'm not to be messed with." One must show a willingness to engage in violent counterattack; otherwise, one appears weak and runs the risk of being "rolled on" or physically assaulted "by any number of others" (Anderson, 1999:73). The felt importance of the street code is likely to be heightened in disadvantaged high-crime neighborhoods, where "there is always someone looking for a fight," and where young people may feel that they cannot rely on the police or other authorities to protect them. And in neighborhoods where the street code is widely accepted, young people may feel that violence is the only response that will gain them the respect of, and proper treatment from, their peers.

An interesting and important aspect of this argument is that in neighborhoods where the street code is prevalent, young people may feel pressure to use violence *even if they do not personally value aggressive behavior.* In their eyes, failure to observe the street code may be too costly, possibly resulting in a loss of status and an increase in victimization. In short, the street code places pressure on all youth to use violence to save face and protect themselves.

This point is illustrated by the following young male from a disadvantaged, high-crime neighborhood in New York City. Following a dispute with a fellow teen, he is pressured by his friends to retaliate:

(Continued)

(Continued)

[M]y boys was telling me, shoot the [guy]. Slice him, stab him. I'm saying, shit was running through my mind. . . . I was gonna do it. [But the cops] pulled up too quick. (Wilkinson and Carr, 2008:1042).

Stewart and Simons (2010) conducted a test of the "neighborhood culture" argument by examining data on a large sample of African American adolescents. Consistent with Anderson's work on the code of the street, they observed that when young people reside in neighborhoods widely accepting of the street code, they are at increased risk of displaying violent behavior, even after taking into account (or controlling for) their personal attitudes toward violence.

This finding highlights the role of neighborhood context in a fairly dramatic way. To fully understand the development of youth violence, it is not enough to examine the individual's personal attitudes or beliefs. Although these beliefs are important, neighborhood factors can impact behavior above and beyond the influence of such beliefs. Also, for young people who hold aggressive beliefs, neighborhood factors can *reinforce* these beliefs, increasing the likelihood that these beliefs will lead to violent behavior (see Stewart and Simons, 2010).

Question for Discussion
1. Eric Stewart and his colleagues (2008:143) argue that the influence of the street code can be reduced by improving "police and community relationships in disadvantaged areas." When residents can trust the police to respond in a fair and effective manner, they will see that violence is not the only option available to them and will feel less need to take the law into their own hands. Do you agree? Do you think this approach may have potential? What might the police do to improve their standing in disadvantaged communities? (Note: For more on policing, see Chapter 20.)

Community Crime Rates Reduce Control, Foster the Social Learning of Crime, and Increase Strain

To sum up, economic deprivation, residential instability, and family disruption increase community crime rates through their effects on control, social learning, and strain. These arguments are illustrated in Figure 12.1.

The community crime rate is the dependent variable Figure 12.1. But research suggests that **the community crime rate may also function as an independent variable.**[16]

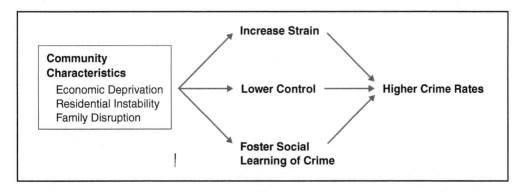

FIGURE 12.1 Community Characteristics Contribute to Higher Crime Rates Through Their Effects on Strain, Control, and Social Learning

Imagine a community in which the crime rate starts to rise. After a certain point, businesses and residents may begin to move out. Property values then start to fall, and poorer individuals begin to move into the community. A rise in community crime rates, then, may contribute to economic deprivation and residential instability, and through these effects, rising crime may indirectly lead to a reduction in control, an increase in the social learning for crime, and an increase in strain. Further, rising crime rates may directly affect levels of control, strain, and social learning. For example, by making residents fearful, rising crime rates may reduce the likelihood that people will exercise direct control over others in the community. Recall the remark quoted near the beginning of this chapter: "If something bad happens around here, you keep quiet, you don't tell on your neighbors for fear of your life" (Longa, 1998). And rising crime rates directly increase the level of strain in the community, since being a crime victim and having close others victimized are major types of strain.

So **community crime rates are involved in a reciprocal relationship with community characteristics.** Community characteristics affect community crime rates, and community crime rates affect community characteristics. The latter effect is, of course, reminiscent of the arguments made by labeling theorists, who state that crime sometimes has consequences that increase the likelihood of further crime (also see Kubrin and Weitzer, 2003a; Piquero et al., 2006).

OVERVIEW OF THE LEADING THEORIES OF DELINQUENCY

This chapter concludes our discussion of the leading theories of delinquency. Four major theories were reviewed: strain theory, social learning theory, control theory, and labeling theory. These theories, which focus on explaining why some juveniles are more likely to engage in delinquency than others, also have been used to answer other major questions about delinquency: Why do individuals exhibit different patterns of offending over the life course? Why are individuals more likely to commit delinquent acts in some situations than in others? And, why do some groups have higher rates of delinquency than other groups? The best way to review these theories is to list their major independent variables and their explanations of why these independent variables cause delinquency.

Strain theory focuses on two major categories of strain: goal blockage and the loss of positive stimuli/presentation of negative stimuli. The experience of strain leads to negative emotions like anger and frustration, and individuals may turn to delinquency in an effort to cope with strain and negative emotions. Delinquency may allow them to reduce or escape from their strain, seek revenge against those who have wronged them, or manage their negative emotions (e.g., through illicit drug use).

Social learning theory focuses on the extent to which individuals associate with others who reinforce delinquency, present beliefs favorable to delinquency, and model delinquent behavior. These activities lead individuals to believe that delinquency is a desirable or at least justifiable response in certain situations.

Control theory focuses on the extent to which individuals are subject to direct control, have a stake in conformity, believe crime is wrong, and are high in self-control. The absence of such controls frees individuals to satisfy their needs and desires in the most expedient way possible, which is often through delinquent acts.

Labeling theory focuses on the extent to which individuals are viewed and treated (labeled) as "bad" or "evil" by others. Such negative labeling leads to a reduction in control, an increase in strain, an increase in the social learning for crime, and a delinquent self-concept.

Each theory presents a different image of the delinquent. In strain theory, the delinquent is **angry and frustrated,** beset with a variety of problems or strains, and unable to cope through legal channels. In social learning theory, the delinquent believes that **delinquency is a desirable or justifiable response in a particular situation.** In control theory, the delinquent is **unrestrained,** free to satisfy personal needs and desires in the most expedient way possible. And in labeling theory, the delinquent is **branded as "bad,"** rejected and mistreated by conventional others.

All four theories have some support, with social learning and control theories dominating the literature. We should emphasize, however, that these theories continue to be tested and revised. They are not "engraved in stone." Rather, they are ongoing creations. In fact, strain, control, and labeling theories have been subject to major modifications in the recent past.

Each theory partly explains why individuals engage in delinquency. One theory may sometimes be more relevant to a particular individual or group than the other theories. For example, you may know a delinquent individual who appears to be high in control, low in strain, and low in labeling. This person's delinquency may best be explained in terms of social learning theory: Perhaps the delinquency is frequently reinforced and seldom punished; perhaps the individual accepts certain beliefs that justify delinquency; or there has been much exposure to delinquent models. Strain, control, and/or labeling theories, however, may provide the best explanation of delinquency for someone else. In most cases, all four theories probably have some relevance to the explanation of delinquency.

A complete explanation of delinquency, therefore, should draw on strain, social learning, control, and labeling theories. Therefore, you might ask about the possibility of combining these theories into a more general theory of delinquency. Many criminologists have, in fact, tried to develop integrated theories of crime that combine all or some of these theories; we present one recent example in Chapter 18, which follows our review of the research inspired by these theories in Chapters 13 through 17.

TEACHING AIDS
Exercise: Increasing Community Control

Earlier we described a study in which Wilkinson (2007) interviewed several hundred active, violent offenders in two very poor, high-crime New York City communities. She asked the offenders what they thought the adults in their neighborhoods would do if they witnessed various types of crime. She also asked her subjects how bystanders reacted to the violent events in which the offenders were involved (42 percent of these events involved guns). Here is what she found:

> In 31.4 percent of the events in which bystanders were present, they reportedly watched without intervening, in 19.9 percent of events they did nothing or ignored the conflict, in 14.1 percent they ran away or took cover for self-protection, in 12.8 percent of events they instigated or "amped up" the situation, in 9.0 percent they yelled to try to stop the violence, in 7.7 percent of events, they broke it up, and in 2.6 percent, they helped the respondent. Bystanders very rarely called the police or got involved by using violence. (Wilkinson, 2007:209)

It should be noted that these "bystanders" were distinct from the offender's associates. When the offender's associates were present, they most often helped the offender by engaging in violence themselves. The bystanders were also distinct from the opponent's associates.

How can we explain this lack of response to violence in these very poor, high-crime communities? Do you think the response would be very different in your community?

If so, why do you think it would be different? What do you think can be done to increase the likelihood that bystanders will intervene in some manner to stop crimes (see Wilkinson, 2007)?

Exercise: Explaining Other Group Differences in Crime

This chapter draws on strain, social learning, control, and labeling theories to explain why some communities have higher crime rates than others. There are, of course, other group differences in delinquency rates that are in need of explanation. Drawing on strain, social learning, control, and labeling theories, **how would you explain the fact that males have higher rates of delinquency than females?**

The best way to answer this question is to outline or briefly describe the essential arguments of each theory. For example, list the major types of strain, state why strain increases the likelihood of delinquency, and name the factors that condition the effect of strain on delinquency. Then review each of the key points you have listed, asking whether it might shed light on the relationship between gender and delinquency. For example, is there reason to believe that males experience more strain than females or that males are more likely to experience the types of strain that are conducive to crime? Is there reason to believe that males are more likely to react to strain with negative emotions like anger? Is there reason to believe that males are more likely to respond to strain and negative emotions with crime (e.g., are males more likely to associate with delinquent peers, whose presence increases the likelihood of a delinquent response to strain?)

Broidy and Agnew (1997) provide a nice illustration of how strain theory might be used to explain gender differences in crime (see Box 6.1 in Chapter 6; also see Piquero and Sealock, 2004). Chapter 18 uses all the delinquency theories in this text, and the research inspired by the theories, to explain gender differences in delinquency—as well as age, class, and race/ethnic differences. But you should try completing this exercise before looking at Chapter 18. Applying the theories is important: it dramatically increases your understanding of the theories, and the theories are of little use to you unless you develop the ability to apply them.

Web-Based Exercise: Societal Differences in Crime and Delinquency

This chapter focuses on differences in delinquency across communities in the United States. You may be wondering about societal differences in delinquency. Unfortunately, we do not have good data in this area. A group of criminologists, however, is attempting to develop such data by administering a common self-report measure of delinquency in a number of cities throughout the world. Initially, these cities were in Western Europe and the United States. But each round of the "International Self-Report Delinquency Study" includes a larger and more diverse set of cities. You can read about the efforts of this group at http://www.northeastern.edu/isrd (Northeastern University, School of Criminology and Criminal Justice).

As indicated in Chapter 2, self-report data provides the best estimate regarding the extent of delinquency. The large majority of delinquent acts do not become known to law enforcement or result in arrest by the police. In addition, using police data to compare crime and delinquency rates across countries is accompanied by other problems. For example, countries may have somewhat different definitions of crime, the police in some countries may be more likely to arrest the offenders they encounter, and the victims in some countries may be more likely to report crimes to the police. But crimes such as homicide are similarly defined and are likely to be reported and result in arrest. And we can make rough cross-national comparisons on the extent of these crimes. The United Nations Office on Drugs and Crime publishes relevant data, which can be viewed at http://www.nodc.org/unodc/en/data-and-analysis/statistics/crime.html. If you click on **Homicide**" for example, you can see the estimated homicide rates in a large number of countries, with some countries having rates many times higher than other countries. (These data cover homicides committed by both juveniles and adults.) Also, the United Nations reports data from the International Crime Victims Survey at http://www.unicri.it/services/library_documentation/publications/icvs (UN Interregional Crime and Justice Research Institute).

As is the case with community differences in crime, cross-national differences have been explained in terms of the leading crime theories. For example, high levels of economic inequality—a source of strain—have been linked to high levels of homicide (see Agnew, 2006a). For further information on cross-national studies of crime, visit Oxford Bibliographies online and search for **Cross-National Crime** (http://www.oxford-bibliographies.com).

TEST YOUR KNOWLEDGE OF THIS CHAPTER

1. How are group differences in crime rates usually explained?
2. What are the major characteristics distinguishing high-crime communities from low-crime communities? Describe one way in which each of these characteristics has been measured.
3. We argue that race and ethnicity are associated with community crime rates, but the association is largely, or perhaps entirely, due to third variables. Describe the argument we make in this area.
4. Why did the number of people living in high-poverty communities increase so much from 1970 to 1990? According to the latest available data (2011), how many people live in high-poverty neighborhoods? How does the number of high-poverty neighborhoods recorded in 2011 compare to previous years?
5. We state that high-crime communities are high in crime for "two fundamental reasons." What are these reasons?
6. What do we mean when we state that the residents of high-crime communities are less likely to exercise control over other residents?
7. Why are the residents of high-crime communities less likely to exercise control? (Your answer should describe the three major ways in which economic deprivation, residential instability, and family disruption undermine control.)
8. What are the two major ways in which deprived communities foster the social learning of crime?
9. Why are delinquent groups and "beliefs favorable to delinquency" more common in such communities?
10. The residents of deprived communities are higher in strain than residents of other communities. List three specific strains that are more common in deprived communities.
11. Why are the residents of deprived communities more likely than those of other communities to cope with strain through delinquency?
12. We argue that not only do community characteristics affect crime rates but that also crime rates affect community characteristics. Describe the ways in which this occurs (i.e., how rising crime rates may affect community characteristics).
13. Briefly describe the major arguments of strain, social learning, control, and labeling theories. What four major questions about delinquency do these theories attempt to answer?

THOUGHT AND DISCUSSION QUESTIONS

1. Describe some of the ways in which the residents of your home community may have exercised control over other residents.

2. What types of government and other programs might be implemented to reduce community crime rates? (See Chapter 24.) What types of programs might inadvertently increase community crime rates?

3. How might you combine two or more of the leading delinquency theories into a more general or integrated theory of delinquency? (Note: Certain ways in which these theories might be combined or integrated have already been discussed. For example, this chapter states that high strain and low control lead to the formation of delinquent groups, which are central to social learning theory. This particular idea is at the heart of the major integrated theory of delinquency developed by Elliott et al., 1979, 1985.)

KEY TERMS

- Residential instability
- Collective efficacy
- Old heads

- Social disorganization theories

- Delinquent or criminal subcultures

ENDNOTES

1. See Bellair and McNulty, 2005; Bellair and Roscigno, 2000; J. Kaufman, 2005; Kornhauser, 1978; McNulty and Bellair, 2003; Ousey and Augustine, 2001; Rosenfeld et al., 2013; Sampson, 1997; Shaw and McKay, 1942.

2. For overviews of the research in this area, see Bursik and Grasmick, 1993, 1995; Byrne and Sampson, 1986; Haynie et al., 2006; Kubrin and Weitzer, 2003a; Kornhauser, 1978; Land et al., 1990; Mears and Bhati, 2006; Office of Juvenile Justice and Delinquency Prevention, 1999a; Pratt and Cullen, 2005; Rosenfeld et al., 2013; Sampson, 1997, 2002, 2006; Sampson and Lauritsen, 1993; Sampson and Wilson, 1995; Sampson et al., 2005; Silver and Miller, 2004; Simons et al., 2005; Stretesky et al., 2004; R. Taylor, 2001a; Thornberry, Krohn et al., (with Porter) 2003; Velez et al., 2003; G. White, 1999.

3. See Rosenfeld et al., 2013; Sampson, 1987; Shihadeh and Steffensmeier, 1994; W. Wilson, 1987.

4. See Bellair and McNulty, 2005; Crutchfield et al., 2006; Hawkins, Herrenkohl et al., 1998; C. Johnson and Chanhatasilpa, 2003; Krivo and Peterson, 1996; McNulty and Bellair, 2003; McNulty and Holloway, 2000; Peeples and Loeber, 1994; Sampson, 1985, 1987, 2002; Sampson and Raudenbush, 1999; Sampson et al., 2005; Titterington and Damphouse, 2003; Velez, 2006; Velez et al., 2003.

5. For overviews, see Hagan, 1994; Jargowsky and Park, 2009; McNulty and Bellair, 2003; Sampson and Wilson, 1995; Simons et al., 2005; Velez et al., 2003; W. Wilson, 1987, 1996.

6. See Bursik and Grasmick, 1996; Elliott et al., 1996; Farrington, 1993a; Jargowsky and Park, 2009; Peeples and Loeber, 1994; Sampson et al., 1997.

7. See Agnew, 1999; Bernard, 1990; Hagan, 1994; J. Kaufman, 2005; Kingston et al., 2009; Rosenfeld et al., 2013; Warner and Fowler, 2003.

8. See Baglivio et al., 2017; Piquero et al., 2006; McNulty and Bellair, 2003; Stewart and Simons, 2006.

9. See Agnew, 1999; Balkwell, 1990; Bernard, 1990.

10. See Bursik, 1988; Bursik and Grasmick, 1993, 1995; Kornhauser, 1978; Kubrin and Weitzer, 2003a; Parker and Reckdenwald, 2008; Rosenfeld et al., 2013; Sampson, 2002, 2006; Sampson and Groves, 1989; Sampson and Raudenbush, 1999; Sampson and Wilson, 1995; Sampson et al., 2005; Sampson et al., 1997; Schreck et al., 2009; Simons et al., 2005; R. Taylor, 2001a.

11. See Berg et al., 2016; Carr et al., 2007; Hirschfield, 2008; Kubrin and Weitzer, 2003a; Silver and Miller, 2004; Warner, 2007; Weitzer et al., 2008.

12. Bellair, 1997, 2000; Bellair and McNulty, 2005; Bellair and Roscigno, 2000; Bellair et al., 2003; Elliott et al., 1996; Hay et al., 2006; Hoffmann, 2003; Kubrin and Weitzer, 2003a; Lee, 2000; Lowenkamp et al., 2003; R. Peterson et al., 2000; Pratt and Cullen, 2005; Pratt et al., 2004; Rosenfeld et al., 2001; 2013; Rountree and Warner, 1999; Sampson, 2002, 2006; Sampson and Groves, 1989; Sampson and Raudenbush, 1999; Sampson et al., 1997; Sampson et al., 2005; Silver and Miller, 2004; Simons et al., 1996; Simons et al., 2005; Stewart, Simons, and Conger, 2002; Velez, 2001; Warner, 2003; Wikstrom and Loeber, 2000.

13. See E. Anderson, 1994, 1999; Bourgois, 2003; Fagan, 1998; Kubrin and Weitzer, 2003a, 2003b; McNulty and Bellair, 2003; Pratt and Cullen, 2005; Sampson and Bartusch, 1999; Simons et al., 2005; Stewart and Simons, 2006, 2010; Veysey and Messner, 1999; Wilkinson, 2003; and Chapter 16.

14. See E. Anderson 1994, 1999; Bourgois, 2003; Brezina et al., 2004; Fagan, 1998; Kubrin and Weitzer, 2003a, 2003b; Majors and Billson, 1992; McNulty and Bellair, 2003; Oliver, 1994; Sampson and Bartusch, 1999; Stewart and Simons, 2006, 2010; Warner, 2003.

15. See note 14.

16. See Bellair, 2000; Hipp, 2010; Liska and Warner, 1991; Liska et al., 1998; Sampson, 2002; Sampson and Raudenbush, 1999.

PART 3

The Causes of Delinquency

RESEARCH

Chapters 6 through 12 described the leading theories of delinquency. These theories have inspired much research on the causes of delinquency, with criminologists testing these theories or ideas derived from them. Criminologists have also conducted research on the causes of delinquency that was not directly inspired by these theories, but this research can nevertheless be interpreted in terms of these theories.

The next six chapters describe the major research on the causes of delinquency. Chapter 13 describes those individual traits that cause delinquency, with a focus on the traits of low intelligence, low self-control, and irritability. Chapters 14 through 17 then describe those features of the social environment that cause delinquency, with a focus on family, school, and peer environments. As you will see, the effects of individual traits and environmental factors on delinquency are readily explained in terms of strain, social learning, control, and/or labeling theories.

Chapter 18 attempts to "pull everything together" by presenting a general or integrated theory of delinquency. This theory lists the key causes of delinquency, describes why the named causes increase delinquency, and discusses the relationships among these causes. The chapter then uses the integrated theory to explain certain basic facts about delinquency, such as why males are more delinquent than females.

But before we describe the research on the causes of delinquency, we want to highlight a few basic points about these causes.

First, **delinquency is caused by a good number of factors.** This may sound obvious, but it is common for politicians and the general public alike to blame delinquency on one or a few factors. For example, it is frequently claimed that delinquency is caused by mass media violence or by a lack of religion. Not only do such claims ignore the many other causes of delinquency, but media violence and the lack of religion are not even among the most important causes of delinquency (see Chapter 17).

Second, **most factors have only small to moderate effects on delinquency, although a few factors have larger effects.** No factor, however, perfectly explains delinquency. So when we state that "factor X causes delinquency," you should not assume that all juveniles with factor X are delinquent and that all juveniles without factor X are nondelinquent. Factor X simply increases the probability that juveniles will engage in delinquency, perhaps by only a small amount. We try to provide some indication of the relative importance of the different causes of delinquency, although this is sometimes difficult because of a lack of good research (i.e., studies that examine large, representative samples of juveniles, employ good measures, examine a wide range of causes, and are longitudinal—see Chapter 5).

Third, **most of the causes of delinquency are related to one another.** For example, individuals with traits conducive to delinquency are more likely to be in environments conducive to delinquency. So, irritable juveniles are more likely to experience poor parenting (in part because they upset and overwhelm their parents). To give another example, juveniles who experience poor parenting are more likely to associate with delinquent peers and belong to gangs. It is difficult to keep track of all the relationships between the causes of delinquency, but we will try to give you a rough sense of how these causes are related in the chapters that follow. And we provide a summary of such relationships in Chapter 18 when we present an integrated theory of delinquency.

Fourth, **not only are the causes of delinquency related to one another, they also sometimes condition the effects of one another on delinquency.** For example, many criminologists now argue that individual traits and the social environment condition the effect of one another on delinquency. So irritable individuals are more likely to engage in delinquency when they are in environments conducive to delinquency, such as abusive families and delinquent peer groups. The limited research that has been done in this area is generally supportive of such effects. In particular, certain data suggest that delinquency is most likely among individuals who possess traits like irritability and low self-control and are in environments conducive to delinquency.

Keep these points in mind when you read the following chapters. While we often discuss the causes of delinquency in isolation from one another, there are **numerous causes, and they usually work together to produce delinquency.**

13 Individual Traits

What Impact Do Individual Traits
Have on Delinquency?

This chapter begins to describe the research on the causes of delinquency, focusing on individual traits that increase the likelihood of delinquency. We first list the most important of these traits and describe why they increase delinquency, drawing on strain, social learning, control, and labeling theories. Then we discuss why some individuals are more likely than others to possess these traits.

After reading this chapter, you should be able to:

- Identify and describe the major traits, or clusters of traits, that are associated with delinquent behavior.
- Draw on the leading theories to explain why these traits affect delinquency.
- Explain why some individuals are more likely to possess these traits.
- Describe the types of studies researchers conduct to examine the role of genes in the development of delinquency.
- Describe how genetic inheritance, biological harm, and environmental factors may contribute to traits conducive to delinquency.
- Summarize the relationship between mental illness and violence.

ARE JUVENILES WITH CERTAIN TRAITS MORE LIKELY TO ENGAGE IN DELINQUENCY?

Think back to some of the people you knew before college—not just your friends but others as well—and think about the ways these people differed from one another. They probably differed in terms of intelligence—some were smart and some were not so smart. Some were probably easygoing and friendly, while others were "touchy" or "irritable." Some liked excitement or adventure, even risky, dangerous activities, while others preferred safer activities. Some were impulsive, engaging in activities without much thought for the consequences, while others were more thoughtful and reflective. Some were socially skilled, getting along well with people, while others had problems in social relations. People often differ in the traits they possess. **By** *traits*, **we mean relatively stable ways of perceiving, thinking about, and behaving toward the environment and oneself** (see Blackburn, 1993). For example, if a person regularly acts without thinking, we say this person possesses the trait of impulsivity.

Research suggests that people with certain traits are more likely to engage in delinquency. Such traits include low intelligence (IQ), learning disabilities (e.g., reading disabilities), attention deficit hyperactivity disorder (ADHD), impulsivity, risk seeking, reduced ability to learn from punishment, irritability, insensitivity to others or low empathy, poor social skills, poor problem-solving skills, immature moral reasoning, amoral beliefs, and beliefs favorable to delinquency.[1]

Researchers are still trying to determine the relative importance of these traits in causing delinquency, although we have good evidence that certain of them do have moderate to strong effects. Researchers are also trying to determine how these traits are related to one another. We know that many of the traits are strongly correlated with one another; that is, they often appear together in juveniles. These clusters of related traits are sometimes called *super-traits*. One super-trait was described in Chapter 8: low self-control. Low self-control comprises several more specific traits, including impulsivity, risk seeking, and a lack of ambition or motivation. There is still some debate, however, over how many super-traits there are and the composition of these traits.[2]

We focus on a few key traits in this chapter, traits whose effect on delinquency is reasonably well established. The first trait is *low verbal IQ*. The remaining traits are grouped together into the super-traits of *low self-control* and *irritability*. Recent data suggest that these super-traits play an especially important role in the explanation of delinquency, particularly high-rate, chronic offending (see Chapter 10).[3]

Low Verbal IQ

Data from multiple sources suggest that **individuals with low IQ scores are more likely to engage in delinquency.**[4] This finding appears when criminologists use official and self-report measures of delinquency. It appears when researchers control for third variables like social class and race. For example, researchers find that IQ is associated with delinquency when they limit their analysis to whites only and to African Americans only. The correlation appears in longitudinal as well as cross-sectional studies. Data suggest that it is primarily a person's **verbal IQ** score that affects delinquency. (One's total IQ score is made up of two components: verbal and performance. The verbal IQ score reflects several subtests, measuring such things as general factual knowledge, vocabulary, memory, abstract thinking, and social comprehension and judgment. All these subtests are administered orally and require oral answers. The performance IQ score reflects several other subtests, which measure such things as attention to detail, visual puzzle solving, and maze completion. Manual rather than oral responses are required.) Individuals with low verbal scores have trouble expressing themselves, remembering information, and thinking abstractly.

How might we explain the effect of low verbal IQ on delinquency? A **strain theorist** would argue that low IQ leads to increased strain, making it more difficult for juveniles to achieve goals like educational success and increasing the likelihood of negative relations with teachers, peers, and others.[5] Low verbal IQ is also associated with low problem-solving ability, so individuals with low verbal scores might be less able to cope with strain through legitimate channels (Moffitt, 1990). **Social learning theorists** argue that low verbal IQ **reduces** the likelihood that individuals will be reinforced for conventional behavior, like schoolwork, which in turn makes crime more appealing. **Control theorists** argue that low IQ leads to poor school performance and negative attitudes toward school, thereby weakening one's stake in conformity.[6] Also, low IQ may lead to offending because it reduces the individual's ability to foresee the consequences of offending and to exercise self-control.[7]

Low Self-Control

Low self-control is a super-trait consisting of several more specific traits.[8] Such traits include the following.

1. *Impulsivity,* or the tendency to act without considering the consequences of one's behavior. Impulsivity is sometimes measured by questions like "I often act on the spur of the moment without thinking" (agree or disagree). (Note: This question and the other questions used to illustrate the specific traits that make up the super-traits of low self-control and irritability are from Grasmick et al., 1993.)
2. A strong **preference for immediate versus delayed rewards,** even if the delayed rewards are larger. This trait is measured with questions like "I often do whatever brings me pleasure here and now, even at the cost of some distant goal."
3. *Risk seeking,* or a strong need for exciting, thrilling, and risky activities. This trait is measured with questions like "Sometimes I will take a risk just for the fun of it."
4. *Hyperactivity,* or high activity levels, restlessness, and a tendency to always be on the go. This trait is measured with questions like "I almost always feel better when I am on the move than when I am sitting and thinking."
5. **Low ambition, motivation, or perseverance.** Individuals with this trait do not finish tasks, have trouble making and carrying out plans, and are easily distracted or diverted. This trait is measured with questions like "When things get complicated, I tend to quit or withdraw."

6. **Amoral beliefs or beliefs favorable to delinquency.** Individuals believe that certain delinquent acts are neither bad nor good (amoral beliefs); they unconditionally approve of certain minor forms of delinquency; they believe more serious forms of delinquency are justifiable or excusable under certain conditions; and/or they hold values conducive to delinquency, like toughness. (Such beliefs are more fully described in Chapters 7 and 8.)

It may be difficult to keep all these traits in mind, but try to imagine what people with these traits are like. Basically, they might be described as **"wild"** or **"out of control."**

How might we explain the effect of low self-control on delinquency? A **strain theorist** would argue that individuals low in self-control have more trouble achieving their goals through legitimate channels, especially given their low motivation. Further, such individuals are more likely to upset others, given that they are "out of control" and prone to risky behavior. Other people might then respond with negative treatment, thereby increasing strain. Finally, individuals with low self-control are more likely to respond to strain with delinquency, given their impulsivity, low motivation, and amoral beliefs or beliefs favorable to delinquency.

A **social learning theorist** would argue that individuals with low self-control are more attracted to the rewards associated with crime, since these rewards are typically immediate and easily achieved (e.g., it is much easier to steal money than to work for it). Further, they often find crime rewarding in and of itself, since crime typically involves risky behavior. Finally, they are more likely to view crime in a favorable light given their beliefs.

A **control theorist** would argue that individuals with low self-control are, by definition, less likely to be constrained by direct controls and by their stake in conformity. Being impulsive, they give less thought to the consequences of their crime. These individuals are also less likely to be constrained by their beliefs, since they hold amoral beliefs. Further, such individuals are less likely to develop a stake in conformity, given their low ambition and their tendency to irritate conventional others like parents and teachers (which undermines their bonds to these individuals).

Finally, a **labeling theorist** would argue that such individuals are more likely to be labeled and treated as "bad" or "evil," with conventional others rejecting them or treating them in a negative manner. And this, in turn, increases their level of strain, reduces their control, fosters the social learning of crime (especially if they come to associate with delinquent peers), and leads to a delinquent self-concept.

Irritability

Irritability is also a super-trait consisting of several more specific traits.[9] A list of such traits would include the following.

1. **A heightened sensitivity to stressors or strains.** Irritable individuals are more easily upset than others and display stronger emotional reactions when upset, including higher levels of anger. Irritability is measured by questions like "I can get very upset when things don't go my way," and "My anger frequently gets the best of me."

2. **The tendency to attribute one's problems to the malicious behavior of others.** Irritable individuals believe others are "out to get them" and tend to blame others for their problems. For example, suppose someone bumps into an irritable person on the street; that person would likely interpret the accident as a deliberate provocation, while others might simply view it as an unintended occurrence.

3. **A tendency to be self-centered and to have little concern for the rights and feelings of others.** This trait is measured by questions like "I will try to get the

things I want even when I know it's causing problems for other people," and "I am not very sympathetic to other people when they are having problems."

4. **An aggressive or antagonistic interactional style.** This trait includes a tendency to respond to conflicts physically.

Again, it may be difficult to keep all these traits in mind. But if you imagine what someone with these traits is like, he or she might be described as **"mean" or "nasty" or "having a short fuse."**

It is easy to explain why this trait increases the likelihood of delinquency, especially if we draw on strain theory. Individuals with this trait are more likely to provoke negative reactions from others, thus increasing their level of strain. They are more sensitive to strains, and they are more inclined to cope with strain through delinquency.

A **social learning theorist** would argue that irritable individuals are more likely to be rejected by conventional others and to associate with delinquent peers, who better tolerate their irritability (and sometimes reinforce it). Also, irritable individuals find crime more rewarding, given their tendency to blame others for their problems and to exhibit an aggressive interactional style.

A **control theorist** would argue that irritable individuals are less responsive to direct controls, since their anger often "gets the best of them." Such individuals are also less likely to develop a stake in conformity; they frequently alienate conventional others like parents and teachers. Furthermore, such individuals are less likely to condemn crime.

A **labeling theorist** would argue that irritable individuals are more likely to be viewed and treated as "bad" people, with all the negative effects we've attributed to such labeling.

Summary

Three major sets of traits increase the likelihood of delinquency: low verbal IQ and, especially, the super-traits of low self-control and irritability. The effect of these traits on delinquency is easily explained via strain, social learning, control, and labeling theories.

Having described these traits, we now turn to a rather important question: Why is it that some individuals are more likely than others to possess these traits?

WHY ARE SOME INDIVIDUALS MORE LIKELY THAN OTHERS TO POSSESS THESE TRAITS?

The traits we've identified as increasing the likelihood of delinquency are a function of biological factors and the social environment. We first discuss the ways in which biological factors may contribute to these traits, and then we examine the role of the social environment.

Biological Influences on Traits

Evidence suggests that **there may be a genetic component to crime** and that **crime may sometimes result from certain types of biological harm,** such as that caused by birth complications, head injury, and exposure to toxic substances such as lead. Researchers, however, do not claim that these factors lead directly to crime. For example, there is no gene for crime. Rather, it is usually claimed that **genetic factors and biological harms create a predisposition for crime** by influencing the likelihood that individuals will develop traits like those mentioned in the preceding section. Such factors are usually said to influence the development of these traits through their effect on the *central nervous system* (the brain and spinal cord) and the *autonomic nervous system* (which controls heart rate and gland secretions, among other things, and influences the emotional reaction to stimuli).

Genetic inheritance of crime. Studies suggest that there is a genetic component to crime.[10] That is, crime is inherited to some extent. Researchers have tried to estimate the extent of genetic inheritance by using several methods, most notably *twin studies, adoption studies*, and *molecular genetic studies*. Twin studies compare identical twins to fraternal twins. Identical twins are genetically identical, while fraternal twins are about 50 percent genetically alike with respect to the genes that vary among people (see Raine, 1993). It is assumed that twins, whether identical or fraternal, are exposed to the same environmental influences. If crime is genetically inherited, we would expect that identical twins would be more similar in criminal behavior than fraternal twins. Most studies indicate that this is the case. Twin studies, however, suffer from certain problems. Most notably, evidence suggests that identical twins are more likely to spend time together and share the same friends than are fraternal twins. These facts, rather than the twins' identical genes, may explain their greater similarity in criminal behavior (see D. Rowe, 2002).

Adoption studies overcome these problems, although such studies are not problem-free. Adoption studies focus on children who were separated from their biological parents early in life. The traits of these children are compared to the traits of their biological parents. If a tendency to commit crime is inherited, there should be more crime among adopted children whose biological parents are criminals than among adopted children whose biological parents are not criminals. Most data suggest that this is the case. For example, one large study in Denmark found the following: When neither adopted nor biological parents were criminals, 13.5 percent of the adopted boys had criminal convictions; when adoptive parents were not criminals and the biological parents were, 20 percent of the adopted boys had criminal convictions (Raine, 1993).

Molecular genetic studies are a more recent development. Here researchers identify specific genes or DNA sequences (which carry genetic information) and try to determine the extent to which they are associated with criminal behavior (see Baker et al., 2006; Guo et al., 2008; Rutter et al., 2006; Simons et al., 2011). Researchers, in particular, examine individuals with varying DNA sequences to determine if those with certain sequences are more likely to engage in crime. In doing so, researchers try to take account of third variables that may affect the association between genes and crime.

Although the evidence suggests that the tendency to commit crime is inherited to some degree, it is difficult to precisely specify the extent to which the tendency is inherited. Genetic factors may be as important as environmental factors for some types of crimes and offenders. At the same time, certain cautions are in order. The extent to which crime is inherited may vary by type of crime (e.g., violent versus property) and type of offender. Evidence suggests that juvenile delinquency may be less heritable than adult crime, although genetic factors may play an influential role in the explanation of high-rate, chronic delinquency (Barnes et al., 2011; Raine, 1993).

In addition, both twin and adoption studies suggest that genetic inheritance only partly explains crime and that environmental factors also play an important role in the explanation of crime. In particular, these studies suggest that crime is most likely when the individual possesses a biological predisposition for crime and is in an environment conducive to crime. For example, crime is most likely when the individual has both biological and adoptive parents who are criminals (see especially Rutter et al., 2006). Further, molecular genetic studies are revealing that the environment shapes or "conditions" the influence of genes on antisocial behavior (Beaver and Connolly, 2013; Simons and Lei, 2013). Studies in this area are finding that genetic factors heighten the risk of offending when the individual is exposed to a "bad" environment—that is, an environment conducive to crime (e.g., exposure to harsh parenting, violent peers, and neighborhood crime).

But when the individual is exposed to a "good" environment, genetic factors play little or no role in offending.

One interpretation of the findings just described is that stressful environments may "trigger" genetic predispositions for problem behavior, while positive environments can suppress or counteract the influence of genes. This raises the possibility that environmental interventions could be used to minimize the risk posed by genetic factors. An alternative interpretation is that, due to their genetic endowment, certain individuals are unusually sensitive to their environment. These individuals are especially prone to trouble when they are in bad environments, but they tend to perform well and may even thrive in good environments (for more on the interpretation of gene-environment interactions, see Beaver and Connolly, 2013; Simons and Lei, 2013).

Related to this line of research, we are discovering that the interaction between genes and the environment is more complex than previously imagined and that the environment can influence the "expression" of genes. Rather than being self-activating, genes are "turned on and off" by an internal regulatory process that is susceptible to environmental influence. There is now some evidence that certain interventions may have this effect. For example, cognitive behavioral therapy, which has been used in the treatment of juvenile offenders and prison inmates, has been linked to subsequent changes in brain structure and gene expression (Levy-Gigi et al., 2013). With these important advances in molecular genetics, it is becoming clear that "trying to study the effects of genes independent of the environment (and vice versa) truly misses the mark" (Beaver and Connolly, 2013:46). The main point, however, is that despite evidence linking genetic factors to crime, environmental factors still play an important role.

Biological harms and crime. Studies also suggest that experiencing certain *biological harms* increases the likelihood of crime. Such harms include (1) the mother's poor health habits during pregnancy, including poor nutrition and alcohol and drug use; (2) delivery complications of certain types; (3) exposure to toxic substances such as lead; (4) certain dietary deficiencies; and (5) head injury.[11] The research in these areas often suffers from one or more of the problems listed in Chapter 5, such as the failure to control for relevant third variables or to conduct longitudinal studies. Nevertheless, the data as a whole suggest that certain types of biological harm may contribute to at least some crime.

The central and autonomic nervous systems. The mechanisms by which genetic inheritance and biological harm contribute to crime are not fully understood. Most researchers in the area, however, suggest that those factors affect the central and autonomic nervous systems. A number of possible effects have been explored. For example, genetic factors and biological harm may contribute to **dysfunctions in the frontal lobe of the brain,** which is involved in abstract thinking, planning, self-monitoring behavior, and behavioral inhibition (Moffitt and Henry, 1989; Raine, 1993; Yang and Raine, 2010). These factors may also contribute to **dysfunctions in the left hemisphere of the brain;** such dysfunctions have been linked to low verbal IQ scores. These factors **may affect the autonomic nervous system,** with data suggesting that criminals show less emotional response to stimuli (they are "physiologically 'drowsy' " in the words of Bartol and Bartol, 1986:69). This condition, called *underarousal,* is reflected in lower resting heart rate, slower alpha brain waves, and below-average skin conductance (an electrical property demonstrated when a person sweats less than normal in response to stimuli). Underarousal, in turn, may contribute to traits such as hyperactivity.

Researchers are now investigating the ways in which genetic inheritance and biological harms may affect the central and autonomic nervous systems. For example, data suggest that some of these factors may result in reduced levels of *serotonin*, a neurotransmitter.[12] Neurotransmitters allow for communication between brain cells and so underlie all of our behavior, thoughts, perceptions, emotions, and the like. Reduced serotonin may lower one's level of inhibition, contributing to such traits as impulsivity.

Biological factors and traits conducive to crime. Genetic factors and certain types of biological harm, then, may increase the likelihood of crime through their effects on the central and autonomic nervous systems. There is still the question, however, of why **"dysfunctions" in the central and autonomic nervous systems** may lead to crime. The most commonly advanced theory is that the dysfunctions increase the likelihood that individuals will develop traits conducive to crime, such as low IQ, impulsivity, and irritability. There is some evidence for this line of argument.[13] In particular, there is good evidence of a genetic effect on IQ, low self-control, and irritability.[14] Related to this, molecular genetic studies are beginning to identify the specific genes related to traits like hyperactivity and impulsivity (see Baker et al., 2006; Fishbein, 2001; D. Rowe, 2002). There is also good evidence that many of the traits listed here are influenced by biological harms, such as birth complications, head injury, and lead poisoning. For example, exposure to lead, a toxic metal, has been linked to such traits as hyperactivity and impulsivity (Reyes, 2015). (Note: You may recall hearing news stories about the city of Flint, Michigan, and its lead-contaminated water supply. Of major concern has been the potential adverse effects on child development of heavy exposure to lead).

Many of the traits often associated with criminality have also been linked to dysfunctions in the central and autonomic nervous systems.[15] Dysfunctions in the frontal lobe of the brain may contribute to such traits as hyperactivity, the preference for immediate rewards, impulsivity, irritability, and insensitivity to others. Underarousal in the autonomic nervous system has been linked to hyperactivity and sensation seeking. It takes more to stimulate underaroused individuals, which may cause them to become overly active and to increase their need of thrills or excitement (see Box 13.1).

Environmental Influences on Traits

The traits discussed here are also a function of the individual's social environment, especially the early family environment.[16] In particular, children are less likely to be irritable and low in self-control when **parents teach them** how to manage their anger and exercise self-control. Parents do this in a number of ways. For example, parents model **high** self-control; parents make clear that the impulsive, risky, and "lazy" behaviors associated with **low** self-control are not acceptable; and parents monitor their children's behavior, consistently sanctioning them when they exhibit low self-control and reinforcing them when they exercise high self-control. (See Chapter 14 for a fuller discussion of effective parenting methods.)

The **resources** possessed by parents also influence the expression of irritability and low self-control. In particular, data suggest that a parent's **social class** has a strong effect on at least some of the individual traits listed here (see, e.g., Meich et al., 1999). At least part of this effect may stem from the impact of social class on parenting practices (see Chapter 14). Further, **social programs** that attempt to compensate for early family problems often lead to changes in these traits. For example, data indicate that children from deprived environments experience a boost in IQ when they are placed in programs that provide intellectual stimulation—such as preschool programs of certain types (Ramey and Ramey, 1995). Likewise, a number of programs aimed at developing social skills have produced increases in children's self-control (Piquero et al., 2010).

Box 13.1   The Beat of a Delinquent Heart: The Relationship between Heart Rate and Offending

A biological factor that has been linked to delinquency in numerous studies is a simple one to assess: a low resting heart rate (in one study, a low resting heart rate was defined as 65 beats per minute or less). Of course, a low resting heart rate does not guarantee delinquent behavior, but it tends to be more common among serious and aggressive juvenile offenders. Further, the relationship between a low resting heart rate and delinquency has not yet been explained away by third variables. In fact, the relationship seems to hold even after taking into account (controlling for) physical height, weight, gender, race, self-control, attachment to parents, delinquent peers, and other variables. Moreover, longitudinal studies find that a low resting heart rate has predictive power; for example, possession of this trait as a child increases the risk of problem behavior later in life (Todd Armstrong et al., 2009; Cauffman et al., 2005).

It is not yet clear why a low resting heart rate places individuals at increased risk for offending, but criminologists are concentrating on three leading explanations. **First,** a low resting heart rate may signal damage or disorder in the areas of the brain that control the rate of the heart. These same areas of the brain may also help regulate emotions and behavior. **Second,** individuals in very risky occupations, such as bomb disposal experts, have been shown to have "particularly low resting heart rates" (Todd Armstrong et al., 2009:1127). Based on this observation, it has been argued that persons with a low resting heart rate may be relatively fearless and thus prone to crime and delinquency. A **third** possibility is that a low resting heart rate is indicative of low internal arousal, which may be a source of physiological discomfort. To increase their arousal level, individuals possessing this trait may seek out risky and exciting activities, including delinquency (Todd Armstrong et al., 2009).

Related to the third possibility, which has received some support (Portnoy et al., 2014), the following offenders describe themselves as needing more stimulation than can be provided by a "straight" conventional life:

> No, I don't think I can take a nine-to-five job. My body hasn't got that in its computer. (quoted in Åkerström, 1985:171)

> What's the damn meaning in sitting in a place and tilting a chair? . . . At best [if you land a legitimate job] you get hold of a TV, and sit there and brood in front of it with a beer. . . . You need some kind of stimulation. (quoted in Åkerström, 1985:186)

Questions for Discussion

1. In light of the preceding research, it should be possible to identify children who are at risk of delinquency by measuring their resting heart rate at a very early age. What would be the advantages and disadvantages of this strategy? What concerns might labeling theorists raise?
2. Assume that some individuals have a need for high levels of external stimulation, as suggested by the offenders quoted previously. From the standpoint of a strain theorist, why would such a need increase the likelihood of crime and delinquency? How would control and social learning theorists explain a link between a high need for external stimulation and delinquency?

Another aspect of the social environment that has received a good deal of attention involves children's exposure to violence. Exposure to violence can also impact traits and is common among youth who later enter the juvenile justice system. For example, many of these youth report that they have "seen or heard someone get hurt very badly or be killed," have been "threatened with a weapon," or have thought they, or someone close to them, "was going to be hurt very badly or die" (Abram et al., 2004:405–406). Studies have linked such experiences to the development of posttraumatic stress disorder (PTSD), which involves fear, horror, or a sense of helplessness in response to past traumatic events. Further, research in this area indicates that exposure to violence and PTSD tends to reduce the individual's ability to regulate emotions and impulses, leading to irritability, low self-control, and a heightened risk of delinquency (Agnew et al., 2011; Allwood and Bell, 2008; Monahan et al., 2015; Turner et al., 2007; Widom, 2014). For more on trauma, see Box 21.1 in Chapter 21.

Traits, then, are a function of the social environment as well as of biological factors. Often, however, it is difficult to separate out the effects of environmental and biological factors in a precise manner. Many types of biological harm are a function of the social environment (like one's social class). Lower-class individuals, for example, are more likely to be exposed to lead and to have had poor prenatal care (Denno, 1990). At the same time, biological factors may shape one's social environment. Children with dysfunctions in their central and autonomic nervous systems, for example, may be more difficult for parents to raise. As a consequence, those parents may be more likely to ignore their children or treat them in a harsh manner.

Further, **environmental and biological factors may condition the effects of one another on the traits discussed** (see the discussion of conditioning effects at the start of Chapter 5). For example, biological factors, like genetic inheritance or birth complications, may be more likely to produce these traits if the individual is in a harsh or chaotic family environment. As we described earlier, a new line of research is exploring the interplay between biological and environmental factors, including the extent to which environmental factors influence the expression of genes (see Burt and Simons, 2014; Rutter et al., 2006). Likewise, such a family environment may be more likely to produce these traits if the individual has a genetic predisposition for them or has experienced certain types of biological harm. The most important point to remember, however, is that some evidence suggests that these traits are a function of both biological and environmental factors.[17]

IS MENTAL ILLNESS RELATED TO VIOLENCE?

Most of the research on mental illness and crime/delinquency has focused on violence. Certain events, such as the shooting deaths of 20 children and 6 adults at Sandy Hook Elementary School in 2012, foster the belief that mental illness is a major cause of violence. The most recent research suggests that most people with mental health problems are *not* violent, but that certain mental health problems are associated with violence. Part of the association between mental illness and violence may be due to third variables, however. Factors such as low socioeconomic status, physical and sexual abuse, other strains or stressors, and drug abuse contribute to both mental illness and violence. But there is evidence that major mental illness has a *modest* effect on violence (for an excellent discussion, see Silver, 2006).

Major mental illness includes thought and mood disorders such as schizophrenia and bipolar disorder. These illnesses are more likely to lead to violence when accompanied by substance abuse and treatment noncompliance (e.g., the failure to take prescribed medication). And there is some evidence that they affect violence for reasons related to the leading delinquency theories. For example, mental illness increases violence partly because it increases strain and reduces bonds to conventional others (see Link et al., 2016; Silver,

2006; Silver and Teasdale, 2005). But given the modest overall effect of mental illness on violence, we do not treat it as one of the major traits contributing to delinquency. Nevertheless, it is important to discuss mental illness, both because it is sometimes viewed as a major cause of violence and because juvenile justice facilities have come to hold a large number of mentally ill individuals (see Box 13.2).

Box 13.2   Therapy or Punishment? Addressing the Mental Health Needs of Juvenile Offenders

Donald attacked a schoolteacher when he was just 5 years old and has been in and out of mental health programs ever since. At age 16, Donald was serving time for a breaking and entering charge. Although he was diagnosed with bipolar disorder and other psychiatric conditions, and although his grandmother begged that he be placed in a mental health facility, a judge sentenced him to a state-run correctional center. There, it was assumed, he would get the best mental health care available. Yet two years into his confinement, this assumption was still being tested:

> Donald's confinement has been repeatedly extended because of his violent outbursts. This year [in 2009] he assaulted a guard here at the prison, the Ohio Valley Juvenile Correctional Facility, and was charged anew with assault. His fists and forearms are striped with scars where he gouged himself with pencils and the bones of a bird he caught and dismembered. (*New York Times*, 2009:A1)

Donald is among the 20 percent of youth in the juvenile justice system who qualify "as having a serious mental health disorder," a figure that is "double the estimated rate in the general youth population" (Pullmann et al., 2006:376). If we were to include other psychiatric conditions, such as affective disorders, anxiety disorders, substance-abuse disorders, and ADHD, the percentage would be much higher. Yet many experts argue that juvenile justice facilities are ill-equipped to meet the mental health needs of these young offenders. In the words of one child psychiatrist, "We're seeing more and more mentally ill kids [in these facilities] who couldn't find community programs that were intensive enough to treat them. . . . Jails and juvenile justice facilities are the new asylums" (*New York Times*, 2009:A1). In fact, mental health experts have described the juvenile justice system as a system in crisis—a crisis compounded by budget cuts to community-based mental health programs, a chronic shortage of child mental health professionals, and the fact that incarceration may exacerbate psychiatric illness (*New York Times*, 2009).

In recent years, attention has focused on the excessive use of solitary confinement to punish juveniles with mental health needs. In March 2014, the U.S. Department of Justice (DOJ) announced that it was seeking a federal court order to stop this practice in Ohio's juvenile correctional facilities. The DOJ alleges that one boy with mental health needs was locked in solitary confinement for 21 days straight. As described by a journalist:

> Seclusion has become the state's modus operandi for handling boys with mental illness. . . . The state punishes the boys with seclusion (i.e., solitary confinement) for days on end, often also depriving them of education, exercise, programming and crucial mental-health care. (A. Johnson, 2014)

In contrast, the Mendota Juvenile Treatment Center in Madison, Wisconsin, offers intensive mental health treatment to serious juvenile offenders and seeks to avoid the cycle of punishment and defiance that often leads to excessive seclusion. The center

(Continued)

(Continued)

was established to treat youth who were too violent or unruly to be housed in the state's traditional correctional facilities. The center recognizes that punishment, by itself, tends to ineffective with this population. In fact, punishment often *increases* defiance in troubled youth. As a result, program staff receives special training in how to respond to disruptive behavior. In addition, the youth participate in individual counseling and group therapy sessions on a weekly basis. These sessions address substance abuse, anger management, social skills, and problem solving. Further, the youth can earn privileges for good behavior. Initial evaluations indicate that the Mendota program is promising and can help prevent violent recidivism (for more on the program, visit: http://www.crimesolutions.gov). These findings are consistent with other studies showing that the provision of adequate mental health care reduces repeat offending among juvenile offenders (Pullmann et al., 2006:378).

Question for Discussion

1. How does the general public view mentally ill offenders, especially young offenders like Donald? Do you think many people are aware of, or care about, the mental health needs of such offenders? Would most people support greater treatment services? Would they support the placement of mentally ill offenders in treatment versus correctional facilities? Would they be willing to pay more in taxes to support community-based mental health programs? What are your own thoughts on these issues?

SUMMARY

Evidence suggests that juveniles with certain traits are more likely to engage in delinquency, especially high-rate, chronic offending. These traits include low verbal IQ and the super-traits of low self-control and irritability. The effect of these traits on delinquency is readily explained in terms of strain, social learning, control, and labeling theories. Moreover, these traits are a function of both biological and environmental factors.

TEACHING AIDS

Controversial Issue: Should Delinquents Be Held Responsible for Their Behavior?

The following exercise is adapted from Raine (1993:309–312). Imagine a hypothetical juvenile named Joe with the following characteristics: Joe's mother is a drug addict, and his father is a life-course persistent offender. Joe's birth was accompanied by serious complications, probably as a result of his mother's drug use and other poor health habits during pregnancy. And Joe experienced a number of additional biological harms through adolescence, including head injuries from accidents and assaults. Joe, then, had a strong biological predisposition to develop traits conducive to crime, like low self-control and irritability.

Joe grew up in a highly aversive (undesirable) environment. Joe never knew his father, who abandoned his mother when she became pregnant. Joe was rejected and abused by his drug-addicted mother and her boyfriends, was surrounded by siblings who regularly engaged in crime, and grew up in a deprived neighborhood with a high crime rate. Not surprisingly, Joe developed the traits of low self-control and irritability. Rejected by conventional peers as a result of his temperament, Joe joined a neighborhood gang. He experienced numerous problems in school and eventually dropped out.

Joe was the subject of some pity and concern while a child. Social welfare agencies made an effort to help him, placing the boy in a series of foster homes—although he ran away from most of them. Joe, however, was shown little pity when he turned into an adolescent and started committing serious crimes. Joe was arrested on several occasions and spent some time in juvenile institutions—but such institutions provided few rehabilitative services. They did, however, provide much exposure to delinquent peers. At age 15, Joe held up a store with a gun, shooting the owner in the arm. Joe was arrested for armed robbery and aggravated assault, tried as an adult under a new "get tough" law, and sentenced to 20 years in prison.

While Joe is not real, elements of his life history are taken from real cases, and he resembles many life-course persistent offenders in the United States. So assume, for the sake of argument, that Joe is a real person. We have two questions for you: **Should we hold Joe responsible for his criminal behavior?** Related to this, **should Joe receive a 20-year sentence for his crimes?**

These questions involve a key issue regarding the causes of crime. Some individuals contend that committing crimes is largely a matter of free choice and, as such, criminals deserve punishment, including serious punishment if they commit serious crimes. This is the underlying idea of the adult criminal justice system—although a very small percentage of offenders are able to escape punishment because they satisfy the legal criteria for mental illness. (Joe did not satisfy these criteria, since he knew what he was doing, knew his crime was considered wrong, and was not overcome by an "irresistible impulse" to commit the crime.) Other individuals, however, contend that crime is largely the result of **forces beyond the individual's control**—like biological factors and poor parenting. On this view, criminals do not deserve serious punishment but rather are in need of help. (For an expanded discussion of these issues, see Box 5.1 in Chapter 5; also see Agnew, 1995c; Brezina and Wright, 2001.)

Web-Based Exercise: Programs for Mentally Ill Offenders

Visit the CrimeSolutions.gov website and, under "**Advanced Search**," find the **Targeted Population** box. Check the **Mentally Ill Offenders** option, type **Needs** in the keyword box, and then click the **Search** button. Based on the results, what types of program are available for offenders with mental health needs? What are some of the specific components of these programs? How effective are these programs?

TEST YOUR KNOWLEDGE OF THIS CHAPTER

1. What is an "individual trait"?
2. List or briefly describe any five traits that appear to increase the likelihood of crime.
3. What is meant by "super-trait"?
4. Describe the characteristics of someone with a low verbal IQ.
5. Drawing on the leading delinquency theories (strain, social learning, control, and labeling), describe why low verbal IQ seems to increase the likelihood of delinquency.
6. Describe any three of the specific traits that make up low self-control. At a general level, describe what someone low in self-control is like.
7. Drawing on the leading delinquency theories, describe why low self-control increases the likelihood of delinquency.
8. Describe any three of the specific traits that make up irritability. At a general level, describe someone who is irritable.
9. Drawing on the leading delinquency theories, describe why irritability increases the likelihood of delinquency.
10. Describe the three major ways in which researchers have tried to determine whether crime is inherited.
11. Describe any three types of biological harm that may increase the likelihood of crime.

12. Genes and biological harms are said to influence the development of traits conducive to crime through their effects on the central nervous system (CNS) and autonomic nervous system (ANS). Describe any two of these effects on the CNS and/or ANS.

13. Describe one piece of evidence suggesting that dysfunctions in the CNS and/or ANS contribute to traits conducive to crime.

14. Traits conducive to crime are also a function of the early family environment. Describe those parenting practices that influence the level of self-control.

15. Why is it often difficult to precisely determine the extent to which crime is caused by biological or social factors?

16. What do we mean when we state that biological and environmental factors may condition the effects of one another on traits conducive to crime? Give an example of such a conditioning effect.

17. Certain high-profile events have fostered the belief that mental illness is a major cause of violence. What does the research indicate? Are most people with mental health problems violent? For individuals suffering from major mental disorders, what circumstances increase the likelihood of violence?

THOUGHT AND DISCUSSION QUESTIONS

1. Describe the ways in which individuals who are irritable and low in self-control may shape their social environment. Consider the reactions they might evoke from others in particular situations, how they might alter their ongoing relations with others such as parents and school officials, and how they might "select themselves into" certain types of environments through their actions. (See Chapter 10.)

2. Do you think the juvenile's school and peer environments may influence his or her levels of self-control and irritability? If so, describe how.

3. Do you think there are gender differences in levels of self-control and irritability? If so, what might be the source of these differences? (See Chapter 18.)

4. Drawing on the arguments in this chapter, what policies or programs would you suggest to reduce delinquency? (Note: Some of these programs, like those designed to reduce exposure to the lead in old paint, might, at first glance, seem far removed from delinquency. See Chapter 24 for examples of programs designed to address the traits that cause delinquency and the biological and social factors that influence these traits.)

KEY TERMS

- Traits
- Super-traits
- Low verbal IQ
- Low self-control
- Impulsivity
- Risk seeking
- Hyperactivity
- Irritability
- Central nervous system (CNS)
- Autonomic nervous system (ANS)
- Twin studies
- Adoption studies
- Molecular genetic studies
- Biological harms
- Serotonin

ENDNOTES

1. For overviews, see Andrews and Bonta, 2006; S. Baron, 2003; S. Bennett et al., 2005; Blackburn, 1993; Caspi et al., 1994; Chapple, 2005; Dodge and Schwartz, 1997; Farrington, 1996b, 1998; Farrington and Welsh, 2007; Goode, 2008; Hollin, 2002; Lahey and Waldman, 2005; Little and Steinberg, 2006; Lynam and Miller, 2004; Matsueda et al., 2006; Joshua Miller and Lynam,

2001; Ogilvie et al., 2011; Peskin et al., 2012; Piquero and Bouffard, 2007; Pratt and Cullen, 2000; Pratt et al., 2002; Ratchford and Beaver, 2009; Rutter et al., 1998; John Paul Wright and Boisvert, 2009.

2. See Arneklev et al., 1999; Caspi et al., 1994; Caspi et al., 2005; Farrington and Welsh, 2007; Lahey and Waldman, 2005; Lynam and Miller, 2004; Joshua Miller and Lynam, 2001; Piquero and Boufford, 2007; B. Wright, Caspi, Moffitt, and Silva, 1999.

3. See Bartusch et al., 1997; Bellair et al., 2016; Caspi et al., 2005; Colder and Stice, 1998; Farrington and Welsh, 2007; Lahey and Waldman, 2005; Lynam and Miller, 2004; McGloin et al., 2004; Joshua Miller and Lynam, 2001; Moffitt, 1993, 1997; Moffitt et al., 2001; Moffitt et al., 1994; Rutter et al., 1998.

4. See Bartusch et al., 1997; Bellair and McNulty, 2005; Bellair et al., 2016; Blackburn, 1993; Denno, 1990; Farrington, 1996b, 1998; Farrington and Welsh, 2007; Hirschi and Hindelang, 1977; Lahey and Waldman, 2005; Loeber, Farrington, Stouthamer-Loeber, Moffitt, and Caspi, 1998; McGloin et al., 2004; Mears and Cochran, 2013; Moffitt, 1990, 1997; Moffitt et al., 1994; Rutter et al., 1998; J. Wilson and Herrnstein, 1985.

5. See Bellair and McNulty, 2005; Bellair et al., 2016; Loeber, Farrington, Stouthamer-Loeber, Moffitt, and Caspi, 1998; McGloin et al., 2004; Moffitt, 1990; Wilson and Herrnstein, 1985:171.

6. See Bellair and McNulty, 2005; Denno, 1990; Farrington and Welsh, 2007; Hirschi and Hindelang, 1977; McGloin et al., 2004; Rutter and Giller, 1983.

7. See Farrington, 1996b; Farrington and Welsh, 2007; McGloin et al., 2004; Moffitt, 1990; Peskin et al., 2012; Wilson and Herrnstein, 1985.

8. See Arneklev et al., 1999; Burt et al., 2014; M. Gottfredson and Hirschi, 1990; Grasmick et al., 1993; Joshua Miller and Lynam, 2001; Moffitt et al., 2001; Pratt and Cullen, 2000; B. Wright, Caspi, Moffitt, and Silva, 1999.

9. See Agnew et al., 2002; Arneklev et al., 1999; Caspi et al., 1994; Caspi et al., 2005; Colder and Stice, 1998; Lahey and Waldman, 2005; Joshua Miller and Lynam, 2001; Moffitt et al., 2001; B. Wright, Caspi, Moffitt, and Silva, 1999.

10. For excellent overviews, see Baker et al., 2006; Beaver and Connolly, 2013; Brennan et al., 1995; Carey and Goldman, 1997; Farrington 1998; Fishbein, 2001; Guo et al., 2008; Lahey and Waldman, 2005; Moffitt, 2006; Raine, 1993, 2002a; Rhee and Waldman, 2002; Rodgers et al., 2001; D. Rowe, 2002; Rutter et al., 1998; Rutter et al., 2006; Walsh, 2002.

11. See Brennan et al., 1995; Denno, 1990; Fishbein, 2001; Gajos and Beaver, 2016; Hawkins, Herrenkohl, Farrington, Brewer, Catalano, and Harachi, 1998; Liu et al., 2009; McGloin et al., 2006; Narag et al., 2009; Peskin et al., 2012; Raine, 1993, 2002a, 2002b; Ratchford and Beaver, 2009; Reyes, 2015; Rutter et al., 1998; Tibbetts and Piquero, 1999.

12. See Baker et al., 2006; Berman et al., 1997; Fishbein, 2001; Moffitt et al., 1997.

13. See Baker et al., 2006; S. Bennett et al., 2005; Brennan et al., 1995; Cauffman et al., 2005; Denno, 1990; Farrington, 1996b, 1998; Farrington and Welsh, 2007; Fishbein, 2001; Gruber and Yurgelun-Todd, 2005; Hollin, 1992; Liu et al., 2009; Moffitt, 1990; Peskin et al., 2012; Raine, 1993, 2002a; D. Rowe, 2002; Rutter et al., 1998; Wilson and Herrnstein, 1985; J. P. Wright and Beaver, 2005; Yang and Raine, 2010.

14. See Baker et al., 2006; Beaver et al., 2008; Caspi, 1998; Caspi et al., 2005; Lahey and Waldman, 2005; Plomin and Petrill, 1997; Rutter et al., 1998; John Paul Wright and Beaver, 2005.

15. See Baker et al., 2006; S. Bennett et al., 2005; Cauffman et al., 2005; Gruber and Yurgelun-Todd, 2005; Lykken, 1996; Moffitt, 1990; Moffitt and Henry, 1989; Peskin et al., 2012; Raine, 1993, 2002a; D. Rowe, 2002; J. P. Wright and Beaver, 2005.

16. See Bartol and Bartol, 1986; Blackburn, 1993; Caspi et al., 2005; Cullen et al., 2008; Gottfredson and Hirschi, 1990; Hay, 2001b; Hay and Forrest, 2006; Lahey and Waldman, 2005; Pratt et al., 2004; Pulkkinen, 1986; Unnever et al., 2003; J. Wilson and Herrnstein, 1985; J. P. Wright and Beaver, 2005.

17. See Baker et al., 2006; Beaver et al., 2008; Caspi et al., 2005; Lahey and Waldman, 2005; Ousey and Wilcox, 2007; Raine, 2002b; Raine, Brennan et al. (with Mednick), 1997; Rowe, 2002; Rutter et al., 1998; Rutter et al., 2006; Rutter and Silberg, 2002; Tibbetts and Piquero, 1999.

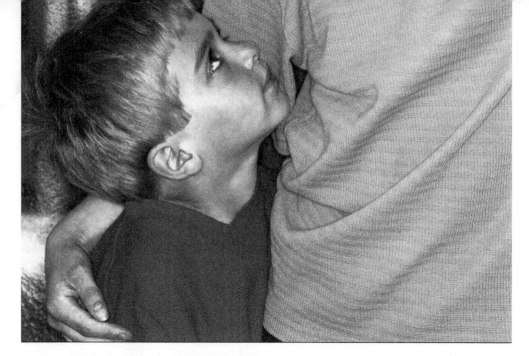

14 The Family

What Impact Does the Family
Have on Delinquency?

Chapter 13 stated that certain individual traits increase the likelihood of delinquency, especially high-rate, chronic delinquency. Delinquency is also caused by the individual's social environment. Individuals in certain types of environments are more likely to engage in delinquency—for reasons explained by strain, social learning, control, and labeling theories. These environments have a relatively large effect on individuals who possess traits conducive to delinquency, but they also lead many "normal" individuals to engage in delinquency.

This chapter begins to examine the effect of the social environment on delinquency. In particular, we ask what types of family increase the likelihood of delinquency. Chapter 15 examines the effect of school experiences and characteristics on delinquency. Subsequent chapters then focus on the effect on delinquency of delinquent peer groups, gangs, religion, work, the mass media, the social media, and the presence of drugs and guns.

After reading this chapter, you should be able to:

- Explain why the family plays a central role in the development of delinquent behavior, according to the major delinquency theories.
- Discuss the effects of family structure on delinquency, including single-parent homes, mother's employment outside the home, teenage motherhood, and family size.
- Discuss the effects of parental and sibling crime/deviance on delinquency.
- Discuss factors related to the quality of family relationships and how they relate to delinquency, especially child-parent attachment, family conflict, and child abuse.
- Identify steps that parents can take to socialize their children against delinquency.
- Describe the major parenting styles and how they relate to delinquency.
- Explain why some parents engage in poor parenting practices.

THE EFFECT OF THE FAMILY ON DELINQUENCY

All major delinquency theories argue that the family plays a central role in determining whether juveniles engage in delinquency. The family—perhaps more than any other social group—influences **(1) the juvenile's level of and reaction to strain, (2) whether the juvenile learns to conform or to deviate, (3) the control to which the juvenile is subject, and (4) the extent to which the juvenile is subject to labeling.** The family sometimes has a **direct effect on delinquency,** and it sometimes has an **indirect effect** through its influence on such things as the juvenile's individual traits, school performance, and selection of friends. Many criminologists have gone so far as to claim that juvenile delinquency is largely a function of the juvenile's family experiences (e.g., M. Gottfredson and Hirschi, 1990; Patterson et al., 1989). Several states have even passed laws that hold parents responsible for the criminal behavior of their children in certain circumstances. These laws are seldom enforced, but one Michigan couple was fined $1,200 for not controlling their 16-year-old son. The son had been arrested for burglarizing several homes and having a 4-foot marijuana plant in his bedroom. According to the verdict, the couple had failed to properly supervise their son after his earlier arrests for burglarizing churches and for attacking his father with a golf club (see Arthur, 2005; Brank et al., 2006; Murphy and Healy, 1999).

What does the research say about the influence of the family? Are family factors a major cause of delinquency? You've already been exposed to the family research in Chapters 6 through 9, where we discussed the evidence on strain, social learning, control, and labeling theories. Much of the research on the family has been directly guided by these theories. As a consequence, portions of the following discussion will sound familiar. The research on the family and delinquency has focused on **four major aspects of the family.** The first aspect is **family structure,** which has to do with the size and composition of the family; it is commonly argued, for example, that single-parent homes (so-called broken homes) cause delinquency. The second aspect is **parental and sibling deviance,** which has to do with the extent to which parents and siblings engage in crime and deviant behavior. The third aspect is the **quality of family relationships,** which has to do with the emotional ties between family members and how well family members get along together. It is commonly argued, for example, that juveniles who love and respect their parents are less delinquent. The fourth aspect is **parental socialization,** which has to do with the extent to which parents teach their children to conform or to deviate. In particular, do parents provide clear rules, monitor behavior, sanction deviance, instruct and model conformity, reinforce conformity, and provide social support? We present here the major research findings in each of these four areas.

FAMILY STRUCTURE

Are Juveniles from Single-Parent Homes More Delinquent?

Many criminologists, politicians, and others argue that single-parent homes (the so-called broken homes) are a major cause of delinquency. An "intact" home is typically defined as one in which both natural parents are present. Historically, homes in which only one natural parent is present have been referred to as "broken homes"; it is said these family units have been broken by divorce, separation, or the death of a spouse. We prefer to use the term "single-parent home" because it avoids the automatic negative connotations associated with "broken home."

The alleged impact of single-parent homes is usually explained in terms of the leading delinquency theories (see especially Rebellon, 2002). Juveniles in single-parent homes are said to be **under more strain,** partly because of the conflict associated with divorce or separation and partly because of the financial and other problems that often follow when someone takes on single parenthood. Juveniles in single-parent homes are also said to be **subject to less control;** among other things, the conflict associated with divorce or separation is said to disrupt the emotional bond between juveniles and their parents, to reduce the parents' ability to exercise effective supervision, and to have a negative impact on a juvenile's school performance. Further, it is said that juveniles in single-parent homes receive **less exposure to conventional role models** and are **more likely to fall prey to delinquent peers,** who encourage delinquent behavior. Finally, it is said that juveniles from single-parent homes are **more likely to be labeled delinquent.**

These arguments have taken on a special urgency in recent years, given the **large percentage of juveniles who now live in single-parent homes.** In 1960, most (85 percent) of all children under 18 were living with two married parents. By 2015, this statistic had decreased to 65 percent. Twenty-seven percent of all children lived in single-parent homes headed by their mother (23 percent) or father (4 percent), and another 4 percent live with neither parent (instead, they live with grandparents, foster parents, or in other family arrangements). About 15 percent of white, non-Hispanic children lived in mother-only families, versus 26 percent of Hispanic children and 49 percent of African American children. **Children in single-parent homes are more likely to suffer from a range of problems, most notably poverty.** In 2014, about 11 percent of the children in married-couple families were living in poverty versus 46 percent of the children in families headed by females with no spouse present (see the 2016 report of the Federal Interagency Forum on Child and Family Statistics, available at http://www.childstats.gov). But are single-parent homes a major cause of delinquency?

The data on single-parent homes and delinquency are somewhat mixed.[1] Some studies find that juveniles from single-parent homes engage in about the same amount of delinquency as juveniles from two-parent homes, while other studies find that juveniles from single-parent homes are somewhat more likely to engage in delinquency. Studies based on official data, like arrest statistics, tend to find that single-parent homes are more strongly related to delinquency than studies based on self-report data. The reason for this difference may be that police and court officials are more likely to arrest and process juveniles from single-parent homes than similarly delinquent juveniles from so-called "intact" homes. This may reflect a **labeling effect,** with officials being more likely to view and treat juveniles from "broken homes" as delinquents in need of intervention. In addition, single-parent homes generally have a stronger effect on status and minor offenses—especially family-related offenses like running away—than on serious offenses. **When one considers the data as a whole, the best conclusion is that being from a single-parent home has a small to moderate effect on delinquency.**

This conclusion is based on a simple comparison of single-parent homes and two-parent homes. You may wonder whether single-parent homes of some types have a bigger effect on delinquency than others. For example, does it make a difference whether the absence of a mother or father is the result of a divorce or separation versus the death of one of the parents? Since divorces and separations are often preceded by much conflict, we might expect that single-parent homes that are the product of divorce/separation would be more strongly related to delinquency. The data provide some support for this view, suggesting that **single-parent homes that result from divorce/separation have a stronger association with delinquency.**

You may also wonder whether delinquency is more likely in mother-only homes (the most common type of single-parent home), mother/stepfather homes (the next most common family type), or father-only homes (rapidly becoming more common). A number of conflicting arguments have been made in this area. For example, some argue that homes with stepfathers should be lower in delinquency, since the stepfather provides an additional source of income and help with discipline. Others argue that homes with stepfathers should be higher in delinquency, since the stepfather may get into frequent conflicts with his stepchildren. Likewise, there are conflicting arguments about whether delinquency should be higher in mother-only versus father-only homes (see Demuth and Brown, 2004; Eitle, 2006). Further, some have argued that the relationship between family type and delinquency may depend on a number of factors, such as race/ethnicity and the sex of the child (see Eitle, 2006). Unfortunately, there has not been much research in these areas, and the research that has been done has produced mixed results. It is therefore **difficult to say at present whether delinquency is higher in single-mother, single-father, or mother/stepfather families.**

Overall, then, **single-parent homes have a small to moderate effect on delinquency.** Limited data suggest that this effect is at least partly attributable to the effect of a single-parent home on the quality of family relationships and parental socialization.[2] The fact that single-parent homes have only a small to moderate effect on delinquency may surprise you, but many studies indicate that the structure of the family (e.g., whether both natural parents are present) is much less important than the behavior and attitudes of family members. To paraphrase Van Voorhis et al. (1988), **what places a juvenile at risk for delinquency is not so much coming from a single-parent home as coming from a bad home.** While single-parent homes have an effect on the behavior and attitudes of family members, there are many single-parent homes with good relationships and many "intact" two-parent homes with poor relationships. A single-parent home with good relationships is less likely to result in delinquency than a two-parent home with bad relationships.

Does the Mother's Employment Outside the Home Increase Delinquency?

It was once the norm for fathers to work outside the home and for mothers to assume major responsibility for child care. In 1950, only 16 percent of all children had working mothers. There has been a dramatic increase in female labor force participation in recent decades, however, and close to three-quarters of all mothers with dependent children work today (U.S. Department of Labor, 2016). As a consequence, some criminologists have asked whether the mother's employment outside the home increases the likelihood of delinquency. (Criminologists seldom ask whether the father's employment has that effect.) It has been argued that the mother's employment outside the home may increase the likelihood of delinquency for several reasons. Among other things, it may reduce maternal supervision of the child and weaken the emotional bond between the mother and child. Data, however, suggest that the mother's employment outside the home has little effect on these factors, and that **there is little or no relationship between delinquency and number of hours worked by the mother.**[3] (Note: Most studies in this area examine data from Western nations. The relationship between mother's employment and delinquency may be stronger in other countries, such as South Korea, where working conditions place greater demands on employees—see Lee et al., 2011.)

Does Placing Juveniles in Childcare Facilities Increase the Likelihood of Delinquency?

Certain news reports have stated that placing juveniles in childcare facilities leads to an increase in behavioral problems, such as aggression (Gilbert, 2003). These reports may have alarmed many parents given that, by 2012, 60 percent of all children between the ages of 3 and 6 (not yet in kindergarten) were enrolled in a childcare center (see the 2016 report of the Federal Interagency Forum on Child and Family Statistics, available at http://www.childstats.gov).

The research in this area is somewhat mixed, but a major research project did find that early childcare placement has lasting effects on problem behavior, though the effects are very small (Vandell et al., 2010; also see Belsky et al., 2007). Specifically, the researchers found that children who had spent a lot of time in care tended to report slightly elevated levels of impulsivity and risk-taking behavior when they were teenagers. In this study, "risk-taking behavior" referred to such acts as theft, property damage, the use of a weapon, the use of drugs and alcohol, and not wearing a seat belt. These findings held even after the researchers took into account a range of other factors, such as the quality of parenting. Other research suggests that these adverse effects are less likely to be seen among children from disadvantaged backgrounds. For such children, spending a lot of time in childcare may help compensate for other disadvantages (Huston et al., 2015).

It is important to note, however, that the quality of childcare is also consequential. Placement in a high-quality childcare environment appears to protect children "against some of the adverse effects of spending a lot of time in care," though it does not eliminate these effects (McCartney et al., 2010:13; Vandell et al., 2010). For example, the effect of childcare on problem behavior is reduced when the childcare setting has a low child-to-caregiver ratio; that is, when caregivers are responsible for supervising a small versus a large group of children (McCartney et al., 2010). In contrast, in large group settings, there is greater potential for the child to be exposed to other children who are impulsive and aggressive, which could lead to the social learning of antisocial behavior (Huston et al., 2015; McCartney et al., 2010).

Moreover, exposure to high-quality care is associated with certain positive outcomes that extend into adolescence, including enhanced cognitive ability and academic achievement (Vandell et al., 2010). These positive outcomes may help offset some of the adverse effects of spending a lot of time in childcare. (Other researchers have found that participation in certain Head Start programs, which provide high-quality care for disadvantaged children, may reduce problem behavior [see Chapter 24]). **In short, the placement of children in childcare centers has the potential to produce some undesirable effects, but** it appears that these effects can be avoided or offset in centers that provide high-quality care in small-group settings.

Are Teenage Parents More Likely to Have Delinquent Children?

Recent estimates suggest that in the United States about one in ten adolescent females (11 percent) will give birth by her 20th birthday. In 2014, approximately 250,000 babies were born to mothers between the ages of 15 and 19, with the vast majority (89 percent) occurring outside marriage. The U.S. teen birthrate has declined steadily over the past two decades, although it remains high in comparison to other developed countries, such as Canada and the United Kingdom. In 1991, the U.S. rate was 61.8 births for every 1,000 adolescent females. By 2014, this rate had been cut by more than half, dropping to 24.2 births for every 1,000 adolescent females. This decline has been attributed to a combination of factors, including greater use of contraceptives by teens and an increase in the percentage of teens who refrain from having sexual intercourse (U.S. Department of Health and Human Services, 2016).

Nevertheless, **teenage mothers** are still a cause for concern. A study compared mothers who gave birth at age 17 and under to mothers who first gave birth at ages 20 or 21 (which, in the United States, is two to three years younger than the average age at first birth). Even after background factors like race/ethnicity and class were controlled, it was found that the teenage mothers obtained less education, had larger families, were more likely to be single parents, were more likely to live in poverty, and were more likely to obtain welfare or public assistance. Further, the children of these teenage mothers were more likely (1) to be born prematurely and low in birth weight (which increases the likelihood that they will develop traits like irritability and low self-control); (2) to be physically abused, neglected, or abandoned; (3) to be poorly supervised; (4) to have trouble in school; and (5) to become teenage mothers themselves (Maynard, 1997; Pogarsky et al., 2003). Given such findings, one might expect that the children of teenage mothers would be more delinquent. The data tend to suggest that this is the case, although **the effect of teenage motherhood on delinquency is moderate.**[4]

Teenage fathers have not received as much research attention as teenage mothers, although recent data suggest that **delinquents are much more likely than nondelinquents to become teenage fathers.** Further, research indicates that teenage fathers often increase rather than decrease their level of delinquency after their child is born (Thornberry et al., 2000; Tremblay et al., 2017). Various studies suggest that teen fathers often have a strong desire to contribute financially to the well-being of their children, but given their youth and lack of education and job skills, they face limited options for legal employment. As a result, some are attracted to drug dealing or other illegal sources of income (see Tremblay et al., 2017).

While the impact of teenage fathers on the delinquency of their children has not been well studied, **there is good reason to expect that teenage fathers increase the likelihood of delinquency.** On average, teenage fathers may be relatively immature and unable to cope with the demands associated with early fatherhood, as indicated by their increased propensity to engage in crime. As a result, they are likely to be poor role models for their children: "Their legacy to their children is likely to be one of socioeconomic disadvantage, poorer health, and poorer education, among other hardships" (Thornberry et al., 2000:7).

Are Juveniles from Large Families More Delinquent?

Data suggest that **juveniles from large families are slightly more likely to engage in delinquency,** even after variables like class are controlled.[5] The reasons for the relationship between family size and delinquency are not entirely clear, but some evidence suggests that the following factors may play a role. Parental supervision, for example, is less adequate in large families: there are more children to supervise, and sometimes as a consequence childrearing responsibilities are delegated to inexperienced siblings. Juveniles in large families tend to be less attached to school and do less well in school. Strain or tension may be higher in large families because of a number of factors: greater likelihood of over-crowding; the stretching of financial resources; and the competition among siblings for limited resources, such as material objects and attention or affection from parents. Finally, juveniles in large families are more likely to be exposed to delinquent siblings.

PARENTAL AND SIBLING CRIME/DEVIANCE
Are Juveniles with Criminal or Deviant Parents and Siblings More Likely to Be Delinquent?

The research on parental criminality and delinquency is easy to summarize: **juveniles with a criminal parent or parents are more likely to be delinquent.**[6] The likelihood is even greater if the parent has multiple convictions and if the convictions occurred after the juvenile was born. Also, juveniles with deviant parents (e.g., those with alcohol or drug problems or personality problems) are more likely to be delinquent. Having a criminal or deviant parent is a better predictor of delinquency than the family structure variables described earlier, but it is not as strongly related to delinquency as family quality and so-cialization variables, which are discussed next.

It is easy to think of reasons for the association of parental criminality and deviance with delinquency. One might draw on social learning theory and argue that criminal par-ents are more likely to model crime, to reinforce crime, and to teach values that favor crime. Limited data, however, suggest that this argument is too simplistic. Criminal parents seldom commit crimes with their children, and they usually disapprove of their children's crime.

Social learning theory, however, may still be of some relevance. While criminal par-ents may not model or directly encourage crime, they may model aggressive behavior and encourage their children to be tough and good fighters. Data also suggest that **control theory** at least partly explains the relationship between parental crime/deviance and de-linquency (Sampson and Laub, 1993a). Criminal/deviant parents are less likely to establish a strong emotional bond with their children, properly supervise their children, or use ef-fective disciplinary techniques. In particular, they are more likely to be erratic, threaten-ing, and harsh or punitive in their discipline. Further, the children of criminal/deviant parents perform less well in school. **Strain theory** may shed some light on the relationship as well, since criminal/deviant parents may be more likely to engage in abusive behaviors and get into conflicts with each other and with other family members. All these effects reflect the greater likelihood that criminal/deviant parents will lack the skills and traits necessary to be effective parents and spouses.

In addition, parental crime and deviance may increase delinquency for reasons re-lated to **labeling theory,** with the children of criminals being more likely to be viewed and treated as "bad." Finally, the effect of criminal/deviant parents on delinquency may be partly genetic (see McCord, 2001; D. Rowe and Farrington, 1997). That is, criminal/deviant parents may pass on a predisposition for traits conducive to delinquency (see Chapter 13).

Not only are juveniles with criminal parents more likely to be delinquent, but so are juveniles with **delinquent siblings.**[7] Since juveniles in the same family are exposed to simi-lar family influences, it is not surprising that siblings tend to exhibit similar levels of delin-quency. Data, however, suggest that this similarity is not simply a function of exposure to similar family influences. Delinquent siblings will often socialize one another in ways that increase the likelihood of crime; for example, they may provide models for delinquency, re-inforce delinquency, and teach beliefs favorable to delinquency. In addition, for many juve-niles, delinquent siblings are a source of verbal and physical abuse (Button and Gealt, 2010).

THE QUALITY OF FAMILY RELATIONSHIPS

Family structure and parental/sibling crime affect delinquency largely through their effects on family relationships—how well family members get along and the extent to which the juvenile is socialized for conformity versus deviance. In this section and the next, we describe family relationship variables related to delinquency. These variables tend to be more strongly related to delinquency than the family structure and parental/sibling crime variables just discussed. First, we consider the *quality of family relationships* and then parental socialization.

Are Juveniles Who Have Warm or Close Relationships with Their Parents Less Delinquent?

Much research suggests that delinquency is lower among juveniles who have a close or warm relationship with their parents. This closeness or warmth involves several related dimensions.[8]

Parental rejection of or indifference to the juvenile. Delinquency is lower when parents love their children and express this love through their actions. Such parents talk with their children, engage in pleasurable activities with them, express interest in them, and provide them with comfort and support. Parents who do not do these things—who reject or ignore their children—are more likely to have delinquent children. In fact, **parental rejection is one of the strongest family correlates of delinquency.** Parents who do not love their children and are unwilling to invest time and effort in them are unlikely either to earn their children's love or to effectively socialize them.

Attachment of juvenile to parents. Delinquency is lower when juveniles have a strong emotional bond or attachment to their parents. Attachment to parents is usually measured by asking juveniles how much they love and respect their parents, care about them, identify with and want to be like them, feel close to them, or engage in intimate communication with them. Not surprisingly, attachment to parents is closely related to parental rejection of the juvenile, although parental attachment and parental rejection are distinct concepts (see Sampson and Laub, 1993a). Data suggest that **attachment to parents is associated with lower delinquency, although the association is often modest.** Attachments to mother and father have similar effects, although individuals who are attached to two parents are lower in delinquency than those attached

to one (which partly explains why delinquency is higher among juveniles from single-parent homes; see Rankin and Kern, 1994).

Attachment may prevent delinquency for reasons related to control, social learning, and strain theories. Most notably, **attachment functions as a form of control.** Juveniles who are attached to their parents do not want to do anything to upset their parents. That is, they have a greater "stake in conformity." Further, juveniles who are attached to their parents will be more likely to model parental behavior, accept parental beliefs, and respond to parental sanctions. Among other things, this **reduces the likelihood that juveniles will fall under the influence of delinquent peers.** (It should be noted that while attachment to conventional parents reduces delinquency, attachment to criminal or deviant parents does not reduce delinquency and may even increase it; see Foshee and Bauman, 1992; Jensen and Brownfield, 1983.) Finally, **juveniles attached to their parents will likely find their home to be a less stressful place** (see Agnew, 2006a).

Family conflict. Parental rejection and parental attachment are closely related to, but distinct from, family conflict. Juveniles may reject and be rejected by their parents, but family conflict may nevertheless be low. Family members, for example, may ignore one another or spend little time together. Data suggest that **delinquency is lower in families with little conflict.** This includes conflict between spouses and between parents and juveniles. Such conflict may assume a number of forms: frequent quarreling, expressions of disapproval, nagging, scolding, threatening, and the like. Family conflict, of course, may be caused by the delinquent or troublesome behavior of the juvenile. Data, however, suggest that conflict also has a causal effect on delinquency. It may weaken the emotional bond between parents and the juvenile, disrupt efforts to socialize the juvenile, expose the juvenile to aggressive models and beliefs, increase the likelihood of association with delinquent peers, and increase the level of strain to which the juvenile is subject.

Child abuse. The quality of family relationships may deteriorate to the point that a child is being abused. Researchers have examined the impact of several types of *child abuse* on delinquency, especially physical abuse, sexual abuse, and neglect (the failure to provide adequate food, shelter, medical care, and affection/attention).[9] There were about 702,000 substantiated cases of abuse in the United States in 2014, representing a rate of 9.4 per 1,000 children. Seventeen percent of these cases involved physical abuse, 8 percent sexual abuse, 75 percent neglect, 6 percent emotional abuse, and 7 percent other types of abuse—like abandonment and parental drug addiction. (Note: Percentages do not add up to 100 because some children experienced more than one type of abuse; see the Child Welfare Information Gateway at http://childwelfare.gov.)

It is widely acknowledged that most cases of abuse are not detected by the authorities. Researchers have tried to estimate the full extent of abuse by surveying parents, juveniles, and community professionals such as doctors and school officials. One of the best surveys in this area focused on a nationally representative sample of 2,030 children ages 2 to 17 (Finkelhor et al., 2005). The researchers interviewed the children if they were 10 to 17 years old; otherwise they interviewed the caregiver most familiar with each child. Interviews were conducted between December 2002 and February 2003. According to the findings of this survey, more than 2 out of every 10 juveniles had been abused by family members during the previous year (a rate of 209 per 1,000). The most common form of abuse was psychological or emotional abuse, which includes name-calling and denigration (144 per 1,000). The rate of physical abuse was 56 per 1,000, or 12 per 1,000 if we focus on instances of physical abuse where the child showed evidence of physical harm (e.g., bruising). The rate of neglect was 29 per 1,000, and the rate of sexual abuse was about 2 per 1,000. (Note: Children are most likely to be sexually abused by acquaintances.)

Early studies on the relationship between child abuse and delinquency suffered from a number of methodological problems, such as the use of small, nonrepresentative samples, cross-sectional designs, and questionable measures of both abuse and delinquency. There is some indication that these studies may have exaggerated the effect of abuse on delinquency, leading many people to conclude that abuse is a very strong predictor of delinquency. More recent studies, however, have begun to overcome such problems. These studies suggest that **abuse increases the likelihood of delinquency by a moderate amount.**

The effect of abuse on delinquency is readily explained by the leading delinquency theories. Abuse is a major type of **strain,** and a child may turn to delinquency in an effort to end or reduce the abuse (e.g., running away from home, assaulting the abuser); to seek revenge against the abuser or related targets; or to manage the negative feelings that result from abuse (perhaps through drug use). A **social learning** theorist would argue that abuse increases the likelihood of delinquency, since it implicitly teaches the child that violence is an appropriate way to deal with problems. Abuse may also drive the child to run away from parents and increase the likelihood of association with delinquent peers (see Chapple, Tyler, and Bersani, 2005). A **control** theorist would argue that abuse decreases all four types of control. Abused juveniles may avoid parents, reducing direct control; they may reduce their emotional bond to parents, reducing stake in conformity; and they may also experience problems at school, further reducing stake in conformity (see Zingraff et al., 1994). In addition, abuse may reduce the effectiveness of parents in transmitting antidelinquent beliefs and in instilling self-control. Finally, parents who abuse their children are implicitly or explicitly **labeling** the children as "bad." Brezina (1998) found evidence for many of these effects.

It is important to emphasize, however, that most abused individuals do not become serious delinquents. It appears that many children are able to escape at least some of the negative consequences of abuse. Researchers are now investigating this topic. For example, abuse is less likely to lead to delinquency among those who do well in school and receive social support from others.[10]

PARENTAL SOCIALIZATION

While it is important for parents to establish warm or close relationships with their children, it is also important for them to teach their children to engage in conventional behavior and avoid delinquency. We discussed some of the steps parents must take in this area in Chapters 7 and 8, where we described social learning and control theories. As a consequence, parts of this discussion will be familiar to you.

What Should Parents Do to Teach Their Children to Avoid Delinquency?

Provide clear rules for behavior. Parents must provide their children with a clear set of rules **that specify what behaviors are unacceptable and restrict opportunities to engage in deviance.** Such rules, for example, may specify who the children can and cannot associate with, where they can and cannot go, and what time they should be home at night. As indicated in Chapter 8, such rules should not be overly strict. Overly strict rules may increase delinquency, perhaps for reasons related to strain theory.

Monitor the juvenile's behavior. Parents must monitor their children's behavior to ensure compliance with the rules the parents have set down. Monitoring may be **direct or indirect.** Direct monitoring consists of direct parental observation of the juvenile. Indirect monitoring may involve talking to the juvenile regularly about his or her activities, talking with the juvenile's teachers and others, and keeping track of what the juvenile is doing—including how well he or she does schoolwork and the character of the juvenile's friends. Patterson et al. (1992:63) state that the "parents of antisocial children have little information about where their children are, who they are with, what they are doing, or when they will be home."

Consistently sanction the juvenile for rule violations. Such sanctions should **not be too harsh or punitive.** In particular, some evidence suggests that parents' verbal abuse and physical punishment may increase their children's delinquency (see Chapter 8). Recommended sanctions include the loss of privileges, the imposition of chores, clear expressions of disapproval, reasoning, and—for younger children—time out.

These parental actions not only provide direct control over the juvenile, they also increase the juvenile's level of internal control. They lead to the internalization of beliefs that condemn delinquency. When rule violations are consistently followed by sanctions, the juvenile soon becomes anxious or nervous at the thought of doing something wrong, which means that the rules have been "internalized," or the juvenile has developed a "conscience." These actions also cause the juvenile to acquire some measure of self-control (see Chapter 8). Data indicate that delinquency is lower in families where parents take these actions; in fact, they are among the most important family variables.[11]

Employ effective techniques for resolving problems/crises. All families occasionally confront problems that threaten to disrupt members' relations with one another. It is important for family members to develop effective techniques for resolving these problems. Otherwise, such problems may interfere with the ability of parents to effectively socialize their children and may increase the level of strain or stress in family members. Families with delinquent children are more likely to employ poor problem-solving techniques: family members tend to blame one another when problems arise, they get angry and argue with one another, and they spend less time trying to define the problem and evaluate solutions as to their likely effectiveness.

The following model for effective problem solving has been suggested:

(1) The problem should be clearly stated in neutral terms; (2) the other person paraphrases to show that he or she has heard the problem correctly; (3) brainstorm a list of possible solutions; (4) choose a solution through a process of negotiation (compromise), and write a contract that describes the terms of the agreement, the positive consequences for following the agreement, and the negative consequences for violating it. (Patterson et al., 1992:78)

Data on the relationship between delinquency and family problem-solving techniques are sparse, but limited data suggest a weak relationship (see Patterson et al., 1992).

Disciplinary styles. Data from Patterson and his associates suggest that the families of delinquent children frequently fall into one of **two types.** In the first type, **supervision and discipline are** *lax.* Parents do not define many objectionable acts as deviant, they do not closely monitor the juvenile, and they seldom punish deviant/delinquent acts (see Box 14.1).

Box 14.1   Are Parents Becoming Too Permissive?

In previous decades, family researchers were mostly concerned with the effects on child development of cold, harsh, "authoritarian" parenting styles. This authoritarian style is illustrated by the experience of Evan, a troubled 11-year-old boy who was exposed to his stepfather's frequent yelling, shouting, and screaming. When Evan misbehaves, he is slapped, is told that his "insubordination" is going to get him "a hook

(Continued)

(Continued)

upside the head," and is forced to spend long periods of time in his room alone. Evan's stepfather demands obedience and responds harshly to rule violations; rarely does he show warmth or affection toward the boy. He refuses to hug Evan, believing that Evan should learn to "be a man" and that "real men" do not show physical affection for each other (see the documentary titled, "The Trouble with Evan" [Filmakers Library, 1994]).

The concerns that family researchers have expressed about authoritarian parenting are warranted, as a link between this style of parenting and adolescent problem behavior has long been established (Hoeve et al., 2009). But the authoritarian style may be less common among today's parents. As Ronald Simons and his colleagues observe, the lax or permissive style of parenting may play a larger role in the overall delinquency problem: "Increasingly, the problem is not harsh disciplinarians who lack warmth, but indulgent parents who fail to exercise control" (Simons et al., 2004:172). They cite recent survey data showing that lax or permissive parents outnumber authoritarian parents.

Though some permissive parents are emotionally cold, many are motivated by a misplaced desire to be their child's "friend." For this reason, they are reluctant to set firm rules, confront misbehavior, and administer punishment for fear of upsetting the child and risking the parent–child relationship. Children need more than parental warmth and support, however. They need to learn patience and self-control, and to be considerate of the needs and feelings of others. Indeed, permissive parenting places children at risk for problem behavior and contributes to the development of selfish and inconsiderate individuals, who are likely to have relationship problems of their own as they grow older (Church et al., 2015; Simons et al., 2004).

Moreover, some family researchers believe that permissive parenting styles are especially detrimental in today's society. In the past, children with permissive parents may have been protected from its adverse effects because they were provided with structure and effective discipline in the school, church, or surrounding neighborhood. But this may no longer be the case. These other institutions have weakened over time and have lost the ability to compensate for inept parenting (Simons et al., 2004).

The preceding observations lend a bit of support to popular claims that permissive parenting has become rampant and that "the problem with kids today is that they lack effective discipline." Unfortunately, these claims are sometimes followed by the recommendation that parents return to harsh physical punishment and the more authoritarian parenting styles of the past—a recommendation that is *not* supported by research on child development. Instead, family researchers recommend a third parenting style that balances the emotional needs of the child with the importance of establishing and enforcing clear rules and limits. This balanced approach (discussed later in the chapter) can be described as a warm-but-firm "authoritative" style of parenting. Unlike the other parenting styles described here, it is associated with healthy emotional development and prosocial behavior (Hoeve et al., 2009).

Questions for Discussion

1. Assume that Evan has children of his own when he grows up. What do you think he has learned about parenting from his stepfather? Do you think it is likely he will use a different style of parenting with his own children? Or is it more likely that he will adopt the same authoritarian approach? Why?
2. The host of the popular talk show *Dr. Phil* frequently describes permissive, overindulgent parenting as "one of the most insidious and destructive forms of child abuse" (Phillip McGraw, quoted in Simons et al., 2004:173). What do you think of Dr. Phil's comments? Is it fair to compare permissive parenting to child maltreatment? Why or why not?

In the second type, **parents frequently punish or threaten to punish, but the punishment is ineffective because it is inconsistently applied.** In particular, parents engage in what Patterson (1982) calls *nattering*. They are quick to condemn even the most trivial deviant acts, and they regularly nag, scold, lecture, and issue commands to the juvenile. Occasionally, they may "explode" and physically abuse the juvenile. On most occasions, however, the parents fail to back up their verbal reprimands with meaningful, nonviolent punishments. In the words of Patterson (1982:225), "They tend to natter, but they do not confront. They do not say, 'No.' They do not say, 'Stop that behavior here and now.' " So the parents complain a lot about the child's behavior, but the child is only occasionally punished for his or her misdeeds.

Often, a negative pattern of interaction develops between family members. Parents treat the child in an aversive way—for example, by threatening or scolding. The child responds by arguing or threatening. The situation escalates, with the parent and child threatening and insulting each other in a series of responses. Eventually, one of the family members— often a parent—backs down. The parent's backing down serves to negatively reinforce the juvenile's aversive behavior. In certain cases, the juvenile's aversive behavior may be positively reinforced, often by attention from the parents. The juvenile's aggressive behavior, then, is inconsistently punished and frequently reinforced. Constant battles between family members have other negative effects. They reduce the emotional bonds between parent and child and the amount of time that family members spend interacting. This decrease in emotional bonds and interaction further reduces parents' control and makes it more difficult for them to effectively socialize the child. Antagonism among family members also creates a high level of strain and anger, which further increases the likelihood of aggression and delinquency.

What Should Parents Do to Teach Their Children to Engage in Conventional Behavior?

The socialization process has two sides. Parents not only need to teach their children to refrain from delinquency; they also need to teach them how to engage in conventional behavior. In particular, parents **need to teach their children social, academic, and problem-solving skills.** Juveniles need these skills if they are to do well in school, become involved in conventional peer groups, and resolve any problems that arise with other people in a nondelinquent manner. The failure to teach such skills may result in school failure, rejection by conventional peers, and association with delinquent peers.[12]

Such skills are taught in several ways. Parents provide direct instruction (e.g., teaching children the alphabet, telling juveniles what they should do if they get into a dispute with a friend). Parents model these skills; for example, parents may model effective problem-solving skills when disputes arise among family members. Parents provide opportunities for juveniles to practice these skills; the parents should choose such opportunities so juveniles have a reasonable chance of successfully exhibiting the skill. And parents reinforce juveniles when they successfully employ these skills.

At the same time, juveniles often face problems or demands they are unequipped to handle. In such cases, it is **important for parents to provide support and assistance.** Support may assume several forms: emotional support, in which parents comfort or reassure the juvenile; informational support, in which parents provide advice on what to do or help clarify issues; and instrumental support, in which parents provide the juvenile with money, goods, or direct assistance. In some cases, parents may have to act on behalf of their children, functioning as their advocates (see especially J. P. Wright and Cullen, 2001).

The activities described in the preceding paragraphs are sometimes referred to as "positive parenting." There has not been much research on the relationship between these activities and delinquency, but limited data suggest that their absence is associated with delinquency. For example, data suggest that the parents of delinquent children are less likely to reinforce conventional behavior and provide social support.[13]

Summary

Most people believe that the family has a major impact on delinquency. The data suggest that they are right in this belief. Many people, however, are misinformed about what aspects of the family are most strongly related to delinquency. They believe, for example, that delinquency is caused by mothers who work or by parents who do not spank their children. The data suggest that these arguments are wrong.

We considered four sets of family variables: those having to do with family structure, parental and sibling crime, the quality of family relationships, and *parental socialization*. Certain variables, like a mother's employment, appear to have little or no effect on delinquency. Other variables have a small to moderate effect on delinquency, such as single-parent homes, placement in childcare, teenage parents, and family size. Still other variables have a moderate effect on delinquency: parental and sibling crime, attachment of juvenile to parent, family conflict, and child abuse. The most important family variables are **parental rejection of the child** and **the nature of parental efforts to socialize the child against delinquency.** The effect of other variables, such as parental efforts to teach the child conforming behavior, are less clear.

Data suggest that our ability to explain delinquency is substantially improved when we consider several family variables together.[14] In particular, data suggest that delinquency is least likely when the quality of family relationships is good and parents attempt to socialize children against delinquency (by setting clear rules, monitoring behavior, and consistently sanctioning deviance). In this style of parenting, sometimes called *warm and authoritative* (or warm but firm), parents have a warm or close relationship with their children, but at the same time they have clear rules, which they consistently enforce. **Delinquency is most common among the children of parents who employ warm and lax and cold and lax styles of parenting.**[15]

There is some evidence that family variables are more important during childhood and early adolescence than during mid- to late adolescence.[16] As children develop, they become more autonomous from parents and more subject to peer and community influences. Also, a person's predisposition to delinquency often forms early in life (Patterson et al., 1992:22–27). Once it is formed, the family may come to exercise less influence over the juvenile.

We explained the effect of family variables on delinquency by using strain, social learning, control, and labeling theories. In most cases, several of these theories can be used to explain the effect of a particular family variable. One can argue, for example, that abuse increases juveniles' level of strain, reduces their level of control (e.g., attachment to parents), teaches them to engage in aggression (e.g., models aggression), and labels them as "bad." As you read the following chapters, you will notice that the impact of most variables on delinquency can usually be explained by most or all of the leading delinquency theories. We return to this point in Chapter 18, where we present a general or integrated theory of delinquency.

WHY DO SOME PARENTS EMPLOY POOR PARENTING PRACTICES?

Several related explanations for poor parenting practices can be given. First, some parents **lack the traits necessary to be successful parents.** For example, parents who are irritable and low in self-control are likely to be quick to anger, and they will tend to employ harsh disciplinary techniques and show little affection or concern for their children. This may partly explain why criminal parents are more likely to be poor parents, since criminal parents are more likely to have traits conducive to crime.[17]

Second, some parents **lack the knowledge to be effective parents.** Perhaps they never experienced good parenting when they were children, so they do not know how to be good parents themselves. In this area, Patterson (1986) found that the poor disciplinary practices of grandparents were associated with the antisocial behavior of both their children and their grandchildren. Some evidence suggests that the grandparents failed to teach their children effective disciplinary techniques, and this partly accounts for the antisocial behavior of the grandchildren (Patterson et al., 1992; also see Thornberry, Freeman-Gallant, et al. [with Smith], 2003). Also, family-training programs that teach parents good parenting skills have shown signs of success. That is, parents enrolled in such programs are often able to reduce the delinquency of their children. (Chapter 24 contains more information on such programs.)

Third, some parents have **"difficult" children,** who possess traits like irritability and low self-control. Children with such traits can challenge even the best of parents. The parents of irritable and impulsive children may come to dislike their "difficult" children and may even stop trying to "parent" them in an effort to avoid conflict and gain some measure of peace. Data suggest that difficult children do have an adverse effect on parenting practices.[18] Further, since traits like irritability and low self-control are inherited to some extent, difficult children are more likely to have parents who are ill equipped to care for them. The most demanding children, then, tend to be matched with the least able parents.

Fourth, many parents may experience **strains or stressors that make it difficult for them to employ good parenting practices.** In this area, poor parenting practices have been linked to low socioeconomic status, unemployment, residence in deprived communities, drug and alcohol use, divorce, teenage motherhood, large family size, and family violence.[19] Also, an observational study revealed that mothers were more likely to engage in poor parenting practices on days when they experienced high stress (Patterson et al., 1989).

Many of these risk factors often converge, and poor parenting appears to be most likely when **unskilled parents facing numerous stressors attempt to raise difficult children.**

A Note on Genes, Parenting, and Delinquency

As we just described, traits like irritability and low self-control are partly inherited, so children with these traits are more likely to have parents who also are irritable and low in self-control. As a result, researchers have wondered whether the "true cause" of delinquency has more to do with the genes that delinquent children share with their parents than with the actual effects of poor parenting. In other words, these shared genes may be the ultimate cause of delinquency, instead of parenting per se.

A growing number of studies on parenting and child problem behavior are estimating the effects of both parenting and genetic factors. These genetically informed studies allow us to gauge the effects of poor parenting after genetic factors are taken into account. Although the studies focus on a variety of outcomes and sometimes produce conflicting results, we attempt to summarize this body of research by highlighting three general (tentative) conclusions. First, there is evidence that part of the association between poor parenting and problem behavior in children is due to genetic factors. For example, children possessing genetically driven tendencies (difficult temperament) sometimes provoke negative reactions from their parents, such as feeling angry and frustrated with the child and wishing the child would go away (Larsson et al., 2008). Second, key studies in this area find that **poor parenting still increases the risk of child problem behavior even when genetic influences are controlled.** So genetic factors do not completely account for the relationship between poor parenting and delinquency. Related to this point, we can note that family-based environmental interventions—such as parent-training programs—have shown promise, reducing the risk of child antisocial behavior and later offending (Piquero et al., 2009). Third, studies in this area, especially molecular genetic studies, are showing that the effects of parenting and genes are intertwined and that genetic factors may influence how children react to parenting. Children with certain genetic endowments, for example, appear especially vulnerable to the effects of poor parenting and are more likely than other children to respond with delinquency. Future research in this area may help us better understand when, and for whom, poor parenting is most likely to lead to delinquent behavior. (For a review of genetic research as it relates to parenting and delinquency, see Simons et al., 2012; for more on the relationship between genes and delinquency, see Chapter 13.)

TEACHING AIDS

Exercise: Putting Your Knowledge to Use

Almost all parents have days when they wonder whether their child might turn out to be delinquent. Parents are often eager to know what they can do to prevent this. In fact, if you encounter any parents who discover that you have had a course in juvenile delinquency, they may well ask you what they should do to prevent their children from becoming delinquent. (Or perhaps you are already a parent, or will be in the near future, and are wondering about the best way to raise your child.) **Draw on the materials in this chapter and put together a brief manual for parents on "How to Prevent Your Child from Becoming a Delinquent."**

The manual should list the things parents should and should not do if they want to prevent their children from becoming delinquents. Further, the manual should provide examples of what parents should and should not do. For example, if you advise parents to avoid sanctions that are overly harsh or punitive, be sure to give examples of appropriate and inappropriate sanctions. Finally, be prepared to justify the advice you give by drawing on the leading delinquency theories. People are more likely to accept your advice if you present a good justification for it.

Web-Based Exercise: An Inside Look at a Troubled Family

This chapter discussed a range of family factors that contribute to delinquency; we brought up family structure, parental and sibling crime/deviance, the quality of family relationships, and parental socialization. The chapter also described why some parents employ poor parenting practices. This web-based exercise asks you to apply the materials in this chapter to a troubled family. Visit YouTube, and watch the video titled "The Trouble with Evan." This amazing and disturbing video provides an inside look at Evan's family life over a period of several months. Evan regularly gets in trouble with his parents, school officials, and the police. Drawing on this chapter and other chapters that are relevant, including the chapters on the theories of delinquency, answer the following questions: Why did Evan get into so much trouble? Why did Evan's parents employ such poor parenting practices?

TEST YOUR KNOWLEDGE OF THIS CHAPTER

1. List and briefly describe the four major aspects of family life covered in this chapter. Which aspects of family life have the greatest effect on delinquency?

2. Briefly describe the relationship between delinquency and (a) single-parent homes, (b) the mother's employment outside the home, (c) childcare, (d) teenage parenthood, and (e) family size. Explain the relationship between delinquency and any two of these factors using strain, control, social learning, and labeling theory (if applicable).

3. Describe recent trends in family life (regarding single-parent homes, teenage parenthood, and mother's employment), and discuss their possible impact on levels of delinquency.

4. Juveniles with criminal parents and siblings are more likely to engage in delinquency. Drawing on the leading delinquency theories, describe why this might be the case.

5. The quality of family relationships includes several dimensions. List these dimensions and briefly describe their relationship to delinquency.

6. Drawing on the leading delinquency theories, explain why child abuse increases the likelihood of delinquency.

7. What major steps must parents take to teach their child to avoid delinquency?

8. What are the two major disciplinary styles that increase the likelihood of delinquency?

9. What should parents do to teach their children to engage in conventional behavior?

10. Briefly describe the warm and authoritative style of parenting that is said to be most effective in preventing delinquency.

11. What are the major reasons for some parents' use of poor parenting practices?

THOUGHT AND DISCUSSION QUESTIONS

1. Suppose you are a researcher investigating the effect of family factors on delinquency. Develop a survey with questions measuring the various dimensions of family life described in this chapter, with at least one question per dimension (e.g., at least one question measuring parental rejection, one on attachment of juveniles to parents, another on parental monitoring, etc.).

2. The effect of a given family factor on delinquency is often explained by using several theories (e.g., the effect of child abuse on delinquency may be explained using all the leading delinquency theories). How might researchers go about determining which of these explanations is correct (or whether all are correct)? For example, how might researchers go about determining whether child abuse affects delinquency for reasons related to strain, control, social learning, and/or labeling theories? (For examples, see Agnew, 1995a; Brezina, 1998.)

3. Drawing on the arguments in this chapter, recommend policies or programs to reduce delinquency (see Chapter 24 for a discussion of delinquency control and prevention programs focusing on the family).

KEY TERMS

- Quality of family relationships
- Child abuse
- Lax and nattering disciplinary styles
- Parental socialization
- Warm but authoritative style of parenting

ENDNOTES

1. For overviews and selected studies on "broken homes" and delinquency, see Apel and Kaukinen, 2008; Chng et al., 2016; Demuth and Brown, 2004; Eitle, 2006; Farrington, 1996a, 1996b, 2002a; Gove and Crutchfield, 1982; Henggeler, 1989; Hirschi, 1995; Hollin, 1992; R. Johnson, 1986; Kierkus and Hewitt, 2009; Loeber, Farrington, Stouthamer-Loeber, and Van Kammen, 1998; Loeber and Stouthamer-Loeber, 1986; Matsueda and Heimer, 1987; McNulty and Bellair, 2003; Nye, 1958; Rankin, 1983; Rankin and Wells, '1994; Rebellon, 2002; Rosen, 1985; Rutter et al., 1998; Sampson and Laub, 1993a; Simons et al., 1993; Theobald et al., 2013; Thornberry et al., 1999; Wells and Rankin, 1991; J. Wilson and Herrnstein, 1985; K. Wright and Wright, 1995.

2. See Demuth and Brown, 2004; Eitle, 2006; Farrington, 2002a; Jang and Smith, 1997; Matsueda and Heimer, 1987; Rankin and Kern, 1994; Rankin and Wells, 1994; Rebellon, 2002; Rutter et al., 1998; Sampson and Laub, 1993a; Simons et al., 2007; Simons et al., 2004; J. Snyder and Patterson, 1987; Van Voorhis et al., 1988.

3. See Farrington, 1995; Loeber and Stouthamer-Loeber, 1986; Vander Ven and Cullen, 2004; Vander Ven et. al., 2001; Wells and Rankin, 1988; K. Wright and Wright, 1995.

4. See Barnes and Morris, 2012; Farrington and Welsh, 2007; Furstenberg et al., 1987; Grogger, 1997; Loeber, Farrington, Stouthamer-Loeber, and Van Kammen, 1998; Maynard and Garry, 1997; K. Moore et al., 1997; Pogarsky et al., 2003; Rutter et al., 1998; Vugt et al., 2016.

5. See Farrington, 1995, 1996a, 2002a; Farrington and Welsh, 2007; Fischer, 1984; Hirschi, 1995; Hollin, 1992; Kierkus and Hewitt, 2009; Loeber and Stouthamer-Loeber, 1986; Patterson et al., 1992; Rutter et al., 1998; Sampson and Laub, 1993a; Tygart, 1991; Wells and Rankin, 1988.

6. For overviews and recent research in this area, see Canter, 1982; Farrington, 1995, 1996a, 1996b, 2002a; Farrington and Welsh, 2007; Henggeler, 1989; Loeber and Stouthamer-Loeber, 1986; Rowe and Farrington, 1997; Rutter and Giller, 1983; Sampson and Laub, 1993a; Snyder and Patterson, 1987; Wilson and Herrnstein, 1985; K. Wright and Wright, 1995; Wu and Kandel, 1995.

7. See Farrington, 1995; Haynie and McHugh, 2003; Hollin, 1992; Loeber and Stouthamer-Loeber, 1986; Rowe and Farrington, 1997; Rowe and Gulley, 1992; Stormshak et al., 2004; also see Button and Gealt, 2010; Sampson and Laub, 1993a.

8. For overviews and recent studies in this area, see Barfield-Cottledge, 2015; Burton et al., 1995; Canter, 1982; Cernkovich and Giordano, 1987; Conger et al., 1992, 1994; Farrington and Welsh, 2007; G. Fox and Benson, 2000; Gove and Crutchfield, 1982; Hay et al., 2006; Henggeler, 1989; Hoeve et al., 2009, 2012; Hollin, 1992; Jang and Smith, 1997; Loeber and Stouthamer-Loeber, 1986; Longshore et al., 2005; Matsueda and Heimer, 1987; McCord, 1991; McNulty and Bellair, 2003; Nye, 1958; Rankin and Kern, 1994; Rankin and Wells, 1990; Rosen, 1985; Sampson and Laub, 1993a; Simons et al., 2007, 2012, Simons et al., 2004; J. Snyder and Patterson, 1987; Thaxton and Agnew, 2004; Wells and Rankin, 1988; Wilson and Herrnstein, 1985; K. Wright and Wright, 1995.

9. For overviews and recent studies, see Chapple, Tyler, and Bersani, 2005; Farrington, 2002a; Farrington and Welsh, 2007; Finkelhor and Hashima, 2001; G. Fox and Benson, 2000; Hirschi, 1995; Ireland et al., 2002; Rebellon and Van Gundy, 2005; Rutter et al., 1998; J. Siegel and Williams, 2002; Simons et al., 2007; Simons et al., 2004; C, Smith and Thornberry, 1995; Thornberry, Krohn et al. (with Porter), 2003; H. Wallace, 2005; Widom, 1989, 1997, 2001; Wilson and Herrnstein, 1985; K. Wright and Wright, 1995; Zingraff et al., 1994; Zingraff et al., 1993.

10. See references cited in note 9.

11. For overviews and selected studies, see Barnes et al., 2006; Burton et al., 1995; Cernkovich and Giordano, 1987; Conger et al., 1995; Cullen et al., 2008; Farrington, 1996a, 1996b, 2002a; Farrington and Welsh, 2007; G. Fox and Benson, 2000; Gove and Crutchfield, 1982; Hay, 2001a; Hay et al., 2006; Henggeler, 1989; Hirschi, 1995; Hoeve et al., 2009; Hollin, 1992; Jang and Smith, 1997; Loeber, Farrington, Stouthamer-Loeber, and Van Kammen, 1998; Loeber and Stouthamer-Loeber, 1986; Matsueda and Heimer, 1987; McCord, 1991; Nye, 1958; Patterson, 1982; 1986; Patterson et al., 1989; Patterson et al., 1992; Rankin and Wells, 1990; Sampson

and Laub, 1993a; Simons et al., 2007; Simons et al., 2004; J. Snyder and Patterson, 1987; Tanner-Smith et al., 2013; Unnever et al., 2003; Wells and Rankin, 1988; K. Wright and Wright, 1995.

12. See Barnes et al., 2006; Patterson, 1982; Patterson et al., 1989; Patterson et al., 1992; J. Snyder and Patterson, 1987.

13. See Cullen's 1994 discussion of social support and crime; Burt et al., 2006; Catalano and Hawkins, 1996; DuBow and Reid, 1994; Hay et al., 2006; Hoeve et al., 2009; Nye, 1958; J. P. Wright and Cullen, 2001; and the work of Patterson and associates cited earlier.

14. See Hay et al., 2006; Loeber and Stouthamer-Loeber, 1986; J. Snyder and Patterson, 1987; K. Wright and Wright, 1995.

15. For a fuller discussion, see Burt et al., 2006; Farrington and Welsh, 2007; Hay, 2001a; Hay and Forrest, 2006; Henggeler, 1989; Hoeve et al., 2009; Loeber and Stouthamer-Loeber, 1986; McCord, 1991; Simons et al., 2005; J. Snyder and Patterson, 1987; Stewart and Simons, 2006; Wilson and Herrnstein, 1985.

16. See Agnew, 1985b; Jang, 1999; Jang and Smith, 1997; Loeber and Stouthamer-Loeber, 1986; Sampson and Laub, 1993a; Thornberry, 1987, 1996; Thornberry et al., 1991, 1999; Thornberry, Krohn et al. (with Porter), 2003.

17. See Patterson et al., 1992; Rutter et al., 1998; Sampson and Laub, 1993a; Snyder and Patterson, 1987; Thornberry, Freeman-Gallant et al., 2003.

18. See Jang and Smith, 1997; Moffitt, 1997; Patterson, 1982; Rutter, 1985; Rutter et al., 1998; Sampson and Laub, 1993a; Thornberry and Krohn, 2005; Wilson and Herrnstein, 1985.

19. See Conger et al., 1992; Conger et al., 1994; Conger et al., 1995; Kaufman, 2005; Larzelere and Patterson, 1990; McNulty and Bellair, 2003; K. Moore et al., 1997; Patterson, 1982, 1986; Patterson et al., 1989; Patterson et al., 1992; Pratt et al., 2004; Rutter et al., 1998; Sampson and Laub, 1993a; Simons et al., 1993; Simons et al., 2004; Simons et al., 2005; Simons et al., 2007; J. Snyder and Patterson, 1987; Thornberry Freeman-Gallant et al., 2003; Tygart, 1991.

15 The School

What Impact Does the School Have on Delinquency?

Schools may contribute to delinquency for reasons related to all the major delinquency theories. Many juveniles do poorly in school and come to dislike or even hate school. School then becomes a source of strain for them it exercises little control over them and provides a context for associating with other dissatisfied, often delinquent, juveniles. Further, school officials may view and treat many juveniles as "bad," particularly those who have trouble adjusting to school routines and are in tracks for "problem" students.

We first discuss school experiences that may contribute to a juvenile's delinquency, including low grades, little involvement in school activities, poor relations with teachers, negative attitudes toward school, low educational and occupational goals, and dropping out of school. As indicated later, there is little dispute that these experiences are **associated** with delinquency. But there is some dispute over the extent to which these experiences **cause** delinquency. Some researchers argue that the association between these school experiences and delinquency is due to third variables and to the causal effect of delinquency on negative school experiences. Others disagree, asserting that such school experiences do have a causal effect on delinquency.

We then examine the extent to which school characteristics, like school size and disciplinary practices, influence levels of delinquency—particularly levels of in-school delinquency. We begin by discussing the amount of delinquency in schools, a topic that has attracted much attention in recent years as a result of several well-publicized school shootings. We then describe the characteristics of those schools with low levels of delinquency.

After reading this chapter, you should be able to:

- Describe the types of school experiences associated with delinquency.
- Explain the association between school experiences and delinquency.
- Indicate why some juveniles have negative school experiences.
- Discuss the types and amounts of delinquency occurring at school.
- Identify three dimensions of bullying and describe the negative consequences of bullying.
- Describe community and student characteristics associated with high rates of in-school delinquency.
- List and explain the characteristics of "effective" schools (i.e., schools that have low delinquency rates).
- Draw on the major theories of delinquency to explain the impact of these school characteristics on delinquent behavior.

WHAT SCHOOL EXPERIENCES CONTRIBUTE TO DELINQUENCY?

Delinquency is **associated** with a range of school experiences, including the following.[1]

1. *Low academic performance.* Delinquents are more likely than nondelinquents to have lower grades and lower scores on tests measuring academic achievement; they are also more likely to be in special education classes or on noncollege tracks, and to be held back. One overview of the research in this area concluded that children with poor academic records (grades of F or D) were about twice as likely to engage in delinquency as children with good academic records (grades of C or above; Maguin and Loeber, 1996).

2. *Little school involvement.* Delinquents are less likely to participate in school activities; in particular, they spend less time on homework and are less involved in extracurricular activities (see Agnew and Petersen, 1989; Osgood et al., 1996).

3. *Low attachment to school.* Delinquents are more likely to dislike school and to feel that school is irrelevant to them. For example, they are more likely to state that they do not like school, that they resent the restrictions at school, that school is boring and a waste of time, and that they would rather be elsewhere.

4. *Poor relationships with teachers.* Delinquents are more likely to report that they dislike their teachers and have unpleasant relationships with them. For example, they are more likely to state that their teachers often lose their tempers, make negative comments, and talk down to students (see Agnew, 1985a).

5. *Low educational/occupational goals.* Delinquents have lower educational and occupational goals. For example, they desire less education than nondelinquents and they expect to receive less education.

6. *Dropping out of school.* Delinquents are more likely to drop out of school.

7. *School misbehavior.* Finally, delinquents are more likely to violate school rules. In particular, they are more likely to cut classes, to be truant from school, and to violate other rules.

Jay MacLeod's classic study of a delinquent group (the "Hallway Hangers") in a Boston public housing project provides a nice illustration of the school experiences of delinquents. In the words of MacLeod (1995:77):

> The Hallway Hangers' attitudes toward the educational system can be summed up in Stoney's words: "Fuck school. I hate fucking school." Most of the Hallway Hangers have dropped out. While officially enrolled, most spent little time in school anyway, preferring the fun, companionship, and drugs at Pop's [a local hangout]. When in class, they generally were disruptive and undisciplined. None of the Hallway Hangers participated in any extracurricular activities. By their own accounts, they were high or drunk much of the time they spent in school . . . they all switched or were switched into different classes, some spiraling down through the array of alternative programs at amazing speed, landing in the last stop on the line. Some stayed there, most dropped out altogether.

Do School Experiences Cause Delinquency?

The association between the school experiences just described and delinquency is often modest, but few criminologists would dispute that it exists. What is in dispute, however, is the meaning of this association.[2] Some researchers suggest that school experiences have little causal effect on delinquency. The association between school experiences and delinquency is said to occur because **both school experiences and delinquency are caused by the same third variables,** in particular, by early family experiences and individual traits like low intelligence and low self-control. This argument has some support. Data suggest that early family experiences and individual traits have a causal effect on both school experiences and delinquency; there is also some evidence that when family experiences and traits are taken into account, the association between school experiences and delinquency is reduced and, in some studies, eliminated.[3] Further, some researchers argue that **delinquency may cause negative school experiences,** which would also help explain the associations just reported. The data also provide some support for this position.[4] So the association between school experiences and delinquency does not necessarily mean that school experiences cause delinquency. Rather, school experiences and delinquency may be caused by the same third variables, and delinquency may have a causal effect on school experiences.

Other researchers acknowledge the foregoing arguments but claim that school experiences still have some causal effect on delinquency. (You should test your knowledge of the leading delinquency theories by using them to explain why the school experiences listed previously might cause delinquency.[5]) The debate over whether school experiences have a causal effect on delinquency has important policy implications. If this is true, then programs designed to improve school experiences should reduce delinquency. But if the association between school experiences and delinquency reflects third variables or the causal effect of delinquency on school experiences, such programs would have little effect. The resolution of this debate requires that researchers examine the effect of school experiences on later delinquency and take account of, or "control for," relevant third variables. Ideally, studies would also test for reciprocal relationships, estimating the extent to which school experiences cause delinquency, and the extent to which delinquency, in turn, causes school experiences (see Hoffmann et al., 2013). Unfortunately, such research is scarce. As a consequence, the debate over whether school experiences have a causal effect on delinquency continues.[6]

Our own reading of the data is that **school experiences have a modest causal effect on delinquency.** The effect is often demonstrated in longitudinal studies that control for at least some relevant third variables, such as social class, family characteristics, certain individual traits, and/or prior delinquency.[7] The effect has also been demonstrated in various "natural experiments" involving school-choice lotteries. In such cases, student lottery winners (by chance) gain admission to desirable, high-performing schools. Research indicates that such students are less likely to develop a criminal record than similar students who lost in the lottery. These results suggest "there is something about schools themselves that is important" in shaping the behavior of young people (see Cook et al., 2010:339). Further, programs designed to improve school experiences often reduce delinquency (see Chapter 24). The effect of school experiences on delinquency, however, is partly indirect. For example, placement in noncollege tracks affects delinquency partly through its impact on other variables, like association with delinquent peers (Colvin, 2000). Juveniles in noncollege tracks are more likely to be exposed to delinquent juveniles, with whom they form friendships. Also, the effect of school experiences on subsequent delinquency is sometimes conditioned by other variables. For example, dropping out of school seems to lead to an increase in delinquency for some individuals, like middle-class students, but not for other individuals, like lower-class students (Jarjoura, 1996).[8] But taken as a whole, we believe the data suggest that negative school experiences of the type listed earlier increase delinquency by a modest amount.

Why Do Some Juveniles Have Negative School Experiences?

Since school experiences may have a modest effect on delinquency, it is important to ask why some juveniles have negative school experiences. We have already mentioned certain potential factors. First, individuals with certain traits, like **low intelligence and low self-control,** are more likely to have negative school experiences. Such individuals have more trouble satisfying the academic demands of school and conforming to school requirements, such as remaining seated and attending to the teacher.[9]

Second, many of the family factors listed in Chapter 14 (such as **family size, parental criminality, parental rejection, and poor discipline)** affect school experiences.[10] Such factors reduce the likelihood that parents will equip their children with the skills and attitudes necessary to do well in school; similarly, it is less likely that parents will effectively monitor their children's school activities and assist their children with schoolwork (see Weishew and Peng, 1993).

Third, **associating with delinquent peers and gang members** negatively affects school experiences. Delinquent peers and gang members place little value on school activities and sometimes actively discourage adolescents from making an effort at school. Based on their field study of St. Louis gangs, Decker and Van Winkle (1996:190) state:

> Attending school, being on time, paying attention to teachers and other staff, getting passing grades—the daily routines and opportunities of our educational system—are not high priorities for most gang members. Truancy, tardiness, skipping classes, [and] leaving school before the end of the day all appear to be popular responses to school discipline and rules. When asked what they did in school, few respondents identified classroom activities.

Fourth, **misbehavior and delinquency** affect school experiences. That is, data suggest that misbehavior has a causal effect on at least certain school experiences, like academic performance and relationships with teachers. Children who misbehave are less attentive to the teacher and spend less time on school tasks, among other things.[11] Misbehavior may also lead to negative labeling by teachers and school officials, thereby contributing to poor relationships with teachers and low attachment to school.

Fifth, school experiences are affected by a range of background factors, including **social class, gender, race/ethnicity, residential mobility** (i.e., frequent moving), and **the type of community the juvenile lives in.**[12] In particular, juveniles from communities with high levels of poverty are more likely to have negative school experiences. The effect of these background factors on school experiences is partly indirect; that is, background factors affect school experiences through their influence on the juvenile's individual traits and behavior, family and other interpersonal experiences, and the type of school the juvenile attends. For example, juveniles from communities with high levels of poverty are more likely to attend inferior schools. And the effect of these factors is partly direct; for example, lower-class parents are less able to provide their children with the resources, skills, and attitudes necessary for school success.

Finally, as discussed next, **certain school characteristics** have an effect on school experiences and delinquency. That is to say, it does make a difference what type of school a child attends.

SCHOOL CHARACTERISTICS AND DELINQUENCY

Students in certain schools are much more likely to engage in delinquency, both within school and without, than students in other schools. The students in some schools, for example, have official rates of delinquency (e.g., court appearances per 100 students) more than 60 times greater than that of students in other schools (Farrington, 1996a). This section first discusses the extent of delinquency in schools and then focuses on the school characteristics that influence levels of school delinquency.

How Much Delinquency Occurs at School?

Crimes involving serious injury and major financial losses are rare in most schools, although **minor crimes are more common.** Each year the Monitoring the Future survey interviews a nationally representative sample of high school seniors from the contiguous United States. The students are asked whether they have been the victims of various crimes at school (inside or outside school or on a school bus) during the previous 12 months. Results from the 2015 survey are reported in Table 15.1.

TABLE 15.1	Percentage of High School Seniors Reporting Various Victimization Experiences at School during the Previous 12 Months
Type of Victimization	**Percent Experiencing Victimization**
Violent Crime	
Injured with a weapon	4.6
Threatened with a weapon	16.3
Injured without a weapon	20.4
Threatened without a weapon	23.4
Property Crime	
Theft of something worth >$50	16.2
Theft of something worth <$50	29.0
Property damaged (vandalized)	20.7

SOURCE: Monitoring the Future Survey, 2015 (visit http://www.monitoringthe future.org; data obtained from the National Addiction & HIV Data Archive Program).

As can be seen, **serious violence was relatively rare:** 4.6 percent of the students were injured with a weapon (and most of these injuries were minor). **Less serious forms of violence were more common.** Nearly one out of four students (23.4 percent) was threatened with injury by an unarmed individual (but not actually injured). Data from 2014 indicate that juveniles are somewhat more likely to be the victims of violence at school than away from school. This is especially true for simple assault. Rates of **serious** violent victimization (rape, robbery, and aggravated assault) are about the same at school as away from school (U.S. Department of Education and Office of Justice Programs, 2016). Homicide is an important exception, however. For example, during the 2012–2013 school year, 31 juveniles were murdered at school. These homicides account for less than 3 percent of all juvenile homicides during that time period. Juveniles were about 50 times more likely to be murdered away from school than at school.

Theft is more common than violence at school. Returning to Table 15.1, we see that about 29 percent of the seniors reported that something worth less than $50 had been stolen from them at school, and 16 percent reported that something worth more than $50 had been stolen. About 21 percent of the seniors reported that someone had deliberately damaged their property (car, clothing, etc.) while they were at school. Juveniles are slightly more likely to be the victims of theft at school than away from school.

Data on trends in school crime are somewhat mixed, but they generally suggest that most forms of school crime have declined since the early to mid-1990s—just as crime in the larger society has declined (U.S. Department of Education and Office of Justice Programs, 2016). This downward trend can be seen, for example, in the data on school-associated youth homicides. Between the 1992–93 and 1998–99 school years, the number of juveniles murdered at school each year hovered consistently near 30, for an average of 31 murders per year. Between the 1999–2000 and 2012–13 school years, the annual total was closer to 20, for an average of 19.6 murders per year.

So, overall, crimes involving serious injury and, to a lesser extent, serious theft are rare in most schools, although minor crimes are more common. As G. Gottfredson and Gottfredson (1985:167) state, "Much of the 'victimization' that occurs in schools involves minor indignities: smart-ass remarks or gestures, one boy forcibly asking another for a quarter, a notebook lifted from someone's desk." Further, most types of school crime have been decreasing over the past decade or so. These assertions regarding school crime are at odds with the impression of school violence conveyed by the mass media. The mass media have devoted extensive coverage to a series of school shootings in recent years, fostering the impression that schools are quite dangerous—even suburban schools populated by middle-class students. But this impression exaggerates the problem of school crime.

At the same time, we do not want to minimize the problem of school crime. As we are painfully aware, serious acts of violence do happen. Certain schools, particularly schools in poor urban areas, do suffer from high rates of serious crime and violence. And the minor crime and violence that occurs in most schools can have a devastating impact on many of its victims, particularly those who are chronically victimized. In this area, much attention has focused on the problem of bullying. This has occurred partly because recent surveys suggest that bullying is extensive and has a range of negative consequences (see later discussion). Also, many of the juveniles who shot others at their schools, like the two students who shot and killed 13 others at Columbine High School in Colorado, were said to be the victims of bullying (although this, of course, does not excuse their behavior). For more on these school shootings, see Box 15.1.

Box 15.1   "I'll Show You One Day": Responding to the Threat of School Violence

In 2001, 15-year-old Andy Williams brought a gun to his suburban high school in Santee, California. When students were on break from their morning classes, Williams opened fire and randomly sprayed bullets into a courtyard where many had gathered, killing 2 students and wounding 13 others.

During the preceding month, Williams repeatedly had told his friends that he was going to "take one of his father's guns to school and shoot people." At the time, his friends thought he was joking. "Everybody would just laugh and tell him to shut up,"

(Continued)

(Continued)

explained one friend. When an adult heard about the threats, he confronted Williams but was told it was all a joke. The adult responded, "You better be [joking]. Or I'll have your ass arrested before you even get to school."

The day before the shooting spree, Williams again repeated his threats, as described by a fellow schoolmate:

> [Williams said,] "Tomorrow, I'm going to have a bunch of guns and I'm going to shoot a bunch of people. I'm going to shoot people down and you're going to watch." We were just making fun of him, just mocking him . . . I called him a stupid ass. I said, "You don't have the guts to do it." Next thing I heard, he shot at my sister. (*Los Angeles Times,* 2001:A1–4)

There are at least two similarities between the tragic killing spree in Santee and other high-profile school shootings. First, like many other school shooters (Strong and Cornell, 2008), Williams was reportedly bullied by his peers. Williams traced the motives for his attack to this experience:

> Williams wrote in a signed statement that his feelings built up "like a cup filling up inside me" as friends in his Santee neighborhood kicked, beat, burned, and spit on him. "I had this sick thought if I shot up the school, it would some way show kids that I could stand up for myself," Williams wrote. (Associated Press, 2002)

Second, like almost all other high-profile school shooters, Williams communicated his violent intentions by making threats and issuing verbal warnings to his peers (Strong and Cornell, 2008). Had his threats been taken seriously and reported to authorities, the Santee attack might have been prevented. In fact, in an earlier study, the FBI had identified a number of "potential school shootings that were prevented because students reported a threat to authorities that was investigated and determined to be serious" (Strong and Cornell, 2008:42).

This crucial piece of information—that most school shooters communicate their intentions in advance—may hold the key to preventing future attacks. In particular, this knowledge has guided the development of a "threat assessment" approach to school violence, which was pioneered by researchers at the University of Virginia. In the threat assessment model, school officials receive special training in responding to and evaluating threats. They also receive training in conflict resolution and make an effort to resolve the conflicts that generate student threats.

Under the Virginia model, all reported threats are assessed, though past experience reveals that the majority of student threats are *not* serious, are voiced in a moment of anger or frustration (e.g., "I'm going to kill him!"), and can be resolved quickly through an apology or other means of conflict resolution. If the student making the threat has also reported a plan to carry it out, however, or has made the threat repeatedly, the circumstances may warrant further action. For instance, the police may be informed of the threat and may seek permission to search the student's home for weapons. School officials may also order a mental health assessment and make referrals for counseling or treatment.

Additional research is needed to determine the effectiveness of the Virginia threat assessment approach, but the results of initial evaluations are promising. In one study, researchers compared schools that had implemented the Virginia model with schools that had not. After taking into account other differences between these schools, the researchers found that schools using the Virginia model reported "less bullying in the

(*Continued*)

past 30 days, greater willingness [among students] to seek help for bullying and threats of violence, . . . more positive perceptions of school climate" and fewer long-term suspensions (Borum et al., 2010:32; Cornell et al., 2009). In another study (Strong and Cornell, 2008), the use of the threat-assessment model by Memphis City Schools was examined over the course of a single school year. Of 110 cases that were assessed by school officials involving threats to "kill, shoot, or stab someone," none of the threats were believed to have been carried out (some threats, however, were deemed serious and led to mental health referrals, placement in alternative schools, or incarceration). For more information on the Virginia model, visit: http://curry.virginia.edu/research/projects/threat assessment.

Questions for Discussion

1. A threat assessment approach can work only if students and parents are willing to report threats to school officials. If you were a school principal, what steps would you take to encourage such reporting?
2. In the immediate aftermath of previous school shootings, media pundits and politicians frequently entertained the imposition of harsher criminal penalties, restrictions on media violence, new gun control measures, and other such responses to school violence. How does the threat assessment approach compare to these other responses? What do evaluations of the threat assessment approach suggest about the power of research to inform promising interventions?
3. Following previous school shootings, people often asked, "How do these kids get their hands on guns?" What have you heard about other school shootings? Where did the shooters obtain their weapons? If they obtained guns in the same manner as the Santee shooter, what does this say about the ability of young people to access firearms? Is there a feasible way to restrict or control such access? (See Chapter 17 for more on guns and delinquency; also see Brezina and Wright, 2000.)

Peer influence

Bullying has three dimensions: It involves behavior designed to harm or disturb others, it occurs on a repeated basis, and it involves a more powerful person or group attacking a less powerful one (Howell, 2003a:115). Estimates of the extent of bullying vary somewhat, but most estimates suggest that about 15 to 20 percent of students are subjected to bullying each year (although see K. Berger, 2007, for the difficulties involved in measuring the extent of bullying).[13] Girls are about as equally likely to be the victims of bullying as boys, although boys are more likely to report that they have engaged in bullying. Related to these findings, girls appear to have greater empathy for the victims of bullying, as they are more likely than boys to report that they "feel sorry for and want to help" others when they see them bullied at school (Limber et al., 2013). Data suggest that the victims of bullying suffer a range of negative psychological and social consequences, including depression, a fear of going to school, trouble making friends, and—in some cases—delinquency (see K. Berger, 2007; Eisenbraun, 2007; Ericson, 2001; Smokowski and Kopasz, 2005). As described in Chapter 24, successful programs have been developed to reduce bullying (for a discussion of cyberbullying, see Chapter 17).

How Can We Explain School Differences in Delinquency?

As indicated earlier, schools differ a good deal in the amount of delinquency they experience. Such differences are largely a function of **differences between the students who attend the schools and the communities in which the schools are located.** Delinquency rates are higher in schools that have a higher percentage of students who are less able, poor, male, and members of minority groups. Delinquency rates are also higher in schools that are located in urban communities with high rates of crime, poverty, unemployment, and female-headed households. However, when researchers take account of student and community characteristics, they find that school characteristics have a small to modest association with delinquency rates—especially rates of within-school delinquency.

Several studies have focused on the association between school characteristics and in-school delinquency rates (for an excellent review, see Cook et al., 2010). These studies are not in full agreement, and there is some evidence that the findings vary by grade level and by type of delinquency (e.g., theft versus violence, delinquency directed at teachers versus that directed at students). Nevertheless, some tentative conclusions can be drawn about the school characteristics associated with in-school delinquency rates.[14]

The characteristics of low-delinquency or effective schools are similar to the characteristics of effective families—both tend to be *warm but firm.* In particular, there is some evidence that rates of in-school delinquency tend to be somewhat lower in schools of the types listed here.

1. *Schools with small class sizes and good resources.* Delinquency in schools tends to be lower when the average teacher instructs a smaller number of students. It is also lower in schools whose teachers are provided with the materials and equipment they need to teach. Drawing on the leading delinquency theories, why do you think class size and resources might be important? (Recall our discussion of family size and delinquency.)

2. *Schools with good discipline.* Delinquency in schools is lower when clear rules for behavior are consistently enforced in a fair manner. Schools with unclear or ambiguous rules have higher rates of delinquency, as do schools that fail to enforce their rules. This finding does not mean that schools should severely punish minor infractions. In fact, there is some evidence that overly punitive discipline contributes to higher rates of delinquency. Certain studies, for example, suggest that delinquency rates are higher in schools that use physical punishment and make frequent use of punishment (note the parallels with the family research here). It is best to spot disruptive behavior early and deal with it in a firm but appropriate manner. In particular, there are techniques for responding to disruptive behavior that are not overly punitive and do not disrupt teaching activities. An early but firm response may prevent more serious problems from developing—problems that may call forth frequent and punitive disciplinary responses.

3. *Schools that provide opportunities for student success and praise student accomplishments.* Delinquency tends to be lower in schools that actively involve students in the learning process and increase the opportunities to achieve success for all students (i.e., including students who do not plan to attend college). Certain teaching techniques that help accomplish these goals are described in Chapter 24. Further, delinquency tends to be lower when teachers praise student accomplishments. As indicated in the discussion of the family, it is important both to punish delinquency and to reinforce conventional behavior.

4. *Schools with high expectations for students.* Delinquency is lower in schools with high standards for success: that is, schools where the teachers have high expectations for their students and make rigorous but not unrealistic work demands on them.

5. *Schools with pleasant working conditions for students.* Delinquency is lower when teachers and other school officials have positive attitudes toward students, allow students some say over school matters, provide support to students who are having

problems, and create a pleasant physical workspace for students (e.g., having trash and graffiti removed, providing attractive decorations).

6. Schools with good cooperation between the administration and teachers. Delinquency is lower in schools when administrators and counselors keep teachers informed of disciplinary problems and support or assist teachers in their disciplinary efforts. Such cooperation probably makes it easier for schools to develop and effectively enforce a clear set of rules.

7. Schools with strong community involvement. Delinquency is lower in schools with high levels of community involvement, especially parental involvement—with parents communicating regularly with teachers and school officials, assisting in the school, and having some say in how the school is run.

We should note that **private schools generally have lower rates of delinquency than public schools,** even after one takes account of differences between the students who attend private and public schools. Some evidence suggests that the rates of delinquency are dissimilar in private and public schools because these school types differ with respect to many of the characteristics just listed. Based on their extensive analysis of public and private schools, J. Coleman et al. (1982:102–103) state that "the Catholic schools are the strictest in discipline; the other private schools are somewhat less strict and appear to nurture the student to a greater degree (as evidenced by perceived teacher interest). The public schools, taken as a whole, are neither strict nor do they nurture the student. In addition, they are least often regarded by their students as fair in the exercise of discipline." Further, private schools tend to be more academically demanding than public schools.

Taken as a whole, these data suggest that on the one hand, the schools with the lowest rates of delinquency are **firm**; they have clear rules that are uniformly enforced, and they are academically demanding. On the other hand, they are **"warm"**; they treat students in a fair manner; teachers are interested in students, provide opportunities for success, and praise student accomplishments; school staff attempt to create a pleasant environment for the students; and parents are available to assist both students and school staff. It is easy to explain the effect of these school characteristics in terms of strain, social learning, control, and labeling theories. Schools with these characteristics should **create less strain.** They are more pleasant; students get along better with their teachers and presumably with other students (since student misbehavior is less tolerated). They are fairer. And students are more likely to achieve their success goals. The students in such schools are also **subject to greater control.** In particular, they are subject to more direct control, they are more likely to form an emotional attachment to teachers and an investment in conventional activities, and they may even be more likely to internalize beliefs condemning delinquency and develop some measure of self-control. Further, drawing on **social learning theory,** these schools are more likely to punish delinquency and reinforce conformity, teach conventional beliefs, and provide exposure to conventional models. Such schools may also be less likely to provide exposure to delinquent others, since the schools likely discourage the formation of delinquent peer groups. Finally, such schools should be **less likely to label** students as "bad."

TEACHING AIDS

Applying Theories and Research

In an article titled "Creating an Action Plan for Effective Schools," Cummings (2014) highlights the importance of school environments that are safe and orderly. Drawing on the body of research reviewed in this chapter, he makes the following recommendations (items not enclosed in quotation marks are paraphrases):

1. "An effective school safety program focuses on prevention, intervention, and emergency response. School leaders can take several steps to create this type of learning environment."

2. "Make sure students have a clear understanding of the behavioral expectations on the campus. Students also should be taught proper behavior. This is a responsibility of all faculty members. Establish personal relationships with students. Personal relationships are especially important on campuses with large numbers of economically disadvantaged students."

3. Teacher and administrators should hold high expectations and communicate these expectations to students on a daily basis. They must be willing to increase the rigor of instruction and then do whatever it takes to help students succeed, providing additional resources and support when needed.

4. "Establish a school-wide program to deal with bullying, violence, and harassment. An effective program is proactive and emphasizes prevention. A safe procedure for reporting incidents should be in place."

5. "Have regular emergency drills and be able to respond quickly to reports of unsafe conditions or emergency incidents. . . ."

6. Parental involvement should be encouraged, and communication between teachers, administrators, and parents should be consistent.

What other steps would you recommend for reducing school crime? (See Chapter 24 for a discussion of school-based delinquency control and prevention programs.)

Web-Based Exercise: More Information on School Violence, Including Bullying

Each year the U.S. Departments of Education and Justice issue a joint report titled "Indicators of School Crime and Safety." The document draws on data from a variety of sources to describe the nature and extent of school crime, including violent deaths, trends in school crime, some consequences of school crime, and some of the ways schools are trying to reduce crime. Find the latest copy of this report on the web by searching for **Indicators of School Crime and Safety**. Then browse through it, using the information to update the statistics in this chapter.

As noted in this chapter, bullying is a major problem in schools; the federal government has joined authorities on the state, county, and school district levels in a concerted effort to reduce bullying. Part of that effort is reflected in the **stopbullying.gov** website created by the U.S. Department of Health and Human Services. Visit this website and browse through it to learn more about the nature and extent of bullying, the risk factors for bullying, and what can be done to reduce bullying (see Chapter 17 for more on cyberbullying).

TEST YOUR KNOWLEDGE OF THIS CHAPTER

1. List those school experiences that are associated with delinquency.
2. Why do some criminologists argue that these school experiences do not cause delinquency? How should researchers go about testing these arguments?
3. Why do we argue that these school experiences have a modest causal effect on delinquency?
4. Why are some juveniles more likely than others to have negative school experiences?

5. Describe the extent of and trends in school crime. Why do we argue that the mass media exaggerate the problem of school crime?

6. What is bullying?

7. Why do some schools have more crime than other schools? List those school characteristics associated with lower levels of school crime. Describe the characteristics of "warm but firm" schools, which tend to have lower levels of school crime.

8. Why do private schools tend to have lower rates of school crime than public schools?

THOUGHT AND DISCUSSION QUESTIONS

1. Use relevant delinquency theories to explain why any three of the major school experiences listed in this chapter increase the likelihood of delinquency.

2. Use any relevant delinquency theories to explain why any three of the school characteristics listed in this chapter reduce the likelihood of school crime.

3. Do you think there was a lot of crime in your high school (or a problem with bullying)? Drawing on this chapter and the major delinquency theories, discuss why there was or was not a lot of crime (or bullying) in your school. Can you think of any factors other than those listed in this chapter that might influence levels of school crime?

4. What recommendations would you make for reducing school crime, including violence and bullying (see the Endnotes section of this chapter and Chapter 24 for further information).

KEY TERMS

- Bullying
- Warm but firm schools

ENDNOTES

1. For overviews and select studies, see Agnew, 1985a; Bellair and McNulty, 2005; Cernkovich and Giordano, 1992; Chapple et al., 2005; Chung et al., 2002; Cook et al., 2010; Farrington and Welsh, 2007; R. Felson and Staff, 2006; D. Gottfredson, 2001; G. Gottfredson, 2012; Hawkins and Lishner, 1987; Henry et al., 2012; Jang, 2002; Jarjoura and Triplett, 1997; Jenkins, 1997; J. Kaufman, 2005; Maguin and Loeber, 1996; McGloin et al., 2004; Moon et al., 2009; A. Payne, 2008; Payne and Welch, 2013; Sampson and Laub, 1993a; Stewart, 2003; Stewart and Simons, 2006; Thaxton and Agnew, 2004; Thornberry, Krohn et al. (with Porter), 2003; Wiatrowski and Anderson, 1987; Wiatrowski et al., 1981, 1982; Wilson and Herrnstein, 1985.

2. See Agnew, 2006a; D. Gottfredson, 2001; Hoffmann et al., 2013; Liljeberg et al., 2011; Maguin and Loeber, 1996; McGloin et al., 2004; Thaxton and Agnew, 2004; Wilson and Herrnstein, 1985.

3. See Felson and Staff, 2006; D. Gottfredson, 2001; Krohn et al., 1995; Maguin and Loeber, 1996; Sweeten et al., 2009; Wiatrowski and Anderson, 1987; Wiatrowski et al., 1982; Wilson and Herrnstein, 1985:267.

4. See J. Hawkins and Lishner, 1987; Krohn et al., 1995; Liljeberg et al., 2011; Sweeten, 2006; Thornberry, 1996; Thornberry, Krohn et al. (with Porter), 2003.

5. See Felson and Staff, 2006; Hawkins and Lishner, 1987; Maguin and Loeber, 1996; Wilson and Herrnstein, 1985.

6. See Felson and Staff, 2006; Jarjoura, 1993, 1996; Krohn et al., 1995; Maguin and Loeber, 1996; Wiatrowski et al., 1982.

7. See Bellair and McNulty, 2005; Chung et al., 2002; G. Gottfredson, 2012; Henry et al., 2012; Liljeberg et al., 2011; Loeber, Farrington, Stouthamer-Loeber, and Van Kammen, 1998; Maguin and Loeber, 1996; Matsueda et al., 2006; McGloin et al., 2004; Moon et al., 2009; Sampson and Laub, 1993a; Thornberry, 1996; Thornberry, Krohn et al. (with Porter), 2003; B. Wright, Caspi, Moffitt, and Silva, 1999.

8. For research on the effect of dropping out of school on delinquency; see Krohn et al., 1995; Jarjoura, 1993, 1996; Sweeten et al., 2009.

9. See Bellair and McNulty, 2005; D. Gottfredson, 2001; Maguin and Loeber, 1996; McGloin et al., 2004; Sampson and Laub, 1993a; Wiatrowski et al., 1981; B. Wright et al., 2001.

10. See Jenkins, 1997; Patterson, 1986; Patterson et al., 1992; Sampson and Laub, 1993a.

11. See Bellair and McNulty, 2005; Hawkins and Lishner, 1987; Patterson, 1986; Patterson et al., 1989; Patterson et al., 1992; Thornberry, 1996; Thornberry, Krohn et al. (with Porter), 2003.

12. See Alexander, 1997; Bellair and McNulty, 2005; D. Gottfredson, 2001; Jenkins, 1997; Maguin and Loeber, 1996; McGloin et al., 2004; Payne et al., 2003; Sampson and Laub, 1993a; T. Wadsworth, 2000.

13. See U.S. Department of Education and Office of Justice Programs, 2006; Eisenbraun, 2007; Ericson, 2001; Howell, 2003a; Limber et al., 2013; Smokowski and Kopasz, 2005.

14. For overviews and select studies, see Catalano and Hawkins, 1996; Coleman et al., 1982; Elliott et al., 1998; Farrington and Welsh, 2007; D. Gottfredson, 2001; G. Gottfredson, 2012; G. Gottfredson and Gottfredson, 1985; G. Gottfredson et al., 2005; Hawkins and Lishner, 1987; Hellman and Beaton, 1986; Lawrence, 1998; A. Payne, 2008; A. Payne et al., 2003; Rutter et al., 1979; Rutter et al., 1998; Stewart, 2003; Weishew and Peng, 1993; W. Welsh, Greene, and Jenkins, 1999; W. Welsh et al., 2000; Wilson and Herrnstein, 1985; also see Alexander, 1997.

16 Delinquent Peers and Gangs

What Impact Do Delinquent Peer Groups and Gangs Have on Delinquency?

As juveniles enter adolescence, the peer group comes to occupy a central—in many cases *the* central—place in their lives. Adolescents start spending much more time with their peers, they attach more importance to their peers, and they are more strongly influenced by their peers (Thornberry, Krohn, et al. [with Porter], 2003; Warr, 2002). It is perhaps no surprise, then, that **many if not most adolescents who commit delinquent offenses do so in the company of peers.** One study, based on a nationally representative sample of adolescents, found that 73 percent of all delinquent offenses were committed in a group. For example, 91 percent of all burglaries and alcohol violations were committed in a group, 79 percent of all drug violations, 71 percent of all assaults, 60 percent of all acts of vandalism, 49 percent of all acts of truancy, and 44 percent of all thefts (Warr, 1996). Other studies produce different percentages (see Stolzenberg and D'Alessio, 2008), but most show that a majority of all delinquent acts are committed with peers.

Based partly on such data, many criminologists argue that **associating with delinquent peers is a major cause of delinquency.** They most often draw on social learning theory when making this argument. As indicated in Chapter 7, delinquent peers are said to reinforce the adolescent's delinquency, model delinquent behavior, and present values conducive to delinquency. This chapter examines the impact of delinquent peers on delinquency. First, we focus on the impact of delinquent peers in general. Then we examine the impact of a particular type of delinquent peer group: the gang.

After reading this chapter you should be able to:

- Describe the association between delinquent peers and delinquent behavior, including some of the possible reasons for this association.
- Describe the conditions under which delinquent peers are most likely to cause delinquency.
- Draw on the major delinquency theories to explain the effect of delinquent peer groups on delinquent behavior.
- Explain why juveniles become involved with delinquent peer groups.
- Distinguish street gangs from other delinquent peer groups.
- Discuss the role of street gangs in serious crime.
- Explain why juveniles join and leave gangs.
- Explain why gangs often develop in lower income, urban communities.
- Describe trends in the growth of street gangs.

WHAT IMPACT DO DELINQUENT PEERS HAVE ON DELINQUENCY?

Is associating with delinquent peers an important cause of delinquency? Cross-sectional data indicate that juveniles with delinquent friends are much more likely to engage in delinquency. In fact, having delinquent friends is typically the strongest correlate of delinquency. But as you know, the fact that delinquent friends and delinquency are associated does not mean that having delinquent friends **causes** delinquency. Both variables may be caused by the same third variable(s). In particular, it has been argued that individual traits (e.g., low self-control), family problems, and negative school experiences cause delinquency on the one hand and association with delinquent peers on the other. It has also been argued that the relationship exists because delinquency causes juveniles to associate with delinquent peers. Most people prefer to associate with people who are like them, so delinquents may choose to associate with fellow delinquents ("birds of a feather flock together"). Until recently, it was not clear **why** having delinquent peers was associated with delinquency.

Data now suggest that **the association between delinquent peers and delinquency is partly due to the causal effect of delinquent peers on the individual's delinquency.** Several longitudinal studies have found that associating with delinquent peers leads to an increase in subsequent delinquency, even when other variables are controlled. In fact, associating with delinquent peers is often the best predictor of subsequent delinquency (other than the juvenile's level of prior delinquency). The results of several laboratory experiments are also relevant here, as they document the causal effect of peers on risky and unethical behaviors. While these experimental studies do not examine criminal or delinquent behaviors in the real world (it would be unethical to conduct such an experiment), the results are revealing. In a driving-simulation study, for example, adolescents were more likely to "run a yellow light" when in the presence of other adolescents than when alone (Gardner and Steinberg, 2005). And in a recent experiment on deviant peer influence, college students were invited to participate in a "test of memory and recall" in which they could earn up to $20 for providing correct answers. Participants who were exposed to a "peer" who cheated on the task were more to likely to cheat themselves, even after being asked not to cheat. In the absence of this cheating peer, no one cheated (Paternoster et al., 2013).

At the same time, studies also indicate that delinquent peers and delinquency are associated (in the real world) partly because delinquent peers and delinquency are caused by the same third variables, such as negative family experiences. Further, delinquency has a causal effect on delinquent peers; that is, delinquent individuals are more likely to select fellow delinquents as friends.[1]

A study by Elliott and Menard (1996) sheds light on the relationship between delinquent peers and delinquency. Their data suggest that the progression from no delinquency to serious delinquency typically proceeds in the following manner: (1) juveniles associate with mildly delinquent peers before they engage in delinquency; (2) this peer association leads to minor delinquency; (3) the minor delinquency leads to association with more delinquent peers; (4) that association leads to more serious delinquency, and so on. Not all juveniles move as far as serious delinquency, and some juveniles do not complete these steps in the order shown. Some juveniles, for example, may engage in delinquency before associating with delinquent peers. Nevertheless, this pattern is the most common pattern of progression. It illustrates that delinquent peers and delinquent acts are **reciprocally** related: each has a causal effect on the other.[2]

Under What Conditions Are Delinquent Peers Most Likely to Cause Delinquency?

Recent data suggest that the effect of delinquent peers on delinquency is not the same in all circumstances.[3] The effect of delinquent peers is greatest when **all the adolescent's friends are delinquent** (versus only some friends). It is greatest when the adolescent's friends form a **cohesive group**—that is, they all know one another and interact together. And it is greatest when these friends hold **beliefs conducive to delinquency, approve of the adolescent's delinquency, and pressure the adolescent to engage in delinquency.** The effect of delinquent peers may also be greater for certain types of offenses, like drug use. These conditional effects are easily explained by social learning and other theories. For example, social learning theory states that we are more likely to model the behavior of a given person when we are frequently exposed to that person's behavior and infrequently exposed to competing behaviors.

It is also the case that the effect of delinquent peers on delinquency is influenced by factors other than the nature of one's peer associations. In particular, there is some evidence that association with delinquent peers is more likely to cause delinquency among those low in control. For example, delinquent peers are more likely to cause delinquency among those who are poorly supervised and weakly attached to their parents (see Barnes et al., 2006; Elliott et al., 1985). Related to this, delinquent peers are more likely to cause delinquency among males than females (Mears et al., 1998; N. Piquero et al., 2005). This may be the case because females are higher in control than males, including direct control, self-control, and the belief that delinquency is bad (see Chapter 18).

What Are Delinquent Peer Groups Like?

Only a small percentage of *delinquent peer groups* **are gangs.** The term "delinquent group," in fact, is somewhat misleading. Most delinquent groups are better described as friendship groups that occasionally engage in delinquency. This will become apparent as we comment on the types of delinquency committed by these groups, the size and composition of the groups, and the quality of relations among group members.

Types of delinquency. Most delinquent peer groups usually engage only in minor delinquency, on an occasional basis, although a significant percentage of groups engage in more frequent and serious delinquency. Warr (1993), for example, found that by mid- to late adolescence, a majority of subjects had close friends who engaged in minor forms of deviance such as marijuana and alcohol use, cheating, and petty theft. Fewer than 20 percent, however, had friends who engaged in serious offenses such as burglary, theft of items worth more than $50, or selling hard drugs.[4]

Size and composition. The groups that engage in delinquency are usually small. The typical size is two to four juveniles, with the groups getting smaller in size as juveniles age. By mid- to late adolescence, the typical offending group consists of only two or three juveniles. (Adults, unlike juveniles, are most likely to commit their offenses alone.) These small groups are subsets of larger groups or cliques of youth (but usually not gangs). Juveniles seldom commit offenses with the same person(s) all the time; rather, they will usually commit offenses with different members of the larger groups or cliques. In this area, Warr (1996:16) states that "it is important to distinguish between *offending groups* (groups that actually commit delinquent acts) and *accomplice networks* (the pool of potential co-offenders available to the adolescent)." Warr found that the average size of accomplice networks was about seven, with the more delinquent youths having larger networks.

Group members are usually similar in terms of age and sex. Most delinquent groups are made up of males (see McCarthy et al., 2004). And membership in such groups peaks at ages 15 to 18. We should note that while males are most likely to offend with males, and females are most likely to offend with females, female offenders are more likely to be a part of mixed-sex groups than are males.

One person in the group will usually suggest or instigate the offense (the "instigator"). Instigators are most often the same age as or a little older than the other group member(s), and they usually have a little more delinquent experience than the others. While the instigator is usually the same sex as the others in the group, females are more likely to report male instigators than males are to report female instigators (see Giordano, 1978; Warr, 1996). Most juveniles who have committed at least a few delinquent offenses report that they have played the role of both instigator and follower. They will often play the role of instigator with one set of friends and follower with another.

Quality of relationships between group members. Some researchers have argued that the members of delinquent groups have poor relationships with one another. One researcher describes these relationships as "cold and brittle" (Hirschi, 1969). In particular, it is said that group members are not very attached to one another and that they frequently exploit one another. Other researchers, however, claim that the members of delinquent groups have great affection for and loyalty to one another. The latter image is often presented in films about gangs, the classic example being *West Side Story*.

Recent data suggest that the quality of peer relations varies a lot from delinquent group to delinquent group, but overall, the **relations in delinquent groups are similar to those found in conventional groups** (see especially Agnew, 1991b; Giordano et al., 1986). One of the best studies in this area found that the members of delinquent groups spend as much time with one another as the members of conventional groups, have similar levels of caring and trust, are more likely to share private thoughts, are more influenced by one another, and find their friendships more rewarding in certain ways (Giordano et al., 1986). Reflecting these facts, the members of delinquent groups usually report that they are close friends or friends with one another (Warr, 1996). The members of delinquent groups, however, are also **more likely to report getting into conflicts with one another** than are the members of conventional groups (Giordano et al., 1986).

Romantic partners are also important. Most of the research on delinquent peers has focused on association with **friends.** Adolescents, however, also associate with romantic partners. And recent research suggests that individuals with delinquent romantic partners are more likely to engage in delinquency themselves. Haynie et al. (2005) examined a sample of adolescents in grades 7 through 12 in a diverse set of schools throughout the United States. These adolescents were asked, "In the past 18 months, have you had a special romantic relationship with someone?" Over half the respondents replied yes. About 90 percent of these respondents said they had only one romantic partner during this time. The average length of a romantic relationship was between eight and nine months, and the relationship involved a high level of romantic involvement (e.g., the romantic partners told each other that they loved one another). The researchers found that individuals with delinquent romantic partners were more likely to engage in delinquency themselves. This was true even after the researchers took account of a range of third variables, including the delinquency of the individual's friends. Friends' delinquency, however, had a stronger relationship to the individual's delinquency than did the romantic partner's delinquency. The researchers also examined whether the romantic partner's delinquency had a stronger effect on males or females. Since males often have more power in a relationship, they thought that the romantic partner's delinquency would have a greater effect on females. This was true when the researchers examined minor delinquency, but not true when they examined serious delinquency.

Why Are Individuals in Delinquent Groups More Likely to Engage in Delinquency?

As indicated, **social learning theory** is most often used to explain the effect of delinquent peers on a juvenile's delinquency. Data indicate that delinquent peers affect delinquency by reinforcing the juvenile's delinquency, providing delinquent models, and fostering beliefs that are conducive to delinquency. Warr (2002) provides an excellent discussion of some of these mechanisms. He states, for example, that juveniles in delinquent peer groups sometimes engage in delinquency because it increases their status or prestige with peers, since risky acts like delinquency often are admired in such groups. This, of course, is an example of the positive reinforcement of delinquency. Warr also states that juveniles in delinquent groups sometimes engage in delinquency because they fear being ridiculed if they abstain. That is, they fear others in the group will laugh at them, tease them, call them derogatory names, or even reject them if they do not engage in delinquency on certain occasions. This is an example of the negative reinforcement of delinquency, with juveniles engaging in delinquency to avoid something bad. Further, Warr (2002:67) states that the juveniles in delinquent groups sometimes engage in delinquency because the group has developed its own "moral code that supplants that of the outside world, granting legitimacy to otherwise illegitimate conduct." Social learning theory, then, sheds much light on the reasons why individuals in delinquent peer groups are more likely to engage in delinquency.

At the same time, **most studies find that delinquent peers affect delinquency even after one takes account of reinforcement, modeling, and beliefs** (although the measures employed in such studies are often poor). And it has been argued that delinquent peers also increase the likelihood of delinquency for reasons related to control, strain, and labeling theories (see especially Agnew, 1995a; Warr, 2002).

Control theory suggests that delinquent peers may reduce a juvenile's fear of direct controls, as well as his or her stake in conformity and level of internal control. Being part of a delinquent peer group may reduce the fear of retaliation by others (a form of direct control), since there is strength in numbers. Also, witnessing one's friends engaging in delinquency without sanction may reduce the fear of official or police sanctions (see R. Johnson, 1979; Meier et al., 1984). Further, delinquent friends may reduce both the juvenile's bonds to conventional others and the amount of effort devoted to conventional activities, like schoolwork (see Decker and Van Winkle, 1996). The result is a lower stake in conformity. Finally, delinquent friends may weaken the juvenile's belief that delinquency is wrong or bad. This occurs partly because the friends often challenge the belief that delinquency is bad. For example, they tell the juvenile that smoking marijuana "is not so bad" (also see Warr, 2002).

Delinquent peers may also affect delinquency for reasons related to **strain theory** (see Agnew, 1995a). Delinquent peers experience more conflict with one another and with others in the community—with such conflict involving the presentation of negative stimuli (see Colvin, 2000; Giordano et al., 1986). And membership in delinquent peer groups may make it more difficult for juveniles to achieve certain of their goals **through legitimate channels,** including their monetary and status goals. Finally, the members of delinquent groups may be more likely to be **labeled** as delinquent by others. Although as Chambliss points out in his discussion of the Saints and Roughnecks, the members of certain delinquent peer groups are able to escape negative labeling (see Chapter 9). Still other explanations have been offered for the effect of delinquent peers on delinquency, although most are related to the leading delinquency theories.[5]

Why Are Some Juveniles More Likely than Others to Get Involved with Delinquent Peers?

It has been argued that juveniles with **the traits of irritability and low self-control are more likely to get involved with delinquent peers.** These traits increase the likelihood that juveniles will be rejected by conventional peers. And they increase the appeal of delinquent groups. Juveniles with a strong need for thrills and excitement (part of low self-control), for example, will probably be more attracted to the activities of delinquent groups. Limited data support these arguments, suggesting that traits like irritability and low self-control increase the likelihood of membership in delinquent groups.[6]

Most of the **family variables that promote delinquency also increase the likelihood of membership in delinquent peer groups.** Factors like large family size, parental criminality, parental rejection, low parental attachment, and poor parental supervision have all been shown to increase association with delinquent peers.[7] Likewise, certain data suggest that many of the **negative school experiences** described in Chapter 15 **increase the likelihood of association with delinquent peers.**[8] These family and school factors reduce the juvenile's level of control. Juveniles low in control are more likely to spend time on the street, increasing their exposure to delinquent peers, and they have less to lose by associating with delinquent peers. These family and school factors also increase the juvenile's level of strain, which makes delinquent peer groups more appealing. Juveniles experiencing problems at school, for example, will probably be more attracted to certain of the activities of delinquent peers—like skipping school.

Further, **juveniles in deprived, inner-city communities are more likely to become involved with delinquent peers.** As indicated in Chapter 12, deprived communities are more likely to develop delinquent peer groups (also see Haynie et al., 2006). So juveniles in such communities will have greater exposure to such groups. Also, juveniles in such communities may be more attracted to delinquent peers, since associating with such peers may be seen as a way to cope with certain of the strains they face—like high levels of violence.

Finally, **delinquent behavior itself increases the likelihood of association with delinquent peers.** This effect may reflect the preference of delinquents to associate with other delinquents. It may also reflect the reluctance of conventional peers to associate with delinquents, which in turn compels delinquents to associate with one another.

WHAT IMPACT DO GANGS HAVE ON DELINQUENCY?

While the most common type of delinquent peer group is the simple friendship group, several authors have pointed to additional types of delinquent or law-violating groups, with the street gang receiving the most attention. This section addresses several basic questions about street gangs: What is a *street gang*? How common are they? What effect do gangs have on crime and delinquency? What are gangs like? And why do some individuals join gangs and some communities develop gangs?[9]

Before proceeding, it is important to emphasize the difficulty of talking about gangs in general. **Gangs often differ greatly from one another.** Gangs in one city, for example, may be large, highly organized, and heavily involved in drug sales. Gangs in another city may be small, loosely organized, and have little or no involvement in drug sales. The gangs within a particular city may also differ from one another. These differences are related to a number of factors, including the race/ethnic and sex composition of the gangs and whether the gangs are newly formed or have a long history.[10] As Short and Hughes observe, "No two gangs are alike, and they change constantly in membership, structure, and behavior; new gangs are formed and old ones fade away or merge with others" (quoted in Howell, 2015:517).

What Is a Street Gang?

There is no generally agreed-upon definition of a street gang.[11] As will become apparent in the discussion that follows, lack of a common definition has created a number of problems. For example, it is difficult to talk about the extent of gangs if the term has no generally accepted definition. Two cities may have similar gang problems, but officials in one city may employ a narrow definition of gangs and claim to have few gangs, while officials in the other city may employ a broad definition and claim to have many.

The definition of gangs employed in this text is the one agreed to by a group of more than 100 American and European gang researchers who held a series of meetings between 1997 and 2005 (see Klein and Maxson, 2006:4). A street gang is **"any durable, street-oriented youth group whose involvement in illegal activity is part of its group identity."** By "durable" the researchers mean that the group has existed for at least several months. By "street-oriented" they mean that the group spends much time in public settings such as the streets, parks, and malls. And by "group identity" they mean that group is viewed at least in part as one that engages in illegal activity. The dividing line between a delinquent peer group and a gang may sometimes be fuzzy, but gangs are distinguished by their stronger group identity and their relatively strong involvement in delinquency.

Certain researchers have offered more elaborate definitions of gangs. They state, for example, that gangs have territories or turfs they protect and that they have formal organizational structures (e.g., they have official positions like president, vice president, and war counselor). Many of the groups commonly thought of as gangs, however, are loosely organized at best and do not claim territories that they protect (Asian gangs, for example, often do not claim territories).

How Common Are Gangs?

Most estimates of the extent of gangs are obtained by surveying police and sometimes other officials in samples of cities around the United States (for an overview, see Curry and Decker, 2003). The estimates from these surveys should be regarded with caution. Not all jurisdictions are surveyed, many jurisdictions do not respond to the surveys, and police estimates of the number of gangs and gang members may be biased. Police departments employ different definitions of gangs, they may deny they have a gang problem (see Klein, 1995), or they may exaggerate their gang problem—perhaps to secure more funding (see Curry et al., 1996). Nevertheless, data suggest that gangs are widespread, being present in all major cities (250,000+ population) and in many smaller areas in the United States.

The most comprehensive survey examining the extent of gangs is carried out by the National Gang Center (see http://www.nationalgangcenter.gov), an agency created by the U.S. Department of Justice. The most recent survey, conducted in 2012, was mailed to 2,538 police and sheriff's departments across the country, including departments in all major cities and suburban areas, and a randomly selected sample of departments in small towns and rural areas (Egley et al., 2014). Based on the 2,199 departments that responded to the survey, it was estimated that 85 percent of cities with populations of more than 50,000 had gangs, and a substantial minority of smaller areas had gangs (e.g., 50 percent of suburban counties and 15 percent of rural counties). Most of the gang problem, however, is concentrated in larger urban areas. Data from the National Gang Center survey suggest that there were 30,700 gangs with 850,000 gang members in 2012.

Several self-report studies have examined the extent of gang membership. For the United States as a whole, these surveys suggest that about 2 percent of juveniles belong to gangs at any given time, and about 5 percent have belonged to a gang at some point in their lives (Klein and Maxson, 2006:21). Other self-report surveys have focused on the extent of gang membership in particular cities, such as Denver, Colorado, and Rochester, New York. These surveys of urban youth suggest that about 5 to 15 percent of adolescents belong to gangs in a given year, and 8 to 30 percent of all adolescents belong to gangs at some point during adolescence.[12] So only a small portion of youths belong to gangs, even in urban areas known to have gang problems. Such youths, however, are responsible for much delinquency, especially serious delinquency, as indicated next.

Are Gangs Becoming More Common?

Data suggest that gangs became much more common from the 1970s to the mid-1990s. Estimates show a steady increase in the number of gangs, gang members, and cities with gang problems during this time (see Curry and Decker, 2003; W. Miller, 2001). Gang activity, however, declined somewhat from 1996 to 2002, especially in smaller areas. In particular, data from the National Gang Center surveys indicate that the number of gang members decreased 14 percent from 1996 to 2002. **Since 2002, the number of gangs and gang members has been rising once again, despite a significant drop in the nation's crime rate over the same period**. This increase has been concentrated in larger, metropolitan areas (Egley et al., 2014).

What Effect Do Gangs Have on Crime and Delinquency?

How much crime and delinquency is gang related? It is not possible at present to give a precise answer to this question. Most cities do not attempt to calculate the proportion of all crimes that are gang related. Cities that do attempt such calculations usually focus only on homicide and maybe a small number of other serious crimes. Further, these cities often employ different methods to determine whether a crime is gang related. One city, for example, may classify a crime as gang related if the offender or victim is a known or suspected gang member. Another city, however, may classify a crime as gang related only if the motive is gang related (e.g., revenge against another gang, protection of turf).

Data, however, suggest that **a sizable share of all crime, particularly serious crime, is gang related in certain cities.** In a typical year, about half of all homicides in Los Angeles and Chicago—the two cities with the worst gang problems—are gang related (National Gang Center, 2013). Self-report studies also indicate that gang members account for a large share of crime, especially serious crime, in certain cities. In Denver, for example, gang members made up 14 percent of all adolescents in high-crime communities, but they accounted for 79 percent of all serious violent crimes and 71 percent of all serious property crimes committed by adolescents (Huizinga et al., 2003). Further, these patterns are not unique to U.S. cities; they have also been observed in Canada and Europe (Maxson and Matsuda, 2012).

While we cannot precisely estimate the share of all delinquency committed by gang members in the United States, it is clear that **gang members commit a substantial share of all delinquency—perhaps the majority of all serious delinquency—in certain cities.** These data, along with other data reported later, indicate that gangs should be a central focus of delinquency control and prevention efforts.

What types of crime do gang members commit? Gang members engage in a wide variety of criminal acts, both serious and minor. While gang members are disproportionately involved in all forms of crime, their disproportionate involvement is greatest for serious and violent offenses—including homicide. There are a number of reasons for this level of involvement in serious crimes like homicide (discussed later), including the fact that gang members are more likely than other juveniles to own and carry firearms, including automatic, high-powered guns.[13] The presence of guns often turns what would otherwise be an assault into a homicide (see Chapter 17).

Certain myths regarding gang crime should be addressed. First, some individuals have the impression that gang members spend most of their time engaged in crime. Although gang members do commit a lot of crime, **they spend the vast majority of their time simply hanging around**—talking and waiting for something to happen. Partying is perhaps their second most frequent activity. When gang members do engage in crime, they commit far more minor than serious crimes, something that is true of delinquents in general.

Second, many commentators claim that street gangs control drug sales in the United States, but data suggest that this belief is mistaken. Many gang members do engage in drug sales—a majority according to some studies. And gang members are more likely than nonmembers to engage in drug sales. But street gangs do not control drug sales in the United States. **Most drug sales are not conducted by gang members,** and when gang members do sell drugs, they usually do so as individuals and sporadically. It is true that some street gangs have been become heavily involved in drug sales, but they by no means control drug sales in the United States.[14] (It should be noted that drug sales in a community may be controlled by **drug gangs.** Drug gangs, however, are distinct from street gangs. Drug gangs are smaller, made up of older members, better organized, and focused on drug sales. Drug gangs sometimes employ the members of street gangs [Klein, 1995].)

Third, many people believe that the victims of gang violence are frequently innocent bystanders. It is true that innocent bystanders are sometimes killed and wounded, **but the members of other gangs are far and away the most frequent targets of gang violence.** Most acts of gang violence involve acts of revenge or turf disputes.

Fourth, it should again be emphasized that **gangs are not all alike.** Among other things, they differ from one another in terms of the extent and nature of their crime. Based on a study of three communities, Fagan (1989) describes four types of gangs: (1) social gangs, whose members engage in high levels of alcohol and marijuana use but little delinquency and other drug use; (2) party gangs, whose members engage in high rates of drug use and drug sales but otherwise engage in little delinquency (their drug sales help support their drug use); (3) serious delinquent gangs, whose members engage in a wide range of serious and minor delinquent acts but have little involvement in drug sales and serious drug use; and (4) "organization" gangs, whose members are heavily involved in delinquency, drug sales, and drug use. Other researchers have reported similar types of gangs (see Shelden et al., 2001; see Klein, 1998, for another typology of gangs).

Does gang membership cause delinquency? It is well established that gang members commit more delinquent acts, especially serious delinquent acts, than nonmembers. In fact, both official and self-report data suggest that gang members have rates of offending that are several times higher than nonmembers.[15] Further, data indicate that gang members also have much higher rates of delinquency than juveniles with delinquent friends.[16] This association, of course, does not mean that gang membership causes delinquency. The association may simply arise because delinquents are more likely to join gangs or because both gang membership and delinquency are caused by the same third variables. And data provide some support for these arguments: delinquent individuals are more likely to join gangs than nondelinquent individuals, and both gang membership and delinquency are caused by many of the same third variables. At the same time, data indicate that individuals experience a dramatic increase in delinquency after they join a gang and a dramatic decrease after they leave the gang. Further, the higher offending rates of gang members appear to hold even when a range of third variables are taken into account.[17] These important data suggest that **there is something about the gang itself that leads to an increase in offending.**

As with peer groups, the effect of gangs on offending can be explained in terms of social learning, strain, control, and labeling theories. With respect to **social learning theory,** researchers report that gang members hold values conducive to delinquency, such as toughness, achieving quick success, and backing fellow gang members. Gang members spend much time talking about their delinquent exploits and occasionally modeling delinquent behavior. And gang members frequently reinforce delinquent behavior and punish certain forms of conventional behavior. With respect to **strain theory,** gang members frequently get into conflicts with one another, the members of rival gangs, the police, and others. Such conflicts often lead to acts of retaliation or revenge (see D. Peterson et al., 2004). Further, gang membership makes it more difficult for individuals to achieve certain goals—like monetary success—through legitimate channels. This is because gang membership increases the likelihood that juveniles will do poorly in school, drop out of school, face employment problems, and become teenage parents (see Decker and Van Winkle, 1996; Thornberry, Krohn et al. [with Tobin], 2003). With respect to **control theory,** gang members have less fear of being sanctioned by others (because there is "power in numbers"). And gang members have a lower stake in conformity, because the gang pulls members away from conventional others and institutions, like school and work. With respect to **labeling theory,** gang members are more likely to be viewed and treated as delinquents or "bad people."[18]

What Are the Characteristics of Gang Members?

Gang members tend to be **poor and to live in lower-income, urban communities,** although gangs exist in some working-class and even middle-class areas.[19]

Gang members are **predominantly male.** The best data suggest that between 20 and 40 percent of gang members are female.[20] Self-report data show a greater percentage of female gang members than official estimates, perhaps because the police are less likely to notice female gang members and keep official statistics on them. Some police departments, for example, have had a policy of not counting females as gang members (Curry and Decker, 2003:111; Esbensen et al., 1999).

Most gang members are **young, typically teenagers.** Gang members tend to range in age from 12 to 30, with 14- and 15-year-olds having the highest rates of participation. There has been an increase in the number of younger and especially older gang members in recent decades. More and more adults are maintaining their gang membership, with some gang members in their 40s and even 50s. In the past, juveniles would quit or drift out of the gang as they got jobs and formed families. There has, however, been a massive loss of manufacturing jobs in inner-city communities, and so it has become more difficult for the young adults in those communities to find decent work. As a consequence, many of these young adults elect to maintain their gang ties—particularly since the gang provides opportunities for obtaining money through illegal channels.

Most gang members **belong to minority groups.** According to one estimate, based on a survey of law enforcement agencies, 35 percent of gang members are African American, 46 percent are Latino, 12 percent are white, and 7 percent belong to "other" racial or ethnic categories (National Gang Center, 2013).[21] These numbers probably underestimate the percentage of white gang members because law enforcement agencies tend **not** to classify many white law-violating groups as street gangs but as, for example, "skinheads" and other hate groups. Disproportionate minority involvement in gangs is also found in self-report studies, however (Esbensen and Osgood, 1997; Esbensen et al., 1999). There is also evidence that mixed-race gangs have become more common (Curry and Decker, 2003; Starbuck et al., 2004).

During the early 1900s, most gang members were white. They were often the children of recent immigrants to the United States—such as Italian, Polish, and Irish immigrants (see Thrasher, 1927, for a classic discussion of such gangs in Chicago). These ethnic groups were the ones that populated the poor inner-city communities, the communities where gangs are most common. As these groups moved up the economic ladder, they were replaced by African Americans migrating from the rural South, Latinos from Mexico and elsewhere, and Asians. Unfortunately, it will be more difficult for today's inner-city residents to move up the economic ladder, given the recent losses in manufacturing jobs that pay a decent wage.

How Are Gangs Organized or Structured?

Gangs are often portrayed as highly organized groups. It is said that they have well-defined roles, such as president, vice president, war counselor, and treasurer; that they have well-defined goals and extensive rules that members are supposed to follow, with these goals and rules being specified in written constitutions or other documents; that they have hundreds or even thousands of members, with smaller gangs being organized into larger gang confederations; and that they are highly cohesive, with members expressing great loyalty to one another and to the larger group. It is true that some gangs are like this, particularly the older, larger gangs that exist in cities like Chicago and Los Angeles. Most gangs, however, do not fit this model.

Most gangs are **loosely organized** (see especially Klein, 1995; Klein and Maxson, 2006). They do not have well-defined roles. There is often a distinction between core members and fringe members, with the fringe members including "wannabes." Wannabes are individuals—often younger juveniles—who want to join or become more involved with the gang. Certain of the core members function as leaders at times; but the leaders may shift from occasion to occasion, and no one may claim to be the leader of the gang. In most gangs, however, members divide into a number of informal cliques or subgroups—and crimes are often committed with the members of these cliques.

There are few well-defined goals or rules for members to follow, beyond the goals and rules that characterize many gang and nongang youth in inner-city communities (e.g., be tough, do not "snitch," "squeal," or "rat" to authorities). The membership of a gang often changes a good deal over time; self-report studies indicate that most gang members belong to the gang for less than a year. Most estimates of gang size are in the 25 to 250 range. The gang itself is not highly cohesive. Some researchers have noted that there is often more conflict between members of the same gang than among members of different gangs. Several observers, in fact, have pointed out that what binds gang members together is not so much their respect and affection for one another as it is their conflict with external groups like other gangs and the police.

What Are Female Gangs Like?

Females are found in **gangs of three types**. Most are in mixed-sex gangs; that is, some members are male and some are female. Many are in female gangs that are affiliated with male gangs (e.g., the Vice Queens are affiliated with the Vice Kings). And a much smaller number are in independent female gangs (see Maxson and Whitlock, 2002; D. Peterson et al., 2001).

The impression is sometimes given that female gang members are largely subservient to male members, with the female members being sexual objects to be used by the male members. Studies, however, suggest that female gang members exercise a good deal of control over their own affairs. And while both male and female gang members may engage in much sexual behavior, female gang members sanction indiscriminate sexual behavior. Further, female gang members engage in a wide range of delinquent acts, including aggressive acts. This is especially true of females in mixed-sex gangs that are predominantly male (see D. Peterson et al., 2001). **Overall, however, female gang members are not as delinquent as male gang members.**

Females join gangs for many of the same reasons that males join (K. Bell, 2009). They often have friends or relatives in the gang. And the gang is often seen as a solution to the problems they face. Many of these problems are shared with males, like class and race discrimination. Data, however, suggest that there are **two problems with special relevance to female gang members. First,** some data indicate that female gang members are more likely than male gang members to have experienced problems like **abuse at home.** Females may join the gang in an effort to cope with such problems: The gang makes it easier to escape from home life and may function as a surrogate family. In this area, some data suggest that females are more likely to join gangs in an effort to form close, family-like ties with their peers, while males are more likely to join because they are attracted to the "action" associated with the gang (see Esbensen et al., 1999). Jody Miller (2001:49–50) illustrates certain of these points in the following description of a female gang member, taken from Miller's field study of female gangs in two cities:

> Brittany described a terrible violent family life. She lived in a household with extended family—twelve people in all—including her mother, grandmother, stepfather, and an adolescent uncle who was physically abusive. Her aunt's boyfriend had sexually assaulted her at the age of five, but family members didn't believe her. Although she didn't know her father, who was in jail, she had early memories of him physically abusing her mother. Moreover, she felt very disconnected and unloved by her family and also described being isolated at school: "I didn't have no friends, used to always get teased. . . . My grades started going down, I started getting real depressed, started skipping school, smoking weed after school and stuff." Brittany saw the gang as a means of finding love. She explained: "I felt that my family didn't care for me . . . that when I was on the streets I felt that I got more love than when I was in the house. So I felt that that's where my love was, on the streets, so that's where I stayed."

Second, females are more likely than males to join gangs in an effort to **partially escape from the gender oppression they encounter or anticipate encountering in the future.** Campbell (1990:172–173) describes the gender oppression that many lower-income females will likely encounter: (1) "a future of meaningless domestic labor with little possibility of educational or occupational escape," (2) "subordination to the man in the house," (3) "responsibility for children," and (4) "the social isolation of the housewife." According to Campbell (1990:172), the gang "represents for its members an idealized collective solution to the bleak future that awaits." That is, the gang represents a source of fun and excitement, although Campbell notes that gang members tend to exaggerate the positive side of gang life and minimize the negative.

This desire to escape from gender oppression does not mean that female gang members hold "liberated" views and that the gang is an effective solution to the problems they face. Female gang members often hold traditional gender role attitudes in many areas (although they are more accepting of the use of violence by females). As Chesney-Lind et al. state, "Girls' gang life is certainly not an expression of 'liberation,' but instead reflects the attempts of young women to cope with a bleak and harsh present as well as a dismal future" (1996:203). Furthermore, female gang members often find that they confront a range of problems when they join the gang, including physical and sexual abuse by the male gang members, many of whom hold sexist attitudes.[22]

Why Do Some Juveniles Join Gangs?

Juveniles give a variety of reasons for joining gangs. Some are **social.** They have friends in the gang with whom they like to socialize. They see the gang as a source of fun and excitement (e.g., the gang holds a lot of parties and helps them meet romantic partners). They like the support, companionship, and sense of belonging they get from the gang; the gang is like a family. These social reasons are emphasized by the following comments of a member of a Chicago street gang:

> People are always putting down gangs because they say we're punks and up to no good, but they don't understand what gangs are all about. [While growing up] I remember seeing these guys; hey, they cared about each other more than a lot of other people who are not in gangs do. . . . [T]hey were always looking out for each other. And that's exactly what we did when we became gang members. . . . They were like my brothers. We did everything together. (Quoted in Padilla, 1992:132)

Some of the other reasons for joining a gang relate to a **desire for a positive identity and status.** The gang makes them feel important, powerful, respected, and feared by others. Some of the reasons reflect a **desire for security or protection from others.** They believe the gang provides them with protection from rival gang members and others. (Note: This belief is mistaken. Individuals are more likely to be victimized after they join gangs [Melde et al., 2009; Ozer and Engel, 2012; D. Peterson et al., 2004].) They may also believe that the gang provides protection for the neighborhood and that it is their duty or responsibility to join. Finally, individuals may join for reasons of **financial gain.** They believe that the gang will help them make money through activities like drug selling, robbery, and burglary. Individuals are forced to join gangs in some cases, but such forced entry is uncommon. Most individuals join gangs because they believe that it will benefit them in some way.

By the time juveniles decide to join a gang, they have usually been hanging around with gang members for a while. They typically go through an **initiation ceremony,** which may involve being "jumped in" or "beaten' in" by other gang members (i.e., enduring a beating by other gang members). The initiation might also involve the commission of a crime or going on a "mission" against a rival gang (e.g., fighting or shooting a rival gang member).

As mentioned earlier, **most gang members leave the gang within a year.** There are a variety of reasons for leaving: witnessing the death or injury of a friend, being the direct victim of violence, being sent to a correctional institution, getting a job, having children, getting married, burnout from frequent arrests, or simply "maturing out" with age. The gang itself may also break up (see Decker and Lauritsen, 1996, for a discussion of leaving the gang). Contrary to certain accounts, most individuals are able to leave gangs without suffering serious reprisals from other gang members.

Applying the theories. At a deeper level, one can explain why individuals join gangs in terms of strain, social learning, and control theories. Individuals may join gangs in an effort to **cope with their strain.** In many cases, they may be unable to achieve their goals through legitimate channels. Most commonly, they cannot make enough money through legitimate work or obtain the respect they feel they deserve. The gang may be seen as a way to make money through illegitimate channels or to achieve status and respect (see Cloward and Ohlin, 1960; A. Cohen, 1955). Their strain may also result from the loss of positive stimuli or the presentation of negative stimuli. For example, juveniles who are neglected or abused by family members may find that the gang allows them to escape from that environment; in fact, the gang may function as a surrogate family, albeit an imperfect one. Juveniles who are harassed by others in their school or community may see the gang as a source of protection. Juveniles who feel that their lives are rather dull or boring may see the gang as a source of excitement. In addition, a juvenile may see the gang as a vehicle for rebelling or retaliating against individuals and groups who have mistreated him or her.

The experience of strain, however, does not guarantee that individuals will join a gang. Strained individuals are more likely to join gangs if they **have friends who are**

gang members and if they live in communities where gang members are respected and reinforced for gang membership. In such cases, strained individuals will be exposed to attractive models who are gang members, will likely be exposed to beliefs favoring gang membership, and will likely conclude that gang membership offers them certain benefits.

Strained individuals with exposure to appealing gang members, however, will not necessarily join gangs. Their parents or others may prevent them from doing so. And they may be concerned about the possible costs of gang membership. Among other things, gang membership may hurt their relations with parents and others, interfere with their schoolwork, and jeopardize their future career goals. Gang membership, then, is more likely when juveniles are **low in direct control (e.g., are not well supervised by parents) and have a low stake in conformity (e.g., dislike their parents, are doing poorly in school, and have low aspirations for future success).**

If these arguments are correct, we would expect gang members to differ from nonmembers in a number of ways. Gang members should be more likely to possess traits that contribute to strain, low control, and a propensity to find delinquency reinforcing. Such traits include low intelligence, irritability, and low self-control. Gang members should be more likely to experience the types of strain described earlier. Gang members should be more likely to have had friends who were gang members before they joined a gang. Gang members should be more likely to experience the family problems described in Chapter 14, such as poor parental supervision, parental rejection, and abuse. And gang members should be more likely to experience the school problems described in Chapter 15, such as poor grades, low attachment to teachers, and dropping out.

Case studies of gang members provide some support for these arguments. Such studies usually report that juveniles join gangs partly because they are experiencing one or more types of strain, that juveniles knew gang members before they joined the gang, and that juveniles were low in at least certain types of control before they joined the gang. Some studies also suggest that gang members are likely to possess the individual traits listed in the preceding paragraph, although there is more disagreement about this point than about the others. These cases studies, however, suffer from certain problems. Most notably, they usually examine only a small number of gang members, and they seldom compare gang members to nongang members. It may be the case, for example, that members of the community who don't belong to gangs are just as high in strain and low in control as gang members.

A few studies have surveyed gang and nongang members in an effort to overcome these methodological problems. Gang members are then compared to nonmembers in the same community. Sometimes a distinction is made between nonmembers who have engaged in certain types of delinquent offenses (nongang delinquents) and those who have not (nongang nondelinquents). These studies focus on some but not all of the variables listed here (e.g., they often fail to measure certain types of strain and certain individual traits).

The results of these studies generally support the preceding arguments; **gang members usually differ from nondelinquents in the ways described.** Some studies, however, find only minimal differences between gang members and nongang delinquents. It may be that discrepant results are found because many of the delinquents in the high-crime communities, which tend to be the ones studied, drift in and out of gangs. As a consequence, many of the nongang delinquents may be former gang members or may join gangs in the future. In any event, we may conclude that there is **some support for the strain, social learning, and control theory explanations of gang membership.**[23]

Why Do Some Communities Develop Gangs?

The same **deprived inner-city communities** that have the highest rates of delinquency are also the **most likely to develop gangs** (see Klein and Maxson, 2006; Jody Miller, 2001; Pyrooz et al., 2010; Thornberry, Krohn et al. [with Tobin], 2003). Not surprisingly, we can explain this in terms of the leading delinquency theories, especially control and strain theories.

As described in Chapter 12, **deprived communities are lower in control.** That is, residents are less likely to effectively supervise and sanction juveniles who engage in deviance, provide juveniles with a stake in conformity, and help juveniles develop strong internal controls. As a consequence, such juveniles frequently hang out on the street together and have little to lose by engaging in crime. Further, **juveniles in these communities experience much strain.** They have trouble achieving their goals through legitimate channels, particularly their monetary and status goals. As indicated in Chapter 12, decent jobs are scarce in such communities. Further, juveniles in these communities are often treated in a negative manner by others, including family members, school officials, peers, and the police. These juveniles, then, experience a number of problems for which the gang might be seen as an effective solution.

The juveniles in deprived communities are ripe for gang involvement (see Curry and Decker, 2003). Several reports suggest that **the triggering factor that turns these juveniles into gangs is conflict with others,** including conflict with other groups of youth, other gangs, and the police. Conflict with others is often an effective mechanism for uniting a group of people, and such conflict is often what turns the unorganized peer group into a gang. It has also been suggested that **many inner-city juveniles may form gangs in response to media portrayals of gang life** (more on this later).

How Can We Explain Long-Term Trends in Gang Activity?

There was a dramatic increase in the number of gangs and gang members from the 1970s to the mid-1990s. Further, gangs spread to many suburban communities, small towns, and even rural areas during this time. These changes have been explained in several ways.

As indicated in Chapter 12, **the number of high-poverty neighborhoods and the number of people living in them increased greatly between the 1970s and the early**

1990s. This occurred for several reasons, including the loss of manufacturing jobs that paid a decent wage, the movement of middle- and working-class African Americans from inner-city to suburban areas, and the concentration of public housing in inner-city communities. For reasons described in the last section, high-poverty communities are more likely to develop gangs. So as high-poverty communities become more common, gangs should become more common as well.

Gangs also spread to many working-class and even middle-class communities, including suburban communities and small towns. How might this be explained? The loss of manufacturing jobs, mentioned earlier, also had some effect on these communities. Many working- and lower-middle-class adolescents, especially those doing poorly in school, found that their economic future was uncertain. They could no longer count on getting blue-collar jobs that paid decent wages. This reduced their stake in conformity and increased their level of strain, making them more amenable to gang involvement. Further, many suburban areas and small towns experienced large increases in population, particularly as urban residents left the city and immigrants settled in the United States. These population increases may have reduced levels of control (recall the discussion of residential instability in Chapter 12). The increases also may have **contributed to conflicts among youth groups.** (For an excellent illustration of these arguments, see the discussion of the rise of skinhead groups among working- and lower-middle-class white youth in Blazak, 1999.)

Yet another factor contributing to the increase in gangs during this period may be the **increase in youth violence between the late 1980s and the mid-1990s,** an increase fueled by the crack trade (see Chapter 3). The rise in violence may have increased the appeal of gangs to youths who viewed gangs as a way to protect themselves from the violence around them (see Rosenfeld et al., 1999).

It has also been argued that the **media and generators of pop culture (e.g., clothing manufacturers, the movie industry) contributed to the spread of gangs by introducing juveniles to gang culture,** including gang dress, talk, hand signals, graffiti, and behavior (see Klein, 1995). That is, the media and manufacturers provided juveniles with gang models to imitate. As Klein and associates (1995:110) point out:

> Baggy pants, Pendleton-style shirts, high-top shoes, ball caps worn backward or at angles, graffiti styles, words like "homey" and "hood" and other signs of affiliations have become part of the larger youth culture. In essence, commercial America has taught youthful America how to walk, talk, dress, and act "gangster-style."

Many juveniles, especially those experiencing the low control and strain described earlier, copied what they saw.[24]

It is sometimes claimed that the rapid growth in gangs was also the result of a plan on the part of certain gangs to increase their influence. Members of these gangs, it is said, deliberately moved to other cities with the intention of setting up new gang chapters, thereby increasing their share of the drug trade and other illegal activities. It is easy to understand the basis of this belief, since the gangs in many cities adopted the names of well-known gangs or gang federations from other cities, such as the Bloods and the Crips from Los Angeles or the People and Folk Nation from Chicago. Data, however, suggest that **the spread of gangs was not deliberately planned by gang members from certain cities.** Most gangs were homegrown, despite the practice of adopting the names and symbols of well-known gangs. When members of gangs like the Bloods and the Crips did move to a new city, it was usually because their families had decided to move, not because the younger relatives had been on a mission to spread gangs (see Howell, 1998a, and Klein, 1995, for a fuller discussion).

The temporary decline in gangs between the mid-1990s and 2002 may also be explained in several ways. It may be partly due to the **strong economy** during this time and the **associated decline in high-poverty communities** (see Chapter 12). It may be due to the **decline in youth violence during this time,** which possibly reduced the appeal of gangs as protective mechanisms. And it may be due to some of the **other factors** that contributed to the general decline in serious crime that began in the mid-1990s (see Chapter 3).

As described earlier, we have witnessed a modest but steady increase in the number of gangs since 2002. The reasons for this latest increase are not fully understood, but possible causes include the economic downturns of the 2000s and a rise, once again, in the number of high-poverty neighborhoods (see Chapter 12).

SUMMARY

Delinquent peer groups and gangs are major causes of delinquency. It is true that delinquent individuals are more likely to associate with other delinquents and to join gangs. It is also true that both delinquency and membership in delinquent groups are caused by many of the same third variables. At the same time, the data suggest that an individual's association with delinquent others, especially gang members, causes a substantial increase in the individual's delinquency. This increase was explained in terms of strain, social learning, control, and labeling theories.

TEACHING AIDS

Controversial Issue: What Is a Gang?

Bursik and Grasmick (1993) described a group allegedly involved in a gang rape in Philadelphia. The group was composed of older adolescents; it was recognized by others and recognized itself as a distinct group, with its own name and symbols; it was heavily involved in deviant and delinquent behavior; it had a reputation in the community as a deviant or troublesome group; it was cohesive and well organized; and it had a "turf" that it protected. According to Bursik and Grasmick:

> Women commonly reported that they had been harassed by members of the gang who hung around drinking beer on benches in the primary street in the area. Since these benches were situated in front of their clubhouse, the group made it clear that this was their "turf" to do with as they pleased. (1993:114)

Based on this description, most people would probably agree that this group was a gang. The group appears to satisfy the criteria of even the more restrictive definitions of gangs. The group, however, was a fraternity on the campus of a prestigious, upper-middle-class university in Philadelphia, and there is some evidence that others did not view the group as a gang. For example, the Gang Crimes Unit of the Philadelphia Police Department was not involved in a rape case against this group.

We do not mean to imply by this example that all fraternities are gangs. Clearly, they are not, although many colleges have at least one fraternity on campus that is heavily involved in deviant and illegal behaviors like drug and alcohol abuse, vandalism, and sexual violence. **Is it appropriate to classify these fraternities—or the fraternity in the example—as gangs?** Defend your position.

Web-Based Exercise: An Examination of Two Major Gangs

There are scores of videos focusing on gangs, but most emphasize the violence and crimes committed by gangs. These videos often fail to give you a good sense of why some communities are more likely than others to develop gangs and why some juveniles are more likely than others to join gangs. A notable exception, the documentary "Crips and Bloods:

Made in America," focuses on two very large, relatively organized gangs in Los Angeles: the Crips and the Bloods. The gangs in this video are not typical of most gangs, which are small and loosely organized. Nevertheless, the Crips and the Bloods are quite important and account for much crime in Los Angeles, including serious crime. This documentary stands out among others because it describes the social conditions that contributed to the development of the gangs and the factors that cause many youth to join. You should watch the documentary; it is available on Netflix, can be rented at Amazon.com, and can sometimes be viewed free of charge at certain websites. When viewing the video, keep the following questions in mind and try to apply materials in this chapter when answering them: Why did the Bloods and the Crips develop in certain communities in Los Angeles? Why do some juveniles join these gangs? What are the characteristics of the gang members? What effect do these gangs have on delinquency? What can be done to reduce the gangs' prevalence and effects?

TEST YOUR KNOWLEDGE OF THIS CHAPTER

1. Having delinquent friends is typically the strongest correlate of delinquency, but this does not prove that delinquent friends cause delinquency. Why not?
2. Describe the evidence suggesting that delinquent friends cause delinquency.
3. Under what conditions are delinquent friends most likely to cause delinquency?
4. Describe the characteristics of a typical delinquent peer group (type and extent of delinquency, size and composition, age and sex, quality of relations between members).
5. How is an "offending group" different from an "accomplice network"?
6. Drawing on the major delinquency theories, explain why associating with delinquent peers increases the likelihood of delinquency.
7. Why are some juveniles more likely than others to associate with delinquent peers?
8. What impact do romantic partners have on delinquency? Is the impact stronger on males or females?
9. Describe the definition of gangs used in this book. How do gangs differ from delinquent peer groups?
10. How have researchers estimated the extent of gangs and gang membership? What major conclusions do they draw in this area?
11. Are gangs becoming more common? Describe trends in gangs and gang membership since the 1970s.
12. How much crime is gang related?
13. List any two "myths" about gangs and describe the evidence on these myths.
14. Drawing on the major delinquency theories, describe why gang membership increases the likelihood of delinquency.
15. Describe the characteristics of gang members (class, gender, age, race, ethnicity).
16. How would you respond to the statement that "gangs are highly organized"?
17. Females join gangs for many of the same reasons as males, although there are two reasons for joining that are more applicable to females than males. What are these reasons?
18. List any three of the major reasons that juveniles give for joining gangs.
19. Drawing on the leading delinquency theories, explain why some juveniles are more likely than others to join gangs.

20. Why are deprived inner-city communities more likely to develop gangs?
21. How might we explain the major trends in gangs and gang membership since the 1970s?

THOUGHT AND DISCUSSION QUESTIONS

1. Did the delinquent peer groups in your high school or community fit the description provided in this chapter (size and composition, reasons for affecting delinquency, etc.)? Were there any gangs in your high school or home community? If so, to what extent did these gangs correspond to the descriptions presented in this chapter (characteristics of members, organization, extent of delinquency, reasons for joining, etc.)?

2. Why do you think street gangs lead to larger increases in delinquency than delinquent peer groups?

3. What policies or programs might we employ to address delinquent peer groups and gangs? (Note: Certain of these policies or programs might try to prevent delinquent peer groups and gangs from forming; others might try to change the nature of these groups, making them more "prosocial" in focus; and others might try to increase the likelihood that individuals will avoid these groups or resist their negative influence. See Chapter 24 for a discussion of delinquency control and prevention programs focusing on delinquent peer groups and gangs.)

KEY TERMS

- Delinquent peer group
- Offending group
- Accomplice network
- Street gang

ENDNOTES

1. For overviews and select studies on peers and delinquency, see Agnew, 1991b; Akers and Jensen, 2003; Barnes et al., 2006; Brame et al., 1999; Brezina et al., 2004; Chapple, 2005; Elliott and Menard, 1996; Elliott et al., 1985; Farrington and Welsh, 2007; Gifford-Smith et al., 2005; Gorman and White, 1995; Haynie, 2001, 2002; Haynie and Osgood, 2005; Haynie et al., 2006; Huizinga et al., 2003; Jang, 1999; Krohn et al., 1995; Matsueda and Anderson, 1998; McGloin, 2009; McGloin and Shermer, 2009; Meier et al., 1984; Meldrum et al., 2009; Patterson and Dishion, 1985; Patterson et al., 1992; N. Piquero et al., 2005; Pratt and Cullen, 2000; Reed and Rountree, 1997; Reiss, 1988; Rutter and Giller, 1983; Sampson and Laub, 1993a; Stewart and Simons, 2006; Thornberry, 1996; Thornberry et al., 1994; Thornberry, Krohn et al. (with Porter), 2003; Warr, 2002; Warr and Stafford, 1991; Wiesner and Capaldi, 2003; Wilson and Herrnstein, 1985; L. Zhang and Messner, 2000.

2. Also see Akers, 1998; Brezina et al., 2004; Matsueda and Anderson, 1998; Rutter et al., 1998; Thornberry, 1996; Thornberry et al., 1994; Thornberry, Krohn et al. (with Porter), 2003; Warr, 2002.

3. See Agnew, 1990a, 1991b, 1993; Elliott et al., 1985; Haynie, 2001, 2002; N. Piquero et al., 2005; Warr, 2002; Warr and Stafford, 1991; Weerman and Smeenk, 2005.

4. Also see Agnew, 1993; Elliott and Menard, 1996; Hagan, 1991.

5. See Agnew, 2006a; Akers and Jensen, 2003; Brezina et al., 2004; Briar and Piliavin, 1965; Gifford-Smith et al., 2005; Hughes and Short, 2005; R. Johnson et al., 1987; McCarthy et al., 2004; McGloin, 2009; Rebellon, 2006; Short and Strodtbeck, 1965; Tittle et al., 1986; Warr, 2002.

6. See Chapple, 2005; R. Johnson, 1979; McGloin and Shermer, 2009; Patterson and Dishion, 1985; Thornberry, 1996; Thornberry et al., 1994; Wright, Caspi, Moffitt, and Silva, 1999, 2001.

7. See Elliott et al., 1985; Jensen, 1972; Patterson and Dishion, 1985; Patterson et al., 1992; Sampson and Laub, 1993a; Warr, 2005.

8. See Elliott et al., 1985; Hawkins and Lishner, 1987; R. Johnson, 1979; Thornberry, 1987, 1996.

9. Several excellent ethnographies or case studies of specific gangs have been listed and briefly summarized by Curry and Decker (2003), Decker et al. (2013), and Shelden et al. (2001). For overviews of the research on street gangs, see Curry and Decker, 2003; Decker et al., 2013; Decker and Van Winkle, 1996; Esbensen et al., 2004; Howell, 1995, 1998a, 2003a; 2015; Howell et al., 2002; Huff, 2002; Klein, 1995, 1998; Klein and Maxson, 2006; Knox, 2000; Maxson and Matsuda, 2012; Jody Miller et al., 2001; Joan Moore and Hagedorn, 2001; National Gang Center, 2013; Office of Juvenile Justice and Delinquency Prevention, 1999a; Shelden et al., 2001; James Short, 1997; Spergel, 1995; Thornberry, Krohn et al. (with Tobin), 2003.

10. See Freng and Winfree, 2004; Howell, 1998a; Klein, 1995; Klein and Maxson, 2006; Spergel, 1995.

11. For discussions of how to define gangs, see Bursik and Grasmick, 1993; Esbensen, Tibbetts, and Gaines, 2004; Esbensen et al., 2001; Howell, 2003a, 2015; Klein and Maxson, 2006; Maxson and Matsuda, 2012.

12. See Esbensen and Deschenes, 1998; Esbensen and Huizinga, 1993; Esbensen et al., 1993, 2001; Hill et al., 1999; Howell, 1995, 1997b, 2015; Klein and Maxson, 2006; Office of Juvenile Justice and Delinquency Prevention, 1999a; Spergel, 1995:31–32; Thornberry and Burch, 1997; Thornberry and Krohn, 2003.

13. See Bjerregaard and Lizotte, 1995; Curry and Decker, 2003; Howell, 1995, 1998a, 1999; Huff, 2002, 2004; Klein and Maxson, 2006; Lizotte et al., 1994.

14. See Curry and Decker, 2003; Howell, 1995, 1998a, 2003a; Howell and Gleason, 1999; Huff, 2002; Klein, 1995; Klein and Maxson, 2006; Klein et al., 1995; Maxson, 1995; Spergel, 1995.

15. See Bjerregaard and Smith, 1993; Curry and Decker, 2003; Esbensen and Huizinga, 1993; Esbensen et al., 2001; Fagan, 1990; Howell, 1995, 1997b, 2004; Huff, 1998, 2002, 2004; Huizinga et al., 2003; Klein and Maxson, 2006; Maxson and Matsuda, 2012; Thornberry, 1998; Thornberry et al., 1993; Thornberry and Krohn, 2003.

16. See Battin et al., 1998; Gatti et al., 2005; Gordon et al., 2004; Howell, 1998a; Huizinga, 1996; Huizinga et al., 2003; Klein and Maxson, 2006; Melde and Esbensen, 2013; Thornberry, 1998; Thornberry and Krohn, 2003; Tita and Ridgeway, 2007.

17. See Bellair and McNulty, 2009; Bjerregaard, 2010; Esbensen et al., 1993; Gatti et al., 2005; Gordon et al., 2004; Huff, 1998; Thornberry, 1998; Thornberry et al., 1993; Thornberry and Krohn, 2003.

18. See Brownfield et al., 2001; Decker and Van Winkle, 1996; Howell, 1998a; Klein and Maxson, 2006; Matsuda et al., 2013; Shelden et al., 2001; Short and Strodtbeck, 1965; Spergel, 1995.

19. See Curry and Decker, 2003; Klein and Maxson, 2006; Jody Miller, 2001; Thornberry and Krohn, 2003.

20. See Bjerregaard and Smith, 1993; Chesney-Lind et al., 1996; Curry and Decker, 2003; Esbensen and Deschenes, 1998; Esbensen and Osgood, 1997; Esbensen et al., 1993, 1999, 2001; Hill et al., 1999; Klein and Maxson, 2006; Jody Miller, 2001; Moore and Hagedorn, 2001; Shelden et al., 2001; Spergel, 1995; Thornberry and Krohn, 2003.

21. See John Moore and Cook, 1999; also see Curry and Decker, 2003; Hill et al., 1999; Howell, 1997b; Klein and Maxson, 2006; Spergel, 1995; Thornberry and Krohn, 2003.

22. For a fuller discussion of female gang involvement, see Bowker and Klein, 1983; Campbell, 1990; Chesney-Lind and Shelden, 2004; Chesney-Lind et al., 1996; Curry, 1998; Curry and Decker, 2003; Esbensen and Deschenes, 1998; Esbensen et al., 1999; Fishman, 1995; Klein, 1995; Maxson and Whitlock, 2002; McGloin and DiPietro, 2013; Jody Miller, 2001; Jody Miller and Brunson, 2004; Joan Moore and Hagedorn, 1996, 2001; Peterson et al., 2001; Shelden et al., 2001.

23. For examples and discussions of the research in this area, see Bell, 2009; Bjerregaard and Smith, 1993; Bowker and Klein, 1983; Brownfield et al., 1997; Curry and Decker, 2003; Esbensen and Deschenes, 1998; Esbensen et al., 1993, 2001, 2009; Esbensen, Tibbetts, and Gaines, 2004; Fagan, 1990; Hill et al., 1999; Hill et al., 2004; Howell, 1998a, 2003a:89–91, 2004; Klein, 1995,

1998; Klein and Maxson, 2006; Klein et al., 1995; Jody Miller et al., 2001; Shelden et al., 2001; James Short, 1997; Spergel, 1995; Thornberry, 1998; Thornberry, Krohn et al. (with Tobin), 2003; Vigil and Yun, 1996; J. Wood and Alleyne, 2010; Yoder et al., 2003.

24. For fuller discussions of these arguments, see Bursik and Grasmick, 1993; Fagan, 1996; Hagedorn, 1988; Pamela Jackson, 1991; Klein, 1995; Klein et al., 1995; Jody Miller, 2001; Shelden et al., 2001; Spergel, 1995.

17 Other Social Influences

What Effects Do Religion, Work, Mass Media Violence, Social Media, Drugs, and Guns Have on Delinquency?

The family, the school, and the peer group constitute the major social environments for most adolescents. Adolescents spend most of their time in these environments and usually develop close relationships with the people in each one. So it is not surprising that family members, peers, and sometimes school officials affect adolescents strongly. But these are not the only influences on adolescents. Adolescents may also be influenced by their religion, their work experiences, their exposure to mass media violence, their involvement with social media, and their exposure to drugs and guns. This chapter examines these other influences. We address several questions that have been receiving a great deal of attention in the media: Does religion reduce delinquency? Does work prevent delinquency among juveniles attending school? Does mass media violence contribute to violent behavior? Does social media engagement increase the risk of delinquency? Do drugs increase delinquency? And does the possession of guns contribute to delinquency?

After reading this chapter, you should have tentative answers to these questions. In particular, you should be able to:

- Summarize the major research findings as they relate to religion and delinquency.
- Discuss the impact of work on delinquency.
- Summarize the major findings and conclusions regarding the effects of media violence exposure, and explain why researchers continue to debate its importance.
- Describe the potential risks and benefits of social media engagement as it relates to crime and delinquency.
- Describe the relationship between drug use and delinquency. Explain how drug use contributes to delinquency and to what extent.
- Discuss the availability of firearms in the United States, and describe the relationship between juvenile access to firearms and violent behavior.

Before reviewing the research, we emphasize an important point. As stated earlier in the book, delinquency is caused by a good number of factors, which usually work together. Despite the tendency of politicians and the general public to single out particular risk factors (e.g., "lack of religion, "media violence," or "guns"), delinquent behavior is rarely the product of a single, isolated risk factor. We will return to this point throughout the chapter, as it helps place the research in perspective and because it has significant policy implications.

DOES RELIGION REDUCE DELINQUENCY?

A letter to the editor of our local newspaper claimed that there was little mystery regarding the causes of crime and delinquency: "The answer is so simple. The answer is this: A lack of religion in these persons' lives has caused them to fail in our society." The letter writer went on to speculate that few delinquents attend church on a regular basis. Like this letter writer, many people believe that a lack of religion is a major cause of delinquency. In fact, many politicians and other people have claimed that the lack of religion is one of the major causes of crime and violence in our society—like the tragic shooting deaths of 20 children and 6 adults at Sandy Hook Elementary School and other well-publicized incidents of school violence. Some commentators say that the root cause of these events is society's rejection of scripture and the exclusion of God from our public schools. Many politicians have been actively searching for ways to increase the role of religion in people's lives—ways like posting the Ten Commandments in public places such as courthouses and schools.

There are good reasons for believing that **religion has an effect on delinquency.**[1] Most notably, **religion may increase control.** Religion may increase direct control, since religious juveniles may come under the watchful eye of those in their religious community. And religion may instill a fear of supernatural sanction in juveniles—punishment by God. Religion may also increase one's stake in conformity, with the result that religious juveniles may develop good reputations and strong emotional bonds to others in their religious community. Further, religion may increase internal control, since religious juveniles may be more likely to learn beliefs that condemn delinquency and to be taught self-control. It is the effect of religion on internal control that is most commonly mentioned in discussions on the topic.

In terms of **social learning theory,** religion may increase the likelihood that juveniles are exposed to conventional models, are taught conventional beliefs, are punished for deviance, and are reinforced for conformity. Further, it has been suggested that religious participation **may reduce strain,** since religious communities may provide the juvenile with social support, and religious beliefs may divert attention from current problems to the rewards of the afterlife. Finally, religious participation may **reduce the likelihood of being labeled** a delinquent. What do the data indicate? Does religion reduce the likelihood of delinquency?

The Evidence

Researchers have produced a moderate number of studies in this area. Religion is most commonly measured by asking respondents how frequently they attend religious services. Many studies also ask respondents what their religion or religious denomination is, how important religion is in their daily lives, and whether they hold certain religious beliefs (e.g., "Is there life after death?" "Will evil people suffer in hell?"). Most studies are cross-sectional, and many fail to control for potentially relevant third variables. Nevertheless, certain conclusions can be drawn from the data.

Most data indicate that **religious juveniles are somewhat less delinquent than nonreligious juveniles, especially when it comes to "victimless crimes" like alcohol and marijuana use.** Recent data, however, suggest that a good part of the association between religion and delinquency is due to third variables, including low self-control, parental supervision, and attachment to parents and school. But even after controlling for these third variables, the data suggest that religion has a modest effect on delinquency, especially on victimless crimes like marijuana use and underage drinking. **This effect is partly indirect.** For example, data suggest that religion affects delinquency partly through its effect on the peers with whom the juvenile associates. Religious individuals are less likely to associate with deviant peers.[2]

Why is it that religion reduces involvement in victimless crimes, whereas no association with serious crimes has been observed? The most commonly offered explanation is that serious crimes are condemned by both religious and nonreligious individuals and groups. Therefore, both religious and nonreligious juveniles are equally likely to refrain from such crimes. Victimless crimes, however, are condemned more strongly by religious groups, so we find that religious individuals are less likely to commit them.

We have been talking about religion in general up to this point. You might be wondering whether different religions or religious denominations have different effects on delinquency. The data in this area are mixed, although studies tend to indicate that **the members of more fundamentalist or**

conservative religious groups commit fewer victimless crimes. Such groups include Baptists and Mormons (as opposed, e.g., to Unitarians and Presbyterians, who tend to be more liberal).

Researchers continue to study the effect of religion on delinquency. One major line of research argues that religion is more likely to affect delinquency in some circumstances than others. Most notably, some researchers argue that religion is more likely to reduce delinquency when adolescents are surrounded by other religious individuals. For example, the adolescent has religious parents, attends a school with a high percentage of religious students, and lives in a community having a high percentage of religiously active residents. If religious youth are surrounded by other religious people, they are more likely to form close bonds to those individuals and to take account of religious considerations in their daily life. But if they are surrounded by people who are indifferent to religion, they are more likely to have conflicts with these others and to ignore or put aside religious considerations. Studies in this area have produced mixed results, but most find support for the argument **that religion is more likely to reduce delinquency when adolescents are surrounded by religious others.**[3]

In sum, religion appears to have a modest inhibiting effect on delinquency, especially when it takes the form of victimless crimes. The effect of religion per se is overshadowed by that of other groups, such as the family, peer group, and school.

DOES WORK REDUCE DELINQUENCY AMONG JUVENILES ATTENDING SCHOOL?

The percentage of juveniles who work while attending school has increased dramatically since World War II. It is estimated that 90 percent of all students now hold jobs at some point, and 80 percent of all students work during the school year at some point. One study of high school students found that during the academic year, employed juniors worked an average of 18.6 hours per week and employed seniors worked an average of 23.5 hours per week. The world of work now occupies a central place in the lives of many adolescents— alongside the family, school, and peer group. It is therefore important to ask whether work has an effect on delinquency among juveniles attending school.[4]

There are **good reasons for expecting work to reduce delinquency,** most of them derived from the leading delinquency theories. Work **may reduce monetary strain,** since it allows adolescents to earn money they can spend on their cars, clothing, social activities, and so on. (Data indicate that juveniles spend most of their wages on personal items and activities rather than giving their money to parents for family expenses or saving it for college.) Work **may increase control,** since adolescents in work settings are supervised by adults and their work provides them with a stake in conformity. Work may also increase the adolescent's acceptance of conventional moral values by increasing interaction with and attachment to adults who transmit such values. Work **may reduce the social learning of crime,** since adolescents who work have less time to interact with delinquent peers. Finally, limited data suggest that employment **often reduces crime among adults.**

It is therefore not surprising that most people believe that work is beneficial for juveniles and reduces the likelihood of delinquency. One often hears, for example, that "work builds character and responsibility" (Williams et al., 1996). Several prominent national commissions during the 1970s and 1980s also argued that work benefits juveniles, and they recommended that society provide adolescents with more work experience (see Paternoster et al., 2003). Many delinquency-control programs followed this recommendation and provided juveniles with work. What do the data show about the effect of work on delinquency?

The Evidence

A number of studies from the mid-1980s to the early 2000s investigated the effect of work on delinquency.[5] These studies challenged the view just described and suggested that adolescents who worked while attending school were somewhat **more** likely to engage in delinquency. This was especially true of adolescents who worked more than 20 hours per week. As a result of such findings, a prominent research group recommended in 1998 that the federal government restrict the number of hours that high school students work during the school year. And efforts were made to implement this recommendation (see Paternoster et al., 2003).

Researchers explained the higher delinquency among working adolescents in several ways. It was said that while work may reduce economic strain, it contributes to other types of strain. The working conditions associated with most adolescent jobs are rather poor, and the long hours worked by many adolescents—in combination with school, family, and social demands—can be stressful. In addition, it was said that the money from work makes it easier for adolescents to purchase drugs and alcohol and to engage in certain other illegal activities. (Data suggest that adolescents with more spending money are somewhat more likely to be delinquent.)[6] Further, it was said that work reduces certain types of control, since working adolescents spend less time with parents and have less time to devote to schoolwork. Finally, it was claimed that work does not reduce association with delinquent peers as much as originally thought, since adolescents often interact with delinquent peers at work (see Wright and Cullen, 2000).

Recent research, however, has challenged the view that work contributes to delinquency. According to this research, the studies mentioned earlier failed to properly take account of third variables that might influence the relationship between work and delinquency (see Chapter 5 for a discussion of *third variables*). In particular, certain of the factors that cause delinquency also increase the likelihood that adolescents will work long hours while in school. It is for this reason that work and delinquency are associated. Researchers, therefore, must adequately take account of, or "control for," the factors that influence both work and delinquency. Several better-controlled studies found that **work has little or no effect on delinquency for most adolescents** (Apel et al., 2007; Paternoster et al., 2003; Rocheleau and Swisher, 2012; for an exception, see Monahan et al., 2011). Perhaps certain of the positive and negative effects of work listed earlier cancel out. **Work,** however, **leads to a reduction in delinquency among those with a strong predisposition for delinquency.** These are adolescents who have traits conducive to delinquency, such as low self-control; are experiencing problems at home and at school; and associate with delinquent peers. Work appears to be of some advantage to these adolescents, perhaps offering them somewhat more supervision and contact with conventional adults than they would otherwise have in their lives. For certain high-risk youth, then, interventions that help them find jobs can be effective, as indicated by a recent evaluation of a summer jobs program in Chicago (Heller, 2014).

The preceding review highlights a key point made in Chapter 5. When evaluating research, it is important to keep in mind the conditions for making causal statements. At the same time, it is important to note that more research is needed in some areas, including the effect of work on delinquency. As Chapter 5 also notes, it can be dangerous to form conclusions based on one or a few studies.

DOES MASS MEDIA VIOLENCE CAUSE VIOLENCE AMONG JUVENILES?

Most research on media violence has focused on television, movies, and video games, although some studies have examined music associated with violent themes. We focus on TV, movies, and violent video games because of their strong presence in our society and the abundant research in the area—although we briefly discuss "violent music" as well.

TV and Movie Violence

About 96 percent of all households in the United States have television receivers, and these TVs are watched a lot. Data from 2016 indicate that, on average, teenagers spend about

15 hours per week watching television. Further, they find much violence on TV. Depictions of violence are pervasive in the most commonly watched television programs, with an average of two acts of physical aggression occurring per hour. Acts of verbal aggression and relationship aggression (e.g., spreading harmful rumors or gossip) are even more frequent (Coyne et al., 2010). Much of the content of movies is also violent. Some movies viewed by millions of youngsters between the ages of 10 and 14 have been rated as "extremely violent"; that is, they contain scenes depicting sadistic, sexualized, or extreme interpersonal violence (Worth et al., 2008). Further, it is estimated that by the time children have finished elementary school, each has seen, on average, more than 8,000 murders and 100,000 other acts of violence on TV. They have seen more than 200,000 acts of violence by the time they leave high school.

Does this extensive exposure to TV and movie violence increase the likelihood that juveniles will engage in violent behavior? Most people believe that TV and movie violence is a major cause of violent behavior, and politicians often make statements to this effect. Further, the federal government has been actively involved in efforts to limit the amount and severity of TV violence or to restrict access to violent programs. As a consequence of such efforts, there is now a ratings system that alerts viewers to the violence content of TV shows. Also, sets manufactured since 2000 are required to contain V-chips, which allow parents to block violent shows.

What do the data show about the effect of TV and movie violence on juvenile violence?[7] There have been literally hundreds of studies in this area. We know that violent juveniles are more likely to watch violent TV shows. That does not, of course, mean that TV and movie violence causes juvenile violence. It might be that both juvenile violence and watching violent TV shows are caused by the same third variables, such as the individual traits or family variables mentioned in earlier chapters. It might also be that engaging in violence causes one to watch violent TV shows. Then, too, violent juveniles may simply prefer violent TV shows. There is, in fact, some evidence for each of these arguments. At the same time, most studies—not all—suggest that TV and movie violence does have a causal effect on violent behavior.

Hundreds of experiments have been conducted in this area. In most such experiments, one group of juveniles is exposed to media violence while a similar group of juveniles is not (members of both groups are similar on relevant third variables like individual traits and family variables). The experimenter then determines whether the juveniles exposed to the media violence engage in more subsequent aggression than the unexposed group (which means that causal order is not a problem). The experimenter, for example, determines whether the juveniles exposed to media violence are more likely to hit a doll in a playroom, press a button that supposedly will result in harm to another person, or play aggressively on the playground (e.g., hit, kick, and push others). Most experiments suggest that exposure to media violence does increase aggressive behavior—although studies that employ more realistic measures of aggression (e.g., aggressive behavior on the playground vs. hitting a doll in the laboratory) often find that the effect of media violence is modest. Some researchers, however, claim that the experiments set up an artificial situation in which it is easy for juveniles to engage in aggression. The juveniles are often presented with an easy opportunity to engage in aggression, and their aggression is rarely punished or condemned. Therefore, the results of these experiments may not apply to the real world.

In response to this criticism, researchers have conducted a number of **studies in the real world** that attempt to take account of relevant third variables and issues of causal order (see Chapter 5). One study, for example, determined whether childhood exposure to TV violence was related to violent behavior in adolescence and adulthood. This study controlled for several relevant third variables, such as social class, intelligence, and parenting practices. Another study examined the levels of juvenile violence in an isolated Canadian community before and after the introduction of television. Still another study asked whether levels of violence might be shown to increase after media coverage of violent events, like championship heavyweight prize fights. These studies are not perfect. Researchers often do not control for all potentially relevant third variables, a sometimes impossible task; an excellent illustration of a flawed study in this area is provided by Jensen (2001). Nevertheless, most—not all—studies in this area suggest that TV violence contributes to violent behavior.

Overall, the most reasonable conclusion to draw from the data is that **TV and movie violence has a modest effect on juvenile violence.** It does not appear to be the major cause of violence as some claim, but it is not an unimportant causal factor either. TV and movie violence is most likely to cause violent behavior when it is committed by attractive characters, when it is rewarded and not punished, when it is presented as justified, when negative consequences of the violence are not shown, and when the scene is realistic. Unfortunately, much of the violence on TV fits that description. For example, as the National Television Violence Study (1997:137) states: "Violence is typically sanitized on television. It is rarely punished in the immediate context in which it occurs and it rarely results in observable harm to the victims. In fact, violence is often funny on television." TV violence is also most likely to lead to violent behavior when the juvenile identifies with the aggressor.

The effect of TV violence is **usually explained in terms of the leading delinquency theories.** Drawing on **social learning theory,** we can note that TV violence exposes juveniles to violent models. These models are often attractive characters, and their violence is frequently rewarded. As a consequence, juveniles may come to feel that violence is an appropriate response in certain situations. Drawing on **control theory,** we can suggest that TV violence may desensitize watchers to violence. That is, heavy exposure to TV violence may make violence seem less bad and reduce concern for the victims of violence. In effect, TV violence may reduce our level of internal control. And drawing on **strain theory,** we can consider that TV violence may cause viewers to see the world as a more dangerous, violent place. They become more fearful and suspicious of others as a result, potentially increasing the likelihood of a violent response. Also, TV violence often arouses or excites individuals. And aroused individuals may be more likely to respond aggressively to certain strainful situations, like provocations by others.

Violent Video Games

Data suggest that most adolescents play video games weekly, with a substantial percentage playing for three or more hours each week. Further, most adolescents prefer violent to nonviolent video games, and large numbers of juveniles have played violent games such as *Grand Theft Auto* and *Mortal Combat* (Anderson and Gentile, 2014). Video game violence can be quite gruesome. For example, in *Grand Theft Auto,* "the player may be rewarded for having sex with a prostitute and kicking her to death to avoid payment. In *Mortal Combat*, a player earns extra points by ripping out the opponent's heart or decapitating him" (Weber et al., 2006:348). These examples highlight the fact that video game players are often **active participants** in the screen violence. They are encouraged to assume the identity of violent characters, they pull the trigger or press the button that results in violence, and they are often directly rewarded for their violence with points and additional playing time (as well as the approval of their friends if they are playing with others). This active involvement has led some to argue that video game violence may have a stronger effect on violent behavior than TV and movie violence (where individuals **passively observe** the screen violence).[8]

A number of surveys have examined the association between playing video games and aggression (or aggressive thoughts and feelings). Most, but not all, find that playing video games (or violent video games) is associated with aggression. This association, however, does not mean that violent video games cause aggression. The association may be due to third variables that cause both video gaming and aggression. In this area, some studies that take into account several third variables find that the association between violent video games and aggression disappears. The association may also be due to the fact that an aggressive disposition causes one to play violent video games. In particular, it is not unreasonable to suppose that aggressive people will be attracted to violent video games, and some evidence supports this possibility.

A number of **experiments** have examined the effect of violent video games on aggression. Typically, a researcher will have one group of juveniles play a violent video game and while another **similar group** of juveniles plays a nonviolent video game (e.g., a sports game with a lot of action but little violence). Then the experimenter will measure the aggressive behavior of the juveniles in each group **after they have finished playing the video games.** Most such studies (but not all) find that the juveniles who play the violent video games are more aggressive. These studies, however, measure only the short-term effect of violent video games. Further, the effect of violent video games on aggression is often small in such studies, especially when more realistic measures of aggression are employed.

More research is clearly needed in this area, particularly research that looks at the **long-term effects** of violent video games on aggression and research conducted in the real world. A growing number of studies are of this type—examining whether individuals who play a lot of violent video games are more likely to engage in **subsequent** aggression, even after taking account of a range of **third variables** that might cause both the playing of violent video games and aggression. In one such study, researchers found that frequent exposure to violent video games was associated, in subsequent months, with a modest increase in youth physical aggression (e.g., "punching or kicking" someone, getting into fights at school), even after taking into account previous levels of aggression and other factors (C. Anderson et al., 2008). These findings are suggestive of longer-term effects. Overall, the observed effects of violent video games are not entirely consistent across studies, and there is still some debate in this area (see Ferguson et al., 2014). Considering the total body of evidence, however, the best conclusion seems to be that **playing violent video games leads to a modest increase in aggression.** This may be especially true of juveniles who are frequent or habitual gamers.

Music with Violent Themes

A smaller body of research examines whether listening to music with violent themes, particularly heavy metal music and certain types of rap music, increases the likelihood of aggression (or aggressive thoughts and feelings). The results of these studies are mixed, although some suggest that there is an **association** between listening to "violent music" and aggression, and that listening to violent music increases aggressive **thoughts and**

feelings (see C. Anderson, Berkowitz, et al., 2003; C. Anderson, Carnagey, and Eubanks, 2003; Kirsh, 2006; Singer et al., 1993). For example, one study found an association between musical preference expressed at age 12 and later delinquency. Early fans of "loud and rebellious" music genres were more likely than nonfans to engage in minor forms of delinquency as they got older, such as shoplifting and vandalism (Ter Bogt et al., 2013). This association remained even after taking into account the child's prior behavior, gender, level of commitment to school, and personality factors.

Thus, while more research is needed, the limited evidence in this area indicates that exposure to certain types of music may have a modest effect on delinquent behavior. Perhaps rebellious or aggressive styles of music encourage teens to test personal and social limits, which is typical of adolescence-limited delinquency (see Chapter 10). Whether such effects last beyond adolescence remains unknown.

Following their review of the evidence in this area, Warburton et al. (2014:317–318) raise an important question: "Can simply listening to music with extreme themes create serial killers or cause acts of mass violence such as school shootings?" They offer the following reply:

> The answer is an emphatic no. Any act of violence results from a convergence of many risk factors that may include access to weapons, home environment, peer influences, mental health issues, substance use, and social isolation, among many others. Violent media, including music, may be one of those factors but is neither sufficient nor necessary for people to commit acts of violence.

Does Media Violence Affect Some Juveniles More than Others?

You may wonder if media violence affects all juveniles the same, or if some are especially susceptible to its effects. The evidence is mixed in this area and, for certain statistical reasons, it can be difficult to detect such differences if they in fact exist. While the effects of media violence may not be limited to any particular group, some studies find that the effects are stronger when other risk factors are present in the lives of juveniles. Generally speaking, media violence is more likely to lead to violent behavior when the juvenile has a history of aggressive behavior, possesses an aggressive or hostile personality, and has parents who fail to monitor his or her activities (Anderson and Gentile, 2014). This is a good example of how risk factors often work together in shaping delinquent behavior.

Summary

There is some reason to believe that mass media violence, particularly TV and movie violence and violent video games, may lead to a small to modest increase in violent behavior. Mass media violence, however, is **not** the major cause of violent behavior that many people claim (see Box 17.1).

Box 17.1   Media Violence in Perspective

Although many people assume that media violence is among the leading causes of youth violence, researchers seem to agree that it is just one of many possible risk factors—probably **not** among the most important, especially when it comes to the development of serious criminal violence. Violent crime, it is argued, typically results "from a combination of multiple risk factors" (Bushman et al., 2010). Individuals differ in their levels of violent behavior for all sorts of reasons—it is usually very difficult to

(Continued)

(Continued)

explain such differences in terms of a single risk factor, such as media violence exposure. In fact, a key question that researchers have been debating is whether the effect of media violence, by itself, is large enough to warrant public concern.

For example, the entire April 2008 issue of *American Behavioral Scientist* was devoted to competing views among the experts, as was much of the March 2010 issue of *Psychological Bulletin*. Based on their individual reviews and interpretation of the evidence, the experts studying these issues seem to agree that, at least for certain people, some types of media violence are harmful and contribute to aggressive behavior (perhaps especially among individuals who are already predisposed to aggression or antisocial behavior). Beyond this point, there is much disagreement.

To illustrate, in an article titled "Much Ado About Nothing," Ferguson and Kilburn (2010) acknowledge that violent video games may contribute to aggressive behavior. But they argue that, at best, the effects are minimal and do not contribute substantially to serious youth violence. To support their position, they highlight recent trends in youth violence. Over the past two decades, video games have exploded in popularity, with many of the best-selling games earning the label "violent." If these games had a meaningful impact on serious aggression, they argue, we should have witnessed a corresponding increase in the rate of youth violence. Instead, the *opposite* has occurred: over the past two decades, rates of youth violence have been *decreasing* and are now at a near historic low (see Chapter 3). In short, Ferguson and Kilburn believe that the harmful effects of violent video games have been greatly exaggerated.

In reply, Bushman and his colleagues (2010) downplay the significance of the trends shown by statistical data. They argue that the violent crime rate is shaped by a wide range of factors—the fact that this rate has been decreasing does not prove that violent video games are inconsequential. Youth violence is still a problem after all. Moreover, while the observed effects of violent video gaming are small, this does not mean they are unimportant. C. Anderson et al. (2010:170), make the following observation:

> When effects accumulate across time, or when large portions of the population are exposed to a risk factor, or when consequences are severe, statistically small effects become much more important. . . . All three of these conditions apply to violent video game effects.

To place the importance of media violence in perspective, it may also be helpful to compare exposure to media violence with other known risk factors, such as low self-control, association with delinquent peers, and exposure to *real-world* violence, including child abuse (see Chapters 7–13). The extensive body of research on these other factors leaves little doubt about their role in the development of youth violence. Moreover, in studies that have examined multiple risk factors simultaneously, the influence of media violence is often shown to be weak in comparison to these other factors, especially delinquent peers (for a good example of such a study, see Ferguson et al., 2009). Researchers argue that these other factors should also be targeted in efforts to prevent violence. Yet in much of the public debate over the causes of youth violence, the importance of these other factors tends to be overshadowed by the attention given to media violence.

Questions for Discussion

1. Why do you think media violence often receives more public attention than other known risk factors for youth violence? The music artist Marilyn Manson, who has been criticized for his violent lyrics, believes that media violence is often the focus because

(Continued)

parents need an easy target—other than themselves—to blame. Do you agree or disagree with this view? Why?

2. As described earlier, not everyone agrees that media violence is a meaningful risk factor. Further, some people may refuse to believe that exposure to media violence has any effect at all on aggression. The prevalence of this attitude continues to frustrate the many researchers who believe that exposure to media violence is a problem and point to hundreds of studies showing that such exposure has, at the very least, modest effects on youth aggression. What may account for the failure of many to accept the results we've been discussing? Could it be that, for many people, the consumption of violent media is a part of their self-identity and that, as Americans, they have a "distaste for anyone telling them" what they should do (Huesmann, 2010:180)? What do you think?

DOES SOCIAL MEDIA ENGAGEMENT INCREASE THE RISK OF DELINQUENT BEHAVIOR?

Social media engagement offers today's teens a number of potential benefits not available to previous generations of youth, such as an enhanced ability to stay connected with friends and family members, make new friends, share pictures with others, acquire knowledge and information, and exchange ideas. Data from 2012 indicate that 95 percent of American teenagers aged 12 to 17 spend time online. Most teens (78 percent) own a cell phone, and about half of these phones are smartphones, which the teens use to access the internet, text-message their friends, and visit social media sites (Madden et al., 2013). Data from 2010 indicate that the average American teen sends or receives 50 text messages a day and that 73 percent of teens visit social media sites. Social media sites include any website that allows for social interaction, such as Facebook, Instagram, Twitter, gaming sites, and blog and "community content" video sites such as YouTube. Twenty-two percent of teens "log on to their favorite social media site more than 10 times a day" (O'Keeffe et al., 2011:800).

At the same time, recent news reports highlight the "dark side" of social media engagement, making it clear that social media sites can also be instruments of harm:

[Twelve-year-old] Rebecca Ann Sedwick jumped to her death on Monday at an old cement business in Lakeland [, Florida]. Investigators say the girl was despondent after others had posted hate messages about her online. The [local newspaper] reported that detectives found multiple social media applications where Rebecca was constantly bullied with messages, including "Go kill yourself," and "Why are you still alive?" Sheriff [Grady] Judd said parents of 15 girls have cooperated in the investigation and several cellphones and laptops have been confiscated. (Associated Press, 2013)

Two girls, ages 12 and 14, were arrested in the case and charged with the felony of "aggravated stalking." One of the girls was the former best friend of the suicide victim. After an investigation, however, the charges were dropped. While evidence indicated that the older girl has posted insults online and called Rebecca ugly names, lawyers close to the case said this behavior did not rise to the level of a crime. Experts on bullying also explained that such cases are difficult to prosecute "because multiple factors are often at play in a suicide" (Alvarez, 2013). Nonetheless, the tragic case of Rebecca Ann Sedwick brought national attention to the phenomenon of online social cruelty, also known as "cyberbullying."

Cyberbullying refers to the use of electronic communication technologies—such as social media sites, email, and text-messaging—to harm or disturb others repeatedly, usually targeting victims who cannot easily defend themselves (Kowalski et al., 2012; compare the definition of traditional bullying we presented in Chapter 15). Given the relative anonymity of the internet and the ability of anyone to assume a false identity on social media sites, there is concern that opportunities for online interaction may lead young people to behave more aggressively than they would otherwise. Consider the following accounts compiled by Robin Kowalski and her colleagues in a book titled *Cyberbullying: Bullying in the Digital Age:*

> [Author and child advocate] Perry Aftab recounted a meeting with a young boy who was what some might call the "perfect child" in real life—well behaved, polite, and a good student. However, online this boy became something completely different— violent and aggressive. When asked why, his response was, "Because I can." (Kowalski et al., 2012:79)

> A 14-year-old girl who had survived breast cancer and the loss of a limb when she was 10 years old was cyberbullied via text messaging for several months. Although the perpetrator's identity remained unknown for some time, it turned out to be the victim's best friend. The perpetrator would talk to the target on Skype while she was sending cyberbullying text messages so that she could witness the target's reactions to the bullying (Kowalski et al., 2012:13)

Further, electronic communication technologies allow perpetrators to attack their victims anywhere and at any time, and to spread rumors to a wide audience. In the words of journalist Bob Sullivan, "Kids can be cruel. And kids with technology can be cruel on a world-wide scale" (quoted in Kowalski et al., 2012:2). Moreover, some criminologists have noted that today's communication technologies may reduce the direct control that adults exercise over juveniles, thereby increasing the likelihood of delinquency (Meldrum and Clark, 2015). Juveniles now have the technological means to spend virtual time with their peers and can often do so discreetly, outside the awareness of parents and teachers. This also means they have greater freedom to discuss, plan, and organize delinquent activities with their peers.

Some of these possibilities overlap with the major delinquency theories covered earlier. From a control theory perspective, the motives that young people have to engage in delinquency are typically held in check by the controls or restraints on their behavior. As suggested in the preceding paragraph, today's communication technologies may weaken some of these constraints. From a social learning perspective, these technologies may allow young people to connect with delinquent peers in new and creative ways. Further, to the extent that social media engagement helps expand their social worlds, juveniles may have increased exposure to delinquent peers as well as deviant content on social media cites. Note, for example, that the percentage of teens who experience unsolicited exposure to pornographic material—via "sexting" and other means—has increased in recent years (Kowalski et al., 2012). Thus from a strain theory perspective, this expanding social world may also increase young people's exposure to victimization, including cyberbullying. Victimization, in turn, is considered an important type of strain, which may generate desires for revenge and retaliation.

The Evidence

What does the evidence show? Does social media engagement cause juveniles to be more delinquent than they would be otherwise? Or are juveniles simply doing the same things they have always done (e.g., bullying their peers), enhanced by the ability to turn to cyberspace? Unfortunately, we cannot yet draw firm conclusions. To date, most of the research in this area is descriptive; it seeks only to determine to extent of cyberbullying and other problems related to social media engagement. Some studies also examine the characteristics of youth who are affected by online delinquency. This research is still valuable and revealing, however, and is a necessary first step in determining the relationship between social media engagement and delinquency.

The existing research yields three important findings. First, studies confirm that social media sites are frequently used as tools for delinquent ends. In a nationwide survey of Canadian youth, for example, 17 percent of the respondents said they had pretended to be someone else online so they could "act mean to people and not get into trouble" (Kowalski et al., 2012:9). In addition, street gangs use social media sites to trade insults with members of rival gangs; to make threats; and to "provoke, perpetrate, and publicize violent acts" (Patton et al., 2013:A59).

Second, the experience of cyberbullying is quite common, although perhaps not as prevalent as many people imagine. The best estimate, based on a review of dozens of published studies in the area, is that 21 percent of adolescents in the United States have been the victims of cyberbullying, and 15 percent admit to participation in cyberbullying at some point in their *lifetimes* (Patchin, 2013). The general consensus is that traditional bullying remains far more common than cyberbullying, however. In a recent study of bullying in the nation's schools, 16 percent of the students reported being bullied at least two or three times *per month*. Of these bullied students, only 4 percent of boys and 6 percent of girls reported that they were the targets of cyberbullying. The perspective of the authors of the study is as follows:

> Although cyberbullying can be devastating to those who experience it, the small number of children it affects compared with other forms of bullying suggests it is important not to sensationalize this phenomenon. Moreover, since empirical research has shown a great overlap between those who are bullied via cyber technology and more traditional means . . . using resources to address more common forms of bullying will also help students who are bullied through cyber technology. (Limber et al., 2013:15)

Third, studies have documented an association between social media engagement and delinquency, including cyberbullying and certain other types of delinquency. The more time juveniles spend online, the more likely they are to engage in delinquency (Kowalski et al., 2012). But as you know, a mere association between the two activities does not necessarily mean that social media engagement *causes* young people to engage in delinquency (e.g., young people who spend a lot of time online may be delinquent for others reasons, including lack of school involvement and low self-control). To determine whether social media engagement causes delinquent behavior we need to control for other factors that may be responsible for the association. On this score, there is *tentative* evidence that the association may represent a real effect of social media engagement on delinquency. In particular, one recent study finds that virtual time spent with peers is associated with higher levels of drug and alcohol use among adolescents, even after controlling for traditional face-to-face time with peers, grades in school, self-control, and parenting factors (Meldrum and Clark, 2015; see also Miller and Morris, 2016). Virtual time spent with peers is also associated with participation in a greater variety of delinquent activities. As stated earlier, virtual interaction with peers can be done discreetly, even when parents are at home or in the same room. And sometimes the content of this interaction involves the discussion and planning of delinquent activities.

Summary

So there is tentative evidence that social media engagement may heighten the risk of delinquent behavior or, at least, facilitate delinquent activity. At the same time, we urge caution. Clearly, more research is needed in this area before any firm conclusions can be drawn. As we saw earlier in this chapter, it can be dangerous to rely on the results of just one or two studies. And it appears that some of the problems associated with social media, such as cyberbullying, are easy to exaggerate. Related to this, there has been a dramatic growth in the number of news stories devoted to cyberbullying (Kowalski et al., 2012), even though traditional bullying remains a larger problem. Most of these news reports link social media use to suicides and other devastating outcomes. Consequently, people are more likely to hear about the risks of social media engagement than the potential benefits, as discussed shortly.

Some of the problems associated with social media may have more to do with adults' ignorance of new communication technology than with the technology itself. Thus young people can circumvent control and supervision by non-tech-savvy parents and teachers, raising the possibility that greater awareness among adults might lead to a reduction in the possible harmful effects of social media engagement. For example, experts recommend that parents learn how to monitor their child's use of the internet, set guidelines for the use of social media, discuss the challenges of cyberspace with their child, and learn what to do, should their child become a victim of cyberbullying (Kowalski et al., 2012). Of course, these parenting strategies assume adequate and ongoing knowledge of the fast-evolving world of social media, which may not be well distributed among busy adults.

Finally, when it comes to crime and technology, we note that technology is often a doubled-edged sword. When new technologies are introduced to society they can be a source of fear and anxiety, especially when they disrupt traditional patterns of interaction or ways of life. As a result, the benefits may be overlooked. You should be aware that new communication technologies can also be used to prevent crime and delinquency. For instance, at least two independent studies indicate that growth in cell phone technology may have contributed to the recent drop in the national crime rate (Klick et al., 2012; Orrick and Piquero, 2015; see Chapter 3 for a discussion of the crime drop). Cell phones allow people of all ages to call the police immediately, at any time of the day or night, when they detect trouble, observe a suspicious person, or witness a crime. Further, smartphones allow observers to capture photos and videos of potential crime suspects, which may serve as a strong deterrent for many would-be offenders. Likewise, social media sites are now being used by neighborhood watch groups to share information and to monitor their communities more effectively in the hopes of preventing crime.

In short, a full account of the effects of social media engagement would have to take into account the ways that it both prevents and facilitates crime and delinquency. This could be an important, if challenging, avenue for future research.

DO DRUGS INCREASE THE LIKELIHOOD OF DELINQUENCY?

It is commonly argued that drug use and sales are a major cause of delinquency. And part of the motivation behind the "war on drugs" is the belief that reducing drug use and sales will have a major impact on other types of delinquency. Drug use and sales are said to contribute to delinquency for at least four reasons.[9]

Reasons that Drugs May Affect Delinquency

The first reason has to do with **pharmacological effects:** drugs, including alcohol, cocaine, amphetamines, and PCP, are said to **weaken self-control and/or increase irritability**—if only temporarily. Also, withdrawal from drugs such as heroin and crack may increase irritability and frustration. As a consequence of these effects, individuals under the influence of certain drugs may be (1) less aware of and concerned about the costs of crime, (2) more likely to become upset with others and respond to provocations in an aggressive manner, and (3) more likely to act in ways that upset or provoke others. Researchers, however, emphasize that not all drugs have those effects. Further, the impact of drugs is influenced by the individual and the social situation. For example, the effect of alcohol on aggression is strongest among individuals already predisposed to aggression (for another example, see Box 17.2).

Box 17.2   Does Marijuana Use Lead to Hard Drug Use and Abuse? A Look at the "Gateway Hypothesis"

While the use and abuse of "hard" drugs—such as heroin and cocaine—continues to be of major public concern, attitudes toward "soft" drugs, such as marijuana, are more ambivalent. According to the 2014 General Social Survey (GSS), a majority of Americans (52%) now support the legalization of marijuana. (Note: The GSS is conducted annually by the National Opinion Research Center and collects sociological data based on a large and representative sample of adults in the United States.) Yet some researches argue that the potential harm of soft drugs should not be minimized. In particular, it is feared that the use of soft drugs may lead to the use and abuse of more dangerous substances. In other words, involvement with soft drugs like marijuana may serve as a "gateway" to more harmful drugs.

What does the research show? Many studies have found an association between teen marijuana use and the later use of other illicit drugs, providing evidence consistent with the gateway hypothesis. We know, for example, that young people rarely use hard drugs without having first tried soft "gateway" drugs like marijuana. This fact, however, does not necessarily mean that soft drug use *causes* people to use hard drugs. To determine whether there is indeed a causal connection between soft and hard drug use, we need to make sure that the association between the two is not due to some third variable (see Chapter 5). For example, high levels of stress or strain could be responsible for the association, causing people to use both soft and hard drugs.

A study by Van Gundy and Rebellon (2010) examined the gateway effect of teen marijuana use while taking into account a number of third variables. Consistent with the gateway hypothesis, they found that the use of marijuana in middle school was associated with the later use of other illicit drugs, even after stress/strain and other factors had been considered. The researchers did **not**, however, find a link between teen marijuana use and the subsequent *abuse* of other illicit drugs. (This study defined drug abuse as use that leads to significant impairment, interpersonal problems, or trouble with the law.) Rather, the abuse of other illicit drugs was predicted by stress/strain and other factors.

Upon closer inspection, the researchers found that the gateway effect is further limited to young people under the age of 21 and to those who are unemployed. It appears that older, working individuals "age out" of marijuana's gateway effect and that such an effect tends to be short-lived. In sum, the effect of teen marijuana use seems to depend on the characteristics of the individual and his or her life situation.

These findings, if supported in future studies, have important policy implications. First, efforts to curb the *abuse* of other illicit drugs may do well to focus on stress and stress management, rather than focusing on the presumed gateway effect of marijuana. Second, as Van Gundy and Rebellon (2010:256) argue, efforts to curb teen marijuana use should be "employed judiciously so as not to interfere with later employment opportunities"— opportunities that could help close the gateway between marijuana and other illicit drugs.

Questions for Discussion

1. In addition to stress or strain, can you think of other third variables that may cause people to use both soft and hard drugs? (Hint: What variables would control and social learning theorists point to as possibilities?)

2. Why would employment as a young adult help "close" the gateway between teen marijuana use and the use of other illicit drugs? Describe some possible reasons why employment would discourage the use of other illicit drugs. (Here again, you could draw on the major delinquency theories).

Second, **juveniles may engage in crime to obtain money to purchase drugs,** especially if they are addicted to expensive drugs like heroin and cocaine. That is, drug use may lead to a particular type of strain—a desperate need for money. Individuals may then engage in a wide range of income-generating crimes, like larceny, burglary, robbery, prostitution, and drug sales. Some of these crimes, such as robbery, may result in violence. In one study of inner-city youth, about a quarter of the respondents who committed burglary said they did so in order to get money for drugs. About 36 percent of the youth who sold drugs and 19 percent who engaged in robbery said they committed these crimes to get money for drugs (Altschuler and Brounstein, 1991).

Third, **the drug trade contributes to crime.** The buyers and sellers of drugs often carry large amounts of money as well as drugs, and they are generally reluctant to involve the police when disputes arise. As a consequence, crime is often the result. Drug sellers may employ violence against one another as they compete for turf or customers. Both drug sellers and customers are often attractive targets for robbers. And drug sellers and their customers often employ violence against one another to settle disputes. These problems were especially severe during the early years of the crack trade, when many young, inexperienced dealers were competing against one another.

Fourth, some researchers argue that **drug use, especially chronic use, may increase the juvenile's predisposition to engage in delinquency by reducing the juvenile's bonds to family and school, lowering academic performance, and increasing the likelihood of association with delinquent peers.** Juveniles are frequently brought into contact with such peers when they buy and use drugs.[10]

It is also argued that drug use not only increases the likelihood that individuals will commit crimes but also increases the likelihood that drug users will be victims of crime. Among other things, drug users may be more likely to be victimized because they are less able to offer effective resistance and because their lifestyles sometimes place them in close contact with offenders. The former argument has been made with respect to Rohypnol, or "roofies," the so-called date rape drug.[11]

The arguments set out in the preceding paragraphs play a central role in a **debate over whether drugs should be legalized.** Individuals who want to legalize drugs claim that drugs are expensive largely because they are illegal. Legalization will lower their cost and thereby reduce much income-generating crime. Further, legalization will also reduce crime associated with the illicit drug trade. Individuals opposed to legalization claim that drug use will increase if drugs are legalized. They point to several negative consequences of this increase, including increased crime arising from the pharmacological effects of drug use and the effects of drug use on such things as family bonds and school performance.[12]

The Evidence

What does the evidence suggest? Do drugs contribute to delinquency? **Individuals who commit crimes are frequently under the influence of drugs (including alcohol).** For example, a 2002 study of arrested male juveniles in five cities around the country found that 60 percent tested positive for drugs other than alcohol. Marijuana was by far the most common drug, followed by cocaine and methamphetamine.[13] Victimization data suggest that nearly 4 in 10 violent crimes involve the use of alcohol (Greenfeld, 1998).

Further, there is a **strong association between drugs and delinquency.** Juveniles who use drugs, and especially those who sell drugs, are much more likely to engage in crime. Some categories of drug users, like heroin addicts and heavy users of crack, engage in enormous amounts of crime. This does not, of course, mean that all drug users are delinquents or that all delinquents are drug users. For example, a self-report study found that a little more than half of the serious delinquents (those who admitted to three or more Part I crimes in the past three years) were also serious drug and/or alcohol users. About a third of the serious drug/alcohol users were serious delinquents.[14]

An association between drugs and delinquency, however, does not mean that drugs cause delinquency. Some researchers argue that the sale/use of drugs and delinquency are associated because both are caused by the same third variables. The data do indicate that drug use/sales and delinquency share many of the same causes, such as individual traits, family problems, school problems, and association with delinquent peers.[15] Also, some researchers argue that drugs and delinquency are associated because delinquency causes drug use and/or sales. Engaging in delinquency increases the likelihood that a person will be exposed to others who possess and use drugs, who reinforce drug use, and who hold values conducive to drug use. Data here indicate that delinquency typically precedes drug use. Also, some studies have found that prior delinquency increases the likelihood of subsequent drug use.[16]

At the same time, the evidence suggests that **drug use, especially serious drug use, does contribute to delinquency.** For example, although drug addicts typically engaged in crime before they became addicts, their level of crime increases during periods of high drug use and decreases during periods of low drug use. Also, longitudinal research suggests that drug use contributes to subsequent delinquency—even after selected third variables are controlled.[17] **The effect of drug use on delinquency, however, is not as large as many imagine or as the associational data suggest.** Much of the association between drugs and delinquency arises because both are caused by the same third variables and because delinquency has an effect on drug use.

DO GUNS INCREASE THE LIKELIHOOD OF DELINQUENCY?

Most criminologists agree that many juveniles own and carry guns and that there is reason to believe that guns contribute to serious violence. There is, however, a major debate over the extent to which guns contribute to crime/delinquency versus the extent to which they prevent crime and delinquency. Some researchers claim that guns prevent more crime and delinquency than they perpetuate. Let us examine the evidence in these areas.[18]

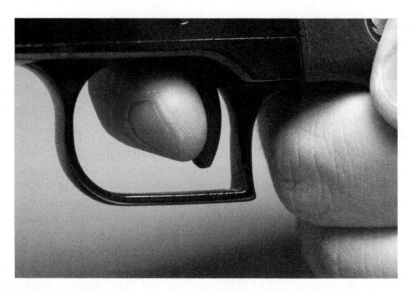

How Common Is Gun Ownership and Possession Among Juveniles?

There are between 270 and 310 million guns in the United States; a third of these are handguns. (Handguns are much more likely to be used in crimes than long guns like rifles and shotguns. For example, about 73 percent of all gun-related homicides are committed with handguns.) According to the 2016 General Social Survey, 36 percent of all households in the United States have guns, with many gun-owning households having more than one gun. This figure represents a steady decline from earlier years; in the 1990s, for example, about 43 percent of all households had guns. This drop in the rate of gun ownership has been attributed to a decrease in hunting (more people now live in urban areas), the overall drop in the violent crime rate (which may have reduced the demand for guns for self-protection), and an increase in single female-headed households, which are less likely to have a gun than households headed by males. Nevertheless, gun ownership is still common in the United States (Tavernise and Gebeloff, 2013).

How common is it for juveniles to own or possess guns? It is illegal for juveniles to purchase guns, and, in most states, it is illegal for juveniles to possess handguns. Several studies have attempted to estimate the extent of gun ownership and possession among juveniles. These studies have focused on institutionalized delinquents, arrested delinquents, gang members, juveniles in high-crime inner-city areas, juveniles in urban areas, and juveniles throughout the country. The large majority of institutionalized delinquents—more than 90 percent in some studies—report having owned guns at some point in their lives (Harcourt, 2003:4). A 1995 survey of arrested male delinquents in seven cities found that 20 percent said they carried a gun all or most of the time—a percentage higher than that for arrested adults. For arrested gang members, the percentage was 31 percent. Five out of 10 of the arrested juveniles said they had been shot at; the figure for gang members was 8 out of 10 (Decker et al., 1997; Sickmund et al., 1997). Other studies have found that anywhere from a quarter to more than half of all gang members own guns, and even more have ready access to guns. A gang, for example, often has a stash of guns that members can use. A 1991 study of males in 10 inner-city high schools throughout the United States found that 22 percent owned guns, and 12 percent carried a gun all or most of the time (Sheley and Wright, 1995). A 1996 survey that interviewed a nationally representative sample of youth ages 12 through 16 found that about 10 percent had carried a handgun in the last year.[19] And a 1995 nationally representative survey found that 10 percent of 15- to 17-year-olds had carried a gun at least once in the last month (Cook and Ludwig, 2004).

These percentages clearly indicate that gun ownership and possession is fairly common among certain categories of juveniles—particularly those involved in serious delinquency.

Many more juveniles have easy access to firearms. In a recent national study of juveniles and guns (Ruback et al., 2011), adolescents in the general population were asked the following survey question: "Is a gun easily available to you in your home?" About one in five juveniles (21%) reported that they had easy access at home to a handgun, shotgun, or rifle. Of these juveniles, about half said they had easy access to more than one type of firearm. (Note: Juveniles may have access to guns outside the home, but Ruback's survey didn't include such a category.) In another national study, focused on the storage of firearms in gun-owning households where juveniles are present, guns were found to be stored unlocked in 42 percent of these households and loaded in 26 percent. In 10 percent of these households, guns were stored both loaded *and* unlocked (Johnson et al., 2006; for more on juvenile access to firearms, see Box 17.3).

Box 17.3   How Do Young Offenders Get Their Hands on Guns?

How do kids get their hands on guns? This question is often posed as if there were some mystery about it. In fact, guns are easy for many young people to obtain, given the high volume of firearms in circulation in the United States. For example, it is estimated that about one-third of all households own at least one gun (Tavernise and Gebeloff, 2013).

The facts behind the infamous shootings at Columbine High School are revealing. On the morning of April 20, 1999, the two teenage shooters in this case—Eric Harris and Dylan Klebold—arrived at their school equipped with explosive devices, knives, and guns: two sawed-off shotguns, a rifle, and a semiautomatic handgun. Within the span of just 16 minutes, the shooters fired more than 100 rounds, killing 13 and wounding 21 more before taking their own lives. They had obtained all the guns illegally through "straw purchases": that is, by using older friends and acquaintances to buy the guns for them.

The fact that such straw purchases are illegal did not stop the Columbine killers from pursuing this method, nor did it stop an older adult from providing guns. Indeed, Mark E. Manes—the 22-year-old man who had provided Klebold and Harris with a semiautomatic handgun—was charged with two felony counts: one for supplying a handgun to a minor, and one for possession of a sawed-off shotgun. He was sentenced to six years in prison. Moreover, in a home video made before the shootings, Harris and Klebold explained that if Manes hadn't come through, they simply would have "found somebody else" (Brezina and Wright, 2000).

In other school shooting sprees, the perpetrators had obtained guns from their own households or from the "usual sources," that is, from parents and grandparents, occasionally from friends, and sometimes through theft. These cases suggest, once again, that it is fairly easy for young people to access guns. This conclusion is supported by various youth surveys. In a large survey of incarcerated juvenile offenders, 70 percent said they would have "no trouble at all" obtaining a gun upon release. Among inner-city high school students, the percentage was 40 percent (Sheley and Wright, 1995). Responses from adolescents in the general population yield somewhat smaller estimates, but the data still suggest that guns are readily accessible to many teenagers.

(Continued)

(Continued)

These observations highlight a troubling fact. So long as hundreds of millions of guns remain in circulation, they will be available to nearly any juvenile who has the means and motive to exploit his or her network of family, friends, and acquaintances for the purpose of obtaining a firearm. Thus, to limit juvenile access to guns, it would be necessary to limit general access to guns, which means doing something about the 300 million guns already in circulation. One quickly sees the enormity of the problem. For some criminologists, it is by no means obvious what could, or should, be done in this regard (but see the following discussion questions).

Questions for Discussion

1. Can you think of any steps that could be taken to restrict juvenile access to firearms, despite the large number of firearms already in circulation? Should gun owners be encouraged or required to take certain precautions, for example? (Note: Earlier in this chapter we described gun-storage practices in households with juveniles.)

2. Some criminologists believe that the passage of new gun control laws would have only limited impact on youth violence, given the 300 million guns already in circulation. These criminologists argue in favor of efforts to tackle the root causes of delinquency, and to address the reasons why many young people carry guns and feel a need to break the law in the first place (see Brezina and Wright, 2000; also see the discussion of school violence in Chapter 15). What do you think? Do you agree or disagree with this view?

Several studies have asked juveniles why they own or carry guns. The most common reason given is **"for protection."** The juveniles most likely to own guns are heavily involved in crime, belong to gangs or delinquent peer groups, and live in dangerous inner-city communities. Most have witnessed violent crimes and have been the victims of violence themselves. Their criminal activity puts them in situations where violence is a very real possibility, and they are surrounded by others who own and carry guns. It is no surprise, then, that they feel they need a gun for protection. Contrary to certain media accounts, juveniles are less likely to say that they own or carry a gun because it is a status symbol or because it makes you popular with peers—although some juveniles do say this. Other juveniles, a minority, say they own guns **for sport or recreational purposes,** such as hunting and target shooting; they are much less likely than other young gun owners to be involved in crime.

The large majority of juveniles with guns get them illegally, primarily from family members, friends, and street sources. In many communities, it is easy to purchase high-quality guns at prices well below retail. Also, the guns currently possessed by juveniles are more lethal than those owned in the past. Juveniles tend to own and carry high-quality, large-caliber automatic or semiautomatic handguns.

A few studies have examined the **factors associated with gun ownership.** Juveniles are more likely to own guns if they are male, their parents own guns, their peers own guns, they belong to gangs, they have been threatened or shot at with a gun, they **sell drugs,** or they engage in most other types of delinquency (although some data suggest that **using drugs** is not very strongly associated with owning or carrying a gun). The dramatic increase in gun-related juvenile homicide from the mid-1980s to the mid-1990s has been tied to the increased involvement of juveniles in drug selling and gangs during these years (see Chapter 3).

Do Guns Contribute to Delinquency?

It is commonly pointed out that **the United States has the highest rates of gun ownership and lethal violence in the industrialized world.** About 22 percent of U.S. households contain *handguns.* In most other industrialized nations, the rate of handgun ownership is

7 percent or lower (Messner and Rosenfeld, 2001). Further, the U.S. homicide rate is several times that of other industrialized countries. Differences in homicide rates are especially pronounced for gun-related homicides; the rate of firearm-related homicides in the United States is 19.5 times higher than the rate in other high-income nations (National Research Council, 2013a). In 2011, firearms were used in 68 percent of the murders in the United States. Of these firearm-related homicides, the majority (73 percent) involved the use of a handgun. During the same year, more than 1,300 juveniles were murdered; about half (48 percent) were killed with firearms (Office of Juvenile Justice and Delinquency Prevention, 2014).

In short, despite recent declines in the rate of gun ownership and violent crime, the United States still has a lot of guns and a lot of gun-related crime, especially in comparison to other industrialized nations. Most studies suggest that there is a **positive association between the rate of gun ownership and the rate of gun-related crime in a country or community.** That is, there is more gun-related crime in countries and communities where guns are more prevalent. It is important to note, however, that this association is far from perfect. Certain communities and countries (e.g., Switzerland) post high rates of gun ownership but low rates of gun-related crime. The rate of gun-related crime is likely dependent on both the availability of guns and the willingness of people to use them. Also, one recent study suggests that it is the availability of **illegal** guns that contributes to violent crime, not the availability of legal guns—although more research is needed on this topic (Stolzenberg and D'Alessio, 2000).

Studies also suggest that **juveniles who own or carry guns are much more likely to engage in most forms of delinquency.** This is most true of juveniles who own guns for protection. It is less true of juveniles who own guns for sport. For example, a study of juveniles in Rochester, New York, found that those who owned guns for protection were **23** times more likely to commit gun crimes than those who did not own guns. Those who owned guns for sport, however, were about 3 times more likely to commit gun crimes than those who did not own guns.[20]

So, most data suggest that **there is an association between guns and crime/delinquency.** But as you know, this association does not prove that guns increase the likelihood of delinquency. The association may be explained in other ways. It may be that gun possession and delinquency are both caused by the same third variables, such as association with delinquent peers. There is some evidence for this position. It may also be that crime/delinquency causes gun ownership. People who live in high-crime countries or communities may purchase guns to protect themselves. Juveniles who engage in delinquency may likewise purchase guns for protection, since their delinquency is often associated with a risky lifestyle. There is also some evidence for this position.

At the same time, some data suggest that **guns contribute to at least certain types of delinquency.** One study, for example, found that the increased availability of guns led to increases in the rate of homicide (Duggan, 2001). The study cited earlier of juveniles in Rochester, New York, found that illegal gun carriers committed about five times more serious, violent crime when they were carrying guns than when they were not (see Lizotte et al., 2002). And a more recent national study finds that easy access to guns among juveniles increases their risk of engaging in future violence even after taking into account a variety of other risk factors, such as prior violent behavior, attitudes, exposure to violence, drug use, and drug dealing (Ruback et al., 2011).

Criminologists argue that **guns contribute to delinquency, especially serious violence, in several ways.** The most prominent argument is that guns increase the likelihood that certain crimes, such as assault and robbery, will result in serious injury or death. For example, it has been argued that the increased availability of guns played a key role in the dramatic increase in juvenile homicides from the late 1980s to the mid-1990s. As guns became more widespread throughout the community, disputes that used to be settled with fists or knives were more likely to be settled with guns. And serious injury and death were more likely to result. Data indicate that gun attacks are more likely to be fatal than attacks with knives, fists, or other weapons. One study, for example, found that attacks with guns were five times more likely to be fatal than attacks with knives. One might argue that gun attacks are more fatal because people who attack with a gun are more intent on killing their victims. Limited data, however, suggest that differences in the intent to kill do not fully explain the higher fatality rate associated with guns. Data, for example, suggest that most offenders who fire guns do not intend to kill their victims.[21] Guns, then, appear to increase the likelihood that crimes like assault and robbery will result in serious injury or death. (At the same time, it should be noted that assaults and robberies with guns have a **lower** likelihood of resulting in **less serious** injuries, partly because victims are less likely to resist.)

It has also been argued that the presence of guns increases the likelihood that certain predisposed adolescents will engage in crimes like assault and robbery. A gun may provide adolescents with the courage or the means to commit a crime they might otherwise avoid. Further, the presence of a gun may trigger an aggressive response in certain individuals—with the gun functioning as an "aggressive cue." Finally, as guns become more common, many adolescents may arm themselves for protection and become more likely to respond to conflicts with gun use. The evidence regarding the latter arguments, however, is less certain.[22]

On the basis of these data and arguments, one might conclude that there would be less delinquency, or at least less delinquency resulting in serious injury and death, if guns were not so widespread. The situation, however, is not so simple.

Do Guns Prevent More Crime than They Contribute To?

Some who acknowledge that guns may contribute to crime assert that guns prevent more crime than they cause (you may have heard the expression that "a well-armed society is a polite society"). Many individuals buy guns for protection, and they may well use their guns to stop crimes from occurring or to subdue criminals. Likewise, many criminals may avoid victimizing people for fear that their targets are armed. Many criminals, in fact, state that they have been scared off by armed targets or that they have avoided victimizing individuals who might have been armed (Sheley and Wright, 1995). (It is unclear, however, whether these criminals then selected victims they thought were unarmed, thus displacing rather than preventing crime.)

Several studies have tried to determine whether guns prevent more crime than they cause. Data from the National Crime Victimization Survey indicate that guns are used for self-defense purposes only about 80,000 times a year. The same survey, however, indicates that guns are used to commit more than 400,000 crimes each year. These data, then, suggest that guns contribute to more crime than they prevent. By contrast, other surveys indicate that guns are more likely to be used for self-defense purposes than to commit crimes. One survey, for example, estimates that guns are used for self-defense purposes at least 2.5 million times per year—far more than the 1 million gun-related crimes that occur each year (Kleck and Gertz, 1995).

There is now a lively debate about the accuracy of these different surveys, and researchers continue to explore the net contribution of guns to the crime problem.[23] According to one leading researcher in this area, "it's really hard to find evidence that where there are more guns [in the United States], there are less crimes, but you can easily find evidence that where there are a lot more guns, there are a lot more gun crimes" (David Hemenway, quoted in Pappas, 2015). At the same time, Kleck (2015:47) argues that most studies in this area suffer from important limitations and that, in the few studies that address these limitations, the observed relationship between gun ownership and crime disappears. According to Kleck, the crime-reducing effects of guns in the hands of victims "may roughly cancel out" the crime-increasing effects of guns in the hands of offenders, "resulting in a near-zero net effect" on the crime rate. The outcome of this debate will allow society to better determine the net impact of guns on crime and delinquency. This debate also has important policy implications: If guns do prevent more crime than they cause, efforts to restrict or control gun ownership in the **general population** may not reduce crime. Even so, virtually everyone agrees that it is desirable to take guns away from criminals and delinquents and to at least restrict handgun possession by juveniles.[24]

Finally, to place the gun issue in larger perspective, we return to a point raised at the outset of this chapter. Delinquency is usually the product of a good number of risk factors working together, and the exact contribution of guns to delinquency likely depends on the presence or absence of other factors. Following their extensive review of gun use among juveniles, Emmert and Lizotte (2015:556) conclude that "drugs, violence, peers, family, and school all play a role in influencing weapon behaviors among adolescents. Policies and interventions focused on single influences will likely miss the bigger picture." In Chapter 24, we will examine delinquency prevention strategies that seek to address multiple risk factors simultaneously.

Likewise, in considering the role of guns in the larger society, it is clear that context matters. As Currie (2015:89) observes:

> The role of guns in violent crime cannot be considered in isolation from other conditions that influence the likelihood of violence, such as the degree of inequality, the depth of social exclusion, and the erosion of community and family supports. In a relatively peaceful, egalitarian, and cohesive country like Switzerland, few people shoot someone else—even [though] . . . guns are widely available. But in a community already wracked by the kinds of adverse social conditions that predictably breed violence, the easy availability of guns adds fuel to the fire.

SUMMARY

In sum, religion, work, mass media violence, social media engagement, drugs, and guns do have an effect on delinquency—although in most cases this effect appears to be modest. Religion reduces delinquency, especially "victimless" crimes, by a small to modest amount. Work—especially long hours of work, by in-school juveniles who are predisposed to delinquency, decreases delinquency by a modest amount. Mass media violence has a modest effect on violent behavior. Initial data indicate that high levels of social media engagement are associated with certain types of delinquent involvement, although the problems associated with social media use do not appear to be as widespread as news reports suggest. Drug use and selling also appear to increase the likelihood of delinquency, although their effect on delinquency is not as large as is commonly portrayed. Finally, there is some evidence suggesting that the possession of guns or easy access to guns increases the likelihood of serious violence, although it is debated whether guns prevent more crime than they cause.

TEACHING AIDS

Controversial Issue: Should Marijuana Be Legalized?

Much of the discussion about how to control delinquency centers on religion, media violence, drugs, and guns (even though individual traits, family, school, and peer factors have larger impacts on delinquency). Such discussion often generates tremendous controversy. Should we expand the role of religion in public life (e.g., display the Ten Commandments in public places, allow school prayer, provide government funding to religious groups involved in social service activities)? And will doing so reduce problems like delinquency? Should the government exercise greater control over media violence? Should drugs be legalized, or should the war on drugs be expanded? Should we expand or restrict our efforts to control gun possession and use?

It is not possible to examine all of these issues in this book (although, see Chapter 24), so in this section we focus on an issue of some concern to many college students: **Should the use of marijuana be legalized?** As you may know, many states have enacted laws that permit medical marijuana use and some states—such as Colorado and Washington State—have legalized the recreational use of marijuana for adults (although the federal government still maintains a ban on the drug). Lawmakers in other states are debating the wisdom of these laws. Drawing on the arguments in this chapter, discuss what impact, if any, you think legalizing marijuana would have on crime and delinquency. What other impacts—positive and/or negative—might legalizing marijuana have? To stimulate your thinking, we present two selections. One is from an editorial by Alison Holcomb, drug policy director of the American Civil Liberties Union, who argues for the legalization of marijuana. The other is by Kevin Sabet, former senior policy adviser to President Obama's drug czar, who argues against the legalization of marijuana (For further information on the legalization debate, see the sources in note 12.)

In an editorial titled "Marijuana Use Should Not Be a Crime," Alison Holcomb (2012) argues:

> Labeling an act a crime is no light matter. At least, it should not be, if we expect our criminal laws and those sworn to enforce them to be respected.... Despite the fact that marijuana arrests have escalated from less than a third of all drug arrests to more than half in the past 20 years, usage rates have not gone down. More than 40 percent of Americans have tried marijuana at some point in their lives, and millions are current users. Clearly, the threat of arrest does little to dissuade, despite its enormous costs both to the individual and to our criminal justice system. Perhaps it even entices with its allure of forbidden fruit.
>
> A more pragmatic approach to the reality of marijuana use in our society would be to replace criminal laws with public health strategies. As we have with tobacco, we could regulate advertising and invest in multimedia information campaigns.... We have relinquished control of the marijuana market to black market profiteers. We could instead take control; regulate price, potency, and advertising; and levy taxes to help pay for prevention, education, and research. It is time for a new approach to marijuana.

Kevin Sabet (2013), by contrast, argues that the risks associated with marijuana legalization outweigh the potential benefits. He believes that the legalization of recreational use in Colorado and Washington State was a mistake. He supports the use of drug courts and expanded treatment services for addicts, civil penalties (such as fines) for recreational users, and aggressive law enforcement efforts to combat drug dealers:

> Because marijuana legalization would expose us to unknown risk...I join both major presidential candidates [Barack Obama and Mitt Romney] and the American Medical Association in opposing marijuana legalization. It is a reckless policy option.... According to the nonpartisan RAND Corporation, legalization would greatly reduce the price of marijuana, thereby significantly increasing use, especially among kids. This is a problem because the brain is developing until age 25, and recently completed research shows that pot can significantly decrease IQ....
>
> Even the supposed benefits of legalization may not pan out.... Marijuana legalization would also do nothing to loosen the cartels' grip on other illegal trades such

human trafficking, kidnapping, extortion, piracy, and other illicit drugs (marijuana accounts for a minority of revenues gained by drug trafficking groups). . . . But these facts do not mean we need to go overboard in our approach. Low-level marijuana users should not be imprisoned for their use. . . . The good news is that we have more choices than merely enforcement or legalization. We can get smarter about our marijuana policy without throwing the next generation under the bus.

In reading the preceding statements, consider how we might evaluate the accuracy of the competing claims that are made. Also, do you think the arguments regarding legalization would be different for other drugs, like cocaine? Further, are the only options in the drug debate complete prohibition and virtually free legal commerce (see Boyum and Kleiman, 2002)? Finally, should our current policies toward **alcohol** be altered, given the contribution that alcohol makes to crime and other social problems? (A study by the National Research Council and Institute of Medicine [2004] recommended higher taxes on alcohol and more limits on alcohol advertising, among other things, in an effort to reduce alcohol consumption, especially teen drinking.)

Web-Based Exercise: Guns Across the Globe

The School of Public Health at the University of Sydney maintains a website titled GunPolicy.org, which seeks to provide researchers, journalists, and officials with accurate information about firearms. The Australian site provides a treasure trove of information, allowing you to look up detailed information on firearms and firearms-related laws in the United States. The site also allows you to compare the United States with other nations. Visit the site and begin by using the **Find Gun Policy Facts** feature on the home page. Select the United States and click on the **Find Facts** button. Then select **Death and Injury** from the menu, and then **Gun Homicides**. After viewing trends in the rate of gun homicide in the United States, click on the **Compare** button and select Canada as the comparison nation. How might we explain the striking differences we see between the United States and Canada? Use the website to conduct further comparisons between these two nations. For each nation, for example, you could compare the total number of guns as well as the rate of gun ownership in the civilian population.

TEST YOUR KNOWLEDGE OF THIS CHAPTER

1. Drawing on the leading delinquency theories, why might we expect religious juveniles to be less delinquent?
2. Describe the major research findings regarding the effect of religion on delinquency. Why does religion have a larger effect on victimless crimes than on serious delinquency? Why does religion have a larger effect when the individual is surrounded by religious others?
3. Why might we expect work to reduce delinquency?
4. What does the research say about the effect of working while attending school on delinquency? How might we explain these results?
5. Violent juveniles are more likely than nonviolent juveniles to watch violent TV shows and movies. Does this mean that TV and movie violence causes violent behavior? If not, why not?
6. Describe a typical experiment examining the effect of TV and movie violence on aggression. Why have some people questioned such experiments?
7. Describe the major research findings regarding the effect of TV and movie violence on violent behavior.

8. Describe the major research findings on the effect of violent video games on aggression.
9. Describe some of the ways in which social media engagement could lead to an increase in delinquent behavior. And then describe how social media engagement could lead to a reduction in crime and delinquency.
10. What are the four major ways in which drug use and sales are said to increase other forms of delinquency?
11. The strong association between drug use and sales and delinquency does not prove that drug use and sales cause other delinquency. Why not?
12. Describe the major research findings on the effect of drug use and sales on delinquency.
13. What reasons do juveniles give for possessing guns? Does the reason for gun possession have any effect on the relation between guns and delinquency?
14. What factors increase the likelihood that juveniles will possess guns?
15. Describe the major research findings on the effect of gun possession on delinquency. Why might gun possession increase the likelihood of certain types of delinquency?
16. Why do some people argue that guns prevent more crime than they contribute to?

THOUGHT AND DISCUSSION QUESTIONS

1. In discussing the causes of delinquency, politicians and others often focus on the lack of religion and on the violence displayed in mass media. Yet data suggest that these factors have only a modest effect on delinquency. Why do you think politicians and others focus on religion and the media rather than more important causes of juvenile crime?
2. Do you think that efforts to restrict juveniles' access to media violence, like the V-chip and the ratings system for TV shows and video games, are effective?
3. There is a major media campaign under way to reduce drug use, with antidrug ads appearing in such places as newspapers, magazines, billboards, TV, and the internet. Find or describe one such ad. What causes of delinquency does it attempt to address, if any? Do you think such ads are effective in reducing juvenile drug use?

ENDNOTES

1. For overviews and recent examples of the research on religion and delinquency, see Baier and Wright, 2001; Burkett and Warren, 1987; Cochran et al., 1994; Desmond et al., 2009; Elifson et al., 1983; Evans et al., 1996; Evans et al., 1995; Giordano et al., 2008; Jang and Johnson, 2001; Jensen and Rojek, 1998; Johnson, Jang, Larson, and Li, 2000; Johnson et al., 2001; Johnson, Li, Larson, and McCullough, 2000; Milot and Ludden, 2009; Pearce and Haynie, 2004; Petts, 2009; Regnerus, 2003; Regnerus and Elder, 2003; Regnerus and Smith, 2005; Schroeder and Frana, 2009; Stark and Bainbridge, 1996; Tittle and Welch, 1983; J. Wallace et al., 2007.
2. For example, see Burkett and Warren, 1987; Evans et al., 1996; Johnson et al., 2001; Regnerus and Elder, 2003.
3. See Adamczyk, 2012; Baier and Wright, 2001; Evans et al., 1995; Pearce and Haynie, 2004; Regnerus, 2003; Stark and Bainbridge, 1996; Tittle and Welch, 1983; J. Wallace et al., 2007.
4. For overviews and selected studies in this area, see Agnew, 1986; Apel et al., 2008; Cullen et al., 1997; Ploeger, 1997; Staff and Schulenberg, 2010; Steinberg, 1996; N. Williams et al., 1996; J. P. Wright and Cullen, 2000; J. P. Wright et al., 1997.
5. See note 4.
6. See Agnew, 1990b; Cullen et al., 1985; J. P. Wright et al., 2001.

7. For overviews of the research on TV and movie violence and violent behavior, see C. Anderson et al., 2007; C. Anderson and Bushman, 2001a, 2002; C. Anderson et al., 2003; Binder et al., 1997; Bloom, 2002; Browne and Hamilton-Giachritsis, 2005; Christensen and Wood, 2007; Donnerstein and Linz, 1995; Donnerstein et al., 1994; Freedman, 2002; Gentile, 2014; Huesmann and Kirwil, 2007; Kirsh, 2006; Levine, 1996; McCord et al., 2001; National Research Council, 2013a; National Television Violence Study, 1997, 1998; Savage and Yancey, 2008; U.S. Department of Health and Human Services, 2001. Also see the entire April 2008 issue of *American Behavioral Scientist.*

8. For overviews of the research on violent video games and aggression, see C. Anderson, 2004; C. Anderson and Bushman, 2001b; C. Anderson and Gentile, 2014; C. Anderson et al., 2003, 2007, 2008, 2010; Bensley and Van Eenwyk, 2001; Browne and Hamilton-Giachritsis, 2005; Dill and Dill, 1998; Greitemeyer and Mügge, 2014; Griffiths, 1999; Kirsh, 2006; National Research Council, 2013a; Sherry, 2001, 2007; Weber et al., 2006.

9. For overviews and examples of the recent research on drugs and delinquency, see Akers, 1992; Altschuler and Brounstein, 1991; Assaad and Exum, 2002; Boyum and Kleiman, 2002; Bureau of Justice Statistics, 1992; Chitwood et al., 1996; Crowe, 1998; D'Amico et al., 2008; Elliott et al., 1989; Fagan 1998; R. Felson, Savolainen, Aaltonen, and Moustgaard, 2008; R. Felson, Teasdale, and Burchfield, 2008; Gentry, 1995; Goldstein, 1985; Goode, 2008a; Huizinga et al., 1989; Inciardi and McElrath, 1998; Kretschmar and Flannery, 2007; McBride and McCoy, 1993; Office of National Drug Control Policy, 1999; Ousey and Lee, 2007; Schroeder et al., 2007; Welte et al., 2001; H. White and Gorman, 2000; H. White and Hansell, 1996; H. White and Labouvie, 1994; H. White et al., 1987, 2002; L. Zhang, Wieczorek, and Welte, 1997.

10. See Crowe, 1998; Schroeder et al., 2007; Thornberry, Krohn et al. (with Porter), 2003; L. Zhang, Wieczorek, and Welte, 1997.

11. See Saum, 1998; also see Crowe, 1998; R. Felson and Burchfield, 2004; Mustaine and Tewksbury, 1998b.

12. For a fuller discussion of these issues, see Boyum and Kleiman, 2002; Gentry, 1995; Goode, 2008a; Inciardi and McElrath, 1998; Meier and Geis, 1997; Sabet, 2013.

13. See Office of National Drug Control Policy, 2003; also see Altschuler and Brounstein, 1991; Elliott et al., 1989; National Institute of Justice, 2003; H. White et al., 2002.

14. See H. White et al., 1987; also see Akers, 1992; Elliott et al., 1989; Huizinga et al., 2003; NSDUH Report, 2006.

15. See D'Amico et al., 2008; Elliott et al., 1989; Neff and Waite, 2007; Passini, 2012; H. White and Gorman, 2000.

16. See D'Amico et al., 2008; Elliott et al., 1989; Goode, 2008a; Huang et al., 2001; Huizinga et al., 1989; Huizinga et al., 2003; Kretschmar and Flannery, 2007; Maldonado-Molina et al., 2011; Messner et al., 2007; Schroeder et al., 2007; Welte et al., 2001; also see R. Felson, Savolainen, Aaltonen, and Moustgaard, 2008; R. Felson, Teasdale, and Burchfield, 2008.

17. See note 16.

18. For overviews and examples of recent research on guns and delinquency/crime, see Berkowitz, 1994; Bjerregaard and Lizotte, 1995; Blumstein, 1995; Cook, 1991; Cook and Ludwig, 1997, 2000, 2004; Cook et al., 2002; Decker et al., 1997; Duggan, 2001; Greenbaum, 1997; Harcourt, 2003; Kleck, 1997; Liberman, 2007; Lizotte and Sheppard, 2001; Lizotte et al., 2002; Lizotte et al., 1994; Ludwig and Cook, 2003; National Research Council, 2013a; Office of Juvenile Justice and Delinquency Prevention, 1996; Reiss and Roth, 1993; Sheley and Wright, 1995, 1998; Siegel et al., 2013; Thornberry and Krohn, 2003; S. Walker, 1998; Wilcox et al., 2006; Wilkinson et al., 2009; Wintemute, 2006; James Wright et al., 1992; James Wright and Vail, 2000; Zawitz, 1995; Zimring, 2005, 2007; Zimring and Hawkins, 1997.

19. See Office of Juvenile Justice and Delinquency Prevention, 2000a; also see Sheley and Wright, 1998; Thornberry and Krohn, 2003.

20. See Lizotte and Sheppard, 2001; also see Sheley and Wright, 1995; Thornberry, Krohn et al. (with Porter), 2003; Wintemute, 2006.

21. See Berkowitz, 1994; Cook et al., 2002; Kleck, 1997; Reiss and Roth, 1993; Wells and Horney, 2002; Zimring and Hawkins, 1997.

22. See Berkowitz, 1994; Blumstein, 1995; Cook and Ludwig, 2000; Kleck, 1997; Wells and Horney, 2002; Wilcox et al., 2006; Zimring and Hawkins, 1997.

23. See Hemenway and Miller, 2004; Kleck, 2015; Kovandzic and Marvell, 2003; McDowall et al., 2000; Monuteaux et al., 2015; National Research Council, 2013a.

24. For discussions of gun control, see Cook and Ludwig, 1997, 1998, 2000; Cook et al., 2002; Harcourt, 2003; Kleck, 1997; Kleck and Gertz, 1995; Lott, 1998; Ludwig and Cook, 2003; McDowall et al., 1991; McDowall et al., 2000; McDowall and Wiersema, 1994; National Research Council, 2013a; Reiss and Roth, 1993; Sherman, 2001; Stolzenberg and D'Alessio, 2000; Wintemute, 2006; James Wright and Vail, 2000; Zimring, 2005, 2007; Zimring and Hawkins, 1997.

18 Pulling It All Together

What Causes Delinquency?

I magine that you are sitting at the dinner table with family or friends, engaged in casual conversation. Someone asks you what classes you are taking, and you mention that you are studying juvenile delinquency. The mention of the topic attracts much interest, and you are then asked, **"So what causes delinquency?"** How would you respond to this question?

We have now reviewed the major theories of delinquency: strain, social learning, control, and labeling theories (Chapters 6–12). We have also reviewed a large body of research that is derived from, or at least compatible with, these theories. This research focused on the individual traits and features of the social environment that cause delinquency, including family, school, and peer environments (Chapters 13–17). So you should be in a very good position to respond to this question. But we expect that you are somewhat uncertain about the reply you would give. There is a good reason for this.

You are probably feeling somewhat overwhelmed and a little confused by now. We have examined several theories and a lot of research based on these theories. You might wonder how everything fits together. In particular, you might wonder whether it is possible to pull all the theories and research together and construct an integrated or general explanation of delinquency.

Several criminologists have tried to do this, and some of their integrated explanations or theories are attracting attention.[1] But none of these theories has gained widespread acceptance among criminologists. In this chapter we present our own integrated explanation of delinquency, to help you pull together the material in Chapters 6 through 17. Our explanation draws heavily on the integrated theories developed by other criminologists, especially Thornberry's (1987) "interactional" theory of delinquency, as well as the first author's own theory (Agnew, 2005).

As you may recall from Chapters 5 through 12, theories try to explain several major facts about delinquency. Most notably, they **try to explain why some individuals engage in more delinquency than others.** This is the focus of the core part of the general theory presented next. After introducing the core part, we show how the general theory can **explain group differences in delinquency.** Since the general theory presented here attempts to pull together the material in Chapters 6 through 17, we begin this chapter by providing a brief overview of the key points in those chapters. We then present the general theory in three stages.

1. We describe the **major direct causes of delinquency** and identify the reasons why these causes affect delinquency. The causes are grouped into *four clusters:* irritability/low self-control, poor parenting practices, negative school experiences, and association with delinquent peers or gang members. It is argued that **the causes in each cluster affect delinquency for reasons related to all the major delinquency theories.**

2. We describe **how these clusters are related. In particular, the clusters have reciprocal effects on one another** (e.g., negative school experiences increase association with delinquent peers, which, in turn, increases negative school experiences).

3. We describe **the ways in which biological factors and the larger social environment affect the clusters,** with a focus on the effects of **gender/sex, age, parental social class, and community characteristics.** This discussion allows us to explain group differences in delinquency.

It is important to stress that the general theory simplifies a complex reality. Among other things, it does not consider many of the less important causes of delinquency, like religion and media violence. The theory is designed to highlight the key causes of delinquency and to describe the major ways in which those causes work together to affect delinquency.

The final section of the chapter illustrates the general theory in action. The theory is used to explain one of the most important facts about delinquency: the fact **that males have higher rates of offending than females.** As indicated in Chapter 4, sex/gender is one of the strongest sociodemographic correlates of delinquency.

After reading this chapter, you should be able to:

- Identify the important direct causes of individual delinquency and describe how these causes group into four clusters.
- Describe the effects of each cluster on delinquency, as well as on other clusters.
- Describe how biological and social environmental factors affect the four clusters.
- Use the general theory to explain patterns of offending over the life course.
- Use the general theory to explain gender differences in delinquency.

A BRIEF REVIEW OF THE THEORIES AND RESEARCH ON THE CAUSES OF DELINQUENCY

Theories

The **major delinquency theories** devote most attention to explaining why some individuals engage in delinquency more than others. These theories describe the independent variables that cause delinquency and explain why these variables cause delinquency.

Strain theory argues that delinquency is caused by stressful events or conditions. The theory focuses on two major types of strain: failure to achieve positively valued goals, and the loss of positive stimuli or presentation of negative stimuli. The experience of strain leads to negative emotions, like anger and frustration, and juveniles may turn to delinquency in an effort to cope with strain and the accompanying emotions. Delinquency may allow juveniles to reduce or escape from their strain, seek revenge against those who have wronged them, or manage their negative emotions (e.g., through illicit drug use).

Social learning theory argues that delinquency is caused by associating with others who present beliefs favorable to delinquency, model delinquency, and reinforce delinquency. These activities lead individuals to conclude that delinquency is a desirable or at least justifiable response in certain situations.

Control theory argues that delinquency results from weak controls: lack of direct controls, few stakes in conformity, neutral beliefs regarding crime, and low self-control. Weak controls free juveniles to satisfy their needs and desires in the most expedient way possible, which is often delinquency.

Labeling theory argues that individuals who are tagged as "delinquent" are often rejected and treated in a harsh manner by others. This harsh/rejecting treatment increases the likelihood of further delinquency by increasing strain, reducing the rejected individual's control, increasing the social learning for crime (since labeled individuals are forced to associate with other delinquents), and fostering a delinquent self-concept.

These theories have also been used to **explain patterns of offending over the life course,** especially the adolescence-limited and life-course persistent patterns of offending. Most individuals **increase their levels of offending during adolescence** because the biological and social changes associated with adolescence lead to increases in strain, reductions in control, and increases in the social learning for crime. For example, the increased autonomy given to adolescents leads to a reduction in direct control and an increase in association with delinquent peers. A small percentage of individuals **offend at high rates**

over much of their lives. They follow this course because they experience poor parenting and develop the traits of irritability/low self-control early in life; these problems tend to persist over time and to contribute to school, peer, marital, and work problems later in life (partly for reasons related to labeling theory). As a consequence, such individuals experience high levels of strain, low control, and much social learning for crime over the greater part of their lives.

Further, these theories have been used to **describe situations most conducive to delinquency.** In particular, delinquency is more likely when the juvenile is provoked by others (a type of strain), with provocations like insults, threats, and attacks being especially conducive to delinquency. Delinquency is also more likely in situations characterized by the use of drugs and alcohol, the availability of attractive targets, the absence of capable guardians, and the presence of delinquent peers. Control is low in such situations, and the likelihood that criminal acts will be reinforced is high. Juveniles who frequently engage in unstructured, unsupervised activities with peers are more likely to encounter these situations.

Finally, these theories have been used to **explain group differences in delinquency,** with Chapter 12 focusing on **community differences in delinquency.** Delinquency is highest in communities that are economically deprived, high in residential instability, and high in family disruption. Such communities are lower in control, higher in strain, and more likely to develop delinquent peer groups and gangs that foster the social learning of crime.

Research

The research derived from these theories focuses on a wide range of independent variables that may cause delinquency. The variables measure strain, the dimensions of control, factors associated with the social learning of crime, and/or labeling. Factors that appear to have at least a small to moderate effect on delinquency include the following.

1. **Individual traits,** including low verbal IQ and, especially, the super-traits of irritability and low self-control. Evidence suggests that these traits are the product of biological and environmental factors, especially poor parenting.

2. **Family experiences,** including broken homes, long hours in childcare, teenage parenthood, large families, criminal parents and siblings, parental rejection, low attachment to parents, family conflict, child abuse, poor parental supervision, poor family problem-solving techniques, and the lack of positive parenting.

3. **School experiences,** including low academic performance, low school involvement, low attachment to school, poor relations with teachers, low educational or occupational goals, and school misbehavior.

4. **School characteristics,** including large schools with poor resources, poor discipline, limited opportunities for student success, low expectations for students, unpleasant working conditions for students, poor cooperation between the administration and teachers, and little community involvement.

5. **Peer group and gang experiences,** including association with delinquent peers and, especially, gang membership.

6. **Religion, mass media, drugs, and guns,** where "religion" means "lack of religion" (mainly for victimless crimes), with the inclusion, as well, of extensive exposure to media violence, drug selling and serious drug use, and gun possession, especially for protection (mainly for serious violence).

It is clear that we have covered much material in this text and, again, it is understandable if you are feeling somewhat overwhelmed and confused. The general theory described next will help you pull a lot of this material together and, hopefully, give a comprehensive and meaningful response when you are asked, "What causes delinquency?"

A GENERAL THEORY OF DELINQUENCY
The Major Direct Causes of Delinquency and Why They Cause It

The first thing a general theory of delinquency should do is list the factors that have relatively large, direct effects on delinquency and explain why these factors affect delinquency. The major theories and the research on these theories provide guidance here.

The leading direct causes of delinquency are listed next. We describe these causes in concrete terms. So, rather than stating that factors like the "presentation of negative stimuli" and "low direct control" cause delinquency, we state that factors like child abuse and poor parental supervision cause delinquency. These concrete descriptions are more meaningful to most people. We group the leading causes into **four clusters: irritability/low self-control, poor parenting practices, negative school experiences, and peer delinquency.** These clusters reflect the four major domains of the juvenile's life: self (individual traits), family, school, and peers. The specific causes in each cluster generally have relatively strong associations with one another, so it is reasonable to group them together (see Agnew, 2005). Grouping causes greatly simplifies the general theory, making it much easier to keep track of the causes and to describe how they work together to affect delinquency.

Finally, we describe why the causes in each cluster affect delinquency. The leading theories have much to say in this area, although relatively little research has been done on this topic. Nevertheless, the limited research that exists tends to affirm one of the central points made in Chapters 13 through 17: namely, that most causes affect delinquency for reasons related to most or all of the leading delinquency theories.[2] We therefore argue that **the causes in each cluster increase delinquency for reasons related to strain, control, social learning, and labeling theories.**

The **four clusters** of variables affecting delinquency are as follows.

1. *Irritability/low self-control.* Recall that individuals with these super-traits are basically out of control and mean, nasty people. They are more likely to engage in delinquency because they are **low in self-control;** in particular, they have trouble restraining themselves from acting on their immediate desires. They are **high in strain,** since they are more sensitive to strains, more likely to blame others for their strains, and more likely to provoke negative responses from others. They are also more disposed to cope with strain in a delinquent manner. They are more likely to **learn to engage in crime,** because they are less sensitive to the punishments for crime and more attracted to the rewards of crime—since crime often provides thrills and excitement and allows for the immediate gratification of one's desires. Finally, they are more likely to be **labeled as bad and treated in a harsh or rejecting manner.**

2. *Poor parenting practices.* Juveniles who experience poor parenting practices are rejected by their parents, dislike or hate their parents, frequently get into conflicts with their parents, are poorly supervised and disciplined by their parents, are abused by their parents, and/or receive little in the way of positive parenting. Other family factors, like having parents who are criminals or are divorced or separated, are important largely because they affect these dimensions of poor parenting (which refer to the quality of family relations and parental socialization).

Poor parenting increases the likelihood of delinquency for reasons related to all the leading theories. Individuals subject to poor parenting are **high in strain** (because, e.g., they are harshly disciplined, abused, and in frequent conflict with parents). They are more likely to cope with strain through delinquency, partly because their parents do not provide much social support or teach legitimate coping skills (these are part of positive parenting). They are **low in direct control** (i.e., are poorly supervised and disciplined) and have a **low stake in conformity** (i.e., are weakly bonded to parents). They **learn to engage in aggressive behavior** from their parents, who often treat them harshly or abuse them. And their parents **label them as bad** and treat them in a harsh or rejecting manner.

3. *Negative school experiences.* Negative school experiences include low academic performance, low school involvement, including little time on homework, low attachment to school, poor relations with teachers, and low educational and occupational goals. Juveniles with negative school experiences are **high in strain**, perhaps because teachers give them low grades and treat them in a negative manner. The juveniles have a **low stake in conformity,** given their low grades, low involvement in school, low attachment to school, and low goals. They are probably **low in direct control,** since they have little involvement in school activities. They are more likely to **learn to engage in crime.** In particular, they are more often in noncollege tracks, a status that increases their exposure to delinquent others. And they are more likely to be **labeled as bad** and treated accordingly.

4. *Association with delinquent peers or gang members (delinquent peer association for short).* Juveniles who score high on this cluster are part of a cohesive group of peers (including friends and siblings) who are heavily involved in delinquency. Further, these peers constitute a gang. Delinquent peer association **increases strain,** since delinquent peers are more likely to get into conflicts with one another and with outsiders. Delinquent peer association **reduces a juvenile's stake in conformity** by reducing bonds to conventional others and minimizing efforts devoted to conventional pursuits, like schoolwork. Delinquent peer association strongly **fosters the social learning of crime,** since the juvenile is exposed to others who differentially reinforce crime, teach beliefs favorable to crime, and model crime. Delinquent peer association increases the likelihood of being **labeled as bad.** And delinquent peer association **increases the amount of time spent in unstructured, unsupervised activities with peers,** which in turn increases exposure to situations conducive to crime.

At this point you should pause for a minute and **test yourself**. Briefly describe each of the four clusters *in your own words*. It is not necessary to describe each and every factor that makes up the cluster; just try to provide a general sense of what the cluster includes. For example, you might say that juveniles who have "negative school experiences" are doing poorly at school, do not like school, and do not want much education. Then draw on the major theories to describe two reasons that would explain why each cluster increases the likelihood of delinquency. For example, you might state that juveniles whose school experiences have been negative are more likely to engage in delinquency because they experience more strain or stress and because they have less to lose (i.e., a low stake in conformity).

How All These Clusters Are Related

A general theory should do more than list the major causes of delinquency and describe why they cause delinquency. It should also describe how these causes are related to one another.

The clusters have *reciprocal effects* on one another. Cluster X causes cluster Y **and** cluster Y causes cluster X. If you read Chapters 13 through 17 closely, you noticed that we argue that each cluster of variables is reciprocally related to the other clusters. For example, in Chapter 13 we argue that poor parenting practices contribute to traits like irritability and low self-control. Then, in Chapter 14, we argue that irritability and low self-control contribute to poor parenting practices. Juveniles who are irritable and low in self-control are difficult to raise, and their frustrated parents often become overly coercive or just give up trying to control their children. To give another example, in Chapter 16, we argue that negative school experiences increase delinquent peer association. People who do poorly in school are more likely to be exposed to delinquent peers (especially in non-college tracks) and to be attracted to them. Then, in Chapter 15, we argue that delinquent peer association increases the likelihood of negative school experiences, since delinquent peers often de-emphasize schoolwork. Similar arguments were made regarding the other combinations of clusters. The reciprocal effects of the clusters on one another are shown in Figure 18.1. Such effects are also emphasized in Thornberry's (1987) integrated theory of delinquency. There has not been much research on reciprocal effects, but data provide some support for their existence.[3]

The reciprocal effects among the clusters shed important light on the causes of delinquency. We see that each cluster not only has a direct effect on delinquency but also has an indirect effect through the other clusters. For example, poor parenting directly affects delinquency and indirectly affects delinquency by contributing to irritability/low self-control, fostering negative school experiences, and increasing delinquent peer associations. Also we see that problems in one cluster tend to create problems in the other clusters. For example, problems at home tend to lead to problems at school. This point has important policy implications. Efforts to reduce problems in one cluster, like the school cluster, will be more effective to the extent that they take into account problems in other clusters, like the family cluster.

How Biological Factors and the Larger Social Environment Affect the Clusters

So far we have described the factors that have relatively large, direct effects on delinquency and how these factors work together to affect delinquency. This information, which sheds much light on why some individuals are more likely than others to engage in delinquency, is useful to those seeking to control delinquency (see Chapter 24). But there is one final issue that a general theory must address: **Why is it that some individuals are more likely than others to possess the traits of irritability and low self-control, and more likely to experience poor parenting, to have negative peer experiences, and to associate with delinquent peers?** A general theory, then, must also describe the *background variables* that affect the major direct causes of delinquency. By providing such descriptions, we allow the theory to explain group differences in offending.

Two sets of background variables have substantial effects on irritability/low self-control, poor parenting, negative school experiences, and/or peer delinquency. **The background variables in the first set affect irritability/low self-control; they include biological factors like genetic inheritance and a range of biological harms,** like poor prenatal care, head injuries, and exposure to lead or other toxic substances. These factors

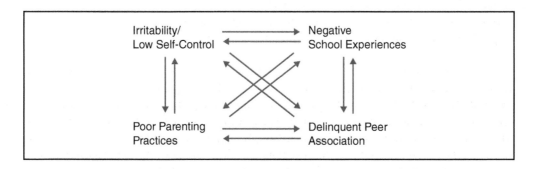

FIGURE 18.1 The Reciprocal Effects of the Clusters on One Another

affect irritability/low self-control through their effects on the central and autonomic nervous systems (described in Chapter 13).

The second set of background variables comprises features of the juvenile's social environment. Certain environmental variables have direct effects on just one or two of the clusters. For example, coming from a so-called broken home and having criminal parents often are related to poor parenting practices, but these variables have little *direct effect* on the other clusters (although they have an *indirect effect* through their influence on poor parenting practices). Other environmental variables, however, affect all or most of the clusters. To keep the general theory simple, we focus on these variables. They include **the type of community in which one lives and one's position in the larger society, as reflected by one's gender, age, and parents' social class.**

In particular, **those in deprived communities, males, adolescents, and lower-class individuals are higher on measures of irritability/low self-control, poor parenting practices, negative school experiences, and delinquent peer associations.** As indicated in Chapters 13 through 17, these variables directly affect irritability/low self-control, poor parenting practices, negative school experiences, and delinquent peer association. Further, these variables indirectly affect the clusters, through their impact on or association with factors like coming from a single-parent home, having criminal parents, or attending an inferior school. For example, juveniles in deprived communities are more likely to live in single-parent homes and attend inferior schools.

The reasons these variables affect the four clusters are described in Chapters 13 through 17. For example, Chapter 15 states that low parental social class increases the likelihood of negative school experiences; this is because lower-class parents are less likely to equip their children with the skills and attitudes necessary to do well in school. To give another example, Chapters 12 and 16 state that juveniles in deprived communities are more likely to join delinquent peer groups, since low control and high strain in such communities foster the development of such groups and increase their appeal to juveniles. And, to give a final example, Chapter 10 explains why adolescents are more likely than children and adults to be irritable and low in self-control, have family problems, have negative school experiences, and associate with delinquent peers.

We should note that **race/ethnicity is associated with the clusters.** However, evidence suggests that this association largely reflects the relation of **race and/or ethnicity to parental social class and community characteristics.** For reasons of past and present discrimination, members of certain races or ethnic groups, such as African Americans, Latinos, and Native Americans, are more likely to be poor and to live in deprived communities. That is the primary reason for the frequent association of race/ethnicity with the clusters. Once we take into account parental social class and community characteristics, the association between race/ethnicity and the clusters is substantially reduced. The association may not be eliminated entirely, likely because race/ethnicity still affects how people treat one another—even after taking account of social class. African Americans, for example, encounter more racial discrimination than whites at all class levels (M. Hughes and Thomas, 1998).

We should also note that **it is possible to describe still other, larger social influences that directly and indirectly affect the clusters.** For example, does the economic system provide adults with decent work at a living wage? The lack of good jobs has far-ranging consequences that may affect the clusters. For example, the lack of decent work increases the economic strain faced by family members, which in turn contributes to poor parenting practices. Does the political system provide sufficient support to those experiencing economic, health, educational, and other problems? Again, the failure to provide such support has far-ranging consequences that affect the clusters. For example, the failure to provide adequate health care may increase the prevalence of biological harms, like birth complications, which contribute to irritability/low self-control. Does the cultural system place a strong emphasis on socializing boys to be aggressive? The impact of these and other larger social forces on crime is discussed in several excellent works.[4]

Explaining Group Differences in Delinquency

Describing the effect of biological factors and the larger social environment on the direct causes allows the general theory to explain group differences in delinquency.

Group differences in delinquency occur mainly because **members of some groups are more likely to score high on the clusters.** So group X has a higher rate of delinquency than group Y largely because the members of group X are more likely to be irritable and low in self-control, to experience poor parenting, to have negative school experiences, and to associate with delinquent peers. However, this may not be the only reason that group X has a higher rate of delinquency. Certain group characteristics beyond those reflected in the four clusters may also have a direct effect on delinquency. For example, the level of direct control that neighborhood residents exercise over one another also helps explain why some communities have higher rates of delinquency than other communities (see Chapter 12). Nevertheless, the general theory predicts that **group differences in the four clusters largely account for group differences in delinquency.** This point is illustrated in the next section, where we use the general theory to explain why males have higher rates of delinquency than females in the next section.

USING THE GENERAL THEORY TO EXPLAIN WHY MALES HAVE HIGHER RATES OF DELINQUENCY THAN FEMALES

As we discussed in Chapter 4, males are more likely than females to engage in most forms of delinquency, especially serious delinquency. According to the general theory, the major reason for this is the greater likelihood that males will score high on the clusters—irritability/low self-control, poor parenting practices, negative school experiences, and delinquent peer association.[5]

Data suggest that **males are more likely than females to possess the traits that make up irritability and low self-control.**[6] Further, the fact that males are higher in irritability/low self-control appears to explain much of the gender difference in delinquency.[7] Gender differences in irritability/low self-control are likely due to both biological and environmental factors (see the biosocial model of gender differences in Udry, 2000).

The role of biological factors in explaining sex differences in irritability/low self-control and offending is suggested by several pieces of evidence. (1) Sex-related differences in temperament have been noted at birth (e.g., newborn females are more likely to smile and cling to their mothers); (2) sex differences in physical aggression and crime emerge very early in life; and (3) historical and cross-cultural studies consistently find that males are more involved than females in most forms of physical aggression and crime (although the extent to which males are more involved varies over time and among societies). Further, evidence suggests that biological factors like genetic inheritance may have a strong impact on irritability/low self-control (Moffitt et al., 2001). The precise biological causes of sex differences in irritability/low self-control and offending, however, are unclear. The most commonly advanced explanation has to do with sex differences in the level of testosterone, a hormone that stimulates the development of masculine characteristics.[8] More research is needed in this area, however.

There is also reason to believe that **sex differences in traits and offending are partly due to environmental factors.** Males and females are treated differently from birth onward. In particular, males and females are socialized differently by family members and others. Among other things, females are more likely to be socialized to be submissive and dependent on others, empathetic with others, and supportive of others. Females are more often exposed to models that exhibit these behaviors, taught beliefs conducive to these behaviors, and reinforced for these behaviors. Males, by contrast, are more likely to be socialized to be aggressive and assertive, to take risks, to be independent, and to be competitive. As a consequence of such differences in socialization, males may be more likely to possess many of the traits that make up irritability and low self-control, like risk seeking, little concern for the feelings and rights of others, and moral beliefs favorable to delinquency.

Gender differences with respect to the other clusters also help explain the fact that **males have higher rates of delinquency.** Among other things, it is argued that males (1) are less closely supervised by family members, (2) are less strongly attached to family members, (3) are less attached to school, (4) spend less time on schoolwork, (5) do less well in school, and (6) are more likely to associate with delinquent peers.[9] These differences may partly reflect sex differences in irritability and low self-control. Because of their greater irritability and lower self-control, for example, males may be more likely to associate with delinquent peers because such peers are more attractive to them. These differences also reflect differences in the way males and females are viewed and treated. Females, for example, are more likely to be seen as submissive and weak, and therefore in need of greater supervision and protection. And females are under greater pressure to maintain their chastity, which again fosters greater supervision and control over their lives.

Data regarding these gender differences in the clusters are somewhat mixed. Some studies, for example, find that males are less strongly bonded to family members, others find that males are more strongly bonded, and still others find that there are no gender differences in family bonding. Perhaps the most consistent findings deal with delinquent peer associations and parental supervision. Females are less likely to associate with delinquent peers and are more likely to be closely supervised by parents. Studies suggest that **gender differences in supervision and especially peer association explain a good portion of the gender difference in delinquency.**[10]

So gender differences in delinquency are due largely to gender differences in standing on the clusters, especially **gender differences in irritability/low self-control, delinquent peer association, and, to a lesser extent, parental supervision.** Some researchers also argue that certain of these clusters are more likely to affect delinquency among males than among females. For example, they note, not only are males more likely than females to associate with delinquent peers but, in addition, delinquent peers are more likely to cause delinquency among males than females (Mears et al., 1998; N. Piquero et al., 2005). The data in this area are somewhat mixed, but most data suggest that, except for the delinquent-peers item, the causes have similar effects on males and females.[11]

The Special Role of Sexual Abuse in Explaining Serious Female Offending

There is, however, one particular cause that may have a larger effect on female offending than on male offending. We single out this cause because it may play an especially important role in the explanation of serious female offending. Chesney-Lind (1989) argues that **abuse by family members, especially sexual abuse, plays a special role in the explanation of female delinquency.** While abuse may lead to delinquency among males, females are much more likely to be the victims of sexual abuse than males, and such abuse is said to have an especially devastating effect on females. Females, in particular, often respond to such abuse by running away from home, and they often find that to survive on the street, they must turn to crime. Their age and runaway status rule out legitimate employment, so they engage in income-generating crimes like prostitution, drug selling, and petty theft. Life on the street, including involvement in activities like prostitution, leads to further abuse and exploitation. The police and juvenile courts often provide little assistance to these females. In fact, such females are frequently arrested and returned to their home environment, where they may suffer further abuse. Interviews with female offenders provide tentative support for this argument.[12]

AN OVERVIEW OF THE GENERAL THEORY OF DELINQUENCY

The general theory of delinquency makes several key arguments.

1. The major direct causes of delinquency can be grouped into four clusters: irritability/low self-control, poor parenting practices, negative school experiences, and delinquent peer association. These clusters affect delinquency by increasing strain, reducing control, increasing the social learning for crime, and increasing labeling.

2. The clusters have reciprocal effects on one another. For example, irritability/low self-control causes poor parenting, and poor parenting causes irritability/low self-control.

3. Biological factors and the larger social environment affect the clusters. In particular, males, adolescents, lower-class people, and the residents of deprived communities are more likely to be high in irritability/low self-control and on measures of poor parenting practices, negative school experiences, and delinquent peer association.

We hope that the general theory helps you keep track of the key points from previous chapters and see how this material fits together. Remember that the theory simplifies a complex reality by, for example, ignoring many of the less important causes of delinquency (see Agnew, 2005, for a more elaborate version of the general theory).

You now know quite a bit about the causes of delinquency. You can list most of its major causes, you can state why the causes increase delinquency, and you know something about how the causes work together to affect delinquency. As you will see in the final chapters of this book, that knowledge can be used to reduce delinquency.

TEACHING AIDS

Web-Based Exercise: Applying the General Theory

Numerous websites provide information on juvenile offenders, including interviews with offenders and background information on them. Two such sites, YouTube and The Crime Report (www.thecrimereport.org), allow you to search for information by using key terms (e.g., juvenile delinquent, juvenile crime, youth crime). Find a report of a juvenile offender that provides at least a moderate amount of information on the offender. Then use the general theory to explain the delinquency of this juvenile. In particular, which causes of delinquency does the report emphasize? Does the report say anything about why these causes increase delinquency and if so, is the explanation related to strain, social learning, control, or labeling theories? Does the report provide any indication that the causes influence one another (e.g., family problems contributed to school problems)? Drawing on the general theory, does the report fail to discuss any potentially important causes of the juvenile's delinquency? Does the report mention any causes that are not part of the general theory?

TEST YOUR KNOWLEDGE OF THIS CHAPTER

1. Briefly describe how the major theories of delinquency explain why some juveniles are more likely to engage in delinquency than others (focus on the strain, control, social learning, and labeling theories).

2. Drawing on these theories, describe the characteristics of situations conducive to crime.

3. How do these theories explain group differences in delinquency, particularly community differences?

4. Briefly describe the four clusters of variables that have a large, direct effect on delinquency.

5. Pick one of these clusters and describe why it increases the likelihood of delinquency, drawing on the major delinquency theories.

6. What do we mean when we state that a variable has a direct effect on delinquency? What do we mean when we state that a variable has an indirect effect on delinquency?

7. Describe how the four clusters are related. Give an example of a reciprocal effect involving the clusters.

8. List the major background variables that affect the clusters. When discussing background variables of an environmental nature, why do we focus on community characteristics, age, gender, and parental social class? Why is it that we do not list race/ethnicity as one of the major causes of the clusters?

9. How does the general theory explain group differences in rates of delinquency?

10. How does the general theory explain the fact that males have higher rates of offending than females? Be sure to identify the key factors accounting for gender differences in offending.

11. Most causes have similar effects on males and females, but one cause of delinquency is said to be especially relevant to females—and may help account for a significant portion of serious female offending. What is that cause, and how does it contribute to female offending?

THOUGHT AND DISCUSSION QUESTIONS

1. How would the general theory explain social class and age differences in delinquency? (For further information, see Agnew, 2005).

2. How would the general theory explain patterns of offending over the life course, including adolescence-limited and life-course persistent offending? (See Chapter 10 and Agnew, 2005).

3. Do you think that the general theory overlooks any important causes of delinquency?

4. Suppose you were to construct your own general theory of delinquency. How would it be similar to and different from the general theory in this chapter?

5. Construct a five-minute explanation of why some juveniles engage in delinquency, an explanation you could present to your family or friends if asked. With the permission of your instructor, several students should present their explanations in class, asking for feedback.

KEY TERMS

- Four clusters
- Irritability/low self-control
- Poor parenting practices
- Negative school experiences
- Delinquent peer association
- Reciprocal effect
- Background variables
- Direct and indirect effects

ENDNOTES

1. For overviews and examples, see Agnew, 2005; Akers and Sellers, 2010; Bernard and Snipes, 1996; Bernard et al., 2010; Braithwaite, 1989; Catalano and Hawkins, 1996; Colvin, 2000; Cullen et al., 2014; Elliott et al., 1985; Farrington, 2006; R. Johnson, 1979; Lilly et al., 2002; Messner et al., 1989; Miethe and Meier, 1994; Pearson and Weiner, 1985; Robinson and Beaver, 2009; Shoemaker, 2004; Thornberry, 1987; Tittle, 1995; Vila, 1994; Wikstrom, 2014.

2. See Agnew, 1993, 1995a, 2005; Brezina, 1998; Farrington, 1993b.

3. See Elliott and Menard, 1996; Thornberry, 1987, 1996; Thornberry et al., 1991, 1994; Thornberry et al., 2003.

4. See Bellair and McNulty, 2005; Colvin, 2000; Cullen and Agnew, 2011; Currie, 1998; Felson, 2002; Hagan 1994; LaFree, 1998; Lynch and Stretesky, 2001; Messner and Rosenfeld, 2001; Pratt and Cullen, 2005; Sampson and Wilson, 1995.

5. For overviews of the research on gender and crime and selected studies, see Agnew, 2009; Bartusch and Matsueda, 1996; R. Berger, 1989; Bottcher, 2001; Canter, 1982; Cernkovich and Giordano, 1987; Chesney-Lind and Shelden, 2004; Cloward and Piven, 1979; Daly, 1998; Daly and Chesney-Lind, 1988; Giordano, 1978; Giordano et al., 1986; Hagan et al., 1996; Hagan et al., 1979; Heidensohn, 2002; Heimer, 1995, 1996; Heimer et al., 2006; Hubbard and Pratt, 2002; Jensen and Eve, 1976; Lanctot and Le Blanc, 2002; Mears et al., 1998; Moffitt et al., 2001; Morash, 1986; D. Rowe et al., 1995; Shoemaker, 2004; Simons et al., 1980; Douglas Smith and Paternoster, 1987; Steffensmeier and Allan, 1996, 2000; J. Wilson and Herrnstein, 1985.

6. See Agnew, 2009; Bartol and Bartol, 1986:120; S. Bennett et al., 2005; R. Berger, 1989; Broidy and Agnew, 1997; Gilligan and Attanucci, 1988; Hagan et al., 1996; Hagan et al., 1979; Heimer, 1996; Mears et al., 1998; Moffitt et al., 2001; Morash, 1983; D. Rowe et al., 1995; Rutter et al., 1998; Slaby and Guerra, 1988; Steffensmeier and Allan, 2000; E. Taylor, 1986; H. White et al., 1985.

7. See Burton et al., 1998; LaGrange and Silverman, 1999; Moffitt et al., 2001.

8. For further information on biological explanations of sex differences in offending, see Archer and McDaniel, 1995; Berkowitz, 1993; Blackburn, 1993; Denno, 1990; Fishbein, 2001; Olweus, 1986; Raine, 1993; D. Rowe, 2002; Rutter et al., 1998; Udry, 2000; Widom and Ames, 1988; Wilson and Herrnstein, 1985.

9. For overviews and selected studies in this area, see Agnew, 2009; Akers, 1998; Bartusch and Matsueda, 1996; R. Berger, 1989; Bottcher, 2001; Canter, 1982; Cernkovich and Giordano, 1987; Chesney-Lind and Shelden, 2004; Cloward and Piven, 1979; Daly, 1998; Daly and Chesney-Lind, 1988; Giordano, 1978; Giordano et al., 1986; Hagan et al., 1996; Hagan et al., 1979; Heidensohn, 2002; Heimer, 1995, 1996; Heimer et al., 2006; Hubbard and Pratt, 2002; Jensen and Eve, 1976; Lanctot and Le Blanc, 2002; Mears et al., 1998; Moffitt et al., 2001; Morash, 1986; D. Rowe et al., 1995; Simons et al., 1980; Douglas Smith and Paternoster, 1987; Steffensmeier and Allan, 1996, 2000; Warr, 2002; J. Wilson and Herrnstein, 1985.

10. See especially Agnew, 2009; Akers, 1998; Chapple, McQuillan et al., 2005; Heimer et al., 2006; Lanctot and Le Blanc, 2002; Moffitt et al., 2001; D. Rowe et al., 1995.

11. See note 10.

12. See Acoca, 1998; Agnew, 2009; Daly, 1992; Gilfus, 1992.

PART 4

The Control and Prevention
of Delinquency

Now that we have examined the causes of delinquency (Chapters 6–18), we are in a good position to ask what can be done to control or reduce delinquency. At one level, the answer is rather simple. **Society can control delinquency by alleviating or eliminating the causes of delinquency.** For example, we know that family factors like parental rejection and poor parental supervision cause delinquency. Therefore, society can control delinquency by reducing parental rejection and improving parental supervision. We can also control delinquency by doing such things as reducing biological harms like head injury and lead exposure, helping juveniles perform better in school, and preventing juveniles from associating with delinquent peers and gang members. More generally, we can reduce delinquency by reducing strain, reducing the social learning of delinquency, increasing control, and reducing labeling. The key question, however, is: How do we accomplish these goals?

Chapters 19 through 25 examine the efforts of public and private agencies to control delinquency. **The focus is on the juvenile justice system: the police, juvenile courts, and juvenile correctional agencies (which run juvenile institutions and community-based programs).** These government agencies have the primary responsibility of controlling delinquency in our society. Chapter 20 focuses on the police, and Chapter 21 focuses on the juvenile courts and juvenile correctional agencies. We explore what these agencies are doing to control delinquency and how effective they are. Chapter 22 then examines whether these agencies discriminate against certain groups in their efforts to control delinquency. Although we want these agencies to do all they can to control delinquency, we also want them to do so in a way that is fair to everyone in our society.

Chapters 23 and 24 examine **four general strategies for controlling delinquency** that are employed by these agencies and other groups. Chapter 23 focuses on the "get tough" strategies of deterrence and incapacitation. **Deterrence** tries to scare potential offenders from committing crimes by increasing the certainty and severity of punishment. **Incapacitation** tries to control delinquency by locking up serious offenders so they cannot commit crimes on the street. These strategies dominated crime control efforts in the late 1980s and 1990s, but they have since come under scrutiny. Chapter 24 examines the strategies of rehabilitation and prevention. **Rehabilitation** tries to reform offenders, while **prevention** tries to stop individuals from becoming offenders by attacking the root causes of crime. In Chapter 25, the final chapter of the book, we attempt to synthesize the preceding material by describing what we think society should do to control delinquency.

Most efforts to control delinquency attempt to eliminate or alleviate the causes of delinquency. **Most commonly, they attempt to increase social control, especially direct control** (see Chapter 8). In particular, one of the major functions of the juvenile justice system today is to catch and punish juvenile offenders for their delinquent acts. The police focus on catching suspected juvenile offenders; the juvenile courts determine whether these suspected offenders have committed delinquent acts and if so, what sanctions they will receive; and juvenile correctional agencies administer many of the sanctions, such as incarceration.

The juvenile justice system and other agencies also attempt to deal with many of the other causes of delinquency. For example, they sometimes attempt to increase other forms of social control, such as the juvenile's stake in conformity and internal control. And they sometimes attempt to reduce strain, labeling, and social learning of crime. In these areas, they often focus on many of the specific causes of delinquency examined in this text, such as those involving individual traits, the family, school, and peer groups. **The juvenile justice system has focused on direct control in recent decades, but this approach is beginning to change.**

The central theme in Chapters 20 through 25 is that **this focus on direct control has been a mistake;** data suggest that efforts to exercise direct control over juveniles have only a moderate effect on delinquency at best. Efforts to deal with the other causes of delinquency will not eliminate delinquency, but data suggest that properly implemented efforts may result in a substantial reduction in delinquency. We argue that the **best approach to reducing delinquency is one that combines the careful use of direct controls with a serious effort to deal with the other causes of delinquency.**

But before we begin this examination of efforts to control delinquency, we must first address the question of how criminologists determine whether a given program or policy is effective in controlling delinquency.

19 Policies and Programs

How Do We Determine the Effectiveness of a Policy or Program in Controlling or Preventing Delinquency?

W e will examine many programs and policies designed to control delinquency, and the central question we'll ask is whether those programs and policies are effective. But how does one go about determining whether a program is effective in controlling delinquency?

Judging effectiveness is an important issue. Politicians and others often claim that some program is or is not effective. They claim, for example, that trying juveniles as adults or placing them in Scared Straight programs is an effective way to reduce delinquency. Or they claim that many rehabilitation and prevention programs are ineffective and a waste of taxpayers' money. Much of what you hear, however, is wrong or has little basis in fact. You will be in a much better position to judge the accuracy of the various claims if you know the proper way to evaluate the effectiveness of a program. You will also have a more solid foundation on which to construct your own views about what society should and should not do to control delinquency.[1]

After reading this chapter, you should be able to:

- Identify the best way to determine whether a policy or program reduces delinquency.
- Identify the essential components of a randomized experiment.
- Explain why it is important to randomly assign individuals to treatment and control groups.
- Describe the major problems that researchers may encounter when they try to implement randomized experiments in the real world.
- Describe two forms of nonrandomized experiments.
- Explain why programs designed to reduce delinquency may be ineffective.
- Indicate the purpose of implementation (or process) evaluations.

THE EXPERIMENTAL MODEL FOR DETERMINING PROGRAM EFFECTIVENESS

What is the best way to determine whether a program is effective in reducing delinquency? The answer is a *randomized experiment*. As you may recall from Chapter 5, experiments involve doing something to a group of people and observing the consequences. In evaluating program effectiveness, we place juveniles in a delinquency control or prevention program and observe the consequences. In particular, we observe whether participation in the program leads to a reduction in delinquency. But the experiment must have certain special features if it is to provide accurate information about the program's effectiveness. Let us describe these features and their importance with an example.

A criminologist develops a program designed to improve the school performance of juvenile offenders. A group of offenders is selected to participate in the program. The criminologist measures the delinquency of these juveniles in the year before they enter the program and in the year following program completion. The criminologist discovers that these juveniles commit 50 percent fewer delinquent acts in the year after they complete the program. Can we conclude that the program is effective? (We should note that many program evaluations are like this. Researchers do a *before-and-after study*, examining levels of delinquency before and after juveniles participate in a program. If the juveniles experience a large drop in delinquency, the program is declared a success.)

In fact, we cannot safely claim that the program is effective. While the juvenile offenders may have reduced their delinquent behavior because of the program, they may have reduced their delinquency for other reasons as well. For example, perhaps most of the juveniles in the program were 16 and 17 years old. One of the things that criminologists know about delinquency is that it peaks around ages 16 and 17 and then declines as juveniles enter adulthood. So the reduction in delinquency detected by the criminologist may not be due to the program. Rather, the reduction may have occurred because the juveniles in the program were entering adulthood and maturing out of delinquency. These juveniles would have reduced their levels of delinquency even if they had not participated in the program. To give another example, suppose the police in the city that ran the program instituted a crackdown against local gangs about the time the program ended. The reduction in delinquency might have been due to this police initiative rather than to the program. Thus, simply comparing levels of delinquency before and after a program is not a good way to determine program effectiveness.

What should be done? **How can researchers and policy makers determine whether the reduction in delinquency is due to the program or to some other factor?** They can compare the delinquency levels of program participants to the delinquency levels of a roughly identical group of juveniles who did not participate in the program. The participants in the program are called the *treatment group*, while the juveniles who do not participate are called the *comparison group* or *control group*. The two groups of juveniles are roughly identical, except that those in the treatment group participate in the program and the controls do not. If the juveniles in the treatment group experience a greater reduction in delinquency than those in the control group, it can only be because they participated in the program. It cannot be because they are older and more likely to mature out of delinquency, since the juveniles in both the treatment and control groups are roughly identical in terms of age. Nor can it be because the juveniles in the treatment group were subject to a police crackdown while those in the control group were not. Both groups of juveniles were subject to the same treatment by the police. The juveniles in the treatment and control groups differ in only one way: the juveniles in the treatment group participated in the program. So the greater reduction in delinquency in the treatment group can be due only to participation in the program. One can then say that the program is effective: it caused a reduction in delinquency.

But **how do researchers ensure that the juveniles in the treatment and control groups are roughly identical?** The best way to do this is through a procedure known as *random assignment*. Researchers start out with a single group of juveniles, and they randomly assign each juvenile to either the treatment group or the control group. For example, they flip a coin. If it comes up heads, the juvenile is in the treatment group. If it comes up tails, the juvenile is in the control group. If they are dealing with a fairly large group of juveniles, they can be reasonably confident that the juveniles in the two groups are roughly identical in terms of age, sex, class, race/ethnicity, prior levels of delinquency, and all other variables.

We should note that the juveniles randomly assigned to the control and treatment groups may or may not be a **random sample** of juveniles (see Chapter 5). In most cases, they are not a random sample. For example, they may be a group of juveniles who were referred to a particular juvenile court for serious offenses. The court may then randomly assign certain of these juveniles to participate in a new treatment program and others to go through normal court processing. But these juveniles do not constitute a random sample of all juveniles or even of juveniles in that particular locale. We will return to this point shortly, because it points to a weakness in many experiments.

You now know the proper way to determine whether a program is effective in reducing delinquency. Let us summarize **the essential elements of a randomized experiment** (these elements are illustrated in Figure 19.1). You begin with a single group of juveniles. You randomly assign each juvenile to either the treatment group or the control group. The juveniles in the treatment group participate in the delinquency control program, while those in the control group do not. You may do nothing to the juveniles in the control

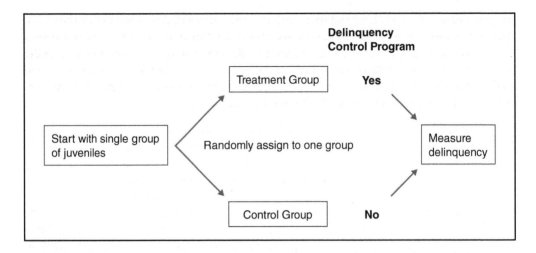

FIGURE 19.1 **Essential Elements of a Simple Randomized Experiment**

group, which would allow you to compare the effectiveness of your program to "doing nothing." Or you may treat the juveniles in the control group the way that such juveniles are normally treated; for example, you might place minor offenders on regular probation. This would allow you to compare the effectiveness of your program to probation. You measure the delinquency of the juveniles in both the treatment group and the control group before the program has begun and after it has ended. You then determine whether those in the treatment group experienced a larger reduction in delinquency. If they have, you can conclude that the treatment or program was effective. (Since juveniles are randomly assigned to the treatment and control groups, you can assume that they are roughly identical in prior levels of delinquency. Many researchers therefore argue that it is necessary to compare only the delinquency levels of those in the treatment and control groups after the program has ended. If those in the treatment group have lower levels of delinquency than those in the control group, they believe you can conclude that the treatment group experienced a larger reduction in delinquency—and that the treatment was effective.)

This model, then, allows criminologists to determine whether a given program caused a reduction in delinquency. If you would like a challenging exercise, we invite you to stop reading and **describe how this experimental model meets the four conditions for making causal statements described in Chapter 5: association, association not due to chance, association not due to third variables, and correct causal order** (now is a good time to review the discussion in Chapter 5).

Let us begin with association. If those in the treatment group are lower in delinquency than those in the control group, it has been demonstrated that the treatment is associated with lower delinquency. This association may be due to chance, but chance is unlikely to explain the association if the treatment and control groups are large and the members of the two groups differ greatly in delinquency. As was the case with survey research, researchers can estimate the probability that the association is due to chance. The association may be due to a third variable, but that is quite unlikely if individuals are randomly assigned to the treatment and control groups. For example, suppose those in the treatment group are found to be lower in delinquency. Someone might claim that this difference is due to the third variable of age: those in the treatment group are older and so are more likely to have matured out of delinquency. But if the researchers have used random assignment, they know that those in the treatment and control groups are roughly identical in terms of age and with respect to all other third variables. Any association they find, therefore, cannot have arisen because those in the treatment and control groups differed in terms of some third variable that causes delinquency. Finally, the experimental model is set up in such a way that researchers administer the treatment or program and then examine subsequent levels of delinquency, so causal order is not a problem: the treatment precedes any change in delinquency that might occur.

The Importance of Doing Randomized Experiments

Let us provide a real-life illustration of the importance of doing randomized experiments. Many communities place juvenile offenders in Scared Straight programs, which usually entail a supervised visit to a prison, where the juveniles hear a presentation by inmates about the horrors of prison life. They are often told that they will probably end up in prison if they continue their current behavior and that there is a good chance they will be raped and assaulted once in prison. Such programs try to deter or scare juvenile offenders from committing further crimes by making them aware of the severe sanctions that await them. These programs were popularized by the *Scared Straight* video that first aired in 1979, and they remain in wide use today. Modern versions of the program are featured in the highly rated television series titled *Beyond Scared Straight*. But are such programs effective at reducing delinquency?

Several studies tried to evaluate the effectiveness of these programs by determining whether the juvenile participants reduced their levels of offending. These before-and-after studies found that the offenders experienced substantial reductions in delinquency after the program had ended. In one study, offenders experienced a 52 percent reduction in delinquency. Based on these results, many people might conclude that Scared Straight programs are quite effective. Several researchers, however, used randomized experiments to evaluate Scared Straight programs. They found that the offenders in the control group—who did not participate in the Scared Straight programs—experienced reductions in delinquency that were as large or larger than the program participants'. So the randomized experiments indicate that Scared Straight programs are **not** effective at reducing delinquency. In fact, some of these experiments suggest that offenders in Scared Straight programs are more likely to engage in subsequent delinquency than those in the control group (for overviews, see Finckenauer and Gavin, 1999; Petrosino et al., 2013). (Among other things, it has been argued that the offenders in the Scared Straight programs may have felt a need to engage in delinquent acts to demonstrate that they were not scared by the program.)

So it is important to properly evaluate programs; the failure to do so can lead to very misleading conclusions about program effectiveness. It is unclear why the before-and-after evaluations of the Scared Straight programs showed reductions in delinquency, but researchers speculate that many of the Scared Straight participants were at an age where they were starting to mature out of delinquency. A before-and-after study is unable to take account of this alternative explanation for the reduction in offending. A randomized experiment, however, can take account of this alternative, since the offenders in the experimental and control groups are of roughly the same age—making them equally likely to mature out of delinquency. (For another real-life illustration, but with a positive outcome, see Box 19.1.)

Given the results of the randomized experiments on Scared Straight programs, you might ask why such programs are still in use. **Unfortunately, program evaluations often have little effect on the extent to which a program is used** (see the discussion of Project DARE in Chapter 20 for another prominent example). Sometimes policy makers and the general public are not aware of the results of program evaluations. And in this area,

Box 19.1   It's Never Too Early to Promote Healthy Development: An Experimental Evaluation of the Nurse–Family Partnership

In the late 1970s, a novel prevention program was implemented in Elmira, New York. The program, developed by Professor David Olds of the University of Colorado Denver, was designed to promote the healthy development of children. This goal was to be achieved by reducing poor birth outcomes (such as premature births and low birthweights), improving the parenting skills of mothers, and reducing the incidence of child abuse and neglect. In particular, nurses would be employed to assist expectant mothers, conducting regular home visits, and providing advice and guidance in prenatal care and childrearing.

Olds and his colleagues recruited 400 pregnant women for the program. The majority were poor, single, teenagers who were expecting their first child. This is also a population that suffers from a high rate of child-related developmental problems. To allow for a proper evaluation of the program, the expectant mothers were **randomly assigned** to one of two groups: (1) the nurse-visited group or (2) a control group that did not receive home visits.

The women in the nurse-visited group received numerous visits during their pregnancies. During this time, for example, the nurses educated the women about the importance of nutrition and encouraged them to avoid smoking and other behaviors that could harm the fetus. After babies were born, the nurses continued to make visits until each child's second birthday, helping the new mothers develop effective childrearing skills (encouraging them to be sensitive, responsive, and engaged parents) and assisting them with plans related to contraceptive use, childcare, and career choices.

The results of follow-up studies indicate that the nurse visitations had a positive impact on various health outcomes, especially among the poor, unmarried teens in the study. In comparison to the women who had been assigned to the control group, the nurse-visited women "provided home environments that were more conducive to their children's emotional and cognitive development" (Olds, 2002:161). In addition, compared with their counterparts in the control group, nurse-visited poor, unmarried teens had fewer substantiated cases of child abuse and neglect, fewer subsequent pregnancies and births, higher levels of employment, and fewer months on welfare. They also described their infants as less fussy and irritable.

The children of these mothers also benefited from the nurse visitations. By age 15, the children from nurse-visited homes reported fewer instances of running away, less frequent use of tobacco and alcohol, and fewer arrests and convictions.

Although a program of this type costs several thousand dollars per family, a study by the Rand Corporation finds that the program is cost effective in the long run, especially when provided to poor, unmarried mothers. Specifically, for every dollar spent on the program, an estimated $4 in savings had been generated, primarily because welfare and criminal justice expenditures were lower and tax revenues from employment were higher.

The nurse–family partnership (NFP) program has since been replicated in Memphis and Denver, again using experimental designs. Early findings indicate that while the impact has been more mixed, nurse visitations improved health- and behavior-related outcomes in these other locations as well. Because these evaluation results are based on randomized experiments and are therefore compelling, NFP has been identified as

(Continued)

(Continued)

a "model" delinquency-prevention program (for more information about NFP, visit the Center for the Study and Prevention of Violence Blueprints website at http://www. blueprintsprograms.com).

Questions for Discussion

1. Although evaluation research clearly favors the NFP program over Scared Straight, Scared Straight has received far more attention over the years and is the focus of a highly rated television series (see our discussion of Scared Straight earlier in this chapter). What may explain this difference in attention? What are some key differences between the two programs that would make one more appealing than the other in the eyes of the general public?
2. A control theorist would likely explain the positive results of NFP in terms of increased parental attachment. The program, for example, is likely to strengthen the social bond between parent and child, thereby reducing the likelihood of delinquency (in fact, one specific goal of the program was to increase parent–child attachment). How would strain and social learning theorists explain the ability of NFP to reduce delinquency?

criminologists need to do a better job of disseminating the results of their evaluations. But program evaluations often have little impact even when the results of the evaluations are known. There are a variety of reasons for this. Among other things, the effectiveness of certain programs seems self-evident to many people (e.g., if you threaten people with severe punishments, of course they are going to reduce their offending). So the program evaluations showing no effect are ignored or said to be flawed. And certain programs are supported by powerful groups—including the groups that sponsor the programs—making politicians reluctant to take action (for further discussion, see Robinson and Slowikowski, 2011; Rosenbaum, 2007; Weiss, 1998).

Problems in Doing Randomized Experiments

Criminologists often encounter difficulties when they attempt to conduct randomized experiments. Some of the more common difficulties are described in the paragraphs that follow.

The people responsible for randomly assigning juveniles to the treatment and control groups are often workers in the juvenile justice system (police, probation officers, judges). **Sometimes these individuals violate the random assignment procedure.** A judge, for example, may refuse to assign someone to the control group because she feels that the juvenile is in desperate need of the treatment. As a consequence, criminologists cannot be sure that the juveniles in the treatment and control groups are roughly identical.

Many of the juveniles randomly assigned to the treatment and control groups may not complete the experiment. Some of the juveniles drop out of the treatment program or fail to successfully complete it. Or the researchers may not be able to locate many of the juveniles when they are collecting follow-up data on delinquency. As a result, the researchers cannot be sure that the juveniles who remain in the treatment and control groups are roughly identical. For example, many treatment programs are very demanding, and individuals with little motivation to change their behavior often drop out. The individuals who successfully complete such programs, then, may be those most motivated to change. Suppose the participants who complete the program experience a greater reduction in delinquency than those in the control group. We have no way of knowing whether this result is due to the treatment or to the participants' personalities (they were more motivated to change to begin with).

Another problem involves the **measurement of delinquency. Delinquency is often measured in terms of arrest rates.** Program evaluations, for example, often report that those in the treatment group were less likely to be arrested during the follow-up period after the treatment ended. Arrest data, however, are not a very accurate measure of delinquency. It may be that those in the treatment group are less likely to be arrested, even though there is no difference in the true rates of delinquency between the treatment and control groups. For example, the police may be more likely to give juveniles in the treatment group a break because they run the program and have a vested interest in its success. On the other hand, those in the treatment group are sometimes more likely to be arrested, even though they are not more delinquent. For example, many delinquency control programs call for the close supervision of juveniles and include features like frequent home visits and random drug tests. Such features increase the likelihood that delinquent acts will be detected and juveniles will be arrested.

Yet another problem with randomized experiments, briefly mentioned earlier, involves **the issue of** *generalizability*. Researchers who evaluate a program almost never begin with a random sample of juveniles or juvenile offenders. Rather, they typically begin with a nonrepresentative group of juveniles in a single location. They might, for example, examine all minor offenders who are referred to a particular juvenile court. They might then find that the program they are evaluating is effective in reducing delinquency among these juveniles. But that single outcome is no guarantee that the same program will be effective for other juveniles. For example, it may not be effective for more serious offenders or for minor offenders in other locations. One cannot, then, necessarily generalize the results of a program evaluation to other juveniles or to other settings.

Other problems in running randomized experiments can be named, but this short list is enough to show that evaluating a program is not as straightforward as it might seem. **Researchers sometimes take steps to deal with these problems.** For example, they try to ensure that random assignment proceeds as planned; they go to great lengths to prevent juveniles from leaving the experiment; they measure delinquency by using self-report data and other methods such as drug testing; and they evaluate the same program with different groups of juveniles in different locations. Many researchers, however, do not go to these lengths; also, the steps just named are not always effective. For example, the juveniles in the treatment program may not be truthful when they are providing self-reports on their delinquency. Given the problems noted, it is often difficult to state with a high degree of certainty that a program is generally effective at reducing delinquency. Rather, researchers must state that a program is "promising" or that it shows "signs of success." **Some programs, however, have received a number of fairly rigorous evaluations, and criminologists are more confident about their effectiveness (or lack of effectiveness).**

WHAT IF ONE IS NOT ABLE TO DO A RANDOMIZED EXPERIMENT?

While randomized experiments are often difficult to carry out, they are the best way to ascertain program effectiveness. However, it is not always possible to do a randomized experiment. Sometimes **ethical problems** present themselves. To illustrate, researchers have developed a number of programs designed to provide alternatives to imprisonment or incarceration. Intensive probation programs, which provide close supervision of juveniles in the community, are an example. Juvenile court judges, however, may feel that it is unethical to randomly send some juveniles to institutions and place others on intensive probation (see Weisburd, 2000). Sometimes the **problems are of a more practical nature.** To illustrate, lawmakers may implement a particular policy that affects everyone in the community, such as a new law that increases the penalties for certain crimes. Random assignment is obviously not possible in this case. One cannot use random assignment procedures to decide that some people in the community are subject to the law and others are not.

Researchers usually deal with these situations by employing **nonrandomized experiments** of various types. For example, researchers may employ *nonequivalent control group designs*. Since they cannot randomly assign individuals to treatment and control groups, they may attempt to create a control group that is similar to the treatment group. To illustrate, imagine a judge who is unwilling to randomly assign people to prison or intensive probation. The researcher can examine the characteristics of the juveniles sent to prison and then attempt to find a similar group of juveniles who were placed on intensive probation. The researcher ideally attempts to **match** the two groups on all relevant variables that may affect subsequent delinquency, such as age and prior delinquency. The researcher can then compare the subsequent delinquency of the two groups. To give another illustration, imagine that a state passes a law increasing the penalties for certain crimes. The researcher may attempt to find a similar state that does not have such a law. The researcher can then compare trends in subsequent delinquency in the two states. This strategy, however, is often difficult to carry out in practice, and **one can never be sure that the treatment and control groups are roughly identical.** Perhaps they differ on some crucial variable that the researcher did not consider.

Another type of nonrandomized experiment is the *time series design*. The researcher periodically measures delinquency before the program or policy takes effect and then after the program or policy has taken effect (so this is a type of before-and-after study). For example, monthly levels of delinquency in a community are measured before a new law takes effect and then again afterward. A noticeable decrease in delinquency after the new law has taken effect might suggest that the new law is effective. However, **the decrease in delinquency might have been due to factors that coincided with the introduction of the new law.** For example, perhaps the economy started to improve around the time the new law was introduced.

There are still other types of nonrandomized experiment. None are as good as randomized experiments, but they do provide us with some information about program effectiveness.

WHY ARE SOME PROGRAMS INEFFECTIVE AT REDUCING DELINQUENCY?

There are **two general reasons why researchers find some programs ineffective.** The first is that **the program does not work.** (In the chapters that follow, we mention several programs for controlling delinquency that do not appear to work, including some programs that are popular now.) The second reason is that **the program is not properly implemented.** It is often the case that programs are not carried out as planned. Perhaps a program was not delivered to the appropriate group of juveniles—it may have been intended for serious offenders but instead was delivered to minor offenders. Or perhaps the services that should have been provided by the program were not provided. The juveniles in the program, for example, might have received less counseling or less supervision than they were supposed to receive. The staff might not have been properly trained or committed to the program, and so they failed to render services in an appropriate manner. As a result of such possibilities, many researchers now do what are known as *implementation or process evaluations*. These evaluations are not designed to determine whether a program is effective. Rather, they are designed **to determine whether the program was properly carried out.** It is sometimes found that programs are not properly carried out, or implemented, which could help explain why they are not effective.

An example illustrating the importance of implementation evaluations is found in Krisberg and Schumann (2000:153). The researchers describe a randomized experiment conducted in the Salt Lake City juvenile court:

> For approximately two years, every youth the judges placed on probation was randomized into [one of] three groups. The first group was called "notification," which meant that the youths were told the rules of probation but never saw a probation officer again. They received nothing more than the admonition "Go forth and sin no more." The second group received essentially supervision services. They came in once a week and met with the probation officer, who did whatever probation officers do. The last group got far more intensive supervision and treatment services. This was supposed to include all the things of which probation staff said, "If only we could do this with every kid, we would get wonderful results."

An evaluation revealed that there were no differences in subsequent delinquency between the groups. This finding was quite shocking to the court staff, because it suggested that just sending kids home and doing nothing yielded about the same results as treatment.

An implementation evaluation, however, helped make sense of these findings. The evaluation revealed that youths in the second and third groups did not receive much in the way of supervision or treatment. In particular, treatment services were limited to informal counseling and/or recreational programs, like camping trips. No educational, vocational, or drug and alcohol addiction services were provided. These findings led the juvenile court to develop better supervision and treatment programs and to more carefully monitor the work of probation officers. Implementation evaluations, then, often suggest that programs may be ineffective in given cases because they were not delivered as intended.

SUMMARY

You now know the proper way to determine whether a program or policy is effective in reducing delinquency. In actual practice, few program evaluations live up to the ideal model we have presented. Researchers conducting randomized experiments often encounter one or more of the problems we've mentioned. And many researchers are unable to do randomized experiments. Good program evaluations are nevertheless occasionally done, and there has been increased pressure in recent years to perform such assessments. A few programs have been the subject of several evaluations involving juveniles of different types, in different locations, and they often complement one another in terms of strengths and weaknesses. For example, some evaluations measure delinquency by using arrest data, but others use self-report data or teacher and parental reports. If these evaluations are in general agreement, one can safely conclude that the program is generally effective (or ineffective).

TEACHING AIDS
Web-Based Exercise: The Importance (and Sometimes Neglect) of Good Evaluation Research

One of the more popular delinquency control programs are Scared Straight–type programs. Their popularity stems in significant part from the *Scared Straight* documentary, first shown in the late 1970s. View this documentary on YouTube (search for "Scared Straight 1978"). It is a riveting, disturbing, and very persuasive video. (Note: Another video is also available: "Scared Straight: 20 Years Later.") After viewing the 1978 version, ask yourself if Scared Straight seems like an effective way to reduce delinquency. If you like, you can also view some contemporary Scared Straight–type programs on the *Beyond Scared Straight* series on the Arts and Entertainment (A&E) channel. The series remains popular. Then visit the CrimeSolutions website at http://www.crimesolutions.gov. This site, maintained by the U.S. Department of Justice, reviews the evaluation research on a range of programs designed to reduce crime and delinquency. Search the site using the term "Scared Straight" or "Juvenile Awareness Programs (Scared Straight)." Read the overview of the evaluations on Scared Straight–type programs. Why do you think these programs remain popular even though the best evaluation research suggests that they *increase* delinquency?

Some Challenges

The three challenges that follow are designed to cultivate your ability to apply the materials in this chapter, so that you will be better able to evaluate the claims you hear about the effectiveness (or ineffectiveness) of programs and policies. (Answers to the challenges are given after the Key Terms.)

    1. Your college likely has an individual or group that administers sanctions to students convicted of cheating or honor code violations. **Ideally,** how would you go about determining whether these sanctions reduce further cheating among the students who are sanctioned? **Realistically,** do you think it would be possible to carry out your ideal evaluation? If not, why not? Describe an alternative way of evaluating the effectiveness of the sanctions, a way that has a better chance of being adopted. Describe the disadvantages of this alternative (compared with a randomized experiment).

    2. Ten thousand juveniles are arrested in City X. A random sample of 1,000 juveniles is drawn from this group and placed in a rehabilitation program. A series of follow-up studies indicates that only 30 percent of the juveniles in the rehabilitation program commit new offenses over the next several years. Can we conclude that the rehabilitation program is effective in reducing delinquency? If not, why not?

    3. A researcher collects data from all juvenile courts in the United States. She finds that 30 percent of the juveniles placed on probation are arrested in the year after their probation ends, while 60 percent of the juveniles sent to institutions are arrested in the year after their release. Can we conclude that probation is more effective at reducing delinquency than placing juveniles in institutions? Why or why not?

TEST YOUR KNOWLEDGE OF THIS CHAPTER

1. What is an experiment?
2. Describe a before-and-after study or evaluation. Describe the major problem with such studies in determining program effectiveness.
3. Describe the essential features of a randomized experiment. Explain why it is important to randomly assign individuals to the treatment and control groups.
4. How does "random assignment" differ from selection of a "random sample"?
5. Why is it that program evaluations often have little effect on the extent to which programs are used?
6. List the major problems in doing randomized experiments.
7. What do we mean when we state that the results of an experiment may not be "generalizable"?
8. Why is it sometimes not possible to evaluate programs by doing randomized experiments?
9. Describe the two major types of nonrandomized experiment (the "nonequivalent control group" design and the "time series" design). Describe the disadvantages of these designs (compared with randomized experiments).

10. What are the two major reasons for the ineffectiveness of some programs at reducing delinquency?

11. What is an "implementation" or "process" evaluation? Why is it important to do such evaluations?

THOUGHT AND DISCUSSION QUESTIONS

1. You are asked to evaluate the effectiveness of a new after-school recreational program in preventing delinquency. Describe the ideal way to conduct such an evaluation, listing the major steps you would take. Describe how you would use one of the alternatives to randomized experiments to evaluate this program.

2. What can be done to increase the impact of program evaluations on policy makers?

KEY TERMS

- Randomized experiment
- Before-and-after study or evaluation
- Treatment group
- Control group or comparison group
- Random assignment
- Generalizability
- Nonequivalent control group design
- Time series design
- Implementation or process evaluation

ANSWERS TO CHALLENGES

1. Ideally, we would evaluate the effectiveness of the sanctions by doing a randomized experiment. For example, we might ask the group that administers sanctions to flip a coin whenever someone is convicted of cheating. If the coin comes up heads, that person would be sanctioned in the traditional manner. If the coin comes up tails, that person would escape sanction. We could then determine whether the sanctioned individuals are less likely to cheat in the following year (which means that we would have to exclude seniors from the experiment). Cheating would ideally be measured in several ways, including formal accusations of cheating by others and self-report data. Realistically, however, for ethical reasons it is unlikely that this experiment could be carried out. A more realistic alternative might involve an experiment employing the nonequivalent control group design. We could collect data on the characteristics of those students sanctioned for cheating, especially characteristics we think might influence the likelihood that they will cheat again. The theories and research on the causes of delinquency can help us here, so we might collect data on their gender, GPA, prior history of cheating, career goals, beliefs regarding cheating, whether their friends cheat, and so on. We could then sample a large group of students at our college, asking them whether they had recently cheated and if so, whether they had been sanctioned for it (the large majority of cheaters escape sanction). We would also collect data on the characteristics of these students. We could then try to match each sanctioned cheater to a nonsanctioned cheater. For example, suppose one of the sanctioned cheaters was a male, had a 2.5 GPA, had no prior history of cheating, and so on. We would try to find a nonsanctioned cheater with the same or similar characteristics. We could then determine whether the sanctioned cheaters were more or less likely to cheat in the future than the nonsanctioned cheaters (see Gold and Williams, 1969, for an example of a similar study). This design,

however, has an important disadvantage. It would be difficult to match sanctioned and nonsanctioned cheaters on more than a few variables. Even if we could match them on all the variables we thought caused cheating, there is still the chance that the sanctioned cheaters would differ from the nonsanctioned cheaters in ways that influenced the likelihood of future cheating.

2. We cannot conclude that the rehabilitation program is effective. This is an example of a before-and-after study. All the 1,000 juveniles had committed offenses before participating in the rehabilitation program, but only 30 percent offended after participating in the program. The problem with this study is that there was no control—no group that did not participate in the rehabilitation program. (The term "random sample" may have thrown you off—remember that selecting a random sample is different from making a "random assignment" to a treatment and control group.) As a consequence, it is impossible to determine whether the reduction in delinquency was due to the rehabilitation program or to some other factor. To properly evaluate this program, we should randomly assign some of the arrested juveniles to the rehabilitation program and randomly assign others to be treated in the traditional manner (e.g., placed on regular probation). We should then compare the rates of reoffending in the two groups. We may find that only 30 percent of the juveniles treated in the traditional manner commit new offenses over the next several years, suggesting that the rehabilitation program is not effective. Perhaps the juveniles in both groups reduced their levels of offending because they were maturing out of delinquency as they aged.

3. We cannot safely conclude that probation is more effective than placing juveniles in institutions. We do have a treatment group (those on probation) and a control or comparison group (those sent to institutions). But juveniles were not randomly assigned to each group. The juveniles in each group may differ from one another in ways that affect the likelihood of future offending. In particular, the juveniles placed on probation are probably less serious offenders than those sent to institutions, and this may be why they are less likely to be rearrested.

ENDNOTE

1. For a fuller discussion of evaluation research in the delinquency field, see Farrington and Welsh, 2007; Gartin, 1995; Kempf-Leonard, 1990; Krisberg and Schumann, 2000; D. MacKenzie, 2006; Sechrest and Rosenblatt, 1987; Sherman et al., 2002; Weisburd, 2000.

20 The Police

What Do the Police Do to Control Delinquency?

I n recent years, the fatal shootings of young black males by police—such as the shooting deaths of 12-year-old Tamir Rice in Cleveland, 17-year old Laquan McDonald in Chicago, and 18-year-old Michael Brown in Ferguson—sparked outrage and protests across the United States. These cases also raised awareness of the deep distrust that has long existed between police and many of the communities they serve. Commenting on the tragedies, President Obama highlighted the importance of good police–community relations for effective crime control:

> When any part of the American family does not feel like it is being treated fairly, that's a problem for all of us. It's not just a problem for some. It's not just a problem for a particular community or a particular demographic. It means that we are not as strong as a country as we can be. And when applied to the criminal justice system, it means we're not as effective in fighting crime as we could be.

In this chapter, we examine various policing strategies, looking at how they impact police–community relations as well as crime. We identify strategies that can strain the relationships between police and members of the public (with a focus on juveniles), and we consider strategies that have potential to increase both trust and public safety.

We begin with a discussion of how the police operate—that is, how they attempt to control delinquency. We then ask how effective the police are in controlling delinquency. Finally, we examine three strategies for improving police effectiveness. The first is hiring more police. The other two strategies call for changing what the police do to control delinquency: by increased use of "police crackdowns" and by greater emphasis on "community policing."[1]

After reading this chapter, you should be able to:

- Describe the major characteristics of preventive patrol.
- Discuss the general effectiveness of preventive patrol in controlling crime.
- List the three major strategies for improving police effectiveness.
- Describe how the police "crack down" on crime and, specify the conditions under which police crackdowns are most effective.
- Explain how community policing addresses the problems of preventive patrol.
- Provide several examples of community policing.
- Discuss the effectiveness of community policing.

HOW DO THE POLICE OPERATE?

What image comes to mind when you think of the police? If you are like most people, your image of the police has been heavily influenced by the mass media which depicts the police as **crime fighters** who spend most of their time dealing with crime, often serious crime. They cruise around in a patrol car, responding to calls for service and discovering crime on their own. They usually end up catching and arresting most offenders.

This image of the police as crime fighters, however, is partly mistaken. Criminologists have spent much time studying the police. They have ridden with the police, interviewed police officers, and analyzed police records such as logbooks. Some criminologists are former police officers; a few have served as police officers for the sake of gaining a better understanding of the police (see Skogan and Frydl, 2004, for an overview). The following points about how the police operate are based on such studies.

Preventive Patrol Is the Major Type of Policing

In *preventive patrol*, a uniformed police officer cruises an assigned beat in a marked patrol car. When the officer is not answering calls or engaged in other activities, he or she usually patrols the beat. It is felt that this patrol prevents crime, since potential offenders never know when a police car might appear. (Most police departments assign just one officer per car. This practice allows them to put more cars on the street, and studies suggest that one-person cars are about as safe and productive as two-person cars.)

Most juveniles who encounter the police deal with officers on preventive patrol. Most police departments, however, also have juvenile officers or divisions (Gaines, 2003; Reaves and Hickman, 2002b; Snyder and Sickmund, 2006). These specialists conduct follow-up investigations on cases referred by patrol officers. They handle special youth problems—like gangs and school crime. And they may run prevention programs, like DARE (Drug Abuse Resistance Education) and PAL (the police athletic leagues).

The Police Spend Only a Small Amount of Their Time Dealing with Crime

The police spend most of their shift cruising their beat, performing administrative tasks like filling out paperwork, and taking breaks. Less than half their time is spent answering calls or on officer-initiated encounters with the public. This pattern varies by police department, police beat, day, and shift, however (officers working the Saturday night shift in a high-crime beat in a major city may spend most of their time answering calls). Further, most calls to the police involve noncriminal matters, such as traffic accidents, medical emergencies, barking dogs, and disputes between neighbors. Finally, most of the calls they do get about criminal matters involve minor crimes. Several studies have found that, on average, **the police spend less than 20 percent of their time on crime-related matters.** Police often complain about this; many enter the job expecting to be crime fighters but find that most of their time is taken up with noncriminal matters. They often feel as if they function more as social workers than as crime fighters.

Policing Is Primarily Reactive in Nature

The police usually do not discover crimes on their own. In fact, it is quite rare for a police officer to encounter a serious crime in progress. Rather, someone else calls the police

and lets them know that a crime has occurred. Usually it is the victim who calls. The police, however, sometimes make special efforts to discover crime on their own, especially for certain "victimless" crimes such as drug crimes and prostitution. The police, for example, may put certain areas under surveillance or employ undercover agents to catch drug offenders or prostitutes. For the most part, however, policing is largely reactive in nature.

When the Police Do Discover or Hear About a Crime, They Usually Do Not Catch the Offender

As you may recall, only about 20 percent of all crimes known to the police result in arrest (see Chapter 2). This percentage varies by type of crime. The police are more likely to make an arrest for violent crimes than for property crimes. For example, 54 percent of all aggravated assaults and

38 percent of all rapes known to the police were cleared by arrest in 2015, while only 13 percent of all burglaries and 22 percent of all larcenies were cleared by arrest.

When the police do make an arrest, it is usually because they have caught someone at the scene or someone is available to identify or help identify the suspect. Violent crimes are more likely to result in arrest because the victims of violence almost always see the offender and often can identify him or her (most violence is committed by relatives, friends, and acquaintances of the victim). The victims of property crimes like burglary and larceny, however, rarely see the offender. Contrary to mass media accounts and popular views, diligent detective work plays only a minor role in solving the large majority of crimes (Chaiken et al., 1977). If the police do not catch the offender at the scene or there is no one who can identify the offender, the crime will probably go unsolved.

The police recognize this problem, and they have tried to increase their speed in responding to crimes—particularly crimes in progress—with the hope of catching offenders at the scene. Unfortunately, such efforts have had only a small effect on arrest rates. The large majority of crime victims do not call the police until well after the crime is over, so response time makes little difference. The victim usually does not discover the crime until after it has occurred (e.g., you arrive home from a long trip and discover that your house has been burglarized). And in almost half the cases where the victim confronts the offender, the victim waits five minutes or longer after the crime is over before calling the police.

If the Police Do Catch a Suspect, They Usually Do Not Arrest the Person

The police do not arrest all suspected offenders they encounter. In fact, only a **minority** of police encounters with suspected juvenile offenders result in arrest—even if the police have adequate legal grounds for making an arrest. Most suspected offenders are handled informally. The police, for example, may lecture the juvenile, call the juvenile's parents, and/or ask the juvenile to make restitution to the victim. But an arrest is not necessarily made. In some cases, the police may refer the juvenile to a social service agency or a diversion program (see Chapter 21). When the police do make an arrest, the juvenile is referred to juvenile court about 70 percent of the time (McGarrell, 2012).

The *police* exercise much *discretion* in deciding whether to arrest suspected offenders. The decision to arrest depends on several factors, including the seriousness of the offense, whether the offender has a prior record, whether the complainant presses for arrest, the offender's demeanor or attitude, whether the offender's parents seem willing and able to help solve the problem, and the norms of the police department and community. Some police departments are more likely to handle matters informally than others (see Eitle et al., 2005; McGarrell, 2012; Skogan and Frydl, 2004; J. Wilson, 1976; also see Chappell et al., 2006), and communities differ in their views about how the police should respond to juvenile offenders. There is also some evidence that the age, race, class, and gender of suspected offenders influence the likelihood of arrest (see Chapter 22).

The police have several reasons for not arresting all suspected offenders (see P. Anderson and Newman, 1998, for a fuller discussion). For one, the police and the courts would soon be overwhelmed if all suspected offenders were arrested. In addition, the police often have a low opinion of the juvenile court, feeling that most offenders only get a "slap on the wrist"; they may therefore believe that arrest and referral would be useless and perhaps even waste their time with paperwork. Further, the police often feel that many offenders are best dealt with in an informal manner. They might encounter a juvenile who has committed a minor offense but otherwise seems like a "good kid." Rather than stigmatizing this juvenile with an arrest record, they handle the matter informally.

HOW EFFECTIVE IS PREVENTIVE PATROL?

Most criminologists acknowledge that **the police are somewhat effective in controlling crime and delinquency.** In particular, they agree that the crime rate would increase if there were no police. Limited data support this conclusion. For example, when the police went on strike in Montreal in 1969, the hourly burglary rate rose by 13,000 percent and the hourly bank robbery rate rose by 50,000 percent (Sherman, 1995:331; Sherman and Eck, 2002). At the same time, criminologists believe that **preventive patrol is not the best policing strategy.** This belief stems from a series of studies evaluating preventive patrol (for excellent overviews, see Eck and Maguire, 2006; Skogan and Frydl, 2004). Most notably, studies suggest that assigning **more police** to preventive patrol has little or no effect on crime rates (see later discussion). Also, studies indicate that preventive patrol is less effective than many alternative policing strategies in reducing crime (discussed later).

HOW CAN THE POLICE INCREASE THEIR EFFECTIVENESS?

Several suggestions for increasing the effectiveness of the police have been offered. Some are designed to increase the ability of the police to catch offenders, thereby increasing direct control. Others are designed to increase the ability of the police to deal with other causes of crime (e.g., reducing strain or the social learning of crime, altering those situations conducive to crime)

Will Hiring More Police Reduce Delinquency?

One obvious suggestion for increasing police effectiveness is to hire more police. And a key provision of the 1994 Violent Crime Control and Law Enforcement Act provided funds to hire about 100,000 additional police (Worrall and Kovandzic, 2007). (Note: The approximately 12,500 local law enforcement agencies in the United States employ about 463,000 police officers. Most officers are assigned to the patrol bureau, where they typically cover a beat in a marked patrol car [see Reaves, 2010; Skogan and Frydl, 2004].)

The effect on crime of hiring more police, however, has been very difficult to determine. You might think that researchers could simply determine whether communities with more police per capita have lower crime rates. However, the reality is much more complicated. Researchers need to take account of third variables that may affect both the number of police and crime rates (see Chapter 5 for a discussion of third variables). Also, researchers must bear in mind that the number of police and the crime rates may have **reciprocal effects.** On the one hand, an increase in the number of police may reduce crime rates. On the other hand, an increase in crime rates may cause communities to hire more police. This latter causal effect probably explains why cities with more police per capita tend to have higher crime rates. Researchers, then, need to estimate these reciprocal effects. This is not easily done, even with longitudinal or overtime data (see Eck and Maguire, 2006:208–217, for an excellent discussion of this issue). A few studies, however, have made decent attempts to estimate these effects. The results of these studies are mixed, with most finding that increasing the number of police has little or no effect on crime rates (for overviews, see Eck and Maguire, 2006; Kleck and Barnes, 2014).[2]

At present, then, we must conclude that there is **no good evidence that increasing the number of police will reduce crime rates.** Researchers, however, argue that while increasing the number of police may not reduce crime, changing what the police do when they are on the street may make a difference. And two major proposals have been made in this area.

Will *Police Crackdowns* Reduce Delinquency?

Police resources are usually spread thin, even in the best of circumstances. As a consequence, many offenders may feel that they can commit crimes with little chance of police detection. Some police departments, however, have tried to increase the likelihood that they will detect crimes by focusing their resources on certain areas, called "hot spots," where crime is common, as well as on crimes of certain types. That is, **they "crack down" on areas of heavy criminal activity, or on selected types of crime.**[3]

Cracking down on the hot spots of crime. Many police departments try to put the most police where there is the most crime. They may assign more patrol cars to beats with the highest crime rates, or they may have more police working on Friday and Saturday nights, when crime is most likely. Such efforts at focused patrol, however, are somewhat crude because there is much variation in crime even within a high-crime area. Some sections of a high-crime area have little or no crime, while other sections—the so-called *hot spots*—have much crime. Less than 3 percent of the addresses in a city produce more than half of all calls to the police (Sherman, 1995; Sherman and Weisburd, 1995). Some of these addresses may produce several hundred calls to the police each year. Further, crime is more likely to occur on certain days and certain times of the day at these addresses.

One recent study finds evidence that juvenile crime, in particular, tends to be highly concentrated in hot spots that develop at and around schools, youth centers, shops, shopping malls, and restaurants (Weisburd et al., 2009). These tend to be areas where unstructured socializing among youth is common and where adult supervision may be inadequate. (In contrast, hot spots for adult crime often include clubs, bars, and taverns.)

Several recent efforts have aggressively targeted known hot spots for crime.[4] Special computer programs have been developed to generate maps showing the location of these hot spots—as well as the days and times of the day when calls for service are most common in these areas. And the police have dramatically increased their presence at hot spots. In some cases, they have saturated a particular area by, for example, establishing mini-precincts, increasing patrols, setting up roadblocks, or mounting undercover operations. In 2002, for example, the Philadelphia Police Department stationed officers at 214 of the city's locations highest drug activity, with an officer at each location 24 hours a day, 7 days a week (Lawton et al., 2005). Such crackdowns attempt to increase the certainty

and sometimes the severity of punishment. **Crackdowns, then, are attempts to deter criminals from committing crime by increasing direct control.**

Data suggest that **crackdowns are often effective at reducing crime,** although their effect is sometimes modest and short-lived.[5] After the crackdown has ended, crime gradually returns to its former level. One solution to this problem is for the police to crack down on all hot spots on a permanent basis, but the necessary resources are not available. However, Sherman and his associates (Sherman, 1995; Sherman and Weisburd, 1995) have proposed another, more realistic solution to this problem. **The police should rotate their crackdowns in an unpredictable manner.** For example, officers might crack down on one hot spot of crime for a period of time and then move on to another. But they would return to the first hot spot before crime had returned to its former level. This rotating series of crackdowns allows the police to reduce crime in a large number of hot spots.

The Minneapolis Hot Spots Patrol Experiment tested this idea (Sherman and Weisburd, 1995). Researchers randomly selected 55 of 110 hot spots for this rotating series of crackdowns. Each hot spot was a small area that had generated a large number of police calls. The typical hot spot consisted of a group of attached buildings clustered around a street corner, with a few businesses like bars, restaurants, and convenience stores. In the year before the experiment began, each hot spot generated, on average, 355 calls for service, with most calls coming between 7 p.m. and 3 a.m. The hot spots that were part of the rotating crackdown were supposed to receive three hours of police presence per day, while the other hot spots were to be patrolled in the usual manner. This heavy allocation was not always achieved, but the police presence in the "crackdown" hot spots was generally much greater than in the other hot spots, usually by a factor of 2 or more. The police would visit the hot spots that were part of the crackdown several times each day, remaining for a few minutes to an hour or more each time. Sometimes they would just sit in their cars; at other times they would get out and walk around. The increased police presence was associated with a modest reduction in crime, as measured by calls to the police and observer ratings of disorders like fights, drug sales, solicitation for prostitution, and playing loud music. Further, the reduction occurred not only when the police were present, but also when they were absent. This finding suggests that the police do not have to have a permanent presence in an area to reduce crime (also see Telep, et al., 2014). **Periodic visits or crackdowns by the police may be an effective strategy for reducing crime.**

Do crackdowns displace crime from one area to another? Some have argued that while crackdowns may reduce crime in particular locations, they do not reduce overall levels of crime. Rather, they simply displace crime from one location to another. For example, if the police increase their presence at a particular intersection, the drug dealers at that location may move to another intersection, and the overall level of drug dealing remains the same. There have been several efforts to determine whether this argument holds water. Researchers measure changes in the level of crime not only in the areas where crackdowns occur but in surrounding areas as well. Such studies usually find no evidence that crime is displaced (Braga et al., 2014; Weisburd and Eck, 2004; Weisburd et al., 2006). There are several possible reasons for this. For example, some offenders state that it would take too much time and effort to reestablish their criminal activities at another location. Also, some state that they might get into conflicts with other offenders if they moved to another location. There is little evidence, then, that crackdowns result in the displacement of crime. In fact, some studies find that crackdowns in one area led to **declines** in crime in surrounding areas—even though there had been no crackdowns in these areas. One suggested explanation is that many offenders **mistakenly** believe that the crackdowns include surrounding areas.

Cracking down on selected crimes. In addition to focusing on hot spots of crime, the police will sometimes target particular crimes. For example, they may focus on drug crimes, drunken driving, prostitution, or juvenile gun violence. The police will intensify patrols and other police activities in the areas where these crimes are most likely to occur, and they will make a special effort to sanction or control individuals who commit these crimes, often, but not always, through arrest. Such crackdowns are often accompanied by media coverage, to help convey the message that the certainty and perhaps the severity of punishment have increased.

One example of this strategy is the **crackdown on gun violence by youth gangs in Boston.**[6] Research indicated that a substantial number of the youth homicides in Boston were the result of gang members killing one another. Most of the gangs and their members were well known to the police and community organizations. The police delivered a clear message to these gangs and gang members: Stop the violence or face intensive police scrutiny. The police said they would saturate the areas in which the gangs congregated and did business, which would disrupt their drug markets, among other things. Severe restrictions would be placed on gang members on probation and parole, including bed checks and room searches. Also, gang members engaged in illegal activities, including disorderly acts like drinking in public, would be severely punished. The police backed up this promise on several occasions; a number of gang members were sentenced to long prison terms. The police did not have the resources to crack down on all gangs at once, but "like an old-West sheriff facing down a band of desperadoes with one bullet in his gun, direct communication with gangs allowed the [police] to say, 'We're ready, we're watching, we're waiting: Who wants to be next?'" (D. Kennedy, 1998:6). Data suggest that **the crackdown resulted in a substantial reduction in youth homicides in Boston** (Braga et al., 2001). Further, other cities have employed this strategy with success (Braga and Weisburd, 2012; McGarrell et al., 2006).

Another example of a police crackdown on selected types of crime has attracted much attention throughout the country. Kelling and his associates have argued that the police should **crack down on visible signs of "disorder" in a neighborhood,** such as aggressive panhandling, public drinking, rowdy teenagers hanging out on the street corner, and prostitution.[7] This disorderly behavior, although not seriously disruptive, inspires much fear in community residents. If the behavior goes unchecked, community residents become less likely to use public spaces like streets and parks. They interact less with one another and play a less active role in their community. Among other things, they become less likely to sanction deviance. Such signs of disorder, then, may lead to a breakdown in direct control at the community level. Further, these signs of disorder may encourage more serious crime, as criminals may assume that it is easier to get away with serious crime in communities that cannot keep minor crimes under control.

The police, then, are encouraged to crack down on minor signs of disorder. This approach is sometimes referred to as *zero-tolerance policing*, since even minor acts of crime are sanctioned. Kelling suggests several strategies for cracking down on minor crimes. Among other things, he says that it is easier to crack down on such crimes when the police are on foot patrol, which puts them in closer contact with minor offenders and allows them to develop a closer relationship with the noncriminal segment of the community. Several cities have followed Kelling's approach, most notably New York. Police were assigned to foot patrol in high-crime areas and told to crack down on all offenses, however minor. And police officials have attributed the large reduction in crime in New York City to the crackdown, although others have offered alternative explanations.[8] Limited evidence, however, suggests that **this strategy may have a modest effect on crime—especially if focused on high-crime areas or hot spots.**[9]

It is important to note, however, that unless carefully managed, such crackdowns may lead to increases in abusive police behavior and strained relations with

community residents.[10] More research is needed in this area, but the likelihood of poorly managed crackdowns appears to be especially high in disadvantaged communities, where the relations between the police and community residents are already problematic.

New York City's experience offers a good illustration of the possible advantages and disadvantages of police crackdowns, and it is worth taking a closer look. As one component of its zero-tolerance approach to policing throughout much of 1990s and 2000s, the New York City Police Department (NYPD) relied heavily on the "stop, question, and frisk" tactic. In practice, this involves stopping persons suspected of an offense (perhaps a minor one), questioning them about their activities, and searching them for weapons or contraband. (Note: The U.S. Supreme Court has ruled that police officers may stop and detain individuals for brief periods of time if they have reason to suspect involvement in criminal activity. They may also conduct a search of the individual's outer garments.) These stops have various purposes—for example, to take weapons off the street before they are used in crimes; and to send an important message to would-be lawbreakers: "You could find yourself being stopped and patted down at any given time." In the course of a stop and frisk, the police may also obtain information that could help them solve or prevent crimes. Following this practice, hundreds of thousands of residents had been stopped and questioned each year by members of the NYPD. To illustrate, journalist Daniel Bergner describes a 2014 stop and frisk:

> On a seedy block, [the officers] heard a *thunk*, glanced over and saw two young black men, and guessed that one of them had noticed the cops and thrown a gun under a parked car. The officers jumped out. "Up against the car! Up against it!" Right away, it became clear that the men had gotten rid of nothing worse than a half-full can of beer, which lay beneath a bumper. "Spread 'em. Keep 'em out." Obediently, the men lifted their arms and parted their legs. When the cops asked whether they worked, one of them . . . said softly that he was an assistant to a dental hygienist and was studying to be a nurse . . . But his warrant check came back positive, so the cops took him to the station house in cuffs. (Bergner, 2014)

An examination found that the NYPD's stop-and-frisk program has mainly targeted high-crime areas and crime hot spots (Weisburd et al., 2014). Although it is difficult to determine the impact of stop-and-frisk policing with any certainty, several prominent criminologists now conclude that, in all likelihood, such proactive policing strategies played a role in New York City's unprecedented crime drop (Weisburd et al., 2014; Zimring, 2011; see also Rosenfeld and Fornango, 2017).

At the same time, stop-and-frisk policing has been the focus of intense public debate, and even those who acknowledge its potential role in public safety have expressed concerns about possible long-term negative consequences. Data indicate that, in 2003, the police made about 160,000 stops in New York City. By 2011, the number of stops approached 700,000. Most of those stopped were African American and Hispanic; at least half were young people, between the ages of 13 and 25. *In the vast majority of cases (89 percent), the police found nothing illegal and took no further action* (Fratello et al., 2013).

Pointing to these statistics, critics argue that the practice unfairly targets minorities and represents a form of racial profiling. Further, it is argued that a great number of law-abiding residents are being stopped and harassed on a regular basis. And a study by the Vera Institute found, as critics had feared, that the stop-and-risk program may have eroded trust and confidence in the criminal justice system and strained police–community relations. Based on a survey of young people who had been stopped by the police in New York City's high-crime areas, the study found that nearly half (44 percent) had been stopped repeatedly—nine times or more. Many report that they had not been informed of the reason for being stopped, that they had been threatened by the police, or that they had been subject to physical force by an officer. Further, the young people who had been stopped repeatedly indicated that they would be "less willing to report crimes, even when they themselves are the victims," and 88 percent of the survey respondents believe that the people in their neighborhood "don't trust the police" (Fratello et al., 2013:2). Notably, a recent study finds that violent crime rates tend to be higher in communities where distrust of the police is extensive, even after taking into account other causes of crime (Corsaro et al., 2015).

In 2013, following public protests and a lawsuit filed by a civil rights organization, a U.S. district court judge determined that the NYPD's stop-and-frisk program was discriminatory, ruled it unconstitutional, and ordered changes to the program. Police officials indicated they would continue to stop, question, and frisk suspicious persons, but would no longer pursue this strategy on a large scale (Hechtman, 2014). Although proponents of the large-scale program had called it essential for fighting crime, the crime rate in New York continued to decline even after the program ended (Grawert and Cullen, 2016).

In terms of reform, policing experts have emphasized the need to focus more narrowly on known serious offenders, such as monitoring repeat offenders and working with communities to identify problem individuals. They have also stressed the need to expand existing police officer training "to encourage respectful policing that makes people feel they are treated fairly (including informing them of the reason for the stop), and emphasize strategies aimed at reducing the number of stops that escalate to the point where officers make threats and use physical force" (Fratello et al., 2013:2). Such steps are important not only because they may prevent abuses of police power, but also because data suggest that people are more likely to obey the law when they believe the police are fair and treat others in a respectful manner (Carr et al., 2007; Kane, 2005; McGarrell, 2012; Sherman, 2002; Skogan and Frydl, 2004).

As illustrated by the New York City experience, there is reason to believe that **police crackdowns focusing on hot spots or on particular types of crime may be effective in reducing crime,** although it can be challenging to execute such crackdowns in a manner that does not create other major problems. However, it should be noted that not all crackdowns are effective, and even when they are, sometimes the effects are modest.[11] Data suggest that crackdowns are most likely to be effective when they are focused and when the police are able to do the following: (1) identify the key individuals or high-crime areas to be targeted; (2) clearly communicate to these individuals or the people in these areas that some, perhaps all, illegal acts will not be tolerated; (3) adequately monitor the behavior of these individuals or the people in these areas; (4) consistently punish illegal acts, with punishments being reasonably swift and meaningful; and (5) coordinate their efforts with other members of the community, including clergy, social workers, and neighborhood organizations that seek to direct youth away from crime.[12] Police crackdowns that incorporate these elements are often referred to as **"pulling levers policing"** or **"focused deterrence policing"** (Braga and Weisburd, 2012).

The police, in short, need to do what effective parents do: state clear rules for behavior, adequately monitor behavior, consistently sanction rule violations in an *appropriate* manner, and support and encourage prosocial behavior. These actions are certainly possible in many cases. Most cities have hot spots of crime and neighborhoods plagued by disorder. Further, the police in some cities can identify and monitor the individuals most likely to commit certain types of crime, such as homicide (e.g., members of violent street gangs, individuals who have been released on probation or parole). But delinquency is less concentrated in some communities than others, making it more difficult to adequately monitor and sanction behavior. And certain types of delinquency—like drug use—are spread widely throughout the community, making crackdowns especially difficult. Nevertheless, properly implemented police crackdowns are a promising strategy for reducing at least some delinquency (see Box 20.1 for a description of police crackdowns in Cincinnati).

Will Community Policing Reduce Delinquency?

There is another major effort under way to transform the nature of policing, and this effort promises to fundamentally alter the nature of police work in the United States. Many researchers and policy makers have argued that the police should move away from preventive patrol and employ a strategy known as *community policing*.[13] As an example, the 1994 Violent Crime Control and Law Enforcement Act mandated that all of the 100,000 new police hired be used for community policing. And the U.S. Department of Justice created a new agency—the Office of Community Oriented Policing Services (COPS)—to assist police departments in the move to community policing (see Zhao et al., 2002; http://www.cops.usdoj.gov). Data suggest that all police departments in large cities now employ community-policing methods to varying degrees, although many departments make only limited efforts in this area.[14] As you will see, community policing efforts are not the same as police crackdowns, although police crackdowns may sometimes emerge from community-policing efforts.

Box 20.1 "We're Coming After You!" The Police Respond to Gang Violence in Cincinnati, Ohio

In early 2006, Cincinnati was rocked by several high-profile murders. Many city residents feared that violent crime was spinning out of control. That summer, in response, the police department implemented a zero-tolerance crackdown. A special squad of officers was assembled to sweep crime hot spots and to make arrests for both serious and minor crimes, including loitering and jaywalking. Within a few months, the squad had made thousands of arrests (Seabrook, 2009).

The zero-tolerance crackdown reduced some types of crime, but it had little effect on the murder rate, which continued to rise. The crackdown also did little to help police–community relations, which had reached a breaking point just a few years earlier. In 2001, civil rights groups had filed a lawsuit against the city for racial profiling and police use of excessive force. Just a few days after the lawsuit was filed, riots erupted in the streets following the police shooting of an unarmed black man.

The assistant police chief, who had played a key role in the zero-tolerance crackdown, acknowledged the limits of this approach:

> "You say, 'O.K., we're going to arrest everyone who jaywalks.' So who do you arrest? Someone's grandmother, or the milkman, or some guy who has just worked a sixteen-hour day and is trying to get home as fast as he can. It's bullshit. Even in high-crime neighborhoods, there are a lot of honest people living there. Meanwhile, the real bad guys—they know the sweep is on, so they just stay inside until things cool off." (quoted in Seabrook, 2009:32)

In 2007, the police implemented a different type of crackdown. It was modeled on the strategy to quell gang violence that had been used with some success in Boston and other cities, also known as Ceasefire programs. Instead of focusing on minor offenders, the police concentrated their efforts on street gangs, which were believed to be responsible for many murders.

(Continued)

(Continued)

The new strategy makes use of "call ins," or group forums, to send a strong message to gang members. Suspected gang members—many of whom are already on probation or parole—are ordered to a courthouse for a special meeting, a "call-in." After presenting surveillance video that shows some of the gang members involved in drug deals or other criminal activity, the police deliver a stern warning to the participants:

> "We know who you are, we know who your friends are, and we know what you're doing. If your boys don't stop shooting people right now, we're coming after everyone in your group." (quoted in Seabrook, 2009:38)

To back up the threat of arrest and punishment, the police have targeted gangs that failed to heed their warning. In one case, they managed to arrest all the key members of a local gang, with some of these arrests resulting in long prison sentences.

There is more to the Ceasefire idea than threats of arrest and punishment, however. A key feature of such programs is the involvement of coordinated partnerships between the police and members of the local community, including clergy, social workers, crime victims, and ex-offenders. These other actors play a critical role because they add credibility and legitimacy to the program, can deliver a persuasive moral message, and can help address some of the root causes of gang involvement. Moreover, some researchers find that police crackdowns tend to be more effective when they include such partnerships (L. Mazerolle et al., 2007).

In the remainder of the call-in session, for example, an attempt is made to highlight the devastating effects of violence on the community. The suspected gang members are exposed to tearful mothers who have lost children to gang violence. And before they leave the session, they receive a phone number to call if they wish to receive help getting a job or obtaining an education.

A participating offender described how the session impacted him. Threats mean little to him, he explained, so he was not impressed by the police warnings. But he continued to think about the session in the weeks that followed, eventually called the phone number, and obtained help landing a job (Seabrook, 2009).

It is difficult to assess the overall effectiveness of the Ceasefire program in Cincinnati, especially without a control or comparison group (see Chapter 19). The murder rate has fluctuated since the beginning of the program, with a substantial decline in the last few years. But the murder rate has also decreased in other cities during the same time period, including cities that do not have a similar program in place. It does appear, however, that homicides involving members of the targeted streets gangs became less frequent following the call-in sessions, whereas homicides involving nonmembers increased. Further, there is reason to believe this strategy helped reduce crime in other cities as well (see Braga and Weisburd, 2012).

Questions for Discussion

1. In Chapter 16, we discussed some of the reasons why young people join gangs. Drawing on this chapter, what interventions would you add to the Ceasefire program to maximize its potential impact?
2. Ideally, how could we redesign the Ceasefire program to allow for a rigorous evaluation of its effectiveness (see Chapter 19)?

What is community policing? The best way to answer this question is to review some of the problems of preventive patrol, because community policing was developed in response to these problems.

Problems of preventive patrol. Preventive patrol has been criticized for several reasons, including the following. First, preventive patrol **isolates the police from the communities they patrol.** Police officers spend much time in a patrol car, cruising a large area. In some areas, they are rotated between beats on a regular basis. Rotation is done to prevent corruption; some departments feel that you can reduce corruption by preventing officers from developing close ties to the people they police. Under strict rotation, however, the officers are isolated from community residents. In fact, police officers often become suspicious of people in the larger community. And in some cases, particularly in minority communities, there may be tension or outright hostility between the police and many community residents. This tension is unfortunate, since residents are more likely to call the police if they know and trust them (see Kessler, 1999). As discussed in Chapter 2, only about 40 percent of all crimes are reported to the police. The police cannot do anything to solve crimes they do not know about. Residents can also function as good information sources, helping the police solve crimes and better understand the community problems that contribute to crime. Further, as indicated earlier, some evidence suggests that community residents are more likely to obey the law if they respect and are well treated by the police (Kane, 2005; McGarrell, 2012; Sherman, 1998, 2002; Sherman and Eck, 2002).

Second, preventive patrol **does not deal with the underlying causes of crime.** Officers on preventive patrol respond to one crime incident after another, typically by arresting or threatening to arrest any suspects they catch. Rarely do they examine the underlying causes of the incidents and ask how such causes might be addressed. That is to say, they deal with the symptoms of the problem but not the underlying problem. For example, over the course of a few months, an officer might get several calls regarding burglaries at an apartment complex. The officer responds to each call in turn and resumes patrol after each one. The officer is not encouraged to step back and ask why this apartment complex has so many burglaries and what can be done about it.

Finally, preventive patrol **does not fully involve community residents in crime control efforts.** Community residents might be asked for information about specific crimes, but the police stress that the fight against crime should be left to the police. The police, however, have limited resources, and criminologists argue that any successful crime control program needs to involve community residents.

1 or 4

What is community policing? Community policing was designed to deal with the problems of preventive patrol. Community policing does not refer to one specific strategy or approach, such as the use of foot patrols. Rather, it encompasses a number of related approaches. At the most general level, community policing tries to do three things (or achieve three goals).

First, it tries to **foster closer ties between the police and community residents.** As indicated earlier, there are a number of advantages to such ties (although efforts must also be made to control police corruption). The police have tried to foster such ties in several ways. Most efforts involve (1) assigning officers to the same community for long periods, so they identify with and become an integral part of the community and (2) having officers spend less time in patrol cars and more time interacting with community residents. The officers may walk a beat, especially in downtown areas or other densely packed locations. They may spend time on bicycles or motor scooters, where interaction with the public is easier. They may increase their accessibility by opening storefront police stations in the community. They may visit community residents in their homes, going door to door. They may serve as substitute teachers in the school system. They may attend community meetings and get involved in community organizations, like the YMCA and Boys and Girls Clubs. They may set up their own community programs, like the Police Athletic League (PAL).

Second, community policing **attempts to solve the underlying problems that lead to crime.** In some cases, special police officers or police units are charged with the task of dealing with the underlying causes of crime. The advocates of community policing, however, argue that regular officers should also be involved in this process. The officer who is assigned to a community on a day-to-day basis has a special advantage when it comes to understanding that community's problems and developing solutions to them. Most police officers usually have some time when they are not responding to calls or engaged in other tasks. They are encouraged to use this time to deal with the underlying causes of crime on their beat. In particular, they are often urged to engage in what is known as problem-oriented policing—discussed later—which provides a model for how one goes about dealing with the underlying causes of crime. The solutions they develop to these problems often involve efforts to increase direct control, but they sometimes entail efforts to increase other forms of social control, reduce the social learning of crime, reduce strain, or alter situations conducive to crime. The police, then, do not simply rely on arrest or the threat of arrest to control crime—they also explore other options for controlling crime.

Third, community policing attempts to **actively involve community residents in the fight against crime.** Such involvement might take the form of neighborhood watch programs, where community residents keep an eye on one another's homes and report suspicious activity to the police. It might also include participation in a range of crime prevention and control programs, such as recreational and mentoring programs. In one city, the police encouraged homeowners, apartment superintendents, landlords, and business owners in a number of crime hot spots to assume a greater role in crime control. In particular, the police advised these individuals on what they could do to reduce crime in their immediate area, providing assistance when necessary. Among other things, individuals in these areas organized citizen patrols, participated in antidrug rallies, held community cleanup campaigns, and formed community groups to deal with local problems. The police assisted in a variety of ways; for example, they arranged for city inspectors to examine problem locations and enforce housing, fire, and safety codes. And they worked with legal authorities to bring suit against the owners of drug-plagued properties. This increased citizen involvement in crime control led to a reduction in several types of crime (P. Mazerolle et al., 1998).

Properly implementing community policing is not easy. Community policing generally requires more police, since the police are asked to do more. They not only respond to crime incidents, but they also try to foster ties with community residents and attempt to deal with the underlying causes of crime. Many police have the time for such extra activities, but some do not (see Famega et al., 2005). Community policing also represents a major change in the police role, and many police resist this change. Community police officers are sometimes referred to as the "grin and wave" squad, and they are often viewed more as social workers than as police. Further, many police administrators resist the idea of community policing, since it means giving more responsibility to regular officers and community residents, who necessarily play a central role in identifying and responding to community problems.

Nevertheless, community policing is becoming increasingly popular. Let us provide a few brief **examples.**

Problem-oriented policing (POP). Many police departments now employ problem-oriented policing (POP), which can be classified as a type of community policing. POP is designed to **deal with the underlying causes of crime** by encouraging police officers to work with community residents and organizations. POP proceeds in four steps:

1. **Scanning:** The police are encouraged to identify problems in their community or across the entire city. These problems might include such things as car thefts in a certain neighborhood, drug sales in an apartment complex, the robbery of tourists, or juveniles who repeatedly run away from home.

2. **Analysis:** The police analyze the problem, in the hope of understanding causes and developing possible solutions. They collect information from a wide range of sources, including community residents, arrested offenders, and organizations that deal with the problem (e.g., social welfare agencies, the local housing authority, and religious institutions).

3. **Response:** The police decide on a solution to the problem and then implement it. The solution may or may not involve a police response. For example, they may decide to launch a police crackdown on drug sales in a particular community, or they may decide to set up a drug education program in the schools. The police often work with community residents, community organizations, and other government agencies in implementing the solution.

4. **Assessment:** The police evaluate the effectiveness of the solution. If it is not effective, they try other solutions.

As an illustration of POP, the residents of a quiet neighborhood in Newport News, Virginia, began to complain about groups of rowdy teenagers in their community on Friday and Saturday nights. While the teenagers were not violent, they played loud music and occasionally engaged in acts of vandalism. The police responded to a number of incidents involving these teenagers, but the problem persisted. Relations between the police, the teenagers, and community residents were deteriorating. The beat officer was asked to examine the underlying causes of this problem and propose a solution. He discovered that a rollerskating rink in the area was trying to increase business by offering lower rates and free bus service to the rink on Friday and Saturday nights. The offer attracted many teenagers to the rink from outside the community. Conversations with these teenagers revealed that there were not enough buses to take them home after the rink closed. As a consequence, the teenagers would walk home through the neighborhood, creating problems. The rink owner was informed of the problem, and he agreed to lease more buses to take the teenagers home. This action effectively ended the problem (see Trojanowicz et al., 1998:174).

Numerous other examples of POP are available, and most—though not all—have been effective in reducing crime.[15] We should note here that the Office of Community Oriented Policing Services (COPS) collects information about the problem-solving efforts of police departments across the country, as well as the results of such efforts. COPS then disseminates information on successful (and not so successful) efforts to deal with a range of problems. You can examine the guides that COPS provides to the police by going to their website (http://www.cops.usdoj.gov), clicking on **Community Policing Topics**, located at the bottom of the page (under **Resources**) and selecting the topic of your choice, such as **Youth Safety: Child Abuse and Bullying**. By further clicking on the resources link, you will find many POP guides for dealing with various problems; topics include **Child Abuse and Neglect in the Home, Domestic Violence, Bullying in Schools**, and **Juvenile Runaways**. And for an excellent manual describing how to do problem-oriented policing, see *Crime Analysis for Problem Solvers in 60 Small Steps* by Clarke and Eck (2005), also available at the COPS website.

Drug abuse resistance education (DARE) programs. Another example of community policing is DARE, the Drug Abuse Resistance Education program. DARE did not emerge out of problem-oriented policing, but it does represent another police effort to work with the community in dealing with the underlying causes of crime (see Carter, 1995). The program, which was developed by the Los Angeles Police Department, has been adopted by police departments all over the country. In fact, police officers run this program in more than half the school districts in the United States. Presented to schoolchildren by a uniformed police officer, DARE focuses on preventing drug abuse, violence, and gang affiliation. The full DARE program begins in kindergarten and continues through high school. The program tries to prevent delinquency in a number of ways. Among other things, it tries to build positive relations with the police, foster antidrug values, and teach kids to resist negative peer pressure. But despite these noble aims, evaluation studies suggest that the DARE program is not effective in reducing drug use (see Chapter 24).

Youth organizations. In yet another example of community policing, the police in many communities have become actively involved in youth organizations that try to prevent delinquency, such as the YMCA, Boys and Girls Clubs, and the Boy Scouts and Girl Scouts. Such organizations provide youths with supervised recreational opportunities and other services, like tutoring and mentoring. The police serve as advisers to these organizations; they participate in a variety of program activities; they help provide security in and around the youth centers; and they help recruit high-risk youth to participate in these organizations. In many cases, the police have started their own youth programs—such as PAL. Data suggest that certain of these youth organizations may be effective at reducing delinquency (see Chaiken, 1998; Chapter 24).

Still other examples of community policing could be provided (see the references in note 12). We encourage you to find out what your hometown police department is doing to implement community policing. (You probably can do this by going to the website of your hometown police department.)

Overall evaluation of community policing. Does community policing work? Is it effective in reducing crime and delinquency? Many claims for its success have been made. Unfortunately, most community-policing efforts have not yet received rigorous evaluation. The limited data that now exist suggest that most community-policing efforts are effective in reducing the fear of crime and in improving police–community relations, but not all efforts reduce crime and delinquency rates. Some do and some do not. As indicated earlier, for example, evaluations suggest that the DARE program does not reduce drug use (see Chapter 24). Neighborhood watch programs and problem-oriented policing, however, appear to reduce crime in at least some circumstances. Certain efforts to establish closer ties to community residents—like door-to-door visits by the police—show some success at reducing crime. Certain of the youth organizations with which the police are affiliated show some success at reducing crime. Taken as a whole, there is reason to believe that **the community-policing movement holds some promise for reducing crime.**[16] However, additional and more rigorous evaluations of community-policing efforts are needed to shed further light on efforts that are and are not effective in reducing crime and delinquency.

SUMMARY

Data suggest that society might lower delinquency rates somewhat by **changing what the police do when they are on the street.** In particular, police crackdowns focusing on hot spots and selected types of crime are often effective. Such crackdowns reduce crime by improving the ability of the police to monitor situations and individuals prone to crime and to sanction crime when it occurs. That is, crackdowns increase direct control by the police. Likewise, certain community-policing efforts are sometimes effective at reducing crime. At the most general level, community policing involves efforts to establish closer ties between the police and the community, to deal with the underlying causes of crime, and to better involve the community in crime control efforts. Community-policing programs sometimes attempt to increase direct control (e.g., neighborhood watch programs) and sometimes address the other causes of crime (e.g., DARE). Criminologists are still in the process of determining which of the many specific types of community policing are most effective, although data are beginning to point to the community-policing programs that do and do not work. Problem-oriented policing, in particular, appears to hold much promise as a crime control strategy. And recent assessments indicate that neighborhood watch programs can also reduce crime (for more on neighborhood watch programs, see Chapter 24).

Drawing on the research cited in the chapter, some have argued that the most successful policing efforts do two things (Clarke and Eck, 2005; Eck and Maguire, 2006; Weisburd and Eck, 2004). First, they **focus on a clearly identifiable crime problem,** such as crime at certain hot spots or a particular type of crime in a community. Second, they **employ a range of strategies to address the problem.** They do not rely solely on a single approach, such as arrest. Rather, they may also attempt to address such underlying causes of the problem as strain or social learning, and to alter situations conducive to crime.

TEACHING AIDS
Web-Based Exercises

Locating the hot spots of crime As noted in this chapter, crime is not evenly spread throughout a city or even within a city's high-crime communities. Rather, crime is concentrated in certain locations, such as shopping malls, parks, and areas around particular bars or clubs. Further, the crimes at these locations are more likely on certain days and at certain times (e.g., Friday and Saturday evenings). The police in many cities use computer-mapping techniques to identify the hot spots of crime and concentrate police patrols there, a strategy that has been successful in reducing crime. You should:

1. Visit the Crime Mapping website (www.crimemapping.com).
2. Pull up the crime map for your hometown, the community in which your college is located, or any other community (not every U.S. community is available on this website).
3. Become familiar with the symbols for the different types of crime.
4. Examine the location of crimes in the community over the last week (the default) or month. Do the crimes cluster in certain areas? Focus on one or a few particularly dense clusters? Are the crimes in this cluster more common on certain days and times (you can find the date and time or each crime by clicking on the icon for the crime). Identify the physical characteristics of the cluster: for example, is it a strip shopping center, a park, a commercial area with several bars? (Once you get a few addresses by clicking on the crime icons, you can use a web service such as earth-scout.com to get visual images of the area.)

Problem-oriented policing: a type of community policing. Problem-oriented policing (or POP) has been one of the more successful community policing initiatives. As noted, the idea behind POP is to examine the underlying causes of similar crime incidents (e.g., acquaintance rapes on college campuses, home invasion robberies), devise strategies for addressing these causes, use them for a given period, and then evaluate their effectiveness. The Center for Problem-Oriented Policing was developed to assist police in this regard. You should:

1. Visit the website of the Center for Problem-Oriented at http://www.popcenter.org.
2. Explore the website, then click on **POP Guides,** then click on **Browse Guides by: Alphabetical.** Skim through the titles of the guides. Each guide provides advice to police departments that want to address a particular type of crime through problem-oriented policing. In particular, the guides describe the steps the police should follow, review research on the causes of the crime, and discuss strategies that have been found to be effective and ineffective in reducing the crime.
3. Focus on one type of crime that is of interest to you, read through the guide for that crime, and then provide an overview of how the police should use problem-oriented policing in responding to it.
4. How does this response differ from the "standard" police response, or preventive patrol?

Community policing. The U.S. Department of Justice created COPS, or Community-Oriented Policing Services, to support community policing through the United States. Visit the COPS website at http://www.cops.usdoj.gov. Explore the website, getting an idea of the different community-policing initiatives and the resources available to police departments.

TEST YOUR KNOWLEDGE OF THIS CHAPTER

1. List the major points made about how the police operate.
2. What is preventive patrol?
3. How do the police spend most of their time?
4. What do we mean when we say that the police are primarily "reactive"?
5. Under what circumstances are the police most likely to catch offenders? Why is it that efforts to improve police response time have had little effect on the likelihood of catching offenders?
6. List any three factors that influence the likelihood that police will arrest the suspects they catch.
7. What is one of the reasons why the police end up releasing (without arrest) most of the suspected offenders they catch?
8. Why do criminologists feel that the police are **somewhat** effective at controlling crime?
9. What major challenge have researchers faced when trying to determine whether hiring more police will reduce crime? What does the most recent evidence in this area indicate?
10. Describe the strategy of "police crackdowns." Indicate what it is that the police crack down on. What causes of crime do police crackdowns address?
11. It is difficult for the police to permanently crack down on all "hot spots" for crime. What alternative strategy do Sherman and associates suggest that the police pursue?
12. Describe Operation Ceasefire, the police crackdown in Boston focusing on gun violence.
13. Police crackdowns do not appear to displace crime from one area to another. Why might this be the case?
14. Describe zero-tolerance policing.

15. What steps are the police taking to reduce abusive police behavior?
16. Under what conditions are police crackdowns most likely to be effective?
17. Community policing was developed to overcome the problems associated with heavy reliance on preventive patrolling. List the three major problems that were identified.
18. List the three major goals of community policing (or the three things that community policing does in trying to overcome the problems arising from preventive patrol). Provide an example of how police departments have tried to achieve each of these goals (e.g., how police departments have tried to foster closer ties between the police and community residents).
19. What is problem-oriented policing (POP)? Describe the four steps in POP.
20. Describe any two community-policing initiatives other than POP (initiatives like DARE, CAPS, and youth organizations). Indicate why these initiatives are said to be examples of community policing.
21. Describe the evaluation research on community policing.

THOUGHT AND DISCUSSION QUESTIONS

1. How do you think an advocate of community policing would feel about the strategy of police crackdowns? (Ask yourself how police crackdowns relate to the three goals of community policing and whether community-policing initiatives might result in police crackdowns.)
2. Most police departments have made efforts to implement community policing, but research suggests that the impact of such efforts on departmental practices often is minimal. (That is, community policing is implemented in name but little more.) Why do you think many police departments resist moving toward the community-policing model?
3. Can you think of any other suggestions beyond those in this chapter for improving police effectiveness?

KEY TERMS

- Preventive patrol
- Police discretion in making arrests
- Police crackdowns
- Hot spots
- Zero-tolerance policing
- "Pulling levers policing" or "focused deterrence policing"
- Community policing
- Problem-oriented policing (POP)
- Drug Abuse Resistance Education (DARE)
- Chicago Alternative Policing Strategy (CAPS)

ENDNOTES

1. For overviews and selected studies on the police, see P. Anderson and Newman, 1998; Brandl and Barlow, 1996; Chaiken, 1998; S. Cox and Conrad, 1996; Eck and Maguire, 2006; Eck and Spelman, 1987; Gaines and Cordner, 1999; Greene, 2000; Kappeler et al., 1996; Kelling, n.d., 1988; Kelling and Coles, 1996; MacDonald, 2002; Mastrofski, 2000; McGarrell, 2012; Messner et al., 2007; Moore et al., 1988; Muraskin, 1998; Petersilia, 1989; Rosenfeld et al., 2007; Sherman, 1998, 2002; Sherman and Eck, 2002; Skogan and Frydl, 2004; Trojanowicz et al., 1998; S. Walker, 1998; Weisburd and Eck, 2004; Worrall and Kovandzic, 2007; Zimring, 2007.

2. For overviews and selected studies, see Eck and Maguire, 2006; Greenberg et al., 1983; Kelling et al., 1974; Kleck and Barnes, 2014; Sherman and Eck, 2002; Skogan and Frydl, 2004; Weisburd and Eck, 2004; Worrall and Kovandzic, 2007; Zimring, 2007.

3. For overviews, see Braga et al., 1999, 2014; J. Cohen et al., 2003; Decker, 2003; Eck and Maguire, 2006; Lawton et al., 2005; McGarrell et al., 2006; M. Scott, 2003; Sherman, 2002; Sherman and Eck, 2002; Weisburd and Eck, 2004; Weisburd et al., 2006; Willis et al., 2004.

4. For overviews and examples, see Braga and Bond, 2008; Braga et al., 1999, 2014; J. Cohen et al., 2003; Eck and Maguire, 2006; Erez, 1995; C. Katz et al., 2001; Sherman, 1990, 2002; Sherman and Eck, 2002; Sherman and Weisburd, 1995; Weisburd and Eck, 2004; Weisburd et al., 2003; Weisburd et al., 2006.

5. See note 4.

6. See Braga et al., 2001; Braga and Weisburd, 2012; D. Kennedy, 1997, 1998; Kleiman, 1999; McGarrell et al., 2006; also see Braga et al., 2008; Corsaro et al., 2013; Decker, 2003, for similar crackdowns in other cities.

7. See Eck and Maguire, 2006; Greene, 2000; C. Katz et al., 2001; Kelling, 1988; Kelling and Coles, 1996; Messner et al., 2007; Rosenfeld et al., 2007; Skogan and Frydl, 2004; Taylor, 2001b; J. Wilson and Kelling, 1982.

8. See Eck and Maguire, 2006; Kelling and Coles, 1996; Messner et al., 2007; Rosenfeld et al., 2007; Sherman et al., 1998; Skogan and Frydl, 2004; S. Walker 1998:82; Weisburd et al., 2014; Zimring, 2011.

9. See Braga and Bond, 2008; Braga et al., 1999, 2014; Eck and Maguire, 2006; Fritsch et al., 1999; C. Katz et al., 2001; Kubrin et al., 2010; MacDonald, 2002; Messner et al., 2007; Rosenfeld et al., 2007; M. Smith, 2001; Xu et al., 2005.

10. See Braga et al., 2014; Eck and Maguire, 2006; Gau and Brunson, 2010; Greene, 2000; Kane, 2005; McGarrell, 2012; M. Scott, 2003; Sherman, 1998, 2002; Sherman and Eck, 2002; Stoutland, 2001.

11. See Braga et al., 2014; J. Cohen et al., 2003; Decker, 2003; M. Scott, 2003; Sherman and Eck, 2002.

12. See J. Cohen et al., 2003; Eck and Maguire, 2006; Kennedy, 1998; Kleiman, 1999; McGarrell et al., 2006; Sherman, 2002; Skogan and Frydl, 2004.

13. For overviews and selected studies on community policing, see Alpert and Piquero, 1998; Braga et al., 1999; Brown, 1989; Cordner, 1999; Eck and Maguire, 2006; Eck and Spelman, 1987; Greene, 2000; Kelling and Coles, 1996; MacDonald, 2002; McEwen, 1994; M. Moore et al., 1988; National Institute of Justice, 1992; Sherman and Eck, 2002; Skogan, 2004; Spelman and Eck, 1987; Trojanowicz et al., 1998; Weisburd and Eck, 2004; Worrall and Kovandzic, 2007.

14. See Burruss and Giblin, 2014; Eck and Maguire, 2006; Engel and Worden, 2003; Famega et al., 2005; He et al., 2005; MacDonald, 2002; Pelfrey, 2004; Reaves and Hickman, 2002b; Skogan, 2004; Zhao et al., 2003.

15. See Braga et al., 1999; Clarke and Eck, 2005; Corsaro et al., 2013; Eck and Maguire, 2006; Eck and Spelman, 1987; Skogan, 2004; Skogan and Frydl, 2004; Spelman and Eck, 1987; Trojanowicz et al., 1998; Weisburd and Eck, 2004; Weisburd et al., 2010.

16. For overviews and examples of the evaluations of community policing, see Bennett et al., 2008; Eck and Maguire, 2006; Greene, 2000; MacDonald, 2002; Sherman and Eck, 2002; Schnebly, 2008; Skogan, 2004; Weisburd and Eck, 2004; Worrall and Kovandzic, 2007; Xu et al., 2005; Zhao et al., 2002.

21 Juvenile Court and Corrections

What Do the Juvenile Court and Juvenile
Correctional Agencies Do to Control Delinquency?

I n this chapter, we first examine what happens when juveniles are sent to juvenile court. Next, we examine the ways in which the juvenile correctional system sanctions and attempts to reform juvenile offenders.[1] We also comment briefly on the effectiveness of these sanctioning and reform efforts. Chapters 22 through 25 also deal with the effectiveness of the juvenile court and correctional system—as well as efforts to increase the effectiveness of these agencies.

After reading this chapter, you should be able to:

- List the major goals of juvenile court.
- Describe the types of cases handled by juvenile court.
- Describe the major stages in the juvenile court process, from intake to disposition.
- Discuss the major ways in which juvenile courts respond to offenders, including diversion, waiver to adult court, and dispositions involving probation, intermediate sanctions, rehabilitation, and out-of-home placements.
- Summarize the research on the effectiveness of these different responses, and indicate what steps juvenile courts are taking to increase their effectiveness.

WHAT HAPPENS WHEN JUVENILES ARE SENT TO JUVENILE COURT?

This section examines the goals of the juvenile court, the number and types of cases handled by the juvenile court, and the major stages in the juvenile court process, beginning with the referral to juvenile court and finishing with the "disposition," or sentence, that is given out by the juvenile court. Not all juvenile courts operate in the same manner. They differ from state to state, for example, but this discussion should give you a general sense of what happens in juvenile court.

What Are the Major Goals of Juvenile Court?

As indicated in Chapter 1, the juvenile court was **originally set up to rehabilitate juveniles rather than to punish them.** It was felt that juveniles were not fully responsible for their behavior, including delinquent behavior, so the court was established to provide them with enough guidance and assistance to lead conventional lives. The court often failed to attain this lofty goal in actual practice, but the major goal of the juvenile court was nevertheless rehabilitation rather than punishment. And rehabilitation was to be achieved by addressing many of the causes of delinquency examined earlier, such as family and school problems.

Rehabilitation is still an important goal of the juvenile court, but in recent decades juvenile courts have also placed an **increased emphasis on holding juveniles accountable for their offenses and punishing them.** Juvenile offenders, particularly serious offenders, were more likely to be severely sanctioned for their offenses. The juvenile court, then, began placing more emphasis on direct control, at least for serious offenders.

There were several reasons for this **shift in focus from rehabilitation to accountability and punishment.** First, a series of studies in the 1970s raised serious doubts about society's ability to rehabilitate delinquents (see Chapter 24 for more information). Second, doubts about the effectiveness of rehabilitation were also raised by the rapid increase in delinquency rates during the 1960s and early 1970s—as well as by the more recent increase in violent delinquency during the late 1980s and early 1990s. Third, conservative politicians began to aggressively attack rehabilitation and prevention programs in the late 1960s. They claimed that crime and serious delinquency were not caused by social problems like poverty but rather were the result of deliberate choices by bad people. It was said that such people deserved punishment and that punishment was the most effective way to stop their crime. The criminal and juvenile justice systems were portrayed as "too lenient," and there were calls to "crack down" or "get tough" on crime. The conservative call to crack down on crime was aided by the extensive and often biased coverage of crime in the news media and entertainment industry (for excellent discussions of these issues, see Beckett and Sasson, 2000, and Garland, 2001).

By the mid-2000s, the view of juvenile offenders began to shift yet again. This latest shift resulted from concerns about the ineffectiveness and expense of get-tough efforts. Further, research began to highlight the differences between juveniles and adults, including the relative immaturity of juveniles and their susceptibility to the adverse effects of violence and abuse. As we describe later in this chapter, many states are retreating from the get-tough experiment and are devoting increased resources to rehabilitation. Although many get-tough laws remain on the books, these states are making efforts to hold juveniles accountable in ways that respect the unique developmental needs of juveniles and the challenges they face. To a certain extent, then, we are witnessing a return to the original goal of the juvenile court.

How Many Cases Does Juvenile Court Handle, and What Types Does the Court Deal With?

In 2013, juvenile courts handled about one million **delinquency** cases—or 3.4 cases for every 100 juveniles age 10 and older who were eligible for juvenile court referral. This does not mean that one million different juveniles were handled by juvenile court. Many juveniles pass through the juvenile court more than once in a given year, and each visit is counted as a separate case (for statistics on juvenile court, see Hockenberry and Puzzanchera, 2015).

Thirty-five percent of the court cases were for **property crimes** like larceny-theft, burglary, vandalism, and motor vehicle theft. **Public order offenses** like disorderly conduct, weapons offenses, and obstruction of justice accounted for 26 percent of all cases. **Violent crimes** like homicide, rape, and assault accounted for another 26 percent of all cases (more than half of these violent crimes involved simple or minor assaults). And **drug offenses,** including sales and use, accounted for 13 percent of all cases. If we focus on specific offenses, the two most common crimes handled by juvenile courts are larceny-theft (accounting for about 17 percent of court cases) and simple assault (accounting for about 18 percent of court cases).

About 72 percent of the juveniles accused of delinquency were **males.** We should note, however, that the percentage of court cases involving females has increased over time. In 1985, females accounted for 19 percent of all delinquency cases handled by juvenile court, versus 28 percent in 2013. **Older juveniles** were much more likely to be processed by the court than younger juveniles, with 16- and 17-year-olds having the highest rates of court processing. For example, 16- and 17-year-old juveniles had rates of court processing that were about 30 times higher than 10-year-olds. **African Americans** had rates of court processing about 2.7 times higher than whites (3.6 times higher for violent crimes). Asian Americans had the lowest rates of court processing. (If we look at the number of delinquency cases processed by the court per 1,000 juveniles ages 10+ in a given racial group, the rate of processing for African Americans in 2013 was 74.3 per 1,000; for whites it was 27.4 per 1,000, and for Asians it was 7.3 per 1,000). We discuss racial differences in court processing in Chapter 23, when we examine evidence of discrimination in the juvenile justice system.

Juvenile courts *formally processed* about 109,000 *status offense* cases in 2013. It is estimated that only about one out of five status offense referrals is formally processed, so the number of status offense cases handled in the juvenile court system is much higher. Most of these cases are handled informally or dismissed. Good data exist only for status offense cases that were formally processed, however. These formally processed cases were for truancy (51 percent), underage liquor law violations (15 percent), ungovernability (being beyond the control of parents) (9 percent), running away (8 percent), curfew violations (9 percent), and "other" (8 percent). Males were involved in 58 percent of the status offense cases (versus 72 percent of the delinquency cases). Males accounted for the majority of all status offense cases except running away: that is, curfew violations, liquor law violations, truancy, and ungovernability. Females accounted for nearly 6 out of 10 runaway cases. We comment on the greater involvement of females in runaway cases in Chapter 22, where we discuss discrimination by the juvenile justice system.

What Are the Major Stages in the Juvenile Court Process?

Referral to juvenile court. The first step in the juvenile court process is *referral*, usually by the police, to the juvenile court. In 2013, 82 percent of all **delinquency** cases handled by the court came from the police. (Fifty-five percent of formally processed status offense cases were referred by the police, with schools and family members referring most of the rest.) Usually the arresting officer physically takes the juvenile to juvenile court or to a juvenile detention center. The officer provides the court staff with a *complaint*, which describes the offense(s) the juvenile is accused of having committed.

The remaining 18 percent of the delinquency cases handled by the court were referred by parents, victims, school officials, probation officers, and others. For example, it is not uncommon for parents to go to juvenile court, claim that they cannot do anything to control their child, and fill out a complaint describing offense(s) the child has committed. Also, probation officers will often file complaints against juveniles under their supervision, stating that these juveniles have committed new offenses or have otherwise violated the conditions of their probation.

Intake screening. Juveniles referred to juvenile court are screened by an *intake officer*, who is usually a probation officer associated with the court. The intake screening typically includes an interview with the juvenile and his or her parent(s) or guardians, although the police, victims, and others are sometimes interviewed as well. The main purpose of the intake screening is to gather information about the case and decide what to do with the juvenile. That is, should the case be dismissed, handled informally, or formally processed by the juvenile court? And if the case is to be formally processed, should the juvenile be released or detained while awaiting trial? The decision of the intake officer is often reviewed by a prosecuting attorney in the court.

The intake officer considers a number of factors about the case. How strong is the evidence against the juvenile: specifically, is there "probable cause" to believe that the juvenile committed the offense? How serious is the offense? Does the juvenile admit to the offense? Does the juvenile have a prior record? How old is the juvenile? Does the juvenile have a good or bad attitude? How is the juvenile doing in school? How strongly is the complainant pressing for action? How concerned are the parents, and what action have they taken or do they plan to take? In reaching a decision about what to do with the juvenile, the intake officer considers not only the offense (what the juvenile may have done), but also the offender (what the juvenile is like).

About 45 percent of the delinquency cases referred to juvenile courts were dismissed or handled informally in 2013, although this percentage varied greatly from court to court. Cases involving minor offenses are especially likely to be dismissed or handled informally, particularly if the juvenile does not have a prior record. And data suggest that the large majority of status offense cases are dismissed or handled informally. Cases are dismissed for a variety of reasons. For example, the evidence against the juvenile may be poor; the offense may be trivial; or the intake officer may feel that the situation is best dealt with outside the court system (e.g., by a social service agency). Usually, before a case is informally processed, the juvenile must admit to the offense. There is strong pressure to do so, since a failure to admit to the offense may result in formal processing, with the possibility of an official record and more severe sanctions.

Informal processing (or diversion). Informally processed cases are dealt with in a number of ways. Most commonly, the juvenile is placed on **informal probation** for a brief period, say, 90 days. The juvenile is supervised in the community by a probation officer, who may provide some counseling to the juvenile and perhaps will require the juvenile to attend school regularly, abide by a curfew, attend a drug treatment program, participate in family counseling, or make restitution to the victim. Some informally processed offenders, though not placed on informal probation, are nevertheless required to apologize and make monetary restitution to the victim of their crime, or otherwise accept responsibility for the offense. If the juvenile successfully completes informal probation or meets the requirements of the court, the case is usually dismissed.

Many juvenile courts have set up *diversion programs* for informally processed offenders. Such programs offer services like individual and family counseling, mentoring, tutoring, treatment for substance abuse, and employment counseling (Lundman, 2001; Mears, 2012; C. Sullivan et al., 2007). The programs may be run by the court, by community organizations, and/or by volunteers in the community (with court supervision). Some communities have established local assessment centers where juveniles and their families can gain access to these programs. The centers offer "one-stop shopping": diverted youth are sent to a center for evaluation, and placement in the appropriate programs can be arranged (see Dembo et al., 2004; Oldenettel and Wordes, 1999).

Diversion programs serve to change the course of youth who have landed in the court system: by avoiding formal processing, they will not be stigmatized with the "delinquent" label. Diversion programs, then, partly derive from labeling theory. Such programs are also designed to save money, since diverting youth from the court is usually cheaper than formally processing them. Further, diversion programs are said to free court staff to focus on more serious cases. Many of the youth diverted into these programs, however, would have been released by the court in the past rather than made to undergo formal processing. So diversion programs often do not save as much money or staff time as expected.

Two examples of diversion programs are presented next.

Teen courts are increasingly popular, with well over a thousand now in existence throughout the United States. Such courts are affiliated with juvenile courts, police departments, schools, and private nonprofit organizations like the YMCA. Teen courts usually receive referrals from intake officers at juvenile courts, although they may also receive referrals from the police and school officials. Referred youth are typically first-time offenders charged with minor offenses like shoplifting, minor assault (fighting), disorderly conduct, and possession of alcohol. And these youth have usually admitted to their offenses. Teen courts, then, usually do not determine whether youth are guilty or innocent of the charged offense. Rather, teen courts hear the facts surrounding the offense and determine the disposition or sentence the youth will receive. Teen courts are run in a variety of ways, but in most cases an adult supervises courtroom activities and oversees the court. Teenagers, however, serve as lawyers and jurors. In particular, teenagers question the youth about the offense and teenagers on the jury determine the youth's disposition. Community service is the most common disposition, followed by apologizing to the victim, writing an essay related to the offense, serving on a teen-court jury, attending drug/alcohol classes, and making monetary restitution. Part of the appeal of teen courts is the belief that many youth are more strongly influenced by their peers than by adult authority figures. Also, teen courts encourage youth to become more involved in crime control.

The initial evaluations of teen courts were promising (Butts and Buck, 2000). But more recent and rigorous evaluations have raised questions about their effectiveness. In fact, several studies find that offenders referred to teen court often have a *higher* rate of recidivism than those who experienced traditional juvenile court sanctions (e.g., Stickle et al., 2008; Denise Wilson et al., 2009). The reasons for this outcome are not yet clear, but one possibility is that, while teen courts may allow young offenders to avoid formal or official labeling, these offenders may experience *informal* labeling by their peers. For example, they may perceive that they are being punished, embarrassed, and negatively labeled by conventional peers, which may increase their attraction to delinquent peers. Teen courts, then, should proceed with caution.[2]

Civil citation has been established in a number of states to deal with the "excessive" number of young persons referred to juvenile court for minor offenses. Civil citation, first adopted by the state of Florida in 2011, expands the options available to police officers. In response to minor offenses, police can make an arrest, file a formal complaint, do nothing, or issue a citation that requires the juvenile to report to a "civil citation coordinator." Provided the juvenile admits guilt, the coordinator places him or her in a diversion program, which may involve community service, participation in a drug treatment program, or other mandated action. Juveniles who successfully complete the terms of a diversion can avoid the acquisition of an arrest record. However, if the juvenile refuses to accept the citation, or fails to comply with the terms of diversion, the result may be arrest and formal processing by the court. As civil citation is a fairly recent development, it is too early to say whether the measure is or is not effective (Mears et al., 2016).

As suggested, existing evaluations of diversion programs have produced mixed results. Certain diversion programs do not appear to reduce subsequent offending. Other programs appear to reduce subsequent offending more than the alternatives of releasing or formally processing juveniles. The more effective programs seem to make a concerted effort to address the known causes of delinquency. Nevertheless, we can cite two reviews that examined a wide range of diversion programs and compared their effectiveness. Petrosina et al. (2010) and Wilson and Hoge (2013) concluded that diversion programs as a whole are more effective in reducing recidivism or reoffending than is formal processing, with some evidence that the more effective diversion programs are those that provide services to juveniles—such as family counseling, educational assistance, or restorative justice conferencing (see Chapter 24). It is not entirely clear why diversion programs are more effective, although the reviews note that participation in these programs makes it easier for some juveniles to avoid negative labeling. Juvenile courts, then, may want to consider making greater use of diversion, although more research is needed here, particularly research that identifies the characteristics of the most successful diversion programs.

Detention hearing. If the case is to be formally processed, the intake officer must also decide whether to release the juvenile to his or her parents or guardians or to detain him or her until trial. If the intake officer decides to detain the juvenile, there must be a detention hearing within a short period of time (one to three days in most states). The hearing is held before a juvenile court judge and is designed to determine whether the juvenile should continue to be held in detention.

The judge considers whether there is probable cause to believe that the juvenile committed the offense and whether there is good reason for continued detention. In particular, the judge asks whether the juvenile poses a threat to the community, whether the juvenile might flee if released, and whether the juvenile would be in any danger if released. (Note: The Supreme Court has ruled that juveniles do not have the right to be released on bail, although certain individual states grant juveniles that right.)

Detention facilities. If the judge decides that detention is warranted, the juvenile may be detained in a secure facility or detention center, which is like an adult jail. For example, juveniles are typically held in locked cells with bars on the windows. The conditions in these detention centers are sometimes quite bad: many centers are overcrowded; many have inadequate educational programs, health services, and/or treatment services; and many are plagued by violence (see Acoca, 1998; Barton, 2012; Holman and Ziedenberg, 2007). In our home state of Georgia, detentions centers have had a history of such problems. A newspaper article reported the following conditions.

> A report issued last week by an independent monitor . . . examined the state's 32 juvenile detention facilities, which housed 33,888 inmates . . . and found that more than half the 105 citations the state agreed to fix two years ago are still incomplete. . . . The facilities lack necessary educational and mental health services and were severely overcrowded—some almost double their capacity; 7,864 incidents in juvenile facilities that could harm juvenile inmates, including the use of force by guards and youth-on-youth assaults, were reported in the first six months of this year . . . state records show that there are hundreds of suicide attempts inside the state's detention facilities each year. . . . The report shows that there are problems everywhere, but nowhere are the problems more severe than in Metro [in the Atlanta area], the largest short-term facility in the state with 217 youths. "You have to watch your back at Metro, because there are boys in there that'll kill you over Oreo cookies," said [a detainee] . . . many of the children incarcerated at detention facilities—particularly at Metro—suffer serious physical and mental trauma inside. (Dyer, 2000:A10)

Some towns or cities lack juvenile detention centers, which means that juveniles may be detained in adult jails. Federal regulations require that such juveniles have no sight or sound contact with the jailed adults. There is some evidence that placement in detention, especially large, secure facilities, increases the likelihood of further delinquency (Barton, 2012). This may be because detained juveniles are exposed to serious offenders and are more subject to negative labeling. Also, juveniles placed in detention tend to receive harsher sanctions by the court, even after taking account of the offense history and other characteristics. This is perhaps a labeling effect, with such juveniles seen as a greater threat by court workers.

Given the problems with detention, there have been efforts to both improve detention facilities and reduce the use of detention (Barton, 2012). Efforts to reduce detention usually involve the development of explicit criteria for detaining youth, with these criteria limiting detention to more serious cases. And they involve the development of alternatives to secure detention. One such alternative is home detention. Juveniles are required to remain at home, except for school, work, or emergencies. They are regularly visited by court staff, and they may be subject to electronic monitoring. That is, they may be fitted with an electronic wrist or ankle bracelet, which alerts authorities if they leave home. Another alternative involves after-school and evening reporting centers, where youth are supervised, provided with positive activities, and sometimes offered counseling and other services. Yet another alternative involves placement in nonsecure facilities, such as group and foster homes. This is especially suitable for youth whose parents refuse to bring them home or might harm them.

Twenty-one percent of all delinquency cases referred to the court in 2013 resulted in detention. About 19 percent of whites and 25 percent of African Americans were detained.

(We discuss possible reasons for this difference in Chapter 22.) And about 23 percent of males and 16 percent of females were detained. A total of 221,600 juveniles were detained for delinquent offenses in 2013. And there were about 17,803 juveniles in detention on October 23, 2013—the date of a census of juveniles in residential placement conducted by the Office of Juvenile Justice and Delinquency Prevention (Hockenberry, 2016).

Status offense cases are much less likely to result in detention than delinquency cases, although some formally processed status offenders are detained. In 2013, 7 percent of formally processed status offense cases resulted in detention. Federal regulations strongly discourage the detention of status offenders, and there has been a dramatic decrease since the 1970s in the number of status offenders who are detained (although see the discussion of status offenders and out-of-home placements later in this chapter).

Petition. If a case is going to be formally processed, the intake officer or prosecutor will prepare a formal petition. The *petition* describes the offense or offenses that brought the youth to juvenile court. The juvenile is often brought to court, is presented with the charges in the formal petition, and is informed of his or her rights, such as the right to have an attorney. Most juveniles end up admitting to the charges in the petition, either at this initial hearing or at a later date.

Waiver. Some juvenile offenders have their cases waived or sent to adult criminal court. This is especially likely to happen to older juveniles who commit serious violent crimes and/or have long prior records. Waiver to adult court can occur in three major ways.

> *Judicial waiver.* In most states, juvenile court judges can transfer cases that meet certain criteria to adult court. The judge must hold a waiver hearing, usually after intake and petition. Guidelines usually limit waivers to juveniles above a certain age who are accused of certain offenses—like felonies or serious crimes. When deciding to waive a case, judges and prosecutors usually ask whether there is probable cause to believe that the juvenile has committed the offense and whether the juvenile is "amenable to treatment" by the juvenile court. That is, can the juvenile court help the juvenile? Among other things, judges consider the juvenile's offense, prior record, prior dispositions or sentences, age, and the resources available to the juvenile court. Juveniles may be ruled not amenable to treatment if they have already committed a number of offenses and have not responded to treatment efforts of the court. About 4,000 cases, or less than 1 percent of all formally processed cases, were judicially waived to adult court in 2013.
>
> *Prosecutor discretion* (also known as concurrent jurisdiction and direct file). In a smaller number of states, prosecutors are allowed to determine whether cases that meet certain criteria will be tried in juvenile or adult court. Typically, the cases involve older juveniles who commit certain serious crimes. Prosecutors decide where to try such cases at intake or shortly thereafter. No special hearing is required when prosecutor discretion is employed. We do not know how many cases are waived to adult court by prosecutors, although the number is believed to greatly exceed the number of judicial waivers in those states where prosecutor discretion exists.[3]
>
> *Statutory waiver.* Many state legislatures have passed laws stating that certain juvenile offenders will automatically be sent to adult court. Typically, such laws state that the juveniles be above a certain age and be accused of certain serious offenses, usually violent offenses. In our home state of Georgia, for example, juveniles age 13 and above who commit one of the "seven deadly sins" are automatically sent to adult court. The seven deadly sins are murder, voluntary manslaughter, rape, aggravated sodomy, aggravated child molestation, aggravated sexual battery, and armed robbery committed with a firearm. Juveniles who commit one of these offenses are taken

directly to the adult system by the police. Once more, it is not known how many cases are waived to adult court through statutory waiver. In certain states, however, the number of cases waived through statutory waiver far exceeds the number of cases waived by judges.[4]

The most extreme form of statutory waiver requires that all "juveniles" of a certain age be tried in adult court. Wisconsin, for example, passed a law in 1996 requiring that all 17-year-old offenders be tried in adult court (they had been under the jurisdiction of the juvenile court). Six other states now exclude 17-year-olds from juvenile court jurisdiction; New York and North Carolina also exclude 16-year-olds. It is has been estimated that each year, well over 100,000 16- and 17-year-old offenders have their cases prosecuted in adult court (Griffin et al., 2011).[5]

As we discuss in Chapter 23, data suggest that trying juveniles in adult court does not necessarily deter them from further offending. In fact, some studies find that juveniles tried as adults have higher rates of reoffending, especially violent offending, than comparable juveniles tried in juvenile court.[6]

Adjudication. Adjudication is the juvenile equivalent of an adult trial. It is a hearing before the juvenile court judge to determine whether the juvenile committed the offense(s) described in the petition. Most juveniles admit to the offense(s), so a full hearing is seldom necessary. Juveniles sometimes admit to the offense(s) as part of a plea bargain; that is, they admit to the offense in exchange for a reduction in sentence (e.g., probation instead of incarceration) and/or a reduction in charges (e.g., simple assault instead of aggravated assault). If it is determined that the juvenile committed the offense, the juvenile is not found "guilty" of that specific offense; rather, he or she is **"adjudicated delinquent."** For example, juveniles are not found guilty of robbery or assault. Guilt implies that one is responsible for the offense and deserves punishment. Rather, juveniles are adjudicated delinquent. (States use the term "delinquent" for juveniles who have committed offenses that would be crimes if committed by adults. Juveniles who commit status offenses are usually referred to by such other terms as "persons in need of supervision" or "children in need of supervision.")

As discussed in Chapter 1, juvenile court hearings used to be relatively informal—very different from proceedings in adult court. In particular, juveniles had few *due process rights*, such as the right to an attorney and the right to present and cross-examine witnesses. Also, the standard of proof was lower in juvenile court than in adult court. Rather than "proof beyond a reasonable doubt," the juvenile court required only a "preponderance of evidence." The rationale behind these differences was that the juvenile court was set up to assist rather than punish the juvenile. Therefore, the legal protections available in adult court were not necessary.

These informal practices changed somewhat during the 1960s and 1970s, when a series of Supreme Court decisions extended several due process rights to juveniles, particularly at the adjudicatory stage. The Supreme Court essentially said that the juvenile court often does punish juveniles; for example, by confining them in institutions that offer little in the way of treatment. Juveniles therefore should receive many of the same due process protections as adults. The most influential of these decisions was the *Gault* **decision** in 1967:

Gerald Gault was a 15-year-old boy living in Arizona. In 1964, he and a friend called his neighbor, Ms. Cook, and asked her: "Do you give any?" "Are your cherries ripe today?" and "Do you have big bombers?" Gerald was arrested and tried in juvenile court. Among other things, Gerald never received notice of the charges against him ("lewd phone calls"), was not advised of his right to counsel, was not advised of his right to remain silent, and did not have the opportunity to confront and cross-examine Ms. Cook. The juvenile court judge adjudicated Gerald a delinquent and committed him to the State Industrial School for a period up to six years. If Gerald had been tried as an adult, the maximum penalty would have been a small fine and two months' imprisonment. The Supreme Court considered Gerald's case and decided that he had been unjustly denied certain due process rights. In particular, the Supreme Court ruled that in adjudicatory hearings that might result in commitment to an institution, juveniles have (1) the right to notification of the charges against them, (2) the right to an attorney—with the state providing an attorney if the juvenile's family cannot afford one, (3) the right to confront and cross-examine witnesses, and (4) the right against self-incrimination (i.e., the right to remain silent).

Juveniles have been extended other due process rights by the Supreme Court, like the right to proof "beyond a reasonable doubt" (see Bernard and Kurlychek, 2010; and Feld, 2012, for overviews of the rights of juveniles). Juvenile court hearings have become more formal, more like those in adult courts, as a result of these Supreme Court decisions.

Juveniles, however, still do not have all the due process rights available to adults. Most notably, they lack the right to a **trial by jury** (although certain individual states grant this right to juveniles). The Supreme Court recognized that there is still some difference between the goals of juvenile and adult courts, with the juvenile court focusing more on the rehabilitation of the child. It was felt that "juries would be highly disruptive of the informal, cooperative atmosphere in which everyone tried to find the child's best interests, and would tend to create an adversarial atmosphere in which each side attempted to win the case" (Bernard and Kurlychek, 2010:112).

Furthermore, research suggests that some juvenile courts fail to provide juveniles with certain rights that have been granted to them; that juveniles often elect not to exercise their rights, often with the encouragement of court officials; and that the quality of legal representation for juveniles is often poor (Feld, 2012). These points were amplified in an editorial in the *New York Times* written decades after the Gault case:

> The American Bar Foundation, in new studies, has found that juvenile defendants have woefully inadequate representation. . . . Young defendants often lack lawyers at key stages, or meet them for the first time in court. The lawyers often have excessive caseloads and inadequate investigative resources. And many of the lawyers are not trained about alternatives to incarceration for their juvenile clients. (*New York Times,* 2003)

In addition, while juvenile court proceedings have become more formal in recent years, they remain less formal than criminal court proceedings. This point was made by Kupchik (2006), who observed several juvenile and adult criminal courts in the Northeast. Kupchik found that the lawyers and judges in juvenile court spend much less time on "legal housekeeping" matters, such as filing formal motions about the admissibility of evidence. Instead, their time goes to simply talking with one another about the juvenile, the juvenile's offense, and possible dispositions (sentences). And in talking with one another, they employ "a far more relaxed conversational style than in criminal court and recognize fewer formalized status distinctions between judge, prosecutor, and defense" (Kupchik, 2006:55). The juvenile court judge also encourages the juvenile and his or her parents to play an active role in the proceedings. The judge, for example, may ask the parents how the child behaves at home, may ask the child about problems at home and school, and may ask the juvenile and parents what they want to happen as a result of the proceedings at hand. So while the juvenile court has become more formal in recent years and juveniles have more due process rights, the juvenile court is still less formal than adult court and places less emphasis on due process rights.

About 55 percent of the cases involving juveniles that are formally processed result in an adjudication of delinquency. The remaining cases are dealt with informally or dismissed.

For example, the judge will sometimes withhold adjudication and place a juvenile on informal probation or require that the juvenile make restitution to the victim. If the juvenile successfully completes probation or makes restitution, the judge will refrain from adjudicating the juvenile a delinquent.

Social history or predisposition report.   Once a juvenile has been adjudicated delinquent, a probation officer will complete a social history or predisposition report. The report is supposed to provide a detailed picture of the juvenile and his or her problems, and to suggest supervision and treatment plans. The judge uses the report to decide on an appropriate sentence, or "disposition." The disposition process is not designed simply to punish juveniles for offenses committed. Rather, it aims to deal with the problems that cause juveniles to get into trouble with the law. The probation officer who writes the social history of each juvenile will explore family environment, school environment, peer relations, neighborhood, and prior history with the court. The juvenile may also undergo a psychological examination.

Risk and needs assessments   Increasingly, juvenile court staff are making use of risk and needs assessment instruments in deciding how to respond to adjudicated offenders. **Risk assessment instruments** attempt to predict the likelihood that a given juvenile will commit offenses in the future. These instruments measure a juvenile's standing on a number of factors found to predict future offending in that particular court or in a sample of juvenile courts. Such instruments are generally more accurate in predicting future offending than the judgments of court workers.[7] Some risk assessment instruments are relatively simple, containing a few predictors, while others contain scores of predictors. Research suggests that the simpler instruments perform as well as or better than the complex instruments (Baird et al., 2013). Some of the factors commonly found to predict future offending include the following:

- Prior court referral or adjudication at a young age.
- Prior record of offenses.
- Parental or sibling criminality.
- Victim of child abuse or neglect.
- Substance abuse.
- Prior out-of-home placements.
- Poor family relations and parental supervision.
- Running away.
- School problems (low grades, poor attendance, behavioral problems).
- Association with delinquent peers.

(Note: The seriousness of the juvenile's current offense is usually not a good predictor of future offending.)

Limited data suggest that there may be some male/female differences in the predictors of offending, with child abuse and neglect, substance abuse, and running away having a stronger effect on female offending (Funk, 1999; Van der Put et al., 2014). Researchers have examined how well risk assessment instruments predict future offending among females, since many of these instruments were developed using male or largely male samples. A recent study suggests that many, although not all, instruments perform well with females—with some instruments having items with special relevance for females (Brumbaugh et al., 2009).

Based on their score on the risk assessment instrument, juveniles are said to be at low risk, medium risk, or high risk for future offending. The high-risk juveniles are then subjected to greater supervision. For example, they may be required to meet with their probation officer twice a week—while the low-risk juveniles may have to meet with their probation officer only once a month. Risk assessment instruments are also starting to be employed at other stages of the court process. For example, these instruments (or variations of them) are sometimes used by intake officials to help determine whether juveniles should be formally or informally processed or whether detainment would be preferable (see Mears and Kelly, 1999). *Needs assessment instruments* **list the factors known to cause delinquency, such as problems with family, school, and peers.** Such instruments help the court staff develop a treatment plan for each juvenile by identifying the areas in which the juvenile is most in need of assistance. There is, of course, some overlap between risk and needs assessment instruments—but there are some differences as well. Some predictors of future offending (e.g., age at first court referral) are not major causes of delinquency, although they are associated with major causes of delinquency (e.g., low self-control).

Risk and needs assessment instruments are said to improve the decisions made by the court staff, since the instruments take explicit account of the research on the causes and prediction of delinquency. Also, these instruments are said to increase the likelihood that juvenile offenders will be treated fairly. For example, risk assessment instruments increase the likelihood that the juvenile's level of supervision will be based on factors known to predict future offending—and not on the personal feelings and possibly the prejudices of the court staff. Such instruments, however, do not eliminate input from the court staff—the staff is typically given the option of modifying or overriding the recommendations derived from these instruments if they can make a compelling case for doing so.

While these instruments are partly designed to reduce the likelihood of discriminatory actions by court staff, concern has been raised about their impact on the treatment of African American offenders (Moore and Padavic, 2011). Certain of the items in risk assessment instruments may be correlated with race. For example, some instruments assign a higher risk score to individuals who live in single-parent versus two-parent families. African American juveniles are more likely to live in single-parent families, so the use of risk instruments may still result in the harsher treatment of African Americans. Consequently, some attention has been devoted to developing instruments that minimize this race effect. For example, instead of asking whether the juvenile lives with one or two parents, instruments might ask if there is a parent willing to assume responsibility for caring for the juvenile.

We have described the major stages in the juvenile court process up to the preparation of the social history or predisposition report. The final stage is the disposition or sentence given to the juvenile, and that brings us to a consideration of the juvenile justice system.

JUVENILE CORRECTIONS: WHAT HAPPENS TO JUVENILES WHO RECEIVE A DISPOSITION OR SENTENCE FROM THE COURT?

The judge has a number of sentencing or disposition options, ranging from verbal reprimand to incarceration. In 2013, 64 percent of adjudicated delinquents were placed on probation; 24 percent were placed in out-of-home facilities; and 12 percent were subject to other sanctions, such as fines, community service, or treatment and counseling of various types (without probation).

Formal Probation

The most commonly used sentencing option is formal *probation*, which involves the supervision and treatment of the juvenile in the community by a probation officer. Well over half of all adjudicated delinquents were placed on formal probation in 2013. As indicated earlier, a large number of juveniles were also placed on informal probation. In particular, many of the juvenile offenders not formally processed by the court are placed on informal probation.

Juveniles placed on formal probation are asked to satisfy certain conditions. Such conditions may include reporting to their probation officer at regular intervals, attending school regularly, being home at a certain hour every day, and not associating with certain people. The juvenile may also be required to participate in counseling programs, drug treatment, after-school, and similar programs that provide a range of services. The conditions of probation must be reasonable and relevant to the juvenile's offense.

A juvenile on probation meets with his or her probation officer anywhere from several times a week to once a month or less often. Probation officers have two major functions or tasks (see Steiner et al., 2003, for information on the functions of probation officers). The first is to supervise the juveniles in their charge, making sure the youth do not commit new offenses or violate the conditions of their probation. If offenses or violations are detected, probation may be revoked and the juveniles may face more severe sanctions, such as being sent to an institution. The second function of probation officers is to assist the juveniles by helping them overcome the problems that contributed to their delinquency. Not surprisingly, many probation officers experience problems reconciling these two functions. On the one hand, they are expected to play the role of law enforcer, supervising juveniles and sanctioning them if they misbehave. On the other hand, they are expected to play the role of social worker, helping juveniles in need. Some probation officers deal with the tension between these roles by emphasizing one function over the other. So some probation officers act more like "tough cops," while others act more like "caring social workers."

Although probation is supposed to offer juveniles supervision and assistance in the community, probation officers often have heavy caseloads, and many provide little in the way of supervision or assistance. In many juvenile courts, formal probation often involves little more than doing nothing to the juvenile. It is therefore not surprising that formal probation does little to lower rates of reoffending (Greenwood and Turner, 2012; Lipsey, 1992; also see Kurlychek et al., 1999).

Intermediate Sanctions

During the 1980s and 1990s, most juvenile courts developed a range of *intermediate sanctions*. These sanctions, designed to provide more control and punishment than juveniles receive on formal probation, were supposed to be less extreme and less costly than confinement in an institution. Sanctions included restitution (e.g., requiring a juvenile to make a monetary payment to the victim) and participation in Scared Straight programs, intensive supervision programs—often combined with home confinement—and military-style boot camps. To illustrate, *intensive supervision programs* (ISPs) are run by probation officers with small caseloads. Juveniles in ISPs are subject to frequent home visits and, in many programs, random drug tests. In some cases, juveniles may be confined to their homes except for school, emergencies, and possibly work. Confinement may be enforced through electronic monitoring. A tamperproof strap with a transmitting device may be attached to the juvenile's wrist or ankle. The device signals a receiver if the juvenile leaves his or her home when this is not supposed to happen.

Although certain intermediate sanctions provide treatment to juveniles, most focus on control and punishment. The sanctions have proved reasonably popular. On the one hand, they satisfy the demand for controlling and punishing juvenile offenders, especially serious offenders. On the other hand, they are much cheaper than incarceration. It now costs more than $100,000 a year, on average, to confine a juvenile offender. Intermediate sanctions can be maintained for a fraction of that amount. Certain sanctions, in fact, were explicitly developed as alternatives to institutions, with the idea that they would

save money and reduce overcrowding in institutions. So, rather than sending an offender to an institution, a judge might place the offender in an intensive supervision program. Intermediate sanctions, however, have not saved as much money as anticipated because they are frequently used for juveniles who otherwise would have been placed on formal or "regular" probation.

Evaluations of intermediate sanctions generally have not produced promising results. Some data suggest that fines and restitution do lower future offending, but only by a small amount. Scared Straight programs actually increase subsequent offending (see Chapter 19). Most data suggest that intensive supervision programs have little effect on rates of reoffending if not combined with rehabilitation efforts. And since data indicate that military-style boot camps do not reduce future offending, this type of ISP has fallen out of favor. In fact, several years ago, our home state of Georgia abandoned the use of boot camps for juveniles because of evidence pointing to their lack of effectiveness.

At a general level, evaluation data suggest that programs that focus on punishing juveniles, scaring them, or controlling them are not effective at reducing offending. When these programs are combined with efforts to treat or rehabilitate juveniles, they do sometimes work. But simply getting tough is no more effective than traditional methods at reducing repeat offending.[8] Chapter 23 discusses some of the reasons why such get-tough programs are not effective in reducing reoffending.

A Renewed Focus on Rehabilitation

As noted in Chapter 1, there has been a renewed focus on rehabilitating juvenile offenders since the early 2000s. This change stems partly from data suggesting that punitive approaches are ineffective and partly from new evaluation research, which suggests that *certain* rehabilitation programs are effective in reducing delinquency. Further, rehabilitation programs typically cost less to run than punitive approaches, and they more than pay for themselves over time by preventing or mitigating delinquency and other problems, such as school failure. Rehab programs address the many causes of delinquency discussed in Chapters 6 through 17, including individual, family, school, and peer problems. For example, they teach juveniles how to better manage their anger and exercise self-control, teach parents how to better supervise their children and build stronger bonds to them, and help juveniles perform better in school.

Rehabilitation programs may be used with youth who are diverted from the juvenile court or are placed on probation. They may be used in conjunction with drug and mental health courts—specialized facilities that focus on responding to youth with problems in those areas (see Butts et al., 2012). And they may be used with juveniles placed in residential facilities. Such programs are discussed further in Chapter 24.

Out-of-Home Placements

In 2013, 24 percent of adjudicated delinquents were placed outside their homes, in residential facilities; that amounts to 78,700 delinquents. These juveniles were placed in a range of public and private residential facilities, including group homes, wilderness programs, and training schools.

A census of juveniles in correctional facilities found that 54,148 delinquents and status offenders were serving sentences in juvenile correctional facilities on October 23, 2013. The census surveyed 991 public and 956 private facilities. Although there are nearly as many private facilities as public facilities, most of the confined juveniles were in public facilities (which are larger, on average, than private facilities). The median length of stay in these institutions on the day of the census was about 4 months (half the juveniles had been in longer, and half for less time).

As indicated earlier, 17,803 juveniles were being **detained** in juvenile facilities on October 23, 2013. So, about 72,000 juveniles were serving sentences or being detained in juvenile correctional facilities on that date. This amounts to about two juveniles for every thousand in the population (about one-fourth the confinement rate for adults).

What offenses are juveniles confined for? According to the 2013 census, about 95 percent of juveniles serving sentences in correctional facilities were there for delinquent offenses. The remaining 5 percent were there for status offenses. About 25 percent of the juveniles were confined for serious violent crimes (homicide, sexual assault, robbery, aggravated assault). Juveniles were also confined for property crimes (24 percent), violations of probation, parole, and court orders (17 percent), and offenses involving simple assault, drugs, alcohol, and weapons. **Contrary to popular belief, most confined juveniles are not being held for violent crimes.**

The confinement of status offenders. Federal guidelines strongly discourage the confinement of status offenders. While these guidelines have been largely adhered to, some status offenders are nevertheless confined (see H. Snyder and Sickmund, 2006:178). Further, juvenile courts will sometimes charge status offenders with minor criminal offenses, for which they can be confined without violating the guidelines. For example, ungovernable children might be charged with simple assault if they have threatened their parents at some point. Also, status offenders who violate the conditions of their probation can be charged with violation of probation, which allows confinement. For example, a truant may be placed on probation, with the requirement that he or she attend school regularly. If the truant fails to attend school, he or she can then be charged with violation of probation and sent to an institution (see Bernard and Kurlychek, 2010). In addition, many nonadjudicated delinquents and status offenders are placed outside the home. Parents, for example, may agree to voluntarily place their sons or daughters in private out-of-home facilities, including mental health facilities. In exchange, the court does not formally process the case, or it withholds adjudication. Many criminologists feel that such "voluntary" placements are becoming increasingly common—especially for females and status offenders (see Chesney-Lind and Shelden, 2004).

What are the demographic characteristics of confined juveniles? In 2013, about 86 percent of all confined juveniles were male. About 40 percent were African

American, 32 percent were non-Hispanic whites, 23 percent were Latino, 1 percent were Asian, and 2 percent were Native American. If we consider custody rates, focusing on juveniles serving sentences in correctional facilities, we find that 2.9 African Americans were confined for every 1,000 African American juveniles, 2.5 Native Americans for every 1,000 Native American juveniles, 1.1 Latinos for every 1,000 Latino juveniles, 0.69 white for every 1,000 white juveniles, and about 0.2 Asian for every 1,000 Asian juveniles. African Americans, then, have the highest rate of confinement, about 2.5 times that of Latinos and about 4 times that of whites. Also, previous research indicates that African Americans and Latinos are more likely than whites to be confined in public facilities. Public facilities tend to be larger, more secure, more crowded, and less oriented to treatment than private facilities (see Sickmund, 2006).

What are juvenile correctional facilities like? Juvenile correctional facilities tend to differ from adult prisons in several important ways (see Caeti et al., 2003; Kupchik, 2007; Snyder and Sickmund, 2006). Most notably, juvenile facilities place more emphasis on treatment and less on punishment and control. Juvenile facilities are also typically smaller than adult prisons and have lower staff-to-resident ratios. It is important to emphasize, however, that juvenile facilities are not all alike; they differ from one another along a number of dimensions. Although some house as few as 10 to 20 juveniles, others can accommodate several hundred. Some provide a moderate amount of freedom, with juveniles attending school in the community and having much liberty to move around the facility. Others are like adult prisons, surrounded by a fence; juveniles are held in secure cells, and their movement about the institution is closely controlled. Some institutions place much emphasis on treatment, while others focus on control and punishment. Some are well run, while others suffer from a host of problems, such as overcrowding, violence, and inadequate educational, health, recreational, and treatment services. Unfortunately, data suggest that a large percentage of offenders are confined in overcrowded institutions that struggle with a range of problems (see especially Krisberg, 2012).[9] For example, data from the 2010 census of juvenile facilities produced the following estimate: that 15 percent of all confined juveniles were in crowded facilities (Hockenberry et al., 2013).

One type of juvenile facility is the *group home or halfway house*, usually a nonsecure facility housing a small number of juveniles. Group homes and halfway houses are quite similar, except that juveniles are typically sent to a group home instead of a more secure institution, and sent to a halfway house after serving time in an institution. Their stay in the halfway house is designed to ease their transition back into the community. Juveniles live in the group home or halfway house, receiving counseling and other services. But they usually attend school in the community. The small size of the house often allows juveniles to build a close relationship with the staff. Forty-four percent of the juveniles who receive out-of-home placements are in group homes.

Wilderness or outdoor programs provide juveniles with physically challenging activities, such as rock climbing and ocean sailing. The participants are usually part of a small group of juveniles; they learn to work together, follow directions, and overcome challenges that are designed to increase their coping skills and self-esteem (see MacKenzie and Freeland, 2012; J. Roberts, 1998). Some wilderness programs last only a week or so, while others last more than a year, often involving outdoor work like maintaining and restoring wilderness areas. About 4 percent of the juveniles who receive out-of-home placements are in wilderness programs.

Training schools are most like adult prisons. (Training schools are called by different names in different states; in your state they may be called youth development centers, youth centers, reformatories, or the like.) Many are large, focus on security, do not offer adequate treatment, and suffer from a host of other problems—including staff-on-inmate violence and inmate-on-inmate violence. The juveniles in such institutions often develop a subculture that discourages cooperation with the staff, encourages the exploitation of weaker inmates, and rewards toughness. Further, as indicated earlier, such institutions are expensive.

Inderbitzin, who studied a maximum-security training school, provides a rough sense of what many such institutions are like:

> The institution in this study is very much a juvenile prison. The perimeter of the campus is clearly defined by a tall fence with razor wire coiled around the top. Specialized security staff monitors the double-gated entrance and all movement within the walls. At the time of this study there were about 200 boys sentenced to this training school. . . . Based on his offense, each youth was assigned to a "cottage" living unit, which would be his home during his incarceration. The boys would attend school, work a job somewhere within the institution, go to recreation for one hour a day at the central gym, and eat their meals in the institution's main cafeteria, but each night they would return to their cottage. Cottages generally consisted of a common living room area where the boys would watch television and hold group meetings and counseling sessions; a small kitchen area where they could fix snacks; a game room which held a pool table and a video game; a small laundry room; a bathroom; and a hallway of sixteen locked rooms. While there was some freedom of movement within the common areas of cottages at designated times, the outside doors of the cottages were locked at all times and windows in the rooms had bars on them. (Inderbitzin, 2005:5)

Occasionally, the public learns of problems in certain training schools (Halbfinger, 2003; Krisberg, 2012; MacKenzie and Freeland, 2012). In New York, a governor-appointed task force highlighted a range of serious problems. The findings of the task force were summarized in the following manner:

> Youngsters in custody were routinely assaulted by staffers. Beatings were so severe that teeth were knocked out, bones were broken, and some kids were rendered unconscious. The assaults were sometimes sparked by infractions no more serious than laughing or stealing a cookie. . . . It would be nice if New York, and its mistreatment of young offenders, were an isolated case. But it's not. Earlier this month the Bureau

of Justice Statistics reported that some 13 percent of juveniles in confinement suffered sexual victimization, the vast majority (80 percent) from the people charged with their care. The BJS report . . . is only one in a growing series of studies pointing out massive flaws in America's juvenile-justice system. (Close, 2010)

About 36 percent of juveniles who receive out-of-home placements are in training schools. (Note: About 11 percent of juveniles who receive out-of-home placements are in detention centers; some are awaiting transfer to other facilities and others are serving brief sentences in the detention centers.)

How do the institutional experiences of males and females compare? Most confined juveniles are male, and they tend to be confined for somewhat different offenses than females. Males are much more likely than females to be confined for serious violent crimes: 28 percent of the institutionalized males are confined for such crimes versus 13 percent of the females. Females, on the other hand, are much more likely than males to be confined for status offenses: 11 percent of the institutionalized females are confined for such offenses versus 4 percent of the males. Females are also more likely to be confined for violations of probation or parole. As indicated earlier, probation violations are sometimes used as a device for confining status offenders (also see Chesney-Lind and Shelden, 2004). These offense differences partly reflect the fact that males are much more likely than females to commit serious violent crimes, while males and females have similar rates of status offending. But, as discussed in Chapter 22, these differences may also reflect discriminatory treatment by criminal justice officials, with males being treated more strictly for violent offenses and females for certain status offenses.

Institutionalized males and females suffer from many of the same problems, although data suggest that the **females are more likely to have been the victims of abuse and to have run away from home.** This reflects one of the key points made about gender and delinquency in Chapter 18: data suggest that abuse and running away from home play an especially important role in the generation of female delinquency, particularly serious delinquency. Females are more likely than males to be sexually abused and to run away from home to escape such mistreatment. Once on the street, female runaways experience further abuse and must often engage in income-generating crimes to survive (since they are too young to work and are wanted by the police). Unfortunately, confined females often receive little help in overcoming the effects of abuse. In fact, they often experience further abuse when institutionalized (see Chesney-Lind and Shelden, 2004; Kempf-Leonard, 2012; Krisberg, 2012; also see Gaarder et al., 2004).

More generally, **treatment programs are less available in female institutions than in those serving males.** And many of the training programs available in female institutions tend to be "limited to traditional feminine options like cosmetology, home economics, and 'business education' (generally simple secretarial training)" (Chesney-Lind and Shelden, 2004; Kempf-Leonard, 2012). At the same time, confined females face more restrictions on their behavior than do confined males, and staff makes a greater effort to influence the sexual practices and peer associations of confined females. These differences reflect a greater desire to regulate the sexual behavior of females.

Female and male offenders, then, may have somewhat different problems; but females' problems are often neglected in correctional institutions. Given these facts, **some criminologists argue that it is important to develop programs specifically geared toward the special needs and problems of females.** Several such programs have been developed, although most focus on at-risk females or females on probation (see Kempf-Leonard, 2012; Krisberg, 2005). And the Office of Juvenile Justice and

Delinquency Prevention (OJJDP) formed the "Girls Study Group," made up of scholars and juvenile justice workers with special expertise in the area of female delinquency. The group was charged with searching for and promoting programs that will more effectively respond to female delinquency. Several such programs were identified, and the OJJDP is supporting efforts to increase their use and to identify new programs. You can learn more about work in this area on an OJJDP website: http://www.ojjdp.gov/programs/girlsdelinquency.html.)

In general, there is growing recognition that childhood adversity can be traumatic for both boys and girls—including physical, sexual, or emotional abuse, as well as experiencing or witnessing violence, homelessness, and neglect. Traumatic experiences increase the risk of becoming involved in the juvenile justice system and influence how youth respond to punishment and confinement. Many organizations now stress the need for the juvenile justice system to respond appropriately to such youth by providing "trauma-informed care" (see Box 21.1).

Box 21.1   The Case for Trauma-Informed Care

Studies indicate that traumatic experiences are prevalent in the lives of youth involved in the juvenile justice system. In a study of nearly 2,000 young people (ages 10–18) who were arrested and detained in Cook County, Chicago, Abram and her colleagues (2004) found that most of them (92.5 percent) had experienced a traumatic event. Further, the prevalence of trauma appears to be higher among justice-involved youth than among adolescents in the general community (Abram et al., 2004) .

Much of this trauma is related to young people's exposure to violence, either witnessing violent acts or being the direct victim of violence. These findings are important because exposure to violence has been linked to the development of post-traumatic stress disorder (PTSD), aggression, juvenile offending, and other negative outcomes. In the Cook County sample, **11 percent of the study participants met the clinical criteria (fear, horror, or a sense of helplessness in response to traumatic events) for PTSD within the previous year.**

Consider the following case.

One former juvenile offender . . . has scars that cover her arms—the only signs of healing from being locked away for half of her life. She is now 27. Each gash comes with its own story of questions, confusion and crisis that started when her brother molested her at the age of 12. The courts determined she was emotionally disturbed from her past, which also included physical abuse and repeated run-ins with the child welfare system, [this former offender] said.

Over six years, [the same woman] says she was placed in 22 facilities. . . . "They were just shipping me here, there, everywhere," she recalled. She says she caught a single charge—for assault—in a residential treatment center where she bloodied a staff member's nose during a fight. After that, she said she was labeled a menace, and it wasn't long before she started acting the part. She fought for sport, lashed out for attention, and did sexual favors for staff to get out of trouble.

From other girls, she said she learned to snort pills and how to feel a sense of relief from cutting her skin — with staplers, the metal ring from pencil erasers, or the broken tile from the floor. "It felt like I was releasing the pain from my insides," she explained. "When the blood comes out, it feels like you're crying." (Green, 2016)

(Continued)

(*Continued*)

The National Council of Juvenile and Family Court Judges published a guide for those working with such youth. The guide discusses the adverse impact of trauma on childhood development and highlights the following points:

1. **"There are mental health treatments that are effective in helping youth who are experiencing child traumatic stress.** . . . Trauma-focused, evidence-based treatments include the following components: psychoeducation, caregiver involvement and support, emotional regulation skills, anxiety management, cognitive processing, construction of a trauma narrative, and personal empowerment training." (quoted in Buffington et al., 2010, p. 9)
2. **"The juvenile justice system needs to be trauma-informed at all levels.** Such a juvenile justice system makes system-level changes to improve a youth's feelings of safety, reduce exposure to traumatic reminders, and help equip youth with supports and tools to cope with traumatic stress reactions. . . [Y]outh are less likely to benefit from rehabilitation services if the system they are involved in does not respond to their issues of safety and victimization." (quoted in Buffington et al., 2010, p. 12)

Question for Discussion

1. Groups and organizations that promote treatment and rehabilitation programs are sometimes accused of being "soft on crime." How would you defend trauma-informed care in the face of such an accusation? (Note: see Chapters 24 and 25 for general arguments in favor of prevention and rehabilitation efforts.)

How effective are juvenile facilities in reducing reoffending? Evaluations suggest that sending juveniles to training schools is no more effective at reducing offending than many community-based alternatives. Some data, in fact, suggest that it may be easier to reduce reoffending in community-based programs than in institutions. Reflecting these unsurprising data, juveniles released from training schools have reoffending rates ranging from 55 percent to 90 percent (Howell, 2003a:135; Krisberg, 2012; Snyder and Sickmund, 2006:234–235). The data on group homes are mixed; they reduce offending in some studies but not in others. Likewise, the data on wilderness programs are mixed. There is, however, some suggestion that wilderness programs and group homes with a strong treatment component may be effective in reducing reoffending (Howell, 2003a; D. MacKenzie, 2006). One example is described in Box 21.2.

A number of individuals and groups have recommended that the justice system reduce or eliminate the use of training schools for juveniles (see Greenwood, 2002; Krisberg, 2012). They point to the problems and expense associated with such schools, and they argue that the juveniles in these schools can be better handled in facilities of other types or in the community. One study of 14 states found that 31 percent of the juveniles confined in secure facilities scored low on a risk assessment scale designed to assess the test takers' likelihood of committing more delinquent acts (Krisberg and Howell, 1998). Based on the recommendations, several states have moved away from the use of large, secure training schools. They have placed most of their confined offenders in smaller, more treatment-oriented facilities in the community. Massachusetts adopted such an approach in the 1970s, and states such as Missouri, Pennsylvania, Vermont, Utah, Maryland, and Florida have followed suit (see Box 21.2). Many states, however, continue to confine substantial percentages of their adjudicated offenders in large, secure training schools.

Box 21.2 The Missouri Model: A Promising Alternative

Given the serious problems that have plagued many large and costly training schools—including violence, abuse, and high rates of recidivism—many states are exploring alternative forms of placement for their serious juvenile offenders. One promising alternative is the Missouri Model of care, which has been described as a "guiding light" for juvenile justice reform.

Like many other states, Missouri had confined its serious young offenders in a large correctional facility, but major problems with the facility came to light in the early 1980s. Adopting an alternative approach, the state embarked on a decades-long effort to overhaul its system of juvenile corrections, eventually developing a large number of small treatment centers dispersed across the state. These centers are designed to create safe, nonpunitive environments that are conducive to rehabilitation. They also allow juvenile offenders to be located near their homes so that family members can visit and stay involved in the treatment process. The philosophy guiding this approach is described by Missouri's former director of youth services:

> Everything we did was guided by a central belief: These are kids, even though they've committed some very adult-like behaviors. Let's find out how they got into this, and help them get out of it and lead productive lives. (Tim Decker quoted in Vestal, 2008)

Further, under the Missouri Model, staff members receive extensive training and are encouraged to adopt the therapeutic orientation of the model. For example, it is emphasized that everyone has a desire for approval, acceptance, and success. However, the juveniles in the care of institutions are often emotionally immature, have poor communication skills, and have difficulty expressing their feelings in a responsible manner. As a result, their opportunities for success have been limited. To encourage positive change it is important to help these juveniles develop their relationship and communication skills. For example, staff may frequently ask them to discuss their feelings and behaviors, help them to identify the emotional "triggers" that lead them to act out, and help them "develop the capacity to express their emotions clearly, calmly, and respectfully—even negative emotions like anger and fear" (Mendel, 2010:41).

Upon entering a treatment center, the juvenile works with trained staff members to develop an individualized treatment program that outlines specific goals to be completed before release. The juvenile may also participate in activities that are not always available in large training schools, such as family therapy, vocational training, educational programs, caring for pets, theater groups, and sporting events.

In addition, under the Missouri Model, an effort is made to assist the juvenile with reentry into the community. Upon release, many juveniles participate in an aftercare program. For example, they may enter a day treatment program and receive guidance and support from a mentor in the community. (To learn more about the many distinctive features of the Missouri Model, see Mendel, 2010.)

By following this model, it appears that Missouri has benefited from a relatively low rate of juvenile recidivism, especially in comparison to states that have maintained large, prison-style facilities (see Mendel, 2010). It is believed that lower rates of juvenile reoffending, in turn, have produced considerable cost savings over the long run, resulting in lower criminal justice expenditures.

Given these advantages, the Missouri Model has attracted much attention. In 2008, it was recognized with a prestigious Innovations in American Government award by

(Continued)

(Continued)

Harvard University's Kennedy School of Government. According to one report, "law-makers and other officials from at least 30 states have visited the Missouri facilities, and several are taking steps to adopt the system" (Vestal, 2008). To learn more about the Missouri Model, visit: http://missouriapproach.org.

Question for Discussion

1. Why would we expect the Missouri Model to produce a relatively low rate of recidivism, especially in comparison to systems that focus on punishment, warehousing juvenile offenders in large, prison-like facilities? How would strain, control, and social learning theorists explain the lower rate of recidivism associated with the Missouri Model?

Aftercare Services

Once juveniles have been released from an institution, they sometimes receive "aftercare" services to ease their transition back into the community. *Aftercare* is similar to probation: the juvenile is supervised by someone associated with the juvenile justice system. The juvenile may receive counseling, as well, and may participate in special treatment programs. Aftercare services, however, are generally viewed as inadequate. The few evaluations of aftercare programs have produced mixed results, but some data suggest that aftercare programs that combine supervision with adequate treatment may reduce reoffending (Howell, 2003a; D. MacKenzie, 2002; Young et al., 2013).

The Office of Juvenile Justice and Delinquency Prevention has helped develop and implement in several jurisdictions a model aftercare program known as the Intensive Aftercare Program. It has several components.[10]

1. It targets juveniles with a high risk for further offending (as determined by risk assessment instruments).

2. It develops an individual treatment plan for each juvenile, based on a careful evaluation of the juvenile's needs. The plan focuses on such known causes of offending as individual, family, school, and peer factors. For example, depending on the juvenile's needs, the juvenile and his or her family may receive anger management training, parent training, educational and vocational skills training, substance abuse treatment, or a combination of these (see Chapter 24 for further information). The treatment begins while the juvenile is still in the institution and continues after release into the community. The treatment program, then, draws on the resources of the correctional institution and a range of community agencies.

3. It closely supervises juveniles after they have been released from institutions. Initially, released juveniles may live in group homes, participate in day treatment programs, or be confined to their own homes, except for school and emergencies. For juveniles who abide by program requirements, the level of supervision is gradually reduced. For example, the juveniles who have been released from home confinement after a period of time may still be required to meet regularly with parole officers and submit to random drug tests.

4. It sanctions inappropriate behavior and rewards progress in the program. Sanctions may include more restrictive curfews, community service, home confinement, and (in extreme cases) the revocation of parole and return to an institution. Rewards may include passes to movies and sporting events, gift certificates, and reduction in the level of supervision.

The Intensive Aftercare Program was implemented in three communities, and its effectiveness was evaluated (Wiebush et al., 2005). In particular, researchers randomly assigned juvenile offenders to either the Intensive Aftercare Program or a control group that received traditional aftercare services. The juveniles in the Intensive Aftercare Program did **not** have lower rates of reoffending. The researchers, however, point out that because of some problems in achieving full implementation, the Intensive Aftercare Program should not be dismissed as ineffective. Rather, there should be additional efforts to refine, better implement, and evaluate the program. A more recent review of research indicates that intensive aftercare has promise and is most effective "when it is well implemented" and targeted at "older youths, at high risk of recidivism" (James et al., 2013:270).

AN OVERVIEW OF THE JUVENILE JUSTICE PROCESS

Figure 21.1 provides an overview of the juvenile justice process (Hockenberry and Puzzanchera, 2015:53). Looking at the process as a whole, one finds that for every 1,000 delinquency cases referred to juvenile court, 551 are formally processed (have a petition filed). Many of the juveniles whose cases are not petitioned, however, are placed on informal probation or receive other sanctions. Of the 551 formally processed cases, 305 end in an adjudication of delinquency; of those juveniles, 194 are placed on probation, 74 are placed out of home, and 37 receive other sanctions (but no probation). Some of the juveniles on probation and some who receive "other sanctions" are subject to the intermediate sanctions listed earlier. If you do the appropriate math, you will find that about 7 percent of the delinquency cases referred to juvenile court are placed out of home. Another 23 percent receive other formal sanctions, including probation, fines, and/or restitution. Many others are informally sanctioned and/or treated.

We briefly commented on the effectiveness of the juvenile court and correctional agencies in controlling delinquency. In particular, we noted that a number of sanctions do not seem to reduce reoffending; these include waiving juveniles to adult court (although evidence is somewhat mixed here); regular probation; intermediate sanctions that focus on punishing, controlling, or scaring juveniles; and placing juveniles in large, secure training schools. Studies, however, suggest that sanctions with a strong treatment component are effective in reducing reoffending. We elaborate on these points in the chapters that follow and ask what the juvenile court and juvenile correctional agencies can do to more effectively control delinquency.

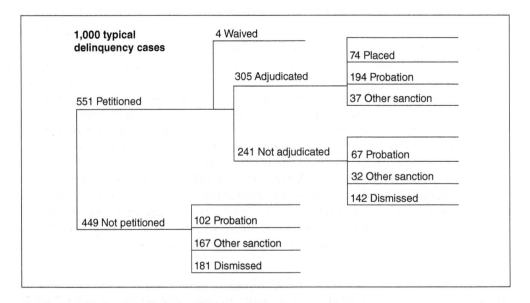

FIGURE 21.1 Overview of the Juvenile Justice Process
SOURCE: Hockenberry and Puzzanchera, 2015:53.

Chapter 23 examines the argument that the juvenile court and the correctional system need to "get tough" with offenders, especially serious juvenile offenders—that is, that the justice system needs to punish more offenders and punish them more severely. Chapter 24 examines the argument for more emphasis on the rehabilitation of offenders and on the prevention of delinquency. One of the central themes in the coming chapters is the ongoing debate between those who favor getting tougher with juvenile offenders (i.e., increasing direct control by the justice system) and those who favor placing more emphasis on rehabilitation and prevention (i.e., addressing the varied causes of delinquency described in Chapters 6–17). In *The Cycle of Juvenile Justice*, Bernard and Kurlychek (2010) point out that the juvenile justice system cycles back and forth between an emphasis on punishing juveniles and an emphasis on rehabilitating them. From the late 1980s to the early 2000s, the focus was on punishment. But this began to change in the early 2000s, with a renewed focus on rehabilitation. Chapter 25, the concluding chapter of the book, argues for a middle ground, one that emphasizes the **smart** use of sanctions, especially for serious offenders, **and** a much increased emphasis on those prevention and rehabilitation programs that **have shown to be effective.**

Before we address these topics, we need to consider the critical issue of whether the juvenile justice system treats fairly the juveniles who come before it. In particular, does the juvenile justice system discriminate against certain groups, and if so, what can be done to reduce such discrimination? Chapter 22 focuses on these questions.

TEACHING AIDS
Controversial Issue
The central issue facing the juvenile justice system is whether to respond to delinquency through tougher punishments, through an increased emphasis on rehabilitation and prevention, or through some combination of the two.

The position one adopts depends, in part, on how one views offenders. Consider the following remarks by former presidents Ronald Reagan and Bill Clinton. The sentiments expressed by Reagan helped propel the crackdown on crime and delinquency that began in the 1970s, while Clinton's statement suggests a different approach to controlling crime. To what extent do you agree with each quotation? Justify your response. (We consider the different approaches to controlling crime and delinquency in some detail in Chapters 23–25.)

> Choosing a career in crime is not the result of poverty or an unhappy childhood or of a misunderstood adolescence; it is the result of a conscious, willful choice made by some who consider themselves above the law, who seek to exploit the hard work and, sometimes, the very lives of their fellow citizens. . . . The crime epidemic threat is [not] some inevitable sociological phenomenon. . . . It is, instead, a cumulative result of too much emphasis on the protection of the rights of the accused and too little concern for our government's responsibility to protect the lives, homes, and rights of our law-abiding citizens. . . . [T]he criminal element now calculates that crime really does pay. (**Ronald Reagan,** quoted in Beckett and Sasson, 2000:61–62)
>
> We have to rebuild families and communities in this country. We've got to take more responsibility for these little kids before they grow up and start shooting each other. I know the budget is tight, but I'm telling you, we have got to deal with family, community and education, and find jobs for members of society's underclass to bring structure to their lives. (**Bill Clinton,** quoted in Beckett and Sasson, 2000:70)

Web-Based Resources and Activities
More information on the juvenile justice system. A great place to obtain more information on the juvenile justice system is the website for the Office of Juvenile Justice and Delinquency Prevention at http://www.ojjdp.gov. The OJJDP is the federal agency responsible

for dealing with juvenile crime and justice, and their website provides a great deal of information on the nature and extent of delinquency, the causes of delinquency, and—especially—the control and prevention of delinquency. The materials include hundreds of publications, the latest statistics, descriptions of a range of programs, answers to frequently asked questions, and so forth. The best place to begin is by clicking on **Tools**, then clicking on **First-Time Visitor** and **Student**. These sections provide brief overviews of the website and instructions on how to best use it. Then go exploring. For example, click on **Programs** and then browse through the **Model Programs Guide**. Click on **Statistics**" then on **Juveniles as Offenders;** click on **Related FAQs**, then read the responses to frequently asked questions about juvenile offenders (e.g., "When are juveniles most likely to commit violent crime?"). Click on **Topics**, then click on **bullying** under **Schools** to see the latest publications and reports on bullying. And if you have a particular topic in mind, use the search feature on the site.

An inside look at the juvenile justice system. Numerous videos available on the web provide an inside look at the juvenile court and corrections. Many of these can be found on YouTube, such as "Juvenile Court Process" (describes what happens in juvenile court) and "Primetime—Juvenile Prisons" (describes traditional juvenile training schools for males and females.) For a video on the Missouri Model, described in Box 21.2, search for "Primetime Crime—New Model for Juvenile Justice" on the web.

TEST YOUR KNOWLEDGE OF THIS CHAPTER

1. Describe the major goals of juvenile court. Indicate how these goals have changed over time and why.
2. Provide a brief overview of the number and types of cases (e.g., property crime, violent crime) handled by juvenile court. Describe the sociodemographic characteristics of the individuals who have the highest rates of court referral.
3. List and briefly describe the major stages in the juvenile court process, from referral to disposition.
4. What are the major purposes of intake screening?
5. How are informally processed cases dealt with? What are diversion programs and the alleged advantages of such programs? Why is it that diversion programs do not save as much money or staff time as expected?
6. Describe how a typical teen court works, from the referral of cases to sentencing. What do you think are the advantages and disadvantages of teen courts? For example, do you think teen courts reduce labeling, increase control, and so on?
7. Describe the evaluation data on diversion programs.
8. What is a petition?
9. Describe the three major ways of waiving cases to adult courts and their relative frequency of use. Does waiver reduce reoffending?
10. What is the purpose of adjudicatory hearings?
11. What major due process rights were granted to juveniles in the Gault decision?
12. Why has the Supreme Court not granted juveniles the right to a jury trial?
13. What is a social history or predisposition report?
14. What do risk and needs assessment instruments try to do? What are their advantages? What special problems might arise when they are used with females and African Americans?

15. List and briefly describe the major dispositions or sentences received by adjudicated delinquents and their relative frequency of use.

16. What happens to juveniles placed on probation? What are the two major functions of probation officers? What do the evaluation data say about the effectiveness of probation?

17. What are intermediate sanctions? List and briefly describe the major intermediate sanctions. What do the evaluation data say about the effectiveness of intermediate sanctions?

18. Why has there been a renewed focus on rehabilitation since the early 2000s?

19. For what types of offenses are juveniles confined? Describe the sociodemographic characteristics of juveniles with high rates of confinement.

20. How is it that many status offenders are still confined?

21. List and briefly describe the major types of juvenile correctional facilities.

22. How do the institutional experiences of females differ from those of males?

23. Describe the evaluation data on the effectiveness of juvenile correctional facilities.

24. What is juvenile aftercare? Briefly describe the model aftercare program developed by the Office of Juvenile Justice and Delinquency Prevention.

THOUGHT AND DISCUSSION QUESTIONS

1. Do you think that offenders in juvenile court should have the same due process rights as those in adult court, including the right to trial by jury? Justify your response.

2. Why do you think that large, secure training schools fail to reduce offending (compared to the alternatives like community treatment)?

3. More generally, why do you think attempts to control or punish juveniles are not very effective at reducing offending? (This issue is discussed further in Chapter 23.)

4. What criteria or standards should be used in determining whether to employ a particular sanctioning or treatment program? (One obvious criterion is the effectiveness of the program, but also consider other criteria, like the relative cost of the program.)

KEY TERMS

- Referral
- Complaint
- Intake screening
- Intake officer
- Informal processing
- Diversion programs
- Teen courts
- Detention hearing
- Petition
- Judicial waiver
- Prosecutor discretion
- Statutory waiver
- Adjudication
- Due process rights
- *Gault* decision
- Social history or predisposition report
- Risk and needs assessments
- Risk and needs assessment instruments
- Probation
- Intermediate sanctions
- Restitution
- Intensive supervision probation (ISP)
- Group home or halfway house
- Wilderness or outdoor programs
- Training schools
- Inmate subculture
- Aftercare

ENDNOTES

1. For overviews of the juvenile court and correctional system, see Altschuler, 1998; Barton, 2012; Bernard, 1992; Butts et al., 2012; Champion, 1998; Chesney-Lind and Shelden, 2004; Clement, 1997; S. Cox and Conrad, 1996; Feld, 1998, 1999; Future of Children, 1996; Howell, 1997a; Inderbitzin, 2005; Kempf-Leonard, 2012; Knoll and Sickmund, 2010; Krisberg, 2005, 2012; Kupchik, 2006; Kurlychek et al., 1999; Lundman, 2001; Mears, 2012; Petersilia, 1997; Puzzanchera et al., 2003, 2010; A. Roberts, 1998, 2004; Rubin, 1998; Sherman et al., 1998; Sickmund, 2006; H. Snyder and Sickmund, 2006.

2. For overviews of teen courts, see Butts and Buck, 2000; Butts et al., 2012; Harrison et al., 2001; Norris et al., 2011; Rasmussen, 2004; Stickle et al., 2008; Denise Wilson et al., 2009.

3. For further information on waivers to adult court, see Bishop and Frazier, 2000; Butts and Mitchell, 2000; Fagan and Zimring, 2000; Feld and Bishop, 2012; Griffin et al., 2011; Howell, 2003a; Kupchik, 2006; Myers, 2003; Rainville and Smith, 2003.

4. See note 3.

5. See Butts and Mitchell, 2000; Feld and Bishop, 2012; Griffin et al., 2011; Howell, 2003a; Kupchik, 2006; Myers, 2003; H. Snyder et al., 2000; Torbet et al., 2000.

6. See Bishop and Frazier, 2000; Butts and Mitchell, 2000; Feld and Bishop, 2012; Myers, 2003; Howell, 2003a; Steiner et al., 2006; Steiner and Wright, 2006; Zane et al., 2016.

7. For overviews, see D. Andrews and Bonta, 2006; Baird et al., 2013; Brumbaugh et al., 2009; Clear, 1988; Funk, 1999; Howell, 2003a:266–271; Le Blanc, 1998; Moore and Padavic, 2011; OJJDP, 2000b; Schwalbe, 2007; Van der Put et al., 2014; Wiebush et al., 1995.

8. For overviews of the evaluation research, see Altschuler, 1998; D. Andrews et al., 1990; Bishop et al., 1996; Cullen and Applegate, 1997; Cullen, Wright, and Applegate, 1996; Fagan, 1995; Greenwood, 2002; Greenwood and Turner, 2012; Greenwood et al., 1996; Howell, 1997a, 2003a; Howell et al., 1995; Krisberg et al., 1995; Krisberg and Howell, 1998; Lipsey, 1992; Lipsey and Cullen, 2008; Lipsey and Wilson, 1998; Lundman, 2001; D. MacKenzie, 2002, 2006; MacKenzie and Freeland, 2012; Schneider, 1990; Sherman et al., 2002.

9. Acoca, 1998; Holman and Ziedenberg, 2007; Krisberg, 2012; A. Roberts, 2004; B. Smith, 1998; H. Snyder and Sickmund, 1999.

10. For discussions of the problems with aftercare and an overview of the model aftercare program, see Troy Armstrong and Altschuler, 1998; Altschuler et al., 1999; Gies, 2003; S. Hawkins et al., 2009; MacKenzie and Freeland, 2012; Wiebush et al., 2000.

22 The Juvenile Justice System

Does the Juvenile Justice System Discriminate
Against Certain Groups in Its Efforts to Control
Delinquency?

The juvenile justice system is not simply supposed to control delinquency; it is supposed to control delinquency in a **fair or just manner.** Among other things, that means that the system is supposed to treat similar offenders in similar ways. It is commonly charged, however, that the system discriminates against certain groups of people. This charge is perhaps most often made with respect to certain race and ethnic groups, but discrimination based on class and gender is also alleged.

Discrimination in the juvenile justice system is sometimes explained in terms of conflict and labeling theories, which argue that powerful groups in our society view minority groups and poor people as a threat to their economic and cultural interests. With respect to race, whites are said to be concerned that minority group members will challenge their privileged position. Some argue that this concern is greatest in communities with large minority populations, high levels of crime, and high levels of racial inequality (i.e,. where whites are much wealthier on average than members of minority groups). Whites respond to this perceived threat by exercising greater social control over minority group members. In particular, the police are more likely to patrol minority communities and arrest minority group members, and the juvenile justice system is more likely to severely sanction minority group members. Lacking power, minority group members often are unable to resist these efforts at control. A similar argument is made with respect to poor people.[1]

Labeling theory also explains discrimination in another, related way. It is argued that the general public and justice officials hold certain stereotypes regarding particular groups, with these stereotypes being derived from the media and other sources. Most notably, it is argued that poor people and certain minority group members are more likely to be seen as dangerous or threatening. This view increases the likelihood that the people so stereotyped will be arrested and severely sanctioned by the courts. The situation with respect to gender is more complex. Males are generally seen as more dangerous than females, leading to the prediction that males who commit **delinquent offenses** will be treated more severely than females who commit such offenses. But females who engage in sexual behavior or acts believed to increase the likelihood of sexual behavior are viewed more seriously than males who engage in the same behaviors. This, of course, reflects the double standard many people hold regarding the sexual behavior of females and males. For example, according to the double standard, females guilty of **certain status offenses**—like running away and incorrigibility—should be sanctioned more severely than males who commit the same offenses.

Now we shall examine the evidence on discrimination by the juvenile justice system, focusing on whether the system discriminates against minorities and, to a lesser extent, certain class and gender groups.[2]

After reading this chapter, you should be able to:

- Describe how criminologists typically study racial discrimination in the juvenile justice system.
- Discuss the major conclusions that criminologists have drawn from these studies of racial discrimination.
- Identify the most important determinants of a juvenile's treatment within the justice system.
- Describe how racial discrimination varies across police departments and juvenile courts, and by type of crime.
- Explain direct and indirect racial discrimination.
- Discuss why and how states are addressing the overrepresentation of minorities in the juvenile justice system.
- Discuss findings regarding class and gender discrimination within the juvenile justice system.

DOES THE JUVENILE JUSTICE SYSTEM DISCRIMINATE AGAINST AFRICAN AMERICANS?

Most of the research on discrimination has focused on racial and ethnic discrimination, particularly discrimination against African Americans. There has been less research on discrimination against other racial and ethnic groups. As a consequence, the discussion that follows focuses on African Americans. Limited data, however, suggest that Latinos and Native Americans face discrimination as well, although not quite to the same extent as African Americans.

As discussed in previous chapters, **African Americans are overrepresented in all aspects of the juvenile justice system.** While African Americans made up 16 percent of the juvenile population, in 2013 they accounted for 34 percent of all juvenile arrests and 35 percent of all delinquency cases handled by the juvenile court. Further, in comparison to other racial groups, the cases of African American youth were more likely to be formally processed by the court and, if adjudicated delinquent, more likely to result in out-of-home placement. In addition, African Americans accounted for 42 percent of all juveniles in detention and about 45 percent of all cases judicially waived to adult courts (see Hockenberry and Puzzanchera, 2015).

These data, however, do not prove that **discrimination** exists. That is, they do not prove that African Americans are treated more severely than whites who commit similar offenses and have similar records. Perhaps African Americans are overrepresented in the juvenile justice system because they commit more delinquent acts and more serious delinquent acts than other groups. As indicated in Chapter 4, evidence suggests that African Americans are involved in more serious delinquency than whites, especially serious violence. A number of studies have tried to determine whether African Americans are overrepresented in the juvenile justice system because they are more likely to engage in delinquency, are discriminated against, or some combination of the two.

The typical study focuses on a state or one or more counties in a state. And it examines one or more decision points in the juvenile justice process, such as the decision to arrest a juvenile, to refer the juvenile to juvenile court, to formally process the juvenile, to detain the juvenile, or to place the juvenile in an institution. It is important to note that discrimination can occur at any one of these points in the process. The criminologist conducting the study will attempt to determine whether the race of the juvenile had influenced each decision that is made. Because other relevant factors must be taken into account as well, most studies, for example, consider the seriousness of the juvenile's offense and the juvenile's prior record. So the criminologist will ask whether African Americans are treated more severely than whites who have committed similar offenses and have similar records. For example, are African Americans more likely to be arrested or detained or institutionalized than similar whites?

Almost all studies find that **the most important determinants of how juveniles are treated in the justice system are the seriousness of the individual's offense and his or her prior record.** At the same time, many studies find that the overrepresentation of African Americans in the juvenile justice system cannot be fully explained in terms of race differences in the extent and seriousness of delinquency. Rather, these studies suggest that this **overrepresentation is partly due to discrimination against African Americans.** Let us provide two examples of such studies. One study examined the impact of race and ethnicity on arrest and referral to the juvenile court system in each of three cities: Rochester, New York; Pittsburgh, Pennsylvania; and Seattle, Washington (Huizinga et al., 2007). The researchers collected extensive data from a sample of juveniles in each city, including information on self-reported delinquency, standing on many of the causes of delinquency (e.g., socioeconomic status, gang membership), and whether the juveniles had been arrested and referred to juvenile court. The researchers found that African Americans were more likely to be arrested and referred to juvenile court in two of the three cities, even when prior self-reported delinquency and the causes of delinquency were accounted for. That is to say, the higher arrest and court referral rates of African Americans could not be explained by their higher rates of offending or race-related differences in the causes of delinquency (e.g. African Americans were more likely to live in poor families).

In a second study, Leiber and Fox (2005) examined the impact of race on the decisions made at various stages in the juvenile court process, including the decisions to detain juveniles, to formally process them, to send them to diversion programs, to adjudicate them delinquent, and to place them in out-of-home settings. The researchers found that African Americans were more likely to be treated severely at certain stages; in particular, African Americans were more likely to be placed in detention, less likely to be diverted, and more likely to be adjudicated delinquent. This was true even after a range of third variables had been accounted for: the severity of the offense, prior record, school problems, family status (single- or two-parent household), and so on. The researchers also found that processing at earlier stages of the court process affected what happened at later stages. In particular, juveniles who were placed in detention were more likely to be treated severely at later stages, even after other factors had been accounted for. This, of course, works to the disadvantage of African Americans, since they were more likely to be placed in detention (see the discussion on indirect discrimination later in this chapter).

The discrimination against African Americans may be explained by a number of factors (see Bishop, 2005). For example, it may occur because the police are more likely to patrol African American communities, complainants are more likely to press for arrest if the offender is African American, and African Americans are less able to afford private attorneys. Recent data, however, suggest that one reason for this discrimination is that juvenile justice officials in certain areas hold negative stereotypes of African Americans. Among other things, these officials believe that African American juveniles are more likely than white juveniles to be dangerous and disrespectful, and to engage in crime because of negative personality traits and bad attitudes—as opposed to blaming negative environmental factors.[3]

On looking at the data as a whole, we can draw several general conclusions about discrimination against African Americans. These are discussed next.

The Extent of Discrimination Varies Across Police Departments and Juvenile Courts

Some police departments and juvenile courts discriminate against African Americans, while others do not seem to engage in direct or overt discrimination. This conclusion should not be too surprising. Police departments and juvenile courts differ from one another in many ways and exist in different community environments. It is reasonable to expect some differences in the extent of discrimination. This conclusion helps explain why studies examining discrimination produce contradictory results. While many studies find evidence of racial discrimination, many do not. The studies on discrimination usually examine different police departments and juvenile courts at different points in time, so we would expect some difference in results.

Criminologists have begun to investigate factors that influence whether police and juvenile justice officials discriminate against African Americans and certain other race and ethnic groups. As indicated earlier, the leading argument in this area is that discrimination is most likely in communities that are likely to view minority group members as a threat to whites. Most studies tend to support this argument, suggesting that discrimination is greater in communities with high percentages of African American and Latino residents, high levels of crime, and high levels of racial inequality— even with a range of other factors taken into account.[4]

The Extent of Discrimination May Vary by Type of Crime

There is also some evidence that discrimination may be greater for less serious crimes, since the police and court officials have more discretion over how to handle the cases. There is little question about whether to arrest someone suspected of homicide or armed robbery (although there may be race differences in the punishments imposed by the courts), but much discretion can be exercised when someone is caught using drugs or shoplifting. There is much evidence, in fact, for the existence of discrimination in the enforcement of drug laws. African Americans, in particular, were especially hard hit by the war on drugs during the 1980s and 1990s. African Americans and whites use drugs at about the same rate overall, but African American juveniles are several times more likely to be arrested for drug abuse violations than white juveniles (see Bishop, 2005; Donziger, 1996; Tonry, 1995). This dramatic difference occurred partly because the war on drugs had a special focus on crack cocaine. Crack is used more by African Americans than whites. Powdered cocaine, however, is used more by whites.

Further, there is some evidence that discrimination may be more likely when African Americans commit crimes against whites (Pope and Snyder, 2003). It is said that the police and others are more likely to ignore or informally deal with crimes committed against members of minority groups, since they have less sympathy for minority victims. Most crime, however, is *intraracial* (e.g., African American on African American, white on white), a condition that may help explain why some studies fail to find evidence of discrimination. Most studies, in particular, fail to take account of the race of the victim.

Small Amounts of Discrimination at Different Points in the Juvenile Justice Process Can Have a Large Overall Effect

Many studies find evidence for small to moderate amounts of discrimination at several points in the juvenile justice process. For example, it may be that African Americans are moderately more likely to be arrested than whites, slightly more likely to be referred to juvenile court when arrested, slightly more likely to be detained, slightly more likely to have their cases formally processed, and slightly more likely to be sent to institutions. These small to moderate amounts of discrimination add up, however, so that in the end we find that a much larger proportion of African Americans than whites are confined in institutions (see especially McCord et al., 2001:254–258).

The likelihood of small to moderate amounts of discrimination at several points in the justice process means that it is important for researchers to examine all major decision points in the process. Some researchers fail to do this by, for example, focusing on just one decision point, such as the adjudicatory hearing. If they find little or no evidence of discrimination at this point, they may conclude that discrimination is not a problem. Nevertheless, discrimination may have occurred at several other points in the process.

Racial Discrimination May Be Direct or Indirect

Researchers examining discrimination usually try to determine whether African Americans are treated more severely than similar whites. So a researcher may compare African Americans and whites who are similar in terms of the seriousness of their offense, their prior record, their social class, their family status, and other variables. The researcher usually includes a range of variables that influence arrest and treatment by the court. **If African Americans are treated more severely than similar whites, that is evidence for** *direct*, **or overt,** *discrimination*. It suggests that the police or court officials may be racist, treating African Americans more harshly solely because of their race. But what if the researcher finds that there is no difference in the way African Americans and whites are treated? Does that mean that discrimination does not exist?

The answer is no. The researcher is comparing African Americans and whites who are similar on a range of variables that influence arrest and court processing. But in the real world, African Americans and whites are **not** similar on many of these variables. Take family status as an example. African American juveniles are more likely than white juveniles to reside in single-parent homes, and some evidence suggests that juveniles from single-parent homes are more likely to be arrested and treated severely by the court. As a consequence, African Americans are treated more severely than whites. This more severe treatment may not stem from direct or overt racial discrimination; African Americans and whites who are similar in terms of family status may be treated the same. Rather, the discrimination occurs because race is associated with a variable that influences treatment by the police and courts—family status in this case. This is *indirect discrimination*. African Americans are treated more severely than whites not because of direct discrimination based on race but because **race is associated with other variables that influence treatment by the police and court.**

Let us give another example of indirect discrimination. While most African Americans are not poor, African Americans are more likely than whites to be poor and to live in poor communities. Some evidence suggests that individuals are more likely to be arrested and treated severely by the court if they are poor or live in poor communities. Among other things, the police may be more likely to patrol poor communities and to stop and question the people there, and the police and court officials may be more likely to discriminate against the poor juveniles they encounter. As a consequence of this association between race and poverty, African Americans are more likely to be arrested and treated severely by the court. The more severe treatment in this case is not due directly to race but rather is due to the indirect effect of race. Race is associated with social class, which in turn affects treatment by the police and courts. Discrimination, then, may be direct or indirect. But the effect is the same in both cases: the overrepresentation of African Americans in the juvenile justice system.

What Can Be Done to Address the Overrepresentation of Minorities in the Juvenile Justice System?

The research described in the preceding section led the federal government to take steps to reduce the overrepresentation of minorities in the juvenile justice system. In 1994, the federal government required each state to determine whether minorities were overrepresented in detention and correctional facilities. And in 2002, the federal government went further, requiring each state to determine whether minorities were overrepresented at all major points in the juvenile justice process. A state in which minorities were overrepresented then had to determine the reason(s) for the overrepresentation, develop and implement programs to reduce the imbalance, and, later, evaluate the effectiveness of those programs. The government said that states that failed to meet its requirements would lose some of their federal funding for delinquency programs.

Following the new mandate, almost all states estimated the extent to which minorities are overrepresented in their juvenile justice systems. African Americans are overrepresented at one or more points in the juvenile justice process in every state that submitted an estimate. Latinos are also overrepresented, although not to the extent of African Americans. Most states also determined the reasons for the overrepresentation they found. Limited data point to one circumstance: African Americans have higher offending rates and are more involved in serious crimes than whites. But most states report that this overrepresentation is also due to discrimination against African Americans (see Leiber, 2002; Pope and Leiber, 2005).

Most states implemented programs to reduce minority overrepresentation, and some states reached the point of evaluating the effectiveness of the programs they had implemented. As indicated, minority overrepresentation exists partly because minorities have higher levels of involvement in delinquency, especially serious delinquency. Programs have been developed to reduce crime by minorities; many of these programs are similar to the prevention and rehabilitation programs discussed in Chapter 24 (see W. Welsh, Jenkins, and Harris, 1999, for an example of one promising program). And evidence suggests that minority overrepresentation is also due to direct and indirect discrimination against minorities. Accordingly, programs are being developed to reduce discrimination. Such programs include sensitivity training for police and court workers; developing more explicit guidelines for making decisions, including the increased use of risk assessment instruments; closer monitoring of police and court decisions for fairness; developing alternatives to secure detention and confinement; and increasing the representation of minorities in the police and court systems.[5]

How much progress has been made since 2002, when the federal government issued its most recent mandate? A review conducted by the National Research Council (NRC, 2013b) finds that limited progress has been made over the past decade, as few states have managed to reduce racial and ethnic disparities in their juvenile justice systems. In practice, the government does not impose a numerical standard or quota on the states, so an actual reduction in these disparities is not necessary to meet the core requirements of the federal mandate (though each state must file annual reports, provide estimates of minority overrepresentation in their systems, and follow through with their plans to address overrepresentation). Further, according to the NRC report, the federal government granted the states considerable leeway in determining their compliance with the mandate; only one state (Mississippi) had lost funding for lack of compliance.

Nevertheless, according to the report, the steps taken by the federal government "have had a positive impact on the states' willingness to address the problem" (NRC, 2013b:298). Despite many challenges, there are some signs of success, with preliminary evaluations indicating that a number of programs throughout the country have substantially reduced the overrepresentation of minorities in the juvenile justice system. Most of these successes have occurred in local jurisdictions, at the county level. For example, a juvenile court in Oregon found that African American and Latino youth were almost twice as likely to be placed in detention as white youth. The court developed a racially and ethnically neutral risk assessment instrument and, within a few years, race and ethnic differences in detention were largely eliminated (Cabaniss et al., 2007:395). The study's authors defined as "race-neutral" risk assessment instruments that do the following:

> [a]ssess a youth's probation status, history of appearing in court, prior record, and the seriousness of the charge, without giving undue weight to social factors that increase the likelihood that minority youth will be detained more often than white youth. For example, instead of asking if a youth resides with both parents, a situation that is less common among African American youth, a race-neutral instrument might ask if two adults capable of supervising a youth live in the home. Based on their responses to intake questions, youth are assigned low, moderate, or high risk scores which suggest their likelihood of reoffending or failing to appear in court. (Cabaniss et al., 2007:397–398)

Other successful efforts to address the overrepresentation of minorities in the juvenile justice system are described in a report from Building Blocks for Youth (2007) and on the Disproportionate Minority Contact webpage of the site maintained by the Office of

Box 22.1   Step by Step: Addressing the Overrepresentation of Minorities in the Juvenile Justice System

In Santa Cruz County, just south of San Francisco, juvenile justice officials recognized they had a problem. Although Latinos represented about 33 percent of the adolescent population, they accounted for a much larger proportion of the young people being held in the county's juvenile detention facility. In fact, in the late 1990s, 64 percent of confined youth in the county were Latino (J. Cox and Bell, 2001).

Initially, Santa Cruz County practitioners believed that there were justifiable reasons for the overrepresentation of Latinos among confined youth and that they could do little about them. For example, data confirmed that, in comparison to the nonminority boys that came into contact with the juvenile justice system, Latino boys tended to be involved in more serious offenses. Latino boys also posted a higher rate of heroin use and gang membership. It was believed that these higher rates of serious delinquency resulted from a greater level of exposure to various risk factors, including factors related to larger social and economic problems over which the juvenile court had little control.

However, upon closer examination, it became clear that certain practices *within* the juvenile justice system may have contributed to the overrepresentation of Latino youths in confinement. In particular, members of the Santa Cruz County probation department recognized that the decision to arrest, detain, or release a child could be affected by race and ethnicity in subtle and unintentional ways.

For example, in comparison to nonminorities, Latino boys were more often described as "gang members"—a label that implies a greater risk of reoffending and could lead to a greater probability of confinement. Yet Santa Cruz County practitioners recognized that such labels involve subjective judgments. They therefore moved toward a method of risk assessment based on "objective, identifiable risk factors such as severity of the current offense or past record of delinquent acts" and did not use gang membership unless it had been proven in court (J. Cox and Bell, 2001:34).

Santa Cruz County also created new diversion programs to reduce the likelihood that youths would be detained unnecessarily (previously, court officials faced a lack of adequate alternatives to secure confinement). For example, given a high rate of substance abuse problems among Latino boys, a culturally sensitive residential drug treatment program was developed. In addition, juvenile probation officers and other staff received ongoing training and education related to cultural sensitivity and the dynamics of minority overrepresentation in the juvenile justice system.

According to Cox and Bell (2001), these system changes resulted in an impressive reduction in the overrepresentation of minorities in the Santa Cruz County juvenile detention facility. By the year 2000, the Latino population in secure detention had dropped from 64 to 46 percent, for a reduction of 18 percent. In the words of Cox and Bell (2001:36), this outcome shows that "one agency can make a difference."

Question for Discussion

1. Although the main purpose of the changes just described was to reduce minority overrepresentation, can you think of any other benefits that might result from such changes? (Consider that before the changes were made, correctional officials in California had recommended that more than "1,200 additional beds be constructed for the detention of young people" [J. Cox and Bell, 2001:31]).

Juvenile Justice and Delinquency Prevention (see http://www.ojjdp.gov/dmc). We detail one such effort in Box 22.1. However, it is clear that we still have a long way to go in our efforts to reduce minority overrepresentation (see Bishop and Leiber, 2012; Leiber, 2006; Piquero, 2008a).

The future role of the federal government in this area is a bit uncertain. In 2016, Congress voted on a bill that would reauthorize the federal mandate to reduce the over-representation of minorities in the juvenile justice system (the original 1994 mandate, which was last reauthorized in 2002, technically expired in 2007). The bill included certain provisions that would reduce the leeway and flexibility previously granted to states. For example, waivers and exceptions to the mandate would be phased out. Certain lawmakers, however, objected to this tightening of requirements, and the reauthorization bill failed to pass. At the time of this writing, the Trump administration had not signaled whether the federal mandate will receive continued support.

DOES THE JUVENILE JUSTICE SYSTEM DISCRIMINATE AGAINST THE POOR AND AGAINST MALES OR FEMALES?

There has been less research on class- and gender-based discrimination, and the research that has been done in these areas has produced somewhat contradictory results. Nevertheless, we can draw a few tentative conclusions.

Although the evidence is somewhat mixed, the data suggest that there is **discrimination against lower-class juveniles in at least certain communities** (see, e.g., Sampson, 1986b; Sealock and Simpson, 1998). Both the individual's social class and the economic status of the neighborhood in which the individual lives may influence treatment by justice officials. In particular, the economic status of the neighborhood may have an important effect on the likelihood of arrest. The police may be more likely to patrol low-income neighborhoods, to stop and question people in such neighborhoods, and to arrest people from such neighborhoods. Also, juveniles in many lower-class neighborhoods are more likely to congregate on the street, where they are more visible to the police. The individual's social class, however, may have a larger effect on how juveniles are treated once they have been referred to juvenile court.

Data on gender suggest that males may be somewhat more likely to be arrested and treated severely for **delinquent offenses** than similar females who engage in such crimes. Among other things, it is argued that males are more likely to be seen as a threat than females. Some data, however, suggest that this attitude may be changing: female delinquents have been treated more like male delinquents in recent years. This new equality of treatment is especially true with respect to females who do not conform to gender stereotypes (e.g., do not act submissive when confronted by the police). This change may partly account for the fact that female arrests for violence are increasing faster than male arrests. However, in some jurisdictions females are more likely than similar males to be arrested and treated severely for many **status offenses**. This is especially true with respect to offenses like running away from home and being incorrigible. It is argued that the police and court officials often associate these status offenses with sexual behavior or the possibility of sexual behavior on the part of females, and that they feel a need to more closely regulate the sexual behavior and "moral life" of females than males (for excellent discussions, see Chesney-Lind and Shelden, 2004; Feld, 2008; F. Sherman, 2012).

SUMMARY

This chapter examined race, class, and gender discrimination by the juvenile justice system and concluded that there is some evidence for such discrimination. The variables of race, class, and gender, however, were examined in isolation from one another. A few recent studies indicate that if we are to fully understand discrimination, researchers must consider these variables together. For example, some data suggest that the court system treats African American females more severely than white females (see Chesney-Lind and Shelden, 2004; Leiber and Mack, 2003; F. Sherman, 2012). Also, some data suggest that the group most likely to experience discrimination is older juveniles who are male and African American (Steffensmeier et al., 1998). Future research will likely focus on the joint effects of race, class, sex, and age, as well as on attempts to reduce discrimination in the juvenile justice system.

TEACHING AIDS
Controversial Issue

There is, of course, no doubt that direct discrimination by the juvenile justice system is wrong. The issue of indirect discrimination, however, is sometimes more controversial. Consider the following: The police often concentrate their patrols in lower-income communities, saying that such communities have higher crime rates and that it makes sense to put the most police where there is the most crime. This policy means that the lower-class individuals come under greater police scrutiny than middle-class individuals. The police may therefore be more likely to detect a criminal act by a lower-class person than one by a middle-class person. It also means that African Americans come under more police scrutiny than whites, since African Americans are more likely to live in lower-class communities (although most African Americans live elsewhere).

Do you think the police are justified in concentrating their patrols in lower-class communities (which tend to have higher crime rates), even though this practice indirectly discriminates against lower-class individuals and African Americans? Justify your response. Are there any negative consequences that might result from this policy? (Hint: Draw on the delinquency theories.) Is there anything that can be done to reduce these negative consequences? (See the discussion of discrimination in L. Sherman, 2002.)

Race and Experiences with the Police

The discussion of discrimination in this chapter is rather abstract. We state, for example, that many studies show that the police are more likely to arrest African Americans than similar whites. This statement, however, does not capture the personal experiences of some individuals with the police. An editorial in the *New York Times* attempted to describe such experiences (Herbert, 2007a:A25). The editorial began:

> No one is paying much attention, but parts of New York City are like a police state for young men, women and children who happen to be black or Hispanic. They are routinely stopped, searched, harassed, intimidated, humiliated and, in many cases, arrested for no good reason. . . . Last Monday in the Bushwick section of Brooklyn, about three dozen grieving young people on their way to a wake for a teenage friend who had been murdered were surrounded by police, cursed at, handcuffed and ordered into paddy wagons. They were taken to the 83rd precinct stationhouse where several were thrown into jail.

The editorial writer goes on to state that the police said these young people were on a rampage, yelling and blocking traffic, but that "every account [he] was able to find described a large group of youngsters, very sad and downcast about the loss of their friend, walking peacefully toward the [wake]."

In one study, a criminologist interviewed 40 African American adolescent males in a disadvantaged urban community to learn more about their interactions with the police. The author of the study published these findings:

> 83% of respondents reported having experienced harassment themselves, and more than nine out of ten reported that someone they knew had been harassed or mistreated. . . . [R]espondents consistently identified frequent pedestrian and vehicle stops as the bedrock of neighborhood policing efforts. . . . [I]t was not simply that young men objected to being routinely stopped, but they took particular exception to the way officers spoke to them during these encounters. . . . [S]everal study participants expressed grave concern about being ordered to sit or lie on the pavement while enduring physically intrusive searches. . . . [A]pproximately two-thirds of the young men said the police are almost never polite, and slightly under half reported that the police often harass and mistreat people in the neighborhood. (Brunson, 2007:81)

These quoted findings do not imply that all police harass African Americans or that all African Americans have negative views of the police. Nevertheless, young African Americans in disadvantaged communities are much more likely than others to report negative experiences with the police, experiences stemming from the aggressive police tactics that are more often used in such communities. And these negative experiences have a range of unfortunate consequences. As indicated earlier, negative treatment by the police may increase the likelihood of crime (see Kane, 2005). And you may have heard about the "Stop Snitching" campaigns in many communities, where songs, websites, and T-shirts urge people to stop cooperating with the police.

What do you think can be done to improve relations between the police and African Americans, particularly young African American males in disadvantaged communities? (Note: See Chapter 20 and the February 2007 issue of *Criminology and Public Policy* for further information and a discussion of possible approaches.)

Web-Based Exercise: The Disproportionate Minority Contact Initiative

As described earlier in this chapter, the federal government has mandated that states make efforts to reduce the disproportionate number of minority juveniles who come in contact with the juvenile justice system. You can learn more about this initiative by visiting the OJJDP's Disproportionate Minority Contact (DMC) webpage, cited earlier, at http://www.ojjdp.gov/dmc/about.html. Click on **Tools** and browse through some of the documents designed to help states and communities comply with this mandate, including the "DMC Reduction Best Practices Database," which describes strategies to reduce disproportionate minority contact within the juvenile justice system. Then get on YouTube and view the video titled "Addressing Disproportionate Minority Contact," which describes the efforts of Connecticut to reduce DMC.

TEST YOUR KNOWLEDGE OF THIS CHAPTER

1. How do conflict and labeling theories explain discrimination against minority groups and the lower class?
2. Why do some criminologists predict that males are more likely than females to be severely punished for serious delinquent acts, while females are more likely to be severely punished for many status offenses?

3. Why did we state that the overrepresentation of African Americans at various points in the juvenile justice process does not by itself prove that discrimination exists?

4. How do researchers try to determine if juvenile justice officials discriminate against minority group members?

5. What are the two most important determinants of how juveniles are treated in the juvenile justice system?

6. Many studies find evidence of discrimination against African Americans. Describe the stereotypes of African American juveniles that contribute to this discrimination.

7. List a major factor said to influence whether the police and juvenile courts in certain areas discriminate against African Americans. Briefly describe what the research says about this factor.

8. Is discrimination by the police and courts more likely for certain types of crime? Describe the research in this area.

9. Why is it important for researchers studying discrimination to examine all the major points in the juvenile justice process?

10. What is meant by direct and indirect discrimination? Give a clear-cut example of direct discrimination. Give two clear-cut examples of indirect discrimination.

11. Describe federal efforts to reduce minority overrepresentation in the juvenile justice system. What have the states found regarding the extent and causes of minority overrepresentation in their juvenile justice systems?

12. List three programs or strategies being used to reduce discrimination against minorities by juvenile justice officials.

13. Describe the evidence on class-based discrimination by juvenile justice officials.

14. Describe the evidence on gender-based discrimination by justice officials.

THOUGHT AND DISCUSSION QUESTIONS

1. What steps would you recommend for reducing discrimination by the juvenile justice system?

2. To what extent do you think the causes of race/ethnic, class, and gender discrimination are similar and different?

3. To what extent do you think race/ethnic, class, and gender discrimination can be addressed by means of programs of the same types? If you think different programs are required to address these types of discrimination, describe the differences you have in mind.

4. This chapter examined race/ethnic, class, and gender discrimination in isolation from one another. Do you think it is important for researchers to consider particular race/ethnic, class, and gender combinations when examining discrimination? For example, do you think African American females face special problems in their treatment by the juvenile justice system (problems not faced by white females or African American males)?

KEY TERMS

- Direct discrimination
- Indirect discrimination

ENDNOTES

1. You may have noticed that this argument is very similar to an argument used in Chapter 1 to explain the "invention" of juvenile delinquency. In particular, it was argued that upper-class people felt threatened by the large concentration of poor people and immigrants in the cities, so they created the juvenile court and juvenile correctional institutions in an effort to exercise more control over the children of the poor and immigrants. For a fuller discussion of the conflict and labeling explanations of discrimination, see G. Armstrong and Rodriquez, 2005; Bishop, 2005; Engen et al., 2002; Kent and Jacobs, 2005; Leiber, 2003; Leiber and Fox, 2005; Parker et al., 2005.

2. For overviews and selected studies in this area, see G. Armstrong and Rodriguez, 2005; Austin, 1995; Bishop, 2005; Bishop and Leiber, 2012; Bishop et al., 2010; Bortner et al., 2000; Bridges and Steen, 1998; Building Blocks For Youth, 2000; Chesney-Lind and Shelden, 2004; Dannefer and Schutt, 1982; DeJong and Jackson, 1998; Donziger, 1996; Engen et al., 2002; Feld, 1995, 2008; Frazier and Bishop, 1995; Guevara et al., 2008; Hsia and Hamparian, 1998; Huizinga and Elliott, 1987; Huizinga et al., 2007; Kempf-Leonard, 2007, 2012; Krisberg, 2005; Lauritsen and Sampson, 1998; Leiber, 2002, 2003; Leiber and Fox, 2005; Leiber and Stairs, 1999; Leonard et al., 1995; Leonard and Sontheimer, 1995; MacDonald and Chesney-Lind, 2001; McCord et al., 2001; Jerome Miller, 1996; National Council on Crime and Delinquency, 2007; National Research Council, 2013b, Peck et al., 2016; Penn, 2006; Piliavin and Briar, 1964; Piquero, 2008a; Pope and Feyerherm, 1993; Pope and Leiber, 2005; Pope and Snyder, 2003; Reiman, 1995; Sampson, 1986b; Sealock and Simpson, 1998; F. Sherman, 2012; Short and Sharp, 2005; Snyder and Sickmund, 1999; Steffensmeier et al., 1998; Tonry, 1995; Tracy, 2005; S. Walker et al., 2004; Zatz, 1987; Zimring, 2005.

3. For example, see Bishop, 2005; Bishop and Leiber, 2012; Bishop et al., 2010; Bridges et al., 1995; Leiber, 2003, 2006; Leiber and Stairs, 1999; Sampson and Laub, 1993b.

4. See note 1.

5. For further information, see J. Bell, 2005; Bishop, 2005; Bishop and Leiber, 2012; Building Blocks for Youth, 2007; Cabaniss et al., 2007; Feyerherm, 1995; Hsia and Hamparian, 1998; Krisberg, 2005; Leiber, 2002, 2003, 2006; Leonard et al., 1995; Pope and Leiber, 2005; Short and Sharp, 2005; also see the MacArthur Foundation's Models for Change website at http://modelsforchange.net.

23 The Strategies of Deterrence and Incapacitation

Is It Possible to Control Delinquency
by Punishing More Offenders and
Punishing Them More Severely?

Perhaps the most common criticism of the juvenile court and correctional system is that neither is tough enough, especially in dealing with serious offenders. This criticism is often voiced by politicians and the media. It is shared by many in the juvenile justice system. Many police, for example, complain that the offenders they send to juvenile court usually receive little more than a "slap on the wrist." Court workers often note that unless juveniles commit a very serious offense, they will not receive a meaningful sanction until they have appeared in court several times (see Stone, 1998). Further, many people in the general public believe that the juvenile justice system is not tough enough in dealing with serious offenders, although they also believe that the system does not place enough emphasis on rehabilitation and prevention (Applegate et al., 2009; Bishop, 2006; Mears et al., 2007; Nagin et al., 2006).

The results of a 2007 poll conducted in our home state of Georgia are illustrative. Among the general public, 48 percent expressed the view that the state's juvenile justice system was too lenient. Among the criminal justice professionals polled, 71 percent said the system was too lenient. In both groups, a majority agreed that juveniles who have committed serious violent crimes should be transferred to the adult criminal justice system (Clark, 2007). In a more recent national poll, 69 percent of registered voters said judges should be allowed to send serious juveniles offenders to correctional facilities—although the poll item did not distinguish between juvenile and adult facilities (Pew Charitable Trusts, 2014).

As a consequence, it is often argued that **the juvenile justice system needs to get tough with offenders, especially serious offenders.** That is, more juvenile offenders should be punished, and punished more severely. In fact, the juvenile justice system made a concerted effort to do just that in the late 1980s and throughout the 1990s.[1] Certain of these efforts were mentioned in Chapter 21. For example, intermediate sanctions were developed, partly with the idea of allowing the courts to inflict more punishment and to impose more supervision than is provided with regular probation. Also, more offenders were waived to adult court, where they were often sentenced to long periods of incarceration. Still other efforts to get tough are described in this chapter. All these efforts, of course, aim to increase the level of **direct control** exercised by the justice system.

Many people would expect these efforts to reduce delinquency. Three arguments are generally made in this area. First, getting tough will deter juveniles who are appropriately punished from committing further delinquency. Second, getting tough will deter juveniles in the general population, including those who were not punished, from committing delinquent acts. Juveniles in the general population will come to realize that the certainty and severity of punishment have increased, and this will increase their fear of engaging in delinquency. And third, getting tough will result in more juvenile offenders being locked up, which will stop them from committing crimes on the street. These arguments appeal both to common sense and to the desire of many people to punish individuals who commit serious crimes.

This chapter has three parts. First, we examine the charge that the juvenile court and correctional system are not tough enough in dealing with offenders, especially serious offenders. Second, we describe the efforts of the juvenile court and correctional system to get tough with offenders. Third, we discuss the effectiveness of these get-tough efforts and consider what can be done to make them more effective. In particular, we ask whether these efforts deter those individuals who were in fact punished from committing further crime (called *specific deterrence*); whether they deter those in the general population from engaging in crime (called *general deterrence*); and whether they reduce crime by locking up or incapacitating offenders, so they cannot commit crimes on the street (called *incapacitation*).

After reading this chapter, you should be able to:

- Express the basic ideas that underlie the strategies of deterrence and incapacitation.
- Distinguish between specific and general deterrence.

- Provide tentative conclusions about the effectiveness of specific and general deterrence.
- Explain the limitations of punishment as a deterrent.
- Discuss the research on incapacitation, including the problems involved in estimating the amount of crime prevented by incapacitation.
- Describe the strategy of selective incapacitation and the difficulties involved in implementing this strategy.
- Describe the tentative conclusions we may draw about the effectiveness of incapacitation in reducing crime.

ARE THE JUVENILE COURT AND CORRECTIONAL SYSTEM TOUGH ENOUGH IN DEALING WITH OFFENDERS, ESPECIALLY SERIOUS OFFENDERS?

As we pointed out in Chapter 21, the cases of the large majority of juveniles who are referred to juvenile court are dismissed, are handled informally, or result in probation. While probation may call for the close supervision of the juvenile and the imposition of meaningful sanctions, it usually does not. In most cases, juvenile offenders have little contact with their probation officers and are subject to only minimal sanctions. Based on these facts, one might conclude that the juvenile court/correctional system is not tough enough in dealing with offenders.

We must keep in mind, however, that most juveniles are referred to juvenile court for minor offenses. It may be that serious offenders are treated differently. Data do, in fact, indicate that serious offenders are more likely to receive severe sanctions. It is still the case, however, that most serious offenders do not receive sanctions beyond probation. Consider two relatively serious violent crimes: aggravated assault and robbery. Data from 2013 indicate that 74 percent of the aggravated assault cases referred to juvenile courts were formally processed. Of these, 56 percent were adjudicated delinquent, and 1 percent were judicially waived to adult court. The rest of the cases were dismissed or informally processed. Of those adjudicated delinquent, 30 percent were placed out-of-home. The rest were placed on probation or, in a small number of cases, were sanctioned in some other way or released. If we do the appropriate math, we find that 13 percent of the aggravated assault cases referred to juvenile courts resulted in out-of-home placement and about 2 percent were waived to adult courts. The numbers for robbery are as follows: 87 percent of the robbery cases referred to juvenile courts were formally processed. Of these, 60 percent resulted in adjudication of delinquency and 4 percent were judicially waived to adult courts. Of the offenders adjudicated delinquent, 43 percent were placed out-of-home. Overall, 25 percent of the robbery cases referred to juvenile court resulted in out-of-home placement and 3 percent were waived to adult court (Hockenberry and Puzzanchera, 2015). **Most serious offenders referred to juvenile court, then, do not receive severe sanctions.** (It should be noted, however, that aggravated assault and robbery cases vary in level of seriousness: while some aggravated assaults involve serious injury, others involve threats to injure someone with a weapon like a bat; and while some robberies involve major thefts at gunpoint, others consist of taking a fellow student's lunch money under threat of violence.)

Further, data suggest that adult courts are generally more likely to incarcerate serious juvenile offenders and to detain them for longer periods of time than juvenile courts, especially when the offenders are charged with violent crimes.[2] One study examined how juveniles charged with felonies were dealt with in the *adult* criminal courts of 40 of the nation's largest urban counties. The researchers found that about two-thirds of the juveniles were convicted of felonies and that about 43 percent of those convicted were sentenced to prison, receiving an average sentence of 7.5 years. Another 20 percent of the convicted juveniles were sentenced to serve much shorter terms of confinement in jails (Rainville and Smith, 2003). Data such as these have led many people to conclude that juvenile court is not tough enough.

The juvenile court often fails to impose severe sanctions for several reasons, some of which can be difficult to address. For example, juvenile courts cannot be expected to sanction a juvenile without good evidence that he or she committed an offense. But other conditions cited as reasons can be addressed. For example, juvenile courts and correctional staffs are often limited, which makes it difficult to formally process and impose meaningful sanctions on most juvenile offenders; and although politicians have devoted enormous sums of money to the control of adult crime, they have been reluctant to make substantial investments in the juvenile justice system. Also, most juvenile courts are still at least partly guided by a philosophy that emphasizes rehabilitation over punishment. This philosophy, in particular, tends to view juvenile offenders as not fully responsible for their behavior and in need of assistance rather than punishment.

However, many people have argued over the years that the juvenile court and correctional system need to place more emphasis on punishment or on getting tough with offenders, especially serious offenders.

EFFORTS TO GET TOUGH WITH SERIOUS OFFENDERS

During the 1990s, the federal government became a leading advocate of taking a tougher stance toward juvenile offenders. In particular, the U.S. Office of Juvenile Justice and Delinquency Prevention (OJJDP) developed a comprehensive strategy for responding to delinquency, particularly serious delinquency. One of the cornerstones of this strategy was the proposition that juvenile offenders need to be held accountable for their offenses and subjected to meaningful sanctions. Specifically, the OJJDP has stated:

> [Y]oung people who violate the law should be held accountable for their offenses through the swift, consistent application of sanctions that are proportionate to the offenses—both as a matter of basic justice and as a way to combat delinquency and improve the quality of life in the nation's communities. (C. Andrews and Marble, 2003:1; also see Beyer, 2003)

Further, the OJJDP recommended that juvenile courts hold offenders accountable by developing a system of *graduated sanctions* that involves

> immediate sanctions in the community for first-time, nonviolent offenders; intermediate sanctions in the community for more serious offenders; and secure care programs for the most violent offenders. Youths should move between different levels of the continuum through a well-structured system of phases. At each level of the continuum, offenders should understand that they will be subject to more severe sanctions if they reoffend. (Krisberg et al., 1995:143; also see Howell, 2003a)

To help juvenile courts and correctional agencies hold offenders accountable for their behavior, the OJJDP provided millions of dollars in grants so that states could hire additional court workers, set up graduated sanctioning systems, and build or expand juvenile correctional facilities (C. Andrews and Marble, 2003; Beyer, 2003). (As discussed later, the OJJDP also encouraged states to combine sanctions with rehabilitation and prevention programs.)

Most states also placed increased emphasis on getting tough with juvenile offenders. For example, many states altered the mission statements for their juvenile court systems to say explicitly that the major purposes of juvenile court include holding offenders accountable for their behavior, punishing offenders, and/or protecting the community from offenders. That is not to say that these states abandoned the goal of rehabilitation but, rather, that they now emphasized accountability and punishment along with rehabilitation. Accordingly, juvenile courts and correctional agencies made systematic efforts to get tough with offenders, especially serious offenders. As described in Chapter 1, several states have begun to retreat from these get-tough efforts in recent years. Nevertheless, get-tough efforts constituted the major trend in juvenile justice and continue to have some influence on the way we respond to juvenile offenders.[3] Indeed, many get-tough laws remain on the books, as revealed in the next section.

Some Get-Tough Measures

Beginning in the late 1980s and early 1990s, many juvenile courts attempted to make more efficient use of their limited court staff so they could better concentrate on serious offenders. One reason for the development of diversion programs was to allow court staff to transfer less serious cases out of the court system and focus on more serious cases. Also, many juvenile courts **tried to better identify serious offenders and then concentrate their resources on those individuals.** For example, many courts now use risk assessment instruments to identify juveniles at greatest risk for future offending (see Chapter 21 for more information).

Juvenile courts also imposed more severe sanctions on offenders, especially serious offenders. The desire for more severe sanctions is one of the reasons for the development of the **intermediate sanctions** described in Chapter 21; the sanctions include restitution, intensive supervision, home confinement, and boot camps. Beyond that, states took a number of steps to increase the certainty and especially the severity of sanctions given out by the juvenile court. The most notable of these steps are as follows.

1. *Mandatory minimum sentences and sentencing guidelines.* Many states have adopted mandatory minimum sentences or sentencing guidelines in their juvenile courts. Mandatory minimum sentences require judges to confine certain offenders, usually older juveniles who commit serious crimes and/or have prior records, for a predetermined amount of time. For example, Delaware required juvenile court judges to "sentence any youth convicted of a second felony within one year to a minimum term of six months' confinement" (Feld, 1999:258). Sentencing guidelines are less common, but a few states provide guidelines for judges to follow in the sentencing of juveniles. The guidelines typically classify juvenile offenders into categories based on the seriousness of their offense, the extent of their prior record, and their age. The guidelines then specify the minimum and maximum sentences for juveniles in each category. For example, the guidelines in Washington State specify that juveniles classified as "serious" offenders receive sentences ranging from confinement for 125 weeks to 3 years (Feld, 1999:255). Judges are strongly encouraged to select a sentence within this range, taking account of certain aggravating and mitigating factors associated with each case.

Mandatory minimum sentences and sentencing guidelines, which were created with the goal of increasing the severity of court sanctions, were supposed to limit the discretion of judges. They represent a significant departure from the original mission of the juvenile court, which was to determine the problems that caused juveniles to offend and to devise individualized treatment plans to address these problems. That is, the court was supposed to focus on *helping offenders* rather than *punishing juveniles for their offenses* (see Chapter 1 of this volume; also see Feld, 1999).

2. *Blended sentences.* Juvenile courts used to be quite limited in the punishments they could impose. Juvenile courts, in particular, were able to confine offenders in juvenile institutions for only short periods of time—usually until the offenders reached adulthood or shortly thereafter. But almost half of all states have passed laws that allow their juvenile

courts to sentence certain serious offenders to long periods of confinement in adult correctional institutions. In some states, the sentenced offenders begin serving their time in juvenile correctional institutions and, upon reaching adulthood, are transferred to adult institutions. In other states, juvenile court judges have the option of sending juvenile offenders directly to adult correctional institutions. And in still other states, juveniles are sentenced to both juvenile and adult correctional facilities, but if they successfully complete the juvenile portion of their sentence and do not reoffend, the adult portion of the sentence is suspended. Sentences of this third type are called blended sentences because, when necessary, a young offender's sentence consists of time in the juvenile correctional system followed by time in the adult system. Such sentences are obviously designed to increase the severity of sanctions administered by the juvenile courts (see Butts and Mitchell, 2000; Redding and Howell, 2000).

3. Waiver to adult court. Almost all states have passed legislation making it easier to try certain juvenile cases in adult court, where the sanctions are generally more severe. Certain of these laws expand the range of cases that judges can waive to juvenile court; some laws, for example, lower the age limit for waiver or increase the number of offenses eligible for waiver. Other laws require or strongly encourage judges to waive cases of certain types to adult court. Still other laws give prosecutors the power to decide whether cases meeting certain criteria should be tried in adult or juvenile courts. Finally, certain laws state that cases that meet certain criteria will automatically be tried in adult court. These laws tend to focus on cases involving older juveniles who commit certain serious crimes and/or have prior records (see Chapter 21 for further information).

The get-tough approach to juvenile offenders has also been reflected in other ways. As indicated in Chapter 1, most juvenile courts **have reduced the confidentiality of juvenile court proceedings.** Juvenile court hearings used to be closed to the public; the names of juvenile offenders were not revealed to the media or made available to the public; court records were rarely shared with agencies outside the juvenile court; and court records were often expunged or destroyed if the juvenile remained crime free for a specified time. The rationale for such actions derived from labeling theory: the juvenile offender was to be protected from the stigma of a delinquent label. There is now less concern with protecting juvenile offenders and more concern with protecting society *from* juvenile offenders. All states now (1) require or permit open court hearings for juveniles accused of certain serious crimes, (2) allow the names of juveniles convicted of certain serious offenses to be released to the public, (3) allow greater access to juvenile court records, and/or (4) make it more difficult for juveniles to expunge or destroy their court records. To give an example, virtually all states now allow adult criminal courts access to juvenile court records. Such records are often taken into account during the sentencing of adults convicted of crimes; in addition, adults with serious juvenile records receive more severe sentences.

The get-tough policies had a significant effect on the treatment of juvenile offenders, especially serious and high-rate offenders. The adoption of get-tough policies peaked during the 1980s and 1990s, partly as a response to the large increase in serious juvenile violence from the mid-1980s to early 1990s (see Chapter 3). And these policies resulted in major changes in the treatment of juvenile offenders, particularly serious and chronic offenders. There was a substantial increase in the rate at which juvenile offenders were incarcerated. This rate peaked in 1997, with 368 juveniles per 100,000 held in juvenile facilities. There was a dramatic increase in the number of juveniles transferred to adult court during the 1980s and 1990s. Reflecting this fact, the number of juveniles serving time in adult jails increased sixfold from the mid-1980s to 1997—when it peaked at 9,105. The number of juveniles admitted to adult prisons more than doubled from 1985 to 1997, when it peaked at 7,400 admissions (Austin et al., 2000). (Note: Individuals serving sentences of more than a year are sent to prisons, while sentences of a year or less are served in jails.) In recent years, however, as discussed in Chapter 1, there has been some reaction against get-tough policies (also see Chapter 24). Partly as a result, the years since the late 1990s have seen significant declines in the juvenile incarceration rate, in the number of juveniles transferred to adult court, and in the number of juveniles in adult prisons and jails. Even so, get-tough policies remain in effect in most places and continue to shape the reaction to juvenile crime.[4]

HOW EFFECTIVE ARE GET-TOUGH MEASURES, AND WHAT CAN BE DONE TO INCREASE THEIR EFFECTIVENESS?

Has the get-tough movement worked? Is it effective? It is difficult to give a definitive answer because not all of the get-tough efforts have been carefully evaluated, and existing evaluations have not always produced consistent results. There are, however, enough evaluation data to draw some tentative conclusions about the effectiveness of these get-tough efforts.

We first examine whether the get-tough strategies have a deterrent effect, that is: Do they deter juveniles from engaging in crime? We then examine whether the get-tough strategies have an incapacitation effect that is: Do they prevent crime by locking people up so they cannot commit crimes on the street? We also discuss what can be done to increase the effectiveness of the get-tough strategies.

Deterrence

Punishing more offenders or punishing them more severely is said to deter juveniles from committing crime.[5] *Deterrence* is based on *the fear of punishment*. By increasing the *certainty and/or severity of punishment*, society aims to increase the fear of punishment among those in the general population as well as among those who are punished. It is this fear that is said to deter juveniles from committing delinquent acts.

This argument is compatible with control and social learning theories. Recall that one of the major types of control is direct control. Direct control refers to the probability that one's criminal acts will be detected and punished by others. The strategy of deterrence tries to increase one type of direct control—direct control by the juvenile justice system. People who advocate deterrence want to increase the likelihood that juvenile offenders will be caught by the police and will receive meaningful sanctions from the juvenile courts. Advocates of deterrence usually pay less attention to direct control exercised by family members, friends, school officials, and others. They also pay less attention to other forms of social control, such as one's stake in conformity and internal control.

Social learning theorists also argue that delinquency is less likely to occur if it is punished. Again, advocates of deterrence focus on one type of punishment—punishment by the juvenile justice system. They pay less attention to the punishments administered by family members, friends, and others. Also, they do not focus on the other causes of crime outlined in social learning theory, such as the reinforcements for crime, beliefs conducive to crime, and exposure to delinquent models.

We next examine whether the get-tough efforts described earlier—which focus primarily on increasing the severity of punishment—deter from further offending those specific others who are punished (specific deterrence). We then examine whether these strategies deter people in the general population, including those who were not punished, from offending (general deterrence).

Specific Deterrence

Do punishments by the juvenile justice system reduce the likelihood of delinquency among those who are punished?

A number of studies have tried to determine whether increasing the severity of punishment reduces delinquency. The studies compare the subsequent delinquency of juveniles who had received more severe and less severe punishments. For example, juveniles on intensive supervision programs are compared with similar juveniles on regular probation. Juveniles tried in adult courts are compared with similar juveniles tried in juvenile courts. The evaluations try to determine whether the get-tough approach reduces the likelihood of future delinquency, with future delinquency most often measured in terms of arrests or court referrals.

One general conclusion emerging from the evaluations is that the **get-tough approaches have little or no effect on future offending.** In certain cases, they may actually increase future offending. The major get-tough initiatives include intermediate sanctions (for those who otherwise would have been placed on regular probation), sending juveniles to institutions or sending them there for longer periods, and trying juveniles as adults, which often results in confinement in adult institutions. As indicated in Chapter 21, evaluations suggest that most intermediate sanctions have little or no effect on future offending. Sending juveniles to institutions is no more effective at reducing offending than many community-based alternatives. Some data, in fact, suggest that it may be easier to reduce reoffending in community-based programs than in institutions. Sending juveniles to institutions for longer periods also does not reduce offending; in fact, some data suggest that longer periods of confinement increase the likelihood of subsequent offending. Finally, although findings are somewhat mixed, data suggest that trying juveniles as adults does not consistently reduce reoffending. In fact, trying juveniles as adults can increase their rates of future offending.[6] Subjecting juveniles to more severe punishments, then, does not seem to deter them from further offending.

Are punished offenders less likely to commit delinquent acts than similar offenders who have not been punished by the juvenile justice system? While most studies have compared more severely to less severely punished offenders, a few studies have compared punished offenders to offenders who have not been punished. These latter studies are somewhat problematic. The ideal way to compare punished to unpunished offenders is to do a randomized experiment. For example, we might ask the police to flip a coin whenever they catch a juvenile offender. If the coin comes up heads, they release the offender. If it comes up tails, they arrest the offender and refer him or her to juvenile court for punishment. We could then determine whether punished offenders have lower rates of subsequent delinquency than released offenders. If the punished offenders do have lower rates, that suggests that punishment does deter those who are punished. But, as you might imagine, a study of this type has never been done.

A few studies, however, have compared arrested or convicted offenders to comparable offenders who have not been arrested or convicted. The two groups are usually comparable in terms of the offenses they have committed and sociodemographic characteristics like age, gender, race, and class. Since random assignment is not used, however, it may be that the two groups differ in important ways that we are not aware of. The results of such studies are mixed, but they tend to suggest that the arrested and convicted offenders do not have lower rates of subsequent delinquency. Some studies, in fact, find that the arrested offenders have higher rates of subsequent delinquency (see Chapter 9).[7] Overall, then, one may tentatively conclude that **formally punishing offenders does not reduce their subsequent delinquency.**

Why doesn't punishing offenders deter them from delinquency? There are at least four possible reasons why punishing offenders may not deter them from committing delinquent acts.

First, **the juvenile justice system does not punish in an effective way.** To be effective, punishments must be reasonably certain, as well as meeting other criteria (see Chapter 8;

D. Andrews and Bonta, 2006). But the certainty or likelihood of punishment is usually very low (see Chapters 3 and 21). As a consequence, punished offenders may feel that they can get away with crime in the future. In fact, some data suggest that punished offenders do not increase their estimates of the certainty of future punishment and may even reduce them.[8]

Second, **many juveniles are not very responsive to punishment.** Those who have a low stake in conformity, or little to lose by engaging in delinquency, may not feel very threatened by the prospect of punishment. Others are not very rational; that is, they do not give much thought to the possible costs of their delinquent acts. Rather, they are impulsive and often act without thinking about the consequences of their behavior (see Chapter 13). Furthermore, many juveniles commit their offenses under the influence of drugs or alcohol or delinquent peers, which also reduces their concern for the costs of crime (see Chapters 16 and 17; also Carmichael and Piquero, 2004; Nagin and Pogarsky, 2004; B. Wright et al., 2004).

Third, there are several **major causes for an individual's delinquency.** However, punishing a person for his or her delinquency does little to address these causes. For example, punishment usually reduces neither the strain the offender may be experiencing nor the extent to which he or she learns crime from others. While punishment does increase one form of direct control, it usually does not increase the other forms of control.

Fourth, **punishments may sometimes backfire and increase the likelihood of subsequent crime.** This issue was discussed in some detail in Chapter 9, which described labeling theory. As stated in that chapter, punishments may increase strain. Punishments that are excessive, overly harsh, or applied in a discriminatory manner may themselves create strain. For example, institutionalized offenders sometimes state that their imprisonment turned them into angry, vengeful individuals. Furthermore, punishment may make it more difficult for individuals to achieve their goals and may increase the likelihood of negative treatment by others. Punishment may also reduce many types of social control and increase the social learning of crime. If you are confined in an institution, you are physically isolated from conventional others and forced to associate with other delinquents, who teach you to be a better delinquent. It is for this reason that institutions are sometimes referred to as "schools for crime." In addition, individuals who have been labeled delinquent through punishment often find that conventional others are reluctant to associate with them. Partly as a consequence, they often end up associating with other delinquents. There is reason to believe that these negative effects are especially likely when juveniles are punished in the adult system and confined in adult institutions (Bishop and Frazier, 2000).

Can we punish in an effective way? A number of criminologists argue that the effect of punishment on delinquency depends on the nature of the punishment and the characteristics of the person being punished. While punished offenders as a whole may not reduce their subsequent delinquency, it may be that some punished offenders will reduce their delinquency, while others will increase their delinquent behavior. A few studies, conducted mostly with adults, provide some support for this argument.

Limited data suggest that punishment is likely to deter offenders from committing additional crimes under the following circumstances. (1) The likelihood of meaningful punishment is reasonably high (e.g., certain studies on police crackdowns demonstrate that it is possible to deter offenders from further crime when the probability of meaningful punishments is high); (2) the individuals who are punished have some concern for the costs of crimes (e.g., they have a stake in conformity, such as a decent job or close ties to their family members); (3) punishment is combined with rehabilitation, so that some of the other causes of delinquency are addressed; and (4) steps are taken to minimize or counteract the negative effects of punishment (e.g., efforts are made to punish in a fair, respectful manner and to reintegrate punished offenders into conventional society).[9]

Combining punishment with rehabilitation. Some criminologists have drawn on the foregoing arguments to propose that punishment be combined with rehabilitation, with rehabilitation addressing the other causes of crime. In particular, it has been argued that the punishment process often provides an opportunity to rehabilitate offenders. Offenders in intensive supervision programs or in institutions, for example, can be required to participate in rehabilitation programs, which can then address many of the other factors that caused the offenders to engage in crime. We now have some knowledge of the types of rehabilitation program that are effective (see Chapter 24). Further, data suggest that such programs are effective even if offenders are forced to participate in them. Such programs are effective in both community and institutional settings, although they are perhaps somewhat more effective in community settings (e.g., used with offenders on intensive probation supervision). The evaluation research supports these arguments, with data indicating that punishments are effective in reducing subsequent offending when they are combined with carefully selected rehabilitation programs.[10] The OJJDP is now encouraging juvenile courts and correctional agencies to combine punishment with rehabilitation (Beyer, 2003; Kurlychek et al., 1999).

Restorative justice. Some criminologists and policy makers are also proposing that we adopt an alternative style of punishment, known as the restorative justice approach, which is designed to address certain of the problems of punishment described earlier.[11] (This approach was discussed briefly in Chapter 9.) Restorative justice has a range of objectives, but one of its central objectives is to sanction offenders in a more effective manner. Advocates of restorative justice argue that it is important to hold delinquents accountable for their offenses and to impose meaningful sanctions on them. At the same time, they say that such sanctions should not be excessive and should not isolate offenders from conventional society. Rather, sanctions should allow offenders to repair the harm they have done, restore their ties with conventional others, and address at least some of the causes of their delinquency.

These ideas have been implemented in different ways (see Bazemore and Umbreit, 2001). Nevertheless, most restorative justice programs share certain features. After the offender has admitted his or her guilt, offender and victim are usually given the opportunity to participate in the restorative justice program. If the parties agree to embark on the program, a *conference* is scheduled. The conference usually includes the offender, the offender's family, perhaps a few supporters of the offender, the victim, a few supporters of the victim, representatives from the community, and possibly the arresting officer. The conference may be held at the local juvenile court or another site, like a school or community center. The conference is typically run by a facilitator or coordinator, perhaps a member of the staff of the juvenile court, but not necessarily.

The conference usually begins with the victim describing the harm that the crime caused. Supporters of the victim may also discuss the harm experienced by the victim. Further, community representatives might talk about the impact of the crime on the local neighborhood. The offender and the offender's supporters may then talk about the crime, the reasons behind the crime, and how the crime has affected them. The victim may then have the opportunity to question the offender. This process helps the offender appreciate how much harm he or she has caused and, perhaps, empathize or identify with the victim. It also helps the victim and others better understand the offender and his or her problems, making them less likely to reject or hate the offender. Participants in the conference— including both the victim and offender—then discuss how the harm caused by the crime might be repaired. Typically, the offender apologizes to the victim, makes restitution to the victim to cover the cost of damaged property, medical expenses, and so on, and performs community service. Community service is a way to make restitution to the larger neighborhood and perhaps establish positive ties with conventional others. Community representatives at the conference may also try to establish positive ties with the offender, as well as deal with certain of the problems that motivated the delinquent act.

The restorative justice approach attempts to sanction offenders without increasing the likelihood of further crime. The sanctions applied are not overly harsh, they do not for the most part involve confinement in an institution, and they do not cut offenders off from conventional others and foster association with delinquent peers. Further, the restorative justice approach **tries to address at least certain of the causes of crime beyond direct control.** Offenders are made aware of the harm caused by their crime, which may increase their internal control. They establish close ties to conventional others and become involved in positive community activities, which may increase their stake in conformity. And efforts may be made to address still other of the causes of crime.

Bazemore (2000:251) provides the following example of how the restorative justice approach often operates. A 14-year-old boy got into an altercation with a teacher, injuring the teacher and breaking the man's glasses. After the boy admitted to the offense, a conference was held in the local school. The conference was directed by a trained facilitator, and conference participants included the offender, his mother, his grandfather, two of the offender's other teachers, the arresting officer, the victim, two friends of the victim, and a small group of members of the community. The victim, the offender, his relatives, and the police officer spoke about the offense and its impact on them. Likewise, people from the community had an opportunity to comment on the impact of the crime. Then the facilitator asked the victim and others—including the offender—how the harm caused by the crime could be repaired. A discussion ensued, and it was decided that the offender should reimburse the victim for his medical expenses and the cost of new glasses. Further, the offender should perform community service work on the school grounds.

The OJJDP is promoting a restorative justice approach to sanctioning that has been implemented, to varying degrees, by several hundred U.S. communities. The approach is usually employed with less serious crimes, although it has been used with more serious crimes in certain areas. Initial evaluations indicate that the restorative justice approach is promising. Data suggest that both victims and offenders much prefer restorative justice to traditional court processing, and some data suggest that the approach may reduce subsequent rates of offending, at least for certain types of offender.[12]

Summary For now, we can draw the following tentative conclusion: overall, punishing juveniles or punishing them more severely does not reduce subsequent delinquency. But there is reason to believe that punishments may reduce delinquency if administered properly. In particular, punishments need to be made more certain, to address at least some of the other causes of crime, and to be administered in ways that do not increase the likelihood of further crime. These goals can be, at least partly, accomplished by combining punishments with rehabilitation and, perhaps, through the use of the restorative justice approach.

General Deterrence

Studies on specific deterrence ask whether punishment deters delinquency among those who are punished. Studies on general deterrence ask whether punishment deters delinquency among juveniles in the general population, including those who were not punished. For example, suppose five students are caught cheating and are punished. Their punishment may deter other students in the class from cheating, even though only five were punished. The unpunished students may come to fear that they too might be caught and punished if they cheat.

Numerous studies have tried to determine whether there is a general deterrent effect; that is, whether increasing the certainty and/or severity of punishment reduces crime in the general population. Some studies compare geographic areas that differ in terms of the certainty and/or severity of punishment. Usually states are compared, but sometimes cities or counties are compared. Certainty of punishment is usually measured in terms of the arrest rate—that is, the number of offenses known to the police that result in arrest. Severity is often measured in terms of the average length of prison sentence served for various crimes. These studies try to determine whether areas with higher certainty and/or severity of punishment have lower crime rates.

Such studies, however, are able to determine only whether there is an association between the certainty and severity of punishment and crime rates. They cannot determine whether certainty and severity of punishment have a causal effect on crime rates. For example, many of these studies find that areas with a high certainty of punishment have lower crime rates. But the association between certainty and crime rates may be due to third variables, like poverty. High levels of poverty may cause crime, on the one hand, and may lead to a low certainty of punishment on the other. Areas high in poverty, for example, may have less money to spend on policing and so may have less effective police forces. Also, the certainty of punishment and crime rates may be associated because crime rates affect the level of certainty. High rates of crime may overwhelm the police, reducing their ability to catch offenders and thereby lowering the certainty of punishment.

Researchers have tried to overcome these problems by taking account of third variables and doing longitudinal studies. In particular, researchers focus on third variables that may influence both the certainty and severity of punishment and crime rates. For example, they may examine the relationship between certainty of punishment and crime rates in areas that have similar levels of poverty. Also, researchers do longitudinal studies that examine whether changes in the certainty and/or severity of punishment affect crime rates at a subsequent point in time. For example, Singer and McDowall (1988) considered a New York law that lowered the age at which juveniles charged with certain crimes could be tried in adult courts. They compared the arrest rates for juveniles affected by the law before and after it took effect and did not find any evidence of a significant reduction in arrest rates that could be attributed to the law. They also compared the arrest rates for juveniles affected by the law to the arrest rates for juveniles of the same age in a nearby jurisdiction not affected by the law, and they again did not find any evidence that the law significantly reduced arrest rates.

These studies, however, have also been criticized. Criminologists argue that the studies are based on the assumption that people are aware of the certainty and severity of punishment in the area where they live. Data, however, suggest that this assumption is often wrong (see Kleck et al., 2005). Many people have little idea of the true certainty and severity of punishment. (Do you know the certainty and severity of punishment for marijuana use in your hometown or state?) In particular, people who are law abiding often greatly overestimate the certainty and severity of punishment. (Officials in our home state of Georgia tried to counter this ignorance of sanctions by making a video describing changes in the law that increased the severity of punishments for certain crimes. The video was then shown to students throughout the state in a deliberate attempt to deter them from committing delinquent acts.)

Some criminologists argue, therefore, that the best way to determine whether people are deterred by the threat of punishment is to ask them to estimate the certainty and severity of punishment—in particular, to ask them to estimate the likelihood that they will be punished if they commit a particular offense and what their punishment will be. If people are deterred by the threat of punishment, their estimates of the certainty and severity of punishment should have an effect on their levels of crime. So people who state that they will be caught and severely punished if they engage in crime should be less likely to engage in crime.

A number of studies have been done in this area. For example, students are asked to estimate the likelihood that they will be caught by the police if they use marijuana, and they are asked what punishment they would probably receive if caught. The responses to these questions allow researchers to measure the students' perceptions about the certainty and severity of punishment. The researchers then determine whether these perceptions are related to delinquency. The more recent and better studies are longitudinal and take into account third variables. So researchers compare the subsequent offending of similar juveniles who differ in terms of their perceptions of certainty and severity of punishment. If deterrence works, the juveniles who believe they will definitely receive severe punishments should have lower levels of subsequent delinquency.

Thus, a range of studies have tried to determine whether the certainty and severity of punishment are related to crime in the general population. These studies do not always agree, but the more recent and best research offers tentative support for the following conclusions.[13]

Most notably, **increasing the certainty of punishment may reduce crime by a moderate amount in some circumstances.** The certainty of punishment, however, is only one of many factors influencing the level of crime. The certainty of punishment is less important than other factors, such as the individual's beliefs regarding delinquency and the threat of informal punishment from family members and others. The severity of punishment is less important than the certainty of punishment. Most studies suggest that changes in the severity of punishment have little or no effect on delinquency. The study by Singer and McDowall (1988) described earlier did not find any evidence that increasing the severity of punishment by making it easier to try juveniles as adults reduced offending in the general population (also see Bishop and Frazier, 2000; Steiner et al., 2006). Certain studies, however, suggest that increasing the severity of punishment may reduce delinquency *if the certainty of punishment is high.*

As indicated, the certainty of punishment reduces delinquency in some circumstances. Limited research suggests that the effect of punishment is short-lived and is confined to the specific geographic area in which the punishment is administered. Punishments administered a year earlier, therefore, have little or no effect on current levels of delinquency. (Likewise, individuals' perception of the certainty of punishment a year earlier often has little effect on their current delinquency.) Also, punishments administered outside one's community appear to have little deterrent effect. This makes sense. People are most responsive to recent punishments administered where they live. Finally, some data suggest that punishments must be reasonably certain if potential offenders are to be deterred. A few studies estimate that the probability of punishment needs to be above 30 to 40 percent if potential offenders are to be deterred, although more research is needed in this area.

Increasing the certainty of punishment, then, may cause a moderate reduction in delinquency in the general population, although this effect tends to be short-lived and confined to the immediate area in which the certainty is increased. And it may be that society will have to substantially increase the certainty of punishment before this measure can have an observable effect on crime. Such an increase cannot easily be achieved. It involves hiring more police and changing how they function (see Chapter 18). It also involves hiring more juvenile court staff. Increasing the severity of punishment appears to have little or no impact on delinquency, unless, perhaps, the certainty of punishment is high.

Unfortunately, most of the get-tough approaches described earlier **focus on increasing the severity of punishment.** It is easy to understand why this is the case. It is a simple matter for politicians to increase severity: they pass a law that raises the penalties for certain crimes. Such laws make them appear tough on crime and may win them votes.

But, as just discussed, it is doubtful whether the laws have a deterrent effect. It is possible, however, to **increase the certainty of punishment and perhaps have something of an effect on delinquency rates.** The discussion of police crackdowns in Chapter 20 describes how this may be done. Recall the evidence suggesting that police crackdowns do result in a moderate reduction in crime in the immediate area where they are instituted. The effect of the crackdowns is typically short-lived, however, and crime returns to its former level soon after the crackdowns end. But a strategy of "rotating crackdowns" (discussed in Chapter 20) has the potential for reducing crime over the long term (Telep et al., 2014). Also, community policing has some potential for increasing the certainty of punishment, since it establishes closer ties between the police and a community and better involves community residents in crime control efforts. Finally, we might increase certainty by providing more resources to juvenile courts and correctional agencies, so that they can impose meaningful sanctions on a higher percentage of juvenile offenders.

Summary. Increasing the certainty of punishment may reduce delinquency by a moderate amount in the general population; increasing the severity of punishment has little or no effect on delinquency in the general population unless, perhaps, the certainty of punishment is high. Most of the get-tough approaches described focus on increasing the severity of punishment; as such, there is good reason to believe that they do little to reduce offending in the general population. Unfortunately, it is much more difficult to increase the certainty of punishment than the severity of punishment.

Incapacitation: Will Locking Up Delinquents Reduce Delinquency?

Deterrence is based on the fear of punishment. Increasing the certainty and severity of punishment is supposed to increase the fear of punishment and thereby deter people from committing crime. However, it is often difficult to deter juveniles from committing crimes—both juveniles who have been punished and those in the general population. Partly as a consequence, many people have come to recommend another get-tough approach to controlling delinquency. They argue that we should lock up serious offenders for long periods. This measure, they claim, will substantially reduce crime. The reason is simple: if you lock up offenders, they cannot commit crimes on the street. Crime is therefore reduced even if no one is deterred from committing crime. This delinquency control strategy is known as incapacitation.[14]

During the past few decades, incapacitation has been the major strategy in the United States for controlling adult crime. The number of adults held in prisons in the United States increased from 200,000 in 1971 to over 1,518,000 in 2008, and the rate of incarceration increased about fivefold during this time. Many more adults were sent to prison and confined for longer periods of time. The average length of confinement for a violent crime, for example, more than tripled over this same time period. The primary reason for this dramatic increase in incarceration rates was the belief that incapacitation would reduce crime. Again, locking up criminals prevents them from committing crimes on the streets. (Note: In recent years, the prison population has begun to decline somewhat, owing partly to a falling crime rate and a retreat from get-tough efforts in many states. Nevertheless, the incarceration rate in the United States is still the highest in the world—see Carson and Golinelli, 2013; National Research Council, 2014.)

Incapacitation has not been the major strategy for controlling juvenile delinquency, but it has been an important strategy. As discussed earlier, there was a movement to increase the number of serious juvenile offenders sent to institutions and to increase the length of time they stay in such institutions. Although this movement was partly designed to deter delinquency, it was also motivated by a desire to protect society by getting serious offenders off the street.

How can one determine how much crime is prevented by incapacitation? The strategy of incapacitation makes much common sense: if you lock people up, you prevent crime on the streets. But how do criminologists go about determining just how much crime is prevented? On the face of it, it should be easy to calculate the amount of crime prevented through incapacitation. One would simply estimate how many crimes incarcerated offenders commit each year when they are free by surveying such offenders or examining their arrest records. (There are, of course, concerns about the accuracy of such estimates: see Zimring and Hawkins, 1997.) Such estimates, then, might be used to determine how many crimes are prevented by locking up criminals.

For example, suppose researchers find that the average juvenile in a training school commits 10 crimes per year when free. And suppose that 100,000 juveniles are in training schools. Incarceration, then, could be said to prevent 1 million offenses per year (10 multiplied by 100,000). If society incarcerates an additional 50,000 offenders, such incapacitation might prevent another 500,000 crimes. Estimates of this sort were offered during the 1970s, when incapacitation was becoming a popular crime control strategy. Several researchers claimed that incapacitating offenders prevents a large amount of crime and that incapacitating additional offenders will prevent much more crime.

It turns out that such claims were exaggerated. Assume that researchers obtain accurate estimates of the number of crimes incarcerated offenders commit each year when free. For example, suppose they had in fact determined that the average incarcerated offender commits 10 crimes per year when free. One might then conclude that locking an offender up prevents 10 crimes per year. But this conclusion is not necessarily correct.

First, it may be that when society locks up one offender, another criminal takes that offender's place. So if we lock up someone for selling drugs on a street corner, someone else may start selling drugs on the same corner the next day. As a result, no crime is prevented. This phenomenon is known as a *substitution effect*. It is difficult to estimate how much substitution occurs; it may be high for certain crimes like drug selling but low for other crimes like robbery.

Second, we know that most juvenile offenses are committed in groups. Locking up one juvenile in the group may have little or no effect on the amount of crime committed by the group. Once again, there is no reduction in crime. This is known as a *group effect*. Again, it is difficult to estimate the size of this effect.

Third, many juvenile offenders substantially reduce their level of offending toward the end of adolescence. This phenomenon, sometimes referred to as "maturing out" of delinquency, occurs as juveniles leave their delinquent peers, get jobs or enter college, and form families of their own. Imprisoning such juveniles for long periods would not prevent a large amount of crime, since many of those individuals would have stopped committing crimes on their own.

Fourth, estimates about the effect of locking up *additional* offenders may be exaggerated, since the additional offenders might not commit as much crime as the offenders who are already locked up. That is, the offenders who are already locked up might commit more crimes per year when free than those who are not locked up; recall that high-rate offenders are probably more likely to be in prison than low-rate offenders. There is no guarantee that locking up additional offenders would prevent enough crimes to match the estimate, since these additional offenders commit crimes at a lower rate.

It is therefore difficult to estimate the amount of crime that is prevented through incapacitation and the amount of crime that will be prevented by incapacitating additional juveniles. Nevertheless, several researchers have tried to estimate the effectiveness of incapacitation as a crime control strategy. Some of the estimates are based on studies that attempt to determine the number of crimes offenders commit each year when free. Such estimates are then used to calculate the amount of crime prevented by incapacitation. As indicated, however, there are serious problems with this strategy, which likely exaggerates the size of the incapacitation effect. As a consequence, some researchers have employed alternative strategies.

In particular, some researchers compare states or other areas that have different rates of incarceration. The objective is to determine whether areas with higher rates of incarceration have lower crime rates. However, one must take account of all the other factors that affect crime rates—something that is not easy to do. Also, any apparent association between incarceration rates and crime rates may be due to the effect of crime rates on incarceration rates. For example, high rates of crime might overwhelm the criminal justice system, leading to low rates of incarceration.

Other researchers examine incarceration rates and crime rates in the same area over time, wishing to determine whether changes in the incarceration rate are associated with changes in the crime rate. For example, what impact has the massive increase in incarceration rates in recent decades had on crime rates? Such studies, however, must also take account of the other factors that might affect the crime rate. Also, such studies are not able to distinguish **incapacitation** effects from **deterrence** effects. That is, they do not allow researchers to determine *why* an increase in incarceration rates reduced crime: because incarcerated offenders could not commit crimes on the street (an incapacitation effect) or because potential offenders were deterred from committing crimes.

What is the impact of incapacitation on crime rates? So none of the studies of the types just discussed is problem free. Taken together, however, they give us a **rough** sense of the effectiveness of incapacitation as a crime control strategy. Most studies have focused on adults and have examined the massive increase in incarceration since the 1970s. The best studies suggest that this increase in incarceration had a moderate effect on crime rates. In particular, the best studies in this area suggest that a 10 percent increase in the incarceration rate is associated with a 2 to 4 percent lower crime rate (see Stemen, 2007:5). However, as the incarceration rate increases, the reduction in crime resulting from further increases is reduced (because more lower-rate offenders are imprisoned). It is estimated that about one-quarter of the crime drop during the 1990s was due to the rapidly increasing rates of incarceration the United States experienced during the 1980s and 1990s.[15]

The studies of the effects of incapacitation are based largely on adults. The extent to which this measure prevents crime among juveniles is not clear, although available data suggest that its impact on youth crime is limited. In one study, researchers compared juvenile crime trends in California and Texas. To combat youth crime, both states pursued a policy of mass incarceration during the 1990s. In Texas, this strategy continued into the 2000s and included the incarceration of both violent and nonviolent offenders. Between 1995 and 2006, for example, Texas increased its juvenile incarceration rate by 48 percent (reflecting a dramatic increase in the number of imprisoned juveniles). Meanwhile, California began to move away from its policy of mass incarceration, *reducing* the juvenile incarceration rate by 75 percent during the same time period—mainly by reserving imprisonment for serious violent offenders. What has been the result? Despite the different crime control strategies in Texas and California—with incarceration rates increasing dramatically in one state and decreasing dramatically in the other—*both states experienced a 51 percent drop in the juvenile crime rate.* The authors of this study conclude that juvenile crime trends are largely unaffected by incarceration or incapacitation strategies. They also argue that the dramatic buildup of the juvenile incarceration rate in Texas may have been "unnecessary" (Stahlkopf et al., 2010:262).

As stated previously, such studies are not problem free. It is still possible, for instance, that the incapacitation of high-risk offenders contributed to the decline in youth crime in both Texas and California. (While California moved toward a more restrictive policy of juvenile incarceration, it continued to imprison violent youth convicted of serious offenses). However, the study does suggest that beyond a certain point, little is gained from "locking up" more and more juveniles.

There may be several reasons for the limited impact of incarceration on juvenile crime. Even in states that have pursued an aggressive policy of juvenile incarceration, the juvenile incarceration rate has not increased as quickly as the adult rate. As indicated earlier, the rate at which juveniles are confined is less than half the adult rate. Also, juveniles are more likely than adults to offend in groups, so incapacitation may have a smaller effect on juvenile crime rates. Further, most incarcerated juveniles will be released from confinement when they are still relatively young. If incarceration increases their level of subsequent offending, the benefits of incarceration may be lost (see Chapter 9, Vieraitis et al., 2007). Some data suggest that this is what happens when juveniles are tried as adults. We prevent some crime by confining these juveniles in adult prisons, but they offend at higher rates when released, which more than wipes out the benefits of confinement. Given these considerations, we may very tentatively conclude that **the strategy of incapacitation has resulted in only a modest reduction in rates of juvenile offending.**

What if we confine more juveniles, especially high-rate offenders? We can, of course, achieve a larger incapacitation effect if we confine more juveniles, especially those who offend at high rates. In particular, we might try to better distinguish between juveniles likely to offend at high and at low rates in the future. Once such a distinction has been made, we might confine those predicted to be high-rate offenders for long periods. This approach is sometimes referred to as *selective incapacitation*, since high-rate offenders are singled out for longer sentences.

It is difficult, however, for juvenile justice officials to accurately distinguish high-rate from low-rate offenders. You might think that high-rate offenders are simply the juveniles with the longest arrest records. But many juveniles with extensive arrest records are not high-rate offenders. They are simply inept. They do not commit that many crimes; they just get caught a lot. Further, most high-rate offenders do not have extensive arrest records. Dunford and Elliott (1984), for example, found that only 19 percent of the juveniles who self-reported more than 200 offenses during a two-year period had been arrested.

Several efforts have been made to develop techniques for distinguishing high-rate from low-rate offenders. These techniques improve our ability to distinguish between offenders by a modest amount, and additional research may result in further improvements. Currently, however, we make a lot of mistakes in our attempts to distinguish among offenders (see Auerhahn, 1999; Gottfredson and Gottfredson, 1994). Many of the individuals predicted to be high-rate offenders turn out to be low-rate offenders. And some of the individuals predicted to be low-rate offenders turn out to be high-rate offenders.

Also, there are ethical issues to consider. For example, an individual predicted to be a high-rate offender might be confined for a much longer period than another individual predicted to be a low-rate offender, even though both had committed the same offense. Do you think it is appropriate to base a juvenile's punishment on the number of crimes he or she *might* commit in the future rather than simply on the crimes the juvenile has already committed? Similar ethical issues were raised in a recent U.S. Supreme Court case that dealt with punishment for juvenile offenders (see Box 23.1).

Box 23.1   Should Serious Juvenile Offenders Die in Prison? The Supreme Court Makes a Historic Ruling

In 2003, 16-year-old Terrance Graham was charged as an adult for several crimes related to the attempted armed robbery of a Florida restaurant, in which the manager was hit on the head with a steel bar (in Florida, juveniles can automatically be tried as adults for certain serious crimes). Terrance pleaded guilty to the charges and declared that this was his "first and last time getting into trouble." In exchange for his guilty plea, the judge withheld adjudication of guilt and sentenced Terrance to a year in jail and several years of probation.

Six months after his release from jail, Terrance was in trouble again. He was arrested in connection with a string of robberies. The judge determined that Terrance had violated the terms of his probation and, for the original charges, sentenced him to life in prison without possibility of parole. As the judge explained to Terrance:

> It is apparent to the court that you have decided that this is the way you are going to live your life and that the only thing I can do now is to try to protect the community from your actions. (quoted in a Florida newspaper, *Herald-Tribune,* 2009)

In effect, without any realistic hope of release, Terrance was sentenced to die in prison. His lawyer claimed that imposing such sentences on juveniles who have not killed anyone violates the Eighth Amendment, which bans cruel and unusual punishment. In 2010, the U.S. Supreme Court ruled on the case in *Graham v. Florida.* In a 5–4 decision, the Court sided with Graham and ruled that sentences of "life without parole" are unconstitutional in nonhomicide juvenile cases (one of the four dissenting justices agreed that Terrance Graham should not have received life without parole, but thought that the overall ruling was too broad).

The justices cited numerous reasons for their decision, but the following should be of special interest to students of juvenile delinquency. First, as the Court had determined in an earlier ruling (which banned the death penalty for juvenile offenders), juveniles are less culpable or responsible than adults for the bad decisions they make (see *Roper v. Simmons,* 543 U.S. 551 [2005]). For example, research indicates that juveniles tend to be more easily influenced by criminal and delinquent peers. In the case of juveniles, poor decisions are often a function of their immaturity and lack of life experience, and less a function of their personality, which has yet to be fully developed. As a result, juveniles "are less deserving of the most serious forms of punishment."

Second, the justices note that life without parole is one of the most severe punishments available and that, for juveniles, it is a particularly harsh penalty. In comparison to an adult, a juvenile who is sentenced to life without parole will spend a greater share of his or her life behind bars.

Third, while some 2,000 juveniles have been sentenced to life without parole, almost all the cases involve homicide (see the Teaching Aids section at the end of this chapter).

(Continued)

(Continued)

Juveniles who have not killed and have not intended to kill cannot be compared to these murderers and are therefore less deserving of the same punishment.

Fourth, as further support for the Court's ruling, the justices note that the United States is the only nation in the world to sentence such youth to die in prison. It is a practice that "has been rejected the world over" (*Graham v. Florida,* No. 08–7412, p. 4).

It is important to note that the Court's ruling does **not** ban long prison terms for such juveniles. Nor does it require Florida or any other state to guarantee the eventual freedom of juvenile inmates. Rather, in nonhomicide cases, the ruling simply requires states to recognize the capacity of juveniles to grow and change by providing "some meaningful opportunity for release based on demonstrated maturity and rehabilitation" (p. 4).

As a result of this historic ruling, Terrance Graham eventually received a new sentence of 25 years in prison. When he is released in the year 2029, he will be 42 years old (Kunerth, 2012).

In 2012, the U.S. Supreme Court further restricted life sentences for juveniles, ruling that *mandatory* sentences of life without parole are unconstitutional when applied to juveniles, even in cases that involve murder (see *Miller v. Alabama,* 567 U.S. 460 [2012]). The court did not *ban* life without parole for juvenile murderers, but required judges to consider mitigating circumstances in their sentencing decisions, such as the age of the juvenile and the nature of the crime (Savage, 2012). Finally, in 2016, the Court applied their 2012 decision retroactively, mandating that all such juveniles have an opportunity for eventual release, regardless of when they committed their offenses:

> Writing for the court's six-justice majority, Justice Anthony Kennedy said that a life-without-parole sentence is always unconstitutionally cruel and unusual punishment for a juvenile offender, unless the defendant is found to be "irreparably corrupt" and "permanently incorrigible." (Totenberg, 2016)

Questions for Discussion

1. Do you agree with the Court's ruling in *Graham v. Florida*? What do you think the chances are that a juvenile who has committed a serious and violent crime will eventually change and avoid crime? What about juveniles who have committed murder (see Box 1.1 in Chapter 1)?
2. Should even these juveniles be given, in the words of the Court, "some meaningful opportunity for release based on demonstrated maturity and rehabilitation?" Or should we "throw away the key?" As you consider these questions, we encourage you to read the related section at the end of this chapter, under Teaching Aids.

Summary. Overall, we can very tentatively conclude that the strategy of incapacitating serious juvenile offenders prevents a modest amount of crime. Efforts to confine additional juvenile offenders, especially high-rate offenders, may prevent more crime. But the amount of additional crime prevented is likely to be modest as well, for reasons indicated in this section.

Furthermore, incapacitation carries a heavy price tag. It is expensive to maintain the juvenile institutions we have now, and it will be expensive to build and maintain additional institutions. Some argue that incapacitation more than pays for itself in terms of the crime it prevents, although there is much debate here (e.g., Fass and Pi, 2002). Also, some data suggest that alternatives to incapacitation, such as prevention and rehabilitation programs, may be more cost effective than incapacitation (see Chapter 24).

In addition, many commentators have pointed to the devastating effect of incapacitation on both the people who are locked up and the larger community (see Stemen, 2007; Tonry, 1995). In particular, large numbers of people who were exposed to the harsh conditions of confinement are labeled "ex-convicts" upon their release, with this label having a negative effect on their future life prospects. The strategy of incapacitation is said to have an especially negative effect on African American communities, since African Americans are much more likely to be confined than other groups. One study estimates that about one in six African American men has been incarcerated (Mauer and King, 2007).

This is not to dismiss incapacitation. No one would deny that there are dangerous offenders who need confinement. Such confinement protects society by preventing such individuals from committing crimes on the street. But incapacitation should not be our major strategy for responding to delinquency. To the extent possible, incapacitation should be limited to serious and high-rate offenders, efforts should be made to improve the conditions of confinement, and some attempt should be made to rehabilitate juveniles during their confinement.

As we indicated earlier, several states have begun to retreat from get-tough efforts in recent years (see Chapter 1). This pullback has been prompted, in part, by the disappointing results of get-tough efforts and the enormous strain they have placed on state budgets. Our home state of Georgia provides a good example. In 2012, Governor Nathan Deal (a former prosecutor) commissioned a task force of criminal justice professionals to review Georgia's juvenile justice system and suggest improvements. The task force made the following observations:

> In recent years, the number of youth in Georgia's juvenile justice system has declined; however, the cost of this system remains substantial and the Georgia taxpayers have not received a sufficient return on their investment. . . . Nearly two-thirds of [the Department of Juvenile Justice] budget is used to operate out-of-home facilities, which can cost more than $90,000 per bed per year. Despite these expenditures, more than half of the youth in the juvenile justice system are re-adjudicated delinquent or convicted of a criminal offense within three years of release, a rate that has held steady since 2003. (Special Council on Criminal Justice Reform for Georgians, 2012:2)

These observations confirmed Governor Deal's own assessment: "When I became governor in 2011, I knew that this state could not continue along the path it was traveling in terms of simply locking people up, throwing away the key to some extent, and then hoping for the best" (Swift, 2013). In 2013, the governor signed into law a bill that reflects the recommendations of the task force to reserve secure detention facilities for the most serious juvenile offenders and to keep lower-level offenders in the community. (Note: The task force had determined that many juveniles in out-of-home facilities were at low risk to reoffend: some had been adjudicated for misdemeanors and status offenses.) The bill also provides funding for community-based programs which, according to the governor, will increase the likelihood that these lower level offenders will receive substance abuse counseling or family therapy. These reforms are expected to reduce juvenile offender recidivism and save taxpayers tens of millions of dollars (Swift, 2013; for more on state-level reform efforts, see Krisberg, 2012; Bishop and Feld, 2012).

SUMMARY

In recent decades, the juvenile court and correctional system focused on getting tough with serious offenders. The get-tough efforts included the increased use of intermediate sanctions (versus regular probation), the increased use of confinement, and procedural changes that made it easier to try serious offenders in adult courts.

Overall, data suggest that these efforts do not deter juveniles who are punished from further offending. The efforts probably do not deter juveniles in the general population from offending either, largely because of the focus on increasing the severity rather than the certainty of punishment. These efforts, however, may prevent a modest amount of crime by confining offenders in institutions so that they cannot commit crimes on the street.

Several strategies for increasing the effectiveness of get-tough efforts were discussed, including strategies designed to increase their specific deterrent effect, general deterrent effect, and incapacitation effect. Such strategies include increasing the certainty of punishment, which involves hiring more police, changing police practices, and devoting more resources to juvenile courts and correctional agencies. Other strategies include combining punishment with rehabilitation programs that address the other causes of crime; employing the restorative justice approach, which minimizes the negative consequences of punishment and attempts to address certain of the other causes of crime; and efforts to improve the conditions of confinement and, to the extent possible, reserve confinement for serious, high-rate offenders. Many states are now pursuing these strategies.

As suggested earlier, however, the ultimate effectiveness of get-tough efforts is limited because they focus on just one of the many causes of crime: low direct control. Any effort to substantially reduce juvenile crime needs to focus on all the major causes of such crime. While it may be appropriate and sometimes useful to sanction juvenile offenders, we also want to make an effort to rehabilitate them, employing programs that address the other causes of delinquency. And we also want to try to stop delinquency from occurring in the first place by means of prevention programs that address the many causes of delinquency. The strategies of rehabilitation and prevention are discussed in Chapter 24.

TEACHING AIDS
Controversial Issue: Life Without Parole for Juvenile Offenders?

The United States now prohibits the execution of individuals who committed their crimes while juveniles (see Chapter 1). Also, as described in Box 23.1, the U.S. Supreme Court has banned sentences of "life without parole" in nonhomicide juvenile cases, and it has banned *mandatory* life terms for juveniles in homicide cases. However, juveniles who have committed murder may still serve life without parole if it is determined they cannot be rehabilitated. According to some prosecutors and victims' rights groups, there are indeed juvenile crimes "so terrible and people so dangerous that only life sentences without the possibility of release are a fit moral and practical response" (Liptak, 2007:A1, A24). Consider the case of Evan Miller, who was 14 years old at the time of his crime:

> Miller was sentenced to life without parole for the July 2003 killing of a neighbor, Cole Cannon. The 52-year-old Cannon was beaten, robbed and left for dead in his mobile home, which Miller and another teen set ablaze to cover up the crime. Most of the account of what happened that night came from a 16-year-old accomplice, Colby Smith, who pleaded guilty to a lesser murder charge in exchange for a life term with a chance of parole. (Smith, 2016)

The U.S. Supreme Court examined the case of Evan Miller before ruling that such juveniles must be considered for eventual release (see *Miller v. Alabama*, 567 U.S. 460 [2012]). Following the decision, a resentencing hearing has been set for Evan Miller. At this hearing, Miller's defense attorney will have an opportunity to highlight mitigating factors in Miller's background, such as a history of abuse, neglect, and mental illness. And prosecutors will have an opportunity to demonstrate that Miller is incapable of rehabilitation. In the end, the judge could either leave the door open for eventual parole or send Miller back to prison for life without parole.

Do you think it is appropriate to sentence juveniles like Evan Miller to life without the possibility of parole? In formulating your response, consider the arguments made in this chapter about deterrence (specific and general) and incapacitation, as well as the arguments made against life sentences in nonhomicide juvenile cases. (Should the same arguments apply to juveniles who have committed murder?—see Box 23.1). Consider, also, the arguments made in Chapter 1 for the abolition of the juvenile death penalty. Finally, how might prosecutors demonstrate that someone with a history like that of Evan Miller is incapable of rehabilitation?

Web-Based Exercise: Restorative Justice in Practice

A number of informative videos can be found online in which police officers, school officials, crime victims, and offenders share their experiences with restorative justice programs in their community. Visit YouTube and search for these videos by using terms such as "restorative justice documentary." View some videos, and then try to answer the following questions: What sets restorative justice programs apart from traditional responses to crime and delinquency? According to the people featured in the videos, what are the major advantages of restorative justice efforts? How do you think the police, school officials, or others authorities in your community would react to restorative justice efforts? Would they be inclined to adopt restorative justice programs? Why or why not?

TEST YOUR KNOWLEDGE OF THIS CHAPTER

1. Many argue that increasing the certainty and severity of punishment will reduce delinquency in three ways (or for three reasons). What are these ways?
2. Many argue that the juvenile court is not tough enough in dealing with serious offenders. What do the data say in this area? (Describe data on the punishments received by serious offenders in juvenile court and on the punishments given out in juvenile versus adult court.)
3. Why doesn't the juvenile court system give out more severe sanctions?
4. The OJJDP advocates a system of "graduated sanctions." Describe this system.
5. Briefly describe the major ways in which juvenile courts have tried to get tough with offenders in recent years. What does the evidence say about the effect of get-tough measures on how juvenile offenders are treated by the justice system?
6. Briefly describe mandatory minimum sentences, sentencing guidelines, and blended sentences.
7. List three ways in which states have tried to increase the number of juvenile offenders waived to adult courts.
8. List two ways in which the confidentiality of juvenile court hearings has been reduced.
9. What is meant by "deterrence"? How is deterrence related to control and social learning theories?
10. What is "specific deterrence"?
11. How have researchers tried to determine whether punishments have a specific deterrent effect?
12. We discussed how punishment often fails to deter juvenile offenders from offending again in the future. Why might this be the case?
13. How can we punish offenders more effectively?
14. What is the restorative justice approach? Describe the goals of restorative justice; tell how the approach is implemented (e.g., the conference) and how the approach tries to sanction in a more effective manner.

15. What does the evaluation research say about the restorative justice approach?
16. What is "general deterrence"?
17. How have researchers tried to determine whether punishments have a general deterrent effect? Summarize the major research findings regarding general deterrence.
18. How might we go about increasing the certainty of punishment?
19. What is meant by an *incapacitation effect*?
20. How have researchers tried to determine the size of the incapacitation effect? Why do researchers sometimes overestimate the size of the incapacitation effect?
21. Why do we suggest that efforts to incapacitate juvenile offenders have only a modest effect on the level of juvenile crime?
22. What is selective incapacitation?
23. What are the disadvantages of incapacitation as a crime control strategy?

THOUGHT AND DISCUSSION QUESTIONS

1. Give an example of a crime control strategy that has an incapacitation effect but little or no deterrent effect. Give an example of a strategy that has a deterrent effect but no incapacitation effect.
2. Many high schools and colleges experience high levels of cheating, with a majority of students having cheated at some point. Drawing on the materials in this chapter, design a sanctioning system to reduce levels of school cheating.
3. One college sanctions cheaters by giving them a failing grade for their first offense and expelling them for their second offense. How would you go about evaluating the effectiveness of this strategy (consider specific deterrence, general deterrence, and the possible incapacitation effect achieved through expulsion—once expelled, people can no longer cheat on campus)?
4. Suppose the governor of your home state seeks your advice about how to control juvenile violence. The governor states that she is thinking of mandating that all juveniles convicted of minor violent crimes serve at least 30 days in a boot camp and that all juveniles charged with serious violent crimes be tried in an adult court. Would you try to discourage the governor from taking these actions? Why or why not? What alternative actions would you recommend?
5. One of the major get-tough strategies employed by states involves making it easier to try juvenile offenders in adult courts, where they are often sanctioned with periods of confinement in prison. Do you think a strain theorist would approve of this strategy? Justify your response. What about a control theorist, a social learning theorist, and a labeling theorist?

KEY TERMS

- Specific deterrence
- General deterrence
- Incapacitation
- Graduated sanctions
- Mandatory minimum sentences
- Sentencing guidelines
- Blended sentences
- Deterrence
- Certainty and severity of punishment
- Restorative justice
- Restorative justice conference
- Substitution effect (regarding incapacitation)
- Group effect
- Selective incapacitation

ENDNOTES

1. For overviews of such efforts, see Bishop and Feld, 2012; Butts and Mitchell, 2000; Campaign for Youth and Justice, 2007; Feld, 1999; Greenwood, 2002, 2006; Howell, 2003a; Krisberg, 2005; Kupchik, 2006; McCord et al., 2001; A. Roberts, 2004; Snyder and Sickmund, 2006; Zimring, 2005.

2. See Bishop and Frazier, 2000; Butts and Mitchell, 2000; Feld and Bishop, 2012; Kupchik, 2006; Kurlychek and Johnson, 2004, 2010; McCord et al., 2001; Steiner et al., 2006.

3. See Bishop and Feld, 2012; Butts and Mitchell, 2000; Campaign for Youth and Justice, 2007; Feld, 1999; Greenwood, 2002; Howell, 2003a; Krisberg, 2005; Krohn and Lane, 2015; McCord et al., 2001; Snyder and Sickmund, 2006; Steiner et al., 2006; Torbet and Szymanski, 1998.

4. See Bishop, 2006; Bishop and Feld, 2012; Bishop and Frazier, 2000; Butts and Mitchell, 2000; Howell, 2003a; Krohn and Lane, 2015; Listwan et al., 2008; Merlo and Benekos, 2010; Puzzanchera et al., 2003.

5. For overviews of the deterrence literature, see Akers et al., 2016; Andrews and Bonta, 2006, 2006; Baron, 2013; Krohn, 2000; Lipsey and Cullen, 2008; Loughran et al., 2016; MacKenzie, 2006; Nagin, 1998a, 1998b; Paternoster, 1987; Piquero and Pogarsky, 2002; Rutter et al., 1998; Schneider, 1990; Sherman et al., 1998; K. Williams and Hawkins, 1986; R. Wright, 1994.

6. See Andrews and Bonta, 2006; Bazemore et al., 2004; Bernburg et al., 2006; Bishop and Frazier, 2000; Bottcher and Ezell, 2005; Butts and Mitchell, 2000; Feld and Bishop, 2012; Greenwood, 2002; Howell, 2003a; L. Johnson et al., 2004; Lin, 2006; Lipsey and Cullen, 2008; D. MacKenzie, 2002, 2006; Matarazzo et al., 2001; McCord et al., 2001; Parent, 2003; Peters et al., 1997; Petrosino et al., 2000; Pratt and Cullen, 2005; Redding and Howell, 2000; Steiner et al., 2006; Zane et al., 2016.

7. See Bernburg et al., 2006; Browning and Huizinga, 1999; Farrington, 1977; Farrington et al., 1978; Gold and Williams, 1969; Huizinga et al., 2003; L. Johnson et al., 2004; Palamara et al., 1986; Paternoster and Iovanni, 1989; Paternoster and Piquero, 1995; Piquero and Pogarsky, 2002; Pogarsky and Piquero, 2003; Schneider, 1990; Sherman, 1993; Sherman et al., 1998; Stewart, Simons, Conger, and Scaramella, 2002; Wolfgang et al., 1972.

8. See Bridges and Stone, 1986; Paternoster and Piquero, 1995; Piquero and Paternoster, 1998; Piquero and Pogarsky, 2002; Pogarsky and Piquero, 2003; Pogarsky et al., 2004; Schneider, 1990; Sedlak and Bruce, 2010.

9. For fuller discussions, see Andrews and Bonta, 2006; Bazemore, 2012; Braithwaite, 1989; Nagin and Paternoster, 1994; Sherman, 1993, 2000; Sherman et al., 1998; Sherman et al., 1992; Wooldredge and Thistlethwaite, 2002.

10. See note 6.

11. For fuller discussions of the philosophy and practice of restorative justice, see Andrews and Bonta, 2006; Bazemore, 2000, 2012; Bazemore and Umbreit, 2001, 2004; Bonta et al., 2006; Braithwaite, 2002, 2005; Levrant et al., 1999; McGarrell and Hipple, 2007; Office of Juvenile Justice and Delinquency Prevention, 1998a; Rodriguez, 2007.

12. See note 11.

13. See Carmichael and Piquero, 2004; Chamlin, 1991; Chamlin et al., 1992; Foglia, 1997; Grasmick and Bursik, 1990; Klepper and Nagin, 1989; Levitt, 2002; Lipsey and Cullen, 2008; D. MacKenzie, 2006; Matsueda et al., 2006; Nagin and Paternoster, 1991, 1993, 1994; Paternoster and Piquero, 1995; Piquero and Pogarsky, 2002; Pratt and Cullen, 2005; Sherman et al., 1992; Steiner et al., 2006; Yu and Liska, 1993; B. Wright et al., 2004.

14. For overviews, see Andrews and Bonta, 2006; Auerhahn, 1999; Blumstein, 1998; Conklin, 2003; Currie, 1998; D. MacKenzie, 2006; Nagin, 1998b; Pratt and Cullen, 2005; Sherman et al., 1998; Spelman, 2000; Stemen, 2007; Visher, 2000; S. Walker, 1998; R. Wright, 1994; Zimring and Hawkins, 1995.

15. Also see Andrews and Bonta, 2006; Conklin, 2003; D. MacKenzie, 2002, 2006; National Research Council, 2014; Pratt and Cullen, 2005; Rosenfeld, 2000; Spelman, 2000; Stemen, 2007; Zimring, 2007.

24 The Strategies of Prevention and Rehabilitation

Is It Possible to Prevent Delinquency and to Rehabilitate Delinquents?

Many criminologists argue that **the juvenile justice system has placed too much emphasis on get-tough approaches.** They point out that such approaches have no effect or only a modest effect on delinquency. While we can increase the effectiveness of such approaches, their ultimate effect on delinquency is limited, since they address only one of the many causes of offending: low direct control. Further, such approaches are frequently expensive, and they expose many juveniles to the often brutal conditions of juvenile institutions. The Georgia Alliance for Children, a child advocacy group, ran a public service advertisement that showed a young juvenile curled up on a concrete floor, with the caption: "You're in an 8 × 10 cell with four thugs twice your size. You would scream, but the underwear your grandmother sent is stuffed in your mouth" (McDevitt, 2000).

It is argued that, rather than simply getting tough, **the justice system should place more emphasis on rehabilitating juvenile offenders and preventing juveniles from becoming delinquent in the first place.** Although the juvenile justice system does emphasize rehabilitation in theory, juvenile offenders often do not receive effective rehabilitation programs **in practice.** And, with certain exceptions, only limited efforts are made to prevent delinquency. As Bernstein (2014:11–12) writes, "The challenge is not simply to build a better mousetrap, but to reexamine every aspect of how we address delinquency, from taking on the racial, educational, social, and economic inequities that feed it to ensuring that relationship-focused, community-inspired responses are not just boutique 'alternatives' but become the status quo—available to everyone."

Prevention and rehabilitation programs do not try to reduce delinquency by increasing the juvenile justice system's direct control. Rather, they try to **reduce delinquency by focusing on the other causes of delinquency.** At the most general level, the more effective prevention and rehabilitation programs attempt to increase the other types of control, reduce strain or the tendency to respond to strain with crime, reduce the social learning of crime, and/or reduce negative labeling. At a more specific level, they try to alter the individual traits that contribute to crime, increase family bonding, improve parental supervision and discipline, reduce family conflict and abuse, increase school attachment and performance, and reduce association with delinquent peers and gangs.

Prevention programs are distinguished from rehabilitation programs in that they try to keep juveniles from becoming delinquent in the first place, whereas rehabilitation programs try to reduce the delinquency of juveniles who already are delinquent. Some prevention programs focus on all or most juveniles. For example, the Partnership for Drug-Free Kids created a major advertising campaign to reduce drug use among juveniles. You may have seen or heard some of these ads ("Live above the influence"; "Life can be hard . . . sometimes I need to be harder"; see the ad gallery at http://abovetheinfluence.com). Other prevention programs target juveniles believed to be at risk for engaging in delinquency. For example, they may target low-birthweight infants, juveniles in high-crime communities, or juveniles described by their teachers or parents as being at risk for delinquency. Prevention and rehabilitation programs are sometimes discussed separately, but we discuss them together because many of the same programs are used for both prevention and rehabilitation purposes.

This chapter has five parts. First, we provide a brief history of prevention and rehabilitation programs. Second, we discuss the effectiveness of prevention and rehabilitation programs and describe the general features of the most successful programs. Third, we describe the characteristics of successful prevention and rehabilitation programs that focus on the early family environment, parent training, the school, individual traits, and delinquent peer groups and gangs. Most prevention and rehabilitation programs focus on these areas. Fourth, we briefly describe prevention and rehabilitation programs in several other areas. Finally, we discuss the crucial role of larger social forces in preventing delinquency. As you will see, the most successful prevention and rehabilitation programs address many of the causes of delinquency described in Chapters 6 through 18.[1]

After reading this chapter, you should be able to:

- Describe the strategies of prevention and rehabilitation.
- Discuss the history of prevention and rehabilitation efforts in the United States.
- Indicate the reasons why most prevention and rehabilitation programs are not properly evaluated.
- Provide tentative conclusions about the effectiveness of prevention and rehabilitation programs.
- Describe the general characteristics of effective prevention and rehabilitation programs.
- Analyze the crucial role of larger social forces, especially the economy, in reducing delinquency.

A BRIEF HISTORY OF PREVENTION AND REHABILITATION

Prevention programs have never played a major role in delinquency control efforts, except for a brief period in the 1960s and early 1970s during the heyday of the War on Poverty (see Empey et al., 1999). The *War on Poverty* was initiated by President Kennedy in the early 1960s and largely implemented by his successor, President Johnson. One of the purposes of the War on Poverty was to reduce crime and delinquency by increasing the opportunities for people to achieve success through legitimate channels. Some of the programs that made up the War on Poverty provided educational assistance and job training to juveniles in disadvantaged communities. The War on Poverty, then, was partly based on strain theory, which views the failure to achieve monetary success as a major cause of crime. Most of the programs that comprised the War on Poverty have been dismantled, but a few remain, like Project Head Start and Job Corps.

You might wonder why prevention does not play a greater role in society's efforts to control delinquency. Prevention seems to make a lot of sense; it seems better to prevent delinquency from developing in the first place than to react to delinquency after it has occurred. But several objections have been raised to prevention programs. For example, they are said to interfere in the private affairs of individuals and families (e.g., "It is none of the government's business how parents raise their children"—unless the parents or children engage in illegal behavior). They are also said to be costly and ineffective. Conservatives often point to the fact that crime and delinquency rates increased dramatically during the 1960s and early 1970s, at the very time that the War on Poverty was being mounted (data on the effectiveness of the War on Poverty are mixed; see Empey et al., 1999). Finally, prevention programs are at odds with the get-tough approach to controlling delinquency, which claims that offenders are responsible for their behavior and deserve punishment. Politicians who advocate prevention programs expose themselves to charges of being soft on crime.

Although prevention has played only a small role in delinquency control in the United States, **rehabilitation was the guiding philosophy of the juvenile justice system from its inception in the 1800s until the 1970s.** That does not mean that the juvenile justice system made a serious effort at rehabilitation; there was often a large gap between philosophy and practice. But the major goal of the juvenile justice system was said to be the rehabilitation of delinquents. And rehabilitation is still part of the guiding philosophy of the juvenile justice system, although get-tough approaches have been popular in recent decades.

Rehabilitation fell out of favor during the 1970s for several reasons. Rising crime rates during the 1960s and early 1970s caused many to question its effectiveness. Doubts about rehabilitation were reinforced by several studies in the 1970s and 1980s claiming that rehabilitation was largely ineffective. The best known of these studies, the Martinson

Report, examined a wide range of rehabilitation programs employed from 1945 to 1967. The author, Robert Martinson, concluded that "with few and isolated exceptions the rehabilitative efforts that have been reported so far have had no appreciable effect on recidivism" (Martinson, 1974:25). Finally, the political climate of the country became more conservative. Criminals, including older delinquents, were said to be responsible for their behavior. And politicians and others argued that such individuals deserved punishment and that punishment was the best way to reduce crime and delinquency. In particular, get-tough advocates said that punishment would reduce crime through deterrence and incapacitation.[2]

Since the early 2000s, however, we have seen **a renewed interest in prevention and rehabilitation,** especially on the part of many criminologists and, increasingly, on the part of the federal government and certain states. The federal strategy for controlling delinquency now emphasizes a balanced approach: that is, efforts to hold juveniles accountable for their actions (which may include punishment) should be balanced with prevention and rehabilitation programs. The federal government has done much to publicize the prevention and rehabilitation programs that show promise. Along with private foundations, such as the MacArthur Foundation and the Annie E. Casey Foundation, the federal government has helped fund the implementation and evaluation of local prevention efforts and rehabilitation programs. The website for the Office of Juvenile Justice and Delinquency Prevention (OJJDP) contains much information on promising prevention and rehabilitation programs—see OJJDP's "Model Programs Guide" at https://www.ojjdp.gov/mpg. Information on promising programs can also be found at other websites, such as CrimeSolutions.gov and Blueprints for Healthy Youth Development (http://www.blueprintsprograms.com). Thanks to the development of these websites, information about prevention and rehabilitation programs is more readily available than ever before.

This renewed interest in prevention and rehabilitation partly stems from the research suggesting that get-tough approaches have no effect or only a modest effect on delinquency. It also stems from the high financial and social costs of many get-tough approaches (see Currie, 1998; Stemen, 2007; Tonry, 1995). Many states, in fact, are doing away with certain of the get-tough approaches they adopted because they can no longer afford to fund them (von Zielbauer, 2003; also see Chapter 23). But perhaps most important of all, the renewed interest in prevention and rehabilitation programs stems from recent research suggesting that some of these programs are effective at reducing delinquency.

Reflecting this renewed interest, several states have also made deliberate efforts to reduce the number of juveniles they incarcerate and/or refer to the adult court system. The state of Connecticut, for example, raised the age at which juvenile offenders are treated as adults from 16 to 18 (*New York Times,* 2007c). More generally, the rate at which juveniles are incarcerated and transferred to adult court has been declining since the late 1990s. Many states are instead placing an increased emphasis on the rehabilitation of offenders and the prevention of delinquency (Bishop and Feld, 2012; Paulson, 2006).

In New York, for example, state officials have implemented significant reforms—increasing the availability of counseling for juvenile offenders, taking steps to curb abuse and mismanagement in juvenile facilities (e.g., by installing surveillance cameras), and encouraging judges to place fewer young offenders in these facilities. A task force appointed by the governor in 2008 suggested further reforms and, overall, recommended that the state adopt a more therapeutic, less punitive approach:

> Wouldn't it make more sense, task-force members reasoned, to reserve incarceration
> for those who posed a threat to public safety? For youngsters who are not deemed

dangerous, other methods seem more reasonable. "The state should treat and rehabilitate them, not hurt and harden them," wrote the task force. (Close, 2010)

In the next section, we discuss the effectiveness of prevention and rehabilitation
strategies.

HOW EFFECTIVE ARE PREVENTION AND REHABILITATION PROGRAMS?

Several researchers have reviewed the evaluations of prevention and rehabilitation programs. One researcher reviewed 443 evaluations (Lipsey, 1992; also see Lipsey et al., 2010).
All of these reviewers faced a major problem: most prevention and rehabilitation programs
had not been properly evaluated. That is, in most cases, researchers did not employ the
procedures for evaluation research described in Chapter 19. Most commonly, they did not
randomly assign juveniles to the treatment and control groups. The evaluations also frequently suffer from other problems such as high dropout rates from the treatment group,
failure to conduct long-term follow-ups, and failure to examine how well the program was
implemented. Further, many of the decent evaluations that have been done are in need of
replication. As noted in Chapter 19, programs should be evaluated across different settings
and populations. A program that works well in one setting or with one group of juveniles
may not work well in other settings or with other groups. As a result of these problems,
criminologists know much less about the effectiveness of prevention and rehabilitation
programs than they would like. Virtually every review of prevention and rehabilitation
programs stresses the need for more and better evaluation research.

At the same time, enough evaluations have been moderately well done to allow us to
draw some conclusions about the effectiveness of prevention and rehabilitation programs.
The reviews suggest that well-designed and well-implemented prevention and rehabilitation programs can reduce rates of delinquency anywhere from 20 percent to 50 percent.[3]
The estimates vary because different reviews look at different programs and employ different definitions of a "well-designed" program. But the evidence is sufficient to suggest
that **prevention and rehabilitation programs have an important role to play in efforts
to control delinquency.** As criminologists learn more about the characteristics of effective
programs and how to best implement them, the role of prevention and rehabilitation will
likely increase. This is not to say that prevention and rehabilitation programs will solve
the delinquency problem in the immediate future. It is clear, however, that society should
make greater use of such programs—along with well-designed efforts to deter delinquency
and incapacitate serious offenders. This strategy is precisely the one that the federal government is now advocating.

General Characteristics of Effective Prevention and Rehabilitation Programs

It is important to emphasize that the reviews of prevention and rehabilitation programs find
that only some programs are effective at reducing delinquency; other programs have little
effect on delinquency or actually increase it. For example, some evaluations suggest that
group discussions involving delinquent and conventional juveniles are counterproductive.
The conventional juveniles are supposed to influence the delinquents in positive ways, but
often the reverse occurs.

Criminologists now have a rough idea of what characteristics distinguish effective from
ineffective programs. Such information, of course, is vital if society is to effectively control delinquency. Many individuals and groups are unaware of this information, and they
continue to invest resources in programs that are likely to have little effect on delinquency.

Drawing on several reviews, we can tentatively state that the most effective prevention and rehabilitation programs have the following characteristics.

1. They focus on the major causes of delinquency in the group being treated. This may sound obvious, but many prevention and rehabilitation programs focus on factors that are not causes, or at least not important causes, of delinquency. For example, they try to increase the juvenile's level of self-esteem. Other programs have no clear focus. Many programs, for example, employ unstructured counseling sessions. Counselors frequently hold "rap sessions" with juveniles where they discuss a wide range of issues. Programs of these types have little effect on delinquency. For a program to be effective, it must address the causes of delinquency described in earlier chapters, such as individual traits, family and school problems, and association with delinquent peers.

Further, programs should attempt to target the causes of delinquency that are most relevant to the group being treated. For example, it makes little sense to target gang membership in a population that is low in gang membership. Programs should also attempt to target all or most of the major causes of delinquency in a group. Delinquency is usually caused by several factors. Programs that focus only on one factor, even if it is an important cause of delinquency, will be less effective. An example of an effective program that targets several causes is multisystemic therapy, or MST (see Box 24.1). MST draws on elements from several of the more focused programs described later.

Box 24.1   Multisystemic Therapy: Addressing the Multiple Causes of Delinquency

As described in earlier chapters, delinquency is a product of multiple risk factors that operate across various life domains, such as the family, school, and neighborhood. It makes sense, then, for interventions to recognize this complexity and address the major risk factors in each of these domains, but often this does not happen. Many interventions, for example, focus only on the individual offender, or focus on just one or two factors that are believed to be responsible for delinquent behavior. Not surprisingly, such interventions have a poor track record.

One important exception involves multisystemic therapy, or MST. This intervention targets serious juvenile offenders, especially those who have experienced trouble with the law and are at risk of out-of-home placement. Recognizing that behavior is influenced not only by individual traits but also by dynamics operating in the multiple "systems" that individuals are a part of, MST targets risk factors that may operate at home, at school, or in the surrounding neighborhood. Moreover, MST focuses on risk factors that have been highlighted by criminological research and are known to have a strong link to offending behavior, such as association with delinquent peers.

To address multiple risk factors, MST typically seeks to empower the parents of troubled adolescents. For example, a therapist may visit the home of a juvenile offender weekly and help his or her parents set limits, enforce curfews, promote school attendance, decrease the child's association with delinquent peers, and promote associations with positive peers. Depending on the needs of a particular case, these weekly visits may go on for four months or more.

To illustrate, before their exposure to MST, the parents of a 15-year-old offender set few limits and rarely monitored his behavior. As a result, the boy spent much of his free time with delinquent friends and eventually dropped out of school. Further, the

(Continued)

(Continued)

parents found items in the home that they suspected had been stolen by the boy. Under the guidance of an MST therapist, the parents began to set limits, encourage school attendance, and discourage delinquent peer associations. For example, they turned over the suspected stolen items to the police and called the boy's delinquent friends, warning them that they were no longer welcome to associate with their child. Further, the parents told the delinquent friends about their cooperation with the police and said that they would report any information about suspected criminal activities. They also contacted the parents of the boy's prosocial friends and obtained their assistance in supervising the at-risk boy's behavior.

The results of several randomized experiments indicate that MST is an effective intervention for serious juvenile offenders. Compared to offenders who received regular child welfare services, MST participants in one recent study had fewer out-of-home placements and reported lower levels of subsequent offending. In addition, parents and teachers reported fewer behavior problems among the MST participants (Ogden and Hagen, 2006; also see Timmons-Mitchell et al., 2006).

Because many evaluation studies have found support for MST, it is listed as an effective program on both the OJJDP's "Model Programs Guide" webpage (https://www.ojjdp.gov/mpg) and the website of Blueprints for Healthy Youth Development website (for more information on MST, visit http://www.blueprintsprograms.com).

Questions for Discussion

1. Although MST shows much promise, it has received little public attention or fanfare. In contrast, Scared Straight has been the focus of a highly rated television series (*Beyond Scared Straight*), even though research indicates the program is ineffective and may even increase delinquency. What might explain this difference in visibility and popularity?
2. What might be done to increase the visibility of programs like MST, or the likelihood that they will be implemented?

2. They are intensive. The most effective programs usually last a long time and employ several techniques to influence the juvenile or group. One cannot change a juvenile's traits or alter his or her social environment in a short period of time, with minimal effort. For example, you cannot change a juvenile's level of irritability in a single counseling session. Likewise, you cannot change family members' ways of relating to one another by simply giving parents a pamphlet to read over the weekend. Individual traits and interactional patterns have developed over many years, and they can be resistant to change. The most effective programs, then, tend to be the most intensive.

Many programs that try to change the behavior of individuals employ the following strategy, sometimes referred to as the *cognitive behavioral approach*. First, instructors describe what they want the juvenile (or parent, or other person) to do. For example, they might advise the juvenile to employ a particular anger management technique when mad at others. The technique and its use are described in detail. The juvenile might also be given reading material on the technique. Second, the instructors display or model what it is that they want the juvenile to do; they may stage several situations in which someone gets angry and then uses the technique. Third, they get the juvenile to practice the technique, often by means of having the juvenile participate in a number of role-playing situations (e.g., someone says or does something to anger the juvenile, and the juvenile then tries out the anger management technique). The instructors provide the juvenile with feedback, taking special care to reinforce successful performances. Fourth, the juvenile begins to apply the technique to situations in the real world. The juvenile might be asked to use the anger management technique the next time someone makes him or her angry. After reporting on the real-world application and receiving feedback, the juvenile applies the technique to additional real-world situations. Still more feedback and reinforcement are provided. Fifth, the juvenile reaches a point where regular instruction is no longer necessary. But the instructors are available for consultation if necessary, and the juvenile may periodically participate in refresher or booster courses. Influencing individuals and groups, then, is not an easy process. You should be suspicious if you hear someone claim that a program can reduce delinquency in a short period of time with minimal effort.

The fact that the most successful programs are intensive poses some problems for policy makers. Although most good programs are cost effective, saving more money than they cost over the long run, intensive programs are expensive to administer (Aos et al., 2001; Greenwood, 2006). Also, the intensive nature of many prevention and rehabilitation programs makes them difficult to implement on a large scale. Most programs have been implemented in small groups, where it is easier to ensure that they are properly run. It is more difficult to ensure that programs are properly run if they are implemented at many sites, serving many thousands of juveniles. Arranging for the large-scale implementation of good prevention and rehabilitation programs, in fact, is perhaps the major challenge facing policy makers (beyond securing support for such programs). Not surprisingly, studies suggest that programs are much less successful when they are poorly implemented (S. Wilson et al., 2003).

3. They focus on juveniles at high risk for subsequent delinquency. Juveniles at high risk for delinquency are the ones who can benefit the most from prevention and rehabilitation programs, and programs focusing on such juveniles achieve the greatest reductions in subsequent delinquency. It makes little sense to provide programs to juveniles at low risk for delinquency; such juveniles will likely refrain from delinquency whether they participate in prevention and rehabilitation programs or not.

4. They are run in the community. Some data suggest that programs may be slightly more effective when they are run in the community rather than in juvenile institutions. It is easy to think of reasons why this might be the case. Juveniles confined in institutions are cut off from the larger community, including family, school, peer group, and neighborhood. As a result, it is more difficult for rehabilitation programs to address the family, school, and other problems that cause delinquency. Further, juveniles confined in institutions are exposed to other delinquents on a regular and intimate basis. These other delinquents often encourage delinquency and discourage cooperation with the staff. The staff, in fact, is often defined as the "enemy." Rehabilitation is obviously difficult under such circumstances. Finally, juveniles in institutions are often preoccupied with the stresses of confinement, including the threat of physical and sexual assault from others. These circumstances also make rehabilitation difficult. It is possible to help juveniles in institutions, but it may be somewhat more difficult.

5. They establish a warm but firm relationship between counselors and juveniles. Some evidence suggests that programs are more effective when counselors establish a warm or close relationship with the juveniles and strongly discourage deviant behavior while encouraging conventional behavior. A close bond between counselors and juveniles reduces strain. Also, the juveniles are more likely to model the counselors' behavior, accept their beliefs, and respond to their sanctions. At the same time, it is important that the counselors clearly promote conventional behavior and condemn deviance. The counselors cannot be lax or let the juveniles take advantage of them. Note that the importance of being warm but firm was also emphasized in the context of the family and school.

WHAT ARE THE CHARACTERISTICS OF SUCCESSFUL PREVENTION/REHABILITATION PROGRAMS IN DIFFERENT AREAS?

Many programs have shown some success at preventing delinquency and rehabilitating delinquents. It is impossible to describe all these programs in this book, but this section describes the key features of programs focusing on several areas: the early family environment, parent training, the school, individual traits, and delinquent peers and gangs. All such programs address one or more of the causes of delinquency described in earlier chapters.

Before we present the program descriptions, a few words of caution are in order. First, many different programs have been employed in each of the areas cited. Rather than describing individual programs, we describe what we believe are the key features of successful programs in an area. Many of the individual programs contain only some of these key features. Second, while the evaluation research provides reason to believe that these programs can reduce delinquency, more and better research is needed. In certain cases, our conclusions are based on a small number of less-than-ideal evaluations. Third, although we describe the programs in each area separately, they are sometimes combined in the real world. As indicated earlier, the most effective way to prevent delinquency or rehabilitate delinquents is to combine several programs, for this allows us to address the multiple causes of delinquency. Fourth, these programs—alone or in combination—should not be viewed as the definitive solution to the delinquency problem. The programs can reduce delinquency in at least some circumstances, but it is unlikely that they will eliminate the problem.

Prevention/rehabilitation programs are unlikely to eliminate delinquency for several reasons. They are often difficult to properly implement, especially on a large scale (see D. Gottfredson and Gottfredson, 2002). Moreover, it is often difficult to ensure that everyone who needs the programs participates in them. In fact, the people who need the programs the most are often the least likely to participate in them—especially prevention programs, where participation is often voluntary. Furthermore, even if the programs are properly administered to the people who need them the most, they are able to help only some of the participants.

Programs Focusing on the Early Family Environment

As you know, the family has a major impact on delinquency, affecting a juvenile's level of control, strain, labeling, and the social learning of crime. Some parents, for example, fail to develop a strong emotional bond with their children, fail to properly supervise them, and abuse and neglect them. These (in)actions directly increase the likelihood of delinquency. Also, they indirectly increase the likelihood of delinquency through their effect on such factors as individual traits, school experiences, and association with delinquent peers and gangs (see Chapter 14 and the other chapters on the causes of delinquency for a full discussion). Juveniles in families of certain types, for example, more often experience biological harms like head injuries, birth complications, and exposure to toxic substances. They are therefore more likely to develop traits conducive to delinquency.

Several early family intervention programs have been developed in an effort to **reduce the likelihood that families will produce delinquent children.** The programs typically target disadvantaged families or families at risk for certain problems, such as child abuse. For example, the programs might target single parents, adolescent mothers, the parents of premature or low-birthweight babies, and/or families having a history of drug abuse or family violence. Some programs begin before the birth of the child, while others begin at or shortly after birth. In the most effective programs, the parents are visited weekly by a nurse, social worker, or trained paraprofessional. When necessary, the home visitors can turn to physicians, psychologists, or teachers for further assistance. The programs last anywhere from a few months to several years, with the longer programs being more successful.[4] Programs focusing on the early family environment address the causes of delinquency in three major ways.

First, they attempt to **reduce the child's exposure to biological harms by providing medical care to the child and mother and by providing health and safety training to the parents.** Expectant mothers may be given prenatal care and advice. For example, they are encouraged to avoid smoking, alcohol use, and drug use during pregnancy. If necessary, the mother will be offered counseling and drug treatment. Such measures help prevent problems like low birthweight and birth complications. After birth, the child receives regular medical care and the parents receive assistance in caring for the child. The child in particular receives regular pediatric exams, and steps are taken to address any developmental or other problems that arise. The parents are also given information on child development and how to best care for their child. Such information and assistance can prevent a range of harmful biological events, such as head injuries and exposure to toxic substances such as lead.

Second, these programs also **attempt to foster good parenting practices by reducing parental stress and providing information on good parenting.** As you may recall from Chapter 14, two of the major determinants of poor parenting are stress and lack of knowledge. It is difficult to be a good parent if you do not have decent housing or a job, if you struggle to put food on the table, or if you are involved in an abusive relationship. One of the first things the programs attempt to do is help parents address some of the basic problems they face. For example, they may help the parents find decent housing, get a job, obtain food, secure medical care, arrange transportation, and end spouse abuse. Sometimes the home visitor provides assistance in these areas. Home visitors often function as counselors to the family, discussing problems, offering advice and assistance, and providing emotional support. The home visitors also refer family members to various social service and treatment programs when necessary. The assistance of the home visitor not only makes it easier for the parents to engage in good parenting, but it also helps foster a bond between the home visitor and the parents.

It is also difficult to be a good parent if you were never exposed to good parenting, so the home visitors attempt to teach good parenting skills. They provide information on child development, offer advice on parenting, model parenting skills, and assist parents when necessary. They also monitor the progress of the child and intervene if necessary. For example, they may provide special assistance if it appears that the parents are not forming an emotional bond with their baby. In some cases, the parents may take special parent training classes or participate in parent-support groups. Also, male home visitors may make a special effort to work with the father if he is present.

It is important to emphasize that home visitors do not attempt to coerce or "talk down" to the parents. Rather, they aim to function as friends and allies to the parents. For example, the home visitor in the Hawaii Healthy Start program introduces herself to the parents by saying something like the following:

> I work with the Healthy Start program. I have new information about babies that I didn't know when I was raising my kids. It can make being a mother easier, but not easy! Also, you can look at me as your information center about this community. I live here, too, and I didn't know about WIC [Special Supplemental Food Program for Women, Infants, and Children] or the well-baby clinic before I started this job. I hope you learn to think of me as your "special" friend, someone here completely for you and the baby. I am here to talk when you need to share something that concerns

you. I know that it is hard to start with a new baby and to have so much on your mind. (Earle, 1995:6)

Third, programs focusing on the early family environment **often provide educational childcare.** Such care better prepares the child for school. Also, it reduces the stress on the parents by giving them a break from constant childcare and by making it easier for them to obtain employment. In addition, the parents are taught how to provide a stimulating environment that will foster their child's cognitive development. Related to this, a toy- and book-lending library is often made available to the parents.

Programs focusing on the early family environment, then, **address several of the most important causes of delinquency. They reduce the likelihood of biological harm,** which in turn reduces the likelihood that juveniles will develop traits conducive to crime. They **address several family factors that are related to delinquency,** including the emotional bond between parents and child, the level of parental supervision, and child abuse and neglect. (For a discussion of programs focusing specifically on child abuse, see J. Barlow et al., 2006; Cronin et al., 2006.) They also supplement the socialization efforts of parents by placing the child in a well-designed preschool program. These efforts, in turn, have an impact on other causes of delinquency, such as poor school performance and association with delinquent peers. It is not surprising that early intervention programs have shown some success at preventing delinquency. Such programs are becoming more common, with a few states implementing them on a large scale (for an example of a successful program that focuses on the early family environment, see Box 19.1 in Chapter 19, where we describe the Nurse–Family Partnership).

Parent Training Programs

One of the most widely used programs for dealing with delinquency is parent training.[5] Parent training programs may be used alone or in combination with other programs— such as programs focusing on the early family environment, school-based programs, and programs that concentrate on individual traits.

Given the central role of the family in delinquency, it is not surprising that parent training programs are so widely used. As indicated, a variety of family factors affect delinquency, including weak emotional bonds between the parent(s) and child, poor supervision, abuse and neglect, and family conflict. These factors are important in and of themselves, and they are important because they affect certain other causes of delinquency, such as individual traits, school performance and attachment, and association with delinquent peers. Programs that can change the way parents relate to their children have much potential for controlling delinquency.

Parent training programs usually target the families of delinquents or juveniles at risk for delinquency. They also target families that are at risk for poor parenting, such as cases of adolescent mothers or families presenting evidence of family violence. These programs are offered in the home, in clinics, or in other settings like schools. Sometimes they are provided to individual families, and sometimes they are provided to several families at once.

Parent training programs **typically have several components.** Most notably, they **teach parents how to more effectively discipline their children.** Poor discipline is not only a major cause of delinquency, it also undermines the emotional bond between the parent and child and contributes to family conflict. Parents are taught how to set clear rules and better monitor their child's behavior; they learn to recognize both deviant and prosocial behavior, as well as how to properly sanction deviant behavior and reinforce prosocial behavior. Parents are encouraged to make more use of positive reinforcers, such as praise, rewards, privileges, and attention; and to make less use of punishers, such as criticism, yelling, and hitting. The preferred strategies of punishment involve time out (for children), loss of privileges, imposition of chores, clear expressions of disapproval, and reasoning. (If you would like to get a better sense of the skills that parent training programs try to teach, conduct a YouTube search using the following key words: "Incredible Years parenting program.")

Parent training programs also **frequently teach family members how to better resolve their conflicts.** While proper disciplinary techniques reduce family conflict, they do not eliminate it. The parents and juvenile, for example, may still disagree over the rules that parents try to enforce or the punishments that parents administer. A common strategy for resolving such conflicts involves the negotiation of a behavioral contract between the parents and the juvenile, particularly an adolescent. The contract clearly specifies the rules that the juvenile must follow and the consequences of both following and breaking rules. For example, adolescents may agree to go to school every day during the week in exchange for the privilege of staying out until midnight on Friday and Saturday nights. The adolescent typically plays a major role in developing behavioral contracts. Parents and juveniles are taught how to negotiate such agreements, and they may call on a therapist for assistance. By reducing conflict, negotiation also helps strengthen family bonds.

Parent training programs may also **teach family members better communication skills, alter parents' expectations for their children** (the unrealistic expectations of parents sometimes contribute to abuse and other problems), and **encourage family members to spend more time together in pleasurable activities.** Parents are taught such skills and practices through a variety of strategies. They might receive reading materials and/or direct instruction; they might be exposed to models who display the desirable practices and rehearse the practices themselves, receiving feedback. In any event, they receive continued guidance when they apply the learned practices in their homes.

Parent training programs have shown much promise in reducing delinquency, although they are not effective with all families. There are difficulties in inducing families to participate, especially the families that need it most (Kazdin, 1994). Also, parent training is often difficult to successfully implement when families face multiple stressors—poverty, poor housing, work problems, and family violence. Efforts, however, are being made to deal with these problems by, for example, trying to reduce family stressors and improve the ability of parents to cope with stressors. Also, there are efforts to provide financial and other incentives to participate in these programs.

The effectiveness of the programs is undoubtedly the result of a number of factors. As indicated, they **strengthen the bond between parent and child, improve parental discipline,** and **reduce family conflict and abuse.** At a more general level, they reduce strain. Adolescents are subject to less negative treatment and receive more positive stimuli from parents. In particular, there is a reduction in family conflict, abuse, and the use of harsh disciplinary techniques. Parent training programs also **promote the social learning of conventional behavior.** Parents clearly state rules that condemn deviance; parents function as conventional role models, avoiding the use of violent disciplinary techniques; conventional behavior is consistently reinforced; and deviant behavior is consistently punished. Further, such programs clearly result in an **increase in control.** Direct control is obviously increased; also, the adolescent's emotional bond to parents is increased, and the adolescent is more likely to internalize beliefs condemning deviance and to develop a high level of self-control. Finally, such programs **reduce negative labeling,** since parents are less likely to abuse their children, either verbally or physically.

Several researchers have suggested that parent training programs be made generally available, incorporating them into the high school curriculum or offering them to the parents of all newborn children. This would reduce the stigma of participating in the programs and might make it easier to secure funding (since the programs would no longer be seen as special programs for the poor or disadvantaged). Many European countries have moved in this direction, but only a few schools and areas in the United States have done so (for more information, see A. Piquero et al., 2009; Sherman et al., 2002).

Programs Focusing on School Factors

As you know, delinquency is also related to a range of negative school experiences, including poor school performance, low attachment to school, low school involvement, low educational goals, and poor relations with teachers. Delinquency is also more common in schools of certain types, including schools that are large, have poor discipline, provide few opportunities for student success, have low expectations for students, have an unpleasant learning environment for students, have poor cooperation between teachers and administrators, and have low community involvement (see Chapter 15 for more information).

Several programs try to address these factors. Some programs focus on the individual, with most such programs attempting to boost school performance. It is felt that individuals who perform well in school will come to like school, get involved in school activities, develop high educational goals, and get along well with teachers. Other programs focus on the larger school environment—including the classroom and entire school—and attempt to change the school in ways that will reduce delinquency.[6]

Preschool programs. Evidence suggests that good preschool programs can both improve school performance and reduce delinquency. Most such programs focus on preschool children in disadvantaged areas, and they attempt to promote the children's social and intellectual development, as well as increase the parents' involvement in the educational process. The best preschool programs begin early in life, last two years or more, have low student-to-teacher ratios, and employ carefully designed curriculums. In addition, the teachers meet regularly with the parents to discuss ways that the parents might foster their children's social and intellectual development. The success of preschool programs is further enhanced if the children continue to receive assistance once they have begun school. Many of the *Head Start* programs throughout the country meet these criteria, with these programs providing preschool to about 1 million disadvantaged children—or about 40 percent of eligible children (for a good summary of Head Start and its impact, see Mongeau, 2016).

In-school programs. Various in-school programs attempt to improve the school performance of individual students and address other school experiences related to delinquency. These programs tend to focus on students doing poorly in school, students rated as disruptive by teachers and others, and delinquents. The most straightforward programs arrange for students to be tutored by other students, community volunteers, trained paraprofessionals, or teachers. Such programs are effective at boosting school performance, but it is not yet known whether they reduce delinquency.

Other programs are more elaborate, and several have been found to affect both school experiences and delinquency. In certain programs, for example, juveniles sign a contract with school officials. The juveniles agree to attend school regularly, do their schoolwork, and behave properly in class. Program staff members provide needed services to the juveniles, such as tutoring and counseling. The program staff also trains teachers and sometimes parents to monitor the juveniles' performance and provide assistance when necessary. The juveniles receive regular feedback about their performance from program staff. Staff members discuss ways in which the juveniles might improve when they receive negative reports, and they reinforce juveniles who meet the terms of their contracts.

For example, they praise the juveniles and provide them with points that can be traded in for school trips and other rewards.

Altering the classroom environment. Other programs attempt to alter the classroom environment in ways that improve classroom performance, increase school attachment and involvement, improve relations with teachers and classmates, and improve discipline.

For example, researchers have attempted to reduce delinquency through the strategies of interactive teaching, proactive classroom management, and cooperative learning groups. Interactive teaching provides students with specific objectives they must master, offers frequent feedback, gives help when necessary, employs objective grading, and bases grades on mastery of material and improvement over past performance—not on comparisons with other students. Such teaching increases the opportunities for the students to succeed, and the grading methods increase perceptions of fairness and decrease competition with other students. Teachers using proactive classroom management are taught to clearly state rules for classroom behavior, recognize and reward attempts to cooperate, make frequent use of encouragement and praise, and minimize the impact of disruptions. Cooperative learning groups consist of small, heterogeneous groups of students who help one another master classroom materials and receive recognition as a team for their accomplishments. The groups serve to reduce alienation, reinforce cooperation, and promote attachment among students.

Another example of a promising program focusing primarily on the classroom environment is the Olweus Bullying Prevention Program. Bullying is an important form of delinquency in itself, and it may contribute to further delinquency, partly for reasons related to strain theory. As described by the developer of the program, "a person is being bullied when he or she is exposed, repeatedly and over time, to negative actions on the part of one or more other persons" (Olweus, 1991:413; also see Chapter 15). Negative actions are defined as intentional actions that inflict or attempt to inflict injury or discomfort upon another. A successful antibullying program has several key features. A school-based team is formed to address bullying, its members including administrators, teachers, counselors, parents, and students. A questionnaire is administered to students to determine the nature and extent of bullying, and the results are publicized to make everyone aware of the problem. Clear rules against bullying are established, and also widely publicized. Teachers and others closely monitor student activities; students are taught to report bullying and help victims; and anonymous reporting procedures are established. Instances of bullying are quickly sanctioned in a nonhostile manner. And the victims of bullying are provided support and taught skills to reduce the likelihood of further bullying (see Whitted and Dupper, 2005, for more information).

Changing the school environment. A number of programs have tried to change the school environment as a whole. They usually employ several strategies, and it is often difficult to determine which one has the greatest impact on delinquency. Most programs try to change schools in ways that improve student performance, increase school attachment and involvement, improve school discipline, and generally make the school environment more satisfying.

The programs often begin by creating teams that include school administrators, teachers, parents, students, and others. These teams evaluate the school and then help plan and implement school improvements. Such improvements often include the following: teachers learn innovative teaching and classroom management techniques; students help develop school disciplinary rules; steps are taken to make sure that the rules are clearly stated, widely publicized through devices like newsletters and posters, and during ceremonies, and enforced in a consistent and fair manner. There is an effort to make greater use of positive reinforcers, like praise and privileges, for conventional behavior. There is better communication with parents about the positive and negative behaviors of their children. An effort is made to involve parents more actively in the school. For example, volunteer opportunities are created for parents, and parental input is solicited on important issues. An effort is made to reduce student "downtime," so that students have less unsupervised and unstructured time. There is increased monitoring of the lunchroom, restrooms, and school grounds. An effort is made to increase the involvement and success experiences of high-risk students, usually through an expansion of extracurricular activities and through special academic and counseling programs featuring career exploration and job-seeking skills. A variety of programs addressing individual traits conducive to delinquency are developed. These include social skills training, anger management, and programs designed to instill conventional beliefs. Students, teachers, and others launch school pride campaigns, which include pep rallies and school cleanup programs. The problems associated with large schools are addressed by creating "schools within schools." That is, small groups of students are assigned to the same homeroom and many of the same classes.

Taken together, such **programs** can have a substantial impact on school factors associated with delinquency. They reduce strain. Students are then better able to achieve their educational goals; they are treated more fairly by school officials; they find school more interesting and pleasant; and they get along better with teachers and fellow students. These programs also **increase control.** Students are better supervised at school; they also develop a stronger bond to teachers and fellow students. They increase their investment in conventional activities, as well—through higher school performance and upgraded educational goals—and they are exposed to conventional beliefs and taught to exercise self-control. Further, these programs **foster the social learning of conventional behavior.** Students are more likely to form close associations with conventional role models, to be exposed to conventional beliefs, and to be consistently reinforced for conventional behavior and punished for deviance. Finally, these programs **reduce negative labeling** by school officials.

Programs Focusing on Individual Traits

As indicated in Chapter 13, the super-traits of low self-control and irritability contribute to delinquency. These super-traits encompass several more specific traits, including the following:

- impulsivity (the tendency to act without thinking)
- risk seeking
- amoral beliefs or beliefs favorable to delinquency
- a tendency to become easily upset or angry
- a tendency to blame one's problems on others
- little concern for the feelings or rights of others
- an aggressive or antagonistic interactional style

Many of the programs described earlier have an impact on these traits. As you may recall, the traits are often a function of biological factors and the early family environment. Many of the family programs just described attempt to reduce biological harms and improve the family environment, so they should affect these traits. Many school-based programs also affect individual traits, including such traits as impulsivity and beliefs regarding delinquency.

The programs described in this section, however, focus directly on individual traits. The programs, which are offered in both preschool and elementary/high school, may be available to all juveniles or just to juveniles at risk for delinquency. Also, these programs are frequently used to rehabilitate juvenile delinquents who are in community treatment programs or institutions. There are several common programs, each targeting a somewhat different set of traits. The programs focus on training in a variety of areas, including social and interpersonal skills, problem solving, anger management, conflict resolution, and violence prevention.[7]

Officials sometimes employ several programs or elements from several programs. They target a range of individual traits and often proceed by teaching juveniles the skills necessary for effective interaction with others. (These include such basic social skills as maintaining eye contact when talking with someone, as well as more advanced skills, such as recognizing and showing sensitivity to the feelings of others.) The programs teach juveniles how to respond to problems without engaging in delinquency. In particular, they teach juveniles how to be assertive (rather than aggressive), how to negotiate with others, how to manage their anger, and how to respond to a range of problematic situations, including teasing from peers and criticism from teachers. Related to this, the programs teach basic problem-solving skills. In particular, juveniles are taught to stop and think before they act rather than responding impulsively. The programs also expose juveniles to beliefs that favor conventional behavior and condemn delinquency: they provide information about the negative consequences of delinquency, let students know that various forms of delinquency are less common among their peers than they might think, and persuading students and classes to take public stands against various types of delinquency, such as drug use and violence. Peer leaders often assist in this process, since students may be more likely to trust and identify with them.

These programs, then, target a range of individual traits conducive to delinquency, such as impulsivity, risk seeking, beliefs favorable to delinquency, anger, lack of concern for others, and aggressive interactional styles. In some cases, properly qualified officials may treat certain traits with medication. Most notably, hyperactivity is often treated with drugs like Ritalin or Adderall, which have shown some success in reducing short-term problem behavior. Certain evidence, however, suggests that drugs are most effective when combined with programs of the type described here (see Wasserman and Miller, 1998; Murray et al., 2008).

Targeting individual traits may reduce strain, reduce negative labeling, increase control, and foster the social learning of conventional behavior. In particular, juveniles will be in a better position to achieve their goals, will be treated in a more positive manner by others, and will be less likely to respond to strain with delinquency. They will less likely be negatively labeled by others. They will be higher in control—particularly self-control and beliefs condemning delinquency. And they will be better able to resist the influence of delinquent peers and act in conventional ways that result in reinforcement.

To give you a better sense of what these programs are like, let us describe the basic components of problem-solving training and anger management programs.

Problem-solving training. Dodge (1986) lists five steps in effective problem-solving: (1) search for cues in the environment; (2) interpret these cues; (3) generate possible responses to the situation; (4) consider the possible consequences of the responses; and (5) enact the chosen response. Data suggest that delinquents have problems at each of these steps because they seem to attend to fewer environmental cues, tend to focus on aggressive cues, often attribute hostile intent when there is none, generate fewer alternative solutions and more aggressive responses, fail to recognize the negative consequences of delinquent behavior, and often lack the social skills to enact prosocial responses (see Kazdin, 1994).

Problem-solving training teaches juveniles to carefully perform each of the steps necessary for effective problem solving and to avoid the mistakes just listed. The instructor describes and models the steps in effective problem solving. The child is then asked to apply these steps to an imaginary problem, often making statements to himself or herself that call attention to the mental tasks to be performed. In the Think Aloud program, for example, children are taught to ask themselves a series of four questions:

"What is my problem?"
"What is my plan?"
"Am I using my plan?"
"How did I do?" (quoted in Hollin, 1990a:66)

The WISER way teaches youth to Wait, Identify the problem, generate Solutions, Evaluate the consequences, and self-Reinforce (Hollin, 1990b:485). The instructor prompts the youth when necessary and provides feedback and reinforcement. Eventually, the program participants apply the steps to real-life problems. Such training addresses several of the specific traits listed earlier, including impulsivity, risk seeking, and aggressive interactional styles.

Anger management. Anger management programs teach juveniles how to limit or control their anger, with the goal of promoting more adaptive behavior. Most programs have several features in common. First, juveniles explore the causes and consequences of their anger. They may do this by keeping a diary or log of events that made them angry and their reaction to these events. The causes of anger include not only external events but also the internal statements made about those events. Aggressive individuals, for example, are more likely to interpret the ambiguous acts of others as indicating hostile intent, so the stare of a stranger may be interpreted as a deliberate challenge. The diary may help identify such self-statements. It may also help identify the early warning signs of anger, such as tensed muscles or flushing. Second, the juveniles learn techniques for more effectively controlling their anger—counting backward, imagining a peaceful scene, deep breathing, muscle relaxation, and self-statements like "Calm down" and "Cool off." Some programs also attempt to increase the juvenile's level of self-efficacy in the interest of further increasing self-control. In addition to teaching juveniles to reduce or more effectively control their anger, the programs often teach social and problem-solving skills that allow for a more adaptive response to situations. Finally, juveniles receive much practice applying the preceding techniques, first in response to imaginary provocations and eventually in real-life settings. And they receive much feedback and reinforcement as they apply these techniques (see Blackburn, 1993; Hollin, 1990a).

The most effective programs focusing on individual traits employ similar training techniques. These techniques include direct instruction; modeling of the desired behaviors by the trainer or others; role playing by the youth, with feedback from the trainer and others; reinforcement for appropriate behavior; and completing homework assignments that require the use of newly acquired traits or skills in real-life settings. Certain programs make special efforts to ensure that these skills will be used in the outside world, such as making the training as similar to real life as possible and attempting to ensure that the new skills are reinforced when used successfully in real-life settings. Many of the parent training and other programs described earlier use similar training techniques, which are part of the cognitive behavioral approach described earlier.

Programs Focusing on Delinquent Peers and Gangs

As you know, associating with delinquent peers and gang members is a major cause of delinquency. Such association creates much strain, since delinquent peers and gang members frequently get into conflicts with one another and others. In addition, such association reduces control, since it draws juveniles away from parents, school, and other conventional groups. Association with delinquent peers or gangs also contributes to the social learning of crime, since juveniles are exposed to delinquent models, taught beliefs favorable to delinquency, and reinforced for delinquency. And such association increases the likelihood of negative labeling by others.

The **family, school, and individual-trait programs** described in the preceding sections **all have an impact on peer relations.** They reduce the likelihood that juveniles will get involved with delinquent peers and gangs; they reduce the negative influence of peers on the juvenile; and they reduce the likelihood that peers will treat one another badly. For example, parent training programs teach parents how to better supervise their children. Well-supervised juveniles are less likely to join delinquent peer groups, are less likely to succumb to negative peer pressures, and are less likely to get into serious disputes with peers. In fact, one might argue that the best way to counter the effect of delinquent peers on delinquency is to strengthen individual traits and the family, school, and community. Delinquent peers and gangs often flourish when these agencies are weak.

This section, however, focuses on programs that directly target delinquent peer groups and gangs—with most such programs targeting gangs. Such programs usually focus on adolescents, since peer influence is greatest at this time. Some programs focus on adolescents in general; others focus on at-risk adolescents, such as adolescents in schools with gang problems; and still others focus on adolescents who belong to delinquent peer groups or gangs. The most common response to delinquent peer groups and gangs involves efforts by the justice system to suppress illegal activities in these groups. Many communities, however, have made an attempt to supplement suppression with crisis intervention, rehabilitation, and prevention programs.[8]

Suppression programs by the police and courts. The police often target gangs in certain areas. They gather information on the gangs, increase patrols in areas where they hang out (gang "hot spots"), and closely monitor gang members. They may also aggressively enforce curfew and truancy laws and conduct "street sweeps," rounding up and searching suspected gang members. And they attempt to severely sanction gang members for their crimes. The police are often supported by prosecutors and probation officers who focus on gang cases, with the prosecutors seeking serious penalties for gang-related crimes. In this connection, many states have passed laws increasing the penalties for gang-related crimes. Probation officers closely supervise gang members, strictly enforcing the conditions of their probation.

These suppression techniques have met with mixed success, although some, when carefully implemented, are sometimes able to reduce gang activity (see the discussion of police crackdowns in Chapter 20; also see Braga and Weisburd, 2012). One example of a successful suppression program was provided in Chapter 20: the crackdown on gun violence by youth gangs in Boston. Most gang researchers, however, argue that suppression techniques will be more effective if they are combined with other efforts to address gang problems—including crisis intervention, rehabilitation, and prevention.

Crisis intervention programs try to prevent disputes from escalating into violence. Much gang crime involves disputes between gangs or gang members. In some communities, mediators make an active effort to learn about disputes or conflicts that might erupt into violence. They patrol the streets in gang areas and encourage gang members and community residents to call them when problems arise. They may attempt to reduce gang conflict by challenging the rumors that sometimes fuel conflict or by trying to discourage gang members from resorting to violence, sometimes enlisting the aid of the families of gang members and others close to the gang. And they mediate disputes between gangs and among gang members. In some cases, they hold "gang summits" and try to negotiate truces among warring gangs. Evidence on the effectiveness of such programs is somewhat encouraging, although further evaluation is needed.

Rehabilitation programs are directed at the members of delinquent peer groups and gangs. Such individuals may be offered a range of rehabilitation services, including counseling, mentoring, programs focusing on family problems, help with school problems, vocational training, and assistance finding a job. The House of Umoja in Philadelphia, for example, provides a sanctuary for gang members, who can receive educational assistance, counseling, and job training and placement. Efforts to rehabilitate gang members have not been evaluated thoroughly, although some carefully constructed programs show signs of success.

We should note, however, that not all efforts to rehabilitate gang members are successful. For example, some programs attempt to place gang members or delinquents in conventional peer groups, with the thought of exposing them to conventional role models. In addition, gang members are taught conventional beliefs, reinforced for conventional behavior, and punished for delinquency. Such programs, however, have shown mixed results. Putting delinquent and conventional juveniles together in the same group can often increase the delinquency of the conventional juveniles—especially when there are more than a few delinquents in the group.[9]

Prevention programs attempt to discourage juveniles from joining gangs and to teach them skills that will help them resist gang and peer influence. For example, a number of educational programs provide information about gang violence and drug use, the negative consequences of gang membership, how gangs recruit individuals, and methods of resisting recruitment. Other programs attempt to counter peer pressure to use drugs by providing juveniles with information about the negative consequences of drug use, letting them know that drug use is less common than they think, teaching them to recognize and resist peer pressure to use drugs, and persuading them to make a public commitment against drug use.

One of the most popular antigang education programs in the country is GREAT, or Gang Resistance Education and Training (Esbensen, Peterson et al., 2004). This program is run in many school systems and has been revised over the years in an effort to increase its limited effectiveness. In its latest form, the program involves a series of 13 lessons in which a uniformed police officer covers conflict resolution, goal setting, resisting peer pressure, and other topics. Results from a recent evaluation indicate that the revised version of GREAT (universally implemented in 2003) is more effective, has lasting effects, and decreases the odds of gang membership by a significant amount (for more information, visit http://www.great-online.org.) The most effective education programs tend to have certain traits in common. They make use of the cognitive behavioral strategies described earlier—as opposed to simply lecturing juveniles or holding discussions with them. They employ individuals with whom the juveniles can identify, often making use of peer instructors. They not only focus on the negative consequences of gang membership or delinquency, they also teach juveniles the skills they need to recognize and resist influence attempts. And they often try to establish a norm against gang membership or delinquency. For example, they may let juveniles know that most kids their age do not use drugs, or they may try to get class members to take a public stand against drug use.

Summary. As you can see, there have been a number of efforts to deal with delinquent peer groups and gangs. Many have failed, although some show promise. To combat gang crime, the federal government has encouraged communities to form coalitions of representatives from the police, other government agencies, and community organizations.

The coalitions are supposed to engage in tasks like collecting information on the extent and nature of the gang problem in their community, designing suppression programs to be implemented by police, developing rehabilitation and prevention programs, and coordinating the delivery of these programs. A number of such coalitions have been formed, although some have been more successful than others at completing their tasks. We lack good evaluation data on the effectiveness of most such coalitions, but some show evidence of success in reducing gang crime. And most gang researchers feel that a coordinated strategy involving the suppression of gang activities and the use of carefully selected rehabilitation and prevention programs is our best hope for reducing gang activity.

SELECTED OTHER PREVENTION AND REHABILITATION PROGRAMS

A variety of other prevention and rehabilitation programs have shown promise. Many are run in the community, with some attempting to change the nature of the community in ways that reduce delinquency. Brief overviews of selected programs are provided next.[10]

Mentoring Mentoring programs match at-risk or delinquent juveniles with nonprofessional volunteers, such as college students, community residents, and business persons. Ideally, the mentors form a close relationship with the juveniles. They function as conventional role models, offer guidance, and help the juveniles deal with a range of problems, including family, school, and peer problems. Mentors, then, have the potential to reduce strain, increase control, and foster the social learning of conventional behavior. Evidence on the effectiveness of mentoring programs is mixed, but data suggest that intensive mentoring programs reduce delinquency by a modest amount when they carefully train volunteers and ensure that volunteers reinforce prosocial behavior and sanction deviant behavior.[11]

Supervised recreational opportunities. A number of programs provide supervised recreational activities for juveniles, especially after school, when incidents of delinquency peak. Such programs increase direct control by attempting to monitor youth who might otherwise be unsupervised. There may be attempts to establish relationships between the conventional adults who run the program and the participants. Evidence on the effectiveness of these programs is also mixed, but data suggest that carefully constructed recreational programs may reduce delinquency. Such programs are small; they provide structured activities, are well supervised, and make an effort to aggressively recruit and retain youth in the community.[12]

Vocational training and employment programs. These programs reduce strain and create a stake in the community by teaching job skills and helping juveniles find employment. Vocational programs typically focus on delinquents and at-risk juveniles, like high school dropouts or juveniles doing poorly in school. Some vocational programs are based in the community, and some are incorporated into the school system. Once again, evidence on the effectiveness of these programs is mixed. Many vocational programs do not appear to reduce delinquency, but certain well-designed programs show much promise—especially those targeting juveniles from high-risk backgrounds (see Chapter 17). Such intensive, long-term programs help juveniles deal with other problems they may be facing and provide incentives for participation. The *Job Corps* program of the federal government is an example.[13]

Situational crime prevention. As indicated in Chapter 11, crime is a function of both a juvenile's predisposition for delinquency and the situations he or she encounters. Predisposed juveniles are more likely to engage in delinquency when they are provoked by others, when drugs and alcohol are present, and when the benefits of delinquency are seen as high and the costs of delinquency as low. A variety of strategies have been developed to reduce the likelihood that individuals will encounter such situations. Two such strategies were mentioned in Chapter 11: installing theft-proof change boxes on buses and placing attendants in parking lots. Clarke (1992, 1995) describes 12 general techniques of situational crime prevention, including "deflecting [potential] offenders" (e.g., separating rival fans at sporting events); "target hardening" (e.g., putting steering locks on cars); "target removal" (e.g., removable car radios); and "formal surveillance" (e.g., cameras to detect speeding). Clarke (1995), Clarke and Eck (2005), Eck (2002), and M. Felson (2002) also provide examples of situational prevention approaches that appear to be successful. These approaches reduce the likelihood that individuals will encounter others who provoke them, reduce the availability of drugs and alcohol, reduce the perceived benefits of crime, or increase the perceived costs of crime.

Programs that address drug use, mental health, and guns. Most of the program types (e.g., family, school, individual, and peer) described in the preceding sections have been employed to reduce drug use as well as delinquency, and they have shown some effect on levels of drug use. In addition, a number of programs focus specifically on drugs (for overviews, see Brochu, 2006; National Institute on Drug Abuse, 2006; Winters, 2007; and the National Drug Control Strategy at http://www.whitehousedrugpolicy.gov).[14] As mentioned earlier, the "Above the Influence" antidrug media campaign targets certain factors known to cause drug use. For example, the campaign tries to convince juveniles that drug use has a number of negative consequences. It has been difficult to evaluate the impact of such media campaigns, but existing data suggest that they are generally not effective in reducing drug use (see Ferri et al., 2013). In a more promising approach, court personnel attempt to identify and refer individuals with drug problems to a *drug court*, which develops a treatment program for these individuals, closely monitors their behavior to ensure compliance with the plan—with frequent drug tests being employed—and rewards individuals for compliance and punishes noncompliance. Drug courts are used extensively with adults, and evidence suggests that they are effective in reducing drug use (M. Gottfredson, 2006). Such courts are becoming more common with juveniles, with juvenile drug courts not only providing drug treatment but also addressing other problems—such as family, school, and peer problems. By 2009, about 500 juvenile drug courts were in place across the United States. Preliminary evidence suggests that such courts can reduce juvenile drug use by a modest amount (Mitchell et al., 2012).

In recent years, a small number of juvenile mental health courts have been established in the United States. The courts address the unmet needs of offenders who have mental health problems, mainly by connecting these youth and their families with appropriate treatment programs in the community. In the context of these courts, "participants are viewed not as criminals but as individuals afflicted with an illness that impairs [their ability to refrain from illegal behavior]" (Sarteschi et al., 2011:19). Additional evaluation research is needed to determine whether the courts are effective for juveniles (see Tanner-Smith et al., 2016), though data on adult mental health courts indicate that they represent a promising approach and can help to reduce repeat offending (Sarteschi et al., 2011).

A number of programs have also tried to reduce the prevalence of guns among juveniles or, at least, the likelihood that juveniles will use guns. Most such programs have not been evaluated thoroughly, or the evidence on the effectiveness of these programs is mixed. However, there is good evidence that a few programs, like gun buybacks, do not work. Certain programs appear promising, especially carefully planned police crackdowns that target individuals who may be illegally carrying or using guns. Such crackdowns are usually instituted in areas with high rates of gun crime ("gun hot spots"). These programs increase the **certainty** of punishment and, sometimes, the severity of punishment as well.[15]

Community crime prevention. Some programs attempt to reduce delinquency by attacking the community problems that contribute to delinquency.[16] As indicated in Chapter 12, economic deprivation and other factors increase community crime rates through their effects on strain, control, and the social learning of crime.

The most common community crime prevention program is Neighborhood Watch. As you may recall, one reason that some communities have higher crime rates is failure of the residents to effectively monitor their communities and sanction deviance. That is, some communities are low in direct control. Neighborhood watch programs try to address this problem by gathering neighbors together, encouraging them to more closely monitor their community, and encouraging them to report suspicious activity to the police. Such programs, however, are difficult to implement in the high-crime communities that need them the most. Neighborhood watch programs are not always effective, perhaps due to the low involvement of program participants in some areas (see Hope, 1995). Nevertheless, a review of the evidence indicates that, on average, neighborhood watch programs help to reduce to crime (Bennett et al., 2008).

More ambitious community crime prevention programs attempt to address a range of local problems that contribute to crime. Although the programs are often initiated by people outside the community, an attempt is usually made to actively involve community residents in the program. Some community programs attempt to provide social services to juveniles and others in the community; services include mentoring, tutoring and other educational programs, vocational programs, counseling, health programs, and recreational programs. Few such programs have been properly evaluated, although some show signs of success. Prevention and rehabilitation programs are discussed further in Chapter 25.

Still other programs attempt to stimulate economic development in struggling communities. This has been done by providing tax breaks and other financial incentives to attract businesses to disadvantaged communities. Also, grants to local governments are used to, for example, improve housing and public services in disadvantaged communities (see Bushway and Reuter, 2002; DePledge, 2002). The impact of these programs on economic development has not been evaluated thoroughly, although some evidence suggests that these programs have had limited success in certain communities.

THE CRITICAL ROLE OF LARGER SOCIAL FORCES IN PREVENTING DELINQUENCY

Most of the prevention and rehabilitation programs described in the foregoing pages focus on the individual and his or her immediate social environment—family, school, peer group, and local community. The nature of one's immediate environment, however, is strongly influenced by larger social forces. These forces play a major role in generating problems such as dysfunctional families, school failure, gangs, and neighborhoods plagued by crime. Further, these forces influence the success or failure of prevention and rehabilitation programs, since they shape the context in which these programs operate. It is difficult for parent training programs to be successful, for example, when parents are unemployed and struggling to survive.

Of all the social forces we might discuss, **economic forces are the most important.** A range of economic forces in the United States have contributed to a high overall level of prosperity, but this prosperity has not been shared by all. Consider the following.

- Although the United States is among the world's most prosperous nations, its prosperity has not been shared by a large portion of the population. According to one report, which compared the earnings of workers in 19 developed nations, the United States has one of the highest levels of income inequality. Despite relatively "high earnings at the top of the U.S. income scale . . . inequality in the United States is so severe that low-earning U.S. workers are actually worse off than low-earning workers in all but seven peer countries" (Gould and Wething, 2012:2).
- The United States also has the highest child poverty rate among affluent countries (the poverty line being set at one-half of each country's median income level). "In 2009, the United States had the highest rate of child poverty among peer countries, at 23.1 percent—meaning that more than one in five children lived in poverty" (Gould and Wething, 2012:4).
- Further, the United States ranks next to last among affluent countries in economic resources devoted to government social programs, such as family assistance and health (Dreier, 2007). Other developed nations "are much more likely than the United States to step in where markets and labor policy fail in order to lift their most disadvantaged citizens out of poverty" (Gould and Wething, 2012:7). Related to this, Americans pay lower taxes than people in all other affluent countries except Japan (taxes calculated as the percentage of gross domestic product; see Dreier, 2007).
- Reasons for the high rate of poverty in the United States in addition to low government spending on social programs include a major loss of manufacturing jobs in recent decades, an increase in service sector jobs that pay poorly and carry few benefits, and an increase in single-parent families (which are more likely to live in poverty).[17]

Poverty contributes to a range of situations conducive to crime and delinquency, including poor health care and problems in the family (like poor parenting and child abuse) and at school, as well as a range of neighborhood problems.[18] The prevention and rehabilitation programs described earlier have shown some success in reducing the negative effects of poverty and, in some cases, helping individuals escape from poverty. But these programs deal largely with the symptoms of the widespread poverty in the United States. Any serious approach to reducing delinquency must devote greater attention to reducing poverty throughout the country—both individual poverty and the concentration of poverty in certain communities.

A range of programs have been suggested in the area of prevention and rehabilitation. Some argue that society should do more to attract jobs to inner-city areas plagued by crime and to induce employers to hire people from such areas. Some argue that we should increase the pay and benefits associated with low-skilled jobs so that all work pays a living wage. Many full-time workers do not make enough to raise a family out of poverty (Herbert, 2007b; Steenland, 2013). And many workers do not receive and cannot afford health care, although the passage of the Affordable Care Act helped to address this issue. Some argue that we should make jobs located in suburban areas more accessible to inner-city residents through improved transportation and new housing policies. Some argue that we should create new jobs in the public sector, particularly in inner-city communities. Such jobs might be in areas like childcare, health care, public safety, and child protection. Some argue that we should provide increased tax benefits and other financial assistance to families with children, and we should do more to help single parents collect child support. Some argue that we should increase social services, including job training, educational programs, childcare, preschool programs like Head Start and Early Head Start, food programs, housing assistance, and a range of pro-family policies like flexible work schedules and stronger family leave policies.[19]

We do not mean to end this chapter on a pessimistic note, but the United States is at a critical point in its efforts to reduce delinquency. We have a reasonably good idea of how to go about reducing delinquency, and a number of states are using this knowledge to reform their juvenile justice systems and implement promising programs. But it remains to be seen whether we will take the steps needed to maximize the potential of these efforts, which are essential to the goal of securing success on a large scale.

SUMMARY

A number of rehabilitation and prevention programs have been reviewed. Not all programs work, but criminologists now have a reasonably good idea of the characteristics that distinguish the most successful programs from the least successful ones. The key feature of the most successful programs is that they address the causes of delinquency, identified in earlier chapters. Further, these programs are cost effective. Data indicate that they more than pay for themselves in terms of preventing crime and other problems, such as dropping out of school and unemployment.[20] One study estimated that several rehabilitation programs for juvenile offenders save $5 to $10 dollars for each dollar of taxpayer cost (Aos et al., 2001). In addition, data suggest that many prevention and rehabilitation programs are more cost effective than get-tough strategies like incapacitation. On average, it costs more than $100,000 a year to confine a juvenile offender. While confining juveniles does stop some crime, many prevention and rehabilitation programs can stop crime at a much lower cost.[21] Finally, these programs have wide popular support. Even though the public wants to get tough with juvenile offenders, especially serious offenders, polls indicate that most people *also* support an increased emphasis on rehabilitation and prevention.[22]

Rehabilitation and prevention programs will not solve the delinquency problem. As indicated, they reduce but do not eliminate delinquency. And, as indicated, we are likely to encounter problems if we try to implement these programs on a large scale. It will be difficult to ensure that the programs are run as designed. And it will be difficult to ensure that the people who need these programs the most participate in them. But it is nevertheless clear that prevention and rehabilitation should be a central part of any serious effort to control delinquency.

TEACHING AIDS

Web-Based Exercise: Finding the Latest Information on Programs and Practices for Reducing Delinquency

Several websites provide excellent overviews of programs and policies that are effective in reducing delinquency, as well as some that are ineffective and others that are "promising" (they may be effective, but haven't been sufficiently evaluated). These sites include the OJJDP's **Model Programs Guide** at http://www.ojjdp.gov/mpg, **Blueprints for Healthy Youth Development** at http://www.blueprintsprograms.com, and **The Campbell Collaboration** at http://www.campbellcollaboration.org. But the website we want to highlight provides the most comprehensive overview of what works and what does not in controlling crime and delinquency: **CrimeSolutions.gov** is sponsored by the National Institute of Justice and is at http://www.crimesolutions.gov. Programs and practices are rated "effective," "promising," or "no effects." Spend some time exploring this site. In the **I would like to** box, click on **Learn how programs and practices are rated**. Explore the various programs and practices under **Juveniles**. Find one "effective" program/practice and one with "no effects." Read about the characteristics of each program/practice, along with the evaluations done of the programs/practice. Then draw on the material in this chapter to describe why one program/practice is effective and the other has no effects. For example, ask yourself whether the effective program/practice addresses major causes of delinquency, is intensive, or focuses on high-risk juveniles.

Exercise: Extend Your Knowledge of Rehabilitation and Prevention Programs

Most of the prevention and rehabilitation programs featured in this chapter (e.g., parent training programs and anger management programs) were described in general terms. Also, space limitations prevented us from describing many other programs. We would like you to add to this chapter. Start by selecting a specific prevention or rehabilitation program, either an example of one of the general programs described in this chapter (e.g., a specific parent training program) or a program not described in this chapter. To make this exercise more interesting, you might select a program that is used in your home community (call your local juvenile court or go to its website for information). Then attempt to answer the following questions about the program (this will be easier for some programs than others, but do the best you can).

1. What happens in the program? That is, what does the program do to rehabilitate offenders and/or prevent delinquency? Does it possess the five general characteristics of effective rehabilitation and prevention programs described at the start of this chapter?
2. What causes of delinquency does the program address?
3. What groups does the program target (e.g., serious juvenile offenders, high school students, teenage mothers)? To what extent is the program being used? For example, is it used in only one location or throughout the United States?
4. Has the program been evaluated? How favorable are the evaluations? What do the evaluations say about the effectiveness of the program in reducing delinquency?
5. Are there any other advantages or disadvantages of the program that people should be aware of? For example, does the program reduce the fear of crime but cost quite a lot?

You can obtain this information from a variety of sources, including books, newspapers and magazines, academic journals, government publications, technical reports issued by research organizations, and websites. We suggest you look at the following sources:

- Relevant references in this text (and the references in these references); for example, the CDC publication titled *Best Practices of Youth Violence Prevention* contains information on many specific programs (available in PDF form at http://www.cdc.gov/ violenceprevention/pub/yv_bestpractices.html).
- Indexes to academic journal articles, like Sociological Abstracts, PsycINFO, Criminal Justice Abstracts, and the National Criminal Justice Reference Service Abstracts Database (http://www.ncjrs.gov/abstractdb/search.asp).
- Indexes to newspaper articles, like the *New York Times Index* and LexisNexis.com.
- The websites for the Office of Juvenile Justice and Delinquency Prevention (OJJDP) and the National Criminal Justice Reference Service (NCJRS). Be sure to look at the

OJJDP Model Programs Guide at http://www.ojjdp.gov/MPG. Also look at the websites for Blueprints for Healthy Youth Development (http://www.blueprintsprograms .com) and CrimeSolutions.gov.

- The website for the program you are interested in (if it has a website) and/or literature produced by the program sponsors.
- Other relevant websites, such as the Resource Links website maintained by the National Center on Education, Disability, and Juvenile Justice (http://www.edjj .org).

Do not overwhelm yourself. Try to focus on recent reports that provide a summary or overview of your program—look at a few such reports if possible. Pay attention to the source of the report. Ask yourself whether the organization producing the report might have a reason to be overly optimistic or overly pessimistic about the program you are examining. If you do not have much success finding information on your program, switch to another program.

TEST YOUR KNOWLEDGE OF THIS CHAPTER

1. Why do many criminologists believe that the United States has placed too much emphasis on get-tough approaches?
2. How do prevention and rehabilitation programs differ from get-tough approaches? How does prevention differ from rehabilitation?
3. Why haven't prevention programs played a greater role in efforts to reduce delinquency in the United States?
4. Why did rehabilitation programs fall out of favor in the 1970s?
5. How might we explain the renewed interest in prevention and rehabilitation programs in the last few years?
6. What are the general characteristics of successful prevention and rehabilitation programs? Describe the cognitive behavioral approach.
7. Why are prevention and rehabilitation programs unlikely to eliminate delinquency?
8. We provided moderately detailed descriptions of prevention and rehabilitation programs in five areas: the early family environment, parent training, school factors, individual traits, and delinquent peers and gangs. For each area, describe what is done to prevent delinquency and rehabilitate delinquents, describe the effectiveness of such efforts, and describe the causes of delinquency that the prevention or rehabilitation programs address.
9. Briefly describe the other prevention and rehabilitation programs that were mentioned (e.g., mentoring, supervised recreational opportunities) and the evidence on their effectiveness.
10. Why do we state that "larger social forces" play a crucial role in the prevention of delinquency? What larger social force do we highlight, and why?
11. List any three proposals that have been made to reduce poverty and/or the concentration of poverty in the United States.

THOUGHT AND DISCUSSION QUESTIONS

1. Can you think of any prevention and/or rehabilitation programs that were not discussed in this chapter—programs you've read or heard about or programs of your own design? What causes of crime do these programs address?

2. As indicated in Chapter 23, many high schools and colleges are experiencing high levels of cheating. Drawing on the materials in this chapter, describe how you would go about preventing school cheating and rehabilitating cheaters.

3. Most people favor placing more emphasis on prevention and rehabilitation programs. Nevertheless, many efforts to reduce delinquency place much more emphasis on getting tough than on rehabilitation and prevention. And politicians who stress rehabilitation and prevention programs are often attacked as being soft on crime. Why do you think public policies differ so notably from the desire of the general public for more emphasis on prevention and rehabilitation?

4. Even though we now have a reasonably good idea about which programs are and are not effective in controlling delinquency, ineffective programs remain popular and continue to receive funding (e.g., Scared Straight, DARE, and programs designed to increase self-esteem). Why do you think this is the case? What can be done to change this?

KEY TERMS

- Prevention programs
- Rehabilitation programs
- War on Poverty
- Cognitive behavioral approach
- Parent training programs
- Head Start
- Problem-solving training
- Crisis intervention programs (for gangs)
- Job Corps
- Situational crime prevention
- Drug courts

ENDNOTES

1. For overviews of rehabilitation and prevention, see Andrews and Bonta, 2006; Aos et al., 2001; H. Barlow, 1995; Blueprints for Healthy Youth Development at http://www.blueprintsprograms.com; Burns et al., 2003; The Campbell Crime and Justice Group at www.campbellcollaboration.org/CCJG/; Coordinating Council on Juvenile Justice and Delinquency Prevention, 1996; CrimeSolutions.gov at https://www.crimesolutions.gov; Cullen, 2002, 2007; Cullen and Applegate, 1997; Cullen and Gendreau, 2000; Currie, 1998; Farrington, 1996a, 1996b, 2002b; Farrington and Welsh, 2007; Greenwood, 1995, 2002, 2006; Guerra et al., 1994; Hawkins, Catalano, and Brewer, 1995; Heyman and Slep, 2007; Howell, 2003a, 2003b; Howell and Hawkins, 1998; Kazdin, 1994; Kellermann et al., 1998; Kumpfer and Alvarado, 1998; Lipsey et al., 2010; Lipsey and Wilson, 1998; Loeber et al., 2003; Losel, 2007; D. MacKenzie, 2006; McCord et al., 2001; McGuire, 1995; Morley et al., 2000; Muller and Mihalic, 1999; Office of Juvenile Justice and Delinquency Prevention, 1995; Rutter et al., 1998; Sawhill, 2003; Sherman et al., 2002; Thornton et al., 2002; Tremblay and Craig, 1995; U.S. Department of Health and Human Services, 2001; Wasserman and Miller, 1998; Weissbourd, 1996; S. Wilson et al., 2003; Welsh, 2012.

2. For discussions of the decline of rehabilitation, see Andrews and Bonta, 2006; Beckett and Sasson, 2000; Cullen 2002; Cullen and Gendreau, 2000; Feld, 2003; Garland, 2001; Greenwood, 2006; Zimring, 2005.

3. See Andrews and Bonta, 2006; D. Andrews et al., 1990; Brewer et al., 1995; Catalano et al., 1998; Cullen, 2002; Cullen and Gendreau, 2000; Currie, 1998; Farrington, 1996a, 1996b; Farrington and Welsh, 2007; D. Gottfredson, 2001; Greenwood, 2006; Guerra, 1997; Guerra et al. 1994; Hawkins, Arthur, and Catalano, 1995; Hawkins, Catalano, and Brewer, 1995; Howell, 2003a, 2003b; Kazdin, 1994; Krisberg et al., 1995; Lipsey, 1992; Lipsey and Wilson, 1998; Losel, 1995; D. MacKenzie, 2006; McCord et al., 2001; McGuire, 1995; Sherman et al., 2002; Thornton et al., 2002; Tremblay and Craig, 1995; Wasserman and Miller, 1998; David Wilson et al., 2001; Yoshikawa, 1994.

4. For overviews of programs focusing on the early family environment, see Bilukha et al., 2005; Currie, 1998; Earle, 1995; Farrington, 1996a, 1996b; Farrington and Welsh, 2002, 2007; Greenwood, 2006; Guerra, 1997; Hawkins, Arthur, and Catalano, 1995; Howell, 2003a; Howell and Hawkins, 1998; Kazdin, 1994; Kumpfer and Alvarado, 1998; McCord et al., 2001; Olds, 2002; Olds et al., 1998; Sherman et al., 2002; Thornton et al., 2002; Tremblay and Craig, 1995; Wasserman and Miller, 1998; Yoshikawa, 1994; Zigler et al., 1992; Welsh, 2012.

5. For overviews of parent training programs, see Andrews and Bonta, 2006; Brewer et al., 1995; Farrington, 1996a, 1996b; Farrington and Welsh, 2002, 2007; Greenwood, 2006; Guerra, 1997; Hollin, 1992; Howell, 2003a; Kaminski et al., 2008; Kazdin, 1994; Kumpfer and Tait, 2000; McCord et al., 2001; McDonald and Frey, 1999; Patterson, 1982; Petrucci and Roberts, 2004; A. Piquero et al., 2009; Rankin and Wells, 1987; Sherman et al., 2002; Thornton et al., 2002; Tremblay and Craig, 1995; Wasserman and Miller, 1998; Welsh, 2012.

6. For overviews of school programs, see Arnette and Walsleben, 1998; Brewer et al., 1995; Catalano et al., 1998; D. Elliott et al., 1998; Farrington and Welsh, 2007; D. Gottfredson, 2001; D. Gottfredson and G. Gottfredson, 2002; D. Gottfredson et al., 2002a, 2002b; Greenwood, 2006; Hawkins and Lishner, 1987; Hawkins, Farrington, and Catalano, 1998; Howell, 2003a; Maguin and Loeber, 1996; McCord et al., 2001; Samples and Aber, 1998; Sherman et al., 2002; Tremblay and Craig, 1995; Wasserman and Miller, 1998; D. Wilson et al., 2001; S. Wilson et al., 2003; Welsh, 2012.

7. For overviews of programs focusing on individual traits, see Blackburn, 1993; Brewer et al., 1995; Farrington, 1996a, 1996b; Farrington and Welsh, 2007; D. Gottfredson, 2001; D. Gottfredson et al., 2002a, 2002b; Guerra, 1997; Guerra et al., 1994; J. Hawkins, Catalano, and Brewer, 1995; Hawkins, Farrington, and Catalano, 1998; Howell, 2003a; Kazdin, 1994; Kellermann et al., 1998; Losel and Beelmann, 2003; Pearson et al., 2002; Samples and Aber, 1998; Sherman et al., 2002; Thornton et al., 2002; Wasserman and Miller, 1998.

8. For overviews and selected examples of peer programs, see Braga et al., 2002; Brewer et al., 1995; Burch and Kane, 1999; Catalano et al., 1998; Decker and Curry, 2000; Esbensen and Osgood, 1999; Farrington, 1996a, 1996b; Farrington and Welsh, 2007; Fearn et al., 2001; Fritsch et al., 1999; Gifford-Smith et al., 2005; Gorman and White, 1995; Guerra, 1997; Howell, 1997b, 1998b, 1999, 2003a; Huff, 2002; Klein, 1998; Klein and Maxson, 2006; Maxson, 2004; McCord et al., 2001; Morley et al., 2000; Shelden et al., 2001; Sherman et al., 2002; Spergel, 1995; U.S. Department of Justice, 2006; Welsh and Hoshi, 2002; Welsh, 2012.

9. See Farrington, 1996a, 1996b; Gifford-Smith et al., 2005; Gorman and White, 1995; Howell, 2003a; McCord et al., 2001.

10. Also see Blueprints for Healthy Youth Development at http://www.blueprintsprograms.com; Brewer et al., 1995; Catalano et al., 1998; CrimeSolutions.gov at https://www.crimesolutions .gov; Kellermann et al., 1998; Sampson, 2002; Sherman et al., 2002.

11. See Blueprints for Healthy Youth Development at http://www.blueprintsprograms.com; Catalano et al., 1998; CrimeSolutions.gov at https://www.crimesolutions.gov; Farrington and Welsh, 2007; Grossman and Garry, 1997; Howell, 2003a; McCord et al., 2001; Morley et al., 2000; Office of Juvenile Justice and Delinquency Prevention, 1998b; Thornton et al., 2002; Tolan et al., 2008; B. Welsh and Hoshi, 2002.

12. See Farrington and Welsh, 2007; D. Gottfredson et al., 2002a, 2002b; D. Gottfredson et al., 2007; McCord et al., 2001; Morley et al., 2000; Welsh and Hoshi, 2002; Welsh, 2012.

13. See Brewer et al., 1995; Bushway and Reuter, 2002; Currie, 1998; and Lipsey, 1992; also see Hamilton and McKinney, 1999.

14. Also see Boyum and Kleiman, 2002; MacCoun and Reuter, 1998; National Institute on Drug Abuse, 2006; Office of National Drug Control Policy, 1999; Orwin et al., 2004; Vander Waal et al., 2001.

15. See Braga and Weisburd, 2012; Brewer et al., 1995; Catalano et al., 1998; Cook and Ludwig, 2000; Cook et al., 2002; Hahn et al., 2005; Harcourt, 2003; Kellermann et al., 1998; Kleck, 1997; Kovandzic and Marvell, 2003; Ludwig and Cook, 2003; McGarrell et al., 2002; Office of Juvenile Justice and Delinquency Prevention, 1996; Sherman, 2001; Sherman and Eck, 2002; Welsh and Hoshi, 2002; Wintemute, 2006; Zimring, 2005, 2007.

16. See Bushway and Reuter, 2002; Hope, 1995; McCord et al., 2001; Sampson, 2002; Sherman et al., 2002; and Welsh and Hoshi, 2002, for excellent overviews of community crime prevention programs.

17. See Currie, 1998; Hagan, 1994; Lewit et al., 1997; Sampson and Wilson, 1995; W. Wilson, 1987, 1996.

18. See Brooks-Gunn and Duncan, 1997; Currie, 1998; Hagan, 1994; Sampson, 1997; Sampson and Wilson, 1995; W. Wilson, 1987, 1996.

19. For fuller discussions of these issues, see Center for American Progress Task Force on Poverty, 2007; Currie, 1998; Lewit et al., 1997; Messner and Rosenfeld, 2001; Plotnick, 1997; Stemen, 2007; W. Wilson, 1987, 1996.

20. See Aos et al., 2001; Burns et al., 2003; Caldwell et al., 2006; Farrington and Welsh, 2007; Greenwood, 2002; McCord et al., 2001; B. Welsh et al., 2001; Welsh, 2012.

21. See Greenwood, 1998, 1999, 2006; Greenwood et al., 1996; also see Fass and Pi, 2002; Welsh, 2012.

22. See Martin and Glantz as cited in Greenwood, 1998; also see Beckett and Sasson, 2000; Bishop, 2006; Cullen, 2006, 2007; Cullen and Applegate, 1997; Cullen et al., 1998; Flanagan and Longmire, 1996; Moon et al., 2000; Nagin et al., 2006; Roberts and Stalans, 1998.

25 What Should We Do to Reduce Delinquency?

I f you tell someone that you have just read a book on delinquency or taken a course in the area, you may well hear: "So what should we do to reduce delinquency?" How would you respond?

If you are like many of the students in our classes, your initial response will be one of silence. You have been exposed to a great deal of material, some of which may have challenged your beliefs about the causes of delinquency and the best ways to control it. There is a lot to reflect on and pull together.

We want to help you in this process by presenting what we think is a reasonable strategy for reducing delinquency—a strategy that we think takes account of the research on the causes and control of delinquency, that is just or fair, that is within our means, and that would be acceptable to most people in this country. This strategy reflects, in large measure, the one advocated by the federal government.[1] First, we believe that society should place much more emphasis on prevention and rehabilitation. And second, we believe that society should hold juveniles accountable for their behavior and protect our communities from dangerous juveniles—but this should be done in a more effective and just manner than is now the case.

After reading this chapter, you should be able to:

- Describe the nature of comprehensive, community-based strategies for preventing and controlling delinquency.
- Discuss the effectiveness of comprehensive, community-based strategies.
- Describe strategies that are designed to sanction juvenile offenders more effectively.
- Describe and justify your own strategy for controlling delinquency in society.

WE SHOULD PLACE MORE EMPHASIS ON PREVENTION AND REHABILITATION

We think it is necessary to place much more emphasis on prevention and rehabilitation programs of the types described in Chapter 24. It makes more sense to prevent individuals from becoming delinquent in the first place than to respond to their delinquency after the fact. And it makes much sense to attempt to reform or rehabilitate the individuals who do become delinquent. The vast majority of these youth are returned to the community after being processed by the juvenile justice system, sometimes immediately and sometimes after an out-of-home placement. We want to do all that we can to ensure that they cease or, at least reduce, their offending.

Most of the prevention and rehabilitation programs described in Chapter 24 work or show much promise for success. The best of them are able to reduce offending rates upward of 50 percent, and there is reason to believe that criminologists will have the tools to design even more effective programs as additional program evaluations are completed and our knowledge of the causes of delinquency increases. **Such programs also represent a fair or just response to delinquency.** Data suggest that delinquency is partly due to forces beyond the individual's control—forces like genetic inheritance, biological harms, the early family environment, the school one attends, the peers one is exposed to, and the community in which one lives. That is not to say that juveniles have no responsibility for their behavior. But it is to say that delinquency is not simply a matter of free choice. Delinquents are to some extent victims of their environment, and they both need and deserve our assistance. Further, **most prevention and rehabilitation programs are cost effective,** as indicated in Chapter 24. In particular, the programs typically save much more money than they cost, and they frequently prevent delinquency at a lower cost than the get-tough approaches that were so popular for decades. Finally, there is **strong public**

support for prevention and rehabilitation programs, as well as for get-tough approaches, to controlling delinquency.

But **how should we go about putting such prevention and rehabilitation programs into place?** The federal government, many states, and a lot of communities have come to place an increased emphasis on prevention and rehabilitation in recent years (although get-tough approaches remain influential). One model for implementing prevention and rehabilitation programs has shown some promise. This model's premises are reflected to varying degrees in several programs sponsored by the National Institute of Justice and other agencies, programs like the Comprehensive Strategy for Serious, Violent, and Chronic Juvenile Offenders; Safe Futures; the Communities That Care model; Weed and Seed; the Strategic Approaches to Community Safety Initiative; Project PACT (Pulling America's Communities Together); the Comprehensive Communities Program; the Comprehensive Anti-Gang Initiative; Project Safe Neighborhoods; and Empowerment Zones/Enterprise Communities.[2] Some of these programs focus specifically on crime and delinquency, while others focus on a broad range of social problems, including crime. The programs are typically run in high-crime communities, sometimes in neighborhoods, and sometimes in entire cities or counties. And several states are attempting to implement these programs in communities statewide. *6 step*

The programs employ a similar strategy. **First,** community leaders are told about the program, and an effort is made to enlist their support. These leaders may include the mayor; the police chief; judges; school superintendents; leaders from business, civic, and religious communities; and sometimes representatives from state and federal agencies. **Second,** if these community leaders support the program, they can put together a team responsible for implementing and running the program. This broad-based team may include representatives from the police and courts, social welfare agencies, the school system, healthcare delivery system, business and religious communities, and community organizations. **Third,** after receiving some training, the team proceeds to identify community problems that contribute to delinquency and community resources that might be used in response. Among other things, the team collects information from community residents, including juveniles, and from experts in the area. **Fourth,** the team takes responsibility for designing a comprehensive approach to addressing the problems they have identified. The team may be provided with a menu of promising programs from which they can choose. And they may appoint task forces in different areas (e.g., family problems).

Fifth, the team helps develop mechanisms to coordinate the delivery of services to at-risk youth and delinquent juveniles, so that each juvenile will be able to receive the full range of services he or she needs. They also attempt to ensure that cases are carefully managed, such that each targeted juvenile's progress is closely tracked and that person's services are adjusted as necessary. One device for accomplishing these goals is the Community Assessment Center, briefly described in Chapter 21. The Community Assessment Center links all the agencies providing services to at-risk and/or delinquent youth. Youth are sent to the center for assessment, referred to the agencies that provide the services that they (and their families) need, and tracked over time to make sure they get those services. **Sixth,** the team assumes responsibility for evaluating the approach they have developed, revising it if necessary. Given the range of prevention and rehabilitation programs provided, it is quite likely that problems will arise: some programs may not be offered to the youths who need them, some programs may not be properly implemented, some programs may not be effective, and so on. Ongoing evaluation is critical.

The federal government and other organizations assist communities in this effort. The federal government, for example, provides technical assistance in a range of areas, such as identifying promising programs and implementing and evaluating selected programs. The federal government also provides information on funding sources, often provides some funding, and facilitates communication with other teams across the country. Many communities, in addition, may develop a group of local experts to assist in the process. The following websites represent efforts that have been supported by the federal government or private foundations: Blueprints for Healthy Youth Development at http://www.blueprintsprograms.com and CrimeSolutions.gov. Also see the *Targeted Community Action Planning Toolkit* (Flores, 2003) and *Best Practices to Address Community Gang Problems*, developed by the Office of Juvenile Justice and Delinquency Prevention (2010). These organizations are designed to spread information about promising programs, funding opportunities, and issues like program implementation and evaluation.

The comprehensive approach that is mounted differs somewhat from community to community, since different communities have different problems and resources. For example, a community that has a serious gang problem may mount a variety of gang intervention programs. Another community may have little or no problem with gangs. At the same time, there are **certain common features in the comprehensive approaches that are developed.** Prevention programs are typically developed in a range of different areas, since delinquency is caused by a range of problems. These programs involve broad segments of the community, including the juvenile justice system, the schools, social service agencies, community organizations, the business community, and religious organizations. These programs usually target juveniles at high risk for delinquency. Efforts are sometimes made to encourage family members and school officials to identify such juveniles (e.g., family members are encouraged to seek help if they are having problems with their children). Likewise, a number of rehabilitation programs are usually developed. The local juvenile court develops a procedure to carefully screen all referred youths so that they can receive the rehabilitation services they need. A special effort is made to target serious, high-rate, and chronic offenders for treatment, since they account for such a large share of the delinquency problem.

Most efforts to implement this strategy have not yet been formally evaluated. But the few evaluations that have been done suggest that communities often have problems carrying out certain of the six tasks described earlier. For example, this strategy requires that a range of different government and community organizations work together to develop needed services and to ensure that juveniles receive the services they need; it can be difficult, however, to get these organizations to coordinate their efforts (steps 4 and 5). Fortunately, the evaluations include advice on how to better implement a community's chosen strategy.[3] The few communities that have been able to carry out the tasks to some degree appear to have had some success at reducing delinquency, although more and better evaluations are called for (see Howell 2003a, 2003b; Office of Juvenile Justice and Delinquency Prevention, 2010).

We Should Hold Juveniles Accountable for Their Behavior and Protect the Community

We also believe that juveniles should be sanctioned for their delinquent acts and that the community should be protected from dangerous offenders. Data indicate that one of the reasons that juveniles engage in delinquency is low direct control. That is, they are not consistently sanctioned for their delinquent acts. Further, most people believe that juveniles, especially older juveniles, have at least some responsibility for their behavior. This issue is the subject of much debate in the social and behavioral sciences and philosophy (see Agnew, 1995c; Brezina and Wright, 2001; Zimring, 1998). It is commonly argued that human behavior is not fully determined by outside forces, so sanctioning juveniles for their behavior may prevent some delinquency and may be viewed as a just approach in some cases. Further, this strategy has much political and public support.

The **juvenile justice system,** of course, **places much emphasis on sanctioning juveniles, but it often fails to sanction them efficiently.** We have laws that increase the severity of punishment, especially for serious offenders. Such laws are easily passed, and the legislation is politically popular. Data, however, indicate that certainty of punishment is much more important than severity. Unfortunately, it is not so easy to **increase the certainty of punishment.** But among other things, we might teach parents, teachers, and others how to better exercise direct control, for they are in the best position to detect and sanction delinquent acts. Also, the juvenile justice system should make a better effort to detect and sanction delinquency. As indicated in Chapter 20, communities can improve strategies of policing in ways that increase the ability of the police to catch offenders. In particular, data suggest that focused police crackdowns and certain types of community policing are effective in this area. And society can provide more resources, to enable the juvenile court and juvenile corrections system to better sanction offenders. In particular, the juvenile justice system should employ a system of "graduated sanctions," such that all offenders receive meaningful sanctions, which increase in severity if offending continues.

In addition to increasing the certainty of punishment, we need to change how we punish. The punishments now employed often have a number of negative effects: they increase strain, isolate juveniles from conventional society, and foster the social learning of crime. The system should punish in ways that minimize these negative effects. Community-based sanctions, which often avoid the negative effects of institutions, should be employed to the extent possible. As indicated in Chapter 21, the community-based sanctions that have been developed recently are more cost effective than institutionalization. We should punish in a way that rebuilds the ties between offenders and the larger community, perhaps employing some of the initiatives associated with the restorative justice movement (see Chapter 23). Our efforts to punish should be combined with efforts to rehabilitate. In particular, data indicate that sanctions are most effective when combined with measures that address the other causes of delinquency. Finally, we should work to eliminate discrimination in the justice system.

It is also important, of course, to **protect the community from dangerous offenders.** This protection is now often accomplished by institutionalizing juveniles in large facilities that place little emphasis on rehabilitation. Data, however, suggest that the juvenile court system institutionalizes more juveniles than is necessary. And data suggest that it is **better to confine juveniles in small-scale institutions that place a strong emphasis on treatment** (for examples, see our description of the Mendota Juvenile Treatment Program in Chapter 13 [Box 13.2] and the Missouri Model in Chapter 21 [Box 21.1]). Such juveniles are less likely to be harmed by their institutional confinement and are more likely to be rehabilitated, which, of course, contributes to the protection of the community. Adjudicated delinquents can be screened for risk of future offending, particularly serious offending. Juveniles who pose some risk to the community can be placed under close supervision or confined in institutions, if warranted. Close supervision and institutional confinement may prevent some delinquency through the "incapacitation effect," as discussed in Chapter 23.

These strategies are described in detail in the publications listed in notes 1 and 2. We also encourage you to examine the websites of the National Institute of Justice (NIJ) and many of the agencies that are part of the NIJ, such as the Office of Juvenile Justice and Delinquency Prevention (see http://www.ojjdp.gov). Also, visit the website of the National Crime Prevention Council (http://www.ncpc.org). The valuable resources on these sites describe what you can do to reduce delinquency. We hope that your examination of delinquency does not end with this book. Rather, we hope that this book represents the beginning of a serious commitment to work toward the reduction of delinquency in our society.

TEACHING AIDS

Exercise: What Should We Do to Reduce Delinquency?

In the exercise for Chapter 18, we asked you to imagine that a family member or friend asked you: "What causes delinquency?" For this chapter's exercise, imagine that a family member or friend asks you: "What should we do to reduce delinquency?" Outline a 5- to 10-minute response to this question—one that draws on the materials in this text and will be meaningful to your audience. With your instructor's permission, several people in your class should share their responses with the class and solicit feedback.

Web-Based Exercise: Interested in a Career in Criminology/Corrections?

Perhaps you would like to do graduate work in criminology or enter a career devoted to the control and prevention of crime and delinquency. If so, several websites offer information on career possibilities and schools that provide further training in criminology and criminal justice, including master's degrees and doctorates. These websites include Discover Criminal Justice at http://discovercriminaljustice.com, Discover Corrections at http://www.discovercorrections.com, and Discover Policing at http://discoverpolicing .org. The American Society of Criminology maintains a list of graduate programs in criminology and criminal justice at https://www.asc41.com/links/gradPrograms.html. And you can visit the websites of these programs to learn more about them. Many graduate programs offer funding in the form of graduate assistantships and tuition waivers. Good luck.

TEST YOUR KNOWLEDGE OF THIS CHAPTER

1. What criteria (e.g., cost, public acceptance) do we employ to evaluate the suitability of delinquency control measures?
2. Why do we argue that more emphasis needs to be placed on prevention and rehabilitation?
3. Describe the strategy that we suggest (and the federal government recommends) for putting prevention and rehabilitation programs into place.
4. Describe the limited evaluation research on the strategy that we suggest.
   5. Why do we argue that juveniles need to be held accountable for their delinquency?
6. Why do we argue that, too often, juvenile offenders are sanctioned inefficiently or ineffectively? What needs to be done to more effectively sanction juveniles?
7. How do we go about protecting the community from dangerous offenders? What steps does this text recommend to better achieve this goal?

THOUGHT AND DISCUSSION QUESTIONS

1. Can you think of any criteria beyond those we have listed that should be used to evaluate the suitability of delinquency control programs?
2. To what extent do you agree and/or disagree with our recommendations for controlling delinquency? How would you alter these recommendations?
3. The exercise for this chapter asks you to develop your own set of recommendations for controlling delinquency. What might you do to help implement these recommendations, both in your local community and beyond?

ENDNOTES

1. See Bilchik, 1998; Caliber Associates, 2006; Coolbough and Monsel, 2000; Coordinating Council on Juvenile Justice and Delinquency Prevention, 1996; David-Ferdon and Simon, 2014; Flores, 2003; Howell, 1997a, 2003a, 2003b; Krisberg et al., 2004; Kurlychek et al., 1999; Morley et al., 2000; Office of Juvenile Justice and Delinquency Prevention, 2006, 2010; U.S. Department of Justice, 2007.

2. See Caliber Associates, 2006; Coleman et al., 1999; Coolbough and Monsel, 2000; Coordinating Council on Juvenile Justice and Delinquency Prevention, 1996; CrimeSolutions.gov (https://www.crimesolutions.gov); David-Ferdon and Simon, 2014; Dunworth and Mills, 1999; Flores, 2003; Howell, 1997a, 2003a, 2003b; Howell and Hawkins, 1998; Kelling et al., 1998; Krisberg et al., 2004; Morley et al., 2000; National Institute of Justice, 1996; Office of Justice Programs, 1999; Office of Juvenile Justice and Delinquency Prevention, 1999b, 2006, 2010; L. Robinson, 1996; Sherman et al., 2002; U.S. Department of Justice, 2007; the Weed and Seed Data Center at http://www.weedandseeddatacenter.org.

3. For example, see Caliber Associates, 2006; Coolbaugh and Monsel, 2000; CrimeSolutions.gov (https://www.crimesolutions.gov); David-Ferdon and Simon, 2014; Howell, 2003a; Krisberg et al., 2004; Morley et al., 2000; Office of Juvenile Justice and Delinquency Prevention, 2010.

References

Abdullah, Halimah
2014 "Minority kids disproportionately impacted by zero-tolerance laws." CNN, January 30. Available at: http://www.cnn.com/2014/01/24/politics/zero-tolerance/

Acoca, Leslie
1998 "Outside/inside: The violation of American girls at home, on the streets, and in the juvenile justice system." Crime and Delinquency 44:561–589.

Adamczyk, Amy
2012 "Understanding delinquency with friendship group religious context." Social Science Quarterly 93:482–505.

Adams, Mike S., and T. David Evans
1996 "Teacher disapproval, delinquent peers, and self-reported delinquency: A longitudinal test of labeling theory." Urban Review 28:199–211.

Adams, Mike S., Craig T. Robertson, Phyllis GrayRay, and Melvin C. Ray
2003 "Labeling and delinquency." Adolescence 38:171–186.

Agnew, Robert
1983 "Physical punishment and delinquency." Youth and Society 15:225–236.
1984 "Autonomy and delinquency." Sociological Perspectives 27:219–240.
1985a "A revised strain theory of delinquency." Social Forces 64:151–167.
1985b "Social control theory and delinquency: A longitudinal test." Criminology 23:47–62.
1986 "Work and delinquency among juveniles attending school." Journal of Crime and Justice 9:19–41.
1990a "The origins of delinquent events: An examination of offender accounts." Journal of Research in Crime and Delinquency 27:267–294.
1990b "Adolescent resources and delinquency." Criminology 28:535–566.
1991a "A longitudinal test of social control theory and delinquency." Journal of Research on Crime and Delinquency 28:126–156.
1991b "The interactive effect of peer variables on delinquency." Criminology 29:47–72.
1992 "Foundation for a general strain theory of crime and delinquency." Criminology 30:47–87.
1993 "Why do they do it? An examination of the intervening mechanisms between 'social control' variables and delinquency." Journal of Research in Crime and Delinquency 30:245–266.
1994a "Delinquency and the desire for money." Justice Quarterly 11:411–427.
1994b "The techniques of neutralization and violence." Criminology 32:555–580.
1995a "Testing the leading crime theories: An alternative strategy focusing on motivational processes." Journal of Research in Crime and Delinquency 32:363–398.
1995b "Strain and subcultural theories of criminality." Pp. 305–327 in Joseph F. Sheley, ed., Criminology: A Contemporary Handbook. Belmont, CA: Wadsworth.
1995c "Determinism, indeterminism, and crime: An empirical exploration." Criminology 33:83–109.
1997 "Stability and change in crime over the life course: A strain theory explanation." Pp. 101–132 in Terence P. Thornberry, ed., Developmental Theories of Crime and Delinquency: Advances in Criminological Theory, Volume 7. New Brunswick, NJ: Transaction.
1999 "A general strain theory of community differences in crime rates." Journal of Research in Crime and Delinquency 36:123–155.
2001a "An overview of general strain theory." Pp. 161–174 in Ray Paternoster and Ronet Bachman, eds., Explaining Criminals and Crime. Los Angeles: Roxbury.

2001b "Building on the foundation of general strain theory: Specifying the types of strain most likely to lead to crime and delinquency." Journal of Research in Crime and Delinquency 38:319–361.

2002 "Experienced, vicarious, and anticipated strain." Justice Quarterly 19:603–632.

2003a "An integrated theory of the adolescent peak in offending." Youth and Society 34:263–299.

2003b "The interactive effects of social control variables on delinquency." In Chester Britt and Michael R. Gottfredson, eds., Control Theories of Crime and Delinquency, Advances in Criminological Theory, Volume 12. New Brunswick, NJ: Transaction.

2005 Why Do Criminals Offend: A General Theory of Crime and Delinquency. Los Angeles: Roxbury.

2006a Pressured Into Crime. New York: Oxford University Press.

2006b "General strain theory: Current status and directions for further research." Pp. 101–123 in Francis T. Cullen, John Paul Wright, and Kristie R. Blevins, eds., Taking Stock: The Status of Criminological Theory. New Brunswick, NJ: Transaction.

2006c "Storylines as a neglected cause of crime." Journal of Research in Crime and Delinquency 43:119–147.

2009 "The contribution of 'mainstream' theories to the explanation of female delinquency." Pp. 7–29 in Margaret Zahn, ed., The Delinquent Girl. Philadelphia: Temple University Press.

2011 Toward a Unified Criminology: Integrating Assumptions about Crime, People, and Society. New York: New York University Press.

2013 "When criminal coping is likely: An extension of general strain theory." Deviant Behavior 34:653–670.

Agnew, Robert, and Timothy Brezina

1997 "Relational problems with peers, gender and delinquency." Youth and Society 29:84–111.

Agnew, Robert, Timothy Brezina, John Paul Wright, and Francis T. Cullen

2002 "Strain, personality traits, and delinquency: Extending general strain theory." Criminology 40:43–72.

Agnew, Robert, Francis T. Cullen, Velmer S. Burton, Jr., T. David Evans, and R. Gregory Dunaway

1996 "A new test of classic strain theory." Justice Quarterly 13:681–704.

Agnew, Robert, Shelley K. Matthews, Jacob Bucher, Adria N. Welcher, and Corey Keyes

2008 "Socioeconomic status, economic problems, and delinquency." Youth and Society 40:159–181.

Agnew, Robert, and Ardith A. R. Peters

1985 "The techniques of neutralization: An analysis of predisposing and situational factors." Criminal Justice and Behavior 13:81–97.

Agnew, Robert, and David M. Petersen

1989 "Leisure and delinquency." Social Problems 36:332–350.

Agnew, Robert, Heather Scheuerman, Jessica Grosholz, Deena Isom, Lesley Watson, and Sherod Thaxton

2011 "Does victimization reduce self-control? A longitudinal analysis." Journal of Criminal Justice 39:169–174.

Agnew, Robert, and Helene Raskin White

1992 "An empirical test of general strain theory." Criminology 30:475–499.

Aguilar, Benjamin, L. Alan Sroufe, Byron Egeland, and Elizabeth Carlson

2000 "Distinguishing the early-onset/persistent and adolescent-onset antisocial behavior types: From birth to 16 years." Development and Psychopathology 12:109–132.

Akers, Ronald L.

1985 Deviant Behavior: A Social Learning Approach. Belmont, CA: Wadsworth.

1990 "Rational choice, deterrence, and social learning theory in criminology: The path not taken." Journal of Criminal Law and Criminology 81:653–676.

1992 Drugs, Alcohol, and Society. Belmont, CA: Wadsworth.

1998 Social Learning and Social Structure: A General Theory of Crime and Deviance. Boston: Northeastern University Press.

1999 "Social learning and social structure: Reply to Sampson, Morash, and Krohn." Theoretical Criminology 3:477–493.

Akers, Ronald L., and Gary F. Jensen
2003 Social Learning Theory and the Explanation of Crime, Advances in Criminological Theory, Volume 11. New Brunswick, NJ: Transaction.

Akers, Ronald L., Marvin D. Krohn, Lonn Lanza-Kaduce, and Marcia Radosevich
1979 "Social learning and deviant behavior: A specific test of a general theory." American Sociological Review 44:635–655.

Akers, Ronald L., James Massey, William Clarke, and Ronald M. Lauer
1983 "Are self-reports of adolescent deviance valid? Biochemical measures, randomized response, and the bogus pipeline in smoking behavior." Social Forces 62:234–251.

Akers, Ronald L., Christine S. Sellers, and Wesley G. Jennings
2016 Criminological Theories, 7th edition. New York: Oxford University Press.

Åkerström, Malin
1985 Crooks and Squares: Lifestyles of Thieves and Addicts in Comparison to Conventional People. New Brunswick, NJ: Transaction.

Alexander, Karl L.
1997 "Public schools and the public good." Social Forces 76:1–30.

Allan, Emile Andersen, and Darrell J. Steffensmeier
1989 "Youth, underemployment, and property crime: Differential effects of job availability and job quality on juvenile and young adult arrest rates." American Sociological Review 54:107–123.

Allwood, Maureen A., and Debora J. Bell
2008 "A preliminary examination of emotional and cognitive mediators in the relations between violence exposure and violent behaviors in youth." Journal of Community Psychology 36:989–1007.

Alpert, Geoffrey P., and Alex Piquero
1998 Community Policing. Prospect Heights, IL: Waveland Press.

Altschuler, David M.
1998 "Intermediate sanctions and community treatment for serious and violent juvenile offenders." Pp. 367–388 in Rolf Loeber and David P. Farrington, eds., Serious and Violent Juvenile Offenders. Thousand Oaks, CA: Sage.

Altschuler, David M., Troy L. Armstrong, and Doris Layton MacKenzie
1999 Reintegration, Supervised Release, and Intensive Aftercare. Washington, DC: Office of Juvenile Justice and Delinquency Prevention.

Altschuler, David M., and Paul J. Brounstein
1991 "Patterns of drug use, drug trafficking, and other delinquency among inner-city adolescent males in Washington, DC." Criminology 29:589–622.

Alvarez, Lizette
2013 "Charges dropped in cyberbullying death, but sheriff isn't backing down." New York Times, November 21. Available at: http://www.nytimes.com/2013/11/22/us/charges-dropped-against-florida-girls-accused-in-cyberbullying-death.html

Alyahri, Abdullah, and Robert Goodman
2008 "Harsh corporal punishment of Yemeni children: Occurrence, type and associations." Child Abuse and Neglect 32:766–773.

Ambert, Anne-Marie
1997 Parents, Children, and Adolescents. New York: Haworth.

Anderson, Amy L., and Lorine A. Hughes
2009 "Exposure to situations conducive to delinquent behavior: The effects of time use, income, and transportation." Journal of Research in Crime and Delinquency 46:5–34.

Anderson, Craig A.
2004 "An update of the effects of playing violent video games." Journal of Adolescence 27:113–122.

Anderson, Craig A., Leonard Berkowitz, Edward Donnerstein, L. Rowell Huesmann, James D. Johnson, Daniel Linz, Neil M. Malamuth, and Ellen Wortella
2003 "The influence of media violence on youth." Psychological Science in the Public Interest 4:81–110.

Anderson, Craig A., and Brad J. Bushman
2001a "Media violence and the American public: Scientific facts versus media misinformation." American Psychologist 56:477–489.
2001b "Effects of violent video games on aggressive behavior, aggressive cognition, aggressive affect, physiological arousal, and prosocial behavior: A meta-analytic review of the scientific literature." Psychological Science 12:353–359.
2002 "The effects of media violence on society." Science 295:2377–2378.

Anderson, Craig A., and Douglas A. Gentile
2014 "Violent video game effects on aggressive thoughts, feelings, physiology, and behavior." Pp. in Douglas Gentile, ed., Media Violence and Children. Santa Barbara, CA: Praeger.

Anderson, Craig A., Nicholas L. Carnagey, and Janie Eubanks
2003 "Exposure to violent media: The effect of songs with violent lyrics on aggressive thoughts and feelings." Journal of Personality and Social Psychology 84:960–971.

Anderson, Craig A., Douglas A. Gentile, and Katherine E. Buckley
2007 Violent Video Game Effects on Children and Adolescents. New York: Oxford University Press.

Anderson, Craig A., Akira Sakamoto, Douglas A. Gentile, Nobuko Ihori, Akiko Shibuya, Shintaro Yukawa, Mayumi Naito, and Kumiko Kobayashi
2008 "Longitudinal effects of violent video games on aggression in Japan and the United States." Pediatrics 122:1067–1072.

Anderson, Craig A., Akiko Shibuya, Nobuko Ihori, Edward L. Swing, Brad J. Bushman, Akira Sakamoto, Hannah R. Rothstein, and Muniba Saleem
2010 "Violent video game effects on aggression, empathy, and prosocial behavior in eastern and western countries: A meta-analytic review." Psychological Bulletin 136:151–173.

Anderson, Elijah
1990 Streetwise: Race, Class and Change in an Urban Community. Chicago: University of Chicago Press.
1994 "The code of the streets." Atlantic Monthly 273 (May):81–94.
1997 "Violence and the inner-city street code." Pp. 1–30 in Joan McCord, ed., Violence and Childhood in the Inner City. Cambridge: Cambridge University Press.
1999 Code of the Street. New York: W. W. Norton.

Anderson, Patrick R., and Donald J. Newman
1998 Introduction to Criminal Justice. Boston: McGraw-Hill.

Andrews, Chyrl, and Lynn Marble
2003 Changes to OJJDP's Juvenile Accountability Program. Washington, DC: Office of Juvenile Justice and Delinquency Prevention.

Andrews, D. A., and James Bonta
2006 The Psychology of Criminal Conduct. New Providence, NJ: LexisNexis.

Andrews, D. A., Ivan Zinger, Robert D. Hoge, James Bonta, Paul Gendreau, and

Francis T. Cullen
1990 "Does correctional treatment work? A clinically relevant and psychologically informed meta-analysis." Criminology 28:369–404.

Aos, Steve, Polly Phipps, Robert Barnoski, and Roxanne Lieb
2001 The Comparative Costs and Benefits of Programs to Reduce Crime. Olympia, WA: Washington State Institute for Public Policy.

Apel, Robert, Shawn Bushway, Robert Brame, Amelia M. Haviland, Daniel S. Nagin, and Ray Paternoster
2007 "Unpacking the relationship between adolescent employment and antisocial behavior." Criminology 45:67–98.

Apel, Robert, Shawn D. Bushway, Raymond Paternoster, Robert Brame, and Gary Sweeten
2008 "Using state child labor laws to identify the causal effect of youth employment on deviant behavior and academic achievement." Journal of Quantitative Criminology 24:337–362.

Apel, Robert, and Catherine Kaukinen
2008 "On the relationship between family structure and antisocial behavior: Parental cohabitation and blended households." Criminology 46:35–70.

Applegate, Brandon K., Robin K. Davis, and Francis T. Cullen
2009 "Reconsidering child saving: The extent and correlates of public support for excluding youths from the juvenile court." Crime and Delinquency 55:51–77.

Aradillas, Elaine
2017 "Why did two 6th graders try to kill their classmate?" People Magazine, January 23.

Archer, Dane, and Patricia McDaniel
1995 "Violence and gender: Differences and similarities across societies." Pp. 63–88 in R. Barry Ruback and Neil Alan Weiner, eds., Interpersonal Violent Behaviors. New York: Springer.

Aries, Philippe
1962 Centuries of Childhood. New York: Vintage Books.

Armstrong, Gaylene S., and Nancy Rodriquez
2005 "Effects of individual and contextual characteristics on preadjudication detention of juvenile delinquents." Justice Quarterly 22:521–539.

Armstrong, Todd A., Shawn Keller, Travis W. Franklin, and Scott N. Macmillan
2009 "Low resting heart rate and antisocial behavior: A brief review of evidence and preliminary results from a new test." Criminal Justice and Behavior 36:1125–1140.

Armstrong, Troy L., and David M. Altschuler
1998 "Recent developments in juvenile aftercare: Assessment, findings, and promising programs." Pp. 448–472 in Albert K. Roberts, ed., Juvenile Justice. Chicago: Nelson-Hall.

Arneklev, Bruce J., Harold G. Grasmick, and Robert J. Bursik, Jr.
1999 "Evaluating the dimensionality and invariance of low self-control." Journal of Quantitative Criminology 15:307–331.

Arnett, Jeffrey J.
1997 "Young people's conceptions of the transition to adulthood." Youth and Society 29:3–23.

Arnette, June L., and Marjorie C. Walsleben
1998 Combating Fear and Restoring Safety in Schools. Washington, DC: Office of Juvenile Justice and Delinquency Prevention.

Arthur, Raymond
2005 "Punishing parents for the crimes of their children." Harvard Journal of Criminal Justice 44:233–253.

Aseltine, Robert H., Jr.
1995 "A reconsideration of the effect of parental and peer influences on deviance." Journal of Health and Social Behavior 36:103–121.

Aseltine, Robert H., Jr., Susan Gore, and Jennifer Gordon
2000 "Life stress, anger and anxiety, and delinquency: An empirical test of general strain theory." Journal of Health and Social Behavior 41:256–275.

Assaad, Jean-Marc, and M. Lyn Exum
2002 "Understanding intoxicated violence from a rational choice perspective." Pp. 65–84 in Alex R. Piquero and Stephen G. Tibbetts, eds., Rational Choice and Criminal Behavior. New York: Routledge.

Associated Press
2002 "Santee teen takes blame for school shooting, worries about future." August, 19. Retrieved from: www.nctimes.net/news/2002/20020819/61337.html
2007 "Teen who plotted N.Y. school rampage was teased for living in trailer park, lawyer says." August 22. Retrieved from: http://www.foxnews.com/story/0,2933,294091,00.html
2013 "Florida: Bullying investigated after girl, 12, kills herself." September 12. Retrieved from: http://www.nytimes.com/2013/09/13/us/florida-bullying-investigated-after-girl-12-kills-herself.html
2016 "Slender Man stabbing: Wisconsin girls to be tried as adults, appeals court rules." July 27. Retrieved from: https://www.theguardian.com/us-news/2016/jul/27/slender-man-stabbing-wisconsin-girls-tried-as-adults-appeals-court

Athens, Lonnie
2005 "Violent encounters." Journal of Contemporary Ethnography 34:1–48.

Atkin, Ross
2003 "Public housing at a crossroads." Christian Science Monitor, March 12, 11.

Atlanta Constitution
2001 "No justice in sentencing kids as adults." March 13, A10.
2003 "Hope VI program is worth keeping." July 25, A14.

Auerhahn, Kathleen
1999 "Selective incapacitation and the problem of prediction." Criminology 37:703–734.

Austin, James
1995 "The overrepresentation of minority youths in the California juvenile justice system." Pp. 153–178 in Kimberly Kempf Leonard, Carl E. Pope, and William H. Feyerherm, eds., Minorities in Juvenile Justice. Thousand Oaks, CA: Sage.

Austin, James, Kelly Dedel Johnson, and Maria Gregoriou
2000 Juveniles in Adult Prisons and Jails. Washington, DC: Bureau of Justice Assistance.

Averdijk, Margit, Jean-Louis van Gelder, Manuel Eisner, and Denis Ribeaud
2016 "Violence begets violence . . . but how? A decision-making perspective on the victim-offender overlap." Criminology 54:282–306.

Babbie, Earl
2016 The Practice of Social Research, 14th edition. Belmont, CA: Wadsworth.

Baglivio, Michael T., Kevin T. Wolff, Nathan Epps, and Randy Nelson
2017 "Predicting adverse childhood experiences: The importance of neighborhood context in youth trauma among delinquent youth." Crime & Delinquency 63:166–188.

Baier, Colin J., and Bradley R. E. Wright
2001 "'If you love me, keep my commandments': A meta-analysis of the effect of religion on crime." Journal of Research in Crime and Delinquency 38:3–21.

Baird, Chris, Theresa Healy, Kristen Johnson, Andrea Bogie, Erin Wicke Dankert, and Chris Scharenbroch
2013 A Comparison of Risk Assessment Instruments in Juvenile Justice. Washington, DC: National Council on Crime and Delinquency.

Baker, Laura A., Serena Bezdjian, and Adrian Raine
2006 "Behavioral genetics: The science of antisocial behavior." Law and Contemporary Problems 69:7–46.

Baldwin, John D.
1990 "The role of sensory stimulation in criminal behavior, with special attention to the age peak in crime." Pp. 204–217 in Lee Ellis and Harry Hoffman, eds., Crime in Biological, Social, and Moral Contexts. New York: Praeger.

Baldwin, John D., and Janice I. Baldwin
1981 Behavior Principles in Everyday Life. Englewood Cliffs, NJ: Prentice-Hall.

Balkwell, James W.
1990 "Ethnic inequality and the rate of homicide." Social Forces 69:53–70.

Bandura, Albert
1973 Aggression: A Social Learning Approach. Englewood Cliffs, NJ: Prentice-Hall.
1986 Social Foundations of Thought and Action: A Social Cognitive Theory. Englewood Cliffs, NJ: Prentice-Hall.
1990 "Selective activation and disengagement of moral control." Journal of Social Issues 46:27–46.

Bao, Wan-Ning, Ain Haas, and Yijun Pi
2007 "Life strain, coping, and delinquency in the People's Republic of China: An empirical test of general strain theory from a matching perspective in social support." International Journal of Offender Therapy and Comparative Criminology 51:9–24.

Barber, Nigel
2008 "Evolutionary social science: A new approach to violent crime." Aggression and Violent Behavior 13:237–250.

Barlow, Hugh D.
1995 Crime and Public Policy. Boulder, CO: Westview.

Barlow, Jane, Doug Simkiss, and Sarah StewartBrown
2006 "Interventions to prevent or ameliorate child physical abuse and neglect." Journal of Children's Services 3:6–28.

Barnes, J. C., Kevin M. Beaver, and Brian B. Boutwell
2011 "Examining the genetic underpinnings to Moffitt's developmental taxonomy: A behavioral genetic analysis." Criminology 49:923–954.

Barnes, Grace M., Joseph H. Hoffman, John W. Welte, Michael Farrell, and Barbara A. Dintcheff
2006 "Effects of parental monitoring and peer deviance on substance use and deliquency." Journal of Marriage and the Family 68:1084–1104.

Barnes, J. C., and Robert G. Morris
2012 "Young mothers, delinquent children: Assessing mediating factors among American youth." Youth Violence and Juvenile Justice 10:172–189.

Baron, Stephen W.
2003 "Self-control, social consequences, and criminal behavior." Journal of Research in Crime and Delinquency 40:403–425.

Baron, Stephen W.
2004 "General strain, street youth and crime: A test of Agnew's revised theory." Criminology 42:457–483.
2007 "Street youth, gender, financial strain, and crime." Deviant Behavior 28:273–302.
2013 "When formal sanctions encourage violent offending: How violent peers and violent codes undermine deterrence." Justice Quarterly 30:926–955.

Baron, Stephen W., and Timothy F. Hartnagel
1997 "Attributions, affect, and crime: Street youth's reactions to unemployment." Criminology 35:409–434.
2002 "Street youth and labor market strain." Journal of Criminal Justice 30:519–533.

Bartol, Curt R., and Anne M. Bartol
1986 Criminal Behavior: A Psychosocial Approach. Englewood Cliffs, NJ: PrenticeHall.

Bartollas, Clemens, Stuart J. Miller, and Simon Dinitz
1976 Juvenile Victimization: The Institutional Paradox. New York: Halsted Press.

Barton, William H.
2012 "Detention." Pp. 636–663 in Barry C. Feld and Donna M. Bishop, eds., The Oxford Handbook of Juvenile Crime and Juvenile Justice. Oxford: Oxford University Press.

Bartusch, Dawn R. Jeglum, Donald R. Lynam, Terrie E. Moffitt, and Phil A. Silva
1997 "Is age important? Testing a general versus a developmental theory of antisocial behavior." Criminology 35:13–48.

Bartusch, Dawn R. Jeglum, and Ross L. Matsueda
1996 "Gender, reflected appraisals, and labeling: A cross-group test of an interactionist theory of delinquency." Social Forces 75:145–177.

Battin, Sara R., Karl G. Hill, Robert D. Abbott, Richard F. Catalano, and J. David Hawkins
1998 "The contribution of gang membership to delinquency beyond delinquent friends." Criminology 36:93–115.

Bazelon, Emily
2013 "We've been measuring rape all wrong." Slate Magazine, November 19. Available at: http://www.slate.com/articles/double_x/doublex/2013/11/national_crime_victimization_survey_a_new_report_finds_that_the_justice.html

Bazemore, Gordon
2000 "Community justice and a vision of collective efficacy: The case of restorative conferencing." Pp. 225–297 in Julie Horney, ed., Policies, Processes, and Decisions of the Criminal Justice System; Criminal Justice 2000, Volume 3. Washington, DC: Office of Justice Programs.
2012. "Restoration, shame, and the future of restorative justice practice." Pp. 695–722 106 in Barry C. Feld and Donna M. Bishop, eds., The Oxford Handbook of Juvenile Crime and Juvenile Justice. New York: Oxford University Press.

Bazemore, Gordon, Jeanne B. Stinchcomb, and Leslie A. Leip

2004 "Scared smart or bored straight?" Justice Quarterly 21:269–300.

2001 A Comparison of Four Restorative Conferencing Models. Washington, DC: Office of Juvenile Justice and Delinquency Prevention.

Bazemore, Gordon, and Mark Umbreit

2004 "Balanced and restorative justice." Pp. 467–510 in Albert R. Roberts, ed., Juvenile Justice Sourcebook. New York: Oxford University Press.

Beaver, Kevin M., and Eric J. Connolly

2013 "Genetic and environmental influences on the development of childhood antisocial behavior." Pp. 43–55 in Chris L. Gibson and Marvin D. Krohn, eds., Handbook of Life-Course Criminology. New York: Springer.

Beaver, Kevin M., Chris L. Gibson, Michael G. Turner, Matt DeLisi, Michael G. Vaughn, and Ashleigh Holand

2011 "Stability of delinquent peer associations: A biosocial test of Warr's sticky-friends hypothesis." Crime and Delinquency 57:907–927.

Beaver, Kevin M., John P. Wright, Matt DeLisi, and Michael G. Vaughn

2008 "Genetic influences on the stability of low self-control: Results from a longitudinal sample of twins." Journal of Criminal Justice 36:478–485.

Becker, Howard S.

1963 Outsiders: Studies in the Sociology of Deviance. New York: Free Press.

Beckett, Lois

2016 "Is the 'Ferguson effect' real? Researcher has second thoughts." The Guardian, May 13. Available at: https://www.theguardian.com/us-news/2016/may/13/ferguson-effect-real-researcher-richard-rosenfield-second-thoughts

Beckett, Katherine, and Theodore Sasson

2000 The Politics of Injustice. Thousand Oaks, CA: Pine Forge.

Begle, Angela M., Rochelle F. Hanson, Carla Kmett Danielson, Michael R. McCart, Kenneth J. Ruggiero, Ananda B. Amstadter, Heidi S. Resnick, Benjamin E. Saunders, and Dean G. Kilpatrick

2011 "Longitudinal pathways of victimization, substance use, and delinquency: Findings from the National Survey of Adolescents." Additive Behaviors 36:682–689.

Bell, Carl C., and Esther J. Jenkins

1993 "Community violence and children on Chicago's South Side." Psychiatry 56:46–54.

Bell, James

2005 "A solvable problem: Reducing the disproportionality of youths of color in juvenile detention facilities." Corrections Today 67:80–83.

Bell, Kerryn E.

2009 "Gender and gangs: A quantitative comparison." Crime and Delinquency 55:363–387.

Bellair, Paul E.

1997 "Social interaction and community crime: Examining the importance of neighborhood networks." Criminology 35:677–704.

2000 "Informal surveillance and street crime: A complex relationship." Criminology 38:137–170.

Bellair, Paul E., and Thomas L. McNulty

2005 "Beyond the bell curve: Community disadvantage and the explanation of black–white differences in adolescent violence." Criminology 43:1135–1168.

2009 "Gang membership, drug selling, and violence in neighborhood context." Justice Quarterly 26:644–669.

Bellair, Paul E., Thomas L. McNulty, and Alex R. Piquero

2016 "Verbal ability and persistent offending: A race-specific test of Moffitt's theory." Justice Quarterly 33:455–480.

Bellair, Paul E., and Vincent J. Roscigno

2000 "Local labor-market opportunity and adolescent delinquency." Social Forces 78:1509–1538.

Bellair, Paul E., Vincent J. Roscigno, and Thomas L. McNulty

2003 "Linking local labor market opportunity to violent adolescent delinquency." Journal of Research in Crime and Delinquency 40:6–33.

Belsky, Joy, Deborah Lowe Vandell, Margaret Burchinal, K. Alison Clarke-Stewart, Kathleen McCartney, and Margaret Tresch Owen

2007 "Are there long-term effects of early child care?" Child Development 78:681–701.

Bennett, Sarah, David P. Farrington, and L. Rowell Huesmann

2005 "Explaining gender differences in crime and violence: The importance of social cognitive skills." Aggression and Violent Behavior 10:263–288.

Bennett, Trevor, Katy Holloway, and David Farrington

2008 "The effectiveness of neighborhood watch." Campbell Systematic Reviews 2008:18. Available at: http://campbellcollaboration.org/lib/project/50/

Bennett, Trevor, and Richard Wright

1984 Burglars on Burglary. Aldershot, England: Gower.

Bennett, William J., John J. DiIulio, Jr., and John P. Walters

1996 Body Count: Moral Poverty and How to Win America's War Against Crime and Drugs. New York: Simon and Schuster.

Bensley, Lillian, and Juliet Van Eenwyk

2001 "Video games and real-life aggression: Review of the literature." Journal of Adolescent Health 29:244–257.

Benson, Michael

2002 Crime and the Life Course. Los Angeles: Roxbury.

Berg, Mark T., Eric A. Stewart, Jonathan Intravia, Patricia Y. Warren, and Ronald L. Simons

2016 "Cynical streets: Neighborhood social processes and perceptions of criminal injustice." Criminology 54:520–547.

Berger, Kathleen Stassen

2007 "Update on bullying at school: Science forgotten?" Developmental Review 27:90–126.

Berger, Ronald J.

1989 "Female delinquency in the emancipation era: A review of the literature." Sex Roles 21:375–399.

Bergner, Daniel

2014 "Is stop-and-frisk worth it?" Atlantic Monthly, March 19. Available at: http://www.theatlantic.com/features/archive/2014/03/is-stop-and-frisk-worth-it/358644

Berkowitz, Leonard

1993 Aggression: Its Causes, Consequences, and Control. New York: McGrawHill.

1994 "Guns and youth." Pp. 251–279 in Leonard D. Eron, Jacquelyn H. Gentry, and Peggy Schlegel, eds., Reason to Hope. Washington, DC: American Psychological Association.

Berman, Mitchell E., Richard J. Kavoussi, and Emil F. Coccaro

1997 "Neurotransmitter correlates of human aggression." Pp. 305–313 in David M. Stoff, James Breiling, and Jack D. Maser, eds., Handbook of Antisocial Behavior. New York: Wiley.

Bernard, Thomas J.

1984 "Control criticisms of strain theories: An assessment of theoretical and empirical adequacy." Journal of Research in Crime and Delinquency 21:353–372.

1990 "Angry aggression among the 'truly disadvantaged.'" Criminology 28:73–96.

1999 "Juvenile crime and the transformation of juvenile justice: Is there a juvenile crime wave?" Justice Quarterly 16:337–356.

Bernard, Thomas J., and Megan C. Kurlychek

2010 The Cycle of Juvenile Justice. New York: Oxford University Press.

Bernard, Thomas J., and Jeffrey B. Snipes

1996 "Theoretical integration in criminology." Pp. 301–348 in Michael Tonry, ed., Crime and Justice, Volume 20. Chicago: University of Chicago Press.

Bernard, Thomas J., Jeffrey B. Snipes, Alexander L. Gerould, and George B. Vold
2015 Vold's Theoretical Criminology, 7th edition. New York: Oxford University Press.

Bernasco, Wim, Stijn Ruiter, Gerben J.N. Bruinsma, Lieven J.R. Pauwels, and Frank M. Weerman
2013 "Situational causes of offending: a fixed-effects analysis of space–time budget data." Criminology 51:895–926.

Bernburg, Jön Gunnar, and Marvin D. Krohn
2003 "Labeling, life chances, and adult crime: The direct and indirect effects of official intervention in adolescence on crime in early adulthood." Criminology 41:1287–1318.

Bernburg, Jön Gunnar, Marvin D. Krohn, and Craig J. Rivera
2006 "Official labeling, criminal embeddedness, and subsequent delinquency: A longitudinal test of labeling theory." Journal of Research in Crime and Delinquency 43:67–88.

Bernstein, Nell
2014 Burning Down the House: The End of Juvenile Prison. New York: New Press.

Bersani, Bianca E., John H. Laub, and Paul Nieuwbeerta
2009 "Marriage and desistance from crime in the Netherlands: Do gender and socio-historical context matter?" Journal of Quantitative Criminology 25:3–24.

Beyer, Marty
2003 Best Practices in Juvenile Accountability: Overview. Washington, DC: Office of Juvenile Justice and Delinquency Prevention.

Bichler, Gisela, Alli Malm, and Janet Enriquez
2014 "Magnetic facilities: Identifying the convergence settings of juvenile delinquents." Crime & Delinquency 60:971–998.

Bierie, David M.
2015 "Enhancing the national incident–based reporting system: A policy proposal." International Journal of Offender Therapy and Comparative Criminology 59:1125–1143.

Bilchik, Shay
1998 A Juvenile Justice System for the 21st Century. Washington, DC: Office of Juvenile Justice and Delinquency Prevention.

Bilukha, Oleg, Robert A. Hahn, Alex Crosby, Mindy T. Fullilove, Akiva Liberman, Eve Moscicki, Susan Snyder, Farris Tuma, Phaedra Corso, Amanda Schofield, and Peter A. Briss
2005 "The effectiveness of early childhood home visitation in preventing violence." American Journal of Preventive Medicine 28:11–39.

Binder, Arnold, Gilbert Geis, and Dickson D. Bruce, Jr.
1997 Juvenile Delinquency. Cincinnati: Anderson.

Birkbeck, Christopher, and Gary LaFree
1993 "The situational analysis of crime and deviance." Annual Review of Sociology 19:113–137.

Bishop, Donna
2005 "The role of race and ethnicity in juvenile justice processing." Pp. 23–82 in Darnell F. Hawkins and Kimberly Kemp-Leonard, eds., Our Children, Their Children. Chicago: University of Chicago Press.

Bishop, Donna M.
2006 "Public opinion and juvenile justice policy: Myths and misconceptions." Criminology and Public Policy 4:653–664.

Bishop, Donna M., and Barry C. Feld
2012 "Trends in juvenile justice policy and practice." Pp. 898–926 in Barry C. Feld and Donna M. Bishop, eds., The Oxford Handbook of Juvenile Crime and Juvenile Justice. New York: Oxford University Press.

Bishop, Donna M., and Charles Frazier
2000 "Consequences of transfer." Pp. 227–276 in Jeffrey Fagan and Franklin E. Zimring, eds., The Changing Borders of Juvenile Justice. Chicago: University of Chicago Press.

Bishop, Donna M., Charles E. Frazier, Lonn Lanza-Kaduce, and Lawrence Winner
1996 "The transfer of juveniles to criminal court: Does it make a difference?" Crime and Delinquency 42:171–191.

Bishop, Donna M., and Michael J. Leiber
2012 "Racial and ethnic differences in delinquency and justice system responses." Pp. 445–484 in Barry C. Feld and Donna M. Bishop, eds., The Oxford Handbook of Juvenile Crime and Juvenile Justice. New York: Oxford University Press.

Bishop, Donna M., Michael Leiber, and Joseph Johnson
2010 "Contexts of decision making in the juvenile justice system: An organizational approach to understanding minority overrepresentation." Youth Violence and Juvenile Justice 8:213–233.

Bjerk, David
2007 "Measuring the relationship between youth criminal participation and household economic resources." Journal of Quantitative Criminology 23:23–39.

Bjerregaard, Beth
2010 "Gang membership and drug involvement: Untangling the complex relationship." Crime and Delinquency 56:3–34.

Bjerregaard, Beth, and Alan J. Lizotte
1995 "Gun ownership and gang membership." Journal of Criminal Law and Criminology 86:37–58.

Bjerregaard, Beth, and Carolyn Smith
1993 "Gender differences in gang participation, delinquency, and substance use." Journal of Quantitative Criminology 4:329–355.

Black, Michele C., Kathleen C. Basile, Matthew J. Breiding, Sharon G. Smith, Mikel L. Walters, Melissa T. Merrick, Jieru Chen, and Mark R. Stevens
2011 The National Intimate Partner and Sexual Violence Survey: 2010 Summary Report. Atlanta, GA: Centers for Disease Control and Prevention.

Blackburn, Ronald
1993 The Psychology of Criminal Conduct. Chichester, England: John Wiley and Sons.

Blazak, Randy
1999 "Hate in the suburbs: The rise of the skinhead counterculture." Pp. 49–56 in Lisa J. McIntyre, ed., The Practical Skeptic: Readings in Sociology. Mountain View, CA: Mayfield.

Blomberg, Thomas G., William D. Bales, and Alex R. Piquero
2012 "Is educational achievement a turning point for incarcerated delinquents across race and sex?" Journal of Youth and Adolescence 41:202–216.

Bloom, Richard W.
2002 "On media violence: Whose facts? Whose misinformation?" American Psychologist 57:447–448.

Blueprints for Violence Prevention http://www.colorado.edu/cspv/blueprints/

Blumstein, Alfred
1995 "Youth violence, guns, and the illicit-drug industry." Journal of Criminal Law and Criminology 86:10–36.
1998 "U.S. criminal justice conundrum: Rising prison populations and stable crime rates." Crime and Delinquency 44:127–135.
2002 "Why is crime falling—or is it?" Pp. 1–34 in National Institute of Justice, ed., Perspectives on Crime and Justice: 2000–2001 Lecture Series. Washington, DC: National Institute of Justice.

Blumstein, Alfred, and Richard Rosenfeld
1998 "Exploring recent trends in U.S. homicide rates." Journal of Criminal Law and Criminology 88:1175–1216.

Blumstein, Alfred, and Joel Wallman
2006 The Crime Drop in America. Cambridge: Cambridge University Press.

Bohm, Robert M.
2003 "Death penalty." Pp. 109–114 in Marilyn D. McShane and Frank P. Williams III, eds., Encyclopedia of Juvenile Justice. Thousand Oaks, CA: Sage.

Bonta, James, Rebecca Jesseman, Tanya Rugge, and Robert Cormier
2006 "Restorative justice and recidivism." Pp. 108–120 in D. Sullivan and L. Tifft, eds., Handbook of Restorative Justice. New York: Routledge.

Bortner, M. A., Marjorie S. Zatz, and Darnell F. Hawkins
2000 "Race and transfer: Empirical research and social context." Pp. 277–320 in Jeffrey Fagan and Franklin E. Zimring, eds., The Changing Borders of Juvenile Justice. Chicago: University of Chicago Press.

Borum, Randy, Dewey G. Cornell, William Modzeleski, and Shane R. Jimerson
2010 "What can be done about school shootings? A review of the evidence." Educational Researcher 39:27–37.

Bosick, Stacey J.
2015 "Crime and the transition to adulthood: A person-centered approach." Crime & Delinquency 61:950–972.

Botchkovar, Ekaterina, Ineke Haen Marshall, Michael Rocque, and Chad Posick
2015 "The importance of parenting in the development of self-control in boys and girls: Results from a multinational study of youth." Journal of Criminal Justice 43:133–141.

Bottcher, Jean
2001 "Social practices of gender: How gender relates to delinquency in the everyday lives of high-risk youth." Criminology 39:893–932.

Bottcher, Jean, and Michael E. Ezell
2005 "Examining the effectiveness of boot camps." Journal of Research in Crime and Delinquency 42:309–332.

Bottoms, Anthony E., and Paul Wiles
2002 "Environmental criminology." Pp. 620–656 in Mike Maguire, Rod Morgan, and Robert Reiner, eds., The Oxford Handbook of Criminology, 3rd edition. Oxford: Oxford University Press.

Bouffard, Leana Allen, and Nicole Leeper Piquero
2010 "Defiance theory and life course explanations of persistent offending." Crime and Delinquency 56:227–252.

Bourgois, Philippe
2003 In Search of Respect. New York: Cambridge University Press.

Bowker, Lee H., and Malcolm W. Klein
1983 "The etiology of female juvenile delinquency and gang membership: A test of psychological and social structural explanations." Adolescence 18:739–751.

Boyum, David, and Mark A. R. Kleiman
2002 "Substance abuse policy from a crime-control perspective." Pp. 331–382 in James Q. Wilson and Joan Petersilia, eds., Crime. Oakland, CA: ICS Press.

Braga, Anthony
2003 "Serious youth gun offenders and the epidemic of youth violence in Boston." Journal of Quantitative Criminology 19:33–54.

Braga, Anthony A., and Brenda J. Bond
2008 "Policing crime and disorder hot spots: A randomized controlled trial." Criminology 46:577–607.

Braga, Anthony A., David M. Kennedy, and George E. Tita
2002 "New approaches to the strategic prevention of gang and group-involved violence." Pp. 271–286 in C. Ronald Huff, ed., Gangs in America III. Thousand Oaks, CA: Sage.

Braga, Anthony A., David M. Kennedy, Elin J. Waring, and Anne Morrison Piehl
2001 "Problem-oriented policing, deterrence, and youth violence: An evaluation of Boston's Operation Ceasefire." Journal of Research in Crime and Delinquency 38:195–225.

Braga, Anthony, Andrew Papachristos, and David Hureau
2014 "The effects of hot spots policing on crime: An updated systematic review and meta-analysis." Justice Quarterly 31:633–663.

Braga, Anthony A., Glenn L. Pierce, Jack McDevitt, Brenda J. Bond, and Shea Cronin
2008 "The strategic prevention of gun violence among gang-involved offenders." Justice Quarterly 25:132–162.

Braga, Anthony, and David Weisburd
2012 "The Effects of 'Pulling Levers' Focused Deterrence Strategies on Crime." A Campbell Collaboration Systematic Review. Available at: http://www.campbellcollaboration.org/lib/project/96

Braga, Anthony A., David L. Weisburd, Elin J. Waring, Lorraine Green Mazerolle, William Spelman, and Francis Gajewski
1999 "Problem-oriented policing in violent crime places: A randomized controlled experiment." Criminology 37:541–580.

Braithwaite, John
1981 "The myth of social class and criminality reconsidered." American Sociological Review 46:36–57.
1989 Crime, Shame and Reintegration. Cambridge: Cambridge University Press.
2002 Restorative Justice and Responsive Regulation. Oxford: Oxford University Press.
2005 "Between proportionality and impunity." Criminology 43:283–306.

Braithwaite, John, Eliza Ahmed, and Valerie Braithwaite
2006 "Shame, restorative justice, and crime." Pp. 397–418 in Francis T. Cullen, John Paul Wright, and Kristie R. Blevins, eds., Taking Stock: The Status of Criminological Theory. New Brunswick, NJ: Transaction.

Brame, Robert, Shawn Bushway, and Raymond Paternoster
1999 "On the use of panel research designs and random effects models to investigate static and dynamic theories of criminal offending." Criminology 37:599–642.

Brame, Robert, and Alex R. Piquero
2003 "Selective attribution and the age–crime relationship." Journal of Quantitative Criminology 19:107–127.

Brandl, Steven G., and David E. Barlow
1996 Classics in Policing. Cincinnati, OH: Anderson.

Brank, Eve M., Stephanie A. Hays, and Victoria Weisz
2006 "All parents are to blame (except this one)." Journal of Applied Social Psychology 36:2670–2684.

Brantingham, Paul, and Patricia Brantingham
1984 Patterns in Crime. New York: Macmillan.

Brauer, Jonathan R.
2009 "Testing social learning theory using reinforcement's residue: A multilevel analysis of self-reported theft and marijuana use in the national youth survey." Criminology 47:929–970.

Brennan, Patricia A., Sarnoff A. Mednick, and Jan Volavka
1995 "Biomedical factors in crime." Pp. 65–90 in James Q. Wilson and Joan Petersilia, eds., Crime. San Francisco: ICS Press.

Brewer, Devon D., J. David Hawkins, Richard F. Catalano, and Holly J. Neckerman
1995 "Preventing serious, violent, and chronic juvenile offending: A review of evaluations of selected strategies in childhood, adolescence, and the community." Pp. 61–141 in James C. Howell, Barry Krisberg, J. David Hawkins, and John J. Wilson, eds., A Sourcebook: Serious, Violent, and Chronic Juvenile Offenders. Thousand Oaks, CA: Sage.

Brezina, Timothy
1998 "Adolescent maltreatment and delinquency: The question of intervening processes." Journal of Research in Crime and Delinquency 35:71–99.
2000a "Delinquent problem-solving: An interpretative framework for criminology theory and research." Journal of Research in Crime and Delinquency 37:3–30.
2000b "Are deviants different than the rest of us? Using student accounts of academic cheating to explore a popular myth." Teaching Sociology 28: 71–78.
2008 "Recognition denial, need for autonomy, and youth violence." New Directions for Youth Development 119:111–128.

2009 "Accounting for variation in the perceived effects of adolescent substance use: Steps towards a variable reinforcement model." Journal of Drug Issues 39:443–475.

2017 "General strain theory." In Henry N. Pontell and Gerben Bruinsma, eds., The Oxford Research Encyclopedia of Criminology and Criminal Justice. New York: Oxford University Press.

Brezina, Timothy, Robert Agnew, Francis T. Cullen, and John Paul Wright
2004 "The code of the street." Youth Violence and Juvenile Justice 2:303–328.

Brezina, Timothy, and Amy A. Aragones
2004 "Devils in disguise: The contribution of positive labeling to 'sneaky thrills' delinquency." Deviant Behavior 25:513–535.

Brezina, Timothy, and Alex R. Piquero
2003 "Exploring the relationship between social and non-social reinforcement in the context of social learning theory." Pp. 265–288 in Ronald L. Akers and Gary F. Jensen, eds., Social Learning Theory and the Explanation of Crime, Advances in Criminological Theory, Volume 11. New Brunswick, NJ: Transaction.

2007 "Moral beliefs, isolation from peers, and abstention from delinquency." Deviant Behavior 28:433–465.

Brezina, Timothy, Alex R. Piquero, and Paul Mazerolle
2001 "Student anger and aggressive behavior in school: An initial test of Agnew's macro-level strain theory." Journal of Research in Crime and Delinquency 38:362–386.

Brezina, Timothy, Erdal Tekin, and Volkan Topalli
2009 "Might not be a tomorrow: A multi-methods approach to anticipated early death and youth crime." Criminology 47:1091–1129.

Brezina, Timothy, and Volkan Topalli
2009 "Criminal self-efficacy: Exploring the correlates and consequences of a 'successful criminal' identity." Paper presented at the 2009 meetings of the American Society of Criminology, Philadelphia.

Brezina, Timothy, and James D. Wright
2000 "Going armed in the school zone." Forum for Applied Research and Public Policy 15:82–87.

2001 "Free will and deviance." Pp. 102–104 in Clifton Bryant, ed., Encyclopedia of Criminology and Deviant Behavior, Volume 1. Philadelphia, PA: Brunner Routledge.

Briar, Scott, and Irving Piliavin
1965 "Delinquency, situational inducements, and commitment to conformity." Social Problems 13:35–45.

Bridges, George S., Darlene J. Conley, Rodney L. Engen, and Townsand Price-Spratlen
1995 "Racial disparities in the confinement of juveniles: Effects of crime and community structure on punishment." Pp. 128–152 in Kimberly Kempf Leonard, Carl E. Pope, and William H. Feyerherm, eds., Minorities in Juvenile Justice. Thousand Oaks, CA: Sage.

Bridges, George S., and Sara Steen
1998 "Racial disparities in official assessments of juvenile offenders: Attributional stereotypes as mediating mechanisms." American Sociological Review 63:554–570.

Bridges, George S., and James A. Stone
1986 "Effects of criminal punishment on perceived threat of punishment: Toward an understanding of specific deterrence." Journal of Research on Crime and Delinquency 23:207–239.

Britt, Chester L., and Michael R. Gottfredson
2003 Control Theories of Crime and Delinquency. New Brunswick, NJ: Transaction.

Brochu, Serge
2006 "Evidence-based drug policies." Journal of Scandinavian Studies in Criminology and Crime Prevention 7:36–45.

Broidy, Lisa M.
2001 "A test of general strain theory." Criminology 39:9–33.

Broidy, Lisa M., and Robert Agnew
1997 "Gender and crime: A general strain theory perspective." Journal of Research in Crime and Delinquency 34:275–306.

Broidy, Lisa M., Daniel S. Nagin, Richard E. Tremblay, John E. Bates, Bobby Baume, Kenneth A. Dodge, David Fergusson, John L. Horwood, Rolf Loeber, Robert Laird, Donald R. Lynam, Terrie E. Moffitt, Gregory S. Pettit, and Frank Vitaro
2003 "Developmental trajectories of childhood disruptive behaviors and adolescent delinquency." Developmental Psychology 39:222–245.

Brooks-Gunn, Jeanne, and Greg J. Duncan
1997 "The effects of poverty on children." Future of Children 7:55–71.

Brown, Lee P.
1989 "Community policing: A practical guide for police officials." Washington, DC: National Institute of Justice.

Browne, Kevin D., and Catherine Hamilton-Giachritsis
2005 "The influence of violent media on children and adolescents." Lancet 365:702–710.

Brownfield, David
1986 "Social class and violent behavior." Criminology 24:421–438.

Brownfield, David, Kevin M. Thompson, and Ann Marie Sorenson
1997 "Correlates of gang membership: A test of strain, social learning, and social control theories." Journal of Gang Research 4:11–22.

Browning, Katharine, and David Huizinga
1999 Highlights of Findings from the Denver Youth Survey. Washington, DC: Office of Juvenile Justice and Delinquency Prevention.

Brownstein, Henry H.
2000 The Social Reality of Violence and Violent Crime. Boston, MA: Allyn and Bacon.

Brumbaugh, Susan, Jennifer L. Hardison Walters, and Laura A. Winterfield
2009 Stability of Assessment Instruments for Delinquent Girls. Washington, DC: Office of Juvenile Justice and Delinquency Prevention.

Brunson, Rod K.
2007 "Police don't like black people: African-American young men's accumulated police experiences." Criminology and Public Policy 6:71–102.

Bucher, Jacob
2011 "General issue (G.I.) strain: Applying strain theory to military offending." Deviant Behavior, 32:846–875.

Buffington, Kristine, Carly B. Dierkhising, and Shawn C. Marsh
2010 Ten Things Every Juvenile Court Judge Should Know About Trauma and Delinquency. National Council of Juvenile and Family Court Judges. Available at: http://www.ncjfcj.org/sites/default/files/trauma%20bulletin_1.pdf

Bui, Hoan N.
2009 "Parent–child conflicts, school troubles, and differences in delinquency across immigrant generations." Crime and Delinquency 55:412–441.

Building Blocks for Youth
2000 And Justice for Some. Available at http://www.buildingblocksforyouth.org
2007 No Turning Back. Available at http://www.buildingblocksforyouth.org

Burch, Jim, and Candice Kane
1999 Implementing the OJJDP Comprehensive Gang Model. Washington, DC: Office of Juvenile Justice and Delinquency Prevention.

Bureau of Justice Statistics
1992 Drugs, Crime, and the Justice System. Washington, DC: Bureau of Justice Statistics.

Burgess, Robert L., and Ronald L. Akers
1966 "A differential association reinforcement theory of criminal behavior." Social Problems 14:128–147.

Burkett, Steven R., and Bruce O. Warren
1987 "Religiosity, peer associations, and adolescent marijuana use: A panel study of underlying causal structures." Criminology 25:109–131.

Burns, Barbara J., James C. Howell, Janet K. Wiig, Leena K. Augimeri, Brendan C. Welsh, Rolf Loeber, and David Petchuck
2003 Treatment, Services, and Intervention Programs for Child Delinquents. Washington, DC: Office of Juvenile Justice and Delinquency Prevention.

Burruss, George W., and Matthew J. Giblin
2014 "Modeling isomorphism on policing innovation: The role of institutional pressures in adopting community-oriented policing." Crime and Delinquency 60:331–355.

Bursik, Robert J., Jr.
1988 "Social disorganization and theories of crime and delinquency: Problems and prospects." Criminology 26:519–551.

Bursik, Robert J., Jr., and Harold G. Grasmick
1993 Neighborhoods and Crime. New York: Lexington.
1995 "Neighborhoodbased networks and the control of crime and delinquency." Pp. 107–130 in Hugh Barlow, ed., Crime and Public Policy. Boulder, CO: Westview.
1996 "The use of contextual analysis in models of criminal behavior." Pp. 236–267 in J. David Hawkins, ed., Delinquency and Crime. Cambridge: Cambridge University Press.

Burt, Callie Harbin, and Ronald L. Simons
2014 "Pulling back the curtain on heritability studies: biosocial criminology in the postgenomic era." Criminology 52:223–262.

Burt, Callie Harbin, Ronald L. Simons, and Leslie G. Simons
2006 "A longitudinal test of the effects of parenting and the stability of self-control." Criminology 44:353–396.

Burt, Callie Harbin, Ronald L. Simons, Leslie G. Simons, and Frederick X. Gibbons
2012 "Racial discrimination, ethnic-racial socialization, and crime: A micro-sociological model of risk and resilience." American Sociological Review 77:648–677.

Burt, Callie, H., Gary Sweeten, and Ronald L. Simons
2014 "Self-control through emerging adulthood: Instability, multidimensionality, and criminological significance." Criminology 52:450–487.

Burton, Velmer S., Jr., and Francis T. Cullen
1992 "The empirical status of strain theory." Journal of Crime and Justice 15:1–30.

Burton, Velmer S., Jr., Francis T. Cullen, T. David Evans, Leanne Fiftal Alarid, and R. Gregory Dunaway
1998 "Gender, self-control, and crime." Journal of Research in Crime and Delinquency 35:123–147.

Burton, Velmer S., Jr., Francis T. Cullen, T. David Evans, R. Gregory Dunaway, Sesha R. Kethineni, and Gary L. Payne
1995 "The impact of parental controls on delinquency." Journal of Criminal Justice 23:111–126.

Burton, Velmer S., Jr., and R. Gregory Dunaway
1994 "Strain, relative deprivation, and middle-class delinquency." Pp. 79–95 in Greg Barak, ed., Varieties of Criminology: Readings from a Dynamic Discipline. New York: Praeger.

Bushman, Brad J., Hannah R. Rothstein, and Craig A. Anderson
2010 "Much ado about something: Violent video game effects and a school of red herring: Reply to Ferguson and Kilburn (2010)." Psychological Bulletin 136:182–187.

Bushway, Shawn D., and Peter Reuter
2002 "Labor markets and crime risk factors." Pp. 198–240 in Lawrence W. Sherman, David P. Farrington, Brandon C. Welsh, and Doris Layton MacKenzie, eds., Evidence-Based Crime Prevention. London: Routledge.

Bushway, Shawn D., Terence P. Thornberry, and Marvin D. Krohn
2003 "Desistance as a developmental process: A comparison of static and dynamic approaches." Journal of Quantitative Criminology 19:129–153.

Button, Deeanna M., and Roberta Gealt
2010 "High risk behaviors among victims of sibling violence." Journal of Family Violence 25:131–140.

Button, Tanya M. M., Robin P. Corley, Soo Hyun Rhee, John K. Hewitt, Susan E. Young, and Michael C. Stallings
2007 "Delinquent peer affiliation and conduct problems: A twin study." Journal of Abnormal Psychology 116:554–564.

Butts, Jeffrey A., and Janeen Buck
2000 Teen Courts: A Focus on Research. Washington, DC: Office of Juvenile Justice and Delinquency Prevention.

Butts, Jeffrey A., and Ojmarrh Mitchell
2000 "Brick by brick: Dismantling the border between juvenile and adult justice." Pp. 167–213 in Charles M. Friel, ed., Criminal Justice 2000, Volume 2, Boundary Changes in Criminal Justice Organizations. Washington, DC: National Institute of Justice.

Butts, Jeffrey A., John K. Roman, and Jennifer Lynn-Whaley
2012 "Varieties of juvenile court." Pp. 606–635 in Barry C. Feld and Donna M. Bishop, eds., The Oxford Handbook of Juvenile Crime and Juvenile Justice. Oxford: Oxford University Press.

Butts, Jeffrey A., and Howard N. Snyder
2006 Too Soon to Tell: Deciphering Recent Trends in Youth Violence. Chicago: Chapin Hall Center for Children, University of Chicago.

Byrne, James M., and Robert J. Sampson
1986 "Key issues in the social ecology of crime." Pp. 1–22 in James M. Byrne and Robert J. Sampson, eds., The Social Ecology of Crime. New York: Springer-Verlag.

Cabaniss, Emily R., James M. Frabutt, Mary H. Kendrick, and Margaret B. Arbuckle
2007 "Reducing disproportionate minority contact in the juvenile justice system." Aggression and Violent Behavior 12:393–401.

Caeti, Tory J., Craig Hemmens, Francis T. Cullen, and Velmer S. Burton, Jr.
2003 "Management of juvenile correctional facilities." Prison Journal 83:383–405.

Caldwell, Michael F., Michael Vitacco, and Gregory J. Van Rybroek
2006 "Are violent delinquents worth treating?" Journal of Research in Crime and Delinquency 43:148–168.

Caliber Associates
2006 National Evaluation of the Title V Community Prevention Grants Program. Washington, DC: Office of Juvenile Justice and Delinquency Prevention.

Campaign for Youth and Justice
2007 The Consequences Aren't Minor. Available at www.campaignforyouthjustice.org

Campbell, Anne
1984 The Girls in the Gang. New York: Basil Blackwell.
1990 "Female participation in gangs." Pp. 163–182 in C. Ronald Huff, ed., Gangs in America. Newbury Park, CA: Sage.

Campbell Crime and Justice Group http://www.campbellcollaboration.org/CCJG/

Canada, Geoffrey
1995 Fist Stick Knife Gun. Boston: Beacon Press.

Canter, Rachelle J.
1982 "Family correlates of male and female delinquency." Criminology 20:149–167.

Cantor, David, and James P. Lynch
2000 "Self-report surveys as measures of crime and criminal victimization." Pp. 85–138 in David Duffee, ed., Criminal Justice 2000, Volume 4, Measurement and Analysis of Crime and Justice. Washington, DC: National Institute of Justice.

Capowich, George P., Paul Mazerolle, and Alex R. Piquero
2001 "General strain theory, situational anger, and social networks: An assessment of conditional influences." Journal of Criminal Justice 29:445–461.

Carey, Gregory, and David Goldman
1997 "The genetics of antisocial behavior." Pp. 243–254 in David M. Stoff, James Breiling, and Jack D. Maser, eds., Handbook of Antisocial Behavior. New York: Wiley.

Carlsson, Christoffer
2013 "Masculinities, persistence, and desistance." Criminology 51:661–693.

Carmichael, Stephanie, and Alex R. Piquero
2004 "Sanctions, perceived anger, and criminal offending." Journal of Quantitative Criminology 20:371–393.

Carr, Patrick J., Laura Napolitano, and Jessica Keating
2007 "We never call the cops and here is why." Criminology 45:445–480.

Carson, Dena C., Christopher J. Sullivan, John K. Cochran, and Kim M. Lersch
2009 "General strain theory and the relationship between early victimization and drug use." Deviant Behavior 30:54–88.

Carson, E. Ann, and Daniela Golinelli
2013 Prisoners in 2012: Trends in Admissions and Releases, 1991–2012. Washington, DC: U.S. Department of Justice.

Carter, David L.
1995 "Community policing and D.A.R.E.: A Practitioner's Perspective." Washington, DC: Bureau of Justice Statistics Bulletin.

Caspi, Avshalom
1998 "Personality development across the life course." Pp. 311–388 in Nancy Eisenberg, ed., Handbook of Child Psychology, Volume 3. New York: Wiley.

Caspi, Avshalom, and Terrie E. Moffitt
1995 "The continuity of maladaptive behavior: From description to understanding in the study of antisocial behavior." Pp. 472–511 in Dante Cicchetti and Donald J. Cohen, eds., Developmental Psychopathology, Volume 2: Risk, Disorder, and Adaptation. New York: Wiley.

Caspi, Avshalom, Terrie E. Moffitt, Phil A. Silva, Magda Stouthamer-Loeber, Robert F. Krueger, and Pamela S. Schmutte
1994 "Are some people crime-prone? Replications of the personality–crime relationship across countries, genders, races, and methods." Criminology 32:163–195.

Caspi, Avshalom, Brent W. Roberts, and Rebecca L. Shiner
2005 "Personality development: Stability and change." Annual Review of Psychology 56:453–484.

Catalano, Richard F., Michael W. Arthur, J. David Hawkins, Lisa Berglund, and Jeffrey J. Olson
1998 "Comprehensive community- and school-based interventions to prevent antisocial behavior." Pp. 248–283 in Rolf Loeber and David P. Farrington, eds., Serious and Violent Juvenile Offenders. Thousand Oaks, CA: Sage.

Catalano, Richard F., and J. David Hawkins
1996 "The social development model: A theory of antisocial behavior." Pp. 149–197 in J. David Hawkins, ed., Delinquency and Crime. Cambridge: Cambridge University Press.

Catalano, Shannan
2013 Intimate Partner Violence: Attributes of Victimization, 1993–2011. Washington, DC: U.S. Department of Justice, Bureau of Justice Statistics.

Cauffman, Elizabeth, Laurence Steinberg, and Alex R. Piquero
2005 "Psychological, neuropsychological and physiological correlates of serious antisocial behavior in adolescence: The role of self-control." Criminology 43:133–176.

Center for American Progress Task Force in Poverty
2007 From Poverty to Prosperity: A National Strategy to Cut Poverty in Half. Available at www.americanprogress.org.

Cerdá, Magdalena., Jeffrey D. Morenoff, Ben B. Hansen, Kimberly J. Tessari Hicks, Luis F. Duque, Alexandra Restrepo, and Ana V. Diez-Roux
2012 "Reducing violence by transforming neighborhoods: A natural experiment in Medellín, Colombia." American Journal of Epidemiology 175:1045–1053.

Cernkovich, Stephen A., and Peggy C. Giordano
1987 "Family relationships and delinquency." Criminology 25:295–321.

1992 "School bonding, race, and delinquency." Criminology 30:261–291.

2001 "Stability and change in antisocial behavior: The transition from adolescence to early adulthood." Criminology 39:371–410.

Cernkovich, Stephen A., Peggy C. Giordano, and Meredith D. Pugh
1985 "Chronic offenders: The missing cases in self-report delinquency research." Journal of Criminal Law and Criminology 76:705–732.

Chaiken, Jan M., Peter W. Greenwood, and Joan Petersilia
1977 "The criminal investigation process: A summary report." Policy Analysis 3:187–217.

Chaiken, Marcia R.
1998 Kids, COPS, and Communities. Washington, DC: National Institute of Justice.

Chambliss, William J.
1973 "The saints and the roughnecks." Society 11(1):24–31.

Chamlin, Mitchell B.
1991 "A longitudinal analysis of the arrest-crime relationship: A further examination of the tipping effect." Justice Quarterly 8:187–199.

Chamlin, Mitchell B., Harold G. Grasmick, Robert J. Bursik, Jr., and John K. Cochran
1992 "Time aggregation and time lag in macro-level deterrence research." Criminology 30:377–395.

Champion, Dean J.
1998 The Juvenile Justice System. Upper Saddle River, NJ: Prentice-Hall.
2005 Research Methods for Criminal Justice and Criminology. Upper Saddle River, NJ: Prentice-Hall.

Chappell, Allison, John M. MacDonald, and Patrick W. Manz
2006 "The organizational determinants of police arrest decisions." Crime and Delinquency 52:287–306.

Chapple, Constance
2005 "Self-control, peer relations, and delinquency." Justice Quarterly 22:89–106.

Chapple, Constance L., Julia A. McQuillan, and Terceira A. Berdahl
2005 "Gender, social bonds, and delinquency: A comparison of boys' and girls' models." Social Science Research 34:357–383.

Chapple, Constance L., Kimberly A. Tyler, and Bianca E. Bersani
2005 "Child neglect and adolescent violence." Violence and Victims 20:39–53.

Chassin, Laurie, Laura McLaughlin Mann, and Kenneth J. Sher
1988 "Self-awareness theory, family history of alcoholism, and adolescent alcohol involvement." Journal of Abnormal Psychology 97:206–217.

Chavez-Garcia, Miroslava
2007 "In retrospect: Anthony M. Platt's the child savers: the invention of delinquency." Reviews in American History 35:464–481.

Chen, Xiaojin
2010 "Desire for autonomy and adolescent delinquency: A latent growth curve analysis." Criminal Justice and Behavior 37:989–1004.

Cherry, Daniel
2013 "Meridian schools, justice department reach deal on discipline policies." Mississippi Public Broadcasting, March 22. Available at: http://mpbonline.org/News/article/991meridian_schools_justice_department_reach_deal_on_discipline_policies#sthash.CSuFZUyc.dpf

Chesney-Lind, Meda
1989 "Girls' crime and woman's place: Toward a feminist model of female delinquency." Crime and Delinquency 35:5–29.
2001 "Girls, violence, and delinquency." Pp. 135–158 in Susan O. White, ed., Handbook of Youth and Justice. New York: Kluwer Academic.

ChesneyLind, Meda, and Randall G. Shelden
2004 Girls, Delinquency, and Juvenile Justice. Belmont, CA: Thomson/Wadsworth.

Chesney-Lind, Meda, Randall G. Shelden, and Karen A. Joe
1996 "Girls, delinquency, and gang membership." Pp. 185–204 in C. Ronald Huff, ed., Gangs in America. Thousand Oaks, CA: Sage.

Chetty, Raj, Nathaniel Hendren, and Lawrence F. Katz
2016 "The effects of exposure to better neighborhoods on children: New evidence from the Moving to Opportunity experiment." American Economic Review 106:855–902.

Cheung, Nicole W. T., and Yuet W. Cheung
2008 "Self-control, social factors, and delinquency: A test of the general theory of crime among adolescents in Hong Kong." Journal of Youth and Adolescence 37:412–430.

Chitwood, Dale E., James E. Rivers, and James A. Inciardi
1996 The American Pipe Dream: Crack Cocaine and the Inner City. Fort Worth. TX: Harcourt Brace.

Chng, Grace S., Chi Meng Chu, Gerald Zeng, Dongdong Li, and Ming Hwa Ting
2016 "A latent class analysis of family characteristics linked to youth offending outcomes." Journal of Research in Crime and Delinquency 53:765–787.

Christensen, P. Niels, and Wendy Wood
2007 "Effects of media violence on viewers' aggression in unconstrained social interaction." Pp. 145–168 in Raymond W. Preiss, Barbara Mae Gayle, Nancy Burrell, Mike Allen, and Jennings Bryant, eds., Mass Media Effects Research. Mahwah, NJ: Lawrence Erlbaum.

Chung, Ick-Joong, Karl G. Hill, J. David Hawkins, Lewayne D. Gilchrist, and Daniel S. Nagin
2002 "Childhood predictors of offense trajectories." Journal of Research in Crime and Delinquency 39:60–90.

Church, Wesley T., Jeremiah W. Jaggers, Sara Tomek, Anneliese C. Bolland, Kathleen A. Bolland, Lisa M. Hooper and John M. Bolland
2015 "Does permissive parenting relate to levels of delinquency? An examination of family management practices in low-income black American families." Journal of Juvenile Justice 4:95–110.

Cintron, Myrna
2006 "Latino delinquency: Defining and counting the problem." Pp. 27–46 in Everette B. Penn, Helen Taylor Greene, and Shaun L. Gabbidon, eds., Race and Juvenile Justice. Durham, NC: Carolina Academic Press.

Clampet-Lundqist, Susan, Kathryn Edin, Jeffrey R. Kling, and Greg J. Duncan
2011 "Moving teenagers out of high-risk neighborhoods: How girls fare better than boys." American Journal of Sociology 116:1154–1189.

Clark, Carol
2007 "Teen brain and mental illness focus of book edited by Emory Expert." Emory Report, June 11.

Clark, John, and Larry Tift
1966 "Polygraph and interview validation of self-reported deviant behavior." American Sociological Review 31:516–523.

Clark, Richard L.
2007 Public and Professionals' Views of the Juvenile Justice System in Georgia. Athens, GA: Carl Vinson Institute of Government.

Clarke, Ronald V.
1992 Situational Crime Prevention. New York: Harrow and Heston.
1995 "Situational crime prevention." Pp. 91–150 in Michael Tonry and David F. Farrington, eds., Crime and Justice: A Review of Research, Volume 19. Chicago: University of Chicago Press.

Clarke, Ronald V., and Derek B. Cornish
1985 "Modeling offenders' decisions: A framework for research and policy." Pp. 147–183 in Michael Tonry and Norval Morris, eds., Crime and Justice: An Annual Review of Research, Volume 6. Chicago: University of Chicago Press.

Clarke, Ronald V., and John E. Eck
2005 Crime Analysis for Problem Solvers. Washington, DC: Office of Community Policing Services, U.S. Department of Justice.

Clear, Todd
1988 "Statistical prediction in correction." Research in Correction 1:1–39.

Clement, Mary
1997 The Juvenile Justice System. Boston: Butterworth–Heinemann.

Close, Ellis
2010 "Rehabilitation Beats Punishment for Juveniles." Newsweek, January 14. Available at: http://www.
newsweek.com/rehabilitation-beats-punishment-juveniles-71201

Cloward, Richard A., and Lloyd E. Ohlin
1960 Delinquency and Opportunity. New York: Free Press.

Cloward, Richard A., and Frances Fox Piven
1979 "Hidden protest: The channeling of female innovation and resistance." Signs 4:651–669.

Cochran, John K., Peter B. Wood, and Bruce J. Arneklev
1994 "Is the religiosity–delinquency relationship spurious? A test of arousal and social control theories."
Journal of Research in Crime and Delinquency 31:92–123.

Cohen, Albert K.
1955 Delinquent Boys. New York: Free Press.

Cohen, Jacqueline, Wilpen Gorr, and Piyusha Singh
2003 "Estimating intervention effects in varying risk settings: Do police raids reduce illegal drug dealing
at nuisance bars?" Criminology 41:257–292.

Cohen, Lawrence E., and Marcus Felson
1979 "Social change and crime rate trends: A routine activity approach." American Sociological Review
44:588–608.

Cohen, Lawrence E., James R. Kluegel, and Kenneth C. Land
1981 "Social inequality and predatory criminal victimization: An exposition and test of a formal theory."
American Sociological Review 46:505–524.

Cohen, Lawrence E., and Bryan J. Vila
1996 "Self-control and social control: An exposition of the Gottfredson–Hirschi/Sampson–Laub debate."
Studies on Crime and Crime Prevention 5:125–150.

Colder, Craig R., and Eric Stice
1998 "A longitudinal study of the interactive effects of impulsivity and anger on adolescent problem
behavior." Journal of Youth and Adolescence 27:255–274.

Coleman, James S., Thomas Hoffer, and Sally Kilgore
1982 High School Achievement. New York: Basic Books.

Colvin, Mark
2000 Crime and Coercion. New York: St. Martin's Press.

Compas, Bruce E.
1987 "Stress and life events during childhood and adolescence." Clinical Psychology Review
7:275–302.

Conger, Rand D.
1976 "Social control and social learning models of delinquent behavior." Criminology 14:17–54.

**Conger, Rand D., Katherine J. Conger, Glen H. Elder, Jr., Frederick O. Lorenz, Ronald L. Simons,
and Les B. Whitbeck**
1992 "A family process model of economic hardship and adjustment of early adolescent boys." Child
Development 63:526–541.

Conger, Rand D., Xiaojia Ge, Glen H. Elder, Jr., Frederick O. Lorenz, and Ronald L. Simons
1994 "Economic stress, coercive family process, and developmental problems of adolescents." Child
Development 65:541–561.

Conger, Rand D., Gerald R. Patterson, and Xiaojia Ge
1995 "It takes two to replicate: A mediational model for the impact of parents' stress on adolescent
adjustment." Child Development 66:80–97.

Conklin, John E.
1992 Criminology. New York: Macmillan.
2003 Why Crime Rates Fell. Boston: Allyn and Bacon.

Cook, Philip J.
1991 "The technology of personal violence." Pp. 1–71 in Michael Tonry, ed., Crime and Justice: A Review of Research, Volume 14. Chicago: University of Chicago Press.

Cook, Philip J., Denise C. Gottfredson, and Chongmin Na
2010 "School crime control and prevention." Crime and Justice 39:313–440.

Cook, Philip J., and John H. Laub
1998 "The unprecedented epidemic in youth violence." Pp. 27–64 in Michael Tonry and Mark H. Moore, eds., Crime and Justice: A Review of Research, Volume 24. Chicago: University of Chicago Press.

Cook, Philip J., and Jens Ludwig
1997 "Guns in America: National Survey on Private Ownership and Use of Firearms." Washington, DC: National Institute of Justice.
1998 "Defensive gun uses: New evidence from a national survey." Journal of Quantitative Criminology 14:111–130.
2000 Gun Violence: The Real Costs. New York: Oxford University Press.
2004 "Does gun prevalence affect teen gun carrying after all?" Criminology 42:27–54.

Cook, Philip J., Mark H. Moore, and Anthony A. Braga
2002 "Gun control." Pp. 291–329 in James Q. Wilson and Joan Petersilia, eds., Crime. Oakland, CA: ICS Press.

Coolbough, Kathleen, and Cynthia J. Monsel
2000 The Comprehensive Strategy: Lessons Learned From the Pilot Sites. Washington, DC: Office of Juvenile Justice and Delinquency Prevention.

Coordinating Council on Juvenile Justice and Delinquency Prevention
1996 Combating Violence and Delinquency: The National Juvenile Justice Action Plan. Washington, DC: U.S. Department of Justice.

Copes, Heith
2003 "Streetlife and the rewards of auto theft." Deviant Behavior 24:309–332.

Cordner, Gary W.
1999 "Elements of community policing." Pp. 137–149 in Larry K. Gaines and Gary W. Cordner, eds., Policing Perspectives. Los Angeles: Roxbury.

Cork, Daniel
1999 "Examining space–time interaction in city-level homicide data: Crack markets and the diffusion of guns among youth." Journal of Quantitative Criminology 15:379–406.

Cornell, Dewey, Peter Sheras, Anne Gregory, and Xitao Fan
2009 "A retrospective study of school safety conditions in high schools using the Virginia threat assessment guidelines versus alternative approaches." School Psychology Quarterly 24:119–129.

Cornish, Derek B., and Ronald V. Clarke
1986 The Reasoning Criminal. New York: Springer-Verlag.

Corsaro, Nicholas, Rod K. Brunson, and Edmund F. McGarrell
2013 "Problem-oriented policing and open-air drug markets: Examining the Rockford pulling levers deterrence strategy." Crime and Delinquency 59:1085–1107.

Corsaro, Nicholas, James Frank, and Murat Ozer
2015 "Perceptions of police practice, cynicism of police performance, and persistent neighborhood violence: An intersecting relationship." Journal of Criminal Justice 43:1–11.

Costello, Barbara J., and Paul R. Vowell
1999 "Testing control theory and differential association: A reanalysis of the Richmond youth project." Criminology 37:815–842.

Cothern, Lynn
2000 Juveniles and the Death Penalty. Washington, DC: Office of Juvenile Justice and Delinquency Prevention.

Cox, Judith A., and James Bell
2001 "Addressing disproportionate representation of youth of color in the juvenile justice system." Journal of the Center for Families, Children and the Courts:31–43.

Cox, Steven M., and John J. Conrad
1996 Juvenile Justice. Madison, WI: Brown and Benchmark.

Coyne, Sarah M., Simon L. Robinson, and David A. Nelson
2010 "Does reality backbite? Physical, verbal, and relational aggression in reality television programs." Journal of Broadcasting & Electronic Media 54:282–298.

Cromwell, Paul, Lee Parker, and Shawna Mobley
1999 "The five-finger discount: An analysis of motivations for shoplifting." Pp. 57–70 in Paul Cromwell, ed., In Their Own Words: Criminals on Crime. Los Angeles: Roxbury.

Cronin, Roberta, Francis Gragg, Dana Schultz, and Karla Eisen
2006 Lessons Learned from Safe Kids/Safe Streets. Washington, DC: Office of Juvenile Justice and Delinquency Prevention.

Crowe, Ann H.
1998 Drug Identification and Testing in the Juvenile Justice System. Washington, DC: Office of Juvenile Justice and Delinquency Prevention.

Crutchfield, Robert D., Ross L. Matsueda, and Kevin Drakulich
2006 "Race, labor markets, and neighborhood violence." Pp. 199–220 in Ruth D. Peterson, Lauren J. Krivo, and John Hagan, eds., The Many Colors of Crime. New York: New York University Press.

Cullen, Francis T.
1994 "Social support as an organizing concept for criminology." Justice Quarterly 11:527–559.
2002 "Rehabilitation and Treatment Programs." Pp. 253–289 in James Q. Wilson and Joan Petersilia, eds., Crime. Oakland, CA: ICS Press.
2006 "It's time to reaffirm rehabilitation." Criminology and Public Policy 4:665–672.
2007 "Make rehabilitation corrections' guiding paradigm." Criminology and Public Policy 6:717–728.
2011 "Beyond adolescence-limited criminology: Choosing our future—The American society of criminology 2010 Sutherland address." Criminology 49:287–330.

Cullen, Francis T., Robert Agnew, and Pamela Wilcox
2014 Criminological Theory: Past to Present. New York: Oxford University Press.

Cullen, Francis T., and Brandon K. Applegate
1997 Offender Rehabilitation. Dartmouth, England: Ashgate.

Cullen, Francis T., and Paul Gendreau
2000 "Assessing correctional rehabilitation: Policy, practice, and prospects." Pp. 109–176 in Julie Horney, ed., Policies, Processes, and Decisions of the Criminal Justice System: Criminal Justice 2000, Volume 3. Washington, DC: National Institute of Justice.

Cullen, Frances T., Martha Todd Larson, and Richard A. Mothers
1985 "Having money and delinquent involvement: The neglect of power in delinquent theory." Criminal Justice and Behavior 12:171–192.

Cullen, Francis T., James D. Unnever, John Paul Wright, and Kevin M. Beaver
2008 "Parenting and self-control." In Erich Goode, ed., Out of Control? Assessing the General Theory of Crime. Palo Alto, CA: Stanford University Press.

Cullen, Francis T., Nicolas Williams, and John Paul Wright
1997 "Work conditions and juvenile delinquency: Is youth employment criminogenic?" Criminal Justice Policy and Research 8:119–143.

Cullen, Francis T., John Paul Wright, and Brandon K. Applegate
1996 "Control in the community: The limits of reform?" Pp. 69–116 in Alan T. Harland, ed., Choosing Correctional Options That Work. Thousand Oaks, CA: Sage.

Cullen, Francis T., John Paul Wright, and Kristie R. Blevins
2006 Taking Stock: The Status of Criminological Theory. New Brunswick, NJ: Transaction.

Cullen, Francis T., John Paul Wright, Shayna Brown, Melissa M. Moon, Michael B. Blankenship, and Brandon K. Applegate
1998 "Public support for early intervention programs: Implications for a progressive policy agenda." Crime and Delinquency 44:187–204.

Cummings, Kenneth
2014 "An Action Plan for Creating Effective Schools." AMLE Magazine, February 2014. Available at: http//:www.amle.org

Currie, Elliott
1998 Crime and Punishment in America. New York: Owl Books.
2015 The Roots of Danger: Violent Crime in Global Perspective. New York: Oxford.

Curry, G. David
1998 "Female gang involvement." Journal of Research in Crime and Delinquency 35:100–118.

Curry, G. David, Richard A. Ball, and Scott H. Decker
1996 Update on Gang Crime and Law Enforcement Record Keeping. Washington, DC: U.S. Department of Justice.

Curry, G. David, and Scott H. Decker
2003 Confronting Gangs. Los Angeles: Roxbury.

Curtis, Lynn A.
1974 Criminal Violence: National Patterns and Behavior. Lexington, MA: Lexington Books.

Daly, Kathleen
1992 "Women's pathways to felony court: Feminist theories of lawbreaking and problems of representation." Review of Law and Women's Studies 2:11–52.
1998 "Gender, crime, and criminology." Pp. 85–108 in Michael Tonry, ed., The Handbook of Crime and Punishment. New York: Oxford University Press.

Daly, Kathleen, and Meda Chesney-Lind
1988 "Feminism and criminology." Justice Quarterly 5:497–538.

D'Amico, Elizabeth J., Maria Orlando Edelen, Jeremy N. V. Miles, and Andrew R. Morral
2008 "The longitudinal association between substance use and delinquency among high-risk youth." Drug and Alcohol Dependence 93:85–92.

Dannefer, Dale, and Russell K. Schutt
1982 "Race and juvenile justice processing in court and police agencies." American Journal of Sociology 87:1113–1132.

David-Ferdon, Corrine and Thomas R. Simon
2014 Preventing Youth Violence: Opportunities for Action. Atlanta, GA: Centers for Disease Control.

Deane, Glenn, David P. Armstrong, and Richard Felson
2005 "An examination of offense specialization using marginal logit models." Criminology 43:955–988.

Decker, Scott H.
2003 Policing Gangs and Youth Violence. Belmont, CA: Wadsworth.

Decker, Scott H., and G. David Curry
2000 "Responding to gangs: Does the dose match the problem?" Pp. 561–575 in Joseph F. Sheley, ed., Criminology: A Contemporary Handbook. Belmont, CA: Wadsworth.

Decker, Scott H., and Janet L. Lauritsen
1996 "Breaking the bonds of membership: Leaving the gang." Pp. 103–136 in C. Ronald Huff, ed., Gangs in America. Thousand Oaks, CA: Sage.

Decker, Scott H., Chris Melde, and David C. Pyrooz
2013 "What do we know about gangs and gang members and where do we go from here?" Justice Quarterly 30:369–402.

Decker, Scott H., Susan Pennell, and Ami Caldwell
1997 "Illegal firearms: Access and use by arrestees." Washington, DC: National Institute of Justice.

Decker, Scott H., and Barrik Van Winkle
1996 Life in the Gang. Cambridge: Cambridge University Press.

De Coster, Stacy, and Lisa Kort-Butler
2006 "How general is general strain theory?" Journal of Research in Crime and Delinquency 43:297–325.

De Coster, Stacey and Maxine S. Thompson
2016 "Race and general strain theory: Microaggressions as mundane extreme environmental stresses." Justice Quarterly. Advanced online publication. DOI: 10.1080/07418825.2016.1236204

De Coster, Stacy, and Rena Cornell Zito
2010 "Gender and general strain theory: The gendering of emotional experiences and expressions." Journal of Contemporary Criminal Justice 26: 224–245.

DeJong, Christina, and Kenneth C. Jackson
1998 "Putting race into context: Race, juvenile justice processing, and urbanization." Justice Quarterly 15:487–504.

De Li, Spencer
1999 "Legal sanctions and youths' status achievement: A longitudinal study." Justice Quarterly 16:377–401.
2004 "The impacts of self-control and social bonds on juvenile deliquency in a national sample of adolescents." Deviant Behavior 25:351–373.

DeLisi, Matt, Tricia K. Neppl, Brenda J. Lohman, Michael G. Vaughn, and Jeffrey J. Shook
2013 "Early starters: Which type of criminal onset matters most for delinquent careers?" Journal of Criminal Justice 41:12–17.

DeMause, Lloyd
1974 The History of Childhood. New York: Harper Books.

Dembo, Richard, James Schmeidler, and Wansley Waters
2004 "Juvenile assessment centers." Pp. 511–536 in Albert R. Roberts, ed., Juvenile Justice Sourcebook. New York: Oxford University Press.

Demuth, Stephen, and Susan L. Brown
2004 "Family structure, family process, and adolescent delinquency." Journal of Research in Crime and Delinquency 41:58–81.

Denno, Deborah W.
1990 Biology and Violence. Cambridge: Cambridge University Press.

DePledge, Derrick
2002 "Plan to stop urban zone grants not based on data." Gannett News Service, May 29, from LexisNexis Database.

Desmond, Scott A., Sarah E. Soper, David J. Purpura, and Elizabeth Smith
2009 "Religiosity, moral beliefs, and delinquency: Does the effect of religiosity on delinquency depend on moral beliefs?" Sociological Spectrum 29:51–71.

De Waal, Frans B. M.
2003 "Morality and the social instincts: Continuity with the other primates." The Tanner Lecture on Human Values, Princeton University. Available at: www.tannerlectures.utah.edu/lectures/documents/volume25/deWaal_2005.pdf

Dill, Karen E., and Jody C. Dill
1998 "Video game violence: A review of the empirical evidence." Aggression and Violent Behavior 3:407–428.

Diniz Filho, P. R., and Giza Lopes
2015 "Youth violence in Brazil: Law, prevalence, and promising initiatives." Pp. 27–39 in Marvin D. Krohn and Jodi Lane, eds., The Handbook of Juvenile Delinquency and Juvenile Justice. Malden, MA: Wiley.

Dodge, Kenneth
1986 Social Competence in Children. Chicago: University of Chicago Press.

Dodge, Kenneth A., and D. Schwartz
1997 "Social information processing mechanisms in aggressive behavior." Pp. 171–180 in David M. Stoff, James Breiling, and Jack D. Maser, eds., Handbook of Antisocial Behavior. New York: Wiley.

Dong, Beidi
2015 "Juvenile delinquency and juvenile justice in China." Pp. 76–84 in Marvin D. Krohn and Jodi Lane, eds., The Handbook of Juvenile Delinquency and Juvenile Justice. Malden, MA: Wiley.

Donnerstein, Edward, and Daniel Linz
1995 "The media." Pp. 237–264 in James Q. Wilson and Joan Petersilia, eds., Crime. San Francisco: ICS Press.

Donnerstein, Edward, Ronald G. Sloby, and Leonard D. Eron
1994 "The mass media and youth aggression." Pp. 219–250 in Leonard D. Eron, Jacquelyn H. Gentry, and Peggy Schlegel, eds., Reason to Hope. Washington, DC: American Psychological Association.

Donziger, Steven R.
1996 The Real War on Crime. New York: HarperCollins.

Dreier, Peter
2007 "The United States in comparative perspective." Contexts 6:38–46.

Dubow, Eric F., and Graham J. Reid
1994 "Risk and resource variables in children's aggressive behavior." Pp. 187–211 in L. Rowell Huesmann, ed., Aggressive Behavior: Current Perspectives. New York: Plenum.

Duggan, Mark
2001 "More guns, more crime." Journal of Political Economy 109:1086–1114.

Duncan, Greg J., and Anita Zuberi
2006 "Mobility lessons from Gautreaux and moving to opportunity." Northwestern Journal of Law and Social Policy 1:110–126.

Dunford, Franklyn W., and Delbert S. Elliott
1984 "Identifying career offenders using self-report data." Journal of Research in Crime and Delinquency 21:57–86.

D'Unger, Amy V., Kenneth C. Land, and Patricia L. McCall
2002 "Sex differences in age patterns of delinquent/criminal careers: Results from Poisson latent class analyses of the Philadelphia cohort study." Journal of Quantitative Criminology 18:349–375.

D'Unger, Amy V., Kenneth C. Land, Patricia L. McCall, and Daniel S. Nagin
1998 "How many latent classes of delinquent/criminal careers? Results from mixed Poisson regression analysis." American Journal of Sociology 103:1593–1630.

Dunworth, Terence, and Gregory Mills
1999 National Evaluation of Weed and Seed. Washington, DC: National Institute of Justice.

Durkin, Keith F., Timothy W. Wolfe, and Gregory A. Clark
2005 "College students and binge drinking: An evaluation of social learning theory." Sociological Spectrum 25:255–272.

Dyer, Jim
2000 "Georgia's youngest inmates often at risk in detention." Atlanta Constitution, August 13, A1, A10.

Earle, Ralph B.
1995 "Helping to prevent child abuse—and future criminal consequences." Washington, DC: National Institute of Justice.

Earleywine, Mitchell
2002 Understanding Marijuana: A New Look at the Scientific Evidence. Oxford: Oxford University Press.

Eck, John E.
2002 "Preventing crime at places." Pp. 241–294 in Lawrence W. Sherman, David P. Farrington, Brandon C. Welsh, and Doris Layton MacKenzie, eds., Evidence-Based Crime Prevention. London: Routledge.

Eck, John E., and Edward R. Maguire
2006 "Have changes in policing reduced violent crime? An assessment of the evidence." Pp. 207–265 in Alfred Blumstein and Joel Wallman, eds., The Crime Drop in America. Cambridge: Cambridge University Press.

Eck, John E., and William Spelman
1987 Problem Solving. Washington, DC: National Institute of Justice.

Egan, Timothy
2002 "Pastoral Poverty: The seeds of decline." New York Times, December 8, A3.

Egley Arlen, Jr., James C. Howell, and Meena Harris
2014 Highlights of the 2012 National Youth Gang Survey. Washington, DC: Office of Juvenile Justice and Delinquency Prevention.

Egley, Arlen, Jr., and Christina E. Ritz
2006 "Highlights of the 2004 National Youth Gang survey." Washington, DC: Office of Juvenile Justice and Delinquency Prevention.

Eisenbraun, Kristin D.
2007 "Violence in schools: Prevalence, prediction, and prevention." Aggression and Violent Behavior 12:459–469.

Eisner, Manuel
2009 "No effects in independent prevention trials: Can we reject the cynical view?" Journal of Experimental Criminology 5:163–183.

Eitle, David J.
2002 "Exploring a source of deviance-producing strain for females: Perceived discrimination and general strain theory." Journal of Criminal Justice 30:429–442.
2006 "Parental gender, single-parent families, and delinquency." Social Science Research 35:727–748.

Eitle, David J., and R. Jay Turner
2002 "Exposure to community violence and young adult crime: The effects of witnessing violence, traumatic victimization, and other stressful life events." Journal of Research in Crime and Delinquency 39:214–237.

Eitle, David, Lisa Stolzenberg, and Stewart J. D'Alessio
2005 "Police organization factors, the racial composition of the police, and the probability of arrest." Justice Quarterly 22:30–57.

Elifson, Kirk W., David M. Petersen, and C. Kirk Hadaway
1983 "Religiosity and delinquency." Criminology 21:505–527.

Elliott, Delbert S.
1982 "Measuring delinquency (a review essay)." Criminology 20:527–538.
1994 "Serious violent offenders: Onset, developmental course, and termination." Criminology 32:1–21.
1995 "Lies, damn lies and arrest statistics." Paper presented at the annual meeting of the American Society of Criminology, Boston.

Elliott, Delbert S., and Suzanne S. Ageton
1980 "Reconciling race and class differences in self-reported and official estimates of delinquency." American Sociological Review 45:95–110.

Elliott, Delbert S., Suzanne Ageton, and Rachel Canter
1979 "An integrated theoretical perspective on delinquent behavior." Journal of Research in Crime and Delinquency 16:3–27.

Elliott, Delbert S., Beatrix A. Hamburg, and Kirk R. Williams
1998 Violence in American Schools. Cambridge: Cambridge University Press.

Elliott, Delbert S., and David Huizinga
1983 "Social class and delinquent behavior in a national youth panel: 1976–1980." Criminology 21:149–177.

Elliott, Delbert S., David Huizinga, and Suzanne S. Ageton
1985 Explaining Delinquency and Drug Use. Beverly Hills, CA: Sage.

Elliott, Delbert S., David Huizinga, and Scott Menard
1989 Multiple Problem Youth. New York: Springer-Verlag.

Elliott, Delbert S., and Scott Menard
1996 "Delinquent friends and delinquent behavior: Temporal and developmental patterns." Pp. 28–67 in J. David Hawkins, ed., Delinquency and Crime: Current Theories. Cambridge: Cambridge University Press.

Elliott, Delbert S., William Julius Wilson, David Huizinga, Robert J. Sampson, Amanda Elliott, and Bruce Rankin
1996 "The effects of neighborhood disadvantage on adolescent development." Journal of Research in Crime and Delinquency 33:389–426.

Ellis, Bruce J., Marco Del Giudice, Thomas J. Dishion, Aurelio José Figueredo, Peter Gray, Vladas Griskevicius, Patricia H. Hawley, W. Jake Jacobs and Jenée James, Anthony A. Volk, and David Sloan Wilson
2012 "The evolutionary basis of risky adolescent behavior: Implications for science, policy, and practice." Developmental Psychology 48:598–623.

Ellis, Lee, and Anthony Walsh
1997 "Genebased evolutionary theories in criminology." Criminology 35:229–276.
1999 "Criminologists' opinions about causes and theories of crime and delinquency." Criminologist 24:1, 4–5.

Ellwanger, Steven J.
2007 "Strain, attribution, and traffic delinquency among young drivers: Measuring and testing general strain theory in the context of driving." Crime and Delinquency 53:523–551.

Emmert, Amanda D., and Alan J. Lizotte
2015 "Weapon carrying and use among juveniles." Pp. 544–561 in Marvin D. Krohn and Jodi Lane, eds., The Handbook of Juvenile Delinquency and Juvenile Justice. Malden, MA: Wiley.

Empey, LaMar T., Mark C. Stafford, and Carter H. Hay
1999 American Delinquency. Belmont, CA: Wadsworth.

Engel, Robin Shepard, and Robert E. Worden
2003 "Police officers' attitudes, behaviors and supervisory influences." Criminology 41:131–166.

Engen, Rodney L., Sara Steen, and George S. Bridges
2002 "Racial disparities in the punishment of youth: A theoretical and empirical assessment of the literature." Social Problems 49:194–220.

England, Ralph W.
1960 "A theory of middle class juvenile delinquency." Journal of Criminal Law, Criminology, and Police Science 50:535–540.

English, Diana J.
1998 "The extent and consequences of child maltreatment." Future of Children 8:39–53.

Enzmann, Dirk, Ineke Haen Marshall, Martin Killias, Josine Junger-Tas, Majone Steketee, and Beata Gruszczynska
2010 "Self-reported youth delinquency in Europe and beyond: First results of the Second International Self-Report Delinquency Study in the context of police and victimization data." European Journal of Criminology 7:159–183.

Erez, Edna, editor
1995 Justice Quarterly 12(4).

Ericson, Nels
2001 Addressing the Problem of Juvenile Bullying. Washington, DC: Office of Juvenile Justice and Delinquency Prevention.

Esbensen, Finn-Aage, and Elizabeth Piper Deschenes
1998 "A multisite examination of youth gang membership: Does gender matter?" Criminology 36:799–828.

Esbensen, Finn-Aage, Elizabeth Piper Deschenes, and L. Thomas Winfree, Jr.
1999 "Differences between gang girls and gang boys." Youth and Society 31:27–53.

Esbensen, Finn-Aage, and David Huizinga
1993 "Gangs, drugs, and delinquency in a survey of urban youth." Criminology 31:565–589.

Esbensen, Finn-Aage, David Huizinga, and Anne W. Weiher
1993 "Gang and non-gang youth: Differences in explanatory factors." Journal of Contemporary Criminal Justice 9:94–116.

Esbensen, Finn-Aage, and D. Wayne Osgood
1997 Research in Brief: National Evaluation of G.R.E.A.T. Washington, DC: Office of Juvenile Justice and Delinquency Prevention.
1999 "Gang resistance education and training (GREAT): Results from the national evaluation." Journal of Research in Crime and Delinquency 36:194–225.

Esbensen, Finn-Aage, Dana Peterson, Terrance J. Taylor, and Adrienne Freng
2009 "Similarities and differences in risk factors for violent offending and gang membership." The Australian and New Zealand Journal of Criminology 42:310–335.

Esbensen, Finn-Aage, Dana Peterson, Terrance J. Taylor, Adrienne Freng, and D. Wayne Osgood
2004 "Gang prevention." Pp. 351–374 in Finn-Aage Esbensen, Stephen G. Tibbetts, and Larry Gaines, eds., American Youth Gangs at the Millennium. Long Grove, IL: Waveland Press.

Esbensen, Finn-Aage, Stephen G. Tibbetts, and Larry Gaines
2004 American Youth Gangs at the Millennium. Long Grove, IL: Waveland Press.

Esbensen, Finn-Aage, L. Thomas Winfree, Jr., Ni He, and Terrance J. Taylor
2001 "Youth gangs and definitional issues: When is a gang a gang, and why does it matter?" Crime and Delinquency 47:105–130.

Evans, Sara Z., Leslie Gordon Simons, and Ronald L. Simons
2012 "The effect of corporal punishment and verbal abuse on delinquency: Mediating mechanisms." Journal of Youth Adolescence 41:1095–1110.

Evans, T. David, Francis T. Cullen, Velmer S. Burton, Jr., and Michael L. Benson
1997 "The social consequences of self-control: Testing the general theory of crime." Criminology 35:475–504.

Evans, T. David, Francis T. Cullen, Velmer S. Burton, Jr., R. Gregory Dunaway, Gary L. Payne, and Sesha R. Kethineni
1996 "Religion, social bonds, and delinquency." Deviant Behavior 17:43–70.

Evans, T. David, Francis T. Cullen, R. Gregory Dunaway, and Velmer S. Burton, Jr.
1995 "Religion and crime reexamined: The impact of religion, secular controls, and social ecology on adult criminality." Criminology 33:195–224.

Fagan, Jeffrey
1989 "The social organization of drug use and drug dealing among urban gangs." Criminology 27:633–669.
1990 "Social processes of delinquency and drug use among urban gangs." Pp. 183–219 in C. Ronald Huff, ed., Gangs in America. Thousand Oaks, CA: Sage.
1995 "Separating the men from the boys: The comparative advantage of juvenile versus criminal court sanctions on recidivism among adolescent felony offenders." Pp. 238–260 in James C. Howell, Barry Krisberg, J. David Hawkins, and John J. Wilson, eds., A Sourcebook: Serious, Violent, and Chronic Juvenile Offenders. Thousand Oaks, CA: Sage.
1996 "Gangs, drugs, and neighborhood change." Pp. 39–74 in C. Ronald Huff, ed., Gangs in America. Thousand Oaks, CA: Sage.
1998 Adolescent Violence: A View from the Street. Washington, DC: National Institute of Justice.

Fagan, Jeffrey, and Franklin E. Zimring
2000 The Changing Borders of Juvenile Justice. Chicago: University of Chicago Press.

Famega, Christine N., James Frank, and Lorraine Mazerolle
2005 "Managing police patrol time." Justice Quarterly 22:540–559.

Farnworth, Margaret, Terence P. Thornberry, Marvin D. Krohn, and Alan J. Lizotte
1994 "Measurement in the study of class and delinquency: Integrating theory and research." Journal of Research in Crime and Delinquency 31:32–61.

Farrington, David P.

1977 "The effects of public labeling." British Journal of Criminology 17:112–125.

1986 "Age and crime." Crime and Justice 7:189–250.

1993a "Have any individual, family or neighborhood influences on offending been demonstrated conclusively?" Pp. 7–37 in David P. Farrington, Robert J. Sampson, and Per-Olof Wikstrom, eds., Integrating Individual and Ecological Aspects of Crime. Stockholm: National Council for Crime Prevention, Sweden.

1993b "Motivations for conduct disorder and delinquency." Development and Psychopathology 5:225–241.

1994 "Human development and criminal careers." Pp. 511–584 in Mike Maguire, Rod Morgan, and Robert Reiner, eds., The Oxford Handbook of Criminology. New York: Oxford University Press.

1995 "The development of offending and antisocial behaviour from childhood: Key findings from the Cambridge study in delinquent development." Journal of Child Psychology and Psychiatry 360:929–964.

1996a "The explanation and prevention of youthful offending." Pp. 68–148 in J. David Hawkins, ed., Delinquency and Crime: Current Theories. Cambridge: Cambridge University Press.

1996b "Criminological psychology: Individual and family factors in the explanation and prevention of offending." Pp. 3–39 in Clive R. Hollin, ed., Working with Offenders. Chichester, England: John Wiley and Sons.

1998 "Individual differences and offending." Pp. 241–268 in Michael Tonry, ed., The Handbook of Crime and Punishment. New York: Oxford.

2002a "Families and crime." Pp. 129–148 in James Q. Wilson and Joan Petersilia, eds., Crime. Oakland, CA: ICS Press.

2002b "Developmental criminology and risk-focused prevention." Pp. 657–701 in Mike Maguire, Rod Morgan, and Robert Reiner, eds., The Oxford Handbook of Criminology, 3rd edition. Oxford: Oxford University Press.

2005 "Introduction to integrated developmental and life-course theories of offending." Pp. 1–14 in David Farrington, ed., Integrated Developmental and Life-Course Theories of Offending. New Brunswick, NJ: Transaction.

2006 "Building developmental and life-course theories of offending." Pp. 335–364 in Francis T. Cullen, John Paul Wright, and Kristie R. Blevins, eds., Taking Stock: The Status of Criminological Theory. New Brunswick, NJ: Transactions.

Farrington, David P., Darrick Jolliffe, Rolf Loeber, and D. Lynn Homish

2007 "How many offenses are really committed per juvenile court offender?" Victims and Offenders 2:227–249.

Farrington, David P., Rolf Loeber, and Magda Stouthamer-Loeber

2003 "How can the relationship between race and violence be explained?" Pp. 213–237 in Darnell F. Hawkins, ed., Violent Crime: Addressing Race and Ethnic Differences. Cambridge: Cambridge University Press.

Farrington, David P., Rolf Loeber, Magda Stouthamer-Loeber, Welmoet B. Van Kammen, and Laura Schmidt

1996 "Self-reported delinquency and a combined delinquency seriousness scale based on boys, mothers, and teachers: Concurrent and predictive validity for African-Americans and Caucasians." Criminology 34:493–517.

Farrington, David P., and Joseph Murray

2014 Labeling Theory: Empirical Tests, Advances in Criminological Theory, Volume 18. New Brunswick, NJ: Transaction.

Farrington, David P., S. G. Soborn, and D. J. West

1978 "The persistence of labeling effects." British Journal of Criminology 18:277–284.

Farrington, David P., Maria M. Ttofi, and Jeremy W. Coid

2009 "Development of adolescence-limited, late-onset, and persistent offenders from age 8 to age 48." Aggressive Behavior 35:150–163.

Farrington, David P., and Brandon C. Welsh

2002 Family-based crime prevention. Pp. 22–55 in Lawrence W. Sherman, David P. Farrington, Brandon C. Welsh, and Doris Layton MacKenzie, eds., Evidence-Based Crime Prevention. New York: Routledge.

2007 Saving Children from a Life of Crime. New York: Oxford University Press.

Fass, Simon M., and Chung-Ron Pi
2002 "Getting tough on juvenile crime: An analysis of costs and benefits." Journal of Research in Crime and Delinquency 39:363–399.

Fearn, Noelle E., Scott H. Decker, and G. David Curry
2001 "Public policy responses to gangs: Evaluating the outcomes." Pp. 330–344 in Jody Miller, Cheryl L. Maxson, and Malcolm W. Klein, eds., The Modern Gang Reader. Los Angeles: Roxbury.

Federal Bureau of Investigation (FBI)
2003 Crime in the United States, 2002. Washington, DC: U.S. Government Printing Office.
2009 Crime in the United States, 2008. Washington, DC: U.S. Government Printing Office.
2012 Crime in the United States, 2011. Available at: http://www.fbi.gov/about-us/cjis/ucr/crime-inthe-u.s/2011/crime-in-the-u.s.-2011
2016 Crime in the United States, 2015. Available at: http://www.fbi.gov/about-us/cjis/ucr/crime-inthe-u.s/2011/crime-in-the-u.s.-2015

Federal Interagency Forum on Child and Family Statistics
2007 America's Children: Key National Indicators of Well-Being 2007. Washington, DC: U.S. Government Printing Office.
2016 America's Children in Brief: Key National Indicators of Well-Being 2016. Available at: http://www.childstats.gov/americaschildren/index.asp

Feld, Barry C.
1995 "The social construction of juvenile justice administration: Racial disparities in an urban juvenile court." Pp. 66–97 in Kimberly Kempf Leonard, Carl E. Pope, and William H. Feyerherm, eds., Minorities in Juvenile Justice. Thousand Oaks, CA: Sage.
1998 "The juvenile court." Pp. 509–541 in Michael Tonry, ed., The Handbook of Crime and Punishment. New York: Oxford University Press.
1999 Bad Kids. New York: Oxford University Press.
2003 "The politics of race and juvenile justice: The 'due process revolution' and the conservative reaction." Justice Quarterly 20:765–800.
2008 "Girls in the juvenile justice system." In Margaret Zahn, ed., Delinquent Girls: Findings from the Girls' Study Group. Philadelphia: Temple University Press.
2009 "Violent girls or relabeled status offenders? An alternative interpretation of the data." Crime and Delinquency 55:241–265.
2012 "Procedural rights in juvenile courts." Pp. 664–691 in Barry C. Feld and Donna M. Bishop, eds., The Oxford Handbook of Juvenile Crime and Juvenile Justice. Oxford: Oxford University Press.

Feld, Barry C., and Donna M. Bishop
2012 "Transfer of juveniles to criminal court." Pp. 801–842 in Barry C. Feld and Donna M. Bishop, eds., The Oxford Handbook of Juvenile Crime and Juvenile Justice. New York: Oxford University Press.

Felson, Marcus
1987 "Routine activities and crime prevention in the developing metropolis." Criminology 25:911–931.
1994 Crime and Everyday Life. Thousand Oaks, CA: Pine Forge.
1998 Crime and Everday Life, 2nd edition. Thousand Oaks, CA: Pine Forge.
2002 Crime and Everyday Life, 3rd edition. Thousand Oaks, CA: Pine Forge.
2006 Crime and Nature. Thousand Oaks, CA: Sage.

Felson, Marcus, and Michael Gottfredson
1984 "Adolescent activities near peers and parents." Journal of Marriage and the Family 46:709–714.

Felson, Richard B.
1993 "Predatory and dispute-related violence: A social interactionist approach." Pp. 103–125 in Ronald V. Clarke and Marcus Felson, eds., Routine Activity and Rational Choice; Advances in Criminological Theory, Volume 5. New Brunswick, NJ: Transaction.
1996 "Big people hit little people: Sex differences in physical power and interpersonal violence." Criminology 34:433–452.
1997 "Routine activities and involvement in violence as actor, witness, or target." Violence and Victims 12:209–221.

Felson, Richard B., and Keri B. Burchfield
2004 "Alcohol and the risk of physical and sexual assault victimization." Criminology 42:837–860.

Felson, Richard B., Glenn Deane, and David P. Armstrong
2008 "Do theories of crime or violence explain race differences in delinquency?" Social Science Research 2008:624–641.

Felson, Richard, Jukka Savolainen, Mikko Aaltonen, and Heta Moustgaard
2008 "Is the association between alcohol use and delinquency causal or spurious?" Criminology 46:785–808.

Felson, Richard B., and Jeremy Staff
2006 "Explaining the academic performance–delinquency relationship." Criminology 44:299–320.

Felson, Richard B., and Henry J. Steadman
1983 "Situations and processes leading to criminal violence." Criminology 21:59–74.

Felson, Richard, Brent Teasdale, and Keri B. Burchfield
2008 "The influence of being under the influence: Alcohol effects on adolescent violence." Journal of Research in Crime and Delinquency 45:119–141.

Ferdinand, Pamela
1997 "San Francisco's 1971 crucifixion murder." PBS. Available at: http://www.pbs.org/wgbh/pages/frontline/shows/little/readings/crucifixion.html

Ferguson, Christopher J., and John Kilburn
2010 "Much ado about nothing: The misestimation and overinterpretation of violent video game effects in eastern and western nations: Comment on Anderson et al. (2010)." Psychological Bulletin 136:174–178.

Ferguson, Christopher J., Claudia San Miguel, and Richard D. Hartley
2009 "A multivariate analysis of youth violence and aggression: The influence of family, peers, depression, and media violence." The Journal of Pediatrics 155:904–908.

Ferguson, Christopher J., Cheryl K. Olson, Lawrence A. Kutner, and Dorothy E. Warner
2014 "Violent video games, catharsis seeking, bullying, and delinquency: A multivariate analysis of effects." Crime & Delinquency 60:764–784.

Fergusson, David M., L. John Horwood, and Daniel S. Nagin
2000 "Offending trajectories in a New Zealand birth cohort." Criminology 38:525–552.

Ferri, Marica, Elias Allara, Alessandra Bo, Antonio Gasparrini, and Fabrizio Faggiano
2013 "Media campaigns for the prevention of illicit drug use in young people." Cochrane Database of Systematic Reviews. DOI: 10.1002/14651858.CD009287.pub2.

Feyerherm, William H.
1995 "The DMC initiative." Pp. 1–15 in Kimberly Kempf Leonard, Carl E. Pope, and William H. Feyerherm, eds., Minorities in Juvenile Justice. Thousand Oaks, CA: Sage.

Filmakers Library
1994 "The Trouble with Evan" (videorecording). New York: Filmakers Library.

Finckenauer, James O., and P. W. Gavin
1999 Scared Straight: The Panacea Phenomenon Revisited. Prospect Heights, IL: Waveland Press.

Finestone, Harold
1976 Victims of Change: Juvenile Delinquents in American Society. Westport, CT: Greenwood.

Finkelhor, David, and Nancy J. Asdigian
1996 "Risk factors for youth victimization: Beyond a lifestyle/routine activities approach." Violence and Victims 11:3–19.

Finkelhor, David, and Patricia Y. Hashima
2001 "The victimization of children and youth: A comprehensive overview." Pp. 49–78 in Susan O. White, ed., Handbook of Youth and Justice. New York: Kluwer Academic.

Finkelhor, David, and Richard Ormond
1999 Reporting Crimes Against Juveniles. Washington, DC: Office of Juvenile Justice and Delinquency Prevention.

Finkelhor, David, Richard Ormrod, Heather Turner, and Sherry L. Hamby
2005 "The victimization of children and youth: A comprehensive national survey." Child Maltreatment 10:5–25.

Finkelhor, David, Heather Turner, Richard Ormrod, Sherry Hamby, and Kristen Kracke
2009 Children's Exposure to Violence: A Comprehensive National Survey. Washington, DC: U.S. Department of Justice, Office of Juvenile Justice and Delinquency Prevention.

Fiorella, Sam
2014 "Cyber-bullying, social media, and parental responsibility." Huffington Post, January 23. Accessed at: http://www.huffingtonpost.com/sam-fiorella/cyber-bullying-social-media-and-parental-responsibility_b_4112802.html

Fischer, Donald G.
1984 "Family size and delinquency." Perceptual and Motor Skills 58:527–534.

Fishbein, Diana
2001 Biobehavioral Perspectives in Criminology. Belmont, CA: Wadsworth.

Fisher, Bonnie S., and Francis T. Cullen
2000 "Measuring the sexual victimization of women: Evolution, current controversies, and future research." Pp. 317–390 in David Duffee, ed., Measurement and Analysis of Crime and Justice, Criminal Justice 2000, Volume 4. Washington, DC: National Institute of Justice.

Fisher, Bonnie S., John J. Sloan, Francis T. Cullen, and Chunmeng Lu
1998 "Crime in the ivory tower: The level and sources of student victimization." Criminology 36:671–710.

Fishman, Laura T.
1995 "The vice queens: An ethnographic study of black female gang behavior." Pp. 83–92 in Malcolm Klein, Cheryl L. Maxson, and Jody Miller, eds., The Modern Gang Reader. Los Angeles: Roxbury.

Flanagan, Timothy, and Dennis Longmire
1996 Americans View Crime and Justice. Thousand Oaks, CA: Sage.

Flores, J. Robert
2003 Targeted Community Action Planning Kit. Washington, DC: Office of Juvenile Justice and Delinquency Prevention.

Florida Times-Union
2010 "Duval inmates, including Riverside rapist, now qualify for resentencing." May 18. Available at: http://jacksonville.com/news/metro/2010–05-18/story/least-6-duval-inmates-qualify-resentencingunder-supreme-court-ruling

Foglia, Wanda D.
1997 "Perceptual deterrence and the mediating effect of internalized norms among inner-city teenagers." Journal of Research in Crime and Delinquency 34:414–442.

Ford, Jason A., and Ryan D. Schroeder
2009 "Academic strain and non-medical use of prescription stimulants among college students." Deviant Behavior 30:26–53.

Foshee, V., and K. E. Bauman
1992 "Parental and peer characteristics as modifiers of the bond-behavior relationship: An elaboration of control theory." Journal of Health and Social Behavior 33:66–76.

Fowler, Deborah
2011 "School discipline feeds the pipeline to prison." Phi Delta Kappan 93:14–19.

Fox, Greer Litton, and Michael L. Benson
2000 Families, Crime and Criminal Justice. New York: JAI.

Fox, James Alan, and Jack Levin
2001 The Will to Kill. Boston, MA: Allyn and Bacon.

Fox, James Alan, and Marianne W. Zawitz
1999 Homicide Trends in the United States. Washington, DC: Bureau of Justice Statistics.

Fratello, Jennifer, Andrés F. Rengifo, and Jennifer Trone
2013 Coming of Age with Stop and Frisk: Experiences, Self-Perceptions, and Public Safety Implications. New York: Vera Institute of Justice.

Frazier, Charles E., and Donna M. Bishop
1995 "Reflections on race effects in juvenile justice." Pp. 16–46 in Kimberly Kempf Leonard, Carl E. Pope, and William H. Feyerherm, eds., Minorities in Juvenile Justice. Thousand Oaks, CA: Sage.

Freedman, Jonathan L.
2002 Media Violence and Its Effects on Aggression. Toronto: University of Toronto Press.

French, Lawrence Armand
2006 "Native American youth and delinquency." Pp. 77–94 in Everette B. Penn, Helen Taylor Greene, and Shaun L. Gabbidon, eds., Race and Juvenile Justice. Durham, NC: Carolina Academic Press.

Freng, Adrienne, and L. Thomas Winfree, Jr.
2004 "Exploring race and ethnic differences in a sample of middle school gang members." Pp. 142–143 in Finn-Aage Esbensen, Stephen G. Tibbetts, and Larry Gaines, eds., American Youth Gangs at the Millennium. Long Grove, IL: Waveland Press.

Fritsch, Eric J., Tory J. Caeti, and Robert W. Taylor
1999 "Gang suppression through saturation patrol, aggressive curfew and truancy enforcement: A quasi-experimental test of the Dallas anti-gang initiative." Crime and Delinquency 45:122–139.

Fulkerson, Jayne A., Keryn E. Pasch, Cheryl L. Perry, and Kelli Komro
2008 "Relationships between alcohol-related informal social control, parental monitoring and adolescent problem behaviors among racially diverse urban youth." Journal of Community Health 33:425–433.

Funk, Stephanie J.
1999 "Risk assessment for juveniles on probation: A focus on gender." Criminal Justice and Behavior 26:44–68.

Furstenberg, Frank F., Jr., J. Brooks-Gunn, and S. P. Morgan
1987 Adolescent Mothers in Later Life. Cambridge: Cambridge University Press.

Future of Children, The
1996 The Juvenile Court, Volume 6, Number 3. Los Altos, CA: Center for the Future of Children.

Gaarder, Emily, Nancy Rodriguez, and Marjorie S. Zatz
2004 "Criers, liars, and manipulators: Probation officers' views of girls." Justice Quarterly 21:547–578.

Gaines, Larry K.
2003 "Police responses to delinquency." Pp. 286–290 in Marilyn D. McShane and Frank Williams III, eds., Encyclopedia of Juvenile Justice. Thousand Oaks, CA: Sage.

Gaines, Larry K., and Gary W. Cordner
1999 Policing Perspectives. Los Angeles: Roxbury.

Ganem, Natasha M.
2010 "The role of negative emotion in general strain theory." Journal of Contemporary Criminal Justice 26:167–185.

Gardner, Margo, and Laurence Steinberg
2005 "Peer influence on risk taking, risk preference, and risky decision making in adolescence and adulthood: An experimental study." Developmental Psychology 41:625–635.

Garland, David
2001 The Culture of Control. Chicago: University of Chicago Press.

Garofalo, James, Leslie Siegel, and John Laub
1987 "School-related victimizations among adolescents: An analysis of national crime survey (NCS) narratives." Journal of Quantitative Criminology 3:321–338.

Gartin, Patrick R.
1995 "Dealing with design failures in randomized field experiments: Analytic issues regarding the evaluation of treatment effects." Journal of Research in Crime and Delinquency 32:425–445.

Gajos, Jamie M., and Kevin M. Beaver
2016 "The effect of omega-3 fatty acids on aggression: A meta-analysis." Neuroscience & Biobehavioral Reviews 69:147–158.

Gatti, Uberto, Richard E. Tremblay, Frank Vitaro, and Pierre McDuff
2005 "Youth gangs, delinquency, and drug use." Journal of Child Psychology and Psychiatry 46:1178–1190.

Gau, Jacinta M., and Rod K. Brunson
2010 "Procedural justice and order maintenance policing: A study of inner-city young men's perceptions of police legitimacy." Justice Quarterly 27:255–279.

Geason, Susan, and Paul R. Wilson
1989 Designing Out Crime. Canberra: Australian Institute of Criminology.

Gennetian, Lisa A., Matthew Sciandra, Lisa Sanbonmatsu, Jens Ludwig, Lawrence F. Katz, Greg J. Duncan, Jeffrey R. Kling, and Ronald C. Kessler
2012 "The long-term effects of moving to opportunity on youth outcomes." Cityscape: A Journal of Policy Development and Research 14:137–168.

Gentile, Douglas
2015 Media Violence and Children. Santa Barbara, CA: Praeger.

Gentry, Cynthia
1995 "Crime control through drug control." Pp. 477–493 in Joseph F. Sheley, ed., Criminology. Belmont, CA: Wadsworth.

Gerber, J., and S. Engelhardt-Greer
1996 "Just and painful: Attitudes toward sentencing criminals." Pp. 62–74 in T. Flanagan and D. Longmire, eds., Americans View Crime and Justice. Thousand Oaks, CA: Sage.

Gershoff, Elizabeth T., and Andrew Grogan-Kaylor
2016 "Spanking and child outcomes: Old controversies and new meta-analyses." Journal of Family Psychology 30:453–469.

Gibson, Chris L., and Marvin D. Krohn, eds.
2013 Handbook of Life-Course Criminology. New York: Springer.

Gies, Steve V.
2003 Aftercare Services. Washington, DC: Office of Juvenile Justice and Delinquency Prevention.

Gifford-Smith, Mary, Kenneth A. Dodge, Thomas J. Dishion, and Joan McCord
2005 "Peer influence in children and adolescents." Journal of Abnormal Child Psychology 33:255–265.

Gilbert, Susan
2003 "Two studies link child care to behavior problems." New York Times, July 16, A12.

Gilfus, Mary E.
1992 "From victims to survivors to offenders: Women's routes of entry and immersion into street crime." Women and Criminal Justice 4:63–89.

Gilligan, Carol, and Jane Attanucci
1988 "Two moral orientations: Gender differences and similarities." Merrill-Palmer Quarterly 34:223–237.

Giordano, Peggy C.
1978 "Girls, guys, and gangs: The changing social context of female delinquency." Journal of Criminal Law and Criminology 69:126–132.

Giordano, Peggy C., Stephen A. Cernkovich, and Donna D. Holland
2003 "Changes in friendship relations over the life course: Implications for desistance from crime." Criminology 41:293–328.

Giordano, Peggy C., Stephen A. Cernkovich, and M. D. Pugh
1986 "Friendships and delinquency." American Journal of Sociology 91:1170–1202.

Giordano, Peggy C., Stephen A. Cernovich, and Jennifer L. Rudolph
2002 "Gender, crime, and desistance: Toward a theory of cognitive transformation." American Journal of Sociology 107:990–1064.

Giordano, Peggy C., Monica A. Longmore, Ryan D. Schroeder, and Patrick M. Seffrin
2008 "A life-course perspective on spirituality and desistance from crime." Criminology 46:99–132.

Giordano, Peggy C., Ryan D. Schroeder, and Stephen A. Cernkovich
2007 "Emotions and crime over life-course: A neo-Meadian perspective on criminal continuity and change." American Journal of Sociology 112:1603–1661.

Glueck, Sheldon, and Eleanor Glueck
1950 Unraveling Juvenile Delinquency. New York: Commonwealth Fund.

Gold, Martin
1966 "Undetected delinquent behavior." Journal of Research in Crime and Delinquency 3:27–46.

Gold, Martin, and Jay R. Williams
1969 "The effect of getting caught: Apprehension of a juvenile offender as a cause of subsequent delinquencies." Prospectus 3:1–12.

Goldsmid, Charles A., and Everett K. Wilson
1980 Passing on Sociology. Washington, DC: American Sociological Association.

Goldstein, Paul J.
1985 "The drugs/violence nexus: A tripartite conceptual framework." Journal of Drug Issues 15:493–506.

Gómez, Anu M.
2011 "Testing the cycle of violence hypothesis: Child abuse and adolescent dating violence as predictors of intimate partner violence in young adulthood." Youth and Society 43:171–192.

Goode, Erich
2008a Drugs in American Society. New York: McGraw-Hill.
2008b "Out of control? Introduction to the general theory of crime." In Erich Goode, ed., Out of Control? Assessing the General Theory of Crime. Palo Alto, CA: Stanford University Press.

Goodkind, Sara, John M. Wallace, Jeffrey J. Shook, Jerald Bachman, and Patrick O'Malley
2009 "Are girls really becoming more delinquent? Testing the gender convergence hypothesis by race and ethnicity, 1976–2005." Children and Youth Services Review 31:885–895.

Gordon, Rachel A., Benjamin B. Lahey, Eriko Kawai, Rolf Loeber, Magda Stouthamer-Loeber, and David Farrington
2004 "Antisocial behavior and gang membership: Selection and socialization." Criminology 42:55–87.

Gorman, D. M., and Helene Raskin White
1995 "You can choose your friends, but do they choose your crime? Implications of differential association theories for crime prevention policy." Pp. 131–155 in Hugh Barlow, ed., Crime and Public Policy. Boulder, CO: Westview.

Gottfredson, Denise C.
2001 Schools and Delinquency. Cambridge: Cambridge University Press.

Gottfredson, Denise C., Amanda Cross, and David A. Soule
2007 "Distinguishing characteristics of effective and ineffective after-school programs." Criminology and Public Policy 6:289–318.

Gottfredson, Denise C., and Gary D. Gottfredson
2002 "Quality of school-based prevention programs: Results from a national survey." Journal of Research in Crime and Delinquency 39:3–35.

Gottfredson, Denise C., and David A. Soule
2005 "The timing of property crime, violent crime, and substance use among juveniles." Journal of Research in Crime and Delinquency 42:110–120.

Gottfredson, Denise C., David B. Wilson, and Stacy Skroban Najaka
2002a "School-based crime prevention." Pp. 56–164 in Lawrence W. Sherman, David P. Farrington, Brandon C. Welsh, and Doris Layton MacKenzie, eds., Evidence-Based Crime Prevention. London: Routledge.
2002b "The Schools." Pp. 149–190 in James Q. Wilson and Joan Petersilia, eds., Crime. Oakland, CA: ICS Press.

Gottfredson, Gary D.
2012 "Schools and delinquency." Pp. 203–225 in Barry C. Feld and Donna M. Bishop, eds., The Oxford Handbook of Juvenile Crime and Juvenile Justice. New York: Oxford University Press.

Gottfredson, Gary D., and Denise C. Gottfredson
1985 Victimization in Schools. New York: Plenum.

Gottfredson, Gary D., Denise C. Gottfredson, Allison Ann Payne, and Nisha C. Gottfredson
2005 "School climate predictors of school disorder." Journal of Research in Crime and Delinquency 42:412–444.

Gottfredson, Michael R.
2006 "The empirical status of control theory in criminology." Pp. 77–100 in Francis T. Cullen, John Paul Wright, and Kristie R. Blevins, eds., Taking Stock: The Status of Criminological Theory. New Brunswick, NJ: Transaction.

Gottfredson, Michael R., and Travis Hirschi
1990 A General Theory of Crime. Stanford, CA: Stanford University Press.

Gottfredson, Stephen D., and Don M. Gottfredson
1994 "Behavioral prediction and the problem of incapacitation." Criminology 32:441–474.

Gould, Elise, and Hilary Wething
2012 "U.S. poverty rates higher, safety net weaker than in peer countries." Economic Policy Institute. Available at: http://s2.epi.org/files/2012/ib339-us-poverty-higher-safety-net-weaker.pdf

Gove, Walter R., and Robert D. Crutchfield
1982 "The family and juvenile delinquency." Sociological Quarterly 23:301–319.

Gove, Walter R., Michael Hughes, and Michael Geerken
1985 "Are uniform crime reports a valid indicator of the index crimes? An affirmative answer with minor qualifications." Criminology 23:451–502.

Gove, Walter R., and Charles Wilmoth.
1990 "Risk, crime, and neurophysiologic highs: A consideration of brain processes that may reinforce delinquent and criminal behavior." Pp. 261–294 in Lee Ellis and Harry Hoffman, eds., Crime in Biological, Social, and Moral Contexts. New York: Praeger.

Grasmick, Harold G., and Robert J. Bursik, Jr.
1990 "Conscience, significant others, and rational choice: Extending the deterrence model." Law and Society Review 24:837–861.

Grasmick, Harold G., Charles R. Tittle, Robert J. Bursik, and Bruce J. Arneklev
1993 "Testing the core empirical implications of Gottfredson and Hirschi's general theory of crime." Journal of Research in Crime and Delinquency 30:5–29.

Grawert, Ames and James Cullen
2016 "Fact sheet: Stop and frisk's effect on crime in New York City." New York: Brennan Center for Justice. Available at: https://www.brennancenter.org/analysis/fact-sheet-stop-and-frisks-effect-crime-new-york-city

Green, Erica L.
2016 "Lost girls: Young women face harsher punishment in Maryland's juvenile justice system." Baltimore Sun, December 16. Available at: http://www.baltimoresun.com/news/maryland/investigations/bal-juvenile-justice-gender-gap-20161216-story.html

Green, Sara J.
2011 "Natalie's story: Life as a child prostitute." Seattle Times, July 24. Available at: http://www.seattletimes.com/seattle-news/natalies-story-life-as-a-child-prostitute

Greenbaum, Stuart
1997 "Kids and guns: From playgrounds to battlegrounds." Juvenile Justice 3:3–10.

Greenberg, David F.
1977 "Delinquency and the age structure of society." Contemporary Crises 1:189–223.
1985 "Age, crime, and social explanation." American Journal of Sociology 91:1–27.

Greenberg, David F., Ronald C. Kessler, and Colin Loftin
1983 "The effect of police employment on crime." Criminology 21:375–394.

Greene, Jack R.
2000 "Community policing in America: Changing the nature, structure, and function of the police." Pp. 299–370 in Julie Horney, ed., Policies, Processes, and Decisions of the Criminal Justice System; Criminal Justice 2000, Volume 3. Washington, DC: National Institute of Justice.

Greenfeld, Lawrence A.
1998 Alcohol and Crime. Washington, DC: Bureau of Justice Statistics.

Greenhouse, Linda
2005 "Supreme Court, 5–4, forbids execution in juvenile crime." New York Times, March 2, A1, A14.

Greenwood, Peter W.
1995 "What works with juvenile offenders: A synthesis of the literature and experience." Federal Probation 58:63–67.
1998 "Investing in prisons or prevention: The state policy makers' dilemma." Crime and Delinquency 44:136–142.
1999 Costs and Benefits of Early Childhood Intervention. Washington, DC: Office of Juvenile Justice and Delinquency Prevention.
2002 "Juvenile crime and juvenile justice." Pp. 75–108 in James Q. Wilson and Joan Petersilia, eds., Crime. Oakland, CA: ICS Press.
2006 Changing Lives: Delinquency Prevention as Crime-Control Policy. Chicago: University of Chicago Press.

Greenwood, Peter W., Karyn E. Model, C. Peter Rydell, and James Chiesa
1996 Diverting Children from a Life of Crime: Measuring Costs and Benefits. Santa Monica, CA: RAND.

Greenwood, Peter W., and Susan Turner
2012 "Probation and other noninstitutional treatment." Pp. 723–747 in Barry C. Feld and Donna M. Bishop, eds., The Oxford Handbook of Juvenile Crime and Juvenile Justice. Oxford: Oxford University Press.

Greitemeyer, Tobias, and Dirk O. Mügge
2014 "Video games do affect social outcomes: A meta-analytic review of the effects of violent and prosocial video game play." Personality and Social Psychology Bulletin 1–12.

Griffin, Patrick, Sean Addie, Benjamin Adams, and Kathy Firestine
2011 Trying Juveniles as Adults: An Analysis of State Transfer Laws and Reporting. Washington, DC: Office of Juvenile Delinquency and Delinquency Prevention.

Griffiths, Mark
1999 "Violent video games and aggression: A review of the literature." Aggression and Violent Behavior 4:203–212.

Grogger, Jeffrey
1997 "Incarceration-related costs of early childbearing." Pp. 231–255 in Rebecca A. Maynard, ed., Kids Having Kids. Washington, DC: Urban Institute Press.
2006 "An economic model of recent trends in violence." Pp. 266–287 in Alfred Blumstein and Joel Wallman, eds., The Crime Drop in America. Cambridge: Cambridge University Press.

Grossman, Jean Baldwin, and Eileen M. Garry
1997 Mentoring: A Proven Delinquency Prevention Strategy. Washington, DC: Office of Juvenile Justice and Delinquency Prevention.

Gruber, Staci A., and Deborah A. Yurgelun-Todd
2005 "Neurobiology and the law: A role in juvenile justice?" Ohio State Journal of Criminal Law 3:321–340.

Guerra, Nancy G.
1997 "Intervening to prevent childhood aggression in the inner city." Pp. 256–312 in Joan McCord, ed., Violence and Childhood in the Inner City. Cambridge: Cambridge University Press.

Guerra, Nancy G., Patrick H. Tolan, and W. Rodney Hammond
1994 "Prevention and treatment of adolescent violence." Pp. 383–403 in Leonard D. Eron, Jacquelyn H. Gentry, and Peggy Schlegel, eds., Reason to Hope. Washington, DC: American Psychological Association.

Guevara, Lori, Denise Herz, and Cassia Spohn
2008 "Race, gender, and legal counsel: Differential outcomes in two juvenile courts." Youth Violence and Juvenile Justice 6:83–104.

Guo, Guang, Michael E. Roettger, and Tianji Cai
2008 "The integration of genetic propensities into social-control models of delinquency and violence among male youths." American Sociological Review 73:543–568.

Hagan, John
1989 Structural Criminology. New Brunswick, NJ: Rutgers University Press.
1991 "Destiny and drift: Subcultural preferences, status attainments, and the risks and rewards of youth." American Sociological Review 56:567–581.
1992 "The poverty of a classless criminology." Criminology 30:1–19.
1994 Crime and Disrepute. Thousand Oaks, CA: Pine Forge Press.

Hagan, John, A. R. Gillis, and David Brownfield
1996 Criminological Controversies. Boulder, CO: Westview.

Hagan, John, and Bill McCarthy
1997a Mean Streets. Cambridge: Cambridge University Press.
1997b "Anomie, social capital, and street criminology." Pp. 124–141 in Nikos Passas and Robert Agnew, eds., The Future of Anomie Theory. Boston: Northeastern University Press.

Hagan, John, and Ruth D. Peterson
1995 "Criminal inequality in America: Patterns and consequences." Pp. 14–36 in John Hagan and Ruth D. Peterson, eds., Crime and Inequality. Stanford, CA: Stanford University Press.

Hagan, John, John H. Simpson, and A. R. Gillis
1979 "The sexual stratification of social control: A gender-based perspective on crime and delinquency." British Journal of Sociology 30:25–38.

Hagedorn, John
1988 People and Folks: Gangs, Crime and the Underclass in a Rustbelt City. Chicago: Lake View Press.

Hahn, Robert A., Oleg Bilukha, Alex Crosby, Mindy T. Fullilove, Akivo Liberman, Eve Moscicki, Susan Snyder, Farris Tuma, and Peter A. Briss
2005 "Firearms laws and the reduction of violence." American Journal of Preventive Medicine 28:40–71.

Halbfinger, David M.
2003 "Care of juvenile offenders in Mississippi is faulted." New York Times, September 1, A11.

Hamilton, Robin, and Kay McKinney
1999 Job Training for Juveniles: Project CRAFT. Washington, DC: Office of Juvenile Justice and Delinquency Prevention.

Harcourt, Bernard E.
2003 Guns, Crime, and Punishment in America. New York: New York University Press.

Harris, Kamala D.
2009 Smart on Crime: A Career Prosecutor's Plan to Make Us Safer. San Francisco, CA: Chronicle Books.

Harris, Anthony R., and James A. W. Shaw
2000 "Looking for patterns: Race, class, and crime." Pp. 128–163 in Joseph F. Sheley, ed., Criminology: A Contemporary Handbook. Belmont, CA: Wadsworth.

Harrison, Paige, James R. Maupin, and G. Larry Mays
2001 "Teen court: An examination of processes and outcomes." Crime and Delinquency 47:243–264.

Hart, Timothy C.
2003 National Crime Victimization Survey, 1995–2000: Violent Victimization of College Students. Washington, DC: Bureau of Justice Statistics.

Hawkins, Darnell F.
2003 Violent Crime: Assessing Race and Ethnic Differences. Cambridge: Cambridge University Press.

Hawkins, Darnell F., John H. Laub, and Janet L. Lauritsen
1998 "Race, ethnicity, and serious and violent juvenile offending." Pp. 30–46 in Rolf Loeber and David P. Farrington, eds., Serious and Violent Juvenile Offenders. Thousand Oaks, CA: Sage.

Hawkins, J. David, Michael W. Arthur, and Richard F. Catalano
1995 "Preventing substance abuse." Pp. 343–347 in Michael Tonry and David P. Farrington, eds., Crime and Justice: A Review of Research, Volume 19. Chicago: University of Chicago Press.

Hawkins, J. David, Richard F. Catalano, and Devon D. Brewer
1995 "Preventing serious, violent, and chronic juvenile offending: Effective strategies from conception to age 6." Pp. 47–60 in James C. Howell, Barry Krisberg, J. David Hawkins, and John J. Wilson, eds., A Sourcebook: Serious, Violent, and Chronic Juvenile Offenders. Thousand Oaks, CA: Sage.

Hawkins, J. David, David P. Farrington, and Richard F. Catalano
1998 "Reducing violence through the schools." Pp. 188–216 in Delbert S. Elliott, Beatrix A. Hamburg, and Kirk R. Williams, eds., Violence in American Schools. Cambridge: Cambridge University Press.

Hawkins, J. David, Todd Herrenkohl, David P. Farrington, Devon Brewer, Richard F. Catalano, and Tracy W. Harachi
1998 "A review of predictors of youth violence." Pp. 106–146 in Rolf Loeber and David P. Farrington, eds., Serious and Violent Juvenile Offenders. Thousand Oaks, CA: Sage.

Hawkins, J. David, and Denise M. Lishner
1987 "Schooling and delinquency." Pp. 179–221 in Elmer H. Johnson, ed., Handbook on Crime and Delinquency Prevention. New York: Greenwood Press.

Hawkins, Stephanie R., Pamela K. Lattimore, Debbie Dawes, and Christy A. Visher
2009 Reentry Experiences of Confined Juvenile Offenders: Characteristics, Service Receipt, and Outcomes of Juvenile Male Participants in the SVORI Multi-site Evaluation. Washington, DC: U.S. Department of Justice.

Hay, Carter
2001a "Parenting, self-control, and delinquency: A test of self-control theory." Criminology 39:707–736.
2001b "An exploratory test of Braithwaite's reintegrative shaming theory." Journal of Research in Crime and Delinquency 38:132–153.
2003 "Family strain, gender, and delinquency." Sociological Perspectives 46:107–136.

Hay, Carter, and Michelle M. Evans
2006 "Violent victimization and involvement in delinquency: Examining predictions from general strain theory." Journal of Criminal Justice 34:261–274.

Hay, Carter, and Walter Forrest
2006 "The development of self-control: Examining self-control theory's stability thesis." Criminology 44:739–774.

Hay, Carter, Edward N. Fortson, Dusten R. Hollist, Irshad Altheimer, and Lonnie M. Schaible
2006 "The impact of community disadvantage on the relationship between the family and juvenile crime." Journal of Research in Crime and Delinquency 43:326–356.
2007 "Compounded risk: The implications for delinquency of coming from a poor family that lives in a poor community." Journal of Youth and Adolescence 36:593–605.

Hay, Carter, Ryan Meldrum, and Karen Mann
2010 "Traditional bullying, cyber bullying, and deviance: A general strain theory approach." Journal of Contemporary Criminal Justice 26: 130–147.

Haynie, Dana L.
2001 "Delinquent peers revisited: Does network structure matter?" American Journal of Sociology 106:1013–1057.
2002 "Friendship networks and delinquency: The relative nature of peer delinquency." Journal of Quantitative Criminology 18:99–134.

Haynie, Dana L., Peggy C. Giordano, Wendy P. Manning, and Monica Longmore
2005 "Adolescent romantic relationships and delinquency involvement." Criminology 43:177–210.

Haynie, Dana L., and Suzanne McHugh
2003 "Sibling deviance: In the shadows of mutual and unique friendship effects." Criminology 41:355–392.

Haynie, Dana L., and D. Wayne Osgood
2005 "Reconsidering peers and delinquency: How do peers matter?" Social Forces 84:1109–1130.

Haynie, Dana L., and Danielle C. Payne
2006 "Race, friendship networks, and violent delinquency." Criminology 44:775–806.

Haynie, Dana L., Eric Silver, and Brent Teasdale
2006 "Neighborhood characteristics, peer networks, and adolescent violence." Journal of Quantitative Criminology 22:147–169.

He, Ai (Phil), Jihong (Solomon) Zhao, and Nicholas P. Lovrich
2005 "Community policing." Crime and Delinquency 51:295–317.

Hechtman, Michael
2014 "Bratton raps Kelly and Bloomberg on stop and frisk." New York Post, March 31. Available at: http://nypost.com/2014/03/31/bratton-raps-kelly-and-bloomberg-on-stop-and-frisk

Hefling, Kimberly
2014 "Obama Administration Recommends Ending 'Zero-Tolerance Policies' in Schools." Associated Press, January 8. Available at: http://www.pbs.org/newshour/rundown/obama-administration-recommends-ending-zero-tolerance-policies-in-schools/

Heidensohn, Frances
2002 "Gender and crime." Pp. 491–530 in Mike Maguire, Rod Morgan, and Robert Reiner, eds., The Oxford Handbook of Criminology, 3rd edition. Oxford: Oxford University Press.

Heimer, Karen
1995 "Gender, race, and the pathways to delinquency." Pp. 140–173 in John Hagan and Ruth D. Peterson, eds., Crime and Inequality. Stanford, CA: Stanford University Press.
1996 "Gender, interaction, and delinquency: Testing a theory of differential social control." Social Psychology Quarterly 59:36–61.
1997 "Socioeconomic status, subcultural definitions, and violent delinquency." Social Forces 75:799–833.

Heimer, Karen, Stacy De Coster, and Haline Unal
2006 "Opening the black box: The social psychology of gender and delinquency." Pp. 109–136 in Mathieu Deflem, ed., Sociological Theory and Criminological Research. Boston: Elsevier.

Heimer, Karen, and Ross L. Matsueda
1994 "Role-taking, role commitment, and delinquency: A theory of differential social control." American Sociological Review 59:365–390.

Heller, Sarah B.
2014 "Summer jobs reduce violence among disadvantaged youth." Science 346: 1219–1223.

Hellman, Daryl A., and Susan Beaton
1986 "The pattern of violence in urban public schools: The influence of school and community." Journal of Research in Crime and Delinquency 23:102–127.

Hemenway, David, and Matthew Miller
2004 "Gun threats against and self-defense gun use by California adolescents." Archives of Pediatrics and Adolescent Medicine 158:395–400.

Henggeler, Scott W.
1989 Delinquency in Adolescence. Newbury Park, CA: Sage.

Henggeler, Scott W., Sonja K. Schoenwald, Charles M. Borduin, and Cynthia C. Swenson
2006 "Methodological critique and meta-analysis as Trojan horse." Children and Youth Services Review 28:447–457.

Henry, Kimberly L., Kelly E. Knight, and Terence P. Thornberry
2012 "School disengagement as a predictor of dropout, delinquency, and problem substance use during adolescence and early adulthood." Journal of Youth Adolescence 41:156–166.

Herald-Tribune
2009 "Florida justice: Tough on youths." August 9. Available at: http://www.heraldtribune.com/article/20090809/ARTICLE/908091068?Title=Florida-justice-Tough-on-youths

Herbert, Bob
2007a "Arrested while grieving." New York Times, May 26, A25.
2007b "The millions left out." New York Times, May 12, A25.

Heyman, Richard E., and Amy M. Smith Slep
2007 "Therapeutic treatment approaches to violent behavior." Pp. 602–617 in Daniel J. Flannery, Alexander T. Vazsonyi, and Irwin D. Waldman, eds., The Cambridge Handbook of Violent Behavior and Aggression. New York: Cambridge.

Hill, Karl G., James C. Howell, J. David Hawkins, and Sara R. Battin-Pearson
1999 "Childhood risk factors for adolescent gang membership: Results from the Seattle social development project." Journal of Research in Crime and Delinquency 36:300–322.

Hill, Karl G., Christina Lui, and J. David Hawkins
2004 "Early precursors of gang membership." Pp. 191–199 in Finn-Aage Esbensen, Stephen G. Tibbitts, and Larry Gaines, eds., American Youth Gangs at the Millennium. Long Grove, IL: Waveland Press.

Hindelang, Michael J.
1978 "Race and involvement in common law personal crimes." American Sociological Review 43:93–109.
1981 "Variations in age-race-sex-specific incidence rates of offending." American Sociological Review 46:461–474.

Hindelang, Michael J., Michael Gottfredson, and James Garofalo
1978 Victims of Personal Crime. Cambridge, MA: Ballinger.

Hindelang, Michael J., Travis Hirschi, and Joseph G. Weis
1979 "Correlates of delinquency: The illusion of discrepancy between self-report and official measures." American Sociological Review 44:99–101.
1981 Measuring Delinquency. Beverly Hills, CA: Sage.

Hipp, John R.
2010 "A dynamic view of neighborhoods: The reciprocal relationship between crime and neighborhood structural characteristics." Social Problems 57:205–230.

Hipwell, Alison, Kate Keenan, Kristen Kasza, Rolf Loeber, Magda Stouthamer-Loeber, and Tammy Beam
2008 "Reciprocal influences between girls' conduct problems and depression, and parental punishment and warmth: A six year prospective analysis." Journal of Abnormal Child Psychology 36:663–677.

Hirschfield, Paul J.
2008 "The declining significance of delinquent labels in disadvantaged urban communities." Sociological Forum 23:575–601.

Hirschi, Travis
1969 Causes of Delinquency. Berkeley: University of California Press.
1977 "Causes and prevention of juvenile delinquency." Sociological Inquiry 47:322–341.
1995 "The family." Pp. 121–140 in James Q. Wilson and Joan Petersilia, eds., Crime. Oakland, CA: ICS Press.
2004 "Self-control and crime." Pp. 537–552 in R. F. Baumeister and K. D. Vohs, eds., Handbook of Self-Regulation. New York: Guilford Press.

Hirschi, Travis, and Michael Gottfredson
1983 "Age and the explanation of crime." American Journal of Sociology 89:552–584.

Hirschi, Travis, and Michael J. Hindelang
1977 "Intelligence and delinquency: A revisionist review." American Sociological Review 42:571–587.

Hirschi, Travis, and Hanan C. Selvin
1967 Delinquency Research: An Appraisal of Analytic Methods. New York: Free Press.

Hirtenlehner, Helmut, Lieven Pauwels, and Gorazd Mesko
2015 "Is the criminogenic effect of exposure to peer delinquency dependent on the ability to exercise self-control? Results from three countries." Journal of Criminal Justice 43:532–543.

Hockenberry, Sarah
2016 Juveniles in Residential Placement, 2013. Washington, DC: Office of Juvenile Justice and Delinquency Prevention.

Hockenberry, Sarah, and Puzzanchera, Charles
2015 "Juvenile Court Statistics 2013. Pittsburgh: National Center for Juvenile Justice.

Hockenberry, Sarah, Melissa Sickmund, and Anthony Sladky
2009 Juvenile Residential Facility Census, 2006: Selected Findings. Washington, DC: Office of Juvenile Justice and Delinquency Prevention.
2013 Juvenile Residential Facility Census, 2010: Selected Findings. Washington, DC: Office of Juvenile Justice and Delinquency Prevention.

Hoeben, Evelien M., and Frank M. Weerman
2016 "Why is involvement in unstructured socializing related to adolescent delinquency?" Criminology 54:242–281.

Hoeve, Machteld, Judith Semon Dubas, Veroni I. Eichelsheim, Peter H. van der Laan, Wilma Smeenk, and Jan R. M. Gerris
2009 "The relationship between parenting and delinquency: A meta-analysis." Journal of Abnormal Child Psychology 37:749–775.

Hoeve, Machteld, Suzanne Jak, Geert Jan J. M. Stams, and Wim H. J. Meeus
2016 "Financial problems and delinquency in adolescents and young adults: A 6-year three-wave study." Crime & Delinquency 62:1488–1509.

Hoeve, Machteld, Geert Jan J. M. Stams, Claudia E. van der Put, Judith Semon Dubas, Peter H. van der Laan, and Jan R. M. Gerris
2012 "A meta-analysis of attachment to parents and delinquency." Journal of Abnormal Child Psychology 40:771–785.

Hoffmann, John P.
2003 "A contextual analysis of differential association, social control, and strain theories of delinquency." Social Forces 81:753–786.
2010 "A life-course perspective on stress, delinquency, and young adult crime." American Journal of Criminal Justice 35:105–120.

Hoffmann, John P., and Felicia Gray Cerbone
1999 "Stressful life events and delinquency escalation in early adolescence." Criminology 37:343–374.

Hoffmann, John P., Lance D. Erickson, and Karen R. Spence
2013 "Modeling the association between academic achievement and delinquency: An application of interactional theory." Criminology 51:629–660.

Hoffmann, John P., and Alan S. Miller
1998 "A latent variable analysis of strain theory." Journal of Quantitative Criminology 14:83–110.

Hoffmann, John P., and S. Susan Su
1997 "The conditional effects of stress on delinquency and drug use: A strain theory assessment of sex differences." Journal of Research in Crime and Delinquency 34:46–78.

Holcomb, Alison
2012 "Marijuana use should not be a crime." USA Today, October 30. Available at: http://www.usnews.com/debate-club/should-marijuana-use-be-legalized/marijuana-use-should-not-be-a-crime

Hollin, Clive R.
1990a Cognitive-Behavioral Interventions with Young Offenders. New York: Pergamon.
1990b "Social skills training with delinquents: A look at the evidence and some recommendations for practice." British Journal of Social Work 20:483–493.
1992 Criminal Behaviour: A Psychological Approach to Explanation and Prevention. London: Falmer Press.
2002 "Criminal Psychology." Pp. 144–174 in Mike Maguire, Rod Morgan, and Robert Reiner, eds., The Oxford Handbook of Criminology, 3rd edition. Oxford: Oxford University Press.

Holman, Barry, and Jason Ziedenberg
2007 The Dangers of Detention: The Impact of Incarcerating Youth in Detention and Other Secure Facilities. Justice Policy Institute. Available at: http://www.justicepolicy.org/images/upload/06-11_rep_dangersofdetention_jj.pdf

Honohan, Michael
2001 "Shootings will continue until bullies are corralled." Atlanta Constitution, March 13.

Hope, Tim
1995 "Community crime prevention." Crime and Justice 19:21–89.

Hornik, Robert, Lela Jacobsohn, Robert Orwin, Andrea Piesse, and Graham Kalton
2008 "Effects of the national youth anti-drug media campaign on youths." American Journal of Public Health 98:2229–2236.

Howell, James C.
1995 "Gangs and youth violence: Recent research." Pp. 261–274 in James C. Howell, Barry Krisberg, J. David Hawkins, and John J. Wilson, eds., A Sourcebook: Serious Violence and Chronic Juvenile Offenders. Thousand Oaks, CA: Sage.
1997a Juvenile Justice and Youth Violence. Thousand Oaks, CA: Sage.
1997b "Youth Gangs." Washington, DC: Office of Juvenile Justice and Delinquency Prevention.
1998a Youth Gangs: An Overview. Washington, DC: Office of Juvenile Justice and Delinquency Prevention.
1998b "Promising programs for youth gang violence prevention and intervention." Pp. 284–312 in Rolf Loeber and David P. Farrington, eds., Serious and Violent Juvenile Offenders. Thousand Oaks, CA: Sage.
1999 "Youth gang homicides: A literature review." Crime and Delinquency 45:208–241.
2003a Preventing and Reducing Juvenile Delinquency. Thousand Oaks, CA: Sage.
2003b "Diffusing research into practice using the comprehensive strategy for serious, violent, and chronic juvenile offenders." Youth Violence and Juvenile Justice 1:219–245.
2004 "Youth gangs: An overview." Pp. 16–51 in Finn-Aage Esbensen, Stephen G. Tibbitts, and Larry Gaines, eds., American Youth Gangs at the Millennium. Long Grove, IL: Waveland Press.
2015 "Gang trends, trajectories, and solutions." Pp. 517–535 in Marvin D. Krohn and Jodi Lane, eds., The Handbook of Juvenile Delinquency and Juvenile Justice. Malden, MA: Wiley.

Howell, James C., Arlen Egley, Jr., and Debra K. Gleason
2002 Modern Day Youth Gangs. Washington, DC: Office of Juvenile Justice and Delinquency Prevention.

Howell, James C., and J. David Hawkins
1998 "Prevention of youth violence." Pp. 263–315 in Michael Tonry and Mark H. Moore, eds., Crime and Justice, Volume 24. Chicago: University of Chicago Press.

Howell, James C., Barry Krisberg, J. David Hawkins, and John J. Wilson
1995 A Sourcebook: Serious, Violent, and Chronic Juvenile Offenders. Thousand Oaks, CA: Sage.

Howell, James C., Barry Krisberg, and Michael Jones
1995 "Trends in juvenile crime and youth violence." Pp. 1–35 in James C. Howell, Barry Krisberg, J. David Hawkins, and John J. Wilson, eds., A Sourcebook: Serious, Violent, and Chronic Juvenile Offenders. Thousand Oaks, CA: Sage.

Hoyt, Dan R., Kimberly D. Ryan, and Ana Mari Cauce
1999 "Personal victimization in a high-risk environment: Homeless and runaway adolescents." Journal of Research in Crime and Delinquency 36:371–392.

Hsia, Heidi, and Donna Hamparian
1998 Disproportionate Minority Confinement: 1997 Update. Washington, DC: Office of Juvenile Justice and Delinquency Prevention.

Huang, Bu, Helene R. White, Rick Kosterman, Richard F. Catalano, and J. David Hawkins
2001 "Developmental associations between alcohol and interpersonal aggression during adolescence." Journal of Research in Crime and Delinquency 38:64–83.

Hubbard, Dana Jones, and Travis C. Pratt
2002 "A meta-analysis of the predictors of delinquency among girls." Journal of Offender Rehabilitation 34:1–13.

Huesmann, L. Rowell
2010 "Nailing the coffin shut on doubts that violent video games stimulate aggression." Psychological Bulletin 136:179–181.

Huesmann, L. Rowell, and Lucyna Kirwil
2007 "Why observing violence increases the risk of violent behavior by the observer." Pp. 545–571 in Daniel J. Flannery, Alexander T. Vazsonyi, and Irwin D. Waldman, eds., The Cambridge Handbook of Violent Behavior and Aggression. Cambridge: Cambridge University Press.

Huff, C. Ronald
1998 Comparing the Criminal Behavior of Youth Gangs and At-Risk Youth. Washington, DC: National Institute of Justice.
2002 Gangs in America III. Thousand Oaks, CA: Sage.
2004 "Comparing the criminal behavior of youth gangs and at-risk youths." Pp. 77–89 in Finn-Aage Esbensen, Stephen G. Tibbitts, and Larry Gaines, eds., American Youth Gangs at the Millennium. Long Grove, IL: Waveland Press.

Hughes, Lorine A., and James F. Short Jr.
2005 "Disputes involving youth street gang members: Micro-social contexts." Criminology 43:43–76.

Hughes, Michael, and Melvin E. Thomas
1998 "The continuing significance of race revisited: A study of race, class, and quality of life in America, 1972 to 1996." American Sociological Review 63:785–795.

Huizinga, David
1995 "Developmental sequences in delinquency: Dynamic typologies." Pp. 15–34 in Lisa J. Crockett and Ann C. Crouter, eds., Pathways Through Adolescence. Mahwah, NJ: Lawrence Erlbaum.
1996 The Influence of Delinquent Peers, Gangs, and Co-offending on Violence. Washington, DC: Office of Juvenile Justice and Delinquency Prevention.

Huizinga, David, and Delbert S. Elliott
1986 "Reassessing the reliability and validity of self-report delinquency measures." Journal of Quantitative Criminology 2:293–327.
1987 "Juvenile offenders: Prevalence, offender incidence, and arrest rates by race." Crime and Delinquency 33:206–223.

Huizinga, David H., Scott Menard, and Delbert S. Elliott
1989 "Delinquency and drug use: Temporal and developmental patterns." Justice Quarterly 6:419–455.

Huizinga, David, Terence Thornberry, Kelly Knight, and Peter Lovegrove
2007 Disproportionate Minority Contact in the Juvenile Justice System. Washington, DC: National Criminal Justice Reference Service.

Huizinga, David, Anne Wylie Weiher, Rachele Espiritu, and Finn-Aage Esbensen
2003 "Delinquency and crime: Some highlights from the Denver youth survey." Pp. 47–91 in Terence P. Thornberry and Marvin D. Krohn, eds., Taking Stock of Delinquency. New York: Kluwer.

Hundleby, John D.
1987 "Adolescent drug use in a behavioral matrix: A conformation and comparison of the sexes." Addictive Behaviors 12:103–112.

Huston, Aletha C., Kaeley C. Bobbitt, and Alison Bentley
2015 "Time spent in child care: How and why does it affect social development?" Developmental Psychology 51:621–634.

Hutchinson, Asa
2002 "Drug Legalization Doesn't Work." Washington Post, October 9, A31.

Inciardi, James A., Rith Horowitz, and Anne E. Pottieger
1993 Street Kids, Street Drugs, Street Crime. Belmont, CA: Wadsworth.

Inciardi, James A., and Karen McElrath
1998 The American Drug Scene. Los Angeles: Roxbury.

Inderbitzen, Michele
2005 "Growing up behind bars." Journal of Offender Rehabilitation 42:1–22.

Ingram, Jason R., Justin W. Patchin, Beth M. Huebner, John D. McCluskey, and Timothy S. Bynum
2007 "Parents, friends, and serious delinquency: An examination of direct and indirect effects among at-risk early adolescents." Criminal Justice Review 32:380–400.

Ireland, Timothy O., Carolyn A. Smith, and Terence P. Thornberry
2002 "Developmental issues in the impact of child maltreatment on later delinquency and drug use." Criminology 40:359–400.

Ispa-Landa, Simone and Charles E. Loeffler
2016 "Indefinite punishment and the criminal record: Stigma reports among expungement-seekers in Illinois." Criminology 54:387–412.

Jackson, Dylan B., and Carter Hay
2013 "The conditional impact of official labeling on subsequent delinquency: Considering the attenuating role of family attachment." Journal of Research in Crime and Delinquency 50:300–322.

Jackson, Mary S., and Paul Knepper
2003 Delinquency and Justice. Boston: Allyn and Bacon.

Jackson, Pamela Irving
1991 "Crime, youth gangs, and urban transition: The social dislocations of postindustrial economic development." Justice Quarterly 8:379–397.

Jackson, Patrick G.
1990 "Sources of data." Pp. 21–50 in Kimberly L. Kempf, ed., Measurement Issues in Criminology. New York: Springer-Verlag.

Jacobs, Bruce A., Volkan Topalli, and Richard Wright
2000 "Managing retaliation: Drug robbery and informal sanction threats." Criminology 38:171–198.

James, Chrissy, Geerty Jan J. M. Stams, Jessica J. Asscher, Anne Katrien De Roo, and Peter H. van der Laan
2013 "Aftercare programs for reducing recidivism among juvenile and young adult offenders: A meta-analytic review." Clinical Psychology Review 33:263–274.

Jang, Sung Joon
1999 "Age-varying effects of family, school, and peers on delinquency: A multilevel modeling test of interactional theory." Criminology 37:643–686.
2002 "Race, ethnicity, and deviance: A study of Asian and non-Asian adolescents in America." Sociological Forum 17:647–680.

Jang, Sung Joon, and Byron R. Johnson
2001 "Neighborhood disorder, individual religiosity, and adolescent use of illicit drugs: A test of multi-level hypotheses." Criminology 39:109–144.
2003 "Strain, negative emotions, and deviant coping among African Americans: A test of general strain theory." Journal of Quantitative Criminology 19:79–105.

Jang, Sung Joon, and Carolyn A. Smith
1997 "A test of reciprocal causal relationships among parental supervision, affective ties, and delinquency." Journal of Research in Crime and Delinquency 34:307–336.

Jang, Sung Joon, and Terence P. Thornberry
1998 "Self-esteem, delinquent peers, and delinquency: A test of the self-enhancement thesis." American Sociological Review 63:586–598.

Jankowski, Martin Sanchez
1995 "Ethnography, inequality, and crime in the low-income community." Pp. 80–94 in John Hagan and Ruth D. Peterson, eds., Crime and Inequality. Stanford, CA: Stanford University Press.

Jargowsky, Paul A.
2003 Stunning Progress, Hidden Problems: The Dramatic Decline of Concentrated Poverty in the 1990s. Washington, DC: Brookings Institution.
2013 Concentration of Poverty in the New Millennium. Washington, DC: Century Foundation.
2015 Architecture of Segregation: Civil Unrest, the Concentration of Poverty, and Public Policy. Washington, DC: Century Foundation.

Jargowsky, Paul A., and Yoonhwan Park
2009 "Cause or consequence? Suburbanization and crime in U.S. metropolitan areas." Crime and Delinquency 55:28–50.

Jarjoura, G. Roger
1993 "Does dropping out of school enhance delinquent involvement? Results from a large-scale national probability sample." Criminology 31:149–172.
1996 "The conditional effect of social class on the dropout–delinquency relationship." Journal of Research in Crime and Delinquency 33:232–255.

Jarjoura, G. Roger, and Ruth A. Triplett
1997 "Delinquency and class: A test of the proximity principle." Justice Quarterly 14:763–792.

Jarjoura, G. Roger, Ruth A. Triplett, and Gregory P. Brinker
2002 "Growing up poor: Examining the link between persistent childhood poverty and delinquency." Journal of Quantitative Criminology 18:159–187.

Jenkins, Patricia H.
1997 "School delinquency and the school social bond." Journal of Research in Crime and Delinquency 34:337–367.

Jensen, Gary F.
1972 "Parents, peers, and delinquent action: A test of the differential association perspective." American Journal of Sociology 78:562–575.
2001 "The invention of television as a cause of homicide: The reification of a spurious relationship." Homicide Studies 5:114–130.

Jensen, Gary F., and David Brownfield
1983 "Parents and drugs: Specifying the consequences of attachment." Criminology 21:543–554.
1986 "Gender, lifestyles, and victimization: Beyond routine activity." Violence and Victims 1:85–99.

Jensen, Gary F., and Raymond Eve
1976 "Sex differences in delinquency." Criminology 13:427–448.

Jensen, Gary F., and Dean G. Rojek
1998 Delinquency and Youth Crime. Prospect Heights, IL: Waveland Press.

Johnson, Allan
2014 "Feds want Ohio to stop secluding mentally ill juvenile offenders." Columbus Dispatch, March 14. Available at: http://www.dispatch.com/content/stories/local/2014/03/13/juvenile-justice.html

Johnson, Byron R., Sung Joon Jang, David B. Larson, and Spencer De Li
2000 "Escaping from the crime of inner cities: Church attendance and religious salience among disadvantaged youth." Justice Quarterly 17:377–391.
2001 "Does adolescent religious commitment matter? A reexamination of the effects of religiosity on delinquency." Journal of Research in Crime and Delinquency 38:22–44.

Johnson, Byron R., Spencer De Li, David B. Larson, and Michael McCullough
2000 "A systematic review of the religiosity and delinquency literature: A research note." Journal of Contemporary Criminal Justice 16:32–52.

Johnson, Calvin C., and Chanchalat Chanhatasilpa
2003 "The race/ethnicity and poverty nexus of violent crime: Reconciling differences in Chicago's community area homicide rates." Pp. 89–113 in Darnell F. Hawkins, ed., Violent Crime: Assessing Race and Ethnic Differences. Cambridge: Cambridge University Press.

Johnson, Lee Michael, Ronald L. Simons, and Rand D. Conger
2004 "Criminal justice system involvement and continuity of youth crime." Youth and Society 36:3–29.

Johnson, Matthew C., and Glen A. Kercher
2007 "ADHD, strain, and criminal behavior: A test of general strain theory." Deviant Behavior 28:131–152.

Johnson, Renee M., Matthew Miller, Mary Vriniotis, Deborah Azrael, and David Hemenway
2006 "Are household firearms stored less safely in homes with adolescents? Analysis of a national random sample of parents." Archives of Pediatrics and Adolescent Medicine 160: 788–792.

Johnson, Richard E.
1979 Juvenile Delinquency and Its Origins. Cambridge: Cambridge University Press.
1986 "Family structure and delinquency: General patterns and gender differences." Criminology 24:65–84.

Johnson, Richard E., Anastasios C. Marcos, and Stephen Bahr
1987 "The role of peers in the complex etiology of adolescent drug use." Criminology 25:323–340.

Kaminski, Jennifer Wyatt, Linda Anne Valle, Jill H. Filene, and Cynthia L. Boyle
2008 "A meta-analytic review of components associated with parent training program effectiveness." Journal of Abnormal Child Psychology 36:567–589.

Kane, Robert J.
2005 "Compromised police legitimacy as a predictor of violent crime in structurally disadvantaged communities." Criminology 43:469–498.

Kappeler, Victor E., Mark Blumberg, and Gary W. Potter
1996 The Mythology of Crime and Criminal Justice. Prospect Heights, IL: Waveland Press.

Katz, Charles M., Vincent J. Webb, and David R. Schaffer
2001 "An assessment of the impact of quality-of-life policing on crime and disorder." Justice Quarterly 18:825–876.

Katz, Jack
1988 Seductions of Crime. New York: Basic Books.

Katz, Lawrence F., Jeffrey R. Kling, and Jeffrey B. Liebman
2001 "Moving to opportunity in Boston: Early results of a randomized mobility experiment." The Quarterly Journal of Economics 116:607–654.

Katz, Rebecca S.
2000 "Explaining girls' and women's crime and desistance in the context of their victimization experiences." Violence Against Women 6:633–660.

Kaufman, Joanne M.
2005 "Explaining the race/ethnicity–violence relationship." Justice Quarterly 22:224–251.
2009 "Gendered responses to serious strain: The argument for a general strain theory of deviance." Justice Quarterly 26:410–444.

Kavish, Daniel R., Christopher W. Mullins, and Danielle A. Soto
2016 "Interactionist labeling: Formal and informal labeling's effects on juvenile delinquency." Crime & Delinquency 62:1313–1336.

Kazdin, Alan E.
1994 "Interventions for aggressive and antisocial children." Pp. 341–382 in Leonard D. Eron, Jacquelin H. Gentry, and Peggy Schlegel, eds., Reason to Hope. Washington, DC: American Psychological Association.

Kellermann, Arthur L., Dawna S. Fuqua-Whitley, Frederick P. Rivara, and James Mercy
1998 "Preventing youth violence: What works?" Annual Review of Public Health 19:271–292.

Kelley, Barbara Tatem, Rolf Loeber, Kate Keenan, and Mary DeLamatre
1997 Developmental Pathways in Boys' Disruptive and Delinquent Behavior. Washington, DC: Office of Juvenile Justice and Delinquency Prevention.

Kelling, George L.
n.d. What Works—Research and the Police. Washington, DC: National Institute of Justice.
1988 Police and Communities: The Quiet Revolution. Washington, DC: National Institute of Justice.

Kelling, George L., and Catherine M. Coles
1996 Fixing Broken Windows. New York: Martin Kessler Books.

Kelling, George L., Mona R. Hochberg, Sandra Lee Kaminska, Ann Marie Rocheleau, Dennis P. Rosenbaum, Jeffrey A. Roth, and Wesley G. Skogan
1998 The Bureau of Justice Assistance Comprehensive Communities Program: A Preliminary Report. Washington, DC: Office of Justice Programs.

Kelling, George L., Tony Plate, Duane Dieckman, and Charles E. Brown
1974 The Kansas City Preventive Patrol Experiment: A Summary Report. Washington, DC: Police Foundation.

Kempf-Leonard, Kimberly
1990 Measurement Issues in Criminology. New York: Springer-Verlag.

1993 "The empirical status of Hirschi's control theory." Pp. 143–185 in Freda Adler and William S. Laufer, eds., New Directions in Criminological Theory; Advances in Criminological Theory, Volume 4. New Brunswick, NJ: Transaction.

2007 "Minority youths and juvenile justice." Youth Violence and Juvenile Justice 5:71–87.

2012 "The conundrum of girls and juvenile justice processing." Pp. 485–525 in Barry C. Feld and Donna M. Bishop, eds., The Oxford Handbook of Juvenile Crime and Juvenile Justice. Oxford: Oxford University Press.

Kennedy, David M.

1997 Juvenile Gun Violence and Gun Markets in Boston. Washington, DC: National Institute of Justice.

1998 "Pulling levers: Getting deterrence right." National Institute of Justice Journal 236:2–8.

Kennedy, Leslie W., and Stephen W. Baron

1993 "Routine activities and a subculture of violence: A study of violence on the street." Journal of Research in Crime and Delinquency 30:88–112.

Kennedy, Leslie W., and David R. Forde

1990 "Routine activities and crime: An analysis of victimization in Canada." Criminology 28:137–152.

1996 "Pathways to aggression: A factorial survey of 'routine conflict'." Journal of Quantitative Criminology 12:417–438.

1999 When Push Comes to Shove. Albany: State University of New York Press.

Kent, Stephanie L., and David Jacobs

2005 "Minority threat and police strength from 1980 to 2000." Criminology 43:731–760.

Kessler, David A.

1999 "The effects of community policing on complaints against officers." Journal of Quantitative Criminology 15:333–372.

Kierkus, Christopher A., and John D. Hewitt

2009 "The contextual nature of the family structure/delinquency relationship." Journal of Criminal Justice 37:123–132.

Kingston, Beverly, David Huizinga, and Delbert S. Elliott

2009 "A test of social disorganization theory in high-risk urban neighborhoods." Youth and Society 41:53–79.

Kirk, David S., and Margaret Hardy

2014 "The acute and enduring consequences of exposure to violence on youth mental health and aggression." Justice Quarterly 31:539–567.

Kirsh, Steven J.

2006 Children, Adolescents, and Media Violence. Thousand Oaks, CA: Sage.

Kleck, Gary

1997 Targeting Guns: Firearms and Their Control. New York: Aldine de Gruyter.

2015 "The impact of gun ownership rates on crime rates: A methodological review of the evidence." Journal of Criminal Justice 43:40–48.

Kleck, Gary, and J. C. Barnes

2014 "Do more police lead to more crime deterrence?" Crime and Delinquency 60:716–738.

Kleck, Gary, and Marc Gertz

1995 "Armed resistance to crime: The prevalence and nature of self-defense with a gun." Journal of Criminal Law and Criminology 86:150–187.

Kleck, Gary, Brian Sever, Spencer Li, and Marc Gertz

2005 "The missing link in general deterrence research." Criminology 43:623–660.

Kleiman, Mark A. R.

1999 "Getting deterrence right: Applying tipping models and behavioral economics to the problems of crime control." Pp. 1–29 in National Institute of Justice (ed.), Perspectives on Crime and Justice: 1998–1999 Lecture Series. Washington, DC: National Institute of Justice.

Klein, Malcolm W.

1995 The American Street Gang. New York: Oxford University Press.

1998 "Street gangs." Pp. 111–132 in Michael Tonry, ed., The Handbook of Crime and Punishment. New York: Oxford University Press.

Klein, Malcolm W., and Cheryl L. Maxson
2006 Street Gang Patterns and Policies. New York: Oxford University Press.

Klein, Malcolm W., Cheryl L. Maxson, and Jody Miller
1995 The Modern Gang Reader. Los Angeles: Roxbury.

Kleinfield, N. R.
2003 "Reputation for trouble fills portrait of boy 10, accused of murder." New York Times, March 30, A18.

Klepper, Steven, and Daniel Nagin
1989 "The deterrent effect of perceived certainty and severity of punishment revisited." Criminology 27:721–746.

Klick, Jonathan, John MacDonald, and Thomas Stratmann
2012 "Mobile phones and crime deterrence: An underappreciated link." Pp. 243–256 in Alon Harel and Keith N. Hylton, eds., Research Handbook on the Economics of Criminal Law. Northampton, MA: Edward Elger.

Kneebone, Elizabeth, and Alan Berube
2008 Reversal of Fortune: A New Look at Concentrated Poverty in the 2000s. Washington, DC: Brookings Institution.

Knoll, Crystal, and Melissa Sickmund
2010 Fact Sheet: Delinquency Cases in Juvenile Court, 2007. Washington, DC: Office of Juvenile Justice and Delinquency Prevention.

Knox, George W.
2000 An Introduction to Gangs. Peotone, IL: New Chicago School Press.

Kocieniewski, David
2003 "A teenage loner, an arsenal and, to the police, a close call." New York Times, July 8, A21.

Kornhauser, Ruth Rosner
1978 Social Sources of Delinquency. Chicago: University of Chicago Press.

Kort-Butler, Lisa A., Kimberly A. Tyle,r and Lisa A. Melander
2011 "Childhood maltreatment, parental monitoring, and self-control among homeless young adults: consequences for negative social outcomes." Criminal Justice and Behavior 38:1244–1264.

Kovandzic, Tomislav V., and Thomas B. Marvell
2003 "Right-to-carry concealed handguns and violent crime: Crime control through gun decontrol." Criminology and Public Policy 2:363–396.

Kowalski, Robin M., Susan P. Limber, and Patrick W. Agatston
2012 Cyberbullying: Bullying in the Digital Age. Malden, MA: Wiley-Blackwell.

Kreager, Derek A.
2007 "Unnecessary Roughness? School sports, peer networks, and male adolescent violence." American Sociological Review 72:705–724.

Kreager, Derek A., Ross L. Matsueda, Elena A. Erosheva
2010 "Motherhood and criminal desistance in disadvantaged neighborhoods." Criminology 48:221–258.

Kretschmar, Jeff M., and Daniel J. Flannery
2007 "Substance use and violent behavior." Pp. 647–663 in Daniel J. Flannery, Alexander T. Vazsonyi, and Irwin D. Waldman, eds., The Cambridge Handbook of Violent Behavior and Aggression. Cambridge: Cambridge University Press.

Krienert, Jessie L.
2003 "Masculinity and crime. A quantitative exploration of Messerschmidt's hypothesis." Electronic Journal of Sociology 7. Available at: http://www.sociology.org/content/vol7.2/01_krienert.html

Krisberg, Barry
2005 Juvenile Justice. Thousand Oaks, CA: Sage.

2012. "Juvenile corrections: An overview." Pp. 748–770 106 in Barry C. Feld and Donna M. Bishop, eds., The Oxford Handbook of Juvenile Crime and Juvenile Justice. New York: Oxford University Press.

Krisberg, Barry, Giselle Barry, and Emily Sharrock
2004 Reforming Juvenile Justice Through Comprehensive Community Planning. Oakland, CA: National Council on Criminal Delinquency.

Krisberg, Barry, Elliott Currie, David Onek, and Richard G. Wiebush
1995 "Graduated sanctions for serious, violent, and chronic juvenile offenders." Pp. 142–170 in James C. Howell, Barry Krisberg, J. David Hawkins, and John J. Wilson, eds., A Sourcebook: Serious, Violent, and Chronic Juvenile Offenders. Thousand Oaks, CA: Sage.

Krisberg, Barry, and James C. Howell
1998 "The impact of the juvenile justice system and prospects for graduated sanctions in a comprehensive strategy." Pp. 346–366 in Rolf Loeber and David P. Farrington, eds., Serious and Violent Juvenile Offenders. Thousand Oaks, CA: Sage.

Krisberg, Barry, and Karl F. Schumann
2000 Crime and Delinquency 46 (April).

Krivo, Lauren J., and Ruth D. Peterson
1996 "Extremely disadvantaged neighborhoods and urban crime." Social Forces 75:619–650.

Krohn, Marvin D.
1999 "Social learning theory: The continuing development of a perspective." Theoretical Criminology 3:462–476.
2000 "Sources of criminality: Control and deterrence theories." Pp. 373–403 in Joseph F. Sheley, ed., Criminology. Belmont, CA: Wadsworth.

Krohn, Marvin D., and Jodi Lane, eds.
2015 The Handbook of Juvenile Delinquency and Juvenile Justice. Malden, MA: Wiley.

Krohn, Marvin D., William F. Skinner, James L. Massey, and Ronald L. Akers
1985 "Social learning theory and adolescent cigarette smoking: A longitudinal study." Social Problems 32:455–473.

Krohn, Marvin D., Terence P. Thornberry, Lori Collins-Hall, and Alan J. Lizotte
1995 "School dropout, delinquent behavior, and drug use." Pp. 163–183 in Howard B. Kaplan, ed., Drugs, Crime, and Other Deviant Adaptations. New York: Plenum.

Kubrin, Charis E., Steven F. Messner, Glenn Deane, Kelly McGeever, and Thomas D. Stucky
2010 "Proactive policing and robbery rates across U.S. cities." Criminology 48:57–97.

Kubrin, Charis E., and Ronald Weitzer
2003a "New directions in social disorganization theory." Journal of Research in Crime and Delinquency 40:374–402.
2003b "Retaliatory violence: Concentrated disadvantage and neighborhood culture." Social Problems 50:157–180.

Kumpfer, Karol L., and Rose Alvarado
1998 Effective Family Strengthening Interventions. Washington, DC: Office of Juvenile Justice and Delinquency Prevention.

Kumpfer, Karol L., and Connie M. Tait.
2000 Family Skills Training for Parents and Children. Washington, DC: Office of Juvenile Justice and Delinquency Prevention.

Kunerth, Jeff
2012 "Life without parole becomes 25 years for Terrance Graham, subject of U.S. Supreme Court case." Orlando Sentinel, February 24. Available at: http://articles.orlandosentinel.com/2012-02-24/features/os-life-without-parole-terrance-graham-20120224-12_1_terrance-graham-resentencing-parole

Kupchik, Aaron
2006 Judging Juveniles. New York: New York University Press.
2007 "The correctional experiences of youth in adult and juvenile prisons." Justice Quarterly 24:247–270.

Kurlychek, Megan, and Brian D. Johnson
2004 "The juvenile penalty." Criminology 42:485–517.
2010 "Juvenility and punishment: Sentencing juveniles in adult criminal court." Criminology 48:725–758.

Kurlychek, Megan, Patricia Torbet, and Melanie Bozynski
1999 Focus on Accountability: Best Practices for Juvenile Court and Probation. Washington, DC: Office of Juvenile Justice and Delinquency Prevention.

LaFree, Gary
1998 Losing Legitimacy. Boulder, CO: Westview.
1999 "Declining violent crime rates in the 1990s: Predicting crime booms and busts." Annual Review of Sociology 25:145–168.

LaGrange, Teresa, and Robert A. Silverman
1999 "Low self-control and opportunity: Testing the general theory of crime as an explanation for gender differences in delinquency." Criminology 37:41–72.

Lahey, Benjamin B., Carol A. Van Hulle, Brian M. D'Onofrio, Joseph Lee Rodgers, and Irwin D. Waldman
2008 "Is parental knowledge of their adolescent offspring's whereabouts and peer associations spuriously associated with offspring delinquency?" Journal of Abnormal Child Psychology 36:807–823.

Lahey, Benjamin B., and Irwin D. Waldman
2005 "A developmental model of the propensity to offend during childhood and adolescence." Pp. 15–50 in David F. Farrington, ed., Integrated Developmental and Life-Course Theories of Offending. New Brunswick, NJ: Transaction.

Lam, Chun Bum, Susan M. McHale, and Ann C. Crouter
2014 "Time with peers from middle childhood to late adolescence: Developmental course and adjustment correlates." Child Development 85:1677–1693.

Lanctôt, Nadine, and Marc Le Blanc
2002 "Explaining deviance by adolescent females." Crime and Justice: A Review of Research 29:113–202.

Land, Kenneth C., Patricia L. McCall, and Lawrence E. Cohen
1990 "Structural covariates of homicide rates: Are there any invariances across time and social space?" American Journal of Sociology 95:922–963.

Landau, Simha F.
1998 "Crime, subjective social stress and support indicators, and ethnic origin: The Israeli experience." Justice Quarterly 15:243–272.

Larson, Reed W., Maryse H. Richards, Giovanni Moneta, Grayson Holmbeck, and Elena Duckett
1996 "Changes in adolescents' daily interactions with their families from ages 10 to 18: Disengagement and transformation." Developmental Psychology 32:744–754.

Larsson, Henrik, Essi Viding, Fruhling V. Rijsdijk, and Robert Plomin
2008 "Relationships between parental negativity and childhood antisocial behavior over time: A bidirectional effects model in a longitudinal genetically informative design." Journal of Abnormal Child Psychology 36:633–645.

Larzelere, Robert E., and Gerald R. Patterson
1990 "Parental management: Mediator of the effect of socioeconomic status on early delinquency." Criminology 28:301–324.

Laub, John H., and Robert J. Sampson
2001 "Understanding desistance from crime." Crime and Justice: A Review of Research 28:1–70.
2003 Shared Beginnings, Divergent Lives: Delinquent Boys to Age 70. Boston, MA: Harvard University Press.

Laub, John H., Robert J. Sampson, and Gary A. Sweeten
2006 "Assessing Sampson and Laub's life-course theory of crime." Pp. 313–334 in Francis T. Cullen, John Paul Wright, and Kristie R. Blevins, eds., Taking Stock: The Status of Criminological Theory. New Brunswick, NJ: Transaction.

Lauritsen, Janet L.
2005 "Racial and ethnic differences in offending." Pp. 83–104 in Darnell F. Hawkins and Kimberly Kempf-Leonard, eds., Our Children, Their Children. Chicago: University of Chicago Press.

Lauritsen, Janet L., and Robert J. Sampson
1998 "Minorities, crime, and criminal justice." Pp. 58–84 in Michael Tonry, ed., The Handbook of Crime and Punishment. New York: Oxford University Press.

Lawrence, Richard
1998 School Crime and Juvenile Justice. New York: Oxford University Press.

Lawton, Brian A., Ralph B. Taylor, and Anthony J. Luongo
2005 "Police officers on drug corners in Philadelphia, drug crime, and violent crime." Justice Quarterly 22:427–451.

Le Blanc, Marc
1993 "Late adolescence deceleration of criminal activity and development of self- and social control." Studies on Crime and Crime Prevention 2:51–68.
1998 "Screening of serious and violent juvenile offenders: Identification, classification, and prediction." Pp. 167–193 in Rolf Loeber and David P. Farrington, eds., Serious and Violent Juvenile Offenders. Thousand Oaks, CA: Sage.

Le Blanc, Marc, and Rolf Loeber
1998 "Developmental criminology updated." Crime and Justice 23:115–198.

Le Corff, Yann, and Jean Toupin
2009 "Comparing persistent juvenile delinquents and normative peers with the five-factor model of personality." Journal of Research in Personality 43:1105–1108.

Lee, Joongyeup, Hyunseok Jang and Leana A. Bouffard
2011 "Maternal employment and juvenile delinquency: A longitudinal study of Korean adolescents." Crime and Delinquency 59:1064–1084.

Lee, Maggie
2013 "Juvenile detention alernatives gain ground in several states, DC." The Crime Report, April 19. Available at: http://www.thecrimereport.org/news/inside-criminal-justice/

Lee, Matthew R.
2000 "Community cohesion and violent predatory victimization: A theoretical extension and cross-national test of opportunity theory." Social Forces 79:683–706.

Leiber, Michael J.
2002 "Disproportionate minority confinement (DMC) of youth: An analysis of state and federal efforts to address the issue." Crime and Delinquency 48:3–45.
2003 The Contexts of Juvenile Justice Decision Making: When Race Matters. Albany: State University of New York Press.
2006 "Disproportionate minority confinement (DMC) of youth." Pp. 141–186 in Everette B. Penn, Helen Taylor Greene, and Shaun L. Gabbidon, eds., Race and Juvenile Justice. Durham, NC: Carolina Academic Press.

Leiber, Michael J., and Kristan C. Fox
2005 "Race and the impact of detention on juvenile justice decision making." Crime and Delinquency 51:470–497.

Leiber, Michael J., and Kristin Y. Mack
2003 "The individual and joint effects of race, gender, and family status on juvenile justice decision-making." Journal of Research in Crime and Delinquency 40:34–70.

Leiber, Michael J., and Jayne M. Stairs
1999 "Race, contexts, and the use of intake diversion." Journal of Research in Crime and Delinquency 36:56–86.

Lemert, Edwin M.
1951 Social Pathology. New York: McGraw-Hill.
1972 Human Deviance, Social Problems, and Social Control. Englewood Cliffs, NJ: Prentice-Hall.

Leonard, Kimberly Kempf, Carl E. Pope, and William H. Feyerherm
1995 Minorities in Juvenile Justice. Thousand Oaks, CA: Sage.

Leonard, Kimberly Kempf, and Henry Sontheimer
1995 "The role of race in juvenile justice in Pennsylvania." Pp. 98–127 in Kimberly Kempf Leonard, Carl E. Pope, and William H. Feyerherm, eds., Minorities in Juvenile Justice. Thousand Oaks, CA: Sage.

Leuck, Thomas J.
2007 "To serve and protect, but politely." New York Times, July 29, A21.

Levine, Madeline
1996 Viewing Violence. New York: Doubleday.

Levitt, Steven D.
2002 "Deterrence." Pp. 435–450 in James Q. Wilson and Joan Petersilia, eds., Crime. Oakland, CA: ICS Press.

Levrant, Sharon, Francis T. Cullen, Betsy Fulton, and John F. Wozniak
1999 "Reconsidering restorative justice: The corruption of benevolence revisited?" Crime and Delinquency 45:3–27.

Levy-Gigi, Einat, Csilla Szabó, Oguz Kelemen, and Szabolcs Kéri
2013 "Association among clinical response, hippocampal volume, and FKBP5 gene expression in individuals with posttraumatic stress disorder receiving cognitive behavioral therapy." Biological Psychiatry 74:793–800.

Lewin, Tamar
2003 "1 in 5 teenagers has sex before 15, study finds." New York Times, May 20, A18.

Lewit, Eugene M., Donna L. Terman, and Richard E. Behrman
1997 "Children and poverty: Analysis and recommendations." Future of Children 7:4–24.

Liberman, Akiva
2007 Adolescents, Neighborhoods, and Violence. Washington, DC: Office of Justice Programs.

Liberman, Akiva M., David S. Kirk, and Kideuk Kim
2014 "Labeling effects of first juvenile arrests: Secondary deviance and secondary sanctioning." Criminology 52:345–370.

Liljeberg, Jenny Freidenfelt, Jenny M. Eklund, Marie Väfors Fritz, and Britt af Klinteberg
2011 "Poor school bonding and delinquency over time: Bidirectional effects and sex differences." Journal of Adolescence 34:1–9.

Lilly, J. Robert, Francis T. Cullen, and Richard Ball
2002 Criminological Theory. Thousand Oaks, CA: Sage.

Limber, Susan P., Dan Olweus, and Harlan Luxenberg
2013 Bullying in U.S. Schools: 2012 Status Report. Center City, MN: Hazelden Foundation.

Lin, Jeffrey
2006 Exploring the Impact of Institutional Placement on the Recidivism of Delinquent Youth. Washington, DC: National Institute of Justice.

Link, Nathan W., Francis T. Cullen, Robert Agnew, and Bruce G. Link
2016 "Can general strain theory help us understand violent behaviors among people with mental illnesses?" Justice Quarterly 33:729–754.

Lipsey, Mark W.
1992 "Juvenile delinquency treatment: A meta-analytic inquiry into the variability of effects." Pp. 83–208 in Thomas D. Cook, Harris Cooper, David S. Cordray, Heidi Hartmann, Larry V. Hedges, Richard J. Light, Thomas A. Louis, and Frederick Mosteller, eds., Meta-Analysis for Explanation. New York: Russell Sage.

Lipsey, Mark W., and Francis T. Cullen
2008 "The effectiveness of correctional rehabilitation." Annual Review of Law and Social Science 3 (December).

Lipsey, Mark W., James C. Howell, Marion R. Kelly, Gabrielle Chapman, and Darin Carver
2010 Improving the Effectiveness of Juvenile Justice Programs. Washington, DC: Center for Juvenile Justice Reform.

Lipsey, Mark W., and David B. Wilson
1998 "Effective intervention for serious juvenile offenders." Pp. 313–345 in Rolf Loeber and David P. Farrington, eds., Serious and Violent Juvenile Offenders. Thousand Oaks, CA: Sage.

Liptak, Adam
2007 "Lifers as teenagers, now seeking a second chance." New York Times, October 17, A1, A24.
2010 "Justices limit life sentences for juveniles." New York Times, May 17. Available at: http://www.nytimes.com/2010/05/18/us/politics/18court.html?_r=0

Liptak, Adam, and Ethan Bronner
2012 "Justices bar mandatory life terms for juveniles." New York Times, June 25. Available at: http://www.nytimes.com/2012/06/26/us/justices-bar-mandatory-life-sentences-for-juveniles.html

Liska, Allen E., John R. Logan, and Paul E. Bellair
1998 "Race and violent crime in the suburbs." American Sociological Review 63:27–39.

Liska, Allen E., and Barbara D. Warner
1991 "Functions of crime: A paradoxical process." American Journal of Sociology 96:1441–1463.

Listwan, Shelley J., Cheryl L. Jonson, Francis T. Cullen, and Edward J. Latessa
2008 "Cracks in the penal harm movement: Evidence from the field." Criminology and Public Policy 7:423–465.

Little, Michelle, and Laurence Steinberg
2006 "Psychosocial correlates of adolescent drug dealing in the inner city." Journal of Research in Crime and Delinquency 43:357–386.

Littell, Julia H.
2006 "The case for multisystemic therapy: Evidence or orthodoxy?" Children and Youth Services Review 28:458–472.

Liu, Jianghong, Adrian Raine, Anne Wuerker, Peter H. Venables, and Sarnoff Mednick
2009 "The association of birth complications and externalizing behavior in early adolescents: Direct and mediating effects." Journal of Research on Adolescence 19:93–111.

Lizotte, Alan J., Trudy J. Bonsell, David McDowall, Marvin D. Krohn, and Terence P. Thornberry
2002 "Carrying guns and involvement in crime." Pp. 153–167 in Robert A. Silverman, Terence P. Thornberry, Bernard Cohen, and Barry Krisberg, eds., Crime and Justice at the Millennium; Essays by and in Honor of Marvin E. Wolfgang. Boston: Kluwer Academic.

Lizotte, Alan J., and David Sheppard
2001 "Gun use by male juveniles: Research and prevention." Washington, DC: Office of Juvenile Justice and Delinquency Prevention.

Lizotte, Alan J., James M. Tesoriero, Terence P. Thornberry, and Marvin Krohn
1994 "Patterns of adolescent firearms ownership and use." Justice Quarterly 11:51–74.

Lockwood, Daniel
1997 "Violence among middle school and high school students: Analysis and implications for prevention." Washington, DC: National Institute of Justice.

Loeber, Rolf, David P. Farrington, and David Petechuk
2003 Child Delinquency: Early Intervention and Prevention. Washington, DC: Office of Juvenile Justice and Delinquency Prevention.

Loeber, Rolf, David P. Farrington, Magda Stouthamer-Loeber, and Welmoet B. Van Kammen
1998 Antisocial Behavior and Mental Health Problems. Mahwah, NJ: Lawrence Erlbaum.

Loeber, Rolf, David P. Farrington, Magda Stouthamer-Loeber, Terrie E. Moffitt, and Avshalom Caspi
1998 "The development of male offending: Key findings from the first decade of the Pittsburgh youth study." Studies on Crime and Crime Prevention 7:141–171.

Loeber, Rolf, David P. Farrington, Magda Stouthamer-Loeber, Terrie E. Moffitt, Avshalom Caspi, Helene Raskin White, Evelyn H. Wei, and Jennifer M. Beyers
2003 "The development of male offending: Key findings from fourteen years of the Pittsburgh youth study." Pp. 93–136 in Terence P. Thornberry and Marvin D. Krohn, eds., Taking Stock of Delinquency. New York: Kluwer Academic.

Loeber, Rolf, David P. Farrington, and Daniel A. Waschbusch
1998 "Serious and violent juvenile offenders." Pp. 13–29 in Rolf Loeber and David P. Farrington, eds., Serious and Violent Juvenile Offenders. Thousand Oaks, CA: Sage.

Loeber, Rolf, and Magda Stouthamer-Loeber
1986 "Family factors as correlates and predictors of juvenile conduct problems and delinquency." Pp. 29–149 in Michael Tonry and Norval Morris, eds., Crime and Justice, Volume 7. Chicago: University of Chicago Press.

Loeber, Rolf, Magda Stouthamer-Loeber, Welmoet Van Kammen, and David P. Farrington
1991 "Initiation, escalation and desistance in juvenile offending and their correlates." Journal of Criminal Law and Criminology 82:36–82.

Lofland, John, and Lyn H. Lofland
1995 Analyzing Social Settings. Belmont, CA: Wadsworth.

Lombroso, Cesare
1911 Criminal Man. New York: G. P. Putnam.

Longa, Lyda
1998 "A bad way to die." Atlanta Journal-Constitution, March 3, B3.

Longshore, Douglas A.
1998 "Self-control and criminal opportunity: A prospective test of the general theory of crime." Social Problems 45:102–113.

Longshore, Douglas, Eunice Chang, and Nena Messina
2005 "Self-control and social bonds: A combined control perspective on juvenile offending." Journal of Quantitative Criminology 21:419–437.

Lopes, Giza, Marvin D. Krohn, Alan J. Lizotte, Nicole M. Schmidt, Bob Edward Vásquez, and Jón Gunnar Bernburg
2012 "Labeling and cumulative disadvantage: The impact of formal police intervention on life chances and crime during emerging adulthood." Crime and Delinquency 58:456–488.

Losel, Friedrich
1995 "The efficacy of correctional treatment: A review and synthesis of meta-evaluations." Pp. 79–111 in James McGuire, ed., What Works: Reducing Reoffending. Chichester, England: Wiley.
2007 "It's never too early and never too late: Towards an integrated science of developmental intervention in criminology." Criminologist 32:1, 3–9.

Losel, Friedrich, and Andreas Beelmann
2003 "Effects of child skills training in preventing antisocial behavior." Annals of the American Academy of Political and Social Science 587:84–109.

Losoncz, Ibolya, and Graham Tyson
2007 "Parental shaming and adolescent delinquency: A partial test of reintegrative shaming theory." Australian and New Zealand Journal of Criminology 40:161–178.

Lott, John R.
1998 More Guns, Less Crime. Chicago: University of Chicago Press.

Lotz, Roy, and Leona Lee
1999 "Sociability, school experience, and delinquency." Youth and Society 31:199–223.

Loughran, Thomas A., Ray Paternoster, Aaron Chalfin, and Theodore Wilson
2016 "Can rational choice be considered a general theory of crime? Evidence from individual-level panel data." Criminology 54:86–112.

Lowenkamp, Christopher T., Francis T. Cullen, and Travis C. Pratt
2003 "Replicating Sampson and Grove's test of social disorganization theory: Revisiting a criminological classic." Journal of Research in Crime and Delinquency 40(4):351–373.

Luckenbill, David F.
1977 "Criminal homicide as a situated transaction." Social Problems 25:176–186.

Ludwig, Jens, and Philip J. Cook
2003 Evaluating Gun Policy. Washington, DC: Brookings Institution Press.

Ludwig, Jens, Greg J. Duncan, and Paul Hirschfield
2001 "Urban poverty and juvenile crime: Evidence from a randomized housing-mobility experiment." Quarterly Journal of Economics 116:655–679.

Lundman, Richard J.
2001 Prevention and Control of Juvenile Delinquency. New York: Oxford University Press.
1996 "Psychopathy, sociopathy, and crime." Society 34(1):29–38.

Lynam, Donald R., and Joshua D. Miller
2004 "Personality pathways to impulsive behavior and their relations to deviance." Journal of Quantitative Criminology 20:319–341.

Lynch, James P.
2002 Trends in Juvenile Violent Offending: An Analysis of Victim Survey Data. Washington, DC: Office of Juvenile Justice and Delinquency Prevention.

Lynch, Michael J., and Paul B. Stretesky
2001 "Radical criminology." Pp. 267–286 in Raymond Paternoster and Ronet Bachman, eds., Explaining Criminals and Crime. Los Angeles: Roxbury.

MacCoun, Robert, and Peter Reuter
1998 "Drug control." Pp. 207–238 in Michael Tonry, ed., The Handbook of Crime and Punishment. New York: Oxford University Press.

MacDonald, John M.
2002 "The effectiveness of community policing in reducing urban violence." Crime and Delinquency 48:592–618.

MacDonald, John M., and Meda Chesney-Lind
2001 "Gender bias and juvenile justice revisited: A multiyear analysis." Crime and Delinquency 47:173–195.

Mack, Kristin Y., Michael J. Leiber, Richard A. Featherstone, and Maria A. Monserud
2007 "Reassessing the family-delinquency association: Do family type, family processes, and economic factors make a difference?" Journal of Criminal Justice 35:51–67.

MacKenzie, Doris Layton
2002 "Reducing the criminal activities of known offenders and delinquents." Pp. 330–404 in Lawrence W. Sherman, David P. Farrington, Brandon C. Welsh, and Doris Layton MacKenzie, eds., Evidence-Based Crime Prevention. London: Routledge.
2006 What Works in Corrections. New York: Cambridge University Press.

MacKenzie, Doris Layton, and Rachel Freeland
2012 "Examining the effectiveness of juvenile residential programs." Pp. 771–798 in Barry C. Feld and Donna M. Bishop, eds., The Oxford Handbook of Juvenile Crime and Juvenile Justice. Oxford: Oxford University Press.

MacLeod, Jay
1995 Ain't No Makin' It. Boulder, CO: Westview Press.

Madden, Mary, Amanda Lenhart, Maeve Duggan, Sandra Cortesi, and Urs Gasser
2013 Teens and Technology 2013. Washington, DC: Pew Research Center. Available at: http://www.pewinternet.org/files/old-media//Files/Reports/2013/PIP_TeensandTechnology2013.pdf

Madero-Hernandez, Arelys, Rusto Deryol, M. Murat Ozer, and Robin S. Engel
2016 "Examining the impact of early childhood school investments on neighborhood crime." Justice Quarterly. Advanced online publication. DOI: 10.1080/07418825.2016.1226935

Madero-Hernandez, Arelys, and Bonnie S. Fisher
2013 "Routine Activity Theory." Pp. 513–534 in Francis T. Cullen and Pamela Wilcox, eds., The Oxford Handbook of Criminological Theory. New York: Oxford University Press.

Maguin, Eugene, and Rolf Loeber
1996 "Academic performance and delinquency." Pp. 145–264 in Michael Tonry, ed., Crime and Justice: A Review of Research, Volume 20. Chicago: University of Chicago Press.

Magura, Stephen
2012 "Failure of intervention or failure of evaluation: A meta-evaluation of the National Youth Anti-Drug Media Campaign evaluation." Substance Use and Misuse, 47:1414–1420.

Maguire, Kathleen, and Ann L. Pastore
2003 Sourcebook of Criminal Justice Statistics. Available at http://www.albany.edu/sourcebook/

Maimon, David, and Christopher R. Browning
2010 "Unstructured socializing, collective efficacy, and violent behavior among urban youth." Criminology 48:443–474.

Majors, Richard, and Janet Mancini Billson
1992 Cool Pose. New York: Lexington Books.

Maldonado-Molina, Mildred M., Jennifer M. Reingle, and Wesley G. Jennings
2011 "Does alcohol use predict violent behaviors? The relationship between alcohol use and violence in a nationally representative longitudinal sample." Youth Violence and Juvenile Justice 9:99–111.

Manasse, Michelle E., and Natasha Morgan Ganem
2009 "Victimization as a cause of delinquency: The role of depression and gender." Journal of Criminal Justice 37:371–378.

Markowitz, Fred E., and Richard B. Felson
1998 "Socio-demographic differences in attitudes and violence." Criminology, 36:117–138.

Martin, Monica J., Bill McCarthy, Rand D. Conger, Frederick X. Gibbons, Ronald L. Simons, Carolyn E. Cutrona, and Gene H. Brody
2010 "The enduring significance of racism: Discrimination and delinquency among Black American youth." Journal of Research on Adolescence, 21:662–676.

Martinez, Ramiro, Jr., and Matthew T. Lee
2000 "On immigration and crime." Pp. 485–524 in Gary LaFree, ed., Criminal Justice 2000, Volume 1: The Nature of Crime: Continuity and Change. Washington, DC: National Institute of Justice.

Martinez, Ramiro, Jr., and Amie L. Nielsen
2006 "Extending ethnicity and violence research in a multiethnic city." Pp. 108–137 in Ruth Peterson, Lauren J. Krivo, and John Hagan, eds., The Many Colors of Crime. New York: New York University Press.

Martinson, Robert
1974 "What works? Questions and answers about prison reform." Public Interest 35:22–54.

Martz, Ron
1999 "Crime stats: Questions linger after Atlanta audit." Atlanta Journal-Constitution, January 28, C1, C4.

Maruna, Shadd, and Heith Copes
2005 "What have we learned from five decades of neutralization research." Crime and Justice 32:221–320.

Massey, James L., Marvin D. Krohn, and Lisa M. Bonati
1989 "Property crime and the routine activities of individuals." Journal of Research in Crime and Delinquency 26:378–400.

Massoglia, Michael, and Christopher Uggen
2010 "Settling down and aging out: Toward an interactionist theory of desistance and the transition to adulthood." American Journal of Sociology 116:543–582.

Mastrofski, Stephen D.
2000 "The police in America." Pp. 405–445 in Joseph F. Sheley, ed., Criminology: A Contemporary Handbook. Belmont, CA: Wadsworth.

Matarazzo, Anthony, Peter J. Carrington, and Robert D. Hiscott
2001 "The effect of prior youth court dispositions on current dispositions: An application of societal-reaction theory." Journal of Quantitative Criminology 17:169–200.

Matsuda, Kristy N., Chris Melde, Terrance J. Taylor, Adrienne Freng, and Finn-Aage Esbensen
2013 "Gang membership and adherence to the 'Code of the Street.'" Justice Quarterly 30:440–468.

Matsueda, Ross L.
1988 "The current state of differential association theory." Crime and Delinquency 34:277–306.
1992 "Reflected appraisals, parental labeling, and delinquency: Specifying a symbolic interactionist theory." American Journal of Sociology 97:1577–1611.
2001. "Labeling theory." Pp. 223–241 in Raymond Paternoster and Ronet Bachman, eds., Explaining Criminals and Crime. Los Angeles, CA: Roxbury.

Matsueda, Ross L., and Kathleen Anderson
1998 "The dynamics of delinquent peers and delinquent behavior." Criminology 36:269–308.

Matsueda, Ross L., and Karen Heimer
1987 "Race, family structure, and delinquency: A test of differential association and social control theories." American Sociological Review 52:826–840.

Matsueda, Ross L., Derek A Kreager, and David Huizinga
2006 "Deterring delinquents: A rational choice model of theft and violence." American Sociological Review 71:95–122.

Matza, David
1964 Delinquency and Drift. New York: Wiley.
1969 Becoming Deviant. Englewood Cliffs, NJ: Prentice-Hall.

Matza, David, and Gresham Sykes
1961 "Juvenile delinquency and subterranean beliefs." American Sociological Review 26:713–719.

Mauer, Marc, and Ryan S. King
2007 Uneven Justice. The Sentencing Project. Available at: www.sentencingproject.org

Maxson, Cheryl L.
1995 "Research in brief: Street gangs and drug sales in two suburban cities." Pp. 228–235 in Malcolm W. Klein, Cherly L. Maxson, and Jody Miller, eds., The Modern Gang Reader. Los Angeles: Roxbury.

Maxson, Cheryl L.
2004 "Civil gang injunctions." Pp. 375–389 in Finn-Aage Esbensen, Stephen G. Tibbitts, and Larry Gaines, eds., American Youth Gangs of the Millennium. Long Grove, IL: Waveland Press.

Maxson, Cheryl L., and Malcolm W. Klein
1990 "Street gang violence: Twice as great, or half as great?" Pp. 71–100 in C. Ronald Huff, ed., Gangs in America. Newbury Park, CA: Sage.
1996 "Defining gang homicide: An updated look at member and motive approaches." Pp. 3–20 in C. Ronald Huff, ed., Gangs in America. Thousand Oaks, CA: Sage.

Maxson, Cheryl L., and Kristy N. Matsuda
2012 "Gang delinquency." Pp. 246–271 in Barry C. Feld and Donna M. Bishop, eds., The Oxford Handbook of Juvenile Crime and Juvenile Justice. New York: Oxford University Press.

Maxson, Cheryl L., and Monica L. Whitlock
2002 Joining the gang: Gender differences in risk factors for gang membership. Pp. 19–36 in C. Ronald Huff, ed., Gangs in America III. Thousand Oaks, CA: Sage.

Maynard, Rebecca A.
1997 Kids Having Kids. Washington, DC: Urban Institute Press.

Maynard, Rebecca A., and Eileen M. Garry
1997 Adolescent Motherhood: Implications for the Juvenile Justice System. Washington, DC: Office of Juvenile Justice and Delinquency Prevention.

Mazerolle, Lorraine, David W. Soole, and Sacha Rombouts
2007 "Street-level drug law enforcement: A meta-analytic review." A Campbell Collaboration Systematic Review. Available at: http://www.aic.gov.au/campbellcj/reviews/titles.html

Mazerolle, Paul
1998 "Gender, general strain, and delinquency: An empirical examination." Justice Quarterly 15:65–91.

Mazerolle, Paul, and Jeff Maahs
2000 "General strain and delinquency: An alternative examination of conditioning influences." Justice Quarterly 17:753–778.

Mazerolle, Paul, and Alex Piquero
1997 "Violent responses to strain: An examination of conditioning influences." Violence and Victims 12:323–343.
1998 "Linking exposure to strain with anger: An investigation of deviant adaptations." Journal of Criminal Justice 26:195–211.

Mazerolle, Paul, Alex Piquero, and George E. Capowich
2003 "Examining the links between strain, situational and dispositional anger, and crime." Youth and Society 35:131–157.

McBride, Duane C., and Clyde B. McCoy
1993 "The drugs–crime relationship: An analytical framework." Prison Journal 73:257–278.

McCabe, Donald L.
1992 "The influence of situational ethics on cheating among college students." Sociological Inquiry 62:365–374.

McCarthy, Bill
1995 "Not just 'for the thrill of it': An instrumentalist elaboration of Katz's explanation of sneaky thrill property crimes." Criminology 33:519–538.

McCarthy, Bill, Diane Felmlee, and John Hagan
2004 "Girl friends are better: Gender, friends, and crime among school and street youth." Criminology 42:805–836.

McCartney, Kathleen, Margaret Burchinal, Alison Clarke-Stewart, Kristen L. Bub, Margaret T. Owen, and Jay Belsky
2010 "Testing a series of causal propositions relating time in child care to children's externalizing behavior." Developmental Psychology 46:1–17.

McCluskey, Cynthia Perez
2002 Understanding Latino Delinquency. New York: LFB Scholarly Publishing.

McCord, Joan
1991 "Family relationships, juvenile delinquency, and adult criminality." Criminology 29:397–417.
2001 "Forging criminals in the family." Pp. 223–236 in Susan O. White, Handbook of Youth and Justice. New York: Kluwer Academic.

McCord, Joan, and Margaret E. Ensminger
2003 "Racial discrimination and violence: A longitudinal perspective." Pp. 319–330 in Darnell F. Hawkins, ed., Violent Crime: Addressing Race and Ethnic Differences. Cambridge: Cambridge University Press.

McCord, Joan, Cathy Spatz Widom, and Nancy A. Crowell
2001 Juvenile Crime, Juvenile Justice. Washington, DC: National Academy Press.

McDevitt, Rick
2000 "Juvenile 'reform' only hurts." Atlanta Journal-Constitution, May 28, Q5.

McDonald, Lynn, and Heather E. Frey
1999 Families and Schools Together: Building Relationships. Washington, DC: Office of Juvenile Justice and Delinquency Prevention.

McDowall, David, Alan J. Lizotte, and Brian Wiersema
1991 "General deterrence through civilian gun ownership: An evaluation of the quasi-experimental evidence." Criminology 29:541–559.

McDowall, David, Colin Loftin, and Stanley Presser
2000 "Measuring civilian defensive firearm use: A methodological experiment." Journal of Quantitative Criminology 16:1–19.

McDowall, David, and Brian Wiersema
1994 "The incidence of defensive firearm use by U.S. crime victims, 1987 through 1990." American Journal of Public Health 84:1982–1984.

McEwen, T.
1994 National Assessment Program: 1994 Survey Results. Washington, DC: National Institute of Justice.

McFarlane, Julie H., and Amy Miller
2005 Promoting Community Protection of Adolescents. Portland, OR: Juvenile Rights Project, Inc.

McGarrell, Edmund F.
2012 "Policing juveniles." Pp. 551–572 in Barry C. Feld and Donna M. Bishop, eds., The Oxford Handbook of Juvenile Crime and Juvenile Justice. New York: Oxford University Press.

McGarrell, Edmund F., Steven M. Chermak, and Alexander Weiss
2002 Reducing Gun Violence: An Evaluation of the Indianapolis Police Department's Directed Patrol Project. Washington, DC: Office of Justice Programs.

McGarrell, Edmund F., Steven Chermak, Jeremy M. Wilson, and Nicholas Corsaro
2006 "Reducing homicide through a 'lever-pulling' strategy." Justice Quarterly 23:188–213.

McGarrell, Edmund F., and Natalie Kroovand Hipple
2007 "Family group conferencing and re-offending among first-time juvenile offenders." Justice Quarterly 24:221–246.

McGloin, Jean M.
2009 "Delinquency balance: Revisiting peer influence." Criminology 47:439–477.

McGloin, Jean Marie, Travis C. Pratt, and Jeff Maaks
2004 "Rethinking the IQ-delinquency relationship." Justice Quarterly 21:603–635.

McGloin, Jean Marie, Travis C. Pratt, and Alex R. Piquero
2006 "A life-course analysis of the criminogenic effects of maternal cigarette smoking during pregnancy." Journal of Research in Crime and Delinquency 43:412–426.

McGloin, Jean Marie, and Lauren O'Neill Shermer
2009 "Self-control and deviant peer network structure." Journal of Research in Crime and Delinquency 46:35–72.

McGuire, James
1995 What Works: Reducing Offending. Chichester, England: Wiley.

McHugh, Donald J.
2003 "Parental guidance required." New York Times, July 12, A23.

McKee, Laura, Erin Roland, Nicole Coffelt, Ardis L. Olson, Rex Forehand, Christina Massari, Deborah Jones, Cecelia A. Gaffney, and Michael S. Zens
2007 "Harsh discipline and child problem behaviors: The roles of positive parenting and gender." Journal of Family Violence 22:187–196.

McNulty, Thomas L., and Paul E. Bellair
2003 "Explaining racial and ethnic differences in serious adolescent violent behavior." Criminology 41:709–748.

McNulty, Thomas L., and Steven R. Holloway
2000 "Race, crime, and public housing in Atlanta: Testing a conditional effect hypothesis." Social Forces 79:707–729.

Mears, Daniel P.
2012 "The front end of the juvenile court." Pp. 573–605 in Barry C. Feld and Donna M. Bishop, eds., The Oxford Handbook of Juvenile Crime and Juvenile Justice. Oxford: Oxford University Press.

Mears, Daniel P., and Avinash S. Bhati
2006 "No community is an island: The effects of resource deprivation on urban violence in spatially and socially proximate communities." Criminology 44:509–548.

Mears, Daniel P., and Cochran, J. C.
2013 "What is the effect of IQ on offending?" Criminal Justice and Behavior 40: 1280–1300.

Mears, Daniel P., Carter Hay, Marc Gertz, and Christina Mancini
2007 "Public opinion and the foundation of the juvenile court." Criminology 45:223–258.

Mears, Daniel P., and William R. Kelly
1999 "Assessments and intake processes in juvenile justice processing: Emerging policy considerations." Crime and Delinquency 45:508–529.

Mears, Daniel P., Joshua J. Kuch, Andrea M. Lindsey, Sonja E. Siennick, Georgia B. Pesta, Mark A. Greenwald, and Thomas G. Blomberg
2016 "Juvenile court and contemporary diversion." Criminology & Public Policy 15: 953–981.

Mears, Daniel P., Matthew Ploeger, and Mark Warr
1998 "Explaining the gender gap in delinquency: Peer influence and moral evaluations of behavior." Journal of Research in Crime and Delinquency 35:251–266.

Megens, Kim C. I. M., and Frank M. Weerman
2012 "The social transmission of delinquency: Effects of peer attitudes and behavior revisited." Journal of Research in Crime and Delinquency 49:420–443.

Meich, Richard A., Avshalom Caspi, Terrie E. Moffitt, Bradley R. Entner Wright, and Phil A. Silva
1999 "Socioeconomic status and mental disorders: A longitudinal study of selection and causation during young adulthood." American Journal of Sociology 104:1096–1131.

Meier, Robert F., Steven R. Burkett, and Carol A. Hickman
1984 "Sanctions, peers, and deviance: Preliminary models of a social control process." Sociological Quarterly 25:76–82.

Meier, Robert F., and Gilbert Geis
1997 Victimless Crime? Los Angeles: Roxbury.

Melde, Chris, and Finn-Aage Esbensen
2012 "Gangs and violence: Disentangling the impact of gang membership on the level and nature of offending." Journal of Quantitative Criminology 29:143–166.

Melde, Chris, Terrance J. Taylor, and Finn-Aage Esbensen
2009 "'I got your back': An examination of the protective function of gang membership in adolescence." Criminology 47:565–594.

Meldrum, Ryan C.
2008 "Beyond parenting: An examination of the etiology of self-control." Journal of Criminal Justice 36:244–251.

Meldrum, Ryan C., and Jim Clark
2015 "Adolescent virtual time spent socializing with peers, substance use, and delinquency." Crime and Delinquency 61:1104–1126.

Meldrum, Ryan C., Jacob T. N. Young, and Frank M. Weerman
2009 "Reconsidering the effect of self-control and delinquent peers: Implications of measurement for theoretical significance." Journal of Research in Crime and Delinquency 46:353–376.

Mendel, Richard A.
2010 The Missouri Model: Reinventing the Practice of Rehabilitating Youthful Offenders. Annie E. Casey Foundation. Baltimore. Available at: http://www.aecf.org/m/resourcedoc/aecf-MissouriModelFull report-2010.pdf

Merlo, Alida V., and Peter J. Benekos
2010 "Is punitive juvenile justice policy declining in the United States? A critique of emergent initiatives." Youth Justice 10:3–24.

Merton, Robert K.
1938 "Social structure and anomie." American Sociological Review 3:672–682.
1968 Social Theory and Social Structure. New York: Free Press.

Messerschmidt, James W.
1993 Masculinities and Crime. Lanham, MD: Rowman and Littlefield.

Messner, Steven F., Glenn D. Deane, Luc Anselin, and Benjamin Pearson-Nelson
2005 "Locating the vanguard in rising and falling homicide rates across U.S. cities." Criminology 43:661–696.

Messner, Steven F., Sandra Galea, Kenneth J. Tardiff, Melissa Tracy, Angela Bucciarelli, Tinka Markham Piper, Victoria Frye, and David Vlahov
2007 "Policing, drugs, and the homicide decline in New York City in the 1970s." Criminology 45:385–414.

Messner, Steven F., Marvin D. Krohn, and Allen E. Liska
1989 Theoretical Integration in the Study of Deviance and Crime: Problems and Prospects. Albany: State University of New York Press.

Messner, Steven F., and Richard Rosenfeld
2001 Crime and the American Dream. Belmont, CA: Wadsworth.

Miethe, Terance D., and Richard McCorkle
2001 Crime Profiles. Los Angeles: Roxbury.

Miethe, Terance D., and Robert F. Meier
1990 "Opportunity, choice, and criminal victimization: A test of a theoretical model." Journal of Research in Crime and Delinquency 27:243–266.
1994 Crime and Its Social Context. Albany: State University of New York Press.

Miller, Brooke, and Robert G. Morris
2016 "Virtual peer effects in social learning theory." Crime & Delinquency 62:1543–1569.

Miller, Holly Ventura
2010 "If your friends jumped off a bridge, would you do it too? Delinquent peers and susceptibility to peer influence." Justice Quarterly 27:473–491.

Miller, Jerome
1996 Search and Destroy. Cambridge: Cambridge University Press.

Miller, Jody
2001 One of the Guys: Girls, Gangs, and Gender. New York: Oxford University Press.

Miller, Jody, and Rod K. Brunson
2004 "Gender dynamics in youth gangs." Pp. 163–190 in Finn-Aage Esbensen, Stephen G. Tibbetts, and Larry Gaines, eds., American Youth Gangs of the Millennium. Long Grove, IL: Waveland Press.

Miller, Jody, Cheryl L. Maxson, and Malcolm W. Klein
2001 The Modern Gang Reader. Los Angeles: Roxbury.

Miller, Joshua D., and Donald Lynam
2001 "Structural models of personality and their relation to antisocial behavior: A meta-analytic review." Criminology 39:765–798.

Miller, Walter B.
1958 "Lower class culture as a generating milieu of gang delinquency." Journal of Social Issues 14:5–19.
2001 The Growth of Youth Gang Problems in the United States: 1970–98. Washington, DC: Office of Juvenile Justice and Delinquency Prevention.

Milot, Alyssa S., and Alison Bryant Ludden
2009 "The effects of religion and gender on well-being, substance use, and academic engagement among rural adolescents." Youth and Society 40:403–425.

Minor, William W.
1981 "Techniques of neutralization: A reconceptualization and empirical examination." Journal of Research in Crime and Delinquency 18:295–318.

Mitchell, Ojmarrh, David B. Wilson, Amy Eggers, and Doris L. MacKenzie
2012. "Drug courts' effects on criminal offending for juveniles and adults." Campbell Systematic Reviews 2012:4. Available at: http://www.campbellcollaboration.org/lib/project/74/

Moffitt, Terrie E.
1990 "The neuropsychology of juvenile delinquency: A critical review." Pp. 99–169 in Michael Tonry and Norval Morris, eds., Crime and Justice, Volume 12. Chicago: University of Chicago Press.
1993 "'Life-course persistent' and 'adolescence-limited' antisocial behavior: A developmental taxonomy." Psychological Review 100:674–701.
1997 "Adolescence-limited and life-course persistent offending: A complementary pair of developmental theories." Pp. 11–54 in Terence P. Thornberry, ed., Developmental Theories of Crime and Delinquency: Advances in Criminological Theory, Volume 7. New Brunswick, NJ: Transaction.

2006 "A review of research on the taxonomy of life-course persistent versus adolescence-limited anti-social behavior." Pp. 277–312 in Francis T. Cullen, John Paul Wright, and Kristie R. Blevins, eds., Taking Stock: The Status of Criminological Theory. New Brunswick, NJ: Transaction.

Moffitt, Terrie E., Louise Arseneault, Daniel Belsky, Nigel Dickson, Robert J. Hancox, and Hona Lee Harrington, Renate Houts, Richie Poulton, Brent W. Roberts, Stephen Ross, Malcolm R. Sears, W. Murray Thomson, and Avshalom Caspi
2011 "A gradient of childhood self-control predicts health, wealth, and public safety." Proceedings of the National Academy of Sciences. Available at http://www.pnas.org/content/early/2011/01/20/1010076108.full.pdf+html

Moffitt, Terrie E., Avshalom Caspi, Paul Fawcett, Gary L. Brammer, Michael Raleigh, Arthur Yuwiler, and Phil Silva
1997 "Whole blood serotonin and family background relate to male violence." Pp. 231–249 in Adrian Raine, Patricia A. Brennan, David P. Farrington, and Sarnoff A. Mednick, eds., Biosocial Bases of Violence. New York: Plenum.

Moffitt, Terrie E., Avshalom Caspi, Michael Rutter, and Phil A. Silva
2001 Sex Differences in Antisocial Behaviour. Cambridge: Cambridge University Press.

Moffitt,, Terrie E., and Hona Lee Harrington
1996 "Delinquency: The natural history of antisocial behaviour." Pp. 163–185 in Phil A. Silva and Warren R. Stanton, eds., From Child to Adult. Oxford: Oxford University Press.

Moffitt, Terrie E., and Bill Henry
1989 "Neuropsychological assessment of executive functions in self-reported delinquents." Development and Psychopathology 1:105–118.

Moffitt, Terrie E., Donald R. Lynam, and Phil A. Silva
1994 "Neuropsychological tests predicting persistent male delinquency." Criminology 32:277–300.

Monahan, Kathryn C., Kevin M. King, Elizabeth P. Shulman, Elizabeth Cauffman, and Laurie Chassin
2015 "The effects of violence exposure on the development of impulse control and future orientation across adolescence and early adulthood: Time-specific and generalized effects in a sample of juvenile offenders." Development and Psychopathology 27:1267–1283.

Monahan, Kathryn C., Joanna M. Lee, and Laurence Steinberg
2011 "Revisiting the impact of part-time work on adolescent adjustment: Distinguishing between selection and socialization using propensity score matching." Child Development 82: 96–112.

Mongeau, Lillian
2016 "Is Head Start a failure?" Hechinger Report, August 9. Available at: http://hechingerreport.org/is-head-start-a-failure

Monuteaux, Michael C., Lois K. Lee, David Hemenway, Rebekah Mannix, and Eric W. Fleegler
2015 "Firearm ownership and violent crime in the US: An ecologic study." American Journal of Preventive Medicine 49:207–214.

Moon, Byongook, Merry Morash, Cynthia Perez McCluskey, and Hye-Won Hwang
2009 "A comprehensive test of general strain theory: Key strains, situational- and trait-based negative emotions, conditioning factors, and delinquency." Journal of Research in Crime and Delinquency 46:182–212.

Moon, Melissa M., Jody L. Sundt, Francis T. Cullen, and John Paul Wright
2000 "Is child saving dead? Public support for juvenile rehabilitation." Crime and Delinquency 46:38–60.

Moore, Joan
1991 Going Down to the Barrio: Homeboys and Homegirls in Change. Philadelphia: Temple University Press.

Moore, Joan, and John M. Hagedorn
1996 "What happens to girls in the gang?" Pp. 205–218 in C. Ronald Huff, ed., Gangs in America. Thousand Oaks, CA: Sage.
2001 Female Gangs: A Focus on Research. Washington, DC: Office of Juvenile Justice and Delinquency Prevention.

Moore, John P., and Ivan L. Cook
1999 Highlights of the 1998 National Youth Gang Survey. Washington, DC: Office of Juvenile Justice and Delinquency Prevention.

Moore, Kristin Anderson, Donna Ruane Morrison, and Angela Dungee Greene
1997 "Effects on the children born to adolescent mothers." Pp. 145–180 in Rebecca A. Maynard, ed., Kids Having Kids. Washington, DC: Urban Institute Press.

Moore, Lori D., and Irene Padavic
2011 "Risk assessment tools and racial/ethnic disparities in the juvenile justice system." Sociology Compass 5:850–858.

Moore, Mark H., Robert C. Trojanowicz, and George L. Kelling
1988 Crime and Policing. Washington, DC: National Institute of Justice.

Morash, Merry
1983 "An explanation of juvenile delinquency: The integration of moral reasoning theory and sociological knowledge." Pp. 385–409 in William S. Laufer and James M. Day, eds., Personality Theory, Moral Development, and Criminal Behavior. Lexington, MA: Lexington.
1986 "Gender, peer group experiences, and seriousness of delinquency." Journal of Research in Crime and Delinquency 23:43–67.

Morenoff, Jeffery D.
2005 "Racial and ethnic disparities in crime and delinquency in the United States." Pp. 139–173 in Michael Rutter and Morta Tienda, eds., Ethnicity and Causal Mechanisms. Cambridge: Cambridge University Press.

Morley, Elaine, Shelli B. Rossman, Mary Kopczynski, Janeen Buck, and Caterina Gouvis
2000 Comprehensive Responses to Youth at Risk: Interim Findings from the SafeFutures Initiative. Washington, DC: Office of Juvenile Justice and Delinquency Prevention.

Morris, Gregory D., Peter B. Wood, and R. Gregory Dunaway
2006 "Self-control, native traditionalism, and native american substance use." Crime and Delinquency 52:572–598.

Morris, Nancy A., and Lee Ann Slocum
2010 "The validity of self-reported prevalence, frequency, and timing of arrest: An evaluation of data collected using a life event calendar." Journal of Research in Crime and Delinquency 47:210–240.

Morris, Robert G., and Heith Copes
2012 "Exploring the temporal dynamics of the neutralization/delinquency relationship." Criminal Justice Review 37:442–460.

Morris, Robert G., and Alex R. Piquero
2013 "For whom do sanctions deter and label?" Justice Quarterly 30:837–868.

Mosher, Clayton J., Terance D. Miethe, and Dretha M. Philips
2002 The Mismeasure of Crime. Thousand Oaks, CA: Sage.

Moule Jr., Richard K., Callie H. Burt, Eric A. Stewart, and Ronald L. Simons
2015 "Developmental trajectories of individuals' code of the street beliefs through emerging adulthood." Journal of Research in Crime and Delinquency 52:342–372.

Mowen, Thomas and John Brent
2016 "School Discipline as a Turning Point: The Cumulative Effect of Suspension on Arrest." Journal of Research in Crime and Delinquency 53:628–653.

Muller, Janice, and Sharon Mihalic
1999 Blueprints: A Violence Prevention Initiative. Washington, DC: Office of Juvenile Justice and Delinquency Prevention.

Mulvey, Edward P., and Carol A. Schubert
2012 "Youth in prison and beyond." Pp. 843–867 in Barry C. Feld and Donna M. Bishop, eds., The Oxford Handbook of Juvenile Crime and Juvenile Justice. New York: Oxford University Press.

Muraskin, Roslyn
1998 "Police work with juveniles." Pp. 151–164 in Albert R. Roberts, ed., Juvenile Justice. Chicago: Nelson-Hall.

Murphy, Kim, and Melissa Healy

1999 "Lawsuits now putting onus of youth crime on parents." Atlanta Constitution, May 2, A15.

Murray, Desiree W., Eugene Arnold, Jim Swanson, Karen Wells, Karen Burns, Peter Jensen, Lily Hechtman, Natalya Paykina, Lauren Legato, and Tara Strauss

2008. "A clinical review of outcomes of the multimodal treatment study of children with attention-deficit/hyperactivity disorder (MTA)." Current Psychiatry Reports 10:424–431.

Muskal, Michael

2014 "Minnesota teen's alleged plot to bomb and open fire at school foiled." Los Angeles Times, May 2. Available at: http://www.latimes.com/nation/nationnow/la-na-nn-minnesota-police-foil-schoolattack-20140502-story.html

Mustaine, Elizabeth Ehrhardt, and Richard Tewksbury

1998a "Predicting risks of larceny theft victimization: A routine activity analysis using refined lifestyle measures." Criminology 36:829–857.

1998b "Specifying the role of alcohol in predatory victimization." Deviant Behavior 19:173–200.

Myers, David L.

2003 "Waiver to adult court." Pp. 387–394 in Marilyn D. McShane and Frank P. Williams III, eds., Encyclopedia of Juvenile Justice. Thousand Oaks, CA: Sage.

Na, Chongmin

2017 "The consequences of school dropout among serious adolescent offenders." Journal of Research in Crime and Delinquency 54:78–110.

Nagin, Daniel S.

1998a "Criminal deterrence research at the outset of the twenty-first century." Pp. 1–42 in Michael Tonry, ed., Crime and Justice: A Review of Research, Volume 23. Chicago: University of Chicago Press.

1998b "Deterrence and incapacitation." Pp. 345–368 in Michael Tonry, ed., The Handbook of Crime and Punishment. New York: Oxford University Press.

Nagin, Daniel S., and Raymond Paternoster

1991 "The preventive effects of the perceived risk of arrest: Testing an expanded conception of deterrence." Criminology 29:561–587.

1993 "Enduring individual differences and rational choice theories of crime." Law and Society Review 27:467–496.

1994 "Personal capital and social control: The deterrence implications of a theory of individual differences in criminal offending." Criminology 32:581–606.

Nagin, Daniel S., Alex R. Piquero, Elizabeth S. Scott, and Laurence Steinberg

2006 "Public preferences for rehabilitation versus incarceration of juvenile offenders." Criminology and Public Policy 5:627–652.

Nagin, Daniel S., and Greg Pogarsky

2004 "Time and punishment: Delayed consequences and criminal behavior." Journal of Quantitative Criminology 20:295–317.

Nagin, Daniel S., and Richard E. Tremblay

2005a "What has been learned from group-based trajectory modeling?" Annals of the American Academy of Political and Social Science 602:82–117.

2005b "Developmental trajectory groups: Fact or useful fiction." Criminology 43:873–904.

Narag, Raymund E., Jesenia Pizarro, and Carole Gibbs

2009 "Lead exposure and its implications for criminological theory." Criminal Justice and Behavior 36:954–973.

National Council on Crime and Delinquency

2007 And Justice for Some. Available at www.nccd-crc.org/nccd/

National Gang Center

2013 National Youth Gang Survey Analysis. Available at: http://www.nationalgangcenter.gov/Survey-Analysis

National Institute on Drug Abuse

2006 Principles of Drug Abuse Treatment for Criminal Justice Populations. Washington, DC: National Institute on Drug Abuse.

National Institute of Justice
1992 National Institute of Justice Journal, Community Policing, No. 225.
1996 National Institute of Justice Journal, August, No. 231.
1998a National Institute of Justice Journal, October, No. 237.
2003 2000 Arrestee Drug Abuse Monitoring: Annual Report. Washington, DC: National Institute of Justice.

National Research Council (NRC)
2013a Priorities for Research to Reduce the Threat of Firearm-Related Violence. Washington, DC: National Academies Press.
2013b Reforming Juvenile Justice: A Developmental Approach. Washington, DC: National Academies Press.
2014 The Growth of Incarceration in the United States: Exploring Causes and Consequences. Washington, DC: National Academies Press.

National Television Violence Study
1997 National Television Violence Study, Volume 1. Thousand Oaks, CA: Sage.
1998 National Television Violence Study, Volume 2. Thousand Oaks, CA: Sage.

National Youth Gang Center
2003 "Frequently asked questions regarding gangs." Available at: http:// www.iir.com/nygc/faq.htm

Nedelec, Jospeh. L., Insun Park, and Ian A. Silver
2016 "The effect of the maturity gap on delinquency and drug use over the life course: A genetically sensitive longitudinal design." Journal of Criminal Justice 47:84–99.

Neff, Joan L., and Dennis E. Waite
2007 "Male versus female substance abuse patterns among incarcerated juvenile offenders." Justice Quarterly 24:106–132.

New York Times
2003 "Lawyers for juveniles." November 3, A18.
2007a "Positive trends recorded in U.S. data on teenagers." July 13, A17.
2007c "Back where they belong." July 5, A12.
2009 "Mentally ill offenders strain juvenile system." August 9, A1.

Ngo, Fawn T., and Raymond Paternoster
2013 "Stalking, gender, and coping strategies: A partial test of Broidy and Agnew's gender/general strain theory hypotheses." Victims and Offenders 8:94–117.

Nielsen, Amie L., Matthew T. Lee, and Ramiro Martinez, Jr.
2005 "Integrating race, place, and motive in social disorganization theory." Criminology 43:837–872.

Nofziger, Stacey
2008 "The 'cause' of low self-control: The influence of maternal self-control." Journal of Research in Crime and Delinquency 45:191–224.

Norris, Michael, Sarah Twill, and Chigon Kim
2011 "Smells like teen spirit: Evaluating a Midwestern teen court." Crime and Delinquency 57:199–221.

Novacek, Jill, Robert Raskin, and Robert Hogan
1991 "Why do adolescents use drugs?" Journal of Youth and Adolescence 20:475–492.

NSDUH (National Survey on Drug Use and Health) Report
2006 Youth Violence and Illicit Drug Use. Washington, DC: Substance Abuse and Mental Health Services Administration.

Nye, Ivan F.
1958 Family Relationships and Delinquent Behavior. New York: Wiley.

O'Brien, Robert M.
2000 "Crime facts: Victim and offender data." Pp. 59–83 in Joseph F. Sheley, ed., Criminology. Belmont, CA: Wadsworth.

Office of Justice Programs
1999 Weed and Seed Best Practices. Washington, DC: Office of Justice Programs.

Office of Juvenile Justice and Delinquency Prevention (OJJDP)

1995 Delinquency Prevention Works. Washington, DC: Office of Juvenile Justice and Delinquency Prevention.

1996 Reducing Youth Gun Violence. Washington, DC: Office of Juvenile Justice and Delinquency Prevention.

1998a Guide for Implementing the Balanced and Restorative Justice Model. Washington, DC: Office of Juvenile Justice and Delinquency Prevention.

1998b Juvenile Mentoring Program: 1998 Report to Congress. Washington, DC: Office of Juvenile Justice and Delinquency Prevention.

1999a Report to Congress on Juvenile Violence Research. Washington, DC: Office of Juvenile Justice and Delinquency Prevention.

1999b Title V Incentive Grants for Local Delinquency Prevention Programs: 1998 Report to Congress. Washington, DC: Office of Juvenile Justice and Delinquency Prevention.

2000a Kids and Guns. Washington, DC: Office of Juvenile Justice and Delinquency Prevention.

2000b Jurisdictional Technical Assistance Package for Juvenile Court. Washington, DC: Office of Juvenile Justice and Delinquency Prevention.

2006 Attorney General's Comprehensive Anti-gang Initiative. Washington, DC: Office of Juvenile Justice and Delinquency Prevention.

2010 Best Practices to Address Community Gang Problems: OJJDP'S Comprehensive Gang Model. Washington, DC: Office of Juvenile Justice and Delinquency Prevention.

2014 Statistical Briefing Book. Office of of Juvenile Justice and Delinquency Prevention. Available at: https://www.ojjdp.gov/ojstatbb/default.asp

2017 Statistical Briefing Book. Office of Juvenile Justice and Delinquency Prevention. Available at: https://www.ojjdp.gov/ojstatbb/default.asp

Office of National Drug Control Policy

1999 The National Drug Control Strategy, 1999. Washington, DC: Office of National Drug Control Policy.

2003 Juveniles and Drugs. Washington, DC: Office of National Drug Control Policy.

2007 The President's National Drug Control Strategy. Washington, DC: Office of National Drug Control Policy.

Ogden, Terje, and Kristine Amlund Hagen

2006 "Multisystemic treatment of serious behaviour problems in youth: Sustainability of effectiveness two years after intake." Child and Adolescent Mental Health 11:142–149.

Ogilvie, James M., Anna L. Stewart, Raymond C. Chan, and David H. K. Shum

2011 "Neuropsychological measures of executive function and antisocial behavior: A meta-analysis." Criminology 49:1063–1107.

O'Keeffe, Gwenn Schurgin, Kathleen Clarke-Pearson, and Council on Communications and Media

2011 "Clinical report: The impact of social media on children, adolescents, and families." Pediatrics 127: 800–804.

Oldenettel, Debra, and Madeline Wordes

1999 Community Assessment Centers. Washington, DC: Office of Juvenile Justice and Delinquency Prevention.

Olds, David

2002 "Prenatal and infancy home visiting by nurses: From randomized trials to community replication." Prevention Science 3:153–172.

Olds, David, Peggy Hill, and Elissa Rumsey

1998 Prenatal and Early Childhood Nurse Home Visitation. Washington, DC: Office of Juvenile Justice and Delinquency Prevention.

Oliver, William

1994 The Violent Social World of Black Men. New York: Lexington.

Olweus, Dan

1986 "Aggression and hormones: Behavioral relationship with testosterone and adrenaline." Pp. 51–72 in Dan Olweus, Jack Block, and Marian Radke-Yarrow, eds., Development of Antisocial and Pro-social Behavior. Orlando, FL: Academic Press.

1991 "Bully/victim problems among schoolchildren: Basic facts and effects of a school-based intervention program." Pp. 411–448 in Debra J. Pepler and Kenneth H. Rubin, eds., The Development and Treatment of Childhood Aggression. Hillsdale, NJ: Lawrence Erlbaum.

Orrick, Erin A., and Alex R. Piquero
2015 "Were cell phones associated with lower crime in the 1990s and 2000s?" Journal of Crime and Justice 38:222–238.

Orwin, Robert, Diane Cadell, Adam Chu, Graham Kalton, David Maklan, Carol Morin, Andrea Piesse, Sanjeev Sridharan, Diane Steele, Kristie Taylor, and Elena Tracy
2004 Evaluation of the National Youth Anti-Drug Media Campaign: 2004 Report of Findings. Rockville, MD: Westat.

Osgood, D. Wayne, and Amy L. Anderson
2004 "Unstructured socializing and rates of delinquency." Criminology 42:519–550.

Osgood, D. Wayne, and Jeff M. Chambers
2000 "Social disorganization outside the metropolis: An analysis of rural youth violence." Criminology 38:81–116.

Osgood, D. Wayne, Patrick M. O'Malley, Jerald G. Bachman, and Lloyd D. Johnston
1989 "Time trends and age trends in arrests and self-reported illegal behavior." Criminology 27:389–417.

Osgood, D. Wayne, and Christopher J. Schreck
2007 "A new method for studying the extent, stability, and predictors of individual specialization in violence." Criminology 45:273–312.

Osgood, D. Wayne, Janet K. Wilson, Patrick M. O'Malley, Jerald G. Bachman, and Lloyd D. Johnston
1996 "Routine activities and individual deviant behavior." American Sociological Review 61:635–655.

Ousey, Graham C., and Michelle Campbell Augustine
2001 "Young guns: Examining alternative explanations of juvenile firearm homicide rates." Criminology 39:933–968.

Ousey, Graham C., and Matthew R. Lee
2004 "Investigating the connections between race, illicit drug markets, and lethal violence, 1984–1997." Journal of Research in Crime and Delinquency 41:352–383.
2007 "Homicide trends and illicit drug markets." Justice Quarterly 24:48–79.

Ousey, Graham C., and Pamela Wilcox
2007 "The interaction of antisocial propensity and life-course varying predictors of delinquent behavior." Criminology 45:313–354.

Owens, Jennifer Gatewood, and Lee Ann Slocum
2015 "Abstainers in adolescence and adulthood: Exploring the correlates of abstention using Moffitt's developmental taxonomy." Crime and Delinquency 61:690–718.

Özbay, Özden, and Yusuf Ziya Özcan
2008 "A test of Hirschi's social bonding theory: A comparison of male and female delinquency." International Journal of Offender Therapy and Comparative Criminology 52:134–157.

Ozer, M. Murat, and Robin S. Engel
2012 "Revisiting the use of propensity score matching to understand the relationship between gang membership and violent victimization: A cautionary note." Justice Quarterly 29:105–124.

Padilla, Felix
1992 The Gang as an American Enterprise. New Brunswick, NJ: Rutgers University Press.

Palamara, Frances, Francis T. Cullen, and Joanne C. Gersten
1986 "The effect of police and mental health intervention on juvenile deviance: Specifying contingencies in the impact of formal evaluation." Journal of Health and Social Behavior 27:90–105.

Pappas, Stephanie
2015 "Guns Don't Deter Crime, Study Finds." Live Science Magazine, July 6. Available at: http://www.livescience.com/51446-guns-do-not-deter-crime.html

Parcell, T. J.
2012 "Behind bars, teenagers become prey." New York Times, June 5. Available at: http://www.nytimes.com/roomfordebate/2012/06/05/when-to-punish-a-young-offender-and-when-to-rehabilitate/in-prison-teenagers-become-prey

Parent, Dale G.
2003 Correctional Boot Camps: Lessons from a Decade of Research. Washington, DC: Office of Justice Programs.

Parker, Karen F., and Amy Reckdenwald
2008 "Concentrated disadvantage, traditional male role models, and African-American juvenile violence." Criminology 46:711–735.

Parker, Karen F., Brian J. Stults, and Stephen K. Rice
2005 "Racial threat, concentrated disadvantage and social control." Criminology 43:1111–1134.

Paschall, Mallie J., Miriam L. Ornstein, and Robert L. Flewelling
2001 "African American male adolescents' involvement in the criminal justice system: The criterion validity of self-report measures in a prospective study." Journal of Research in Crime and Delinquency 38:174–187.

Passini, Stefano
2012 "The delinquency–drug relationship: The influence of social reputation and moral disengagement." Addictive Behaviors 37:577–579.

Pastore, Ann L., and Kathleen Maguire
2003 Sourcebook of Criminal Justice Statistics. Available at http://www.albany.edu/sourcebook/

Patchin, Justin W.
2013 "Cyberbullying research: 2013 update." Available at: http://cyberbullying.us/cyberbullyingresearch-2013-update/

Paternoster, Raymond
1987 "The deterrent effect of the perceived certainty and severity of punishment: A review of the evidence and issues." Justice Quarterly 4:173–217.

Paternoster, Raymond, and Ronet Bachman
2001 Explaining Criminals and Crime. Los Angeles: Roxbury.

Paternoster, Raymond, Robert Brame, Ronet Bachman, and Lawrence W. Sherman
1997 "Do fair procedures matter? The effect of procedural justice on spouse assault." Law and Society Review 57:163–204.

Paternoster, Raymond, Shawn Bushway, Robert Brame, and Robert Apel
2003 "The effect of teenage employment on delinquency and problem behaviors." Social Forces 82:297–335.

Paternoster, Raymond, and Leeann Iovanni
1989 "The labeling perspective and delinquency: An elaboration of the theory and an assessment of the evidence." Justice Quarterly 6:359–394.

Paternoster, Raymond, Jean Marie McGloin, Holly Nguyen, and Kyle J. Thomas
2013 "The causal impact of exposure to deviant peers: An experimental investigation." Journal of Research in Crime and Delinquency 50:476–503.

Paternoster, Raymond, and Paul Mazerolle
1994 "General strain theory and delinquency: A replication and extension." Journal of Research in Crime and Delinquency 31:235–263.

Paternoster, Raymond, and Alex Piquero
1995 "Reconceptualizing deterrence: An empirical test of personal and vicarious experiences." Journal of Research in Crime and Delinquency 32:251–286.

Patterson, Gerald R.
1982 Coercive Family Process. Eugene, OR: Castalia.
1986 "Performance models for antisocial boys." American Psychologist 41:432–444.

Patterson, Gerald R., Barbara D. DeBaryshe, and Elizabeth Ramsey
1989 "A developmental perspective on antisocial behavior." American Psychologist 44:329–335.

Patterson, Gerald R., and Thomas J. Dishion
1985 "Contributions of families and peers to delinquency." Criminology 23:63–79.

Patterson, Gerald R., Marion S. Forgatch, Karen L. Yoerger, and Mike Stoolmiller
1998 "Variables that initiate and maintain an early-onset trajectory for juvenile offending." Development and Psychopathology 10:531–547.

Patterson, Gerald R., and M. Elizabeth Gullion
1977 Living with Children. Champaign, IL: Research Press Company.

Patterson, Gerald R., John B. Reid, and Thomas J. Dishion
1992 Antisocial Boys. Eugene, OR: Castalia.

Patton, Desmond Upton, Robert D. Eschmann, and Dirk A. Butler
2013 "Internet banging: New trends in social media, gang violence, masculinity and hip hop." Computers in Human Behavior 29:A54–A59.

Paulson, Amanda
2006 "New tack on teen justice: A push away from prisons." Christian Science Monitor, December 8, 2.

Payne, Allison Ann
2008 "A multilevel analysis of the relationships among communal school organization, student bonding, and delinquency." Journal of Research in Crime and Delinquency 45:429–455.

Payne, Allison Ann, Denise C. Gottfredson, and Gary D. Gottfredson
2003 "Schools as communities." Criminology 41:749–778.

Payne, Allison A., and Kelly Welch
2013 "The impact of schools and education on antisocial behavior over the lifecourse." Pp. 93–110 in Chris L. Gibson and Marvin D. Krohn, eds., Handbook of Life-Course Criminology. New York: Springer.

Payne, Danielle C., and Benjamin Cornwell
2007 "Reconsidering peer influences on delinquency: Do less proximate contacts matter?" Journal of Quantitative Criminology 23:127–149.

Pearce, Lisa D., and Dana L. Haynie
2004 "Intergenerational religious dynamics and adolescent delinquency." Social Forces 82:1553–1572.

Pearson, Frank S., Douglas S. Lipton, Charles M. Cleland, and Dorline S. Lee
2002 "The effects of behavioral/cognitive-behavioral programs on recidivism." Crime and Delinquency 48:476–496.

Pearson, Frank S., and Neil Alan Weiner
1985 "Toward an integration of criminological theories." Journal of Criminal Law and Criminology 76:116–150.

Peck, Jennifer H., Michael J. Leiber, Maude Beaudry-Cyr, and Elisa L. Toman
2016 "The conditioning effects of race and gender on the juvenile court outcomes of delinquent and 'neglected' types of offenders." Justice Quarterly 33:1210–1236.

Peeples, Faith, and Rolf Loeber
1994 "Do individual factors and neighborhood context explain ethnic differences in juvenile delinquency?" Journal of Quantitative Criminology 10:141–157.

Pelfrey, Jr., William V.
2004 "The inchoate nature of community policing." Justice Quarterly 21:579–602.

Penn, Everette B.
2006 "Black youth: Disproportionality and delinquency." Pp. 47–64 in Everette B. Penn, Helen Taylor Greene, and Shaun L. Gabbidon, eds., Race and Juvenile Justice. Durham, NC: Carolina Academic Press.

Peskin, Melissa, Andrea L. Glenn, Yu Gao, Jianghong Liu, Robert A. Schug, Yaling Yang, and Adriane Raine
2012 "Personal characteristics of delinquents: Neurobiology, genetic predispositions, individual psychosocial attributes." Pp. 73–106 in Barry C. Feld and Donna M. Bishop, eds., The Oxford Handbook of Juvenile Crime and Juvenile Justice. New York: Oxford University Press.

Peters, Michael, David Thomas, Christopher Zamberlan, and Caliber Associates
1997 Boot Camps for Juvenile Offenders. Washington, DC: Office of Juvenile Justice and Delinquency Prevention.

Petersilia, Joan
1989 "The influence of research on policing." Pp. 230–247 in Roger G. Dunham and Geoffrey P. Alpert, eds., Critical Issues in Policing. Prospect Heights, IL: Waveland.
1997 "Probation in the United States." Pp. 149–200 in Michael Tonry, ed., Crime and Justice: A Review of Research, Volume 22. Chicago: University of Chicago Press.

Peterson, Bryce E., Dalwon Lee, Alana M. Henninger, and Michelle A. Cubellis
2016 "Social bonds, juvenile delinquency, and Korean adolescents: Intra-and inter-individual implications of Hirschi's social bonds theory using panel data." Crime & Delinquency 62:1337–1363.

Peterson, Dana, Jody Miller, and Finn-Aage Esbensen
2001 "The impact of sex composition on gangs and gang member delinquency." Criminology 39:411–440.

Peterson, Dana, Terrance J. Taylor, and Finn-Aage Esbensen
2004 "Gang membership and violent victimization." Justice Quarterly 21:793–816.

Peterson, Ruth D., Lauren J. Krivo, and Mark A. Harris
2000 "Disadvantage and neighborhood violent crime: Do local institutions matter?" Journal of Research in Crime and Delinquency 37:31–63.

Petrosino, Anthony, Carolyn Turpin-Petrosino, and James O. Finkenauer
2000 "Well-meaning programs can have harmful effects! Lessons from experiments of programs such as Scared Straight." Crime and Delinquency 46:354–379.

Petrosino, Anthony, Carolyn Turpin-Petrosino, and Sarah Guckenburg
2010 "Formal system processing of juveniles: Effects on delinquency." Campbell Systematic Reviews 1:1–88.

Petrosino, Anthony, Carolyn Turpin-Petrosino, Meghan E. Hollis-Peel, and Julia G. Lavenberg
2013 "'Scared Straight' and other juvenile awareness programs for preventing juvenile delinquency." Cochrane Database of Systematic Reviews. Available at: http://www.cochranelibrary.com

Petrosino, Anthony, and Haluk Soydan
2005 "The impact of program developers as evaluators on criminal recidivism: Results from meta-analyses of experimental and quasi-experimental research." Journal of Experimental Criminology 1:435–450.

Petrucci, Carrie J., and Albert R. Roberts
2004 "Principles and evidence on the effectiveness of family treatment." Pp. 339–364 in Albert R. Roberts ed., Juvenile Justice Sourcebook. New York: Oxford University Press.

Petts, Richard J.
2009 "Family and religious characteristics' influence on delinquency trajectories from adolescence to young adulthood." American Sociological Review 74:465–483.

Pew Charitable Trusts
2014 Public Opinion of Juvenile Justice. Washington, DC: Pew Charitable Trusts.

Pickett, Justin T., and Ted Chiricos
2012 "Controlling other people's children: Racialized views of delinquency and whites' punitive attitudes toward juvenile offenders." Criminology 50:673–710.

Piliavin, Irving, and Scott Briar
1964 "Police encounters with juveniles." American Journal of Sociology 51:101–119.

Piquero, Alex
2000 "Frequency, specialization, and violence in offending careers." Journal of Research in Crime and Delinquency 37:392–418.
2008a "Disproportionate minority contact." Future of Children 18:59–79.
2008b "Measuring self-control." In Erich Goode, ed., Out of Control? Assessing the General Theory of Crime. Palo Alto, CA: Stanford University Press.
2016 "'Take my license n'all that jive, I can't see. . . 35': Little hope for the future encourages offending over time." Justice Quarterly 33:73–99.

Piquero, Alex R., and Jeff A. Bouffard
2007 "Something old, something new: A preliminary investigation of Hirschi's redefined self-control." Justice Quarterly 24:1–27.

Piquero, Alex R., and Timothy Brezina
2001 "Testing Moffitt's account of adolescence-limited delinquency." Criminology 39:353–370.

Piquero, Alex R., Timothy Brezina, and Michael G. Turner
2005 "Testing Moffitt's theory of delinquency abstention." Journal of Research in Crime and Delinquency 42:27–54.

Piquero, Alex R., David P. Farrington, and Alfred Blumstein
2003 "The criminal career paradigm." Crime and Justice 30:359–506.

Piquero, Alex R., David P. Farrington, Brandon C. Welsh, Richard Tremblay, and Wesley G. Jennings
2009 "Effects of early family/parent training programs on antisocial behavior and delinquency." Journal of Experimental Criminology 5:83–120.

Piquero, Alex, Wesley G. Jennings, and David P. Farrington
2010 "On the malleability of self-control: Theoretical and policy implications regarding a general theory of crime." Justice Quarterly 27:803–834.

Piquero, Alex, and Paul Mazerolle
2001 Life-Course Criminology. Belmont, CA: Wadsworth.

Piquero, Alex, and Raymond Paternoster
1998 "An application of Stafford and Warr's reconceptualization of deterrence to drinking and driving." Journal of Research in Crime and Delinquency 35:3–39.

Piquero, Alex, Raymond Paternoster, Paul Mazerolle, Robert Brame, and Charles W. Dean
1999 "Onset age and offense specialization." Journal of Research in Crime and Delinquency 36:275–299.

Piquero, Alex R., and Greg Pogarsky
2002 "Beyond Stafford and Warr's reconceptualization of deterrence: Personal and vicarious experiences, impulsivity, and offending behavior." Journal of Research in Crime and Delinquency 39:153–186.

Piquero, Alex R., Carol A. Schubert, and Robert Brame
2014 "Comparing official and self-report records of offending across gender and race/ethnicity in a longitudinal study of serious youthful offenders." Journal of Research in Crime and Delinquency 51:526–556.

Piquero, Alex, and Stephen G. Tibbetts
1996 "Specifying the direct and indirect effects of low self-control and situational factors in an offender's decision making: Toward a more complete model of rational offending." Justice Quarterly 13:481–510.

Piquero, Alex R., Valerie West, Jeffrey Fagan, and Jan Holland
2006 "Neighborhood, race, and the economic consequences of incarceration in New York City, 1985–1996." Pp. 256–273 in Ruth D. Peterson, Lauren J. Krivo, and John Hagan, eds., The Many Colors of Crime. New York: New York University Press.

Piquero, Nicole Leeper, Angela R. Gover, John M. MacDonald, and Alex R. Piquero
2005 "The influence of delinquent peers on delinquency: Does gender matter?" Youth and Society 36:251–275.

Piquero, Nicole Leeper, and Miriam D. Sealock
2000 "Generalizing general strain theory: An examination of an offending population." Justice Quarterly 17:449–484.
2004 "Gender and general strain theory [GST]: A preliminary test of Broidy and Agnew's gender/GST hypotheses." Justice Quarterly 21:125–157.

Platt, Anthony M.
1969 The Child Savers. Chicago: University of Chicago Press.

Ploeger, Matthew
1997 "Youth unemployment and delinquency: Reconsidering a problematic relationship." Criminology 35:659–675.

Plomin, Robert, and Stephen A. Petrill
1997 "Genetics and intelligence: What's new?" Intelligence 24:53–77.

Plotnick, Robert D.
1997 "Child poverty can be reduced." Future of Children 7:72–87.

Poe-Yamagata, Eileen, and Jeffrey A. Butts
1996 Female Offenders in the Juvenile Justice System. Washington, DC: Office of Juvenile Justice and Delinquency Prevention.

Pogarsky, Greg, Alan J. Lizotte, and Terence P. Thornberry
2003 "The delinquency of children born to young mothers." Criminology 41:1249–1286.

Pogarsky, Greg, and Alex R. Piquero
2003 "Can punishment encourage offending? Investigating the 'resetting' effect." Journal of Research in Crime and Delinquency 40:95–120.

Pogarsky, Greg, Alex R. Piquero, and Ray Paternoster
2004 "Modeling change in perceptions about sanction threats." Journal of Quantitative Criminology 20:343–369.

Polakowski, Michael
1994 "Linking self- and social control with deviance: Illuminating the structure underlying a general theory of crime and its relation to deviant activity." Journal of Quantitative Criminology 10:41–78.

Pope, Carl E., and William Feyerherm
1993 Minorities and the Juvenile Justice System. Washington, DC: Office of Juvenile Justice and Delinquency Prevention.

Pope, Carl E., and Michael J. Leiber
2005 "Disproportionate minority confinement/contact (DMC): The federal initiative." Pp. 351–389 in Darnell F. Hawkins and Kimberly Kempf-Leonard, eds., Our Children, Their Children. Chicago: University of Chicago Press.

Pope, Carl E., and Howard N. Snyder
2003 Race as a Factor in Juvenile Arrests. Washington, DC: Office of Juvenile Justice and Delinquency Prevention.

Portnoy, Jill, Adrian Raine, Frances R. Chen, Dustin Pardini, Rolf Loeber, and J. Richard Jennings
2014 "Heart rate and antisocial behavior: The mediating role of impulsive sensation seeking." Criminology 52:292–311.

Pratt, Travis C., and Francis T. Cullen
2000 "The empirical status of Gottfredson and Hirschi's general theory of crime." Criminology 38:931–964.
2005 "Assessing macro-level predictors and theories of crime: A meta-analysis." Crime and Justice 32:373–450.

Pratt, Travis C., Francis T. Cullen, Kristie R. Blevins, Leah Daigle, and James Unnever
2002 "The relationship of attention deficit hyperactivity disorder to crime and delinquency: A meta-analysis." International Journal of Police Science and Management 4:344–360.

Pratt, Travis C., Francis T. Cullen, Christine S. Sellers, L. Thomas Winfree Jr., Tamara D.

Madensen, Leah E. Daigle, Noelle E. Fearn, and Jacinta M. Gau
2010 "The empirical status of social learning theory: A meta-analysis." Justice Quarterly 27:765–802.

Pratt, Travis C., Michael G. Turner, and Alex Piquero
2004 "Parental socialization and community context: A longitudinal analysis of the structural sources of low self-control." Journal of Research in Crime and Delinquency 41:219–243.

Press, Eyal
2006 "Do immigrants make us safer?" New York Times Magazine, December 3, 20–24.

Pulkkinen, Lea
1986 "The role of impulse control in the development of antisocial and prosocial behavior." Pp. 149–175 in Dan Olweus, Jack Block, and Marian Radke-Yarrow, eds., Development of Antisocial and Prosocial Behavior. Orlando, FL: Academic Press.

Pullmann, Michael D., Jodi Kerbs, Nancy Koroloff, Ernie Veach-White, Rita Gaylor, and DeDe Sieler
2006 "Juvenile offenders with mental health needs: Reducing recidivism using wraparound." Crime and Delinquency 52:375–397.

Puzzanchera, Charles
2009 Juvenile Arrests 2008. Washington, DC: Office of Juvenile Justice and Delinquency Prevention.
2013 Juvenile Arrests 2011. Washington, DC: Office of Juvenile Justice and Delinquency Prevention.

Puzzanchera, Charles, Benjamin Adams, and Melissa Sickmund
2010 Juvenile Court Statistics 2006–2007. Washington, DC: National Center for Juvenile Justice.

Puzzanchera, Charles, and Sarah Hockenberry
2013 Juvenile Court Statistics 2010. Washington, DC: National Center for Juvenile Justice.

Puzzanchera, Charles, Anne L. Stahl, Terrence A. Finnegan, Nancy Tierney, and Howard N. Snyder
2003 Juvenile Court Statistics 1999. Washington, DC: Office of Juvenile Justice and Delinquency Prevention.

Pyrooz, David C, Andrew M. Fox, and Scott H. Decker
2010 "Racial and ethnic heterogeneity, economic disadvantage, and gangs: A macro-level study of gang membership in urban America." Justice Quarterly 27:867–892.

Quay, Herbert C.
1983 "Psychological theories." Pp. 330–342 in Sanford H. Kadish, ed., Encyclopedia of Crime and Justice. New York: Free Press.

Quillian, Lincoln
1999 "Migration patterns and the growth of high-poverty neighborhoods." American Journal of Sociology 105:1–37.

Quillian, Lincoln, and Devah Pager
2001 "Black neighbors, higher crime? The role of racial stereotypes in evaluations of neighborhood crime." American Journal of Sociology 107:717–767.

Rafter, Nicole Hahn
1997 Creating Born Criminals. Urbana: University of Illinois Press.

Raine, Adrian
1993 The Psychopathology of Crime. San Diego, CA: Academic Press.
2002a "Biosocial studies of antisocial behavior in children and adults: A review." Journal of Abnormal Child Psychology 30:311–326.
2002b "The biological basis of crime." Pp. 43–74 in James Q. Wilson and Joan Petersilia, eds., Crime. Oakland, CA: ICS Press.

Raine, Adrian, Patricia A. Brennan, and David P. Farrington
1997 "Biosocial bases of violence." Pp. 1–20 in Adrian Raine, Patricia A. Brennan, David P. Farrington, and Sarnoff A. Mednick, eds., Biosocial Bases of Violence. New York: Plenum.

Raine, Adrian, Patricia A. Brennan, David P. Farrington, and Sarnoff A. Mednick
1997 Biosocial Bases of Violence. New York: Plenum.

Rainville, Gerald A., and Steven K. Smith
2003 Juvenile Felony Defendants in Criminal Courts: Survey of 40 Counties, 1998. Washington, DC: Bureau of Justice Statistics.

Ramey, Craig T., and Sharon Landesman Ramey
1995 "Successful early interventions for children at high risk for failure in school." Pp. 129–145 in George J. Demko and Michael C. Jackson, eds., Populations at Risk in America. Boulder, CO: Westview.

Ramey, David M.
2016 "The influence of early school punishment and therapy/medication on social control experiences during young adulthood." Criminology 54:113–141.

Rankin, Joseph H.
1983 "The family context of delinquency." Social Problems 30:466–479.

Rankin, Joseph H., and Roger Kern
1994 "Parental attachments and delinquency." Criminology 32:495–515.

Rankin, Joseph H., and L. Edward Wells

1987 "The preventive effects of the family on delinquency." Pp. 257–277 in Elmer H. Johnson, ed., Handbook on Crime and Delinquency Prevention. New York: Greenwood.

1990 "The effect of parental attachments and direct controls on delinquency." Journal of Research in Crime and Delinquency 27:140–165.

1994 "Social control, family structure, and delinquency." Pp. 97–116 in Greg Barak, ed., Varieties of Criminology. Westport, CT: Praeger.

Rashbaum, William K.

2003 "Crime data manipulated in precinct, officials say." New York Times, June 20, A23.

Rasmussen, Andrew

2004 "Teen court referral, sentencing, and subsequent recidivism." Crime and Delinquency 50:615–635.

Ratchford, Marie, and Kevin M. Beaver

2009 "Neuropsychological deficits, low self-control, and delinquent involvement: Toward a biosocial explanation of delinquency." Criminal Justice and Behavior 36:147–162.

2002b Police Departments in Large Cities, 1990–2000. Washington, DC: Bureau of Justice Statistics.

Reaves, Brian A.

2010 Local Police Departments, 2007. Washington, DC: U.S. Department of Justice.

Rebellon, Cesar

2002 "Reconsidering the broken homes/delinquency relationship and exploring its mediating mechanisms." Criminology 40:103–136.

2006 "Do adolescents engage in delinquency to attract the social attention of peers?" Journal of Research in Crime and Delinquency 43:387–411.

Rebellon, Cesar J., and Michelle Manasse

2004 "Do 'bad boys' really get the girls? Delinquency as a cause and consequence of dating behavior among adolescents." Justice Quarterly 21:355–389.

Rebellon, Cesar J., Nicole Leeper Piquero, Alex R. Piquero, and Sherod Thaxton

2009 "Do frustrated economic expectations and objective economic inequity promote crime? A randomized experiment testing Agnew's general strain theory." European Journal of Criminology 6:47–71.

Rebellon, Cesar J., Murray A. Straus, and Rose Medeiros

2008 "Self-control in global perspective: An empirical assessment of Gottfredson and Hirschi's general theory within and across 32 national settings." European Journal of Criminology 5:331–362.

Rebellon, Cesar J., and Karen Van Gundy

2005 "Can control theory explain the link between parental physical abuse and delinquency?" Journal of Research in Crime and Delinquency 42:247–274.

Reckless, Walter C.

1961 "A new theory of crime and delinquency." Federal Probation 25:42–46.

Redding, Richard E., and James C. Howell

2000 "Blended sentencing in American juvenile courts." Pp. 145–179 in Jeffrey Fagan and Franklin E. Zimring, eds., The Changing Borders of Juvenile Justice. Chicago: University of Chicago Press.

Reed, Mark D., and Pamela Wilcox Rountree

1997 "Peer pressure and adolescent substance use." Journal of Quantitative Criminology 13:143–180.

Regnerus, Mark

2003 "Moral communities and adolescent delinquency." Sociological Quarterly 44:523–554.

Regnerus, Mark D., and Glen H. Elder

2003 "Religion and vulnerability among low-risk adolescents." Social Science Research 32:633–658.

Regnerus, Mark D., and Christian Smith

2005 "Selection effects in studies of religious influence." Review of Religious Research 47:23–50.

Reiman, Jeffrey

1995 The Rich Get Richer and the Poor Get Prison. Boston: Allyn and Bacon.

Reiss, Albert J., Jr.

1951 "Delinquency as the failure of personal and social controls." American Sociological Review 16:196–207.

1988 "Cooffending and criminal careers." Pp. 117–170 in Michael Tonry and Norval Morris, eds., Crime and Justice: A Review of Research, Volume 10. Chicago: University of Chicago Press.

Reiss, Albert J., Jr., and Jeffrey A. Roth
1993 Understanding and Preventing Violence. Washington, DC: National Academy Press.

Rennison, Callie Marie
2001 Violent Victimization and Race, 1993–98. Washington, DC: Office of Justice Programs.

Restivo, Emily, and Mark M. Lanier
2015 "Measuring the contextual effects and mitigating factors of labeling theory." Justice Quarterly 32:116–141.

Reyes, Jessica W.
2015 "Lead exposure and behavior: Effects on antisocial and risky behavior among children and adolescents." Economic Inquiry 53:1580–1605.

Rhee, Soo Hyun, and Irwin Waldman
2002 "Genetic and environmental influences on anti-social behavior." Psychological Bulletin 128:490–529.

Riedel, Marc
2003 "Homicide in Los Angeles County: A study of Latino victimization." Pp. 44–66 in Darnell F. Hawkins, ed., Violent Crime: Assessing Race and Ethnic Differences. Cambridge: Cambridge University Press.

Riley, David
1987 "Time and crime: The link between teenage lifestyle and delinquency." Journal of Quantitative Criminology 3:339–354.

Roberts, Albert R.
1998 Juvenile Justice. Chicago: Nelson-Hall.
2004 Juvenile Justice Sourcebook. New York: Oxford University Press.

Roberts, Julian
2004 "Public opinion and youth justice." Crime and Justice 31:495–542.

Roberts, Julian V., and Loretta J. Stalans
1997 Public Opinion, Crime, and Criminal Justice. Boulder, CO: Westview.
1998 "Crime, criminal justice, and public opinion." Pp. 31–57 in Michael Tonry, ed., The Handbook of Crime and Punishment. New York: Oxford University Press.

Robinson, Laurie
1996 "Linking community-based initiatives and community justice: The Office of Justice programs." National Institute of Justice Journal 231(August):4–7.

Robinson, Laurie O., and Jeff Slowikowski
2011 "Scary—and ineffective: Traumatizing at-risk kids is not the way to lead them away from crime and drugs." Baltimore Sun, January, 31. Available at: http://articles.baltimoresun.com/2011-01-31/news/bs-ed-scared-straight-20110131_1_straight-type-programs-straight-program-youths

Robinson, Matthew B., and Kevin M. Beaver
2009 Why Crime? An Interdisciplinary Approach to Explaining Criminal Behavior. Durham, NC: Carolina Academic Press.

Robinson, Matthew B., and Barbara H. Zaitzow
1999 "Criminologists: Are we what we study? A national self-report study of crime experts." Criminologist 24(2):1, 4, 17.

Rocheleau, Gregory C., and Raymond R. Swisher
2012 "Adolescent work and alcohol use revisited: Variations by family structure." Journal of Research on Adolescence 22:694–703.

Rocque, Michael, Chad Posick, and Ray Paternoster
2016 "Identities through time: An exploration of identity change as a cause of desistance." Justice Quarterly 33:45–72.

Rodgers, Joseph Lee, Maury Buster, and David C. Rowe
2001 "Genetic and environmental influences on delinquency: DF Analysis of NLSY kinship data." Journal of Quantitative Criminology 17:145–168.

Rodriquez, Nancy
2007 "Restorative justice at work." Crime and Delinquency 53:355–379.

Rodriquez, Nancy, and Vincent J. Webb
2004 "Multiple measures of juvenile drug court effectiveness." Crime and Delinquency 50:292–314.

Rogers, Joseph W., and M. D. Buffalo
1974 "Fighting back: Nine modes of adaptation to a deviant label." Social Problems 22:101–118.

Rogosch, Fred, Laurie Chassin, and Kenneth J. Sherr
1990 "Personality variables as mediators and moderators of family history risk for alcoholism: Conceptual and methodological issues." Journal of Studies on Alcohol 51:310–318.

Rosen, Lawrence
1985 "Family and delinquency: Structure or function?" Criminology 23:553–573.

Rosenbaum, Dennis P.
2007 "Just say no to D.A.R.E." Criminology and Public Policy 6:815–824.

Rosenfeld, Richard
2000 "Patterns in adult homicide: 1980–1995." Pp. 130–163 in Alfred Blumstein and Joel Wallman, eds., The Crime Drop in America. Cambridge: Cambridge University Press.

Rosenfeld, Richard, Timothy M. Bray, and Arlen Egley
1999 "Facilitating violence: A comparison of gang-motivated, gang-affiliated, and nongang youth homicides." Journal of Quantitative Criminology 15:495–516.

Rosenfeld, Richard, Mark Edberg, Xiangming Fang, and Curtis S. Florence
2013 Economics and Youth Violence: Crime, Disadvantage, and Community. New York: New York University Press.

Rosenfeld, Richard, and Robert Fornango
2017 "The relationship between crime and stop, question, and frisk rates in New York City neighborhoods." Justice Quarterly. Advance online publication. DOI: 10.1080/07418825.2016.1275748

Rosenfeld, Richard, Robert Fornango, and Andres F. Rengifo
2007 "The impact of order-maintenance policing on New York City homicide and robbery rates: 1988–2001." Criminology 45:355–384.

Rosenfeld, Richard, Steven F. Messner, and Eric P. Baumer
2001 "Social capital and homicide." Social Forces 80:283–309.

Rosenheim, Margaret K., Frankin E. Zimring, David S. Tanenhaus, and Bernardine Dohrn
2002 A Century of Juvenile Justice. Chicago: University of Chicago Press.

Rountree, Pamela Wilcox, and Barbara D. Warner
1999 "Social ties and crime: Is the relationship gendered?" Criminology 37:789–814.

Rowe, Alan R., and Charles R. Tittle
1977 "Life cycle changes and criminal propensity." Sociological Quarterly 18:223–236.

Rowe, David C.
1996 "An adaptive strategy theory of crime and delinquency." Pp. 268–314 in J. David Hawkins, ed., Delinquency and Crime. New York: Cambridge University Press. 2002 Biology and Crime. Los Angeles: Roxbury.

Rowe, David C., and David P. Farrington
1997 "The familial transmission of criminal convictions." Criminology 35:177–201.

Rowe, David C., and Bill L. Gulley
1992 "Sibling effects on substance use and delinquency." Criminology 30:217–233.

Rowe, David C., Alexander T. Vazsonyi, and Daniel J. Flannery
1995 "Sex differences in crime: Do means and within-sex variation have similar causes?" Journal of Research in Crime and Delinquency 32:84–100.

Ruback, R. Barry, Jennifer N. Shaffer, and Valerie A. Clark
2011 "Easy access to firearms: Juveniles' risks for violent offending and violent victimization." Journal of Interpersonal Violence 26:2111–2138.

Rubin, H. Ted
1998 "The juvenile court landscape." Pp. 205–230 in Albert R. Roberts, ed., Juvenile Justice. Chicago: Nelson-Hall.

Rusby, Julie C., Kathleen K. Forrester, Anthony Biglan, and Carol W. Metzler
2005 "Relationships between peer harassment and adolescent problem behaviors." Journal of Early Adolescence 25:453–477.

Rutter, Michael
1985 "Family and school influences on behavioural development." Journal of Child Psychology and Psychiatry 26:349–368.

Rutter, Michael, and Henri Giller
1983 Juvenile Delinquency. New York: Guilford Press.

Rutter, Michael, Henri Giller, and Ann Hagell
1998 Antisocial Behavior by Young People. Cambridge: Cambridge University Press.

Rutter, Michael, Barbara Maughan, Peter Mortimore, Janet Ouston, and Alan Smith
1979 Fifteen Thousand Hours. Cambridge, MA: Harvard University Press.

Rutter, Michael, Terrie D. Moffitt, and Avshalom Caspi
2006 "Gene–environment interplay and psychopathology." Journal of Child Psychology and Psychiatry 47:226–261.

Rutter, Michael, and Judy Silberg
2002 "Gene–environment interplay in relation to emotional and behavioral disturbance." Annual Review of Psychology 53:463–490.

Sabet, Kevin A.
2012 "There are smarter ways to deal with marijuana than legalization." USA Today, October 30. Available at: http://www.usnews.com/debate-club/should-marijuana-use-be-legalized/there-aresmarter-ways-to-deal-with-marijuana-than-legalization 2013 "The changing face of marijuana and marijuana policy." Public Sector Digest, Winter 2013. Available at: http://kevinsabet.com/wp-content/uploads/2013/12/Marijuana-Legalization.pdf

Salerno, Anthony W.
1991 "The child saver movement: Altruism or a conspiracy?" Juvenile and Family Court Journal 42:37–49.

Samples, Faith, and Larry Aber
1998 "Evaluations of school-based violence prevention programs." Pp. 217–252 in Delbert S. Elliott, Beatrix A. Hamburg, and Kirk R. Williams, eds., Violence in American Schools. Cambridge: Cambridge University Press.

Sampson, Robert J.
1985 "Neighborhood and crime: The structural determinants of personal victimization." Journal of Research in Crime and Delinquency 22:7–40.
1986a "Neighborhood family structure and the risk of personal victimization." Pp. 25–46 in James M. Byrne and Robert J. Sampson, eds., The Social Ecology of Crime. New York: Springer-Verlag.
1986b "Effects of socioeconomic context on official reaction to juvenile delinquency." American Sociological Review 51:876–885.
1987 "Urban black violence: The effect of male joblessness and family disruption." American Journal of Sociology 93:348–382.
1997 "The embeddedness of child and adolescent development: A community-level perspective on urban violence." Pp. 31–77 in Joan McCord, ed., Violence and Childhood in the Inner City. Cambridge: Cambridge University Press.
2002 "The Community." Pp. 225–252 in James Q. Wilson and Joan Petersilia, eds., Crime. Oakland, CA: ICS Press.
2006 "Collective efficacy theory: Lessons learned and directions for future inquiry." Pp. 149–168 in Francis T. Cullen, John Paul Wright, and Kristie R. Blevins, eds., Taking Stock: The Status of Criminological Theory. New Brunswick, NJ: Transaction.

2008 "Rethinking crime and immigration." Contexts 7(1):28–33.

2008 "Moving to inequality: Neighborhood effects and experiments meet social structure." American Journal of Sociology 114:189–231.

Sampson, Robert J., and Dawn Jeglum Bartusch

1999 Attitudes Toward Crime, Police, and the Law: Individual and Neighborhood Differences. Washington, DC: National Institute of Justice.

Sampson, Robert J., and Lydia Bean

2006 "Cultural mechanisms and killing fields: A revised theory of community-level racial inequality." Pp. 8–38 in Ruth D. Peterson, Lauren J. Krivo, and John Hagan, eds., The Many Colors of Crime. New York: New York University Press.

Sampson, Robert J., and W. Byron Groves

1989 "Community structure and crime: Testing social-disorganization theory." American Journal of Sociology 94:774–802.

Sampson, Robert J., and John H. Laub

1993a Crime in the Making. Cambridge, MA: Harvard University Press.

1993b "Structural variations in juvenile court processing: Inequality, the underclass, and social control." Law and Society Review 27:285–311.

1997 "A lifecourse theory of cumulative disadvantage and the stability of delinquency." Pp. 133–161 in Terence P. Thornberry, ed., Developmental Theories of Crime and Delinquency, Advances in Criminological Theory, Volume 7. New Brunswick, NJ: Transaction.

Sampson, Robert J., and Janet L. Lauritsen

1993 "Violent victimization and offending: Individual-, situational-, and community-level risk factors." Pp. 1–114 in National Research Council, ed., Understanding and Preventing Violence, Volume 3, Social Influences. Washington, DC: National Research Council.

1997 "Racial and ethnic disparities in crime and criminal justice in the United States." Crime and Justice 21:311–374.

Sampson, Robert J., Jeffrey D. Morenoff, and Stephen Raudenbush

2005 "Social anatomy of racial and ethnic disparities in violence." American Journal of Public Health 95:224–232.

Sampson, Robert J., and Stephen W. Raudenbush

1999 "Systematic social observation of public spaces: A new look at disorder in urban neighborhoods." American Journal of Sociology 105:603–651.

Sampson, Robert J., Stephen W. Raudenbush, and Felton Earls

1997 "Neighborhoods and violent crime: A multilevel study of collective efficacy." Science 277:918–924.

Sampson, Robert J., and William Julius Wilson

1995 "Toward a theory of race, crime and urban inequality." Pp. 37–54 in John Hagan and Ruth Peterson, eds., Crime and Inequality. Stanford, CA: Stanford University Press.

Sampson, Robert J., and John D. Wooldredge

1987 "Linking the micro- and macrolevel dimensions of lifestyle-routine activity and opportunity models of predatory victimization." Journal of Quantitative Criminology 3:371–393.

Sarteschi, Christine M., Michael G. Vaughn, and Kevin Kim

2011 "Assessing the effectiveness of mental health courts: A quantitative review." Journal of Criminal Justice 39:12–20.

Saum, Christine A.

1998 "Rohypnol: The date-rape drug?" Pp. 254–261 in James A. Inciardi and Karen McElrath, eds., The American Drug Scene. Los Angeles: Roxbury.

Savage, David G.

2012 "Supreme Court rules mandatory juvenile life without parole cruel and unusual." Los Angeles Times, June 25. Available at: http://articles.latimes.com/2012/jun/25/news/la-pn-supreme-court-rules-juvenile-life-without-parole-cruel-and-unusual-20120625

Savage, Joanne, and Christina Yancey

2008 "The effects of media violence exposure on criminal aggression: A meta-analysis." Criminal Justice and Behavior 35:772–791.

Sawhill, Isabel V.
2003 One Percent for the Kids. Washington, DC: Brookings Institution Press.

Schaefer, David R., Nancy Rodriguez, and Scott H. Decker
2014 "The role of neighborhood context in youth co-offending." Criminology 52: 117–139.

Schlossman, Steven
1977 Love and the American Delinquent. Chicago: University of Chicago Press.

Schnebly, Stephen M.
2008 "The influence of community-oriented policing on crime-reporting behavior." Justice Quarterly 25:223–251.

Schneider, Anne L.
1990 Deterrence and Juvenile Crime. New York: SpringerVerlag.

Schreck, Christopher J., Jean Marie McGloin, and David S. Kirk
2009 "On the origins of the violent neighborhood: A study of the nature and predictors of crime-type differentiation across Chicago neighborhoods." Justice Quarterly 26:771–794.

Schroeder, Ryan D., and John F. Frana
2009 "Spirituality and religion, emotional coping, and criminal desistance: A qualitative study of men undergoing change." Sociological Spectrum 29:718–741.

Schroeder, Ryan D., Peggy C. Giordano, and Stephen A. Cernkovich
2007 "Drug use and desistance process." Criminology 45:191–222.

Schubert, Carol. A., Edward P. Mulvey, and Lindsay Pitzer
2016 "Differentiating serious adolescent offenders who exit the justice system from those who do not." Criminology 54:56–85.

Schur, Edwin M.
1973 Radical Nonintervention: Rethinking the Delinquency Problem. Englewood Cliffs, NJ: Prentice-Hall.

Schwalbe, Craig S.
2007 "Risk assessment for juvenile justice: A meta-analysis." Law and Human Behavior 34:449–462.

Schwartz, John
2013 "A bid to keep youths out of adult prisons." New York Times, October 28. Available at: http://www.nytimes.com/2013/10/29/us/a-bid-to-keep-youths-out-of-adult-prisons.html

Scott, Elizabeth S.
2002 "The legal construction of childhood." Pp. 113–141 in Margaret K. Rosenheim, Frankin E. Zimring, David S. Tanenhaus, and Bernardine Dohrn, eds., A Century of Juvenile Justice. Chicago: University of Chicago Press.

Scott, Michael S.
2003 The Benefits and Consequences of Police Crackdowns. Washington, DC: Office of Community Oriented Policing Services.

Seabrook, John
2009 "Don't shoot: A radical approach to the problem of gang violence." The New Yorker, June 22, 32–41.

Sealock, Miriam, and Sally S. Simpson
1998 "Unraveling bias in arrest decisions: The role of juvenile offender type-scripts." Justice Quarterly 15:427–457.

Sechrest, Lee, and Abram Rosenblatt
1987 "Research methods." Pp. 417–450 in Herbert C. Quay, ed., Handbook of Juvenile Delinquency. New York: Wiley.

Sedlak, Andrea J., and Carol Bruce
2010 Youth's Characteristics and Backgrounds: Findings from the Survey of Youth in Residential Placement. Washington, DC: Office of Juvenile Justice and Delinquency Prevention.

Sellers, Christine S., John K. Cochran, and L. Thomas Winfree, Jr.
2003 "Social learning theory and courtship violence: An empirical test." Pp. 109–127 in Ronald L. Akers and Gary F. Jensen, eds., Social Learning Theory and the Explanation of Crime, Advances in Criminological Theory, Volume 11. New Brunswick, NJ: Transaction.

Shaffer, Jennifer N., and R. Barry Ruback

2002 Violent Victimization as a Risk Factor for Violent Offending Among Juveniles. Washington, DC: Office of Juvenile Justice and Delinquency Prevention.

Shaw, Clifford R., and Henry D. McKay

1942 Juvenile Delinquency and Urban Areas. Chicago: University of Chicago Press.

Shelden, Randall G., and Lynn T. Osborne

1989 "'For their own good': Class interests and the child saving movement in Memphis, Tennessee, 1900–1917." Criminology 27:747–767.

Shelden, Randall G., Sharon K. Tracy, and William B. Brown

2001 Youth Gangs in American Society. Belmont, CA: Wadsworth.

Sheley, Joseph F., and James D. Wright

1995 In the Line of Fire. New York: Aldine De Gruyter.

1998 High School Youths, Weapons, and Violence: A National Survey. Washington, DC: National Institute of Justice.

Sherman, Francine T.

2012 "Justice for girls: Are we making progress?" UCLA Law Review 59:1584–1628.

Sherman, Lawrence W.

1990 "Police crackdowns." National Institute of Justice Reports 219:2–6.

1993 "Defiance, deterrence, and irrelevance: A theory of the criminal sanction." Journal of Research in Crime and Delinquency 30:445–473.

1995 "The police." Pp. 327–348 in James Q. Wilson and Joan Petersilia, eds., Crime. Oakland, CA: ICS Press.

1998 "American policing." Pp. 429–456 in Michael Tonry, ed., The Handbook of Crime and Punishment. New York: Oxford University Press.

2000 The Defiant Imagination. The Albert M. Greenfield Chair Inaugural Lecture, University of Pennsylvania.

2001 "Reducing gun violence: What works, what doesn't, what's promising." Criminal Justice 1:11–25.

2002 "Fair and effective policing." Pp. 383–412 in James Q. Wilson and Joan Petersilia, eds., Crime. Oakland, CA: ICS Press.

Sherman, Lawrence W., and John E. Eck

2002 "Policing for crime prevention." Pp. 295–329 in Lawrence W. Sherman, David P. Farrington, Brandon C. Welsh, and Doris Layton MacKenzie, eds., Evidence-Based Crime Prevention. London: Routledge.

Sherman, Lawrence W., David P. Farrington, Brandon C. Welsh, and Doris Layton MacKenzie

2002 Evidence-Based Crime Prevention. London: Routledge.

Sherman, Lawrence W., Patrick R. Gartin, and Michael E. Buerger

1989 "Hot spots of predatory crime: Routine activities and the criminology of place." Criminology 27:27–55.

Sherman, Lawrence W., Denise Gottfredson, Doris MacKenzie, John Eck, Peter Reuter, and Shawn Bushway

1998 Preventing Crime: What Works, What Doesn't, What's Promising. Available at http://www.preventingcrime.org/

Sherman, Lawrence W., Douglas A. Smith, Janell D. Schmidt, and Dennis P. Rogan

1992 "Crime, punishment, and stake in conformity: Legal and informal control of domestic violence." American Sociological Review 57:680–690.

Sherman, Lawrence W., and David Weisburd

1995 "General deterrent effects of police patrol in crime 'hot spots': A randomized, controlled trial." Justice Quarterly 12:625–648.

Sherry, John L.

2001 "The effects of violent video games on aggression: A meta-analysis." Human Communication Research 27:409–431.

2007 "Violent video games and aggression." Pp. 245–262 in Raymond W. Preiss, Barbara Mae Gayle, Nancy Burrell, Mike Allen, and Jennings Bryant, eds., Mass Media Effects Research. Mahwah, NJ: Lawrence Erlbaum.

Shihadeh, Edward S., and Darrell J. Steffensmeier
1994 "Economic inequality, family disruption, and urban black violence: Cities as units of stratification and social control." Social Forces 73:729–751.

Shoemaker, Donald J.
2004 Theories of Delinquency. New York: Oxford University Press.

Short, James F., Jr.
1997 Poverty, Ethnicity, and Violent Crime. Boulder, CO: Westview.

Short, James F., Jr., and F. Ivan Nye
1958 "Extent of unrecorded juvenile delinquency: Tentative conclusions." Journal of Criminal Law, Criminology, and Police Science 49:296–302.

Short, James F., Jr., and Fred L. Strodtbeck
1965 Group Process and Gang Delinquency. Chicago: University of Chicago Press.

Short, Jessica, and Christy Sharp
2005 Disproportionate Minority Contact in the Juvenile Justice System. Washington, DC: Child Welfare League of America.

Shover, Neal
1996 Great Pretenders: Pursuits and Careers of Persistent Thieves. Boulder, CO: Westview.

Sibley, Margaret H., William E. Pelham, Brooke S. G. Molina, Daniel A. Waschbusch, Elizabeth M. Gnagy, Dara E. Babinski, and Aparajita Biswas
2010 "Inconsistent self-report of delinquency by adolescents and young adults with ADHD." Journal of Abnormal Child Psychology 38:645–656.

Sickmund, Melissa
2006 Juvenile Residential Facility Census, 2002: Selected Findings. Washington, DC: Office of Juvenile Justice and Delinquency Prevention.
2010 Juveniles in Residential Placement, 1997–2008. Washington, DC: Office of Juvenile Justice and Delinquency Prevention.

Sickmund, Melissa, T. J. Sladky, and Wei Kang
2008 Census of Juveniles in Residential Placement Databook. Available at: http://www.ojjdp.ncjrs.gov/ojstatbb/cjrp

Sickmund, Melissa, Howard N. Snyder, and Eileen Poe-Yamagata
1997 Juvenile Offenders and Victims: 1997 Update on Violence. Washington, DC: National Center for Juvenile Justice.

Siegel, Jane A., and Linda M. Williams
2002 "The relationship between child sexual abuse and female delinquency and crime: A prospective study." Journal of Research in Crime and Delinquency 40:71–94.

Siegel, Larry J., Brandon C. Welsh, and Joseph J. Senna
2003 Juvenile Delinquency. Belmont, CA: Wadsworth.

Siegel, Michael, Craig S. Ross, and Charles King III
2013 "The relationship between gun ownership and firearm homicide rates in the United States, 1981–2010." American Journal of Public Health 103:2098–2105.

Silver, Eric
2006 "Understanding the relationship between mental disorder and delinquency: The need for a criminological perspective." Law and Human Behavior 30:685–706.

Silver, Eric, and Lisa L. Miller
2004 "Sources of informal social control in Chicago neighborhoods." Criminology 42:551–583.

Silver, Eric, and Brent Teasdale
2005 "Mental disorder and violence: An examination of stressful life events and impaired social support." Social Problems 52:60–78.

Simons, Ronald L., Steven R.H. Beach, and Ashley B. Barr
2012 "Differential susceptibility to context: A promising model of the interplay of genes and the social environment." Pp. 139–163 in Will Kalkhoff, Shane R. Thye, Edward J. Lawler, eds., Biosociology

and Neurosociology (Advances in Group Processes, Volume 29). Bingley, UK: Emerald Group Publishing Limited.

Simons, Ronald L., Jay Beaman, Rand D. Conger, and Wei Chao
1993 "Stress, support, and antisocial behavior trait as determinants of emotional well-being and parenting practices among single mothers." Journal of Marriage and the Family 55:385–398.

Simons, Ronald L., Callie H. Burt, Ashley B. Barr, Man-Kit Lei, and Eric Stewart
2014 "Incorporating routine activities, activity spaces, and situational definitions into the social schematic theory of crime." Criminology 52:655–687.

Simons, Ronald L., YiFu Chen, Eric A. Stewart, and Gene H. Brody
2003 "Incidents of discrimination and risk for delinquency: A longitudinal test of strain theory with an African American sample." Justice Quarterly 20:827–854.

Simons, Ronald L., Joanne Christine, Jay Beaman, Rand D. Conger, and Les B. Whitbeck
1996 "Parents and peers as mediators of the effect of community structure on adolescent problem behavior." American Journal of Community Psychology 24:145–171.

Simons, Ronald L., and Man Kit Lei
2013 "Enhanced susceptibility to context: A promising perspective on the interplay of genes and the social environment." Pp. 57–68 in Chris L. Gibson and Marvin D. Krohn, eds., Handbook of Life-Course Criminology. New York: Springer.

Simons, Ronald L., Man Kit Lei, Steven R. H. Beach, Gene H. Brody, Robert A. Philibert, and Frederick X. Gibbons
2011 "Social environment, genes, and aggression: Evidence supporting the differential susceptibility perspective." American Sociological Review 76:883–912.

Simons, Ronald L., Martin G. Miller, and Stephen M. Aigner
1980 "Contemporary theories of deviance and female delinquency: An empirical test." Journal of Research in Crime and Delinquency 17:42–53.

Simons, Ronald L., Leslie Gordon Simons, Callie Harbin Burt, Gene H. Brody, and Carolyn Cutrona
2005 "Collective efficacy, authoritative parenting, and delinquency." Criminology 43:989–1030.

Simons, Ronald L., Leslie Gordon Simons, Yi-Fu Chen, Gene H. Brody, and Kuei-Hsiu Lin
2007 "Identifying the psychological factors that mediate the association between parenting practices and delinquency." Criminology 45:481–517.

Simons, Ronald L., Leslie G. Simons, and Donna Hancock
2012 "Linking family processes and adolescent delinquency: Issues, theories, and research findings." Pp. 175–202 in Barry C. Feld and Donna M. Bishop, eds., The Oxford Handbook of Juvenile Crime and Juvenile Justice. New York: Oxford University Press.

Simons, Ronald L., Leslie Gordon Simons, and Lora Ebert Wallace
2004 Families, Delinquency, and Crime. New York: Oxford University Press.

Simons, Ronald L., Eric Stewart, Leslie C. Gordon, Rand D. Conger, and Glen H. Elder, Jr.
2002 "A test of life-course explanations for stability and change in antisocial behavior from adolescence to young adulthood." Criminology 40:401–434.

Simons, Ronald L., Chyi-In Wu, Rand D. Conger, and Frederick O. Lorenz
1994 "Two routes to delinquency: Differences between early and late starters in the impact of parenting and deviant peers." Criminology 32:247–276.

Singer, Mark I., Trina M. Anglin, Li Yusong, and Lisa Lunghofer.
1995 "Adolescents' exposure to violence and associated symptoms of psychological trauma." Journal of the American Medical Association 273: 477–82.

Singer, Simon I.
2001 "Juvenile court and its systems of juvenile justice." Pp. 349–366 in Susan O. White, ed., Handbook of Youth and Justice. New York: Kluwer.

Singer, Simon I., Murray Levine, and Susan Jou
1993 "Heavy metal music preference, delinquent friends, social control, and delinquency." Journal of Research in Crime and Delinquency 30:317–329.

Singer, Simon I., and David McDowall
1988 "Criminalizing delinquency: The deterrent effects of the New York juvenile offender law." Law and Society Review 22:521–535.

Skiba, Russell, Cecil R. Reynolds, Sandra Graham, Peter Sheras, Jane Close Conoley, and Enedina Garcia-Vázquez
2008 "Are zero tolerance policies effective in the schools?" American Psychologist 63:852–862.

Skogan, Wesley
2004 Community Policing: Can It Work? Belmont, CA: Wadsworth.

Skogan, Wesley, and Kathleen Frydl
2004 Fairness and Effectiveness in Policing. Washington, DC: National Academies Press.

Skogan, Wesley G., Lynn Steiner, Jill DuBois, J. Erik Gudell, and Aimee Fagan
2002 Taking Stock: Community Policing in Chicago. Washington, DC: Office of Justice Programs.

Slaby, Ronald G., and Nancy G. Guerra
1988 "Cognitive mediators of aggression in adolescent offenders: 1. Assessment." Developmental Psychology 24:580–588.

Smallbone, Stephen, and Susan Rayment-McHugh
2013 "Preventing youth sexual violence and abuse: Problems and solutions in the Australian context." Australian Psychologist 48:3–13.

Smith, Bradford
1998 "Children in custody: 20-year trends in juvenile detention, correctional, and shelter facilities." Crime and Delinquency 44:526–543.

Smith, Carolyn, and Marvin D. Krohn
1995 "Delinquency and family life among male adolescents: The role of ethnicity." Journal of Youth and Adolescence 24:69–93.

Smith, Carolyn, and Terence P. Thornberry
1995 "The relationship between childhood maltreatment and adolescent involvement in delinquency." Criminology 33:451–481.

Smith, David A.
1984 "The organizational context of legal control." Criminology 22:19–38.

Smith, David J.
2002 "Crime and the life course." Pp. 702–745 in Mike Maguire, Rod Morgan, and Robert Reiner, eds., The Oxford Handbook of Criminology, 3rd edition. Oxford: Oxford University Press.

Smith, Douglas A., and Robert Brame
1994 "On the initiation and continuation of delinquency." Criminology 32:607–629.

Smith, Douglas A., and Raymond Paternoster
1987 "The gender gap in theories of deviance: Issues and evidence." Journal of Research in Crime and Delinquency 24:140–172.

Smith, Matt
2016 "Judge sets date for resentencing Evan Miller's 'very old case.'" Juvenile Justice Information Exchange, November 15. Available at: http://jjie.org/2016/11/15/judge-sets-date-for-resentencing-evan-millers-very-old-case

Smith, Michael R.
2001 "Police-led crackdowns and cleanups: An evaluation of a crime control initiative in Richmond, Virginia." Crime and Delinquency 47:60–83.

Smokowski, Paul R., and Kelly Holland Kopasz
2005 "Bullying in school." Children and Schools 27:101–110.

Snyder, Howard N.
1999 "The overrepresentation of juvenile crime proportions in robbery clearance statistics." Journal of Quantitative Criminology 15:151–161.
2003 Juvenile Arrests 2001. Washington, DC: Office of Juvenile Justice and Delinquency Prevention.

2012. "Juvenile delinquency and juvenile justice clientele: trends and patterns in crime and justice system response." Pp. 3–30 in Barry C. Feld and Donna M. Bishop, eds., The Oxford Handbook of Juvenile Crime and Juvenile Justice. New York: Oxford University Press.

Snyder, Howard N., and Melissa Sickmund
1999 Juvenile Offenders and Victims: 1999 National Report. Pittsburgh: National Center for Juvenile Justice.
2006 Juvenile Offenders and Victims: 2006 National Report. Pittsburgh: National Center for Juvenile Justice.

Snyder, Howard N., Melissa Sickmund, and Eileen Poe-Yamagata
2000 Juvenile Transfers to Criminal Court in the 1990s: Lessons Learned from Four Studies. Washington, DC: Office of Juvenile Justice and Delinquency Prevention.

Snyder, James, and Gerald R. Patterson
1987 "Family interaction and delinquent behavior." Pp. 216–243 in Herberet C. Quay, ed., Handbook of Juvenile Delinquency. New York: Wiley.

Soulé, Dave, Denise Gottfredson, and Erin Bauer
2008 "It's 3 p.m. Do you know where your child is? A study on the timing of juvenile victimization and delinquency." Justice Quarterly, 25:623–646.

Spano, Richard, Craig Rivera, and John Bolland
2006 "The impact of timing of exposure to violence on violent behavior in a high poverty sample of inner city African American youth." Journal of Youth and Adolescence 35:681–692.

Special Council on Criminal Justice Reform for Georgians
2012 Report of the Special Council on Criminal Justice Reform for Georgians. Atlanta: State of Georgia. Available at: http://www.georgiacourts.org/files/Report%20of%20the%20Special%20 Council%20 on%20Criminal%20Justice%20Reform%20for%20Georgians%202012%20-%20 FINAL.pdf

Spelman, William
2000 "The limited importance of prison expansion." Pp. 97–129 in Alfred Blumstein and Joel Wallman, eds., The Crime Drop in America. Cambridge: Cambridge University Press.

Spelman, William, and John E. Eck
1987 Newport News Tests Problem-Oriented Policing. Washington, DC: National Institute of Justice.

Spergel, Irving A.
1995 The Youth Gang Problem. New York: Oxford University Press.

Staff, Jeremy, and John E. Schulenberg
2010 "Millennials and the world of work: Experiences in paid work during adolescence." Journal of Business and Psychology 25:247–255.

Stafford, Leon
1999 "Lawyers: Teen shooter needs psychiatric hospital." Atlanta Constitution, August 10, C1, 6.

Stahlkopf, Christina, Mike Males, and Daniel Macallair
2010 "Testing incapacitation theory: Youth crime and incarceration in California." Crime and Delinquency 56:253–268.

Starbuck, David, James C. Howell, and Donna J. Lindquist
2004 "Hybrid and other modern gangs." Pp. 200–217 in Finn-Aage Esbensen, Stephen G. Tibbitts, and Larry Gaines, eds., American Youth Gangs at the Millennium. Long Grove, IL: Waveland Press.

Stark, Rodney, and William Sims Bainbridge
1996 Religion, Deviance, and Social Control. New York: Routledge.

Steenland, Sally
2013 "Working full-time but still poor." Center for American Progress, February 20. Available at: https://www.americanprogress.org/issues/religion/news/2013/02/20/53929/working-full-time-and-still-poor/

Steffensmeier, Darrell
1993 "National trends in female arrests, 1969–1990: Assessment and recommendations for research." Journal of Quantitative Criminology 9:411–441.

Steffensmeier, Darrell, and Emilie Allan

1995 "Age-inequality and property crime: The effects of age-linked stratification and status attainment processes on patterns of criminality across the life course." Pp. 95–115 in John Hagan and Ruth D. Peterson, eds., Crime and Inequality. Stanford, CA: Stanford University Press.

1996 "Gender and crime: Toward a gendered theory of female offending." Annual Review of Sociology 22:459–487.

2000 "Looking for patterns: Gender, age, and crime." Pp. 85–127 in Joseph F. Sheley, ed., Criminology. Belmont, CA: Wadsworth.

Steffensmeier, Darrell, Emilie Allan, Miles Harer, and Cathy Streifel

1989 "Age and the distribution of crime." American Journal of Sociology 94:803–831.

Steffensmeier, Darrell, and Miles D. Harer

1999 "Making sense of recent U.S. crime trends, 1980 to 1996/1998: Age composition effects and other explanations." Journal of Research in Crime and Delinquency 36:235–274.

Steffensmeier, Darrell, and Jennifer Schwartz

2009 "Trends in girls' delinquency and the gender gap." Pp. 50–83 in Margaret A. Zahn, ed., The Delinquent Girl. Philadelphia: Temple University Press.

Steffensmeier, Darrell, Jennifer Schwartz, Hua Zhong, and Jeff Ackerman

2005 "An assessment of recent trends in girls' violence using diverse longitudinal sources: Is the gender gap closing?" Criminology 43:355–406.

Steffensmeier, Darrell, Jeffrey Ulmer, and John Kramer

1998 "The interaction of race, gender, and age in criminal sentencing: The punishment cost of being young, black, and male." Criminology 36:763–798.

Steinberg, Laurence

1996 Beyond the Classroom. New York: Simon and Schuster.

Steinberg, Laurence, and Elizabeth Cauffman

2000 "A developmental perspective on jurisdictional boundary." Pp. 379–406 in Jeffrey Fagan and Franklin E. Zimring, eds., The Changing Borders of Juvenile Justice. Chicago: University of Chicago Press.

Steiner, Benjamin, Craig Hemmens, and Valerie Bell

2006 "Legislative waiver reconsidered." Justice Quarterly 23:34–59.

Steiner, Benjamin, Elizabeth Roberts, and Craig Hemmens

2003 "Where is juvenile probation today?" Criminal Justice Studies 16:267–281.

Steiner, Benjamin, and Emily Wright

2006 "Assessing the relative effects of state direct file laws on violent juvenile crime." Journal of Criminal Law and Criminology 96:1451–1478.

Stemen, Don

2007 Reconsidering Incarceration. New York: Vera Institute of Justice.

Stewart, Eric A.

2003 "School social bonds, school climate, and school misbehavior: A multilevel analysis." Justice Quarterly 20:575–604.

Stewart, Eric A., Christopher J. Schreck, and Rod K. Brunson

2008 "Lessons of the street code: Policy implications for reducing violent victimization among disadvantaged citizens." Journal of Contemporary Criminal Justice 24:137–147.

Stewart, Eric A., and Ronald L. Simons

2006 "Structure and culture in African American adolescent violence: A partial test of the 'code of the streets' thesis." Justice Quarterly 23:1–33.

2010 "Race, code of the street, and violent delinquency: A multilevel investigation of neighborhood street culture and individual norms of violence." Criminology 48:569–605.

Stewart, Eric A., Ronald L. Simons, and Rand D. Conger

2000 "The effects of delinquency and legal sanctions on parenting behaviors." Pp. 257–279 in Greer Litton Fox and Michael L. Benson, eds., Families, Crime, and Criminal Justice. New York: JAI.

2002 "Assessing neighborhood and social psychological influences on childhood violence in an African-American sample." Criminology 40:801–830.

Stewart, Eric A., Ronald L. Simons, Rand D. Conger, and Laura V. Scaramella
2002 "Beyond the interactional relationship between delinquency and parenting practices: The contribution of legal sanctions." Journal of Research in Crime and Delinquency 39:36–59.

Stickle, Wendy Povitsky, Nadine M. Connell, Denise M. Wilson, and Denise Gottfredson
2008 "An experimental evaluation of teen courts." Journal of Experimental Criminology 4:137–163.

Stolzenberg, Lisa, and Stewart J. D'Alessio
2000 "Gun availability and violent crime: New evidence from the national incident-based reporting system." Social Forces 78:1461–1482.
2008 "Co-offending and the age-crime curve." Journal of Research in Crime and Delinquency 45:65–86.

Stone, Sandra
1998 "Should the juvenile justice system get tougher on juvenile offenders?" Pp. 199–295 in John R. Fuller and Eric W. Hickey, eds., Controversial Issues in Criminology. Boston: Allyn and Bacon.

Stormshak, Elizabeth A., Colleen A. Comeau, and Stephanie A. Shepard
2004 "The relative contribution of sibling deviance and peer deviance in the prediction of substance use across middle childhood." Journal of Abnormal Child Psychology 32:635–647.

Stoutland, Sara E.
2001 "The multiple dimensions of trust in resident/police relations in Boston." Journal of Research in Crime and Delinquency 38:226–256.

Stowell, Jacob I., Steven F. Messner, Kelly F. McGeever, and Lawrence E. Raffalovich
2009 "Immigration and the recent violent crime drop in the United States: A pooled, cross-sectional time-series analysis of metropolitan areas." Criminology 47:889–928.

Straus, Murray
1994 Beating the Devil Out of Them. New York: Lexington.

Stretesky, Paul B., Arnie M. Schuck, and Michael J. Hogan
2004 "Space matters: An analysis of poverty, poverty clustering, and violent crime." Justice Quarterly 21:817–841.

Strong, Ken, and Dewey Cornell
2008 "Student threat assessment in Memphis city schools: A descriptive report." Behavioral Disorders 34:42–54.

Sullivan, Christopher J., and Jean M. McGloin
2014 "Looking back to move forward: Some thoughts on measuring crime and delinquency over the past 50 years." Journal of Research in Crime and Delinquency 51:445–466.

Sullivan, Christopher J., Jean Marie McGloin, Travis C. Pratt, and Alex R. Piquero
2006 "Rethinking the 'norm' of offender generality: Investigating specialization in the short term." Criminology 44:199–234.

Sullivan, Christopher J., Bonita M. Veysey, Zachary K. Hamilton, and Michele Grillo
2007 "Reducing out-of-community placement and recidivism: Diversion of delinquent youth with mental health and substance use problems from the justice system." International Journal of Offender Therapy and Comparative Criminology 51:555–577.

Sullivan, Mercer L.
1989 Getting Paid. Ithaca, NY: Cornell University Press.

Sutherland, Edwin H., Donald R. Cressey, and David F. Luckenbill
1992 Principles of Criminology. Dix Hills, NY: General Hall.

Sutton, John R.
1988 Stubborn Children: Controlling Delinquency in the United States. Berkeley: University of California Press.

Sweeten, Gary
2006 "Who will graduate? Disruption of high school education by arrest and court involvement." Justice Quarterly 23:462–480.

Sweeten, Gary, Shawn D. Bushway, and Raymond Paternoster
2009 "Does dropping out of school mean dropping into delinquency?" Criminology 47:47–91.

Swift, James
2013 "Georgia juvenile justice reform bill a 'win-win-win'." Juvenile Justice Information Exchange, May 2. Available at: http://jjie.org/georgia-juvenile-justice-reform-bill-a-win-win-win/

Sykes, Gresham M., and David Matza
1957 "Techniques of neutralization: A theory of delinquency." American Sociological Review 22:664–670.

Tannenbaum, Frank
1938 Crime and the Community. New York: Columbia University Press.

Tanenhaus, David S.
2012 "The elusive juvenile court: Its origins, practices, and re-inventions." Pp. 419–444 in Barry C. Feld and Donna M. Bishop, eds., The Oxford Handbook of Juvenile Crime and Juvenile Justice. New York: Oxford University Press.

Tanner-Smith, Emily E., Sandra J. Wilson, and Mark W. Lipsey
2013 "Risk factors and crime." Pp. 89–111 in Francis T. Cullen and Pamela Wilcox, eds., The Oxford Handbook of Criminological Theory. New York: Oxford University Press.

Tanner-Smith, Emily E., Mark W. Lipsey, and David B. Wilson
2016 "Juvenile drug court effects on recidivism and drug use: A systematic review and meta-analysis." Journal of Experimental Criminology 12:477–513.

Tark, Jongyeon, and Gary Kleck
2004 "Resisting crime: The effects of victim action on the outcomes of crimes." Criminology 42:861–909.

Tavernise, Sabrina, and Robert Gebeloff
2013 "Share of homes with guns shows 4-decade decline." New York Times, March 9. Available at: http://www.nytimes.com/2013/03/10/us/rate-of-gun-ownership-is-down-survey-shows.html?_r=0

Taylor, E. A.
1986 "Childhood hyperactivity." British Journal of Psychiatry 149:562–573.

Taylor, Ralph B.
2001a "The ecology of crime, fear, and delinquency." Pp. 124–139 in Raymond Paternoster and Ronet Bachman, eds., Explaining Criminals and Crime. Los Angeles: Roxbury.
2001b Breaking Away from Broken Windows: Baltimore Neighborhoods and the Nationwide Fight Against Crime, Grime, Fear, and Decline. Boulder, CO: Westview.

Teasdale, Brent, and Eric Silver
2009 "Neighborhoods and self-control: Toward an expanded view of socialization." Social Problems 56:205–222.

Tedeschi, James T., and Richard B. Felson
1994 Violence, Aggression, and Coercive Actions. Washington DC: American Psychological Association.

Telep, Cody W., Renée J. Mitchell, and David Weisburd
2014 "How much time should the police spend at crime hot spots?" Justice Quarterly 31:905–933.

Ter Bogt, Tom F. M., Loes Keijsers, and Wim H. J. Meeus
2013 "Early adolescent music preferences and minor delinquency." Pediatrics 131:e380–e389.

Thaxton, Sherod, and Robert Agnew
2004 "The nonlinear effects of parental control and teacher attachment on delinquency." Justice Quarterly 21:763–792.

Theobald, Delphine, David P. Farrington, and Alex R. Piquero
2013 "Childhood broken homes and adult violence: An analysis of moderators and mediators." Journal of Criminal Justice 41:44–52.

Thornberry, Terence P.
1987 "Toward an interactional theory of delinquency." Criminology 25:863–891.
1996 "Empirical support for interactional theory: A review of the literature." Pp. 198–235 in J. David Hawkins, ed., Delinquency and Crime. Cambridge: Cambridge University Press.

1997 Developmental Theories of Crime and Delinquency: Advances in Criminological Theory, Volume 7. New Brunswick, NJ: Transaction.

1998 "Membership in youth gangs and involvement in serious and violent offending." Pp. 147–166 in Rolf Loeber and David P. Farrington, eds., Serious and Violent Juvenile Offenders. Thousand Oaks, CA: Sage.

Thornberry, Terence P., and James H. Burch II

1997 Gang Members and Delinquent Behavior. Washington, DC: Office of Juvenile Justice and Delinquency Prevention.

Thornberry, Terence P., and Margaret Farnworth

1982 "Social correlates of criminal involvement: Further evidence on the relationship between social status and criminal behavior." American Sociological Review 47:505–517.

Thornberry, Terence P., Adrienne Freeman-Gallant, Alan J. Lizotte, Marvin D. Krohn, and Carolyn A. Smith

2003 "Linkedlives: The intergenerational transmission of antisocial behavior." Journal of Abnormal Child Psychology 31:171–184.

Thornberry, Terence P., David Huizinga, and Rolf Loeber

1995 "The prevention of serious delinquency and violence: Implications from the program of research on the causes and correlates of delinquency." Pp. 213–237 in James C. Howell, Barry Krisberg, J. David Hawkins, and John J. Wilson, eds., A Sourcebook: Serious, Violent, and Chronic Juvenile Offenders. Thousand Oaks, CA: Sage.

Thornberry, Terence P., and Marvin D. Krohn

2000 "The self-reporting method for measuring delinquency and crime." Pp. 33–83 in David Duffee, ed., Criminal Justice 2000, Volume 4: Measurement and Analysis of Crime and Justice. Washington, DC: National Institute of Justice.

2001 "The development of delinquency." Pp. 289–305 in Susan O. White, ed., Handbook of Youth and Justice. New York: Kluwer Academic/Plenum.

2003 Taking Stock of Delinquency. New York: Kluwer Academic/Plenum.

2005 "Applying interactional theory to the explanation of continuity and change in antisocial behavior." Pp. 183–210 in David P. Farrington, ed., Integrated Developmental and Life-Course Theories of Offending. New Brunswick, NJ: Transaction.

Thornberry, Terence P., Marvin D. Krohn, Alan J. Lizotte, and Deborah Chard-Wierschem

1993 "The role of juvenile gangs in facilitating delinquent behavior." Journal of Research in Crime and Delinquency 30:55–87.

Thornberry, Terence P., Marvin D. Krohn, Alan J. Lizotte, Carolyn A. Smith, and Pamela K. Porter

2003 "Causes and consequences of delinquency: Findings from the Rochester youth development study." Pp. 11–46 in Terence P. Thornberry and Marvin D. Krohn, eds., Taking Stock of Delinquency. New York: Kluwer Academic/Plenum.

Thornberry, Terence P., Marvin D. Krohn, Alan J. Lizotte, Carolyn A. Smith, and Kimberly Tobin

2003 Gangs and Delinquency in Developmental Perspective. Cambridge: Cambridge University Press.

Thornberry, Terence P., Alan J. Lizotte, Marvin D. Krohn, Margaret Farnworth, and Sung Joon Jang

1991 "Testing interactional theory: An examination of reciprocal causal relationships among family, school, and delinquency." Journal of Criminal Law and Criminology 82:3–35.

1994 "Delinquent peers, beliefs, and delinquent behavior: A longitudinal test of interactional theory." Criminology 32:47–83.

Thornberry, Terence P., Carolyn A. Smith, Craig Rivera, David Huizinga, and Magda Stouthamer-Loeber

1999 Family Disruption and Delinquency. Washington, DC: Office of Juvenile Justice and Delinquency Prevention.

Thornberry, Terence P., Evelyn H. Wei, Magda Stouthamer-Loeber, and Joyce Van Dyke

2000 Teenage Fatherhood and Delinquent Behavior. Washington, DC: Office of Juvenile Justice and Delinquency Prevention.

Thornton, Timothy N., Carole A. Craft, Linda L. Dahlberg, Barbara S. Lynch, and Katie Baer

2002 Best Practices of Youth Violence Prevention: A Sourcebook for Community Action. Atlanta: Centers for Disease Control and Prevention.

Thrasher, Federic M.
1927 The Gang. Chicago: University of Chicago Press.

Tibbetts, Stephen G., and Chris L. Gibson
2002 "Individual propensities and rational decision-making: Recent findings and promising approaches." Pp. 3–24 in Alex R. Piquero and Stephen G. Tibbetts, eds., Rational Choice and Criminal Behavior. New York: Routledge.

Tibbetts, Stephen G., and Alex Piquero
1999 "The influence of gender, low birth weight, and disadvantaged environment in predicting early onset of offending: A test of Moffitt's interactional hypothesis." Criminology 37:843–878.

Tilton-Weaver, Lauree C., William J. Burk, Margaret Kerr, and Håkan Stattin
2013 "Can parental monitoring and peer management reduce the selection or influence of delinquent peers? Testing the question using a dynamic social network approach." Developmental Psychology 49:2057–2070.

Timmons-Mitchell, Jane, Monica B. Bender, Maureen A. Kishna, and Clare C. Mitchell
2006 "An independent effectiveness trial of multisystemic therapy with juvenile justice youth." Journal of Clinical Child and Adolescent Psychology 35:227–236.

Tita, George, and Greg Ridgeway
2007 "The impact of gang formation on local patterns of crime." Journal of Research in Crime and Delinquency 44:208–237.

Titterington, Victoria E., and Kelly R. Damphousse
2003 "Economic correlates of racial and ethnic disparity in homicide: Houston, 1945–1994." Pp. 67–88 in Darnell F. Hawkins, ed., Violent Crime: Assessing Race and Ethnic Differences. Cambridge: Cambridge University Press.

Tittle, Charles R.
1995 Control Balance: Toward a General Theory of Deviance. Boulder, CO: Westview.
2000 "Theoretical developments in criminology." Pp. 51–101 in Gary LaFree, ed., Criminal Justice 2000, Volume 1: The Nature of Crime: Continuity and Change. Washington, DC: National Institute of Justice.

Tittle, Charles R., Marty Jean Burke, and Elton F. Jackson
1986 "Modeling Sutherland's theory of differential association: Toward an empirical classification." Social Forces 65:405–432.

Tittle, Charles R., and Robert F. Meier
1990 "Specifying the sex/delinquency relationship." Criminology 28:271–299.

Tittle, Charles R., Wayne J. Villemez, and Douglas A. Smith
1978 "The myth of social class and criminality: An empirical assessment of the empirical evidence." American Sociological Review 43:643–656.

Tittle, Charles R., David A. Ward, and Harold G. Grosmick
2004 "Capacity for self-control and individuals' interest in exercising control." Journal of Quantitative Criminology 20:143–172.

Tittle, Charles R., and Michael R. Welch
1983 "Religiosity and deviance: Toward a contingency theory of constraining effects." Social Forces 61:653–682.

Tjaden, Patricia, and Nancy Thoennes
1999 "Prevalence and incidence of violence against women: Findings from the National Violence Against Women survey." Criminologist 24(3):1, 4, 12, 14, 17–19.
2006 Extent, Nature, and Consequences of Rape Victimization: Findings from the National Violence Against Women Survey. Washington, DC: U. S. Department of Justice.

Toby, Jackson
1957 "Social disorganization and stake in conformity: Complementary factors in the predatory behavior of hoodlums." Journal of Criminal Law, Criminology, and Police Science 48:12–17.

Tolan, Patrick, and Deborah Gorman-Smith
1998 "Development of serious and violent offending careers." Pp. 68–85 in Rolf Loeber and David P. Farrington, eds., Serious and Violent Juvenile Offenders. Thousand Oaks, CA: Sage.

Tolan, Patrick, David Henry, Michael Schoeny, and Arin Bass
2008 "Mentoring interventions to affect juvenile delinquency and associated problems." A Campbell Collaboration Systematic Review. Available at: www.campbellcollaboration.org/lib/download/238

Tonry, Michael
1995 Malign Neglect. New York: Oxford University Press.

Topalli, Volkan, George E. Higgins, and Heith Copes
2014 "A causal model of neutralization acceptance and delinquency: Making the case for an individual difference model." Criminal Justice and Behavior 41:553–573.

Torbet, Patricia, Patrick Griffin, Hunter Hurst, Jr., and Lynn Ryan MacKenzie
2000 Juveniles Facing Criminal Sanctions: Three States That Changed the Rules. Washington, DC: Office of Juvenile Justice and Delinquency Prevention.

Torbet, Patricia, and Linda Szymanski
1998 State Legislative Responses to Violent Juvenile Crime: 1996–97 Update. Washington, DC: Office of Juvenile Justice and Delinquency Prevention.

Totenberg, Nina
2016 "Supreme Court opens door to parole for juveniles given life sentences." National Public Radio, January, 25. Available at: http://www.npr.org/2016/01/25/464338364/supreme-court-opens-door-to-parole-for-juvenile-lifers

Tracy, Paul E., Jr.
1990 "Prevalence, incidence, rates, and other descriptive measures." Pp. 51–77 in Kimberly Kempf, ed., Measurement Issues in Criminology. New York: Springer-Verlag.
2005 "Race, ethnicity, and juvenile justice." Pp. 300–350 in Darnell F. Hawkins and Kimberly Kempf-Leonard, eds., Our Children, Their Children. Chicago: University of Chicago Press.

Tracy, Paul E., Jr., Marvin E. Wolfgang, and Robert M. Figlio
1990 Delinquency Careers in Two Birth Cohorts. New York: Plenum.

Traver, Marsha, Steve Walker, and Harvey Wallace
2002 Multicultural Issues in the Criminal Justice System. Boston: Allyn and Bacon.

Tremblay, Richard E., and Wendy M. Craig
1995 "Developmental Crime Prevention." Crime and Justice 19:151–236.

Tremblay, Monique D., Jessica E. Sutherland, and David M. Day
2017 "Fatherhood and delinquency: An examination of risk factors and offending patterns associated with fatherhood status among serious juvenile offenders." Journal of Child and Family Studies 26:677–689.

Triplett, Ruth A.
1996 "The growing threat: Gangs and juvenile offenders." Pp. 137–150 in Timothy J. Flanagan and Dennis R. Longmire, ed., Americans View Crime and Justice. Thousand Oaks, CA: Sage.

Triplett, Ruth A., and G. Roger Jarjoura
1994 "Theoretical and empirical specification of a model of informal labeling." Journal of Quantitative Criminology 10:241–276.

Trojanowicz, Robert, Victor E. Kappeler, Larry K. Gaines, and Bonnie Bucqueroux
1998 Community Policing: A Contemporary Perspective. Cincinnati, OH: Anderson.

Truman, Jennifer L., and Lynn Langton
2015 Criminal Victimization, 2014. Washington, DC: Bureau of Justice Statistics.

Truman, Jennifer L., and Rachel E. Morgan
2016 Criminal Victimization, 2015. Washington, DC: Bureau of Justice Statistics.

Truman, Jennifer L., and Michael Planty
2012 Criminal Victimization, 2011. Washington, DC: Bureau of Justice Statistics.

Truman, Jennifer, Lynn Langton, and Michael Planty
2013 Criminal Victimization, 2012. Washington, DC: Bureau of Justice Statistics.

Truman, Jennifer L., and Michael R. Rand
2010 Criminal Victimization, 2009. Washington, DC: Bureau of Justice Statistics.

Turner, C. F., L. Ku, S. M. Rogers, L. D. Lindberg, J. H. Pleck, and F. L. Sonenstein
1998 "Adolescent sexual behavior, drug use and violence: Increased reporting with computer survey technology." Science 280:867–873.

Turner, R. Jay, David Russell, Regan Glover, and Pam Hutto
2007 "The social antecedents of anger proneness in young adulthood." Journal of Health and Social Behavior 48:68–83.

Tygart, C. E.
1991 "Juvenile delinquency and number of children in a family." Youth and Society 22:525–536.

Turner, Michael G., Jennifer L. Hartman, and Donna M. Bishop
2007 "The effects of prenatal problems, family functioning, and neighborhood disadvantage in predicting life-course-persistent offending." Criminal Justice and Behavior 34:1241–1261.

Udry, J. Richard
2000 "Biological limits of gender construction." American Sociological Review 65:443–457.

UNICEF
2007 Child Poverty in Perspective. Florence: UNICEF Innocenti Research Center.

Unnever, James D., Francis T. Cullen, and J. C. Barnes
2016 "Racial discrimination, weakened school bonds, and problematic behaviors: Testing a theory of African American offending." Journal of Research in Crime and Delinquency 53:139–164.

Unnever, James D., Francis T. Cullen, and Travis C. Pratt
2003 "Parental management, ADHD, and delinquent involvement: Reassessing Gottfredson and Hirschi's general theory." Justice Quarterly 20:471–500.

Unnever, James D., Francis T. Cullen, Scott A. Mathers, Timothy E. McClure, and Marisa C. Allison
2009 "Racial discrimination and Hirschi's criminological classic: A chapter in the sociology of knowledge." Justice Quarterly 26:377–409.

Unnithan, N. Prabha
2006 "Asian Americans and juvenile justice." Pp. 65–66 in Everette B. Penn, Helen Taylor Greene, and Shaun L. Gabbidon, eds., Race and Juvenile Justice. Durham, NC: Carolina Academic Press.

U.S. Department of Education and Office of Justice Programs
2016 Indicators of School Crime and Safety 2015. Washington, DC: U.S. Government Printing Office.

U.S. Department of Health and Human Services
2001 Youth Violence Prevention: A Report of the Surgeon General. Rockville, MD: U.S. Department of Health and Human Services.
2016. Trends in Teen Pregnancy and Childbearing. Washington, DC: U.S. Department of Health and Human Services. Available at https://www.hhs.gov/ash/oah/adolescent-development/reproductive-health-and-teen-pregnancy/teen-pregnancy-and-childbearing/trends/index.html

U.S. Department of Justice
2006 Fact Sheet: Department of Justice Initiative to Combat Gangs. Washington, DC: U. S. Department of Justice.
2007 Fact Sheet: Project Safe Neighborhoods. Washington, DC: U. S. Department of Justice.
2013 "Justice Department files consent decree to prevent and address racial discrimination in student discipline in Meridian, Miss." U.S. Department of Justice, May 22. Available at: http://www.justice.gov/opa/pr/2013/March/13-crt-338.html

U.S. Department of Labor
2016 Employment Characteristics of Families Summary. Washington, DC: U.S. Department of Labor. Available at: http://www.bls.gov/news.release/famee.nr0.htm

Van der Put, Claudia E., Maja Dekovic, Machteld Hoeve, Geert Jan J. M. Stams, Peter H. van der Laan, and Femke E. M. Langewouters
2014 "Risk assessment of girls: Are there any sex differences in risk factors for re-offending and in risk profiles?" Crime and Delinquency 60:1033–1056.

Van Gundy, Karen, and Cesar J. Rebellon
2010 "A life-course perspective on the 'gateway hypothesis.'" Journal of Health and Social Behavior 51:244–259.

Van Voorhis, Patricia, Francis T. Cullen, Richard A. Mathers, and Connie Chenoweth Garner
1988 "The impact of family structure and quality on delinquency: A comparative assessment of structural and functional factors." Criminology 26:235–261.

Vandell, Deborah Lowe, Jay Belsky, Margaret Burchinal, Laurence Steinberg, and Nathan Vandergrift
2010 "Do effects of early child care extend to age 15 years? Results from the NICHD study of early child care and youth development." Child Development 81:737–756.

Vander Ven, Thomas, and Francis T. Cullen
2004 "The impact of maternal employment on serious youth crime." Crime and Delinquency 50:272–291.

Vander Ven, Thomas M., Francis T. Cullen, Mark A. Corrozza, and John Paul Wright
2001 "Home alone: The impact of maternal employment on delinquency." Social Problems 48:236–257.

Vander Waal, Curtis J., Duane C. McBride, Yvonne M. Terry-McElrath, and Holly Van Buren
2001 Breaking the Juvenile Drug-Crime Cycle: A Guide for Practitioners and Policymakers. Washington, DC: Office of Justice Programs.

Vaz, Edmund W.
1967 "Juvenile delinquency in the middle class youth culture." Pp. 131–147 in Edmund W. Vaz, ed., Middle-Class Juvenile Delinquency. New York: Harper and Row.

Vazsonyi, Alexander T., and Lara M. Belliston
2007 "The family, low self-control, deviance: A cross-cultural and cross-national test of self-control theory." Criminal Justice and Behavior 34: 505–530.

Vazsonyi, Alexander T., Lloyd E. Pickering, Lara M. Belliston, Dick Hessing, and Marianne Junger
2002 "Routine activities and deviant behaviors: American, Dutch, Hungarian, and Swiss youth." Journal of Quantitative Criminology 18:397–422.

Velez, Maria B.
2001 "The role of public social control in urban neighborhoods: A multi-level analysis of victimization risk." Criminology 39:837–864.
2006 "Toward an understanding of the lower rates of homicide in Latino versus black neighborhoods: A look at Chicago." Pp. 91–107 in Ruth D. Peterson, Lauren J. Krivo, and John Hagan, eds., The Many Colors of Crime. New York: New York University Press.

Velez, Maria B., Lauren J. Krivo, and Ruth D. Peterson
2003 "Structural inequality and homicide." Criminology 41:645–672.

Vermeersch, Hans, Guy T'Sjoen, J. M. Kaufman, and J. Vincke
2008 "Gender, parental control, and adolescent risk-taking." Deviant Behavior 29:690–725.

Vestal, Christine
2008 "States adopt Missouri youth justice model." Stateline.org, March 7. Available at: http://www.stateline.org/live/details/story?contentId=288904

Veysey, Bonita M., and Steven F. Messner
1999 "Further testing of social disorganization theory: An elaboration of Sampson and Grove's 'community structure and crime.'" Journal of Research in Crime and Delinquency 36:156–174.

Vieraitis, Lynne M., Tomislav V. Kovandzic, and Thomas B. Marvell
2007 "The criminogenic effects of imprisonment." Criminology and Public Policy 6:589–624.

Vigil, James Diego, and Steve C. Yun
1996 "Southern California gangs: Comparative ethnicity and social control." Pp. 139–156 in C. Ronald Huff, ed., Gangs in America. Thousand Oaks, CA: Sage.

Vila, Bryan
1994 "A general paradigm for understanding criminal behavior: Extending evolutionary ecological theory." Criminology 32:311–359.

Visher, Christy A.
2000 "Career offenders and crime control." Pp. 601–619 in Joseph H. Sheley, ed., Criminology. Belmont, CA: Wadsworth.

Vitaro, Frank, Patricia L. Dobkin, René Carbonneau, and Richard E. Tremblay
1996 "Personal and familial characteristics of resilient sons of male alcoholics." Addiction 91:1161–1177.

Volkow, Nora D., Ruben D. Baler, Wilson M. Compton, and Susan R. B. Weiss
2014 "Adverse health effects of marijuana use." New England Journal of Medicine 370:2219–227.

Von Zielbauer, Paul
2003 "The American agenda for fighting crime: More prison time . . . and less." New York Times, September 28, A25.

Wadsworth, Ted
2000 Labor markets, delinquency, and social control theory: An empirical assessment of the mediating processes. Social Forces 78:1041–1066.

Wadsworth, Tim
2010 "Is immigration responsible for the crime drop? An assessment of the influence of immigration on changes in violent crime between 1990 and 2000." Social Science Quarterly 91:531–553.

Walker, Elaine, and Daniel Romer
2006 Adolescent Psychopathology and the Developing Brain. New York: Oxford University Press.

Walker, John P., and Robert E. Lee
1998 "Uncovering strengths of children of alcoholic parents." Contemporary Family Therapy 20:521–538.

Walker, Samuel
1998 Sense and Nonsense About Crime and Drugs. Belmont, CA: West/Wadsworth.

Walker, Samuel, Cassia Spohn, and Miriam DeLone
2004 The Color of Justice. Belmont, CA: Wadsworth.

Wallace, Harvey
2005 Family Violence. Boston: Allyn and Bacon.

Wallace, John M., Jr., Ryoka Yamaguchi, Jerald G. Bachman, Patrick M. O'Malley, John E. Schulenberg, and Lloyd D. Johnston
2007 "Religiosity and adolescent substance use." Social Problems 54:308–327.

Wallace, Lisa Hutchinson, Justin W. Patchin, and Jeff D. May
2005 "Reactions of victimized youth: Strain as an explanation of school delinquency." Western Criminology Review 6:104–116.

Walsh, Anthony
2002 Biosocial Criminology. Cincinnati, OH: Anderson.

Warburton, Wayne A., Donald F. Roberts, and Peter G. Christenson
2014 "The effects of violent and antisocial music on children and adolescents." Pp. 301–328 in Douglas Gentile, ed., Media Violence and Children. Santa Barbara, CA: Praeger.

Ward, David A., and Charles R. Tittle
1993 "Deterrence or labeling: The effects of informal sanctions." Deviant Behavior 14:43–64.

Ward, Jeffrey T., Marvin D. Krohn, and Chris L. Gibson
2014 "The effects of police contact on trajectories of violence: A group-based, propensity score matching analysis." Journal of Interpersonal Violence 29:440–475.

Wareham, Jennefer, Denise Paquette Boots, and Jorge M. Chavez
2009 "A test of social learning and intergenerational transmission among batterers." Journal of Criminal Justice 37:163–173.

Ward, Geoff K.
2012 The Black Child Savers: Racial Democracy and Juvenile Justice. Chicago: University of Chicago Press.

Warner, Barbara D.
2003 "The role of attenuated culture in social disorganization theory." Criminology 41:73–98.
2007 "Directly intervene or call the authorities?" Criminology 45:99–130.

Warner, Barbara D., and Shannon K. Fowler
2003 "Strain and violence: Testing a general strain theory model of community violence." Journal of Criminal Justice 31:511–521.

Warr, Mark
1993 "Age, peers, and delinquency." Criminology 31:17–40.
1996 "Organization and instigation in delinquent groups." Criminology 34:11–37.
2002 Companions in Crime. Cambridge: Cambridge University Press.
2005 "Making delinquent friends: Adult supervision and children's affiliations." Criminology 43:77–106.

Warr, Mark, and Mark Stafford
1991 "The influence of delinquent peers: What they think or what they do?" Criminology 29:851–866.

Wasserman, Gail A., and Laurie S. Miller
1998 "The prevention of serious and violent juvenile offending." Pp. 197–247 in Rolf Loeber and David P. Farrington, eds., Serious and Violent Juvenile Offenders. Thousand Oaks, CA: Sage.

Watkins, Adam M.
2005 "Examining the disparity between juvenile and adult victims in notifying the police." Journal of Research in Crime and Delinquency 42:333–353.

Weber, Rene, Ute Ritlerfeld, and Anna Kostygina
2006 "Aggression and violence as effects of playing violent video games." Pp. 347–361 in Peter Vorderer and Jennings Bryant, eds., Playing Violent Video Games. Mahwah, NJ: Lawrence Erlbaum Associates.

Weerman, Frank M.
2011 "Delinquent peers in context: A longitudinal network analysis of selection and influence effects." Criminology 49:253–286.

Weerman, Frank M., Wim Bernasco, Gerben J. N. Bruinsma, and Lieven J. R. Pauwels
2015 "When is spending time with peers related to delinquency? The importance of where, what, and with whom." Crime and Delinquency 61:1386–1413.

Weerman, Frank M., and Wilma M. Smeenk
2005 "Peer similarity in delinquency for different types of friends." Criminology 43:499–524.

Weis, Joseph G.
1986 "Issues in the measurement of criminal careers." Pp. 1–51 in Alfred Blumstein, Jacqueline Cohen, Jeffrey A. Roth, and Christy A. Visher, eds., Criminal Careers and Career Criminals, Volume 2. Washington, DC: National Academy Press.
1987 "Social class and crime." Pp. 71–90 in Michael Gottfredson and Travis Hirschi, eds., Positive Criminology. Newbury Park, CA: Sage.

Weisburd, David
2000 "Randomized experiments in criminal justice policy: Prospects and problems." Crime and Delinquency 46:181–193.

Weisburd, David, and John E. Eck
2004 "What can police do to reduce crime, disorder, and fear?" Annals of the American Academy of Political and Social Science 593:42–65.

Weisburd, David, Stephen D. Mastrofski, Ann Marie McNally, Rosann Greenspan, and James J. Willis
2003 "Reforming to preserve: COMPSTAT and strategic problem solving in American policing." Criminology and Public Policy 3:421–456.

Weisburd, David, Nancy A. Morris, and Elizabeth R. Groff
2009 "Hot spots of juvenile crime: A longitudinal study of arrest incidents at street segments in Seattle, Washington." Journal of Quantitative Criminology 25:443–467.

Weisburd, David, Cody W. Telep, Joshua C. Hinkle, and John E. Eck
2010 "Is problem-oriented policing effective in reducing crime and disorder? Findings from a Campbell systematic review." Criminology and Public Policy 9:139–172.

Weisburd, David, Cody W. Telep, and Brian A. Lawton
2014 "Could innovations in policing have contributed to the New York City crime drop even in a period of declining police strength?: The case of stop, question and frisk as a hot spots policing strategy." Justice Quarterly 31:129–153.

Weisburd, David, Laura A. Wyckoff, Justin Ready, John E. Eck, Joshua C. Hinkle, and Frank Gajewski
2006 "Does crime just move around the corner? A controlled study of spatial displacement and diffusion of crime control benefits." Criminology 44:549–592.

Weishew, Nancy L., and Samuel S. Peng
1993 "Variables predicting students' problem behaviors." Journal of Educational Research 87:5–17.

Weiss, C. H.
1998 Evaluation. Englewood Cliffs, NJ: PrenticeHall.

Weissbourd, Richard
1996 The Vulnerable Child. Reading, MA: AddisonWesley.

Weitzer, Ronald, Steven A. Tuch, and Wesley G. Skogan
2008 "Police-community relations in a majority-black city." Journal of Research in Crime and Delinquency 45:398–428.

Wells, Edward L., and Joseph H. Rankin
1988 "Direct parental controls and delinquency." Criminology 26:263–284.
1991 "Families and delinquency: A meta-analysis of the impact of broken homes." Social Problems 38:71–93.
1995 "Juvenile victimization: Convergent validation of alternative measurements." Journal of Research in Crime and Delinquency 32:287–307.

Wells, William, and Julie Horney
2002 "Weapon effects and individual intent to do harm: Influences on the escalation of violence." Criminology 40:265–296.

Welsh, Brandon C.
2012 "Delinquency prevention." Pp. 395–418 in Barry C. Feld and Donna M. Bishop, eds., The Oxford Handbook of Juvenile Crime and Juvenile Justice. New York: Oxford University Press.

Welsh, Brandon C., David P. Farrington, and Lawrence W. Sherman
2001 Costs and Benefits of Crime Prevention. Boulder, CO: Westview.

Welsh, Brandon C., and Akemi Hoshi
2002 "Communities and crime prevention." Pp. 165–197 in Lawrence W. Sherman, David P. Farrington, Brandon C. Welsh, and Doris Layton MacKenzie, eds., Evidence-Based Crime Prevention. London: Routledge.

Welsh, Wayne N., Jack R. Greene, and Patricia H. Jenkins
1999 "School disorder: The influence of individual, institutional, and community factors." Criminology 37:73–116.

Welsh, Wayne N., Patricia H. Jenkins, and Philip W. Harris
1999 "Reducing minority overrepresentation in juvenile justice: Results of communitybased delinquency prevention in Harrisburg." Journal of Research in Crime and Delinquency 36:87–110.

Welsh, Wayne N., Robert Stokes, and Jack R. Greene
2000 "A macro-level model of school disorder." Journal of Research in Crime and Delinquency 37:243–283.

Welte, John W., Lening Zhang, and William F. Wieczorek
2001 "The effects of substance use on specific types of criminal offending in young men." Journal of Research in Crime and Delinquency 38:416–438.

White, Garland
1999 "Crime and the decline of manufacturing, 1970–1990." Justice Quarterly 16:81–97.

White, Helene Raskin, and D. M. Gorman
2000 "Dynamics of the drug–crime relationship." Pp. 151–218 in Gary LaFree, ed., The Nature of Crime: Continuity and Change, Criminal Justice 2000, Volume 1. Washington, DC: National Institute of Justice.

White, Helene Raskin, and Stephen Hansell
1996 "The moderating effects of gender and hostility on the alcohol–aggression relationship." Journal of Research in Crime and Delinquency 33:450–470.

White, Helene Raskin, and Erich W. Labouvie
1994 "Generality versus specificity of problem behavior: Psychological and functional differences." Journal of Drug Issues 24:55–74.

White, Helene Raskin, Erich W. Labouvie, and Marsha E. Bates
1985 "The relationship between sensation seeking and delinquency: A longitudinal analysis." Journal of Research in Crime and Delinquency 22:197–211.

White, Helene Raskin, Robert J. Pandina, and Randy L. LaGrange
1987 "Longitudinal predictors of serious substance use and delinquency." Criminology 25:715–740.

White, Helene Raskin, Peter C. Tice, Rolf Loeber, and Magda Stouthamer-Loeber
2002 "Illegal acts committed by adolescents under the influence of alcohol and drugs." Journal of Research in Crime and Delinquency 39:131–152.

Whitted, Kathryn S., and David R. Dupper
2005 "Best practices for preventing or reducing bullying in schools." Children and Schools 27:167–175.

Wiatrowski, Michael D., and Kristine L. Anderson
1987 "The dimensionality of the social bond." Journal of Quantitative Criminology 3:65–81.

Wiatrowski, Michael D., David B. Griswold, and Mary K. Roberts
1981 "Social control theory and delinquency." American Sociological Review 46:525–541.

Wiatrowski, Michael D., Stephen Hansell, Charles R. Massey, and David L. Wilson
1982 "Curriculum tracking and delinquency." American Sociological Review 47:151–160.

Widdowson, Alex O., Sonja. E. Siennick, and Carter Hay
2016 "The implications of arrest for college enrollment: An analysis of long-term effects and mediating mechanisms." Criminology 54:621–652.

Widom, Cathy Spatz
1989 "Does violence beget violence? A critical examination of the literature." Psychological Bulletin 106:3–28.
1997 "Child abuse, neglect, and witnessing violence." Pp. 159–170 in D. M. Stoff, J. Breiling, and J. D. Maser, eds., Handbook of Antisocial Behavior. New York: Wiley.
2001 "Child abuse and neglect." Pp. 31–48 in Susan O. White, ed., Handbook of Youth and Justice. New York: Kluwer Academic.
2014 "Varieties of violent behavior." Criminology 52:313–344.

Widom, Cathy Spatz, and Ashley Ames
1988 "Biology and female crime." Pp. 308–331 in Terrie E. Moffitt and Sarnoff A. Mednick, eds., Biological Contributions to Crime Causation. Dordrecht, The Netherlands: Martinus Nijhoff.

Wiebush, Richard G., Christopher Baird, Barry Krisberg, and David Onek
1995 "Risk assessment and classification for serious, violent, and chronic juvenile offenders." Pp. 171–212 in James C. Howell, Barry Krisberg, J. David Hawkins, and John J. Wilson, eds., A Sourcebook: Serious, Violent, and Chronic Juvenile Offenders. Thousand Oaks, CA: Sage.

Wiebush, Richard G., Betsie McNulty, and Thao Le
2000 Implementation of the Intensive Community-Based Aftercare Program. Washington, DC: Office of Juvenile Justice and Delinquency Prevention.

Wiebush, Richard G., Dennis Wagner, Betsie McNulty, Yanging Wang, and Thao N. Le
2005 Implementation and Outcome Evaluation of the Intensive Aftercare Program. Washington, DC: Office of Juvenile Justice and Delinquency Prevention.

Wiesner, Margit, and Deborah M. Capaldi
2003 "Relations of childhood and adolescent factors to offending trajectories of young men." Journal of Research in Crime and Delinquency 40:231–262.

Wikstrom, Per-Olof H.
2014 "Why crime happens: A situational action theory." Pp. 74–94 in Gianluca Manzo, ed., Analytical Sociology: Actions and Networks. New York: John Wiley.

Wikstrom, Per-Olof H., and Rolf Loeber
2000 "Do disadvantaged neighborhoods cause well-adjusted children to become adolescent delinquents? A study of male juvenile serious offending, individual risk and protective factors, and neighborhood context." Criminology 38:1109–1142.

Wikström, Per-Olof H., and Robert Svensson
2008 "Why are English youths more violent than Swedish youths? A comparative study of the role of crime propensity, lifestyles and their interactions in two cities." European Journal of Criminology 5:309–330.

Wilcox, Pamela, Kenneth C. Land, and Scott A. Hunt
2003 Criminal Circumstance. New York: Aldine de Gruyter.

Wilcox, Pamela, David C. May, and Staci D. Roberts
2006 "Student weapon possession and the 'fear of victimization hypothesis.'" Justice Quarterly 23:502–529.

Wiley, Stephanie A., Dena C. Carson, and Finn-Aage Esbensen
2016 "Arrest and the Amplification of Deviance: Does Gang Membership Moderate the Relationship?" Justice Quarterly. Advance online publication. DOI: 10.1080/07418825.2016.1226936

Wiley, Stephanie A., and Finn-Aage Esbensen
2016 "The effect of police contact: Does official intervention result in deviance amplification?" Crime & Delinquency 62:283–307.

Wiley, Stephanie Ann, Lee Ann Slocum, and Finn-Aage Esbensen
2013 "The unintended consequences of being stopped or arrested: An exploration of the labeling mechanisms through which police contact leads to subsequent delinquency." Criminology 51:927–966.

Wilkinson, Deanna L.
2002 "Decision making in violent events among adolescent males: An examination of sparks and other motivational factors." Pp. 163–196 in Alex R. Piquero and Stephen G. Tibbetts, eds., Rational Choice and Criminal Behavior. New York: Routledge.
2003 Guns, Violence, and Identity Among African American and Latino Youth. New York: LFB Scholarly Publishing.
2007 "Local social ties and willingness to intervene: Textured views among violent urban youth of neighborhood social control dynamics and situations." Justice Quarterly 24:185–220.

Wilkinson, Deanna L., and Patrick J. Carr
2008 "Violent youths' responses to high levels of exposure to community violence: What violent events reveal about youth violence." Journal of Community Psychology 36:1026–1051.

Wilkinson, Deanna L., Marquette S. McBryde, Brice Williams, Shelly Bloom, and Kerryn Bell
2009 "Peers and gun use among urban adolescent males: An examination of social embeddedness." Journal of Contemporary Criminal Justice 25:20–44.

Williams, Kirk R., and Richard Hawkins
1986 "Perceptual research on general deterrence: A critical review." Law and Society Review 20:545–572.

Williams, Nicolas, Francis T. Cullen, and John Paul Wright
1996 "Labor market participation and youth crime: The neglect of working in delinquency research." Social Pathology 2:195–217.

Willis, James J., Stephen D. Mastrofski, and David Weisburd
2004 "COMPSTAT and bureaucracy." Justice Quarterly 21:463–496.

Wilson, David B., Denise C. Gottfredson, and Stacy S. Najaka
2001 "School-based prevention of problem behaviors: A meta-analysis." Journal of Quantitative Criminology 17:247–272.

Wilson, David B., Ojmarrh Mitchell, and Doris L. MacKenzie
2006 "A systematic review of drug court effects on recidivism." Journal of Experimental Criminology 2:459–487.

Wilson, Denise M., Denise C. Gottfredson, and Wendy Povitsky Stickle
2009 "Gender differences in effects of teen courts on delinquency: A theory-guided evaluation." Journal of Criminal Justice 37:21–27.

Wilson, Holly A., and Robert D. Hoge
2013 "The effect of youth diversion programs on recidivism." Criminal Justice and Behavior 40:497–518.

Wilson, James Q.
1976 Varieties of Police Behavior. New York: Atheneum.

Wilson, James Q., and Richard Herrnstein
1985 Crime and Human Nature. New York: Simon and Schuster.

Wilson, James Q., and George L. Kelling
1982 "Broken windows: Police and neighborhood safety." Atlantic Monthly 249 (March):29–38.

Wilson, Sandra Jo, Mark W. Lipsey, and James H. Derzon
2003 "The effects of school-based intervention programs on aggressive behavior." Journal of Consulting and Clinical Psychology 71:136–149.

Wilson, William Julius
1987 The Truly Disadvantaged. Chicago: University of Chicago Press.
1996 When Work Disappears. Chicago: University of Chicago Press.

Winfree, L. Thomas, Jr., Terrance J. Taylor, Ni He, and Finn-Aage Esbensen
2006 "Self-control and variability over time: Multivariate results using a 5-year, multisite panel of youths." Crime and Delinquency 52:253–286.

Wintemute, Garen J.
2006 "Guns and gun violence." Pp. 45–96 in Alfred Blumstein and Joel Wallman, eds., The Crime Drop in America. New York: Cambridge University Press.

Winters, Ken C.
2007 Treatment of Adolescents with Substance Abuse Disorders. Rockville, MD: U.S. Department of Health and Human Services.

Wolf, Kerrin C. and Aaron Kupchik
2017. "School Suspensions and Adverse Experiences in Adulthood." Justice Quarterly 34:407–430.

Wolff, Kevin T., Michael T. Baglivio, Jonathan Intravia, and Alex R. Piquero
2015 "The protective impact of immigrant concentration on juvenile recidivism: A statewide analysis of youth offenders." Journal of Criminal Justice 43:522–531.

Wolfgang, Marvin E., and Franco Ferracuti
1982 The Subculture of Violence. Beverly Hills, CA: Sage.

Wolfgang, Marvin E., Robert M. Figlio, and Thorsten Sellin
1972 Delinquency in a Birth Cohort. Chicago: University of Chicago Press.

Wood, Jane, and Emma Alleyne
2010 "Street gang theory and research: Where are we now and where do we go from here?" Aggression and Violent Behavior 15:100–111.

Wood, Peter B., Walter R. Gove, James A. Wilson, and John K. Cochran
1997 "Nonsocial reinforcement and habitual criminal conduct: An extension of learning theory." Criminology 35:335–366.

Wood, Peter B., Betty Pfefferbaum, and Bruce J. Arneklev
1993 "Risk-taking and self-control: Social psychological correlates of delinquency." Journal of Crime and Justice 16:111–130.

Wooldredge, John, and Amy Thistlethwaite
2002 "Reconsidering domestic violence recidivism: Conditional effects of legal controls by individual and aggregate levels of stake in conformity." Journal of Quantitative Criminology 18:45–70.

Worrall, John L., and Tomislav V. Kovandzic
2007 "COPS grants and crime revisited." Criminology 45:159–190.

Worth, Keilah A., Jennifer Gibson Chambers, Daniel H. Nassau, Balvinder K. Rakhra, and James D. Sargent
2008 "Exposure of US adolescents to extremely violent movies." Pediatrics 122:306–312.

Wright, Bradley R. E., Avshalom Caspi, Terrie E. Moffitt, Richard A. Meich, and Phil A. Silva
1999 "Reconsidering the relationship between SES and delinquency: Causation but not correlation." Criminology 37:175–194.

Wright, Bradley R. E., Avshalom Caspi, Terrie E.Moffitt, and Ray Paternoster
2004 "Does the perceived risk of punishment deter criminally prone individuals?" Journal of Research in Crime and Delinquency 41:180–213.

Wright, Bradley R. Entner, Avshalom Caspi, Terrie E.Moffitt, and Phil A. Silva
1999 "Low self-control, social bonds, and crime: Social causation, social selection, or both?" Criminology 37:479–514.
2001 "The effects of social ties on crime vary by criminal propensity: A life-course model of interdependence." Criminology 39:321–352.

Wright, James D., Joseph F. Sheley, and M. Dwayne Smith
1992 "Kids, guns, and killing fields." Society 30:84–89.

Wright, James D., and Teri E. Vail
2000 "The guns–crime connection." Pp. 577–599 in Joseph F. Sheley, ed., Criminology: A Contemporary Handbook. Belmont, CA: Wadsworth.

Wright, John Paul, and Kevin M. Beaver
2005 "Do parents matter in creating self-control in their children?" Criminology 43:1169–1202.

Wright, John Paul, Kevin Beaver, Matt Delisi, and Michael Vaughn
2008 "Evidence of negligible parenting influences on self-control, delinquent peers, and delinquency in a sample of twins." Justice Quarterly 25:544–569.

Wright, John Paul, and Danielle Boisvert
2009 "What biosocial criminology offers criminology." Criminal Justice and Behavior 36:1228–1240.

Wright, John Paul, and Francis T. Cullen
2000 "Juvenile involvement in occupational delinquency." Criminology 38:863–896.
2001 "Parental efficacy and delinquent behavior: Do control and support matter?" Criminology 39:707–736.

Wright, John Paul, Francis T. Cullen, Robert Agnew, and Timothy Brezina
2001 "The root of all evil: An exploratory study of money and delinquent involvement." Justice Quarterly 18:239–268.

Wright, John Paul, Francis T. Cullen, and Nicolas Williams
1997 "Working while in school and delinquent involvement: Implications for social policy." Crime and Delinquency 43:203–221.

Wright, John Paul, Mark A. Morgana, Michelle A. Coynea, Kevin M. Beaver, and J.C. Barnes
2014 "Prior problem behavior accounts for the racial gap in school suspensions." Journal of Criminal Justice 42:257–266.

Wright, John Paul, Stephen G. Tibbetts, and Leah E. Daigle
2008 Criminals in the Making: Criminality Across the Life Course. Thousand Oaks, CA: Sage.

Wright, Kevin N., and Karen E. Wright
1995 Family Life, Delinquency, and Crime: A Policymaker's Guide. Washington, DC: Office of Juvenile Justice and Delinquency Prevention.

Wright, Richard A.
1994 In Defense of Prisons. Westport, CT: Greenwood.

Wright, Richard T., and Scott Decker
1997 Armed Robbers in Action. Boston: Northeastern University Press.

Wu, Ping, and Denise B. Kandel
1995 "The role of mothers and fathers in intergenerational behavioral transmission: The case of smoking and delinquency." Pp. 49–81 in Howard B. Kaplan, ed., Drugs, Crime, and Other Deviant Adaptations. New York: Plenum.

Yoder, Kevin A., Les B. Whitbeck, and Dan R. Hoyt
2003 "Gang involvement and membership among homeless and runaway youth." Youth and Society 34:441–467.

Xu, Yili, Mora L. Fiedler, and Karl H. Flaming
2005 "Discovering the impact of community policing." Journal of Research in Crime and Delinquency 42:147–186.

Yang, Yaling, and Adrian Raine
2010 "Neurology and crime." Pp. 662–664 in Francis T. Cullen and Pamela Wilcox, eds., Encyclopedia of Criminological Theory, Volume 2. Thousand Oaks, CA: Sage.

Yoshikawa, Hirokazu
1994 "Prevention as cumulative protection: Effects of early family support and education on chronic delinquency and its risks." Psychological Bulletin 115:28–54.

Young, Douglas W., Jill L. Farrell, and Faye S. Taxman
2013 "Impacts of juvenile probation training models on youth recidivism." Justice Quarterly 30:1068–1089.

Yu, Jiang, and Allen E. Liska
1993 "The certainty of punishment: A reference group effect and its functional form." Criminology 31:447–464.

Zahn, Margaret A., Susan Brumbaugh, Darrell Steffensmeier, Barry C. Feld, Merry Morash, Meda Chesney-Lind, Jody Miller, Allison Ann Payne, Denise C. Gottfredson, and Candace Kruttschnitt
2008 Violence by Teenage Girls: Trends and Context. Washington, DC: U.S. Department of Justice, Office of Juvenile Justice and Delinquency Prevention.

Zane, Steven N., Brandon C. Welsh, and Daniel P. Mears
2016 "Juvenile transfer and the specific deterrence hypothesis." Criminology & Public Policy 15:901–925.

Zatz, Marjorie S.
1987 "The changing forms of racial/ethnic biases in sentencing." Journal of Research in Crime and Delinquency 24:69–92.

Zawitz, Marianne W.
1995 "Guns used in crime: Firearms, crime, and criminal justice." Washington, DC: Bureau of Justice Statistics.

Zhang, Lening, and Steven F. Messner
2000 "The effects of alternative measures of delinquent peers on self-reported delinquency." Journal of Research in Crime and Delinquency 37:323–337.

Zhang, Lening, William F. Wieczorek, and John W. Welte
1997 "The impact of age of onset of substance use on delinquency." Journal of Research in Crime and Delinquency 34:253–268.

Zhang, Lening, and Sheldon Zhang
2004 "Reintegrative shaming and predatory delinquency." Journal of Research in Crime and Delinquency 41:433–453.

Zhang, Quauwu, Rolf Loeber, and Magda Stouthamer-Loeber
1997 "Developmental trends of delinquent attitudes and behaviors: Replications and synthesis across domains, time, and samples." Journal of Quantitative Criminology 13:181–215.

Zhao, Jihong Solomon, Ni He, and Nicholas P. Lovrich
2003 "Community policing: Did it change the basic functions of policing in the 1990s? A national follow-up study." Justice Quarterly 20:697–724.

Zhao, Jihong Solomon, Matthew C. Scheider, and Quint Thurman
2002 "Funding community policing to reduce crime: Have COPS grants made a difference?" Criminology and Public Policy 2:7–32.

Zigler, Edward, Cara Taussig, and Kathryn Black
1992 "Early childhood intervention: A promising preventative for juvenile delinquency." American Psychologist 47:997–1006.

Zimring, Franklin E.
1998 American Youth Violence. New York: Oxford University Press.
2005 American Juvenile Justice. New York: Oxford University Press.

2007 The Great American Crime Decline. New York: Oxford University Press.

2011 "How New York beat crime." Scientific American, 305:74–79.

Zimring, Franklin E., and Gordon Hawkins

1995 Incapacitation: Penal Confinement and the Restraint of Crime. New York: Oxford University Press.

1997 Crime Is Not the Problem: Lethal Violence in America. New York: Oxford University Press.

Zimring, Franklin E., and Hannah Laqueur

2015 "Kids, groups, and crime: In defense of conventional wisdom." Journal of Research in Crime and Delinquency 52:403–413.

Zingraff, Matthew T., Jeffrey Leiter, Matthew C. Johnsen, and Kristen A. Myers

1994 "The mediating effect of good school performance on the maltreatment–delinquency relationship." Journal of Research in Crime and Delinquency 31:62–91.

Zingraff, Matthew T., Jeffrey Leiter, Kristen A. Meyers, and Matthew C. Johnsen

1993 "Child maltreatment and youthful problem behavior." Criminology 31:173–202.

Zoutewelle-Terovan, Mioara, Victor van der Geest, Aart Liefbroer, and Catrien Bijleveld

2014 "Criminality and family formation: Effects of marriage and parenthood on criminal behavior for men and women." Crime & Delinquency 60:1209–1234.

Photo Credits

Author Index

Subject Index